Aristophanes (Volume I)

Benjamin Bickley Rogers

Alpha Editions

This edition published in 2020

ISBN : 9789354049392 (Hardback)
ISBN : 9789354049897 (Paperback)

Design and Setting By
Alpha Editions
www.alphaedis.com
email - alphaedis@gmail.com

As per information held with us this book is in Public Domain.
This book is a reproduction of an important historical work.
Alpha Editions uses the best technology to reproduce historical work in the same manner it was first published to preserve its original nature. Any marks or number seen are left intentionally to preserve its true form.

PREFACE

By the assistance of Messrs. G. Bell & Sons the Editors are enabled to include in the Library the famous version of Aristophanes made by Dr. Rogers. His complete edition with its full Introductions, Notes, and Appendices, will remain indispensable to large libraries and scholars, but it is hoped that the present edition will make his work more accessible to the general reader.

Introductions and explanatory notes have been added by the Editors. These for the most part contain only information which can readily be found elsewhere, but in cases where it seemed wise to give Dr. Rogers' exact view of a passage, short extracts from his notes are given in his own words.

CONTENTS OF VOLUME I

	PAGE
GENERAL INTRODUCTION	ix
THE ACHARNIANS—	
Introduction	3
Text and Translation	6
THE KNIGHTS—	
Introduction	120
Text and Translation	124
THE CLOUDS—	
Introduction	262
Text and Translation	266
THE WASPS—	
Introduction	404
Text and Translation	408
INDEX	551

GENERAL INTRODUCTION

ARISTOPHANES is an elusive poet. The main religious convictions of Aeschylus may be determined with certainty from his extant plays; attentive study of the dramas of Euripides reveals his cardinal opinions on politics, society and religion, and his philosophic attitude; but who can affirm with confidence that he has penetrated the comic mask of Aristophanes and knows his beliefs? The poet's mocking irony baffles and perplexes his reader at almost every turn.

ξυνήκαθ' ὃ λέγει;—μὰ τὸν Ἀπόλλω 'γὼ μὲν οὔ.

One element of the poet's irony is his apparent frankness. He has at times the air of desiring to be taken seriously and seems to be expressing honest convictions. He is very suggestive and provokes reflection, but the attempt to reduce his opinions to system reveals the illusion. We become uneasily conscious that the great satirist is laughing behind his mask.

A proof of this deceptive quality of the poet's humour is found in the diversity of the opinions that have been held as to his purpose in writing. It was once the fashion among modern interpreters to take him very seriously,—the comic poet disappeared in the reformer. He was eulogized as a moralist and patriot, whose lofty purpose was to instruct his fellow-countrymen; as an earnest thinker, who had

GENERAL INTRODUCTION

reflected deeply on the problems of society and government and had made Comedy simply the vehicle of his reforming ideas ; as a wise and discerning counsellor, who was competent to advise the citizens of Athens at a critical time on political questions and whose judgement of men and measures was sound ; as a stern man withal, resolute in the performance of duty, the implacable and victorious foe of all, wherever found, who undermined the glory of Athens. This view, which Grote combated (*History of Greece*, lxvii), finds vigorous expression in the *Apology* of Robert Browning :

> Next, whom thrash ?
> Only the coarse fool and the clownish knave ?
> No ! strike malpractice that affects the State,
> The common weal—intriguer or poltroon,
> Venality, corruption, what care I
> If shrewd or witless merely ?—so the thing
> Lay sap to aught that made Athenai bright
> And happy, change her customs, lead astray
> Youth or age, play the demagogue at Pnux,
> The sophist in Palaistra, or—what's worst,
> As widest mischief,—from the Theatre
> Preach innovation, bring contempt on oaths,
> Adorn licentiousness, despise the Cult. . . .
>   But my soul bade " Fight !
> Prove arms efficient on real heads and hearts ! "
> I wield the Comic weapon rather—hate !
> Hate ! honest, earnest and directest hate—
> Warfare wherein I close with enemy. . . .
> Such was my purpose : it succeeds, I say !
> Have we not beaten Kallicratidas,
> Not humbled Sparté ?   Peace awaits our word.
> Since my previsions,—warranted too well
> By the long war now waged and worn to end—
> Had spared such heritage of misery,
> My after-counsels scarce need fear repulse.
> Athenai, taught prosperity has wings,
> Cages the glad recapture.

GENERAL INTRODUCTION

Thus vaunts the poet, as Browning interprets him, just after the great victory won at Arginusae. "Sparta is at our feet, a new day dawns, the War is at an end. For Athens has at length learnt the bitter lesson she might have been spared had she yielded to my pleas for peace." The actual history of the next twelve months is pathetic. The battle at Arginusae, in which Callicratidas fell, restored the maritime supremacy of Athens, but peace was not secured. The Spartans made overtures, but the Athenian people, paying small heed to the "good counsels" that their Poet had given them in the *Acharnians*, the *Peace*, the *Lysistrata*, and in other comedies no longer extant, followed the lead of drunken Cleophon and rejected the Spartan proposals, just as five years before they had committed the grave error of accepting his advice after the Athenian victory at Cyzicus. Sparta bestirred herself, Lysander was sent out, and within a year Athenian arms suffered irretrievable reverse at Aegospotami.

The poet's counsels of peace were rejected. Peace came only with disaster. His "sage" solutions of many other burning questions were equally ineffective. If Aristophanes was working for reform, as a long line of learned interpreters of the poet have maintained, the result was lamentably disappointing: he succeeded in effecting not a single change. He wings the shafts of his incomparable wit at all the popular leaders of the day—Cleon, Hyperbolus, Peisander, Cleophon, Agyrrhius, in succession, and is reluctant to unstring his bow even when they are dead. But he drove no one of them from power; there is little evidence, indeed, that

GENERAL INTRODUCTION

he damaged their influence or even disturbed their brazen self-confidence. Cleon, when the poet's libellous personal abuse became even in his judgement indecent, promptly brought him to his knees. " When Cleon pressed me hard and tanned my hide, and outsiders laughed to see the sport, I confess "— Aristophanes says in the *Wasps*—" I played the ape a bit." He adds significantly that he failed to get popular support in this quarrel. The inference is that the people did not think badly of Cleon; but modern opinion of the popular leaders in Athens, formed on the evidence that Aristophanes is supposed to furnish, has been persistently unfavourable, and Cleon's rehabilitation as a sagacious, if turbulent, statesman who consistently maintained the imperial policy of Pericles has been slow.

The poet vehemently protested, it has been said, against the New Education, and viewing the whole intellectual tendency of his time with alarm, pleaded for a restoration of the simple discipline that had moulded the morals and minds and manners of the hardy men who fought at Marathon. Furthermore, he clearly apprehended the evils inherent in the Athenian system of judicature, which committed the administration of justice to a horde of common men, ignorant of the law, swayed by the impulse of the moment, " monsters of caprice and injustice," and ruthlessly exposed the unrighteousness of its proceedings. Finally, reverent of the best traditions of the stage, he stood forth, it is alleged, as their uncompromising defender, and sternly resisted the innovations that were gradually changing the spirit and the form of tragedy during the last third of the century, and for a generation relentlessly pursued

GENERAL INTRODUCTION

their chief exponent, concealing an attack that was meant to ruin him under the veil of caricature, parody, burlesque, and satire. But Socrates still frequented, winter and summer, the gymnasia, the market and the schools, and the Sophists continued to discourse and draw their pay; Philocleon, after a single experience of the pleasures of polite society, again forgathered with his cronies before the dawn of day and trudged away to Court; and Euripides, calmly disregarding the malicious strictures of his youthful critic, continued to write tragedy in his own manner and to present on the stage plays that were heard by the young men of Athens with wild acclaim.

This extreme conception of the function of Greek comedy as chiefly censorial and monitory has been modified with larger and more exact knowledge of the times in which the poet lived and of the conditions of life under which he wrote, but it has had unfortunate consequences. These plays have been regarded as a trustworthy source of information in establishing the facts of Greek history, biography, and institutions. So serious an interpretation of a form of literature of which the primary intention must always be entertainment and amusement inevitably obscured the poet's elusive humour. A jest became a statement of fact, a caricature a portrait, a satire a document. The poet's conception, clothed in a fantastical disguise that rivalled the grotesque dress of his own actors, has been essentially misapprehended in an entire play.

On the other hand the mistaken disposition, recently manifested, to regard Aristophanes simply as a jester and to deny that he had any other purpose than to provoke laughter is an extreme, though

GENERAL INTRODUCTION

natural, reaction. This view denies at the same time, as might have been expected, the cathartic efficacy of Greek tragedy. The highest comedy, typed in the earlier plays of Aristophanes, and in some of the comedies of Molière, is regenerative. The purpose of Aristophanes in the *Acharnians*, in which the action turns upon the impossible and fantastic whimsy of an Athenian farmer securing peace with Sparta for himself and his family alone, is to ridicule the war-party. Nobody would have been more amused than the poet if he had been told that his play was to stop the fighting, but he did believe that the War was an evil, and so far his heart was honestly in his theme; and I have no doubt that many a man who had laughed uproariously at the peace-loving farmer set single-handed in the comedy against a quarrelsome chorus, a powerful general, the whole tribe of sycophants, and the demagogue Cleon in the background, went home from the play less content with the course of his political leaders and longing in his heart for the good old days of peace. The instrument by which the poet probed the popular discontent was that most effective of all means when skilfully used—a laugh.

To regard Aristophanes as merely a jester is to mistake the man. Ridicule of contemporary persons, that is generally good-natured, or systems or prevailing ideas is his main purpose, I think, in his plays. His praise is for the dead. This ridicule, which ranges from satire to airy conceit, is made humorous by centering it in a far-fetched fantastic conception that is not the less available if it is impossible. Facts are exaggerated or invented with superb nonchalance and bewildering semblance of

GENERAL INTRODUCTION

:ality. In these mad revels of unrestrained fancy is difficult to lay hands upon Aristophanes the man. Nevertheless we do discover probable indications of is attachments and beliefs. He lived in an age of intellectual unrest when many vital questions pressed or solution. That a man of his intelligence did not give them consideration and reach conclusions is impossible. No doubt he detested a debauchee—et Ariphrades bear witness,—but he must have sympathized with the revolt of the young men of his day against the severe and meagre discipline in which youth were trained during the first half of the century, and must have shared in their eager interest in the new subjects of knowledge. No doubt he deprecated the vicious use of the skill for which Strepsiades clamours in the *Clouds*, but he had too keen a mind to fail to distinguish between the right and the wrong use of this power or to reject all study of the art of persuasion because it might be abused. He was himself a skilful dialectician, as the Debates found in nearly all his comedies prove. He was acquainted with Socrates and must have known that he never misused his wonderful dialectical power, and must have felt an expert's special thrill of pleasure in observing with what skill he employed it. Furthermore, the times in which the poet lived were troublous; the fate of Athens again and again stood on the razor's edge. He was not indifferent to the welfare of his country nor of his fellow-countrymen. There is a serious undertone in the *Acharnians* that gives it an indescribable elevation, and in the *Lysistrata*, a Rabelaisian play written after the disaster to Athenian arms in Sicily, in which, Thucydides records, fleet and army utterly perished, and of the

GENERAL INTRODUCTION

many who went forth few returned home, there are verses of intensest pathos that betray the poet's poignant sympathy :

οὐκ ἔστιν ἀνὴρ ἐν τῇ χώρᾳ ; μὰ Δί' οὐ δῆτ', εἰφ' ἕτερός τις.

Aristophanes, then, was a man of quick sympathies and settled convictions, although positive expression of belief and feeling is naturally rare in his plays, since he was a writer of comedy. Despite this reticence, it is both interesting and important to determine, so far as this may be done, his opinions on the questions that in his day were pressing for answer, and among these especially his political position. Was he an aristocrat ? Was he, in particular, as M. Couat believed, a pamphleteer in the pay of the aristocrats ? Or was he a democrat ? And if a democrat, how is the satirical—but extremely comical—characterization of Athenian Demus in the *Knights*, which his countrymen viewed with good-natured amusement, to be interpreted ? To these weighty and significant questions the reader may find an answer by studying the plays for himself.

JOHN WILLIAMS WHITE.

[This Introduction is reprinted from Dr. Loeb's translation of *Aristophanes and the Political Parties at Athens* by Maurice Croiset. It was originally arranged that the translation of Aristophanes for the Loeb Classical Library should be made by Professor John Williams White of Harvard University, but as he died before his work was completed it was thought that the printing of the above as an Introduction to the volumes which were to have been his work would be a fitting tribute to the memory of one who, while he was alive, took the deepest interest in the welfare of the Library.]

THE ACHARNIANS

INTRODUCTION

The *Acharnians* was produced at the Lenaean Dionysia in February 425 B.C., and like the *Banqueters* in 427 and the *Babylonians* in 426, it was in the name of Callistratus that it was brought out. The prize was awarded to Aristophanes; Cratinus with his *Storm-Tossed* (Χειμαζόμενοι) was second, and Eupolis with his *New Moons* (Νουμηνίαι) last. It is the oldest Greek comedy which has survived.

The general idea of the play is so simple that it needs no special Introduction. "An honest citizen, finding it impossible to get the State to conclude a peace with Sparta, makes a private peace on his own account; and thenceforward is represented as living in all the joys and comforts of Peace, whilst the rest of the City continues to suffer the straits and the miseries of War. But this simple plot is worked out and illustrated with an abundance of laughable and picturesque incidents."[a] Indeed Mr. Rogers considers that "if only one of his Comedies had survived to our day, I think that this is the one which would have given us the most comprehensive idea of the range of Aristophanic satire," and he adds: "If it has not the concentrated power of his later plays, yet no other Comedy exhibits the same variety of incident. With the

[a] Rogers, Introduction, p. xxvi.

ARISTOPHANES

prodigality of youth, the poet runs through the whole gamut of his likes and dislikes; his longing for Panhellenic unity, as in the great days of Marathon and Salamis; his efforts for right and justice, τὸ εὖ καὶ τὸ δίκαιον, in Athenian public life; and again the special objects of his aversion, as contravening these aims — the demagogues, the Informers, the war-party, the sophists, the lowering of the old heroic tragedy by Euripides — are all brought before us in turn; the germs of almost all his later efforts are discoverable in this early production."[a]

The Chorus consists of old men from Acharnae, a town which had especially suffered from the invasion of Archidamus, and which was celebrated for the "manly and soldier-like qualities" of its inhabitants who "at the commencement of the Peloponnesian War furnished a contingent of no less than 3000 hoplites" (*cf.* l. 180 and note).

[a] Introduction, p. xxvi.

ΤΑ ΤΟΥ ΔΡΑΜΑΤΟΣ ΠΡΟΣΩΠΑ

ΔΙΚΑΙΟΠΟΛΙΣ
ΚΗΡΥΞ
ΑΜΦΙΘΕΟΣ
ΠΡΕΣΒΕΙΣ
ΨΕΥΔΑΡΤΑΒΑΣ
ΘΕΩΡΟΣ
ΧΟΡΟΣ ΑΧΑΡΝΕΩΝ
ΓΥΝΗ Δικαιοπόλιδος
ΘΥΓΑΤΗΡ Δικαιοπόλιδος
ΚΗΦΙΣΟΦΩΝ θεράπων Εὐριπίδου
ΕΥΡΙΠΙΔΗΣ
ΛΑΜΑΧΟΣ
ΜΕΓΑΡΕΥΣ
ΚΟΡΑ Α καὶ Β θυγατέρε τοῦ Μεγαρέως
ΣΥΚΟΦΑΝΤΗΣ
ΒΟΙΩΤΟΣ
ΝΙΚΑΡΧΟΣ
ΘΕΡΑΠΩΝ Λαμάχου
ΓΕΩΡΓΟΣ
ΠΑΡΑΝΥΜΦΟΣ
ΑΓΓΕΛΟΙ

ΑΧΑΡΝΕΙΣ

ΔΙΚΑΙΟΠΟΛΙΣ. Ὅσα δὴ δέδηγμαι τὴν ἐμαυτοῦ καρδίαν,
ἤσθην δὲ βαιά· πάνυ δὲ βαιά· τέτταρα·
ἃ δ' ὠδυνήθην, ψαμμοκοσιογάργαρα.
φέρ' ἴδω, τί δ' ἤσθην ἄξιον χαιρηδόνος;
ἐγᾦδ' ἐφ' ᾧ γε τὸ κέαρ εὐφράνθην ἰδών, 5
τοῖς πέντε ταλάντοις οἷς Κλέων ἐξήμεσεν.
ταῦθ' ὡς ἐγανώθην, καὶ φιλῶ τοὺς ἱππέας
διὰ τοῦτο τοὔργον· ἄξιον γὰρ Ἑλλάδι.
ἀλλ' ὠδυνήθην ἕτερον αὖ τραγῳδικόν,
ὅτε δὴ 'κεχήνη προσδοκῶν τὸν Αἰσχύλον, 10
ὁ δ' ἀνεῖπεν " εἴσαγ', ὦ Θέογνι, τὸν χορόν."
πῶς τοῦτ' ἔσεισέ μου, δοκεῖς, τὴν καρδίαν;
ἀλλ' ἕτερον ἥσθην, ἡνίκ' ἐπὶ Μόσχῳ ποτὲ
Δεξίθεος εἰσῆλθ' ἀσόμενος Βοιώτιον.
τῆτες δ' ἀπέθανον καὶ διεστράφην ἰδών, 15
ὅτε δὴ παρέκυψε Χαῖρις ἐπὶ τὸν ὄρθιον.
ἀλλ' οὐδεπώποτ' ἐξ ὅτου 'γὼ ῥύπτομαι
οὕτως ἐδήχθην ὑπὸ κονίας τὰς ὀφρῦς

---

[a] In the background are three houses : the central one that of Dicaeopolis, the other two those of Euripides and Lamachus. In the foreground is a rough representation of the Pnyx where D. is awaiting the opening of the Assembly.

[b] Received as a bribe from certain of the allies to get their tribute-assessment lowered. The Knights compelled him to disgorge.

THE ACHARNIANS

DICAEOPOLIS.[a] What heaps of things have bitten me
    to the heart !
A small few pleased me, very few, just four ;
But those that vexed were sand - dune-
    hundredfold.
Let's see : what pleased me, worth my
    gladfulness ?
I know a thing it cheered my heart to see ;
'Twas those five talents[b] vomited up by Cleon.
At that I brightened ; and I love the Knights
For that performance ; 'twas of price to Hellas.
Then I'd a tragic sorrow, when I looked
With open mouth for Aeschylus, and lo,
The Crier called, *Bring on your play, Theognis.*[c]
Judge what an icy shock that gave my heart !
Next ; pleased I was when Moschus left, and in
Dexitheus came with his Boeotian song.[d]
But oh this year I nearly cracked my neck,
When in slipped Chaeris for the Orthian Nome.
But never yet since first I washed my face
Was I so bitten—in my brows with soap,[e]

[c] A very dull, frigid poet, *cf. T.* 170 and note.
[d] One of the famous lyrical nomes of Terpander ; the Orthian was another ; a spirit-stirring strain as of soldiers marching to victory. Chaeris was a Theban piper, who used to slink in to feasts uninvited.
[e] ὑπὸ κον. τ. ὁ. unexpectedly for ὑπ' ὀδύνης τὴν καρδίαν or the like.

ARISTOPHANES

ὡς νῦν, ὁπότ' οὔσης κυρίας ἐκκλησίας
ἑωθινῆς ἔρημος ἡ πνὺξ αὑτηί· 20
οἱ δ' ἐν ἀγορᾷ λαλοῦσι, κἄνω καὶ κάτω
τὸ σχοινίον φεύγουσι τὸ μεμιλτωμένον
οὐδ' οἱ πρυτάνεις ἥκουσιν, ἀλλ' ἀωρίαν
ἥκοντες, εἶτα δ' ὠστιοῦνται πῶς δοκεῖς
ἐλθόντες ἀλλήλοισι περὶ πρώτου ξύλου, 25
ἀθρόοι καταρρέοντες· εἰρήνη δ' ὅπως
ἔσται προτιμῶσ' οὐδέν· ὦ πόλις, πόλις.
ἐγὼ δ' ἀεὶ πρώτιστος εἰς ἐκκλησίαν
νοστῶν κάθημαι· κᾆτ' ἐπειδὰν ὦ μόνος,
στένω, κέχηνα, σκορδινῶμαι, πέρδομαι, 30
ἀπορῶ, γράφω, παρατίλλομαι, λογίζομαι,
ἀποβλέπων ἐς τὸν ἀγρόν, εἰρήνης ἐρῶν,
στυγῶν μὲν ἄστυ, τὸν δ' ἐμὸν δῆμον ποθῶν,
ὃς οὐδεπώποτ' εἶπεν, ἄνθρακας πρίω,
οὐκ ὄξος, οὐκ ἔλαιον, οὐδ' ᾔδει πρίω, 35
ἀλλ' αὐτὸς ἔφερε πάντα χὠ πρίων ἀπῆν.
νῦν οὖν ἀτεχνῶς ἥκω παρεσκευασμένος
βοᾶν, ὑποκρούειν, λοιδορεῖν τοὺς ῥήτορας,
ἐάν τις ἄλλο πλὴν περὶ εἰρήνης λέγῃ.
ἀλλ' οἱ πρυτάνεις γὰρ οὑτοιὶ μεσημβρινοί. 40
οὐκ ἠγόρευον; τοῦτ' ἐκεῖν' οὑγὼ 'λεγον·
εἰς τὴν προεδρίαν πᾶς ἀνὴρ ὠστίζεται.

ΚΗΡΥΞ.   πάριτ' εἰς τὸ πρόσθεν,
πάριθ', ὡς ἂν ἐντὸς ἦτε τοῦ καθάρματος.

ΑΜΦΙΘΕΟΣ. ἤδη τις εἶπε;

ΚΗΡ.   τίς ἀγορεύειν βούλεται; 45

ΑΜ. ἐγώ.

---

[a] A rope dripping with ruddle, used to sweep in loiterers from the Agora.

THE ACHARNIANS, 19–46

As now, when here's the fixed Assembly Day,
And morning come, and no one in the Pnyx.
They're in the Agora chattering, up and down
Scurrying to dodge the vermeil-tinctured cord.[a]
Why even the Prytanes are not here! They'll
    come
Long after time, elbowing each other, jostling
For the front bench, streaming down all together
You can't think how. But as for making Peace
They do not care one jot. O City! City!
But I am always first of all to come,
And here I take my seat; then, all alone,
I pass the time complaining, yawning, stretching,
I fidget, write, twitch hairs out, do my sums,
Gaze fondly country-wards, longing for Peace,
Loathing the town, sick for my village-home,
Which never cried, *Come, buy my charcoal*, or
My vinegar, my oil, my anything;[b]
But freely gave us all; no *buy*-word there.
So here I'm waiting, thoroughly prepared
To riot, wrangle, interrupt the speakers
Whene'er they speak of anything but Peace.
—But here they come, our noon-day Prytanes!
Aye, there they go! I told you how 'twould be;
Every one jostling for the foremost place.

CRIER.   Move forward all,
    Move up, within the consecrated line.
AMPHITHEUS.[c] Speaking begun?
CR.   Who will address the meeting?
AM. I.

  [b] These are all *city* cries. In l. 36 the pun in πρίων (lit. " saw " or " sawyer ") is obscure: it may mean " that grating rasping word."
  [c] *Entering in a violent hurry.*

ARISTOPHANES

ΚΗΡ. τίς ὤν;
ΑΜ. Ἀμφίθεος.
ΚΗΡ. οὐκ ἄνθρωπος;
ΑΜ. οὔ,
ἀλλ' ἀθάνατος. ὁ γὰρ Ἀμφίθεος Δήμητρος ἦν
καὶ Τριπτολέμου· τούτου δὲ Κελεὸς γίγνεται·
γαμεῖ δὲ Κελεὸς Φαιναρέτην τήθην ἐμήν,
ἐξ ἧς Λυκῖνος ἐγένετ'· ἐκ τούτου δ' ἐγὼ 50
ἀθάνατός εἰμ'· ἐμοὶ δ' ἐπέτρεψαν οἱ θεοὶ
σπονδὰς ποιεῖσθαι πρὸς Λακεδαιμονίους μόνῳ.
ἀλλ' ἀθάνατος ὤν, ὦνδρες, ἐφόδι' οὐκ ἔχω·
οὐ γὰρ διδόασιν οἱ πρυτάνεις.
ΚΗΡ. οἱ τοξόται.
ΑΜ. ὦ Τριπτόλεμε καὶ Κελεέ, περιόψεσθέ με; 55
ΔΙ. ὦνδρες πρυτάνεις, ἀδικεῖτε τὴν ἐκκλησίαν
τὸν ἄνδρ' ἀπάγοντες, ὅστις ἡμῖν ἤθελε
σπονδὰς ποιῆσαι καὶ κρεμάσαι τὰς ἀσπίδας.
ΚΗΡ. κάθησο σῖγα.
ΔΙ. μὰ τὸν Ἀπόλλω 'γὼ μὲν οὔ,
ἢν μὴ περὶ εἰρήνης γε πρυτανεύσητέ μοι. 60

ΚΗΡ. οἱ πρέσβεις οἱ παρὰ βασιλέως.
ΔΙ. ποίου βασιλέως; ἄχθομαι 'γὼ πρέσβεσι
καὶ τοῖς ταῶσι τοῖς τ' ἀλαζονεύμασιν.
ΚΗΡ. σίγα.
ΔΙ. βαβαιάξ, ὠκβάτανα, τοῦ σχήματος.
ΠΡΕΣΒΥΣ. ἐπέμψαθ' ἡμᾶς ὡς βασιλέα τὸν μέγαν, 65
μισθὸν φέροντας δύο δραχμὰς τῆς ἡμέρας
ἐπ' Εὐθυμένους ἄρχοντος·

---

[a] Scythian archers were the regular police at Athens. A. is ejected as not being an Athenian citizen when he begins to talk of " peace " and complain of the magistrates.

THE ACHARNIANS, 46-67

CR. Who are *you* ?
AM. Amphitheus.
CR. Not a man ?
AM. No, an immortal. For the first Amphitheus
Was of Demeter and Triptolemus
The son : his son was Celeus ; Celeus married
Phaenarete, who bare my sire Lycinus.
Hence I'm immortal ; and the gods committed
To me alone the making peace with Sparta.
But, though immortal, I've no journey-money;
The Prytanes won't provide it.
CR. Archers,[a] there !
AM. O help me, Celeus ! help, Triptolemus !
DI. Ye wrong the Assembly, Prytanes, ye do wrong it,
Haling away a man who only wants
To give us Peace, and hanging up of shields.
CR. St ! Take your seat.
DI. By Apollo, no, not I,
Unless ye prytanize about the Peace.

CR. O yes ! The Ambassadors from the Great King ! [b]
DI. What King ! I'm sick to death of embassies,
And all their peacocks and their impositions.
CR. Keep silence !
DI. Hey ! ! ! Ecbatana, here's a show.
AMBASSADOR. Ye sent us, envoys to the Great King's Court,
Receiving each two drachmas daily, when
Euthymenes was Archon.

[b] *Enter, clad in gorgeous oriental apparel, the envoys sent to the Persian court eleven years previously in the archonship of Euthymenes* 437-6 B.C.

ARISTOPHANES

ΔΙ. οἴμοι τῶν δραχμῶν.
ΠΡ. καὶ δῆτ' ἐτρυχόμεθα διὰ τῶν Καϋστρίων
πεδίων ὁδοιπλανοῦντες ἐσκηνημένοι,
ἐφ' ἁρμαμαξῶν μαλθακῶς κατακείμενοι,   70
ἀπολλύμενοι.
ΔΙ. σφόδρα γὰρ ἐσωζόμην ἐγὼ
παρὰ τὴν ἔπαλξιν ἐν φορυτῷ κατακείμενος;
ΠΡ. ξενιζόμενοι δὲ πρὸς βίαν ἐπίνομεν
ἐξ ὑαλίνων ἐκπωμάτων καὶ χρυσίδων
ἄκρατον οἶνον ἡδύν.
ΔΙ. ὦ Κραναὰ πόλις,   75
ἆρ' αἰσθάνει τὸν κατάγελων τῶν πρέσβεων;
ΠΡ. οἱ βάρβαροι γὰρ ἄνδρας ἡγοῦνται μόνους
τοὺς πλεῖστα δυναμένους καταφαγεῖν καὶ πιεῖν.
ΔΙ. ἡμεῖς δὲ λαικαστάς τε καὶ καταπύγονας.
ΠΡ. ἔτει τετάρτῳ δ' ἐς τὰ βασίλει' ἤλθομεν·   80
ἀλλ' εἰς ἀπόπατον ᾤχετο, στρατιὰν λαβών,
κἄχεζεν ὀκτὼ μῆνας ἐπὶ χρυσῶν ὀρῶν.
ΔΙ. πόσου δὲ τὸν πρωκτὸν χρόνου ξυνήγαγεν;
ΠΡ. τῇ πανσελήνῳ· κᾆτ' ἀπῆλθεν οἴκαδε.
εἶτ' ἐξένιζε· παρετίθει δ' ἡμῖν ὅλους   85
ἐκ κριβάνου βοῦς.
ΔΙ. καὶ τίς εἶδε πώποτε
βοῦς κριβανίτας; τῶν ἀλαζονευμάτων.
ΠΡ. καὶ ναὶ μὰ Δί' ὄρνιν τριπλάσιον Κλεωνύμου
παρέθηκεν ἡμῖν· ὄνομα δ' ἦν αὐτῷ φέναξ.
ΔΙ. ταῦτ' ἄρ' ἐφενάκιζες σύ, δύο δραχμὰς φέρων. 90

---

[a] He calls the Acropolis by this special title (κραναός = "rugged") because it suggests a contrast with the luxury of these envoys.
[b] For these mythical hills cf. Plaut. *Stich.* i. 1, 26 "Persarum | Montes, qui esse Aurei perhibentur." εἰς ἀπόπ., "to the

THE ACHARNIANS, 67-90

DI.   O me, the drachmas!
AMB. And weary work we found it, sauntering on,
Supinely stretched in our luxurious litters
With awnings o'er us, through Caÿstrian
    plains.
'Twas a bad time.
DI.   Aye, the good time was mine,
Stretched in the litter on the ramparts here!
AMB. And oft they fêted us, and we perforce
Out of their gold and crystal cups must drink
The pure sweet wine.
DI.   O Cranaan[a] city, mark you
The insolent airs of these ambassadors?
AMB. For only those are *there* accounted MEN
Who drink the hardest, and who eat the most.
DI. As *here* the most debauched and dissolute.
AMB. In the fourth year we reached the Great
    King's Court.
But he, with all his troops, had gone to sit
An eight-months' session on the Golden
    Hills [b]!
DI. Pray, at what time did he conclude his session?
AMB. At the full moon; and so came home again.
Then he too fêted us, and set before us
Whole pot-baked oxen—
DI.   And who ever heard
Of pot-baked oxen? Out upon your lies!
AMB. And an enormous bird, three times the size
Of our Cleonymus [c]: its name was—Gull.
DI. That's why you gulled us out of all those
    drachmas!

latrines," is substituted παρὰ προσδοκίαν for εἰς πόλεμον or the like.

   [c] See Index: he was very fat and a rascal; in φέναξ there is a play on φοῖνιξ.

13

ARISTOPHANES

ΑΜ. καὶ νῦν ἄγοντες ἥκομεν Ψευδαρτάβαν,
τὸν βασιλέως ὀφθαλμόν.
ΔΙ. ἐκκόψειέ γε
κόραξ πατάξας τόν γε σὸν τοῦ πρέσβεως.
ΚΗΡ. ὁ βασιλέως ὀφθαλμός.
ΔΙ. ὦναξ Ἡράκλεις·
πρὸς τῶν θεῶν, ἄνθρωπε, ναύφρακτον βλέπεις; 95
ἢ περὶ ἄκραν κάμπτων νεώσοικον σκοπεῖς;
ἄσκωμ' ἔχεις που περὶ τὸν ὀφθαλμὸν κάτω;
ΠΡ. ἄγε δὴ σύ, βασιλεὺς ἅττα σ' ἀπέπεμψεν
φράσον
λέξοντ' Ἀθηναίοισιν, ὦ Ψευδαρτάβα.
ΨΕΥΔΑΡΤΑΒΑΣ. ἰαρταμὰν ἔξαρξ' ἀναπισσόναι σάτρα. 100
ΠΡ. ξυνήκαθ' ὃ λέγει;
ΔΙ. μὰ τὸν Ἀπόλλω 'γὼ μὲν οὔ.
ΠΡ. πέμψειν βασιλέα φησὶν ὑμῖν χρυσίον.
λέγε δὴ σὺ μεῖζον καὶ σαφῶς τὸ χρυσίον.
ΨΕΥ. οὐ λῆψι χρῦσο, χαυνόπρωκτ' Ἰαοναῦ.
ΔΙ. οἴμοι κακοδαίμων, ὡς σαφῶς.
ΠΡ. τί δαὶ λέγει; 105
ΔΙ. ὅ τι; χαυνοπρώκτους τοὺς Ἰάονας λέγει,
εἰ προσδοκῶσι χρυσίον ἐκ τῶν βαρβάρων.
ΠΡ. οὔκ, ἀλλ' ἀχάνας ὅδε γε χρυσίου λέγει.
ΔΙ. ποίας ἀχάνας; σὺ μὲν ἀλαζὼν εἶ μέγας.
ἀλλ' ἄπιθ'· ἐγὼ δὲ βασανιῶ τοῦτον μόνον. 110
ἄγε δὴ σὺ φράσον ἐμοὶ σαφῶς, πρὸς τουτονί,

[a] " A fellow who will give you false measure," ἀρτάβη being a Persian measure.
[b] The Scholiast says : ἔξεισι τερατώδης τις γελοίως ἐσκευασμένος, καὶ ὀφθαλμὸν ἔχων ἕνα ἐπὶ παντὸς τοῦ προσώπου.
[c] Because an eye was commonly painted on each side of a ship's bow.
[d] This jumble is generally supposed to mean *I have just begun to repair what is rotten.*

THE ACHARNIANS, 91-111

AMB. And now we bring you Pseudo-Artabas [a]
 The Great King's Eye.[b]
DI. O how I wish some raven
 Would come and strike out yours, the
 Ambassador's.
CRIER. O yes! the Great King's Eye!
DI. O Heracles!
 By Heaven, my man, you wear a war-ship
 look [c]!
 What! Do you round the point, and spy the
 docks?
 Is that an oar-pad underneath your eye?
AMB. Now tell the Athenians, Pseudo-Artabas,
 What the Great King commissioned you to
 say.
PSEUDO-ARTABAS. Ijisti boutti furbiss upde rotti.[d]
AMB. Do you understand?
DI. By Apollo, no not I.
AMB. He says the King is going to send you gold.
 (*To Pseudo.*) Be more distinct and clear about
 the gold.
PSEUD. No getti goldi, nincompoop Iawny.
DI. Wow, but that's clear enough!
AMB. What does he say?
DI. He says the Ionians must be nincompoops
 If they're expecting any gold from Persia.
AMB. No, no: he spoke of golden income-coupons.[e]
DI. What income-coupons? You're a great big
 liar!
 You, get away; I'll test the man myself.
 (*To Pseudo.*)
 Now look at this (*showing his fist*): and answer
 Yes, or No!

[e] ἀχάνη is apparently a large provision-basket.

ARISTOPHANES

ἵνα μή σε βάψω βάμμα Σαρδιανικόν·
βασιλεὺς ὁ μέγας ἡμῖν ἀποπέμψει χρυσίον;
(ἀνανεύει.)
ἄλλως ἄρ' ἐξαπατώμεθ' ὑπὸ τῶν πρέσβεων;
(ἐπινεύει.)
Ἑλληνικόν γ' ἐπένευσαν ἄνδρες οὑτοιί, 115
κοὐκ ἔσθ' ὅπως οὐκ εἰσὶν ἐνθένδ' αὐτόθεν.
καὶ τοῖν μὲν εὐνούχοιν τὸν ἕτερον τουτονὶ
ἐγᾦδ' ὅς ἐστι, Κλεισθένης ὁ Σιβυρτίου.
ὦ θερμόβουλον πρωκτὸν ἐξυρημένε,
τοιόνδε γ', ὦ πίθηκε, τὸν πώγων' ἔχων 120
εὐνοῦχος ἡμῖν ἦλθες ἐσκευασμένος;
ὁδὶ δὲ τίς ποτ' ἐστίν; οὐ δήπου Στράτων.

KHP. σίγα, κάθιζε.
τὸν βασιλέως ὀφθαλμὸν ἡ βουλὴ καλεῖ
εἰς τὸ πρυτανεῖον.

ΔΙ. ταῦτα δῆτ' οὐκ ἀγχόνη; 125
κἄπειτ' ἐγὼ δῆτ' ἐνθαδὶ στρατεύομαι,
τοὺς δὲ ξενίζειν οὐδέποτ' ἴσχει γ' ἡ θύρα.
ἀλλ' ἐργάσομαί τι δεινὸν ἔργον καὶ μέγα.
ἀλλ' Ἀμφίθεός μοι ποῦ 'στιν;

AM. οὑτοσὶ πάρα.

ΔΙ. ἐμοὶ σὺ ταυτασὶ λαβὼν ὀκτὼ δραχμὰς 130
σπονδὰς ποίησαι πρὸς Λακεδαιμονίους μόνῳ
καὶ τοῖσι παιδίοισι καὶ τῇ πλάτιδι·
ὑμεῖς δὲ πρεσβεύεσθε καὶ κεχήνετε.

---

[a] *i.e.* red, the colour of blood ; *cf.* P. 1174.
[b] The two eunuchs in attendance on Pseudo-Artabas.
[c] See Index. D. hurls against the effeminate youth two lines parodied, the first from Euripides, πρωκτόν being substituted for πρᾶγος or the like, the second from Archilochus, who for τὸν πώγων' has τὴν πυγήν.
[d] Another beardless effeminate.

THE ACHARNIANS, 112-133

Or else I'll dye you with a Sardian dye.[a]
Does the Great King intend to send us gold?
(*Pseudo-Artabas nods dissent.*)
Then are our envoys here bamboozling us?
(*He nods assent.*)
These fellows [b] nod in pure Hellenic style;
I do believe they come from hereabouts.
Aye, to be sure; why, one of these two eunuchs
Is Cleisthenes,[c] Sibyrtius's son!
O thou young shaver of the hot-souled rump,
With such a beard, thou monkey, dost thou come
Tricked out amongst us in a eunuch's guise?
And who's this other chap? Not Straton,[d] surely?

CRIER. St! Take your seat! O yes!
The Council ask the Great King's Eye to dinner
At the Town Hall.[e]

DI. Now is not that a throttler?
Here must I drudge at soldiering; while these rogues,
The Town-Hall door is never closed to *them.*
Now then, I'll do a great and startling deed.
Amphitheus! Where's Amphitheus?

AM. Here am I.
DI. Here be eight drachmas; take them; and with all
The Lacedaemonians make a private peace
For me, my wife and children: none besides.
(*To the Prytanes and citizens*)
Stick to your embassies and befoolings, you.

[e] State guests, and other persons worthy of honour, were entertained in the Town Hall daily.

VOL. I   C   17

ARISTOPHANES

ΚΗΡ. προσίτω Θέωρος ὁ παρὰ Σιτάλκους.
ΘΕΩΡΟΣ.   ὁδί.
ΔΙ. ἕτερος ἀλαζὼν οὗτος εἰσκηρύττεται.
ΘΕΩ. χρόνον μὲν οὐκ ἂν ἦμεν ἐν Θράκῃ πολύν,
ΔΙ. μὰ Δί᾽ οὐκ ἄν, εἰ μισθόν γε μὴ ᾽φερες πολύν.
ΘΕΩ. εἰ μὴ κατένιψε χιόνι τὴν Θρᾴκην ὅλην,
καὶ τοὺς ποταμοὺς ἔπηξ᾽ ὑπ᾽ αὐτὸν τὸν χρόνον
ὅτ᾽ ἐνθαδὶ Θέογνις ἠγωνίζετο.
τοῦτον μετὰ Σιτάλκους ἔπινον τὸν χρόνον·
καὶ δῆτα φιλαθήναιος ἦν ὑπερφυῶς,
ὑμῶν τ᾽ ἐραστὴς ἦν ἀληθής, ὥστε καὶ
ἐν τοῖσι τοίχοις ἔγραφ᾽, Ἀθηναῖοι καλοί.
ὁ δ᾽ υἱός, ὃν Ἀθηναῖον ἐπεποιήμεθα,
ἤρα φαγεῖν ἀλλᾶντας ἐξ Ἀπατουρίων,
καὶ τὸν πατέρ᾽ ἠντιβόλει βοηθεῖν τῇ πάτρᾳ·
ὁ δ᾽ ὤμοσε σπένδων βοηθήσειν, ἔχων
στρατιὰν τοσαύτην ὥστ᾽ Ἀθηναίους ἐρεῖν,
ὅσον τὸ χρῆμα παρνόπων προσέρχεται.
ΔΙ. κάκιστ᾽ ἀπολοίμην, εἴ τι τούτων πείθομαι
ὧν εἶπας ἐνταυθοῖ σύ, πλὴν τῶν παρνόπων.
ΘΕΩ. καὶ νῦν ὅπερ μαχιμώτατον Θρακῶν ἔθνος
ἔπεμψεν ὑμῖν.
ΔΙ.   τοῦτο μέντ᾽ ἤδη σαφές.
ΚΗΡ. οἱ Θρᾷκες ἴτε δεῦρ᾽, οὓς Θέωρος ἤγαγεν.
ΔΙ. τουτὶ τί ἐστι τὸ κακόν;
ΘΕΩ.   Ὀδομάντων στρατός.

---

[a] King of the Odrysians in Thrace. Theorus had gone on an embassy to them.
[b] So frigid a poet that he was nicknamed Χιών; cf. 11; T. 170.
[c] In the first year of the war Athens entered into alliance with Sitalces and made his son Σάδοκος a citizen (Thuc. ii.

THE ACHARNIANS, 134-156

CRIER. O yes! Theorus from Sitalces [a]!
THEORUS. Here!
DI. O here's another humbug introduced.
THE. We should not, sirs, have tarried long in Thrace—
DI. But for the salary you kept on drawing.
THE. But for the storms, which covered Thrace with snow
And froze the rivers. 'Twas about the season
At which Theognis [b] was performing here.
I all that time was drinking with Sitalces;
A most prodigious Athens-lover he,
Yea such a true admirer, he would scribble
On every wall *My beautiful Athenians* !
His son,[c] our newly-made Athenian, longed
To taste his Apaturian sausages,
And bade his father help his fatherland.
And *he*, with deep libations, vowed to help us
With such an host that every one would say
Heavens! what a swarm of locusts comes this way !
DI. Hang me, if I believe a single word
Of all that speech, except about the locusts.[d]
THE. And here he sends you the most warlike tribe
Of all in Thrace.
DI. Come, here's proof positive.
CRIER. The Thracians whom Theorus brought, come forward!
DI. What the plague's this?
THE. The Odomantian host.[e]

27). The Apaturia was a family or clan festival, to which only those enrolled in a phratry (φρατρία) could be admitted.
  [d] D. fears that they will eat up their allies no less than their foes.
  [e] A Thracian tribe on the Strymon.

ARISTOPHANES

ΔΙ. ποίων Ὀδομάντων; εἰπέ μοι, τουτὶ τί ἦν;
τίς τῶν Ὀδομάντων τὸ πέος ἀποτεθρίακεν;
ΘΕΩ. τούτοις ἐάν τις δύο δραχμὰς μισθὸν διδῷ,
καταπελτάσονται τὴν Βοιωτίαν ὅλην. 160
ΔΙ. τοισδὶ δύο δραχμὰς τοῖς ἀπεψωλημένοις;
ὑποστένοι μέντἂν ὁ θρανίτης λεώς,
ὁ σωσίπολις. οἴμοι τάλας, ἀπόλλυμαι,
ὑπὸ τῶν Ὀδομάντων τὰ σκόροδα πορθούμενος.
οὐ καταβαλεῖτε τὰ σκόροδ';
ΘΕΩ. ὦ μόχθηρε σύ, 165
οὐ μὴ πρόσει τούτοισιν ἐσκοροδισμένοις;
ΔΙ. ταυτὶ περιείδεθ' οἱ πρυτάνεις πάσχοντά με
ἐν τῇ πατρίδι καὶ ταῦθ' ὑπ' ἀνδρῶν βαρβάρων;
ἀλλ' ἀπαγορεύω μὴ ποιεῖν ἐκκλησίαν
τοῖς Θραξὶ περὶ μισθοῦ· λέγω δ' ὑμῖν ὅτι 170
διοσημία 'στὶ καὶ ῥανὶς βέβληκέ με.
ΚΗΡ. τοὺς Θρᾷκας ἀπιέναι, παρεῖναι δ' εἰς ἔνην.
οἱ γὰρ πρυτάνεις λύουσι τὴν ἐκκλησίαν.

ΔΙ. οἴμοι τάλας, μυττωτὸν ὅσον ἀπώλεσα.
ἀλλ' ἐκ Λακεδαίμονος γὰρ Ἀμφίθεος ὁδί. 175
χαῖρ', Ἀμφίθεε.
ΑΜ. μήπω, πρὶν ἄν γε στῶ τρέχων·
δεῖ γάρ με φεύγοντ' ἐκφυγεῖν Ἀχαρνέας.
ΔΙ. τί δ' ἔστιν;
ΑΜ. ἐγὼ μὲν δεῦρό σοι σπονδὰς φέρων
ἔσπευδον· οἱ δ' ὤσφροντο πρεσβῦταί τινες

---

^a The little round πέλτη (*targe*) was distinctly Thracian.
^b The ordinary pay of a rower was *one* drachma a day. The θρανῖται who sat on the highest bench and worked the longest oars would be picked men.
^c Like cocks which were supposed to fight better when primed with garlic; *cf. K.* 494.

THE ACHARNIANS, 157-179

DI. The Odomantians, pho! Hallo, look here.
Are Odomantians all equipped like this?
THE. Give them two drachmas each a day, and these
Will targeteer ^{a} Boeotia all to bits.
DI. Two drachmas ^{b} for THESE scarecrows! Oh,
   our tars,
Our noble tars, the safeguard of our state,
Well may they groan at this. O! Murder! O!
These Odomantian thieves have sacked my
   garlic.
Put down the garlic! drop it!
THE. You rapscallion,
How dare you touch them, when they're
   garlic-primed.^{c}
DI. O will you let them, Prytanes, use me thus,
Barbarians too, in this my fatherland?
But stop! I warn you not to hold the
   Assembly
About the Thracians' pay. I tell you there's
A portent ^{d} come; I felt a drop of rain!
CRIER. The Thracians are to go, and two days hence
Come here again. The Assembly is dissolved.
DI. O me, the salad I have lost this day!^{e}
But here's Amphitheus, back from Lace-
   daemon.
Well met, Amphitheus!
AM. Not till I've done running.
I needs must flee the Acharnians, clean away.
DI. What mean you?
AM. I was bringing back in haste
The treaties, when some veterans smelt them
   out,

^{d} Lit. "A sign from Zeus."
^{e} The loss of the garlic had ruined it.

ARISTOPHANES

Ἀχαρνικοί, στιπτοὶ γέροντες, πρίνινοι, 180
ἀτεράμονες, Μαραθωνομάχαι, σφενδάμνινοι.
ἔπειτ᾽ ἀνέκραγον πάντες, " ὦ μιαρώτατε,
σπονδὰς φέρεις, τῶν ἀμπελίων τετμημένων; "
κἆς τοὺς τρίβωνας ξυνελέγοντο τῶν λίθων·
ἐγὼ δ᾽ ἔφευγον· οἱ δ᾽ ἐδίωκον κἀβόων. 185
ΔΙ. οἱ δ᾽ οὖν βοώντων· ἀλλὰ τὰς σπονδὰς φέρεις;
ΑΜ. ἔγωγέ φημι, τρία γε ταυτὶ γεύματα.
αὗται μέν εἰσι πεντέτεις. γεῦσαι λαβών.
ΔΙ. αἰβοῖ.
ΑΜ. τί ἔστιν;
ΔΙ. οὐκ ἀρέσκουσίν μ᾽, ὅτι
ὄζουσι πίττης καὶ παρασκευῆς νεῶν. 190
ΑΜ. σὺ δ᾽ ἀλλὰ τασδὶ τὰς δεκέτεις γεῦσαι λαβών.
ΔΙ. ὄζουσι χαὗται πρέσβεων ἐς τὰς πόλεις
ὀξύτατον, ὥσπερ διατριβῆς τῶν ξυμμάχων.
ΑΜ. ἀλλ᾽ αὑταιὶ σπονδαὶ τριακοντούτιδες
κατὰ γῆν τε καὶ θάλατταν.
ΔΙ. ὦ Διονύσια, 195
αὗται μὲν ὄζουσ᾽ ἀμβροσίας καὶ νέκταρος,
καὶ μὴ 'πιτηρεῖν Σιτί' ἡμερῶν τριῶν,
κἂν τῷ στόματι λέγουσι, Βαῖν᾽ ὅπῃ θέλεις.
ταύτας δέχομαι καὶ σπένδομαι κἀκπίομαι,
χαίρειν κελεύων πολλὰ τοὺς Ἀχαρνέας· 200
ἐγὼ δὲ πολέμου καὶ κακῶν ἀπαλλαγεὶς
ἄξω τὰ κατ᾽ ἀγροὺς εἰσιὼν Διονύσια.

---

[a] Acharnae is a short distance to the S. of Mt. Parnes, and its inhabitants mainly occupied themselves with the manufacture of charcoal from its forests of evergreen oak (πρῖνος), maple (σφένδαμνος), and other trees. Archidamus in his first invasion of Attica (431 B.C.) made it his headquarters when ravaging the district; cf. Thuc. ii. 19-23.

THE ACHARNIANS, 180–202

    Acharnians, men of Marathon, hard in grain
As their own oak and maple,*a* rough and tough;
And all at once they cried, *O villain, dare you
Bring treaties when our vineyards are cut down?*
Then in their lappets up they gathered stones;
I fled away: they followed roaring after.
DI. So let them roar. But have you got the treaties?
AM. O yes, I have. Three samples; here they are.
    These are the *five-year* treaties; take and taste*b*
    them.
DI. Pheugh!
AM.   What's the matter?
DI.   I don't like the things,
    They smell of tar and naval preparations.
AM. Then taste the *ten-year* samples; here they are.
DI. These smell of embassies to all the states,
    Urgent, as if the Allies are hanging back.
AM. Then here are treaties both by land and sea
    For *thirty* years.
DI.   O Feast of Dionysus!
    These have a smell of nectar and ambrosia,
And *never mind about the three days' rations*,*c*
And in your mouth they say, *Go where you please.*
These do I welcome, these I pour, and drain,
Nor care a hang about your old Acharnians.
But I, released from War and War's alarms,
Will hold, within, the Rural Dionysia.*d*

  b As if they were samples of wine for σπονδαί = not only "a treaty," but also "libations of wine"; hence the reference to the "smell of pitch" in 190 and "of vinegar" 193.
  c *Cf. P.* 312.
  d Otherwise known as τὰ μικρά as opposed to τὰ μέγαλα, τὰ ἐν ἄστει, and celebrated all over Attica in December.

ARISTOPHANES

ΑΜ. ἐγὼ δὲ φευξοῦμαί γε τοὺς Ἀχαρνέας.

ΧΟΡΟΣ. τῇδε πᾶς ἕπου, δίωκε, καὶ τὸν ἄνδρα
πυνθάνου
τῶν ὁδοιπόρων ἁπάντων· τῇ πόλει γὰρ ἄξιον 205
ξυλλαβεῖν τὸν ἄνδρα τοῦτον. ἀλλά μοι μηνύ-
σατε,
εἴ τις οἶδ᾽ ὅποι τέτραπται γῆς ὁ τὰς σπονδὰς
φέρων.

ἐκπέφευγ᾽, οἴχεται φροῦδος. οἴμοι τάλας τῶν
ἐτῶν τῶν ἐμῶν· [στρ. 210
οὐκ ἂν ἐπ᾽ ἐμῆς γε νεότητος, ὅτ᾽ ἐγὼ φέρων
ἀνθράκων φορτίον
ἠκολούθουν Φαΰλλῳ τρέχων, ὧδε φαύλως ἂν ὁ 215
σπονδοφόρος οὗτος ὑπ᾽ ἐμοῦ τότε διωκόμενος
ἐξέφυγεν οὐδ᾽ ἂν ἐλαφρῶς ἂν ἀπεπλίξατο.

νῦν δ᾽ ἐπειδὴ στερρὸν ἤδη τοὐμὸν ἀντικνήμιον
καὶ παλαιῷ Λακρατείδῃ τὸ σκέλος βαρύνεται, 220
οἴχεται. διωκτέος δέ· μὴ γὰρ ἐγχάνῃ ποτὲ
μηδέ περ γέροντας ὄντας ἐκφυγὼν Ἀχαρνέας.

ὅστις, ὦ Ζεῦ πάτερ καὶ θεοί, τοῖσιν ἐχθροῖσιν
ἐσπείσατο, [ἀντ. 225

---

[a] *Enter, running in pursuit of Amphitheus, twenty-four old Acharnians who constitute the Chorus.*

[b] A celebrated Olympic victor; the adverb φαύλως is a play on his name.

THE ACHARNIANS, 203–225

AM. And I will flee those peppery old Acharnians.
CHORUS.[a] Here's the trail ; pursue, pursue him ;
        follow, follow, every man ;
  Question whosoever meets you
        whitherwards the fellow ran.
Much it boots the state to catch him !
  (*To the audience*) O inform me, if ye know,
Where the man who bears the treaties
        managed from my sight to go.

Fled and gone !   Disappears !
        O this weary weight of years !
O were I   Now as spry
        As in youthful days gone by,
When I stuck   Like a man
        To Phaÿllus [b] as he ran,
And achieved   Second place   In the race,
Though a great   Charcoal freight
        I was bearing on my head,—
Not so light   From my sight
        Had this treaty-bearer fled,
Nor escaped   With such ease   From the chase.

Now because my joints have stiffened,
        and my shins are young no more,
And the legs of Lacrateides
        by old age are burdened sore,
He's escaped us !   But we'll follow :
        but he shall not boast that he
Got away from us Acharnians,
        howsoever old we be.

Who has dared   Father Zeus !
        Gods of heaven ! to make a truce,

ARISTOPHANES

οἶσι παρ' ἐμοῦ πόλεμος ἐχθοδοπὸς αὔξεται
τῶν ἐμῶν χωρίων·
κοὐκ ἀνήσω πρὶν ἂν σχοῖνος αὐτοῖσιν ἀντεμ-
παγῶ   230
ὀξύς, ὀδυνηρός, * * * * ἐπίκωπος, ἵνα
μήποτε πατῶσιν ἔτι τὰς ἐμὰς ἀμπέλους.
ἀλλὰ δεῖ ζητεῖν τὸν ἄνδρα καὶ βλέπειν
Βαλλήναδε
καὶ διώκειν γῆν πρὸ γῆς, ἕως ἂν εὑρεθῇ ποτέ· 235
ὡς ἐγὼ βάλλων ἐκεῖνον οὐκ ἂν ἐμπλήμην
λίθοις.
ΔΙ. εὐφημεῖτε, εὐφημεῖτε.
ΧΟ. σῖγα πᾶς. ἠκούσατ', ἄνδρες, ἆρα τῆς εὐ-
φημίας;
οὗτος αὐτός ἐστιν ὃν ζητοῦμεν. ἀλλὰ δεῦρο
πᾶς
ἐκποδών· θύσων γὰρ ἀνήρ, ὡς ἔοικ', ἐξ- 240
έρχεται.

ΔΙ. εὐφημεῖτε, εὐφημεῖτε.
πρόϊτω 's τὸ πρόσθεν ὀλίγον ἡ κανηφόρος·
ὁ Ξανθίας τὸν φαλλὸν ὀρθὸν στησάτω.
ΜΗΤΗΡ. κατάθου τὸ κανοῦν, ὦ θύγατερ, ἵν' ἀπ-
αρξώμεθα.
ΘΥΓΑΤΗΡ. ὦ μῆτερ, ἀνάδος δεῦρο τὴν ἐτνήρυσιν, 245
ἵν' ἔτνος καταχέω τοὐλατῆρος τουτουί.

---

[a] σχοῖνος = *Schoenus mucronatus*, the *Dagger-pointed Bulrush*, common on all the coasts of the Mediterranean. The spike is supposed to run well up (ἐπίκωπος="up to the hilt") into the heels of the Lacedaemonians as they trample down the vines.
[b] There is a play on Pallene, or Pellene, a famous Attic deme.

THE ACHARNIANS, 226-246

    Who has pledged   Faith with those
                    Who are evermore my foes ;
Upon whom   War I make
              For my ruined vineyard's sake ;
And I ne'er From the strife Will give o'er,
No, I ne'er   Will forbear,
            Till I pierce them in return,
Like a reed,[a]   Sharply barbed
           Dagger-pointed, and they learn
Not to tread   Down my vines   Any more.
Now 'tis ours to seek the fellow,
            and Pelténe-wards [b] to look,
And from land to land to chase him,
            till we bring the rogue to book.
Never shall I tire of pelting,
            pelting him to death with stones.
DI. (*Within*) Keep ye all the holy silence !
CHOR. Hush ! we've got him. Heard ye, comrades,
    " silence " called in solemn tones ?
This is he, the man we're seeking.
            Stand aside, and in a trice
He, methinks, will stand before us,
            coming out to sacrifice !

DI. (*Coming out*) Keep ye all the holy silence !
Now, basket-bearer, go you on in front,[c]
You, Xanthias, hold the phallus-pole erect.
WIFE. Set down the basket, girl : and we'll begin.
DAUGHTER. O mother, hand me here the gravy-spoon,
    To ladle out the gravy o'er the cake.

   [c] Dic. celebrates the Rural Dionysia on a small scale with his daughter (who acts as κανηφόρος) and two slaves, while his wife represents the spectators.

ARISTOPHANES

ΔΙ. καὶ μὴν καλόν γ' ἔστ'. ὦ Διόνυσε δέσποτα,
κεχαρισμένως σοι τήνδε τὴν πομπὴν ἐμὲ
πέμψαντα καὶ θύσαντα μετὰ τῶν οἰκετῶν
ἀγαγεῖν τυχηρῶς τὰ κατ' ἀγροὺς Διονύσια, 250
στρατιᾶς ἀπαλλαχθέντα· τὰς σπονδὰς δέ μοι
καλῶς ξυνενεγκεῖν τὰς τριακοντούτιδας.
ΜΗ. ἄγ', ὦ θύγατερ, ὅπως τὸ κανοῦν καλὴ καλῶς
οἴσεις, βλέπουσα θυμβροφάγον. ὡς μακάριος
ὅστις σ' ὀπύσει, κἀκποιήσεται γαλᾶς 255
σοῦ μηδὲν ἥττους βδεῖν, ἐπειδὰν ὄρθρος ᾖ.
πρόβαινε, κἀν τὤχλῳ φυλάττεσθαι σφόδρα
μή τις λαθών σου περιτράγῃ τὰ χρυσία.
ΔΙ. ὦ Ξανθία, σφῷν δ' ἐστὶν ὀρθὸς ἑκτέος
ὁ φαλλὸς ἐξόπισθε τῆς κανηφόρου· 260
ἐγὼ δ' ἀκολουθῶν ἄσομαι τὸ φαλλικόν·
σὺ δ', ὦ γύναι, θεῶ μ' ἀπὸ τοῦ τέγους. πρόβα.

Φαλῆς, ἑταῖρε Βακχίου,
ξύγκωμε, νυκτοπεριπλάνη-
τε, μοιχέ, παιδεραστά, 265
ἕκτῳ σ' ἔτει προσεῖπον ἐς
τὸν δῆμον ἐλθὼν ἄσμενος,
σπονδὰς ποιησάμενος ἐμαυ-
τῷ, πραγμάτων τε καὶ μαχῶν
καὶ Λαμάχων ἀπαλλαγείς. 270

πολλῷ γάρ ἐσθ' ἥδιον, ὦ
Φαλῆς, Φαλῆς, κλέπτουσαν εὑ-
ρόνθ' ὡρικὴν ὑληφόρον
τὴν Στρυμοδώρου Θρᾷτταν ἐκ

---
[a] θυμβροφάγον : demure, δριμύ.—Photius.
[b] She would wear her best ornaments; cf. L. 1189 seq.

THE ACHARNIANS, 247-274

DI. 'Tis well. Lord Dionysus, grant me now
To show the show and make the sacrifice
As thou would'st have me, I and all my house ;
Then keep with joy the Rural Dionysia ;
No more of soldiering now. And may this Peace
Of thirty summers answer to my hopes.

WIFE. O daughter, bear the basket sweetly, sweet,
With savory-eating [a] look. Happy the man,
Whoe'er he is, who weds thee and begets
Kittens as fair and saucy as thyself.
Move on ! but heed lest any in the crowd
Should nibble off, unseen, thy bits of gold.[b]

DI. O Xanthias, walk behind the basket-bearer,
Holding, you two, the phallus-pole erect.
And I'll bring up the rear, and sing the hymn :
Wife, watch me from the roof. Now then, proceed.

(*Singing*) O Phales,[c] comrade revel-roaming
Of Bacchus, wanderer of the gloaming,
Of wives and boys the naugthy lover,
Here in my home I gladly greet ye,
Six weary years of absence over ;
For I have made a private treaty
And said good-bye to toils and fusses,
And fights, and fighting Lamachuses.[d]

Far happier 'tis to me and sweeter,
O Phales, Phales, some soft glade in,
To woo the saucy, arch, deceiving,
Young Thratta (Strymodore his maiden),

[c] Phales is the φαλλός personified.
[d] For Lamachus see Index ; his very name suggests fighting.

ARISTOPHANES

τοῦ φελλέως, μέσην λαβόντ',
ἄραντα, καταβαλόντα, κατα- 275
γιγαρτίσ' ὦ Φαλῆς, Φαλῆς.
ἐὰν μεθ' ἡμῶν ξυμπίῃς,
ἐκ κραιπάλης ἕωθεν εἰ-
ρήνης ῥοφήσεις τρύβλιον.
ἡ δ' ἀσπὶς ἐν τῷ φεψάλῳ κρεμήσεται.

ΧΟ. οὗτος αὐτός ἐστιν, οὗτος. 280
βάλλε βάλλε βάλλε βάλλε,
παῖε πᾶς τὸν μιαρόν.
οὐ βαλεῖς, οὐ βαλεῖς;
ΔΙ. Ἡράκλεις, τουτὶ τί ἐστι; τὴν χύτραν συν-
τρίψετε. [στρ.
ΧΟ. σὲ μὲν οὖν καταλεύσομεν, ὦ μιαρὰ κεφαλή. 285
ΔΙ. ἀντὶ ποίας αἰτίας, ὠχαρνέων γεραίτατοι;
ΧΟ. τοῦτ' ἐρωτᾷς; ἀναίσχυντος εἶ καὶ βδελυρός,
ὦ προδότα τῆς πατρίδος, ὅστις ἡμῶν μόνος 290
σπεισάμενος εἶτα δύνασαι πρὸς ἔμ' ἀπο-
βλέπειν.
ΔΙ. ἀντὶ δ' ὧν ἐσπεισάμην οὐκ ἴστε γ'· ἀλλ'
ἀκούσατε.
ΧΟ. σοῦ γ' ἀκούσωμεν, ἀπολεῖ· κατά σε χώσομεν
τοῖς λίθοις. 295
ΔΙ. μηδαμῶς, πρὶν ἄν γ' ἀκούσητ'· ἀλλ' ἀνά-
σχεσθ', ὦγαθοί.
ΧΟ. οὐκ ἀνασχήσομαι· μηδὲ λέγε μοι σὺ λόγον·

[a] Lit. "after the night's debauch."

THE ACHARNIANS, 274-299

   As from my woodland fells I meet her
   Descending with my fagots laden,
   And catch her up, and ill entreat her,
   And make her pay the fine for thieving.

   O Phales, Phales, come and sup,
   And in the morn, to brace you up,[a]
   Of Peace you'll quaff a jovial cup;
  And mid the chimney sparks our useless shield
   we'll hang.

CHOR.   That's the man who made the treaty;
    There he stands Full in view;
   Pelt him, pelt him, pelt him, pelt him,
    Pelt him you! Pelt him you!
DI. Heracles! what ails the fellows?
    Hang it all, ye'll smash the pot!
CHOR. It is *you* we will smash with our
    stones, you detestable head.
DI. O most worshipful Acharnians,
    why? what reason have ye got?
CHOR. Dare you ask? Traitor base!
    Dare you look me in the face?
 You who make, You alone,
    Private treaties of your own!
 Shameless heart! Shameless hand!
    Traitor to your fatherland!
DI. But ye know not why I did it:
    hear me now the facts declare.
CHOR. Hear you? No! You're to die;
    'Neath a stony cairn to lie!
DI. Not, O not until ye've heard me;
    worthy sirs, forbear, forbear!
CHOR. No delay! Thee to slay
    We'll immediately begin.

ARISTOPHANES

ὡς μεμίσηκά σε Κλέωνος ἔτι μᾶλλον, ὃν ἐ- 300
γὼ τεμῶ τοῖσιν ἱππεῦσι καττύματα.
σοῦ δ' ἐγὼ λόγους λέγοντος οὐκ ἀκούσομαι
μακρούς,
ὅστις ἐσπείσω Λάκωσιν, ἀλλὰ τιμωρήσομαι.

ΔΙ. ὠγαθοί, τοὺς μὲν Λάκωνας ἐκποδὼν ἐάσατε, 305
τῶν δ' ἐμῶν σπονδῶν ἀκούσατ', εἰ καλῶς
ἐσπεισάμην.

ΧΟ. πῶς δέ γ' ἂν καλῶς λέγοις ἄν, εἴπερ ἐσπείσω
γ' ἅπαξ
οἷσιν οὔτε βωμὸς οὔτε πίστις οὔθ' ὅρκος μένει;

ΔΙ. οἶδ' ἐγὼ καὶ τοὺς Λάκωνας, οἷς ἄγαν ἐγκεί-
μεθα,
οὐχ ἁπάντων ὄντας ἡμῖν αἰτίους τῶν πραγμάτων. 310

ΧΟ. οὐχ ἁπάντων, ὦ πανοῦργε; ταῦτα δὴ τολμᾷς
λέγειν
ἐμφανῶς ἤδη πρὸς ἡμᾶς; εἶτ' ἐγὼ σοῦ
φείσομαι;

ΔΙ. οὐχ ἁπάντων, οὐχ ἁπάντων· ἀλλ' ἐγὼ λέγων
ὁδὶ
πόλλ' ἂν ἀποφήναιμ' ἐκείνους ἔσθ' ἃ κἀδι-
κουμένους.

ΧΟ. τοῦτο τοὔπος δεινὸν ἤδη καὶ ταραξικάρδιον, 315
εἰ σὺ τολμήσεις ὑπὲρ τῶν πολεμίων ἡμῖν
λέγειν.

ΔΙ. κἄν γε μὴ λέγω δίκαια, μηδὲ τῷ πλήθει δοκῶ,

---

[a] For Cleon see Index; the Knights were his special enemies, and καττύματα refers to his trade as a tanner.

THE ACHARNIANS, 300-317

No debate! Thee we hate
    Worse than Cleon's *a* self, whose skin
I'll ere long Cut to shoes
    For the worthy Knights to use.
But from *you*, who made a treaty
    with the false Laconian crew,
I will hear no long orations,
    I will surely punish you.

DI. Worthy fellows, for the moment
    those Laconians pretermit;
'Tis a question of my treaty,
    was I right in making it.

CHOR. Right to make it! when with Sparta
    no engagement sacred stands,
Not the altar, not the oath-pledge,
    not the faith of clasped right hands!

DI. Yet I know that these our foemen,
    who our bitter wrath excite,
Were not always wrong entirely,
    nor ourselves entirely right.

CHOR. Not entirely, shameless rascal?
    Do you such opinions dare
Openly to flaunt before me?
    Shall I then a traitor spare?

DI. Not entirely, not entirely!
    I can prove by reasons strong
That in many points the Spartans
    at our hands have suffered wrong.

CHOR. This is quite a heart-perplexing,
    terrible affair indeed,
If you mean that you will venture
    for our enemies to plead.

DI. Aye, and if I plead not truly,
    or the people doubt display,

ARISTOPHANES

ὑπὲρ ἐπιξήνου 'θελήσω τὴν κεφαλὴν ἔχων λέγειν.
ΧΟ. εἰπέ μοι, τί φειδόμεσθα τῶν λίθων, ὦ δημόται,
μὴ οὐ καταξαίνειν τὸν ἄνδρα τοῦτον ἐς φοινικίδα; 320
ΔΙ. οἷον αὖ μέλας τις ὑμῖν θυμάλωψ ἐπέζεσεν.
οὐκ ἀκούσεσθ', οὐκ ἀκούσεσθ' ἐτεόν, ὦχαρνηίδαι;
ΧΟ. οὐκ ἀκουσόμεσθα δῆτα.
ΔΙ. δεινά τἄρα πείσομαι.
ΧΟ. ἐξολοίμην, ἢν ἀκούσω.
ΔΙ. μηδαμῶς, ὦχαρνικοί.
ΧΟ. ὡς τεθνήξων ἴσθι νυνί.
ΔΙ. δήξομἄρ' ὑμᾶς ἐγώ. 325
ἀνταποκτενῶ γὰρ ὑμῶν τῶν φίλων τοὺς φιλτάτους·
ὡς ἔχω γ' ὑμῶν ὁμήρους, οὓς ἀποσφάξω λαβών.
ΧΟ. εἰπέ μοι, τί τοῦτ' ἀπειλεῖ τοὔπος, ἄνδρες δημόται,
τοῖς Ἀχαρνικοῖσιν ἡμῖν; μῶν ἔχει του παιδίον
τῶν παρόντων ἔνδον εἴρξας; ἢ 'πὶ τῷ θρασύνεται; 330
ΔΙ. βάλλετ', εἰ βούλεσθ'. ἐγὼ γὰρ τουτονὶ διαφθερῶ.
εἴσομαι δ' ὑμῶν τάχ' ὅστις ἀνθράκων τι κήδεται.
ΧΟ. ὡς ἀπωλόμεσθ'. ὁ λάρκος δημότης ὅδ' ἔστ' ἐμός.

---

[a] Dic. goes into the house and returns three lines later carrying in one hand a hamper (λάρκος) full of charcoal and in the other a drawn sword. The Scholiast says that the ensuing scene is parodied from the Telephus of Euripides.

THE ACHARNIANS, 318-333

   On a chopping-block I'm willing,
     whilst I speak, my head to lay.
CHOR. Why so slack, my fellow-burghers?
     Let us stone the naughty varlet,
   Let us scarify and shred him
     to an uniform of scarlet.
DI. What a red and dangerous ember
     sparkled up within you then!
   Won't you hear me, won't you hear me,
     good Acharnians, worthy men?
CHOR. Never, never, will we hear you.
DI.   That will cause me bitter woe.
CHOR. If I do, perdition seize me!
DI.   O Acharnians, say not so.
CHOR. Know that you must die this instant.
DI.   Then I'll make you suffer too.
   For my safety I've a hostage,
     one that's very dear to you.
   Now I'll bring him out and slay him;
     you shall see your darling's end.[a]
CHOR. O Acharnian fellow-burghers,
     what can words like these portend
   To our noble band of brethren?
     Think you that the man can hold
   Any child of ours in durance?
     What can make him wax so bold?
DI. Now then pelt me; here's the hostage!
     I will slay and will not spare.
   I shall speedily discover
     which of you for charcoal care.
CHOR. Heaven preserve us! 'tis a scuttle,
     'tis my fellow-burgher true!

ARISTOPHANES

ἀλλὰ μὴ δράσῃς ὃ μέλλεις. μηδαμῶς, ὦ
μηδαμῶς.
ΔΙ. ὡς ἀποκτενῶ, κέκραχθ'· ἐγὼ γὰρ οὐκ ἀκούσομαι. [ἀντ. 335
ΧΟ. ἀπολεῖς ἄρ' ὁμήλικα τόνδε φιλανθρακέα;
ΔΙ. οὐδ' ἐμοῦ λέγοντος ὑμεῖς ἀρτίως ἠκούσατε.
ΧΟ. ἀλλὰ νυνὶ λέγ', εἴ σοι δοκεῖ, τόν τε Λακε-
δαιμόνιον αὐτὸν ὅτι τῷ τρόπῳ σου 'στὶ φίλος·
ὡς τόδε τὸ λαρκίδιον οὐ προδώσω ποτέ. 340
ΔΙ. τοὺς λίθους νῦν μοι χαμᾶζε πρῶτον ἐξεράσατε.
ΧΟ. οὑτοιί σοι χαμαί, καὶ σὺ κατάθου πάλιν τὸ
ξίφος.
ΔΙ. ἀλλ' ὅπως μὴ 'ν τοῖς τρίβωσιν ἐγκάθηνταί
που λίθοι.
ΧΟ. ἐκσέσεισται χαμᾶζ'. οὐχ ὁρᾷς σειόμενον;
ἀλλὰ μή μοι πρόφασιν, ἀλλὰ κατάθου τὸ
βέλος. 345
ὡς ὅδε γε σειστὸς ἅμα τῇ στροφῇ γίγνεται.
ΔΙ. ἐμέλλετ' ἄρ' ἅπαντες ἀνασείειν βοήν,
ὀλίγου τ' ἀπέθανον ἄνθρακες Παρνήσιοι,
καὶ ταῦτα διὰ τὴν ἀτοπίαν τῶν δημοτῶν.
ὑπὸ τοῦ δέους δὲ τῆς μαρίλης μοι συχνὴν 350
ὁ λάρκος ἐνετίλησεν ὥσπερ σηπία.
δεινὸν γὰρ οὕτως ὀμφακίαν πεφυκέναι
τὸν θυμὸν ἀνδρῶν ὥστε βάλλειν καὶ βοᾶν

---
[a] *i.e.* himself.
[b] *i.e.* provided you release the λάρκος.
[c] Dic. employs the peculiar word ἀνασείειν because the preceding speech of the Chorus is full of " shakes."
[d] μαρίλη is the *black dust* of the charcoal.

THE ACHARNIANS, 334-353

          Never do the thing you mention :
                    never do, O never do !
DI.   Cry aloud ! I'm going to slay him ;
              I shall neither hear nor heed.
CHOR. You will slay then this charcoal-adorer,[a]
                    its equal in years !
DI.   Aye, for when I craved a hearing
              you refused to hear me plead.
CHOR. Ah ! but now ! Now you may !
                Whatsoever suits you say.
      Say you love, Say you prize,
                Our detested enemies.[b]
    Ne'er will I Faithless prove
              To the scuttle which I love.
DI.   Well then first, the stones you gathered,
             throw them out upon the ground.
CHOR. Out they go ! All my hoard !
              Prithee, lay aside the sword.
DI.   But I fear that in your lappets
              other missiles may be found.
CHOR. All are gone ! Every one !
              See my garment shaken wide !
    Don't evade Promise made.
            Lay, O lay the sword aside.
    Here's my robe Shaken out,
            As I twist and twirl about.
DI.   You would then, would you, shake [c] your
      cries aloft,
      And this Parnesian charcoal all but died,
      Slain by the madness of its fellow-burghers.
      And in its fright this scuttle, cuttle-wise,
      Voided its inky blackness [d] on my clothes.
      Alas that men should carry hearts as sour
      As unripe grapes, to pelt and roar, nor hear

ARISTOPHANES

ἐθέλειν τ' ἀκοῦσαι μηδὲν ἴσον ἴσῳ φέρον,
ἐμοῦ θέλοντος ὑπὲρ ἐπιξήνου λέγειν 355
ὑπὲρ Λακεδαιμονίων ἅπανθ' ὅσ' ἂν λέγω·
καίτοι φιλῶ γε τὴν ἐμὴν ψυχὴν ἐγώ.

ΧΟ. τί οὖν οὐ λέγεις, ἐπίξηνον ἐξενεγκὼν θύραζ', [στρ
ὅ τι ποτ', ὦ σχέτλιε, τὸ μέγα τοῦτ' ἔχεις; 360
πάνυ γὰρ ἐμέ γε πόθος ὅ τι φρονεῖς ἔχει.
ἀλλ' ἧπερ αὐτὸς τὴν δίκην διωρίσω,
θεὶς δεῦρο τοὐπίξηνον ἐγχείρει λέγειν. 365

ΔΙ. ἰδοὺ θεᾶσθε, τὸ μὲν ἐπίξηνον τοδί,
ὁ δ' ἀνὴρ ὁ λέξων οὑτοσὶ τυννουτοσί.
ἀμέλει μὰ τὸν Δί' οὐκ ἐνασπιδώσομαι,
λέξω δ' ὑπὲρ Λακεδαιμονίων ἅ μοι δοκεῖ.
καίτοι δέδοικα πολλά· τούς τε γὰρ τρόπους 370
τοὺς τῶν ἀγροίκων οἶδα χαίροντας σφόδρα
ἐάν τις αὐτοὺς εὐλογῇ καὶ τὴν πόλιν
ἀνὴρ ἀλαζὼν καὶ δίκαια κἄδικα·
κἀνταῦθα λανθάνουσ' ἀπεμπολώμενοι·
τῶν τ' αὖ γερόντων οἶδα τὰς ψυχὰς ὅτι 375
οὐδὲν βλέπουσιν ἄλλο πλὴν ψήφῳ δακεῖν·
αὐτός τ' ἐμαυτὸν ὑπὸ Κλέωνος ἄπαθον
ἐπίσταμαι διὰ τὴν πέρυσι κωμῳδίαν.

---

^a A metaphor from wine mingled with an equal quantity of water.

^b i.e. I will come out into the open, not skulk behind a shield; cf. Hom. Il. 267 seq., where the archer Teucer keeps dodging behind the shield of Ajax.

^c Dic. fears (1) the simple country folk who were deluded by the demagogues, (2) the old dicasts (for whom see the *Wasps*), and (3) Cleon. Aristophanes had apparently made fun of Cleon and certain officials in the *Babylonians* which

THE ACHARNIANS, 354-378

        A tempered statement mingled half and half;[a]
        Not though I'm willing o'er a chopping-block
        To say my say for Lacedaemon's folk.
        And yet I love, be sure, my own dear life.

CHOR. O why not bring the block
                out of doors without delay,
        And speak the mighty speech
                which you think will win the day?
        For really I've a longing
                to hear what you will say!
        So in the fashion you yourself prescribed,
        Place here the chopping-block and start your speech.

DI.   Well look and see, the chopping-block is here,
        And I'm to speak, poor little friendless I.
        Still never mind; I won't enshield myself,[b]
        I'll speak my mind for Lacedaemon's folk.
        And yet I fear;[c] for well I know the moods
        Of our good country people, how they love
        To hear the City and themselves bepraised
        By some intriguing humbug, right or wrong,
        Nor ever dream they are being bought and sold.
        And well I know the minds of those old men
        Looking for nothing but a verdict-bite.
        Aye and I know what I myself endured
        At Cleon's hands for last year's Comedy.

he had produced at the Great Dionysia the year before, and Cleon had denounced him for "defaming the State in the presence of strangers," cf. 503.

ARISTOPHANES

εἰσελκύσας γάρ μ' εἰς τὸ βουλευτήριον
διέβαλλε καὶ ψευδῆ κατεγλώττιζέ μου   380
κἀκυκλοβόρει κἄπλυνεν, ὥστ' ὀλίγου πάνυ
ἀπωλόμην μολυνοπραγμονούμενος.
νῦν οὖν με πρῶτον πρὶν λέγειν ἐάσατε
ἐνσκευάσασθαί μ' οἷον ἀθλιώτατον.

ΧΟ. τί ταῦτα στρέφει τεχνάζεις τε καὶ πορίζεις
    τριβάς;   [ἀντ. 385
λαβὲ δ' ἐμοῦ γ' ἕνεκα παρ' Ἱερωνύμου
σκοτοδασυπυκνότριχά τιν' Ἄϊδος κυνῆν·   390
εἶτ' ἐξάνοιγε μηχανὰς τὰς Σισύφου,
ὡς σκῆψιν ἀγὼν οὗτος οὐκ εἰσδέξεται.

ΔΙ. ὥρα 'στὶν ἄρα μοι καρτερὰν ψυχὴν λαβεῖν,
καί μοι βαδιστέ' ἐστὶν ὡς Εὐριπίδην.
παῖ παῖ.

ΚΗΦΙΣΟΦΩΝ. τίς οὗτος;

ΔΙ.   ἔνδον ἔστ' Εὐριπίδης;   395

ΚΗ. οὐκ ἔνδον, ἔνδον ἐστίν, εἰ γνώμην ἔχεις.

ΔΙ. πῶς ἔνδον, εἶτ' οὐκ ἔνδον;

ΚΗ.   ὀρθῶς, ὦ γέρον.
ὁ νοῦς μὲν ἔξω ξυλλέγων ἐπύλλια
οὐκ ἔνδον, αὐτὸς δ' ἔνδον ἀναβάδην ποιεῖ
τραγῳδίαν.

ΔΙ.   ὦ τρισμακάρι' Εὐριπίδη,   400
ὅθ' ὁ δοῦλος οὑτωσὶ σοφῶς ὑποκρίνεται.
ἐκκάλεσον αὐτόν.

---

[a] Κυκλόβορος· ποταμὸς ἐν Ἀθήναις χείμαρρος, ἄγαν ἠχῶν. Schol.

[b] Lit. "helmet of Hades," *i.e.* of invisibility; *cf. Il.* v.

THE ACHARNIANS, 379-402

      How to the Council-house he haled me off,
      And slanged, and lied, and slandered, and betongued me,
      Roaring Cycloborus [a]-wise ; till I well nigh
      Was done to death, bemiryslushified.
      Now therefore suffer me, before I start,
      To dress me up the loathliest way I can.

CHOR. O why keep putting off with that shilly-shally air ?
      Hieronymus may lend you, for anything I care,
      The shaggy " Cap of Darkness " [b] from his tangle-matted hair.
      Then open all the wiles of Sisyphus,
      Since this encounter will not brook delay.

DI.   Now must my heart be strong, and I depart
      To find Euripides.[c] Boy ! Ho there, boy !
CEPHISOPHON. Who calls me ?
DI.   Is Euripides within ?
CE. Within and not within,[d] if you conceive me.
DI. Within and not within ?
CE.   'Tis even so.
      His mind, without, is culling flowers of song,
      But he, within, is sitting up aloft
      Writing a play.
DI.   O lucky, lucky poet,
      Whose very servant says such clever things !
      But call him.

845. H. was a poet with a mop of unkempt hair which almost hid his face ; *cf. L.* 349.

[c] Wanting some beggarly rags Dic. resorts to Euripides, who often dresses his characters in them ; *cf.* 412 ; *F.* 842 ῥακιοσυρραπτάδης.

[d] A skit on E.'s style, *e.g. Alc.* 521 ἔστιν τε κοὐκ ἔτ' ἔστιν.

ARISTOPHANES

ΚΗ. ἀλλ' ἀδύνατον.
ΔΙ. ἀλλ' ὅμως.
οὐ γὰρ ἂν ἀπέλθοιμ', ἀλλὰ κόψω τὴν θύραν,
Εὐριπίδη, Εὐριπίδιον,
ὑπάκουσον, εἴπερ πώποτ' ἀνθρώπων τινί· 405
Δικαιόπολις καλεῖ σε Χολλείδης, ἐγώ.
ΕΥΡΙΠΙΔΗΣ. ἀλλ' οὐ σχολή.
ΔΙ. ἀλλ' ἐκκυκλήθητ'.
ΕΥ. ἀλλ' ἀδύνατον.
ΔΙ. ἀλλ' ὅμως.
ΕΥ. ἀλλ' ἐκκυκλήσομαι· καταβαίνειν δ' οὐ σχολή.
ΔΙ. Εὐριπίδη,
ΕΥ. τί λέλακας;
ΔΙ. ἀναβάδην ποιεῖς, 410
ἐξὸν καταβάδην· οὐκ ἐτὸς χωλοὺς ποιεῖς.
ἀτὰρ τί τὰ ῥάκι' ἐκ τραγῳδίας ἔχεις,
ἐσθῆτ' ἐλεεινήν; οὐκ ἐτὸς πτωχοὺς ποιεῖς.
ἀλλ' ἀντιβολῶ πρὸς τῶν γονάτων σ', Εὐριπίδη,
δός μοι ῥάκιόν τι τοῦ παλαιοῦ δράματος. 415
δεῖ γάρ με λέξαι τῷ χορῷ ῥῆσιν μακράν·
αὕτη δὲ θάνατον, ἢν κακῶς λέξω, φέρει.
ΕΥ. τὰ ποῖα τρύχη; μῶν ἐν οἷς Οἰνεὺς ὁδὶ
ὁ δύσποτμος γεραιὸς ἠγωνίζετο;
ΔΙ. οὐκ Οἰνέως ἦν, ἀλλ' ἔτ' ἀθλιωτέρου. 420
ΕΥ. τὰ τοῦ τυφλοῦ Φοίνικος;
ΔΙ. οὐ Φοίνικος, οὔ,

---

[a] The adjective marks his deme.
[b] *i.e.* " show yourself by means of the eccyclema," a piece of machinery by which the wall of a house is turned as if on a pivot, disclosing the interior.
[c] Because you bring them into being on such a dangerous height.

THE ACHARNIANS, 402–421

CE. But it can't be done.
DI. But still . . . !
For go I won't. I'll hammer at the door.
Euripides, my sweet one!
O if you ever hearkened, hearken now.
'Tis I, Cholleidian [a] Dicaeopolis.
EURIPIDES. But I've no time.
DI. But pivot.[b]
EUR. But it can't be done.
DI. But still . . . !
EUR. Well then, I'll pivot, but I can't come down.
DI. Euripides!
EUR. Aye.
DI. Why do you write up there,
And not down here? That's why you make
    lame heroes.[c]
And wherefore sit you robed in tragic rags,
A pitiful garb? That's why you make them
    beggars.
But by your knees, Euripides, I pray,
Lend me some rags from that old play of
    yours;[d]
For to the Chorus I to-day must speak
A lengthy speech; and if I fail, 'tis DEATH.
EUR. Rags! Rags! what rags? Mean you the
    rags wherein
This poor old Oeneus [e] came upon the stage?
DI. Not Oeneus, no; a wretcheder man than he.
EUR. Those that blind Phoenix [f] wore?
DI. Not Phoenix, no;

[d] τοῦ Τηλέφου; for this play, to which there are frequent references here, see Index *s.v.*
[e] King of Calydon, deprived of his throne by his nephews.
[f] According to this legend P. was accused by his father Amyntor of seducing his mistress and blinded by him.

ARISTOPHANES

ἀλλ' ἕτερος ἦν Φοίνικος ἀθλιώτερος.
ΕΥ. ποίας ποθ' ἀνὴρ λακίδας αἰτεῖται πέπλων;
ἀλλ' ἢ Φιλοκτήτου τὰ τοῦ πτωχοῦ λέγεις;
ΔΙ. οὔκ, ἀλλὰ τούτου πολὺ πολὺ πτωχιστέρου. 425
ΕΥ. ἀλλ' ἦ τὰ δυσπινῆ θέλεις πεπλώματα
ἃ Βελλεροφόντης εἶχ' ὁ χωλὸς οὑτοσί;
ΔΙ. οὐ Βελλεροφόντης· ἀλλὰ κἀκεῖνος μὲν ἦν
χωλός, προσαιτῶν, στωμύλος, δεινὸς λέγειν.
ΕΥ. οἶδ' ἄνδρα, Μυσὸν Τήλεφον.
ΔΙ. ναί, Τήλεφον· 430
τούτου δὸς ἀντιβολῶ σέ μοι τὰ σπάργανα.
ΕΥ. ὦ παῖ, δὸς αὐτῷ Τηλέφου ῥακώματα.
κεῖται δ' ἄνωθεν τῶν Θυεστείων ῥακῶν,
μεταξὺ τῶν Ἰνοῦς.
ΚΗ. ἰδού, ταυτὶ λαβέ.
ΔΙ. ὦ Ζεῦ διόπτα καὶ κατόπτα πανταχῇ, 435
ἐνσκευάσασθαί μ' οἷον ἀθλιώτατον.
Εὐριπίδη, 'πειδήπερ ἐχαρίσω ταδί,
κἀκεῖνά μοι δὸς τἀκόλουθα τῶν ῥακῶν,
τὸ πιλίδιον περὶ τὴν κεφαλὴν τὸ Μύσιον.
δεῖ γάρ με δόξαι πτωχὸν εἶναι τήμερον, 440
εἶναι μὲν ὅσπερ εἰμί, φαίνεσθαι δὲ μή·
τοὺς μὲν θεατὰς εἰδέναι μ' ὃς εἴμ' ἐγώ,
τοὺς δ' αὖ χορευτὰς ἠλιθίους παρεστάναι,
ὅπως ἂν αὐτοὺς ῥηματίοις σκιμαλίσω.
ΕΥ. δώσω· πυκνῇ γὰρ λεπτὰ μηχανᾷ φρενί. 445
ΔΙ. εὐδαιμονοίης, Τηλέφῳ δ' ἁγὼ φρονῶ.

---

[a] This play was produced by Euripides in 431 B.C.
[b] "lame," i.e., after being thrown from Pegasus.
[c] It is not known how Thyestes and Ino came to wear rags.
[d] ll. 441 and 442 are said by the Scholiast to be taken from the *Telephus*.

	Some other man still wretcheder than Phoenix.
EUR.	What shreds of raiment can the fellow mean ?
	Can it be those of beggarly Philoctetes [a] ?
DI.	One far, far, far, more beggarly than he.
EUR.	Can it be then the loathly gaberdine
	Wherein the lame [b] Bellerophon was clad ?
DI.	Bellerophon ? no ; yet mine too limped and begged,
	A terrible chap to talk.
EUR.	I know the man.
	The Mysian Telephus.
DI.	Telephus it is !
	Lend me, I pray, that hero's swaddling-clothes.
EUR.	Boy, fetch him out the rags of Telephus.
	They lie above the Thyesteian rags,
	'Twixt those and Ino's.[c]
CE.	(*To Di.*) Take them ; here they are.
DI.	(*Holding up the tattered garment against the light*)
	Lord Zeus, whose eyes can pierce through everywhere,
	Let me be dressed the loathliest way I can.
	Euripides, you have freely given the rags,
	Now give, I pray you, what pertains to these,
	The Mysian cap to set upon my head.
	For I've to-day to act a beggar's part,[d]
	To be myself, yet not to seem myself ;
	The audience there will know me who I am,
	Whilst all the Chorus stand like idiots by,
	The while I fillip them with cunning words.[e]
EUR.	Take it ; you subtly plan ingenious schemes.
DI.	To thee, good luck ; to Telephus—what I wish him !

[a] Or "little phraselets" such as E. was fond of.

ARISTOPHANES

εὖ γ'· οἷον ἤδη ῥηματίων ἐμπίπλαμαι.
ἀτὰρ δέομαί γε πτωχικοῦ βακτηρίου.
ΕΥ. τουτὶ λαβὼν ἄπελθε λαΐνων σταθμῶν.
ΔΙ. ὦ θύμ', ὁρᾷς γὰρ ὡς ἀπωθοῦμαι δόμων, 450
πολλῶν δεόμενος σκευαρίων· νῦν δὴ γενοῦ
γλίσχρος προσαιτῶν λιπαρῶν τ'. Εὐριπίδη,
δός μοι σπυρίδιον διακεκαυμένον λύχνῳ.
ΕΥ. τί δ', ὦ τάλας, σε τοῦδ' ἔχει πλέκους χρέος;
ΔΙ. χρέος μὲν οὐδέν, βούλομαι δ' ὅμως λαβεῖν. 455
ΕΥ. λυπηρὸς ἴσθ' ὢν κἀποχώρησον δόμων.
ΔΙ. φεῦ· εὐδαιμονοίης, ὥσπερ ἡ μήτηρ ποτέ.
ΕΥ. ἄπελθε νῦν μοι.
ΔΙ. μἀλλά μοι δὸς ἓν μόνον,
κοτυλίσκιον τὸ χεῖλος ἀποκεκρουσμένον.
ΕΥ. φθείρου λαβὼν τόδ'· ἴσθι δ' ὀχληρὸς ὢν
δόμοις. 460
ΔΙ. οὔπω μὰ Δί' οἶσθ' οἷ' αὐτὸς ἐργάζει κακά.
ἀλλ', ὦ γλυκύτατ' Εὐριπίδη, τουτὶ μόνον,
δός μοι χυτρίδιον σπογγίῳ βεβυσμένον.
ΕΥ. ἄνθρωπ', ἀφαιρήσει με τὴν τραγῳδίαν.
ἄπελθε ταυτηνὶ λαβών.
ΔΙ. ἀπέρχομαι. 465
καίτοι τί δράσω; δεῖ γὰρ ἑνός, οὗ μὴ τυχὼν
ἀπόλωλ'. ἄκουσον, ὦ γλυκύτατ' Εὐριπίδη·
τουτὶ λαβὼν ἄπειμι κοὐ πρόσειμ' ἔτι·
εἰς τὸ σπυρίδιον ἰσχνά μοι φυλλεῖα δός.
ΕΥ. ἀπολεῖς μ'. ἰδού σοι. φροῦδά μοι τὰ δρά-
ματα. 470

---

[a] *i.e.*, wearing the rags of T. he feels himself able to talk like him.
[b] Probably for carrying scraps; *cf. sportula*. Telephus is said to have carried one " in a tragedy " (Diog. Laert. vi. 87).

EUR.	Yah! why I'm full of cunning words already.[a] But now, methinks, I need a beggar's staff. Take this, and get thee from the marble halls.
DI.	O Soul, thou seest me from the mansion thrust, Still wanting many a boon. Now in thy prayer Be close and instant. Give, Euripides, A little basket [b] with a hole burnt through it.
EUR.	What need you, hapless one, of this poor wicker?
DI.	No need perchance; but O I want it so.
EUR.	Know that you're wearisome, and get you gone.
DI.	Alas! Heaven bless you, as it blessed your mother.[c]
EUR.	Leave me in peace.
DI.	Just one thing more, but one, A little tankard with a broken rim.
EUR.	Here. Now be off. You trouble us; begone.
DI.	You know not yet what ill you do yourself. Sweet, dear Euripides, but one thing more, Give me a little pitcher, plugged with sponge.
EUR.	Fellow, you're taking the whole tragedy. Here, take it and begone.
DI.	I'm going now. And yet! there's one thing more, which if I get not I'm ruined. Sweetest, best Euripides, With this I'll go, and never come again; Give me some withered leaves to fill my basket.
EUR.	You'll slay me! Here! My plays are disappearing.

[c] Said to be a seller of potherbs; cf. 478.

ARISTOPHANES

ΔΙ. ἀλλ' οὐκέτ', ἀλλ' ἄπειμι. καὶ γάρ εἰμ' ἄγαν
ὀχληρός, οὐ δοκῶν με κοιράνους στυγεῖν.
οἴμοι κακοδαίμων, ὡς ἀπόλωλ'. ἐπελαθόμην
ἐν ᾧπέρ ἐστι πάντα μοι τὰ πράγματα.
Εὐριπίδιον, ὦ φιλτάτιον καὶ γλυκύτατον,   475
κάκιστ' ἀπολοίμην, εἴ τί σ' αἰτήσαιμ' ἔτι,
πλὴν ἓν μόνον, τουτὶ μόνον, τουτὶ μόνον,
σκάνδικά μοι δός, μητρόθεν δεδεγμένος.
ΕΥ. ἁνὴρ ὑβρίζει· κλεῖε πηκτὰ δωμάτων.
ΔΙ. ὦ θύμ', ἄνευ σκάνδικος ἐμπορευτέα.   480
ἆρ' οἶσθ' ὅσον τὸν ἀγῶν' ἀγωνιεῖ τάχα,
μέλλων ὑπὲρ Λακεδαιμονίων ἀνδρῶν λέγειν;
πρόβαινέ νυν, ὦ θυμέ· γραμμὴ δ' αὑτηί.
ἕστηκας; οὐκ εἶ καταπιὼν Εὐριπίδην;
ἐπῄνεσ'· ἄγε νυν, ὦ τάλαινα καρδία,   485
ἄπελθ' ἐκεῖσε, κᾆτα τὴν κεφαλὴν ἐκεῖ
παράσχες, εἰποῦσ' ἅττ' ἂν αὐτῇ σοι δοκῇ.
τόλμησον, ἴθι, χώρησον, ἄγαμαι καρδίας.
   490
ΧΟ. τί δράσεις; τί φήσεις; ἀλλ' ἴσθι νυν
ἀναίσχυντος ὢν σιδηροῦς τ' ἀνήρ,
ὅστις παρασχὼν τῇ πόλει τὸν αὐχένα
ἅπασι μέλλεις εἷς λέγειν τἀναντία.
ἁνὴρ οὐ τρέμει τὸ πρᾶγμ'. εἶά νυν,   495
ἐπειδήπερ αὐτὸς αἱρεῖ, λέγε.

ΔΙ. μή μοι φθονήσητ', ἄνδρες οἱ θεώμενοι,
εἰ πτωχὸς ὢν ἔπειτ' ἐν Ἀθηναίοις λέγειν

---

[a] " Parodied from the *Oeneus* of Euripides ": Schol.
[b] *Here Euripides is wheeled in again, and Dic. advances to the block to make his speech.*
[c] *i.e.*, from which the racers started. Dic. being now well primed with Euripides feels he ought to go ahead.

THE ACHARNIANS, 471-497

DI. Enough! I go. Too troublesome by far
Am I, not witting that the chieftains hate me![a]
Good Heavens! I'm ruined. I had clean for-
   gotten
The thing whereon my whole success depends.
My own Euripides, my best and sweetest,
Perdition seize me if I ask aught else
Save this one thing, this only, only this,
Give me some chervil, borrowing from your mother.
EUR. The man insults us. Shut the palace up.[b]
DI. O Soul, without our chervil we must go.
Knowest thou the perilous strife thou hast to
   strive,
Speaking in favour of Laconian men?
On, on, my Soul! Here is the line.[c] How?
   What?
Swallow Euripides, and yet not budge?
Oh, good! Advance, O long-enduring heart,
Go thither, lay thine head upon the block,
And say whatever to thyself seems good.
Take courage! Forward! March! O well
   done, heart!

CHOR. What will you say? What will you do?
   Man, is it true
You are made up of iron and of shameless-
   ness too?
You who will, one against us all, debate,
Offering your neck a hostage to the State!
   Nought does he fear.
Since you will have it so, speak, we will hear

DI. Bear me no grudge, spectators, if, a beggar,
I dare to speak before the Athenian people

ARISTOPHANES

μέλλω περὶ τῆς πόλεως, τρυγῳδίαν ποιῶν.
τὸ γὰρ δίκαιον οἶδε καὶ τρυγῳδία. 500
ἐγὼ δὲ λέξω δεινὰ μέν, δίκαια δέ.
οὐ γάρ με νῦν γε διαβαλεῖ Κλέων ὅτι
ξένων παρόντων τὴν πόλιν κακῶς λέγω.
αὐτοὶ γάρ ἐσμεν οὑπὶ Ληναίῳ τ' ἀγών,
κοὔπω ξένοι πάρεισιν· οὔτε γὰρ φόροι 505
ἥκουσιν οὔτ' ἐκ τῶν πόλεων οἱ ξύμμαχοι·
ἀλλ' ἐσμὲν αὐτοὶ νῦν γε περιεπτισμένοι·
τοὺς γὰρ μετοίκους ἄχυρα τῶν ἀστῶν λέγω.
ἐγὼ δὲ μισῶ μὲν Λακεδαιμονίους σφόδρα,
καὐτοῖς ὁ Ποσειδῶν, οὑπὶ Ταινάρῳ θεός, 510
σείσας ἅπασιν ἐμβάλοι τὰς οἰκίας·
κἀμοὶ γάρ ἐστιν ἀμπέλια κεκομμένα.
ἀτάρ, φίλοι γὰρ οἱ παρόντες ἐν λόγῳ,'
τί ταῦτα τοὺς Λάκωνας αἰτιώμεθα;
ἡμῶν γὰρ ἄνδρες, οὐχὶ τὴν πόλιν λέγω, 515
μέμνησθε τοῦθ', ὅτι οὐχὶ τὴν πόλιν λέγω,
ἀλλ' ἀνδράρια μοχθηρά, παρακεκομμένα,
ἄτιμα καὶ παράσημα καὶ παράξενα,
ἐσυκοφάντει Μεγαρέων τὰ χλανίσκια·
κεἴ που σίκυον ἴδοιεν ἢ λαγῴδιον 520
ἢ χοιρίδιον ἢ σκόροδον ἢ χονδροὺς ἅλας,
ταῦτ' ἦν Μεγαρικὰ κἀπέπρατ' αὐθημερόν.

---

[a] The speech throughout is probably a parody of one in the *Telephus*, and for ll. 497, 498 the Scholiast quotes the original as—

μή μοι φθονήσητ', ἄνδρες Ἑλλήνων ἄκροι,
εἰ πτωχὸς ὢν τέτληκ' ἐν ἐσθλοῖσιν λέγειν.

[b] Only citizens and μέτοικοι were present at the "Lenaea."
[c] They are "clean-winnowed," only the grain being left, of which the ἀστοί are the flour and the μέτοικοι the bran.

THE ACHARNIANS, 499-522

About the city in a comic play.[a]
For what is true even comedy can tell.
And I shall utter startling things but true.
Nor now can Cleon slander me because,
With strangers present, I defame the State.
'Tis the Lenaea, and we're all alone ; [b]
No strangers yet have come ; nor from the states
Have yet arrived the tribute and allies.
We're quite alone clean-winnowed ; for I count
Our alien residents the civic bran.[c]
The Lacedaemonians I detest entirely ;
And may Poseidon, Lord of Taenarum,
Shake [d] all their houses down about their ears ;
For I, like you, have had my vines cut down.
But after all—for none but friends are here—
Why the Laconians do we blame for this ?
For men of ours, I do not say the State,
Remember this, I do not say the State,[e]
But worthless fellows of a worthless stamp,
Ill-coined, ill-minted, spurious little chaps,
Kept on denouncing Megara's little coats.[f]
And if a cucumber or hare they saw,
Or sucking-pig, or garlic, or lump-salt,[g]
All were Megarian, and were sold off-hand.[h]

[d] *i.e.* as Ἐννοσίγαιος, the Earth-Shaker. Sparta suffered from earthquakes ; *cf.* Thuc. i. 128. 2 ; Paus. vii. 25. 1.
[e] He emphasizes this because that was the exact charge; *cf.* 503.
[f] "The ἐξωμίδες which formed the staple manufacture of Megara; *cf.* Xen. *Mem.* ii. 7. 6 " : R.
[g] *i.e.* rock-salt.
[h] *i.e.* after being denounced as Megarian and confiscated ; *cf.* 542. The exclusion of the Megarians from the " market of Athens and Athenian harbours " was put forward by Sparta in 431 B.C. as one of the chief grounds for war ; *cf.* Thuc. i. 139. 1.

ARISTOPHANES

καὶ ταῦτα μὲν δὴ σμικρὰ κἀπιχώρια,
πόρνην δὲ Σιμαίθαν ἰόντες Μεγαράδε
νεανίαι κλέπτουσι μεθυσοκότταβοι· 525
κᾆθ' οἱ Μεγαρῆς ὀδύναις πεφυσιγγωμένοι \
ἀντεξέκλεψαν Ἀσπασίας πόρνα δύο·
κἀντεῦθεν ἀρχὴ τοῦ πολέμου κατερράγη
Ἕλλησι πᾶσιν ἐκ τριῶν λαικαστριῶν.
ἐντεῦθεν ὀργῇ Περικλέης Οὐλύμπιος 530
ἤστραπτ', ἐβρόντα, ξυνεκύκα τὴν Ἑλλάδα,
ἐτίθει νόμους ὥσπερ σκόλια γεγραμμένους,
ὡς χρὴ Μεγαρέας μήτε γῇ μήτ' ἐν ἀγορᾷ
μήτ' ἐν θαλάττῃ μήτ' ἐν ἠπείρῳ μένειν.
ἐντεῦθεν οἱ Μεγαρῆς, ὅτε δὴ 'πείνων βάδην, 535
Λακεδαιμονίων ἐδέοντο τὸ ψήφισμ' ὅπως
μεταστραφείη τὸ διὰ τὰς λαικαστρίας·
οὐκ ἠθέλομεν δ' ἡμεῖς δεομένων πολλάκις.
κἀντεῦθεν ἤδη πάταγος ἦν τῶν ἀσπίδων.
ἐρεῖ τις, οὐ χρῆν· ἀλλὰ τί ἐχρῆν εἴπατε. 540
φέρ', εἰ Λακεδαιμονίων τις ἐκπλεύσας σκάφει
ἀπέδοτο φήνας κυνίδιον Σεριφίων,
καθῆσθ' ἂν ἐν δόμοισιν; ἦ πολλοῦ γε δεῖ·
καὶ κάρτα μεντἂν εὐθέως καθείλκετε
τριακοσίας ναῦς, ἦν δ' ἂν ἡ πόλις πλέα 545
θορύβου στρατιωτῶν, περὶ τριηράρχου βοῆς,
μισθοῦ διδομένου, Παλλαδίων χρυσουμένων,
στοᾶς στεναχούσης, σιτίων μετρουμένων,

ΑΧΑΡΝΗΣ
THE ACHARNIANS, 523-548

Still these were trifles, and our country's way.
But some young tipsy cottabus-players went
And stole from Megara-town the fair Simaetha.
Then the Megarians, garlicked with the smart,
Stole, in return, two of Aspasia's ^a hussies.
From these three Wantons o'er the Hellenic race
Burst forth the first beginnings of the War.
For then, in wrath, the Olympian Pericles
Thundered and lightened, and confounded Hellas,
Enacting laws which ran like drinking-songs,^b
*That the Megarians presently depart
From earth and sea, the mainland, and the mart.*
Then the Megarians, slowly famishing,
Besought their Spartan friends to get the Law
Of the three Wantons cancelled and withdrawn.
And oft they asked us, but we yielded not.
Then followed instantly the clash of shields.
Ye'll say *They should not*; but what should they, then?
Come now, had some Laconian, sailing out,
Denounced and sold a small Seriphian^c dog,
Would you have sat unmoved? Far, far from that!
Ye would have launched three hundred ships of war,
And all the City had at once been full
Of shouting troops, of fuss with trierarchs,
Of paying wages, gilding Pallases,^d
Of rations measured, roaring colonnades,

---

^a The famous mistress of Pericles.
^b The σκόλιον it resembles was by Timocreon of Rhodes:
' ὤφελέν σ', ὦ τυφλὲ Πλοῦτε, | μήτε γῇ μήτ' ἐν θαλάσσῃ | μήτ' ἐν ἠπείρῳ φανῆναι . . .
^c Seriphus is a very small island, one of the Cyclades, due east from Sparta. The smallest injury to the smallest " island " would have roused Athens to fury.
^d *i.e.* for figure-heads or the like.

ARISTOPHANES

ἀσκῶν, τροπωτήρων, κάδους ὠνουμένων,
σκορόδων, ἐλαῶν, κρομμύων ἐν δικτύοις, 550
στεφάνων, τριχίδων, αὐλητρίδων, ὑπωπίων·
τὸ νεώριον δ' αὖ κωπέων πλατουμένων,
τύλων ψοφούντων, θαλαμιῶν τροπουμένων,
αὐλῶν, κελευστῶν, νιγλάρων, συριγμάτων.
ταῦτ' οἶδ' ὅτι ἂν ἐδρᾶτε· τὸν δὲ Τήλεφον 555
οὐκ οἰόμεσθα; νοῦς ἄρ' ἡμῖν οὐκ ἔνι.

ΗΜ. Α. ἄληθες, ὠπίτριπτε καὶ μιαρώτατε;
ταυτὶ σὺ τολμᾷς πτωχὸς ὢν ἡμᾶς λέγειν,
καὶ συκοφάντης εἴ τις ἦν, ὠνείδισας;

ΗΜ. Β. νὴ τὸν Ποσειδῶ, καὶ λέγει γ' ἅπερ λέγει 560
δίκαια πάντα κοὐδὲν αὐτῶν ψεύδεται.

ΗΜ. Α. εἶτ' εἰ δίκαια, τοῦτον εἰπεῖν αὔτ' ἐχρῆν;
ἀλλ' οὔ τι χαίρων ταῦτα τολμήσει λέγειν.

ΗΜ. Β. οὗτος σὺ ποῖ θεῖς; οὐ μενεῖς; ὡς εἰ θενεῖς
τὸν ἄνδρα τοῦτον, αὐτὸς ἀρθήσει τάχα. 565

ΗΜ. Α. ἰὼ Λάμαχ', ὦ βλέπων ἀστραπάς,
βοήθησον, ὦ γοργολόφα, φανείς,
ἰὼ Λάμαχ', ὦ φίλ', ὦ φυλέτα·
εἴτε τις ἔστι ταξί-
αρχος, ἢ στρατηγός, ἢ
τειχομάχας ἀνήρ, βοηθησάτω 570
τις ἀνύσας. ἐγὼ γὰρ ἔχομαι μέσος.

---

^a καὶ ταῦτα ἐκ Τηλέφου : Schol. The speech ends, as it began, with a quotation, and its effect is to split the Chorus into two hostile sections.

THE ACHARNIANS, 549–571

    Of wineskins, oarloops, bargaining for casks,
    Of nets of onions, olives, garlic-heads,
    Of chaplets, pilchards, flute-girls, and black
        eyes.
    And all the arsenal had rung with noise
    Of oar-spars planed, pegs hammered, oar-
        loops fitted,
    Of boatswains' calls, and flutes, and trills, and
        whistles.
    This had ye done ; and shall not Telephus,[a]
    Think we, do this ? we've got no brains at all.
SEMICHORUS I. Aye, say you so, you rascally villain
        you ?
    And this from you, a beggar ? Dare you
        blame us
    Because, perchance, we've got informers here?
SEMICHORUS II. Aye, by Poseidon, every word he says
    Is true and right ; he tells no lies at all.
S.C. I. True or untrue, is he the man to say it ?
    I'll pay him out, though, for his insolent speech.
S.C. II. Whither away ? I pray you stay. If him you
        hurt,
    You'll find your own self hoisted up directly.[b]
S.C. I. Lamachus ! Help ! with thy glances of light-
        ning ;
    Terrible-crested, appear in thy pride,
    Come, O Lamachus, tribesman and friend to
        us ;
    Is there a stormer of cities beside ?
    Is there a captain ? O come ye in haste,
    Help me, O help ! I am caught by the waist.

[b] *A scuffle takes place in the orchestra, in which the leader of the first semichorus is worsted.*

ARISTOPHANES

ΛΑΜΑΧΟΣ. πόθεν βοῆς ἤκουσα πολεμιστηρίας;
ποῖ χρὴ βοηθεῖν; ποῖ κυδοιμὸν ἐμβαλεῖν;
τίς Γοργόν' ἐξήγειρεν ἐκ τοῦ σάγματος;
ΔΙ. ὦ Λάμαχ' ἥρως, τῶν λόφων καὶ τῶν λόχων. 575
ΗΜ. Α. ὦ Λάμαχ', οὐ γὰρ οὗτος ἄνθρωπος πάλαι
ἅπασαν ἡμῶν τὴν πόλιν κακορροθεῖ;
ΛΑ. οὗτος σὺ τολμᾷς πτωχὸς ὢν λέγειν τάδε;
ΔΙ. ὦ Λάμαχ' ἥρως, ἀλλὰ συγγνώμην ἔχε,
εἰ πτωχὸς ὢν εἶπόν τι κἀστωμυλάμην.
ΛΑ. τί δ' εἶπας ἡμᾶς; οὐκ ἐρεῖς;
ΔΙ. οὐκ οἶδά πω· 580
ὑπὸ τοῦ δέους γὰρ τῶν ὅπλων ἰλιγγιῶ.
ἀλλ' ἀντιβολῶ σ', ἀπένεγκέ μου τὴν μορμόνα.
ΛΑ. ἰδού.
ΔΙ. παράθες νυν ὑπτίαν αὐτὴν ἐμοί.
ΛΑ. κεῖται.
ΔΙ. φέρε νυν ἀπὸ τοῦ κράνους μοι τὸ πτερόν.
ΛΑ. τουτὶ πτίλον σοι.
ΔΙ. τῆς κεφαλῆς νύν μου λαβοῦ, 585
ἵν' ἐξεμέσω· βδελύττομαι γὰρ τοὺς λόφους.
ΛΑ. οὗτος, τί δράσεις; τῷ πτίλῳ μέλλεις ἐμεῖν;
ΔΙ. πτίλον γάρ ἐστιν; εἰπέ μοι, τίνος ποτὲ
ὄρνιθός ἐστιν; ἆρα κομπολακύθου;
ΛΑ. οἴμ' ὡς τεθνήξει.
ΔΙ. μηδαμῶς, ὦ Λάμαχε· 590
οὐ γὰρ κατ' ἰσχύν ἐστιν· εἰ δ' ἰσχυρὸς εἶ,
τί μ' οὐκ ἀπεψώλησας; εὔοπλος γὰρ εἶ.
ΛΑ. ταυτὶ λέγεις σὺ τὸν στρατηγὸν πτωχὸς ὤν;

---

[a] Emblazoned on his shield.
[b] "L. superciliously calls the huge ostrich feather πτίλον, a term used of the soft and downy plumage of the breast": R.

LAMACHUS. Whence came the cry of battle to my ears?
    Where shall I charge? where cast the battle-
        din?
    Who roused the sleeping Gorgon[a] from its
        case?
DI. O Lamachus hero, O those crests and cohorts!
S.C. I. O Lamachus, here has this fellow been
    With frothy words abusing all the State.
LAM. You dare, you beggar, say such things as
        those?
DI. O Lamachus hero, grant me pardon true
    If I, a beggar, spake or chattered aught.
LAM. What said you? Hey?
DI.   I can't remember yet.
    I get so dizzy at the sight of arms.
    I pray you lay that terrible shield aside.
LAM. There then.
DI.   Now set it upside down before me.
LAM. 'Tis done.
DI.   Now give me from your crest that plume.
LAM. Here; take the feather.[b]
DI.   Now then, hold my head,
    And let me vomit. I so loathe those crests.
LAM. What! use my feather, rogue, to make you
        vomit?
DI. A feather is it, Lamachus? Pray what bird
    Produced it? Is it a Great Boastard's plume?
LAM. Death and Destruction!
DI.   No, no, Lamachus.
    That's not for strength like yours. If strong
        you are
    Why don't you circumcise me? You're well
        armed.
LAM. What! you, a beggar, beard the general so?

ARISTOPHANES

ΔΙ. ἐγὼ γάρ εἰμι πτωχός;
ΛΑ. ἀλλὰ τίς γὰρ εἶ;
ΔΙ. ὅστις; πολίτης χρηστός, οὐ σπουδαρχίδης, 595
ἀλλ' ἐξ ὅτου περ ὁ πόλεμος, στρατωνίδης,
σὺ δ' ἐξ ὅτου περ ὁ πόλεμος, μισθαρχίδης.
ΛΑ. ἐχειροτόνησαν γάρ με—
ΔΙ. κόκκυγές γε τρεῖς.
ταῦτ' οὖν ἐγὼ βδελυττόμενος ἐσπεισάμην,
ὁρῶν πολιοὺς μὲν ἄνδρας ἐν ταῖς τάξεσιν, 600
νεανίας δ' οἵους σὺ διαδεδρακότας
τοὺς μὲν ἐπὶ Θρᾴκης μισθοφοροῦντας τρεῖς
δραχμάς,
Τισαμενοφαινίππους, Πανουργιππαρχίδας·
ἑτέρους δὲ παρὰ Χάρητι, τοὺς δ' ἐν Χάοσι
Γερητοθεοδώρους, Διομειαλαζόνας, 605
τοὺς δ' ἐν Καμαρίνῃ κἀν Γέλᾳ κἀν Καταγέλᾳ.
ΛΑ. ἐχειροτονήθησαν γάρ.
ΔΙ. αἴτιον δὲ τί
ὑμᾶς μὲν ἀεὶ μισθοφορεῖν ἁμηγέπῃ,
τωνδὶ δὲ μηδέν'; ἐτεόν, ὦ Μαριλάδη,
ἤδη πεπρέσβευκας σὺ πολιὸς ὢν ἔνη; 610
ἀνένευσε· καίτοι γ' ἐστὶ σώφρων κἀργάτης.
τί δαὶ Δράκυλλος κΕὐφορίδης ἢ Πρινίδης;
εἶδέν τις ὑμῶν τἀκβάταν' ἢ τοὺς Χάονας;
οὔ φασιν. ἀλλ' ὁ Κοισύρας καὶ Λάμαχος,
οἷς ὑπ' ἐράνου τε καὶ χρεῶν πρώην ποτέ, 615

---

[a] Silly, empty-headed fellows; "gowks."
[b] The personal allusions in these names are obscure.
[c] The name is a mere pun on Γέλᾳ.
[d] One of the Chorus; so too with the names in 612.
[e] ἔνη: the Scholiasts did not understand this, but one renders it "long ago"; no one has explained it satisfactorily.

THE ACHARNIANS, 594-615

DI. A beggar am I, Lamachus?
LAM. What else?
DI. An honest townsman, not an office-seekrian,
Since war began, an active-service-seekrian,
But you're, since war began, a full-pay-seekrian.
LAM. The people chose me—
DI. Aye, three cuckoo-birds.[a]
That's what I loathe; that's why I made my treaty,
When grey-haired veterans in the ranks I saw,
And boys like you, paltry malingering boys,
Off, some to Thrace—their daily pay three drachmas—
Phaenippuses, Hipparchidreprobatians,[b]
And some with Chares, to Chaonia some,
Geretotheodores, Diomirogues, and some
To Camarina, Gela, and Grineela.[c]
LAM. The people chose them—
DI. And how comes it, pray,
That you are always in receipt of pay,
And these are NEVER? Come, Marilades,[d]
You are old and grey[e]; when have you served as envoy?
NEVER! Yet he's a steady, active man.
Well then, Euphorides, Prinides, Dracyllus,
Have *you* Ecbatana or Chaonia seen?
NEVER! But Coesyra's son[f] and Lamachus,
They have; to whom, for debts and calls unpaid,[g]

[f] *i.e.* any young nobleman. Coesyra belonged to the great family of the Alcmaeonidae; *cf. C.* 800.
[g] In Dem. 821. 14 ἐράνους λέλοιπε (" he has left his subscription unpaid ") is used to describe a rascal; and see L. & S. *s.v.*

59

ARISTOPHANES

ὥσπερ ἀπόνιπτρον ἐκχέοντες ἑσπέρας,
ἅπαντες ἐξίστω παρῄνουν οἱ φίλοι.
ΛΑ. ὦ δημοκρατία, ταῦτα δῆτ' ἀνασχετά;
ΔΙ. οὐ δῆτ', ἐὰν μὴ μισθοφορῇ γε Λάμαχος.
ΛΑ. ἀλλ' οὖν ἐγὼ μὲν πᾶσι Πελοποννησίοις 620
ἀεὶ πολεμήσω, καὶ ταράξω πανταχῇ,
καὶ ναυσὶ καὶ πεζοῖσι, κατὰ τὸ καρτερόν.
ΔΙ. ἐγὼ δὲ κηρύττω γε Πελοποννησίοις
ἅπασι καὶ Μεγαρεῦσι καὶ Βοιωτίοις
πωλεῖν ἀγοράζειν πρὸς ἐμέ, Λαμάχῳ δὲ μή. 625

ΧΟ. ἁνὴρ νικᾷ τοῖσι λόγοισιν, καὶ τὸν δῆμον μεταπείθει
περὶ τῶν σπονδῶν. ἀλλ' ἀποδύντες τοῖς
ἀναπαίστοις ἐπίωμεν.

Ἐξ οὗ γε χοροῖσιν ἐφέστηκεν τρυγικοῖς ὁ
διδάσκαλος ἡμῶν,
οὔπω παρέβη πρὸς τὸ θέατρον λέξων ὡς
δεξιός ἐστιν·
διαβαλλόμενος δ' ὑπὸ τῶν ἐχθρῶν ἐν Ἀθηναίοις ταχυβούλοις, 630
ὡς κωμῳδεῖ τὴν πόλιν ἡμῶν καὶ τὸν δῆμον
καθυβρίζει,
ἀποκρίνεσθαι δεῖται νυνὶ πρὸς Ἀθηναίους
μεταβούλους.
φησὶν δ' εἶναι πολλῶν ἀγαθῶν ἄξιος ὑμῖν ὁ
ποιητής,
παύσας ὑμᾶς ξενικοῖσι λόγοις μὴ λίαν ἐξαπατᾶσθαι,

---

[a] The leader of the Chorus speaks as though the poet in person had " come forth " (παρέβη) to deliver the Parabasis.

THE ACHARNIANS, 616-634

      Their friends but now, like people throwing
          out
      Their slops at eve, were crying " Stand away! "
LAM. O me! Democracy! can this be borne?
DI. No, not if Lamachus receive no pay.
LAM. But I with all the Peloponnesian folk
      Will always fight, and vex them everyway,
      By land, by sea, with all my might and main.
                                          [*Exit*
DI. And I to all the Peloponnesian folk,
      Megarians and Boeotians, give full leave
      To trade with me; but not to Lamachus.
                                             [*Exit*
CHOR. The man has the best of the wordy debate,
         and the hearts of the people is winning
    To his plea for the truce. Now doff we our robes,
         our own anapaestics beginning.

SINCE first to exhibit his plays he began,
                    our chorus-instructor has never
Come forth *a* to confess in this public address
                    how tactful he is and how clever.
But now that he knows he is slandered by foes
                    before Athens so quick to assent,
Pretending he jeers our City and sneers
                    at the people with evil intent,
He is ready and fain his cause to maintain
                  before Athens so quick to repent.
Let honour and praise be the guerdon, he says,
                  of the poet whose satire has stayed you
From believing the orators' novel conceits
                  wherewith they cajoled and betrayed you;

which is the first that has come down to us "a Parabasis complete in all its seven parts"; see note on *W*. 1009.

ARISTOPHANES

μηδ' ἥδεσθαι θωπευομένους μηδ' εἶναι χαυνοπολίτας.
πρότερον δ' ὑμᾶς ἀπὸ τῶν πόλεων οἱ πρέσβεις ἐξαπατῶντες
πρῶτον μὲν ἰοστεφάνους ἐκάλουν· κἀπειδὴ τοῦτό τίς εἴποι,
εὐθὺς διὰ τοὺς στεφάνους ἐπ' ἄκρων τῶν πυγιδίων ἐκάθησθε.
εἰ δέ τις ὑμᾶς ὑποθωπεύσας λιπαρὰς καλέσειεν Ἀθήνας,
εὕρετο πᾶν ἂν διὰ τὰς λιπαράς, ἀφύων τιμὴν περιάψας.
ταῦτα ποιήσας πολλῶν ἀγαθῶν αἴτιος ὑμῖν γεγένηται,
καὶ τοὺς δήμους ἐν ταῖς πόλεσιν δείξας, ὡς δημοκρατοῦνται.
τοιγάρτοι νῦν ἐκ τῶν πόλεων τὸν φόρον ὑμῖν ἀπάγοντες
ἥξουσιν, ἰδεῖν ἐπιθυμοῦντες τὸν ποιητὴν τὸν ἄριστον,
ὅστις παρεκινδύνευσ' εἰπεῖν ἐν Ἀθηναίοις τὰ δίκαια.
οὕτω δ' αὐτοῦ περὶ τῆς τόλμης ἤδη πόρρω κλέος ἥκει,
ὅτε καὶ βασιλεύς, Λακεδαιμονίων τὴν πρεσβείαν βασανίζων,
ἠρώτησεν πρῶτα μὲν αὐτοὺς πότεροι ταῖς ναυσὶ κρατοῦσιν·
εἶτα δὲ τοῦτον τὸν ποιητὴν ποτέρους εἴποι κακὰ πολλά·
τούτους γὰρ ἔφη τοὺς ἀνθρώπους πολὺ βελτίους γεγενῆσθαι

635

640

645

650

THE ACHARNIANS, 635-650

Who bids you despise adulation and lies
    nor be citizens Vacant and Vain.
For before, when an embassy came from the states
    intriguing your favour to gain,
And called you the town of the VIOLET CROWN,[a]
    so grand and exalted ye grew,
That at once on your tiptails erect ye would sit,
    those CROWNS were so pleasant to you.
And then, if they added the SHINY, they got
    whatever they asked for their praises,
Though apter, I ween, for an oily sardine
    than for you and your City the phrase is.
By this he's a true benefactor to you,
    and by showing with humour dramatic
The way that our wise democratic allies
    are ruled by our State democratic.
And therefore their people will come oversea,
    their tribute to bring to the City,
Consumed with desire to behold and admire
    the poet so fearless and witty,
Who dared in the presence of Athens to speak
    the thing that is rightful and true.
And truly the fame of his prowess, by this,
    has been bruited the universe through,
When the Sovereign of Persia, desiring to test
    what the end of our warfare will be,
Inquired of the Spartan ambassadors, first,
    which nation is queen of the sea,
And next, which the wonderful Poet has got,
    as its stern and unsparing adviser ;
For those who are lashed by his satire, he said,
    must surely be better and wiser,

[a] The famous epithet applied to Athens by Pindar (Frag. 76), αἵ τε λιπαραὶ καὶ ἰοστέφανοι καὶ ἀοίδιμοι Ἑλλάδος ἔρεισμα, κλεινὰὶ Ἀθᾶναι.

κἄν τῷ πολέμῳ πολὺ νικήσειν, τοῦτον ξύμβουλον
ἔχοντας.
διὰ ταῦθ' ὑμᾶς Λακεδαιμόνιοι τὴν εἰρήνην προ-
καλοῦνται,
καὶ τὴν Αἴγιναν ἀπαιτοῦσιν· καὶ τῆς νήσου μὲν
ἐκείνης
οὐ φροντίζουσ', ἀλλ' ἵνα τοῦτον τὸν ποιητὴν ἀφ-
έλωνται.
ἀλλ' ὑμεῖς τοι μή ποτ' ἀφῆθ'· ὡς κωμῳδήσει τὰ
δίκαια· 655
φησὶν δ' ὑμᾶς πολλὰ διδάξειν ἀγάθ', ὥστ' εὐδαί-
μονας εἶναι,
οὐ θωπεύων, οὔθ' ὑποτείνων μισθούς, οὐδ' ἐξαπ-
ατύλλων,
οὐδὲ πανουργῶν, οὐδὲ κατάρδων, ἀλλὰ τὰ βέλτιστα
διδάσκων.

πρὸς ταῦτα Κλέων καὶ παλαμάσθω
καὶ πᾶν ἐπ' ἐμοὶ τεκταινέσθω. 660
τὸ γὰρ εὖ μετ' ἐμοῦ καὶ τὸ δίκαιον
ξύμμαχον ἔσται, κοὐ μή ποθ' ἁλῶ
περὶ τὴν πόλιν ὢν ὥσπερ ἐκεῖνος
δειλὸς καὶ λακαταπύγων.

δεῦρο Μοῦσ' ἐλθὲ φλεγυρά, πυρὸς ἔχουσα μένος, ἔν-
τονος, Ἀχαρνική. 665
οἷον ἐξ ἀνθράκων πρινίνων φέψαλος ἀνήλατ', ἐρεθι-
ζόμενος οὐρίᾳ ῥιπίδι,
ἡνίκ' ἂν ἐπανθρακίδες ὦσι παρακείμεναι, 670

---

[a] Aegina had become tributary to Athens about 455 B.C.;
its autonomy was demanded by Sparta at the outset of the

THE ACHARNIANS, 651-670

And they'll in the war be the stronger by far,
        enjoying his counsel and skill.
And therefore the Spartans approach you to-day
        with proffers of Peace and Goodwill,
Just asking indeed that Aegina [a] ye cede ;
        and nought do they care for the isle,
But you of the Poet who serves you so well
        they fain would despoil and beguile.
But be *you* on your guard nor surrender the bard ;
        for his Art shall be righteous and true.
Rare blessings and great will he work for the State,
        rare happiness shower upon you ;
Not fawning, or bribing, or striving to cheat
        with an empty unprincipled jest ;
Not seeking your favour to curry or nurse,
        but teaching the things that are best.

    AND THEREFORE I say to the people to-day,
    Let Cleon the worst of his villainies try,
    His anger I fear not, his threats I defy !
    For Honour and Right beside me will fight,
        And never shall I
    In ought that relates to the city be found
    Such a craven as he, such a profligate hound.

O MUSE, fiery-flashing, with temper of flame,
        energetic, Acharnian, come to my gaze,
Like the wild spark that leaps from the evergreen oak,
        when its red-glowing charcoal is fanned to a blaze,
And the small fish are lying all in order for the
    frying ;

war, 431 B.C., but the Athenians at once expelled all the inhabitants and colonized it (Thuc. ii. 27). Aristophanes may have been of Aeginetan origin ; see Rogers' Introd p. ix.

ARISTOPHANES

οἱ δὲ Θασίαν ἀνακυκῶσι λιπαράμπυκα,
οἱ δὲ βάπτωσιν, οὕτω σοβαρὸν ἐλθὲ μέλος εὔτονον
   ἀγροικότονον,
ὡς ἐμὲ λαβοῦσα τὸν δημότην.   675

οἱ γέροντες οἱ παλαιοὶ μεμφόμεσθα τῇ πόλει.
οὐ γὰρ ἀξίως ἐκείνων ὧν ἐναυμαχήσαμεν
γηροβοσκούμεσθ' ὑφ' ὑμῶν, ἀλλὰ δεινὰ πάσχομεν.
οἵτινες γέροντας ἄνδρας ἐμβαλόντες ἐς γραφὰς
ὑπὸ νεανίσκων ἐᾶτε καταγελᾶσθαι ῥητόρων,   680
οὐδὲν ὄντας, ἀλλὰ κωφοὺς καὶ παρεξηυλημένους,
οἷς Ποσειδῶν ἀσφάλειός ἐστιν ἡ βακτηρία·
τονθορύζοντες δὲ γήρᾳ τῷ λίθῳ προσέσταμεν,
οὐχ ὁρῶντες οὐδὲν εἰ μὴ τῆς δίκης τὴν ἠλύγην.
ὁ δὲ νεανίας, ἑαυτῷ σπουδάσας ξυνηγορεῖν,   685
ἐς τάχος παίει ξυνάπτων στρογγύλοις τοῖς ῥήμασι·
κᾆτ' ἀνελκύσας ἐρωτᾷ, σκανδάληθρ' ἱστὰς ἐπῶν,
ἄνδρα Τιθωνὸν σπαράττων καὶ ταράττων καὶ κυκῶν.

[a] Θασία, sc. ἄλμη, is a sort of pickle, and perhaps the Pindaric epithet λιπαράμπυκα (" with shining frontlet ") refers to the gleam of the fish as they are dipped in it.

[b] The Scholiast explains as = τῷ βήματι (cf. P. 690), "the orator's stand"; but Rogers thinks there " would be in every dicastery a sort of stone altar on which the witnesses and others took their oaths."

[c] i.e. the fog in which it had become enveloped.

THE ACHARNIANS, 671-688

 And some are mixing Thasian,*a* richly dight, shiny-bright,
  And some dip the small fish therein ;
 Come, fiery-flashing Maid, to thy fellow-burgher's aid,
 With exactly such a song, so glowing and so strong,
  To our old rustic melodies akin.

WE the veterans blame the City.
      Is it meet and right that we,
Who of old, in manhood's vigour,
      fought your battles on the sea,
Should in age be left untended,
      yea exposed to shame and ill ?
Is it right to let the youngsters
      air their pert forensic skill,
Grappling us with writs and warrants,
      holding up our age to scorn ?
We who now have lost our music,
      feeble nothings, dull, forlorn,
We whose only " Safe Poseidon "
      is the staff we lean upon,
There we stand, decayed and muttering,
      hard beside the Court-house Stone,*b*
Nought discerning all around us
      save the darkness of our case.*c*
Comes the youngster, who has compassed
      for himself the accuser's place,
Slings his tight and nipping phrases,
      tackling us with legal scraps,
Pulls us up and cross-examines,
      setting little verbal traps,
Rends and rattles old Tithonus
      till the man is dazed and blind ;

ARISTOPHANES

ὁ δ' ὑπὸ γήρως μασταρύζει, κᾆτ' ὀφλὼν ἀπέρχεται·
εἶτα λύζει καὶ δακρύει, καὶ λέγει πρὸς τοὺς φίλους, 690
οὗ μ' ἐχρῆν σορὸν πρίασθαι, τοῦτ' ὀφλὼν ἀπέρχομαι.

ταῦτα πῶς εἰκότα, γέροντ' ἀπολέσαι, πολιὸν ἄνδρα,
  περὶ κλεψύδραν,
πολλὰ δὴ ξυμπονήσαντα, καὶ θερμὸν ἀπομορξάμενον
  ἀνδρικὸν ἱδρῶτα δὴ καὶ πολύν,
ἄνδρ' ἀγαθὸν ὄντα Μαραθῶνι περὶ τὴν πόλιν;
εἶτα Μαραθῶνι μὲν ὅτ' ἦμεν, ἐδιώκομεν·
νῦν δ' ὑπ' ἀνδρῶν πονηρῶν σφόδρα διωκόμεθα,
  κᾆτα προσαλισκόμεθα.   701
πρὸς τάδε τί ἀντερεῖ Μαρψίας;

τῷ γὰρ εἰκὸς ἄνδρα κυφόν, ἡλίκον Θουκυδίδην
ἐξολέσθαι συμπλακέντα τῇ Σκυθῶν ἐρημίᾳ,
τῷδε τῷ Κηφισοδήμῳ, τῷ λάλῳ ξυνηγόρῳ;   705
ὥστ' ἐγὼ μὲν ἠλέησα κἀπεμορξάμην ἰδὼν
ἄνδρα πρεσβύτην ὑπ' ἀνδρὸς τοξότου κυκώμενον,
ὃς μὰ τὴν Δήμητρ', ἐκεῖνος ἡνίκ' ἦν Θουκυδίδης,

---

[a] Here in the sense of "prosecutors."
[b] φιλόνεικος καὶ φλύαρος καὶ θορυβώδης ῥήτωρ : Schol.
[c] An aristocratic leader, the rival of Pericles, ostracized 444 B.C. Cephisodemus and Evathlus (710) were two of his accusers; the former probably "had some Scythian blood in his veins," and "a Scythian wilderness" seems to stand for something barbarous, inhuman; cf. Aesch. P.V. 2 Σκύθην ἐς οἷμον, ἄβατον εἰς ἐρημίαν.

THE ACHARNIANS, 689-708

Till with toothless gums he mumbles,
                then departs condemned and fined ;
Sobbing, weeping, as he passes,
                to his friends he murmurs low,
All I've saved to buy a coffin
                now to pay the fine must go.

How CAN it be seemly a grey-headed man by the
    Water-clock's stream to decoy and to slay,
Who of old, young and bold, laboured hard for the
    State, who would wipe off his sweat and return
    to the fray ?
  At Marathon arrayed, to the battle-shock we ran,
  And our mettle we displayed, foot to foot, man to
    man,
        And our name and our fame shall not die.
  Aye in youth we were Pursuers on the Marathonian
    plain,
  But in age Pursuers [a] vex us, and our best defence
    is vain.
        To this what can Marpsias [b] reply ?

OH, THUCYDIDES [c] to witness,
              bowed with age, in sore distress,
Feebly struggling in the clutches
              of that Scythian wilderness
Fluent glib Cephisodemus,—
              Oh the sorrowful display !
I myself was moved with pity,
              yea and wiped a tear away,
Grieved at heart the gallant veteran
              by an archer mauled to view ;
Him who, were he, by Demeter,
              that Thucydides we knew,

ARISTOPHANES

οὐδ' ἂν αὐτὴν τὴν Ἀχαίαν ῥᾳδίως ἠνέσχετο,
ἀλλὰ κατεπάλαισε μέν γ' ἂν πρῶτον Εὐάθλους
    δέκα, 710
κατεβόησε δ' ἂν κεκραγὼς τοξότας τρισ-
    χιλίους,
περιετόξευσεν δ' ἂν αὐτοῦ τοῦ πατρὸς τοὺς
    ξυγγενεῖς.
ἀλλ' ἐπειδὴ τοὺς γέροντας οὐκ ἐᾷθ' ὕπνου
    τυχεῖν,
ψηφίσασθε χωρὶς εἶναι τὰς γραφάς, ὅπως ἂν ᾖ
τῷ γέροντι μὲν γέρων καὶ νωδὸς ὁ ξυνήγορος, 715
τοῖς νέοισι δ' εὐρύπρωκτος καὶ λάλος χὠ
    Κλεινίου.
κἀξελαύνειν χρὴ τὸ λοιπόν, κἂν φύγῃ τις,
    ζημιοῦν
τὸν γέροντα τῷ γέροντι, τὸν νέον δὲ τῷ νέῳ.

ΔΙ. ὅροι μὲν ἀγορᾶς εἰσιν οἵδε τῆς ἐμῆς.
ἐνταῦθ' ἀγοράζειν πᾶσι Πελοποννησίοις 720
ἔξεστι καὶ Μεγαρεῦσι καὶ Βοιωτίοις
ἐφ' ᾧτε πωλεῖν πρὸς ἐμέ, Λαμάχῳ δὲ μή.
ἀγορανόμους δὲ τῆς ἀγορᾶς καθίσταμαι
τρεῖς τοὺς λαχόντας τούσδ' ἱμάντας ἐκ
    Λεπρῶν.
ἐνταῦθα μήτε συκοφάντης εἰσίτω 725

---

[a] *i.e.* Demeter. Plutarch and Hesychius derive the title Ἀχαία from ἄχη, *sorrows*, but though this is doubtful, "it may perhaps explain the epithet given in the translation": R.
[b] Evathlus was a pugnacious orator whose name suggests that he was "a good fighter."
[c] Alcibiades.
[d] *In this new scene what was the Pnyx somehow becomes the market-place of Dicaeopolis.*

THE ACHARNIANS, 709-725

Would have stood no airs or nonsense
    from the Goddess Travel-sore,[a]
Would have thrown, the mighty wrestler,
    ten Evathluses [b] or more,
Shouted down three thousand archers
    with his accents of command,
Shot his own accuser's kinsmen
    in their Scythian fatherland.
Nay, but if ye will not leave us
    to our hardly earned repose,
Sort the writs, divide the actions,
    separating these from those ;
Who assails the old and toothless
    should be old and toothless too ;
For a youngster, wantons, gabblers,
    Cleinias' son [c] the trick may do.
So for future fines and exiles,
    fair and square the balance hold,
Let the youngster sue the youngster,
    and the old man sue the old.

DI. These are the boundaries of my market-
   place ; [d]
 And here may all the Peloponnesian folk,
 Megarians and Boeotians, freely trade
 Selling to me, but Lamachus may not.
 And these three thongs, of Leprous make, I
   set
 As market-clerks,[e] elected by the lot.
 Within these bounds may no informer come,

 [e] Officers who kept order in the market ; *cf.* 824, 968. The allusion in ἐκ Λεπρῶν is obscure. Some read λεπρῶν (*sc.* βοῶν) and quote the Scholiast τὰ τῶν λεπρῶν βοῶν δέρματα ἰσχυρά.

ARISTOPHANES

μήτ' ἄλλος ὅστις Φασιανός ἐστ' ἀνήρ.
ἐγὼ δὲ τὴν στήλην καθ' ἣν ἐσπεισάμην
μέτειμ', ἵνα στήσω φανερὰν ἐν τἀγορᾷ.

ΜΕΓΑΡΕΤΣ. ἀγορὰ 'ν 'Αθάναις χαῖρε, Μεγαρεῦσιν φίλα.
ἐπόθουν τυ ναὶ τὸν Φίλιον ἇπερ ματέρα.   730
ἀλλ', ὦ πονηρὰ κώριχ' ἀθλίου πατρός,
ἄμβατε ποττὰν μάδδαν, αἴ χ' εὕρητέ πᾳ.
ἀκούετε δή, ποτέχετ' ἐμὶν τὰν γαστέρα·
πότερα πεπρᾶσθαι χρῄδδετ', ἢ πεινῆν κακῶς;
ΚΟΡΑ. πεπρᾶσθαι πεπρᾶσθαι.   735
ΜΕ. ἐγώνγα καὐτός φαμι. τίς δ' οὕτως ἄνους
ὃς ὑμέ κα πρίαιτο, φανερὰν ζαμίαν;
ἀλλ' ἔστι γάρ μοι Μεγαρικά τις μαχανά.
χοίρους γὰρ ὑμὲ σκευάσας φασῶ φέρειν.
περίθεσθε τάσδε τὰς ὁπλὰς τῶν χοιρίων.   740
ὅπως δὲ δοξεῖτ' ἦμεν ἐξ ἀγαθᾶς ὑός·
ὡς ναὶ τὸν Ἑρμᾶν, αἴπερ ἰξεῖτ' οἴκαδις
ἄπρατα, πειρασεῖσθε τᾶς λιμῷ κακῶς.
ἀλλ' ἀμφίθεσθε καὶ ταδὶ τὰ ῥυγχία,
κἤπειτεν ἐς τὸν σάκκον ὧδ' ἐσβαίνετε.   745
ὅπως δὲ γρυλιξεῖτε καὶ κοΐξετε
χῆσεῖτε φωνὰν χοιρίων μυστηρικῶν.
ἐγὼν δὲ καρυξῶ Δικαιόπολιν ὅπᾳ.
Δικαιόπολι, ἦ λῇς πρίασθαι χοιρία;
ΔΙ. τί ἀνὴρ Μεγαρικός;

[a] Lit. "from the river Phasis" in Colchis, but here the word is taken as derived from φάσις = "an information," cf. φαρῶ 827.
[b] Treaties were regularly inscribed on στῆλαι.
[c] Exit Dicaeopolis and a half-starved Megarian enters, followed by two little girls whom he bids "mount" (cf. ἄμβατε) the stage from the side-scenes.

THE ACHARNIANS, 726–750

Or any other syco-Phasian [a] man.
But I'll go fetch the Treaty-Pillar [b] here,
And set it up in some conspicuous place.[c]

MEGARIAN. Guid day, Athanian market, Megara's luve!
By Frien'ly Zeus, I've miss't ye like my mither.
But ye, puir bairnies o' a waefu' father,
Speel up, ye'll aiblins fin' a barley-bannock.
Now listen, bairns; atten' wi' a' ycre-paineh;[d]
Whilk wad ye liefer, to be sellt or clemmed?
GIRLS. Liefer be sellt! Liefer be sellt!
MEG. An' sae say I mysel'! But wha sae doited
As to gie aught for *you*, a sicker skaith?
Aweel, I ken a pawkie Megara-trick,[e]
I'se busk ye up, an' say I'm bringin' piggies.
Here, slip these wee bit clooties on yere nieves,
An' shaw yeresells a decent grumphie's weans.
For gin' I tak' ye hame unsellt, by Hairmes
Ye'll thole the warst extremities o' clemmin'.
Ne'est, pit thir lang pig-snowties owre yere nebs,
An' stech yere bodies in this sackie. Sae.
An' min' ye grunt an' grane an' g-r-r awa',
An' mak' the skirls o' little Mystery piggies.[f]
Mysel' will ca' for Dicaeopolis.
Hae! Dicaeopolis!
Are ye for buyin' onie pigs the day?
DI. How now, Megarian?

[d] τὸν νοῦν was expected for τὴν γάστερα.
[e] The Megarians claimed to be the inventors of Comedy; cf. W. 57.
[f] Sucking-pigs sacrificed to Demeter before initiation; cf. P. 374, 375.

ARISTOPHANES

ΜΕ. ἀγοράσοντες ἵκομες. 750
ΔΙ. πῶς ἔχετε;
ΜΕ. διαπειναμες ἀεὶ ποττὸ πῦρ.
ΔΙ. ἀλλ' ἡδύ τοι νὴ τὸν Δί', ἢν αὐλὸς παρῇ.
τί δ' ἄλλο πράττεθ' οἱ Μεγαρεῖς νῦν;
ΜΕ. οἷα δή.
ὅκα μὲν ἐγὼ τηνῶθεν ἐμπορευόμαν,
ἄνδρες πρόβουλοι τοῦτ' ἔπρασσον τᾷ πόλει, 755
ὅπως τάχιστα καὶ κάκιστ' ἀπολοίμεθα.
ΔΙ. αὐτίκ' ἄρ' ἀπαλλάξεσθε πραγμάτων.
ΜΕ. σά μάν;
ΔΙ. τί δ' ἄλλο Μεγαροῖ; πῶς ὁ σῖτος ὤνιος;
ΜΕ. παρ' ἀμὲ πολυτίματος ἅπερ τοὶ θεοί.
ΔΙ. ἅλας οὖν φέρεις;
ΜΕ. οὐχ ὑμὲς αὐτῶν ἄρχετε; 760
ΔΙ. οὐδὲ σκόροδα;
ΜΕ. ποῖα σκόροδ'; ὑμὲς τῶν ἀεί,
ὅκκ' ἐσβάλητε, τὼς ἀρωραῖοι μύες,
πάσσακι τὰς ἄγλιθας ἐξορύσσετε.
ΔΙ. τί δαὶ φέρεις;
ΜΕ. χοίρους ἐγώνγα μυστικάς.
ΔΙ. καλῶς λέγεις· ἐπίδειξον.
ΜΕ. ἀλλὰ μὰν καλαί. 765
ἄντεινον, αἰ λῇς· ὡς παχεῖα καὶ καλά.
ΔΙ. τουτὶ τί ἦν τὸ πρᾶγμα;
ΜΕ. χοῖρος ναὶ Δία.
ΔΙ. τί λέγεις σύ; ποδαπὴ χοῖρος ἥδε;

---

[a] Lit. "We have starving-bouts by the fire." But Dic. is supposed to hear διαπίνομεν, "have *drinking*-bouts." "In the translation the Megarian uses 'greeting' in the Scotch sense of *weeping*; the Athenian understands it in the sense of exchanging greetings": R.

THE ACHARNIANS, 750–768

MEG.   Come to niffer, guidman.
DI. How fare ye all?
MEG.   A' greetin' by the fire.[a]
DI. And very jolly too if there's a piper.
What do your people do besides?
MEG.   Sae sae.
For when I cam' frae Megara toun the morn,
Our Lairds o' Council were in gran' debate
How we might quickliest perish, but an' ben.
DI. So ye'll lose all your troubles.
MEG.   What for no?
DI. What else at Megara? What's the price of wheat?
MEG. Och! high eneugh: high as the Gudes, an' higher.[b]
DI. Got any salt?
MEG.   Ye're maisters o' our saut.[c]
DI. Or garlic?
MEG.   Garlic, quotha! when yeresells,
Makin' yere raids like onie swarm o' mice,
Howkit up a' the rooties wi' a stak'.
DI. What *have* you got then?
MEG.   Mystery piggies, I.
DI. That's good; let's see them.
MEG.   Hae! They're bonnie piggies.
Lift it, an't please you; 'tis sae sleek an' bonnie.
DI. What on earth's this?
MEG.   A piggie that, by Zeus.
DI. A pig! What sort of pig?

[b] πολυτίματος=(1) "much-honoured," *cf*. 807; or (2) "high-priced."

[c] Their salt-works were at Nisaea; but the Athenians in 427 B.C. had seized Minoa, the island or promontory which commands it (Thuc. iii. 51).

ARISTOPHANES

ΜΕ. Μεγαρικά.
ἦ οὐ χοῖρός ἐσθ' ἄδ';
ΔΙ. οὐκ ἔμοιγε φαίνεται.
ΜΕ. οὐ δεινά; θᾶσθε τοῦδε τὰς ἀπιστίας· 770
οὔ φατι τάνδε χοῖρον ἦμεν. ἀλλὰ μάν,
αἰ λῇς, περίδου μοι περὶ θυμητιδᾶν ἁλῶν,
αἰ μή 'στιν οὗτος χοῖρος Ἑλλάνων νόμῳ.
ΔΙ. ἀλλ' ἔστιν ἀνθρώπου γε.
ΜΕ. ναὶ τὸν Διοκλέα,
ἐμά γα. τὺ δέ νιν εἴμεναι τίνος δοκεῖς; 775
ἦ λῇς ἀκοῦσαι φθεγγομένας;
ΔΙ. νὴ τοὺς θεοὺς
ἔγωγε.
ΜΕ. φώνει δὴ τὺ ταχέως, χοιρίον.
οὐ χρῇσθα; σιγᾷς, ὦ κάκιστ' ἀπολουμένα;
πάλιν τυ ἀποισῶ ναὶ τὸν Ἑρμᾶν οἴκαδις.
ΚΟ. κοΐ, κοΐ. 780
ΜΕ. αὗτα 'στὶ χοῖρος;
ΔΙ. νῦν γε χοῖρος φαίνεται.
ἀτὰρ ἐκτραφείς γε κύσθος ἔσται πέντ' ἐτῶν.
ΜΕ. σάφ' ἴσθι, ποττὰν ματέρ' εἰκασθήσεται.
ΔΙ. ἀλλ' οὐδὲ θύσιμός ἐστιν αὐτηγί.
ΜΕ. σά μάν;
πᾷ δ' οὐχὶ θύσιμός ἐστι;
ΔΙ. κέρκον οὐκ ἔχει. 785
ΜΕ. νέα γάρ ἐστιν· ἀλλὰ δελφακουμένα
ἑξεῖ μεγάλαν τε καὶ παχεῖαν κἠρυθράν.

[a] " The next twenty-six lines are largely occupied with a play on the double meaning of χοῖρος, (1) a pig, and (2) τὸ γυναικεῖον αἰδοῖον, doubtless portrayed on the σάκκος ": R.
[b] i.e. flavoured with thyme.

MEG.   A Megara piggie.
         What ! no a piggie that ? [a]
DI.   It doesn't seem so.
MEG.   'Tis awfu' ! Och the disbelievin' carle !
         Uphaudin' she's na piggie ! Will ye wad,
         My eantie frien', a pinch o' thymy [b] saut
         She's no a piggie in the Hellanian use [c] ?
DI.   A human being's—
MEG.   Weel, by Diocles,
         She's mine ; wha's piggie did ye think she
             was ?
         Mon ? wad ye hear them skirlin' ?
DI.   By the Powers,
         I would indeed.
MEG.   Now piggies, skirl awa'.
         Ye winna ? winna skirl, ye graceless hizzies ?
         By Hairmes then I 'se tak' ye hame again.
GIRLS.   Wee ! wee ! wee !
MEG.   This no a piggie ?
DI.   Faith, it seems so now,
         But 'twont remain so for five years I'm think-
             ing.
MEG.   Trowth, tak' my word for't, she'll be like her
             mither.
DI.   But she's no good for offerings.
MEG.   What for no ?
         What for nae guid for offerins ?
DI.   She's no tail.[d]
MEG.   Aweel, the puir wee thing, she's owre young
             yet.
         But when she's auld, she'll have a gawcie tail.

   [c] *i.e.* in the Hellenic tongue.
   [d] Therefore not " without blemish " and so unfit for
sacrifice.

77

ARISTOPHANES

ΔΙ. ἀλλ' αἰ τράφεν λῆς, ἅδε τοι χοῖρος καλά.
ΔΙ. ὡς ξυγγενὴς ὁ κύσθος αὐτῆς θατέρᾳ.
ΜΕ. ὁμοματρία γάρ ἐστι κἠκ τωὐτῶ πατρός. 790
αἰ δ' ἂν παχυνθῇ κἀναχνοιανθῇ τριχί,
κάλλιστος ἔσται χοῖρος Ἀφροδίτᾳ θύειν.
ΔΙ. ἀλλ' οὐχὶ χοῖρος τἀφροδίτῃ θύεται.
ΜΕ. οὐ χοῖρος Ἀφροδίτᾳ; μόνᾳ γα δαιμόνων.
καὶ γίγνεταί γα τᾶνδε τᾶν χοίρων τὸ κρῆς 795
ἅδιστον ἂν τὸν ὀδελὸν ἀμπεπαρμένον.
ΔΙ. ἤδη δ' ἄνευ τῆς μητρὸς ἐσθίοιεν ἄν;
ΜΕ. ναὶ τὸν Ποτειδᾶ, κἂν ἄνευ γα τῶ πατρός.
ΔΙ. τί δ' ἐσθίει μάλιστα;
ΜΕ. πάνθ' ἅ κα διδῷς.
αὐτὸς δ' ἐρώτη.
ΔΙ. χοῖρε χοῖρε.
ΚΟ. Α. κοΐ, κοΐ. 800
ΔΙ. τρώγοις ἂν ἐρεβίνθους;
ΚΟ. Α. κοΐ, κοΐ, κοΐ.
ΔΙ. τί δαί; Φιβάλεως ἰσχάδας;
ΚΟ. Α. κοΐ, κοΐ.
ΔΙ. τί δαὶ σύ; τρώγοις ἄν;
ΚΟ. Β. κοΐ, κοΐ, κοΐ.
ΔΙ. ὡς ὀξὺ πρὸς τὰς ἰσχάδας κεκράγατε.
ἐνεγκάτω τις ἔνδοθεν τῶν ἰσχάδων 805
τοῖς χοιριδίοισιν. ἆρα τρώξονται; βαβαί,
οἷον ῥοθιάζουσ', ὦ πολυτίμηθ' Ἡράκλεις.
ποδαπὰ τὰ χοιρί'; ὡς Τραγασαῖα φαίνεται.
ΜΕ. ἀλλ' οὔτι πάσας κατέτραγον τὰς ἰσχάδας,
ἐγὼ γὰρ αὐτῶν τάνδε μίαν ἀνειλόμαν. 810

[a] Phibalis was a low-lying district of Megara bordering on Attica.
[b] Τραγασαῖα with a play on τραγεῖν, to eat; Tragassae was

	But wad ye rear them, here's a bonnie piggie!
DI.	Why she's the staring image of the other.
MEG.	They're o' ane father an' ane mither, baith.
	But bide a wee, an' when she's fat an' curlie
	She'll be an offerin' gran' for Aphrodite.
DI.	A pig's no sacrifice for Aphrodite.
MEG.	What, no for Her! Mon, for hirsel' the lane.
	Why there's nae flesh sae tastie as the flesh
	O' thae sma piggies, roastit on a spit.
DI.	But can they feed without their mother yet?
MEG.	Poteidan, yes! withouten father too.
DI.	What will they eat most freely?
MEG.	Aught ye gie them.
	But spier yoursel'.
DI.	Hey, piggy, piggy!
FIRST GIRL.	Wee!
DI.	Do you like pease, you piggy?
FIRST GIRL.	Wee, wee, wee!
DI.	What, and Phibalean [a] figs as well?
FIRST GIRL.	Wee, wee!
DI.	What, and you other piggy?
SECOND GIRL.	Wee, wee, wee!
DI.	Eh, but ye're squealing bravely for the figs.
	Bring out some figs here, one of you within,
	For these small piggies. Will they eat them?
	Yah!
	Worshipful Heracles! how they are gobbling now.
	Whence come the pigs? They seem to me Aetallian.[b]
MEG.	Na, na; they haena eaten a' thae figs.
	See here; here's ane I pickit up mysel'.

a small town near Troy. "'Eat-all-ians' in the translation is intended to recall *Aetolians*": R.

ARISTOPHANES

ΔΙ. νὴ τὸν Δί' ἀστείω γε τὼ βοσκήματε·
πόσου πρίωμαί σοι τὰ χοιρίδια; λέγε.
ΜΕ. τὸ μὲν ἅτερον τούτων, σκορόδων τροπαλλίδος,
τὸ δ' ἅτερον, αἰ λῇς, χοίνικος μόνας ἁλῶν.
ΔΙ. ὠνήσομαί σοι· περίμεν' αὐτοῦ.
ΜΕ. ταῦτα δή. 815
Ἑρμᾶ 'μπολαῖε, τὰν γυναῖκα τὰν ἐμὰν
οὕτω μ' ἀποδόσθαι τάν τ' ἐμαυτῶ ματέρα.
ΣΥΚΟΦΑΝΤΗΣ. ὤνθρωπε, ποδαπός;
ΜΕ. χοιροπώλας Μεγαρικός.
ΣΥ. τὰ χοιρίδια τοίνυν ἐγὼ φανῶ ταδὶ
πολέμια καὶ σέ.
ΜΕ. τοῦτ' ἐκεῖν', ἵκει πάλιν 820
ὅθενπερ ἀρχὰ τῶν κακῶν ἁμῖν ἔφυ.
ΣΥ. κλάων Μεγαριεῖς. οὐκ ἀφήσεις τὸν σάκον;
ΜΕ. Δικαιόπολι Δικαιόπολι, φαντάζομαι.
ΔΙ. ὑπὸ τοῦ; τίς ὁ φαίνων σ' ἐστίν; Ἀγορανόμοι,
τοὺς συκοφάντας οὐ θύραζ' ἐξείρξετε; 825
τιὴ μαθὼν φαίνεις ἄνευ θρυαλλίδος;
ΣΥ. οὐ γὰρ φανῶ τοὺς πολεμίους;
ΔΙ. κλάων γε σύ,
εἰ μὴ 'τέρωσε συκοφαντήσεις τρέχων.
ΜΕ. οἷον τὸ κακὸν ἐν ταῖς Ἀθάναις τοῦτ' ἔνι.
ΔΙ. θάρρει, Μεγαρίκ'· ἀλλ' ἧς τὰ χοιρίδι' ἀπέδου 830
τιμῆς, λαβὲ ταυτὶ τὰ σκόροδα καὶ τοὺς ἅλας,
καὶ χαῖρε πόλλ'.
ΜΕ. ἀλλ' ἁμὶν οὐκ ἐπιχώριον.
ΔΙ. πολυπραγμοσύνη νυν ἐς κεφαλὴν τρέποιτ'
ἐμοί.
ΜΕ. ὦ χοιρίδια, πειρῆσθε κἄνευ τῶ πατρὸς
παίειν ἐφ' ἁλὶ τὰν μᾶδδαν, αἴ κά τις διδῷ. 835

80

THE ACHARNIANS, 811-835

DI. Upon my word, they are jolly little beasts.
   What shall I give you for the pair? let's hear.
MEG. Gie me for ane a tie o' garlic, will ye,
   An' for the tither half a peck o' saut.
DI. I'll buy them: stay you here awhile.
MEG.   Aye, aye.
   Traffickin' Hairmes, wad that I could swap
   Baith wife an' mither on sic terms as thae.
INFORMER. Man! who are *you*?
MEG.   Ane Megara piggie-seller.
INF. Then I'll denounce your goods and you yourself
   As enemies!
MEG.   Hech, here it comes again,
   The vera primal source of a' our wae.
INF. You'll Megarize to your cost. Let go the sack.
MEG. Dicaeopolis! Dicaeopolis! Here's a chiel
   Denouncin' me.
DI. (*Re-entering*) Where is he? Market-clerks,
   Why don't you keep these sycophants away?
   What! show him up without a lantern-wick?[a]
INF. Not show our enemies up?
DI.   You had better not.
   Get out, and do your showing other-where.
MEG. The pest thae birkies are in Athans toun!
DI. Well never mind, Megarian, take the things,
   Garlic and salt, for which you sold the pigs.
   Fare well!
MEG.   That's na our way in Megara toun.[b]
DI. Then on MY head the officious wish return!
MEG. O piggies, try withouten father now
   To eat wi' saut yere bannock, an' ye git ane.

---

[a] There is a play on the double meaning of φαίνω, (1) "give light," (2) "lay an information."
[b] *i.e.* we always "fare ill."

ARISTOPHANES

ΧΟ. εὐδαιμονεῖ γ' ἄνθρωπος. οὐκ ἤκουσας οἷ προ-
βαίνει
τὸ πρᾶγμα τοῦ βουλεύματος; καρπώσεται
γὰρ ἀνὴρ
ἐν τἀγορᾷ καθήμενος·
κἂν εἰσίῃ τις Κτησίας,
ἢ συκοφάντης ἄλλος, οἰ-   840
μώζων καθεδεῖται·
οὐδ' ἄλλος ἀνθρώπων ὑποψωνῶν σε πημανεῖ τι·
οὐδ' ἐξομόρξεται Πρέπις τὴν εὐρυπρωκτίαν σοι,
οὐδ' ὠστιεῖ Κλεωνύμῳ·
χλαῖναν δ' ἔχων φανὴν δίει·   845
κοὐ ξυντυχών σ' Ὑπέρβολος
δικῶν ἀναπλήσει·
οὐδ' ἐντυχὼν ἐν τἀγορᾷ πρόσεισί σοι βαδίζων
Κρατῖνος ἀποκεκαρμένος μοιχὸν μιᾷ μαχαίρᾳ,
ὁ περιπόνηρος Ἀρτέμων,   850
ὁ ταχὺς ἄγαν τὴν μουσικήν,
ὄζων κακὸν τῶν μασχαλῶν
πατρὸς Τραγασαίου·
οὐδ' αὖθις αὖ σε σκώψεται Παύσων ὁ
παμπόνηρος,
Λυσίστρατός τ' ἐν τἀγορᾷ, Χολαργέων ὄνειδος, 855

[a] καταπυγών : Schol.   [b] See Index.
[c] Not the great Cr., but some young dandy, whose hair was "trimmed adulterer-wise" with a razor (μιᾷ μ. as opposed to "double-bladed scissors"); see R. But L. & S. (s.v. μοιχός) explain κείρεσθαι μοῖχον μ. μ. as a *punishment* for adultery.
[d] Artemon was an engineer employed by Pericles in sieges. Being lame, he had to be carried to the works in a litter, and so was nicknamed ὁ περιφόρητος, which περιπόνηρος recalls. But the phrase Περιφόρητος Ἀρτέμων was also a proverbial saying derived from an earlier Artemon, satirized by Anacreon

THE ACHARNIANS, 836–855

CHOR. A happy lot the man has got :
   his scheme devised with wondrous art
Proceeds and prospers as you see ;
   and now he'll sit in his private Mart
The fruit of his bold design to reap.
And O if a Ctesias come this way,
Or other informers vex us, they
Will soon for their trespass weep.
No sneak shall grieve you buying first
   the fish you wanted to possess,
No Prepis [a] on your dainty robes
   wipe off his utter loathsomeness.
You'll no Cleonymus jostle there ;
But all unsoiled through the Mart you'll go,
And no Hyperbolus [b] work you woe
With writs enough and to spare.

Never within these bounds shall walk
   the little fop we all despise,
The young Cratinus [c] neatly shorn
   with single razor wanton-wise,
That Artemon-engineer of ill,[d]
Whose father sprang from an old he-goat,[e]
And father and son, as ye all may note,
Are rank with its fragrance still.

No Pauson,[f] scurvy knave, shall here
   insult you in the market-place,
No vile Lysistratus, to all
   Cholargian folk a dire disgrace,

as a rascal (πόνηρος) who, having become wealthy, was noted for his luxury and never moved except on a litter; see Plut. *Pericles*, ch. 27.
[e] For Τραγασαίου see 808 ; here the name is only introduced to suggest τράγος " a he-goat."
[f] A starveling painter and caricaturist.

ARISTOPHANES

ὁ περιαλουργὸς τοῖς κακοῖς,
ῥιγῶν τε καὶ πεινῶν ἀεὶ
πλεῖν ἢ τριάκονθ᾽ ἡμέρας
τοῦ μηνὸς ἑκάστου.

ΒΟΙΩΤΟΣ. ἴττω Ἡρακλῆς, ἔκαμόν γα τὰν τύλαν κακῶς. 860
κατάθου τὺ τὰν γλάχων᾽ ἀτρέμας, Ἰσμήνιχε·
ὑμὲς δ᾽, ὅσοι Θείβαθεν αὐληταὶ πάρα,
τοῖς ὀστίνοις φυσεῖτε τὸν πρωκτὸν κυνός.
ΔΙ. παῦ᾽ ἐς κόρακας. οἱ σφῆκες οὐκ ἀπὸ τῶν
θυρῶν;
πόθεν προσέπτανθ᾽ οἱ κακῶς ἀπολούμενοι 865
ἐπὶ τὴν θύραν μοι Χαιριδεῖς βομβαύλιοι;
ΒΟΙ. νεὶ τὸν Ἰόλαον, ἐπιχαρίττως γ᾽, ὦ ξένε·
Θείβαθε γὰρ φυσᾶντες ἐξόπισθέ μου
τἄνθεια τᾶς γλάχωνος ἀπέκιξαν χαμαί.
ἀλλ᾽ εἴ τι βούλει, πρίασο, τῶν ἐγὼ φέρω, 870
τῶν ὀρταλίχων, ἢ τῶν τετραπτερυλλίδων.
ΔΙ. ὦ χαῖρε, κολλικοφάγε Βοιωτίδιον.
τί φέρεις;
ΒΟΙ. ὅσ᾽ ἐστὶν ἀγαθὰ Βοιωτοῖς ἁπλῶς,
ὀρίγανον, γλαχώ, ψιάθως, θρυαλλίδας,
νάσσας, κολοιώς, ἀτταγᾶς, φαλαρίδας, 875
τροχίλως, κολύμβως.
ΔΙ. ὡσπερεὶ χειμὼν ἄρα
ὀρνιθίας εἰς τὴν ἀγορὰν ἐλήλυθας.

---

[a] ὀστίνοις, sc. αὐλοῖς, the pipes being made of bone. Many suppose τὸν π. κυνός to describe the tune they are to strike up, but R. thinks that they play a sort of bagpipes made of dog-skin, so that π. κυνός may be taken literally.
[b] See Index, s.v. Chaeris.
[c] ὀρταλίχων = ἀλεκτρυόνων in the Bocotian dialect : Schol.

THE ACHARNIANS, 856–877

    That deep-dyed sinner, that low buffoon,
    Who always shivers and hungers sore
    Full thirty days, or it may be more,
    In every course of the moon.

BOEOTIAN. Hech sirs, my shouther's sair, wat Heracles!
    Ismeny lad, pit doon thae pennyroyal
    Wi' tentie care. Pipers wha cam' frae Thaibes
    Blaw oop the auld tyke's hurdies wi' the banes.[a]

DI. Hang you! shut up! Off from my doors, you wasps!
    Whence flew these curst Chaeridian[b] bumble-drones
    Here, to my door? Get to the ravens! Hence!

BOE. An' recht ye are, by Iolaus, stranger.
    They've blawn behint me a' the wa' frae Thaibes,
    An' danged the blossom aff my pennyroyal.
    But buy, an't please you, onie thing I've got,
    Some o' thae cleckin'[c] or thae four-winged gear.[d]

DI. O welcome, dear Boeotian muffin-eater,
    What have you there?

BOE.   A' that Boeoty gies us.
    Mats, dittany, pennyroyal, lantern-wicks,
    An' dooks, an' kaes, an' francolins, an' coots,
    Plivers an' divers.

DI.   Eh? Why then, methinks,
    You've brought fowl weather to my market-place.

[d] τετραπτερυλλίδων is a surprise for τετραπόδων.

ARISTOPHANES

ΒΟΙ. καὶ μὰν φέρω χᾶνας, λαγώς, ἀλώπεκας,
σκάλοπας, ἐχίνως, αἰελούρως, πικτίδας,
ἰκτίδας, ἐνύδριας, ἐγχέλεις Κωπαΐδας. 880
ΔΙ. ὦ τερπνότατον σὺ τέμαχος ἀνθρώποις φέρων,
δός μοι προσειπεῖν, εἰ φέρεις, τὰς ἐγχέλεις.
ΒΟΙ. πρέσβειρα πεντήκοντα Κωπᾴδων κορᾶν,
ἔκβαθι τῶδε, κἠπιχάριτται τῷ ξένῳ.
ΔΙ. ὦ φιλτάτη σὺ καὶ πάλαι ποθουμένη, 885
ἦλθες ποθεινὴ μὲν τρυγῳδικοῖς χοροῖς,
φίλη δὲ Μορύχῳ. δμῶες, ἐξενέγκατε
τὴν ἐσχάραν μοι δεῦρο καὶ τὴν ῥιπίδα.
σκέψασθε, παῖδες, τὴν ἀρίστην ἔγχελυν,
ἥκουσαν ἕκτῳ μόλις ἔτει ποθουμένην· 890
προσείπατ' αὐτήν, ὦ τέκν'· ἄνθρακας δ' ἐγὼ
ὑμῖν παρέξω τῆσδε τῆς ξένης χάριν.
ἀλλ' ἔκφερ' αὐτήν· μηδὲ γὰρ θανών ποτε
σοῦ χωρὶς εἴην ἐντετευτλανωμένης.
ΒΟΙ. ἐμοὶ δὲ τιμὰ τᾶσδε πᾷ γενήσεται; 895
ΔΙ. ἀγορᾶς τέλος ταύτην γέ που δώσεις ἐμοί·
ἀλλ' εἴ τι πωλεῖς τῶνδε τῶν ἄλλων, λέγε.
ΒΟΙ. ἰώγα ταῦτα πάντα.
ΔΙ. φέρε, πόσου λέγεις;
ἢ φορτί' ἕτερ' ἐντεῦθεν ἐκεῖσ' ἄξεις;
ΒΟΙ. ἰὼ
ὅ τι γ' ἔστ' ἐν Ἀθάναις, ἐν Βοιωτοῖσιν δὲ μή. 900

---

[a] A parody of Aesch. Fr. 174 δέσποινα πεντήκοντα Νηρῄδων κορῶν.

[b] " He is thinking of the ἐπινίκια, the triumphal banquet to which the Chorus would presently be invited by the Choregus ": R.

THE ACHARNIANS, 878–900

BOE. Aye, an' I'm bringin' maukins, geese, an' tods.
Easels an' weasels, urchins, moles, an' cats,
An' otters too, an' eels frae Loch Copaïs.
DI. O man, to men their daintiest morsel bringing,
Let me salute the eels, if eels you bring.
BOE. Primest o' Loch Copaïs' fifty dochters *a*
Come oot o' that; an' mak' the stranger welcome.
DI. O loved, and lost, and longed for, thou art come,
A presence grateful to the Comic choirs,*b*
And dear to Morychus.*c* Bring me out at once,
O kitchen-knaves, the brasier and the fan.
Behold, my lads, this best of all the eels,
Six years a truant,*d* scarce returning now.
O children, welcome her; to you I'll give
A charcoal fire for this sweet stranger's sake.
Out with her! Never may I lose again,
Not even in death, my darling dressed in— beet.*e*
BOE. Whaur sall I get the siller for the feesh?
DI. This you shall give me as a market-toll.
But tell me, are these other things for sale?
BOE. Aye are they, a' thae goods.
DI. And at what price?
Or would you swap for something else?
BOE. I'se swap
For gear we haena, but ye Attics hae.

c A famous epicure; cf. *W.* 506, *P.* 1008.
d *i.e.* since the beginning of the war.
e A parody of the conclusion of Admetus's address to his wife who is giving her life for his, Eur. *Alc.* 367 μηδὲ γὰρ θανών ποτε | σοῦ χωρὶς εἴην, τῆς μόνης πιστῆς ἐμοί.

ΔΙ. ἀφύας ἄρ' ἄξεις πριάμενος Φαληρικὰς
ἢ κέραμον.
ΒΟΙ. ἀφύας ἢ κέραμον; ἀλλ' ἔντ' ἐκεῖ·
ἀλλ' ὅ τι παρ' ἁμῖν μή 'στι, τᾷδε δ' αὖ πολύ.
ΔΙ. ἐγᾦδα τοίνυν· συκοφάντην ἔξαγε,
ὥσπερ κέραμον ἐνδησάμενος.
ΒΟΙ. νεὶ τὼ Σιώ, 905
λάβοιμι μέντἂν κέρδος ἀγαγὼν καὶ πολύ,
ᾇπερ πίθακον ἀλιτρίας πολλᾶς πλέων.
ΔΙ. καὶ μὴν ὁδὶ Νίκαρχος ἔρχεται φανῶν.
ΒΟΙ. μικκός γα μᾶκος οὗτος.
ΔΙ. ἀλλ' ἅπαν κακόν.
ΝΙΚΑΡΧΟΣ. ταυτὶ τίνος τὰ φορτί' ἐστί;
ΒΟΙ. τῶδ' ἐμὰ 910
Θείβαθεν, ἴττω Δεύς.
ΝΙ. ἐγὼ τοίνυν ὁδὶ
φαίνω πολέμια ταῦτα.
ΒΟΙ. τί δαὶ κακὸν παθὼν
ὀρναπετίοισι πόλεμον ἤρω καὶ μάχαν;
ΝΙ. καὶ σέ γε φανῶ πρὸς τοῖσδε.
ΒΟΙ. τί ἀδικειμένος;
ΝΙ. ἐγὼ φράσω σοι τῶν περιεστώτων χάριν. 915
ἐκ τῶν πολεμίων γ' εἰσάγεις θρυαλλίδας.
ΔΙ. ἔπειτα φαίνεις δῆτα διὰ θρυαλλίδος;
ΝΙ. αὕτη γὰρ ἐμπρήσειεν ἂν τὸ νεώριον.
ΔΙ. νεώριον θρυαλλίς; οἴμοι, τίνι τρόπῳ;
ΝΙ. ἐνθεὶς ἂν ἐς τίφην ἀνὴρ Βοιώτιος 920
ἅψας ἂν εἰσπέμψειεν ἐς τὸ νεώριον

---

[a] Lit. "anchovies"; the Phaleric ones were noted, cf.
B. 76.

THE ACHARNIANS, 901–921

DI. Well then, what say you to Phaleric sprats,[a]
    Or earthenware?

BOE.   Sprats! ware! we've thae at hame.
    Gie us some gear we lack, an' ye've a rowth o'.

DI. I'll tell you what; pack an INFORMER up,
    Like ware for exportation.

BOE.   Mon! that's guid.
    By the Twa Gudes,[b] an' unco gain I'se mak'.
    Takin' a monkey fu' o' plaguy tricks.

DI. And here's Nicarchus[c] coming to denounce
    you!

BOE. He's sma' in bouk.

DI.   But every inch is bad.

NICARCHUS. Whose is this merchandise?

BOE.   'Tis a' mine here.
    Frae Thaibes, wat Zeus, I bure it.

NIC.   Then I here
    Denounce it all as enemies!

BOE.   Hout awa!
    Do ye mak' war an' enmity wi' the burdies?

NIC. Them and you too.

BOE.   What hae I dune ye wrang?

NIC. That will I say for the bystanders' sake.[d]
    A lantern-wick you are bringing from the foe.

DI. Show him up, would you, for a lantern-wick?

NIC. Aye, for that lantern-wick will fire the docks.

DI. A lantern-wick the docks! O dear, and how?

NIC. If a Boeotian stuck it in a beetle,
    And sent it, lighted, down a watercourse[e]

---

[b] The two gods (τὼ θεώ) of a Boeotian are Zethus and Amphion.   [c] Some unknown sycophant.

[d] τῶν περ. χάριν: apparently a favourite phrase with the orators.

[e] "A water-channel by which the superfluous water was carried down from the city into the sea at the Peiraeus": R.

ARISTOPHANES

δι' ὑδρορρόας, βορέαν ἐπιτηρήσας μέγαν.
κεἴπερ λάβοιτο τῶν νεῶν τὸ πῦρ ἅπαξ,
σελαγοῖντ' ἂν αἴφνης.

ΔΙ. ὦ κάκιστ' ἀπολούμενε,
σελαγοῖντ' ἂν ὑπὸ τίφης τε καὶ θρυαλλίδος; 925
ΝΙ. μαρτύρομαι.
ΔΙ. ξυλλάμβαν' αὐτοῦ τὸ στόμα·
δός μοι φορυτόν, ἵν' αὐτὸν ἐνδήσας φέρω,
ὥσπερ κέραμον, ἵνα μὴ καταγῇ φορούμενος.

ΧΟ. ἔνδησον, ὦ βέλτιστε, τῷ [στρ.
ξένῳ καλῶς τὴν ἐμπολὴν 930
οὕτως ὅπως
ἂν μὴ φέρων κατάξῃ.

ΔΙ. ἐμοὶ μελήσει ταῦτ', ἐπεί
τοι καὶ ψοφεῖ λάλον τι καὶ
πυρορραγὲς
κἄλλως θεοῖσιν ἐχθρόν.

ΧΟ. τί χρήσεταί ποτ' αὐτῷ; 935
ΔΙ. πάγχρηστον ἄγγος ἔσται,

κρατὴρ κακῶν, τριπτὴρ δικῶν,
φαίνειν ὑπευθύνους λυχνοῦ-
χος, καὶ κύλιξ
τὰ πράγματ' ἐγκυκᾶσθαι.

ΧΟ. πῶς δ' ἂν πεποιθοίη τις ἀγ- [ἀντ. 940
γείῳ τοιούτῳ χρώμενος

---
[a] Dic. lays hands on Nicarchus who calls the world to witness the assault.
[b] δικῶν, unexpectedly for ἐλαῶν. τριπτήρ is the vat into which the oil pressed from olives ran : the Informer squeezes "oil" from lawsuits.

	Straight to the docks, watching when Boreas blew
	His stiffest breeze, then if the ships caught fire,
	They'd blaze up in an instant.
DI.	Blaze, you rascal!
	What, with a beetle and a lantern-wick?
NIC.	Bear witness![a]
DI.	Stop his mouth, and bring me litter.
	I'll pack him up, like earthenware, for carriage,
	So they mayn't crack him on their journey home.
CHOR.	Tie up, O best of men, with care
	The honest stranger's piece of ware,
	For fear they break it,
	As homeward on their backs they take it.
DI.	To that, be sure, I'll have regard;
	Indeed it creaks as though 'twere charred,
	By cracks molested,
	And altogether God-detested.
CHOR.	How shall he deal with it?
DI.	For every use 'tis fit,
	A cup of ills, a lawsuit [b] can,
	For audits an informing pan,[c]
	A poisoned chalice
	Full filled with every kind of malice
CHOR.	But who can safely use, I pray,
	A thing like this from day to day

[c] Lit. "a lampstand to show up (*cf.* 826 *n.*) those who had to give in their accounts."

ARISTOPHANES

κατ' οἰκίαν
τοσόνδ' ἀεὶ ψοφοῦντι;

ΔΙ. ἰσχυρόν ἐστιν, ὠγάθ', ὥστ'
οὐκ ἂν καταγείη ποτ', εἴ-
περ ἐκ ποδῶν 945
κατωκάρα κρέμαιτο.

ΧΟ. ἤδη καλῶς ἔχει σοι.
ΒΟΙ. μέλλω γέ τοι θερίδδειν.

ΧΟ. ἀλλ', ὦ ξένων βέλτιστε, συν-
θέριζε, καὶ πρόσβαλλ' ὅπου
βούλει φέρων 950
πρὸς πάντα συκοφάντην.

ΔΙ. μόλις γ' ἐνέδησα τὸν κακῶς ἀπολούμενον.
αἴρου λαβὼν τὸν κέραμον, ὦ Βοιώτιε.
ΒΟΙ. ὑπόκυπτε τὰν τύλαν ἰών, Ἰσμήνιχε.
ΔΙ. χὤπως κατοίσεις αὐτὸν εὐλαβούμενος. 955
πάντως μὲν οἴσεις οὐδὲν ὑγιές, ἀλλ' ὅμως·
κἂν τοῦτο κερδάνῃς ἄγων τὸ φορτίον,
εὐδαιμονήσεις συκοφαντῶν γ' οὕνεκα.

ΘΕΡΑΠΩΝ. Δικαιόπολι.
ΔΙ. τίς ἔστι; τί με βωστρεῖς;
ΘΕΡ. ὅ τι;
ἐκέλευε Λάμαχός σε ταύτης τῆς δραχμῆς 960
εἰς τοὺς Χόας αὐτῷ μεταδοῦναι τῶν κιχλῶν,
τριῶν δραχμῶν δ' ἐκέλευε Κωπᾷδ' ἔγχελυν.

---
[a] He had been warned off the markets, 722.
[b] The second day of the Anthesteria, which R. would

In household matters,
A thing that always creaks and clatters?

DI. He's strong, my worthy friend, and tough:
He will not break for usage rough,
    Not though you shove him
Head foremost down, his heels above him.

CHOR. (*To Boeotian*) You've got a lovely pack.
BOE. A bonnie hairst I'se mak'.
CHOR. Aye, best of friends, your harvest make,
And whereso'er it please you take
    This artful, knowing
And best equipped informer going.

DI. 'Twas a tough business, but I've packed the scamp.
Lift up and take your piece of ware, Boeotian.
BOE. Gae, pit your shouther underneath, Ismeny.
DI. And pray be careful as you take him home.
You've got a rotten bale of goods, but still!
And if you make a harvest out of *him*,
You'll be in luck's way, as regards informers.

SERVANT. Dicaeopolis!
DI.   Well? why are you shouting?
SERV.   Why?
Lamachus [a] bids you, towards the Pitcher-feast,[b]
Give him some thrushes for this drachma here,
And for three drachmas one Copaïc eel.

identify with the Lenaea, at which this play was presented. Those who attended the feast seem to have brought their own provisions.

ARISTOPHANES

ΔΙ. ὁ ποῖος οὗτος Λάμαχος τὴν ἔγχελυν;
ΘΕΡ. ὁ δεινός, ὁ ταλαύρινος, ὃς τὴν Γοργόνα
πάλλει, κραδαίνων τρεῖς κατασκίους λόφους. 965
ΔΙ. οὐκ ἂν μὰ Δί', εἰ δοίη γέ μοι τὴν ἀσπίδα·
ἀλλ' ἐπὶ ταρίχει τοὺς λόφους κραδαινέτω·
ἢν δ' ἀπολιγαίνῃ, τοὺς ἀγορανόμους καλῶ.
ἐγὼ δ' ἐμαυτῷ τόδε λαβὼν τὸ φορτίον
εἴσειμ' ὑπαὶ πτερύγων κιχλᾶν καὶ κοψίχων. 970

ΧΟ.   εἶδες ὦ, εἶδες, ὦ   [στρ.
πᾶσα πόλι, τὸν φρόνιμον ἄνδρα, τὸν ὑπέρσοφον,
οἷ' ἔχει σπεισάμενος ἐμπορικὰ χρήματα δι-
     εμπολᾶν,
ὧν τὰ μὲν ἐν οἰκίᾳ
χρήσιμα, τὰ δ' αὖ πρέπει   975
χλιαρὰ κατεσθίειν.
αὐτόματα πάντ' ἀγαθὰ τῷδέ γε πορίζεται.

οὐδέποτ' ἐγὼ Πόλεμον οἴκαδ' ὑποδέξομαι,
οὐδὲ παρ' ἐμοί ποτε τὸν Ἁρμόδιον ᾄσεται
ξυγκατακλινείς, ὅτι παροίνιος ἀνὴρ ἔφυ,   980
ὅστις ἐπὶ πάντ' ἀγάθ' ἔχοντας ἐπικωμάσας,
εἰργάσατο πάντα κακὰ κἀνέτρεπε κἀξέχει,
κἀμάχετο, καὶ προσέτι πολλὰ προκαλουμένου,

---

[a] A soldier's fare, cf. 1101.
[b] i.e. the thongs described 724.
[c] "Between the marketing scenes and the banqueting scenes A. interposes an idyllic description of War and Peace": R.
[d] For this drinking-song cf. 1093 n.

DI. Who is this Lamachus that wants the eel?
SERV. The dread, the tough, the terrible, who wields
The Gorgon targe, and shakes three shadowy
plumes.
DI. An eel for HIM? Not though his targe he
gave me!
Let him go shake his plumes at his salt fish.[a]
If he demur, I'll call the Market clerks.[b]
Now for myself I'll carry all these things
Indoors, to the tune o' *merles an' mavises wings.*

CHOR.[c] Have ye seen him, all ye people,
    seen the man of matchless art,
Seen him, by his private treaty,
    traffic gain from every mart,
  Goods from every neighbour;
Some required for household uses;
    some 'twere pleasant warm to eat;
All the wealth of all the cities
    lavished here before his feet,
  Free from toil and labour.

War I'll never welcome in
    to share my hospitality,
Never shall the fellow sing
    Harmodius [d] in my company,
Always in his cups he acts
    so rudely and offensively.
Tipsily he burst upon
    our happy quiet family,
Breaking this, upsetting that,
    and brawling most pugnaciously.
Yea when we entreated him
    with hospitable courtesy,

ARISTOPHANES

πῖνε, κατάκεισο, λαβὲ τήνδε φιλοτησίαν,
τὰς χάρακας ἧπτε πολὺ μᾶλλον ἔτι τῷ πυρί, 985
ἐξέχει θ' ἡμῶν βίᾳ τὸν οἶνον ἐκ τῶν ἀμπέλων.

εἶδες ὡς ἐπτέρω- [ἀντ.
ταί τ' ἐπὶ τὸ δεῖπνον ἅμα καὶ μεγάλα δὴ φρονεῖ
τοῦ βίου δ' ἐξέβαλε δεῖγμα τάδε τὰ πτερὰ πρὸ τῶν
θυρῶν.
ὦ Κύπριδι τῇ καλῇ
καὶ Χάρισι ταῖς φίλαις
ξύντροφε Διαλλαγή,
ὡς καλὸν ἔχουσα τὸ πρόσωπον ἄρ' ἐλάνθανες. 990

πῶς ἂν ἐμὲ καὶ σέ τις Ἔρως ξυναγάγοι λαβών,
ὥσπερ ὁ γεγραμμένος, ἔχων στέφανον ἀνθέμων;
ἢ πάνυ γερόντιον ἴσως νενόμικάς με σύ;
ἀλλά σε λαβὼν τρία δοκῶ γ' ἂν ἔτι προσβαλεῖν·
πρῶτα μὲν ἂν ἀμπελίδος ὄρχον ἐλάσαι μακρόν, 995
εἶτα παρὰ τόνδε νέα μοσχίδια συκίδων,
καὶ τὸ τρίτον ἡμερίδος ὄρχον, ὁ γέρων ὁδί,
καὶ περὶ τὸ χωρίον ἐλᾷδας ἅπαν ἐν κύκλῳ,

---

^a The κύλιξ φιλοτησία (cf. L. 203) was exactly our "loving-cup."
^b i.e. vine-props.
^c Though he is old he thinks that, if she marries him, he can " still throw into the bargain three things " which he then describes.
^d ἡμερίς seems to have been grown on lofty trellis-work, and originally on the walls of the dwelling-house; see lt.

THE ACHARNIANS, 985-998

Sit you down, and drink a cup,
                a Cup of Love and Harmony,[a]
All the more he burnt the poles [b]
             we wanted for our husbandry,
Aye and spilt perforce the liquor
             treasured up within our vines.

Proudly he prepares to banquet.
             Did ye mark him, all elate,
As a sample of his living
             cast these plumes before his gate?
Grand his ostentation!
O of Cypris foster-sister,
             and of every heavenly Grace,
Never knew I till this moment
             all the glory of thy face,
RECONCILIATION!

O that Love would you and me
             unite in endless harmony,
Love as he is pictured with
             the wreath of roses smilingly.
Maybe you regard me as
             a fragment of antiquity:
Ah, but if I get you, dear,
             I'll show my triple husbandry.[c]
First a row of vinelets will I
             plant prolonged and orderly,
Next the little fig-tree shoots
             beside them, growing lustily,
Thirdly the domestic vine ;[d]
             although I am so elderly.
Round them all shall olives grow,
             to form a pleasant boundary.

ARISTOPHANES

ὥστ' ἀλείφεσθαί σ' ἀπ' αὐτῶν κἀμὲ ταῖς νου-
μηνίαις.

ΚΗΡ. ἀκούετε λεῴ· κατὰ τὰ πάτρια τοὺς χόας 1000
πίνειν ὑπὸ τῆς σάλπιγγος· ὃς δ' ἂν ἐκπίῃ
πρώτιστος, ἀσκὸν Κτησιφῶντος λήψεται.
ΔΙ. ὦ παῖδες, ὦ γυναῖκες, οὐκ ἠκούσατε;
τί δρᾶτε; τοῦ κήρυκος οὐκ ἀκούετε;
ἀναβράττετ', ἐξοπτᾶτε, τρέπετ', ἀφέλκετε 1005
τὰ λαγῷα ταχέως, τοὺς στεφάνους ἀνείρετε.
φέρε τοὺς ὀβελίσκους, ἵν' ἀναπείρω τὰς κίχλας.

ΧΟ. ζηλῶ σε τῆς εὐβουλίας,
μᾶλλον δὲ τῆς εὐωχίας,
ἄνθρωπε, τῆς παρούσης. 1010
ΔΙ. τί δῆτ', ἐπειδὰν τὰς κίχλας ὀπτωμένας ἴδητε;
ΧΟ. οἶμαί σε καὶ τοῦτ' εὖ λέγειν.
ΔΙ.   τὸ πῦρ ὑποσκάλευε.
ΧΟ. ἤκουσας ὡς μαγειρικῶς 1015
κομψῶς τε καὶ δειπνητικῶς
αὑτῷ διακονεῖται;
ΓΕΩΡΓΟΣ. οἴμοι τάλας.
ΔΙ.   ὦ Ἡράκλεις, τίς οὑτοσί;
ΓΕ. ἀνὴρ κακοδαίμων.
ΔΙ.   κατὰ σεαυτόν νυν τρέπου.

---

[a] *Enter Crier, while the eccyclema exposes to view the interior of D.'s house.*

[b] *i.e.* not an ordinary ἀσκὸς οἴνου, but a huge one made out of the skin of Ctesiphon who was παχὺς καὶ προγάστωρ: Schol.

[c] "The unwonted savour of the roasting and stewing meat has quite subdued the hearts of the old Acharnians": R.

Thence will you and I anoint us,
  darling, when the New Moon shines.

CRIER.[a] O yes! O yes!
 Come, drain your pitchers to the trumpet's
  sound,
 In our old fashion. Whoso drains *his* first,
 Shall have, for prize, a skin of—Ctesiphon.[b]

DI. Lads! Lassies! heard ye not the words he
  said?
 What are ye at? Do ye not hear the Crier?
 Quick! stew and roast, and turn the roasting
  flesh,
 Unspit the haremeat, weave the coronals,
 Bring the spits here, and I'll impale the
  thrushes.

CHOR. I envy much your happy plan,[c]
  I envy more, you lucky man,
   The joys you're now possessing.
DI. What, when around the spits you see
   the thrushes roasting gloriously?
CHOR. And that's a saying I admire.
DI.   Boy, poke me up the charcoal fire.
CHOR. O listen with what cookly art
  And gracious care, so trim and smart,
   His own repast he's dressing.
FARMER.[d] Alas! Alas!
DI.   O Heracles, who's there?
FAR. An ill-starred man.
DI.   Then keep it to yourself.

[d] *Enter Dercetes an Athenian farmer.* His farm was at Phyle just on the Attic side of a pass between Boeotia and Attica.

ΓΕ. ὦ φίλτατε, σπονδαὶ γάρ εἰσι σοὶ μόνῳ, 1020
μέτρησον εἰρήνης τί μοι, κἂν πέντ᾽ ἔτη.
ΔΙ. τί δ᾽ ἔπαθες;
ΓΕ. ἐπετρίβην ἀπολέσας τὼ βόε.
ΔΙ. πόθεν;
ΓΕ. ἀπὸ Φυλῆς ἔλαβον οἱ Βοιώτιοι.
ΔΙ. ὦ τρισκακόδαιμον, εἶτα λευκὸν ἀμπέχει;
ΓΕ. καὶ ταῦτα μέντοι νὴ Δί᾽ ὥπερ μ᾽ ἐτρεφέτην 1025
ἐν πᾶσι βολίτοις.
ΔΙ. εἶτα ιυνὶ τοῦ δέει;
ΓΕ. ἀπόλωλα τὠφθαλμὼ δακρύων τὼ βόε.
ἀλλ᾽ εἴ τι κήδει Δερκέτου Φυλασίου,
ὑπάλειψον εἰρήνῃ με τὠφθαλμὼ ταχύ.
ΔΙ. ἀλλ᾽, ὦ πόνηρ᾽, οὐ δημοσιεύων τυγχάνω. 1030
ΓΕ. ἴθ᾽ ἀντιβολῶ σ᾽, ἤν πως κομίσωμαι τὼ βόε.
ΔΙ. οὐκ ἔστιν, ἀλλὰ κλᾶε πρὸς τοῦ Πιττάλου.
ΓΕ. σὺ δ᾽ ἀλλά μοι σταλαγμὸν εἰρήνης ἕνα
εἰς τὸν καλαμίσκον ἐνστάλαξον τουτονί.
ΔΙ. οὐδ᾽ ἂν στριβιλικίγξ· ἀλλ᾽ ἀπιὼν οἴμωζέ ποι. 1035
ΓΕ. οἴμοι κακοδαίμων τοῖν γεωργοῖν βοιδίοιν.

ΧΟ. ἀνὴρ ἐνεύρηκέν τι ταῖς
σπονδαῖσιν ἡδύ, κοὐκ ἔοι-
κεν οὐδενὶ μεταδώσειν.
ΔΙ. κατάχει σὺ τῆς χορδῆς τὸ μέλι· τὰς σηπίας
στάθευε· 1041
ΧΟ. ἤκουσας ὀρθιασμάτων;
ΔΙ. ὀπτᾶτε τἀγχέλεια.

[a] ἐν πᾶσι βολίτοις (lit. *in the midst of every kind of cow dung*) is substituted for the expected ἐν πᾶσιν ἀγαθοῖς.
[b] For δημοσιεύειν thus used cf. Plato, *Gorg.* 514 D.
[c] Probably one of the state doctors.

THE ACHARNIANS, 1020–1043

FAR. O—for you only hold the truces, dear—
Measure me out though but five years of Peace.
DI. What ails you?
FAR. Ruined! Lost my oxen twain.
DI. Where from?
FAR. From Phyle. The Boeotians stole them.
DI. And yet you are clad in white, you ill-starred loon!
FAR. They twain maintained me in the very lap
Of affluent muckery.[a]
DI. Well, what want you now?
FAR. Lost my two eyes, weeping my oxen twain.
Come, if you care for Dercetes of Phyle,
Rub some Peace-ointment, do, on my two eyes.
DI. Why, bless the fool, I'm not a public surgeon.[b]
FAR. *Do* now; I'll maybe find my oxen twain.
DI. No, go and weep at Pittalus's[c] door.
FAR. Do, just one single drop. Just drop me here
Into this quill one little drop of Peace.
DI. No, not one twitterlet; take your tears elsewhere.
FAR. Alas! Alas! my darling yoke of oxen.

CHOR. He loves the Treaty's pleasant taste;
He will not be, methinks, in haste
To let another share it.
DI. Pour on the tripe the honey, you!
And you, the cuttle richly stew!
CHOR. How trumpet-like his orders sound.
DI. Be sure the bits of eel are browned.

101

ARISTOPHANES

ΧΟ. ἀποκτενεῖς λιμῷ με καὶ
τοὺς γείτονας κνίσῃ τε καὶ 1045
φωνῇ τοιαῦτα λάσκων.

ΔΙ. ὀπτᾶτε ταυτὶ καὶ καλῶς ξανθίζετε.
ΠΑΡΑΝΥΜΦΟΣ.ᵃ Δικαιόπολι.
ΔΙ. τίς οὑτοσί; τίς οὑτοσί;
ΠΑ. ἔπεμψέ τίς σοι νυμφίος ταυτὶ κρέα
ἐκ τῶν γάμων.
ΔΙ. καλῶς γε ποιῶν, ὅστις ἦν. 1050
ΠΑ. ἐκέλευε δ' ἐγχέαι σε, τῶν κρεῶν χάριν,
ἵνα μὴ στρατεύοιτ', ἀλλὰ βινοίη μένων,
ἐς τὸν ἀλάβαστον κύαθον εἰρήνης ἕνα.
ΔΙ. ἀπόφερ' ἀπόφερε τὰ κρέα καὶ μή μοι δίδου,
ὡς οὐκ ἂν ἐγχέαιμι μυρίων δραχμῶν. 1055
ἀλλ' αὑτηὶ τίς ἐστίν;
ΠΑ. ἡ νυμφεύτρια
δεῖται παρὰ τῆς νύμφης τί σοι λέξαι μόνῳ.
ΔΙ. φέρε δή, τί σὺ λέγεις; ὡς γέλοιον, ὦ θεοί,
τὸ δέημα τῆς νύμφης, ὃ δεῖταί μου σφόδρα,
ὅπως ἂν οἰκουρῇ τὸ πέος τοῦ νυμφίου. 1060
φέρε δεῦρο τὰς σπονδάς, ἵν' αὐτῇ δῶ μόνῃ.
ὁτιὴ γυνή 'στι τοῦ πολέμου τ' οὐκ ἀξία.
ὕπεχ' ὧδε δεῦρο τοὐξάλειπτρον, ὦ γύναι.
οἶσθ' ὡς ποιεῖτε τοῦτο; τῇ νύμφῃ φράσον,
ὅταν στρατιώτας καταλέγωσι, τουτωὶ 1065
νύκτωρ ἀλειφέτω τὸ πέος τοῦ νυμφίου.
ἀπόφερε τὰς σπονδάς. φέρε τὴν οἰνήρυσιν,
ἵν' οἶνον ἐγχέω λαβὼν ἐς τοὺς χόας.

ᵃ παράνυμφος or πάροχος.

THE ACHARNIANS, 1044–1068

CHOR. The words you speak, your savoury rites,
Keep sharpening so our appetites
That we can hardly bear it.

DI. Now roast these other things and brown them nicely.
GROOMSMAN.^a O Dicaeopolis!
DI. Who's there? who's there?
GR. A bridegroom sends you from his wedding-banquet
These bits of meat.
DI. Well done, whoe'er he is.
GR. And in return he bids you pour him out,
To keep him safely with his bride at home,
Into this ointment-pot one dram of Peace.
DI. Take, take your meat away; I can't abide it.
Not for ten thousand drachmas would I give him
One drop of Peace. Hey, who comes here?
GR. The bridesmaid
Bringing a private message from the bride.
DI. Well, what have *you* to say? What wants the bride?
Affects to listen.
O heaven, the laughable request she makes
To keep her bridegroom safely by her side.
I'll do it; bring the truces; she's a woman,
Unfit to bear the burdens of the war.
Now, hold the myrrh-box underneath, my girl.
Know you the way to use it? Tell the bride,
When they're enrolling soldiers for the war,
To rub the bridegroom every night with this.
Now take the truces back, and bring the ladle.
I'll fill the winecups for the Pitcher-feast.

ARISTOPHANES

ΧΟ. καὶ μὴν ὁδί τις τὰς ὀφρῦς ἀνεσπακὼς
ὥσπερ τι δεινὸν ἀγγελῶν ἐπείγεται. 1070

ΚΗΡ. ἰὼ πόνοι τε καὶ μάχαι καὶ Λάμαχοι.
ΛΑ. τίς ἀμφὶ χαλκοφάλαρα δώματα κτυπεῖ;
ΚΗΡ. ἰέναι σ' ἐκέλευον οἱ στρατηγοὶ τήμερον
ταχέως λαβόντα τοὺς λόχους καὶ τοὺς λόφους·
κἄπειτα τηρεῖν νιφόμενον τὰς εἰσβολάς. 1075
ὑπὸ τοὺς Χόας γὰρ καὶ Χύτρους αὐτοῖσί τις
ἤγγειλε λῃστὰς ἐμβαλεῖν Βοιωτίους.
ΛΑ. ἰὼ στρατηγοὶ πλείονες ἢ βελτίονες.
οὐ δεινὰ μὴ 'ξεῖναί με μηδ' ἑορτάσαι;
ΔΙ. ἰὼ στράτευμα πολεμολαμαχαϊκόν. 1080
ΛΑ. οἴμοι κακοδαίμων, καταγελᾷς ἤδη σύ μου;
ΔΙ. βούλει μάχεσθαι Γηρυόνῃ τετραπτίλῳ;
ΛΑ. αἰαῖ,
οἵαν ὁ κῆρυξ ἀγγελίαν ἤγγειλέ μοι.
ΔΙ. αἰαῖ, τίνα δ' αὖ μοι προστρέχει τις ἀγγελῶν;

ΑΓΓΕΛΟΣ. Δικαιόπολι.
ΔΙ. τί ἔστιν;
ΑΓΓ. ἐπὶ δεῖπνον ταχὺ 1085
βάδιζε, τὴν κίστην λαβὼν καὶ τὸν χόα.
ὁ τοῦ Διονύσου γάρ σ' ἱερεὺς μεταπέμπεται.
ἀλλ' ἐγκόνει· δειπνεῖν κατακωλύεις πάλαι.
τὰ δ' ἄλλα πάντ' ἐστὶν παρεσκευασμένα,

---

[a] The meaning is: "Do you wish to fight with such a Geryon as I am, one who would encounter Hercules?" τετραπτίλῳ is substituted for the expected τρικεφάλῳ, and Dic. must have tricked himself with four plumes to outdo the "three crests" (1109) of Lamachus.

[b] The vessel in which he carried his provisions; cf. Hom. Od. vi. 76. "Those who invited to a feast," says the

THE ACHARNIANS, 1069-1089

CHOR. But here runs one with eyebrows puckered up.
  Methinks he comes a messenger of woe.

CRIER. O toils, and fights, and fighting Lamachuses!
LAM. Who clangs around my bronze-accoutred halls?
CRIER. The generals bid you take your crests and cohorts,
  And hurry off this instant; to keep watch
  Amongst the mountain passes in the snow.
  For news has come that at this Pitcher-feast
  Boeotian bandits mean to raid our lands.
LAM. O generals, great in numbers, small in worth!
  Shame that I may not even enjoy the feast.
DI. O expedition battle-Lamachaean!
LAM. O dear, what YOU! Do *you* insult me too?
DI. What would you fight with Geryon, the four-winged?[a]
LAM. O woe!
  O what a message has this Crier brought me!
DI. Oho! what message will this runner bring me?

MESSENGER. Dicaeopolis!
DI.   Well?
MESS.   Come at once to supper,
  And bring your pitcher, and your supper-chest.[b]
  The priest of Bacchus sends to fetch you thither.
  And do be quick: you keep the supper waiting.
  For all things else are ready and prepared,

Scholiast, "furnished garlands, perfumes, sweetmeats, etc., and the guests brought provisions (ἐψήματα)."

ARISTOPHANES

κλῖναι, τράπεζαι, προσκεφάλαια, στρώματα, 1090
στέφανοι, μύρον, τραγήμαθ', αἱ πόρναι πάρα,
ἄμυλοι, πλακοῦντες, σησαμοῦντες, ἴτρια,
ὀρχηστρίδες, τὰ φίλταθ' Ἁρμοδίου, καλαί.
ἀλλ' ὡς τάχιστα σπεῦδε.
ΛΑ.   κακοδαίμων ἐγώ.
ΔΙ. καὶ γὰρ σὺ μεγάλην ἐπεγράφου τὴν Γοργόνα. 1095
σύγκλειε, καὶ δεῖπνόν τις ἐνσκευαζέτω.
ΛΑ. παῖ παῖ, φέρ' ἔξω δεῦρο τὸν γύλιον ἐμοί.
ΔΙ. παῖ παῖ, φέρ' ἔξω δεῦρο τὴν κίστην ἐμοί.
ΛΑ. ἅλας θυμίτας οἶσε, παῖ, καὶ κρόμμυα.
ΔΙ. ἐμοὶ δὲ τεμάχη· κρομμύοις γὰρ ἄχθομαι. 1100
ΛΑ. θρῖον ταρίχους οἶσε δεῦρο, παῖ, σαπροῦ.
ΔΙ. κἀμοὶ σὺ δημοῦ θρῖον· ὀπτήσω δ' ἐκεῖ.
ΛΑ. ἔνεγκε δεῦρο τὼ πτερὼ τὼ 'κ τοῦ κράνους.
ΔΙ. ἐμοὶ δὲ τὰς φάττας γε φέρε καὶ τὰς κίχλας.
ΛΑ. καλόν γε καὶ λευκὸν τὸ τῆς στρουθοῦ πτερόν. 1105
ΔΙ. καλόν γε καὶ ξανθὸν τὸ τῆς φάττης κρέας.
ΛΑ. ὤνθρωπε, παῦσαι καταγελῶν μου τῶν ὅπλων.
ΔΙ. ὤνθρωπε, βούλει μὴ βλέπειν εἰς τὰς κίχλας;
ΛΑ. τὸ λοφεῖον ἐξένεγκε τῶν τριῶν λόφων.
ΔΙ. κἀμοὶ λεκάνιον τῶν λαγῴων δὸς κρεῶν. 1110
ΛΑ. ἀλλ' ἦ τριχόβρωτες τοὺς λόφους μου κατ-
        έφαγον;
ΔΙ. ἀλλ' ἦ πρὸ δείπνου τὴν μίμαρκυν κατέδομαι;
ΛΑ. ὤνθρωπε, βούλει μὴ προσαγορεύειν ἐμέ;
ΔΙ. οὔκ, ἀλλ' ἐγὼ χὡ παῖς ἐρίζομεν πάλαι.
    βούλει περιδόσθαι, κἀπιτρέψαι Λαμάχῳ, 1115

[a] The Scolium began Φίλταθ' Ἁρμόδι', οὔ τί πω τέθνηκας, but A., "reading φίλταθ' as the neuter plural and combining Ἁρμόδι' οὐ into Ἁρμοδίου contrives to hint at the irregularities of this popular favourite": R.

THE ACHARNIANS, 1090-1115

The couches, tables, sofa-cushions, rugs,
Wreaths, sweetmeats, myrrh, the harlotry are
  there,
Whole-meal cakes, cheese-cakes, sesame-,
  honey-cakes,
And dancing-girls, *Harmodius' dearest* ones.[a]
So pray make haste.

LAM. O wretched, wretched me!
DI. Aye the great Gorgon 'twas you chose for
  patron.
  Now close the house, and pack the supper up.
LAM. Boy, bring me out my soldier's knapsack here.
DI. Boy, bring me out my supper-basket here.
LAM. Boy, bring me onions, with some thymy salt.
DI. For me, fish-fillets : onions I detest.
LAM. Boy, bring me here a leaf of rotten fish.
DI. A tit-bit leaf for me ; I'll toast it there.
LAM. Now bring me here my helmet's double plume.
DI. And bring me here my thrushes and ring-
  doves.
LAM. How nice and white this ostrich-plume to
  view.
DI. How nice and brown this pigeon's flesh to eat.
LAM. Man, don't keep jeering at my armour so.
DI. Man, don't keep peering at my thrushes so.
LAM. Bring me the casket with the three crests in it.
DI. Bring me the basket with the hare's flesh in it.
LAM. Surely the moths my crest have eaten up.
DI. Sure this hare-soup I'll eat before I sup.
LAM. Fellow, I'll thank you not to talk to ME.
DI. Nay, but the boy and I, we can't agree.
  Come will you [b] bet, and Lamachus decide,

[b] He addresses the "boy."

ARISTOPHANES

πότερον ἀκρίδες ἥδιόν ἐστιν, ἢ κίχλαι;
ΛΑ. οἴμ' ὡς ὑβρίζεις.
ΔΙ. τὰς ἀκρίδας κρίνει πολύ.
ΛΑ. παῖ παῖ, καθελών μοι τὸ δόρυ δεῦρ' ἔξω φέρε.
ΔΙ. παῖ παῖ, σὺ δ' ἀφελὼν δεῦρο τὴν χορδὴν φέρε.
ΛΑ. φέρε, τοῦ δόρατος ἀφελκύσωμαι τοὔλυτρον. 1120
ἔχ', ἀντέχου, παῖ.
ΔΙ. καὶ σύ, παῖ, τοῦδ' ἀντέχου.
ΛΑ. τοὺς κιλλίβαντας οἶσε, παῖ, τῆς ἀσπίδος.
ΔΙ. καὶ τῆς ἐμῆς τοὺς κριβανίτας ἔκφερε.
ΛΑ. φέρε δεῦρο γοργόνωτον ἀσπίδος κύκλον 1125
ΔΙ. κἀμοὶ πλακοῦντος τυρόνωτον δὸς κύκλον.
ΛΑ. ταῦτ' οὐ κατάγελώς ἐστιν ἀνθρώποις πλατύς;
ΔΙ. ταῦτ' οὐ πλακοῦς δῆτ' ἐστὶν ἀνθρώποις γλυκύς;
ΛΑ. κατάχει σύ, παῖ, τοὔλαιον. ἐν τῷ χαλκίῳ
ἐνορῶ γέροντα δειλίας φευξούμενον.
ΔΙ. κατάχει σὺ τὸ μέλι. κἀνθάδ' ἔνδηλος γέρων 1130
κλάειν κελεύων Λάμαχον τὸν Γοργάσου.[b]
ΛΑ. φέρε δεῦρο, παῖ, θώρακα πολεμιστήριον.
ΔΙ. ἔξαιρε, παῖ, θώρακα κἀμοὶ τὸν χόα.
ΛΑ. ἐν τῷδε πρὸς τοὺς πολεμίους θωρήξομαι.
ΔΙ. ἐν τῷδε πρὸς τοὺς συμπότας θωρήξομαι. 1135
ΛΑ. τὰ στρώματ', ὦ παῖ, δῆσον ἐκ τῆς ἀσπίδος.
ΔΙ. τὸ δεῖπνον, ὦ παῖ, δῆσον ἐκ τῆς κιστίδος.
ΛΑ. ἐγὼ δ' ἐμαυτῷ τὸν γύλιον οἴσω λαβών.
ΔΙ. ἐγὼ δὲ θοἰμάτιον λαβὼν ἐξέρχομαι.
ΛΑ. τὴν ἀσπίδ' αἴρου, καὶ βάδιζ', ὦ παῖ, λαβών. 1140
νίφει. βαβαιάξ· χειμέρια τὰ πράγματα.

---

[a] To which L. when at war will be reduced.
[b] τὸν Γοργάσου, "son of Gorgasus" is merely another reference to his Gorgon shield.

THE ACHARNIANS, 1116-1141

	Locusts ^a or thrushes, which the daintier are?
LAM.	Insolent knave!
DI.	(*To the boy*) Locusts, he says, by far.
LAM.	Boy, boy, take down the spear, and bring it here.
DI.	Boy, take the sweetbread off and bring it here.
LAM.	Hold firmly to the spear whilst I pull off The case.
DI.	And you, hold firmly to the spit.
LAM.	Boy, bring the framework to support my shield.
DI.	Boy, bring the bakemeats to support my frame.
LAM.	Bring here the grim-backed circle of the shield.
DI.	And here the cheese-backed circle of the cake.
LAM.	Is not this—mockery, plain for men to see?
DI.	Is not this—cheese-cake, sweet for men to eat?
LAM.	Pour on the oil, boy. Gazing on my shield, I see an old man tried for cowardliness.
DI.	Pour on the honey. Gazing on my cake, I see an old man mocking Lamachus.^b
LAM.	Bring me a casque, to arm the outer man.
DI.	Bring me a cask to warm the inner man.
LAM.	With this I'll arm myself against the foe.
DI.	With this I'll warm myself against the feast.^c
LAM.	Boy, lash the blankets up against the shield.
DI.	Boy, lash the supper up against the chest.
LAM.	Myself will bear my knapsack for myself.
DI.	Myself will wear my wraps, and haste away.
LAM.	Take up the shield, my boy, and bring it on. Snowing! good lack, a wintry prospect mine.

^a θωρήσσεσθαι means either (1) "put on a breast-plate," or (2) "get drunk."

ARISTOPHANES

ΔΙ. αἶρου τὸ δεῖπνον· συμποτικὰ τὰ πράγματα.

ΧΟ. ἴτε δὴ χαίροντες ἐπὶ στρατιάν.
ὡς ἀνομοίαν ἔρχεσθον ὁδόν·
τῷ μὲν πίνειν στεφανωσαμένῳ, 1145
σοὶ δὲ ῥιγῶν καὶ προφυλάττειν,
τῷ δὲ καθεύδειν
μετὰ παιδίσκης ὡραιοτάτης,
ἀνατριβομένῳ τε τὸ δεῖνα.

Ἀντίμαχον τὸν Ψακάδος, ξυγγραφέα, τῶν
μελέων ποιητήν, [στρ. 1150
ὡς μὲν ἁπλῷ λόγῳ κακῶς ἐξολέσειεν ὁ Ζεύς.
ὅς γ᾽ ἐμὲ τὸν τλήμονα Λήναια χορηγῶν ἀπ-
έκλεισε δείπνων.
ὃν ἔτ᾽ ἐπίδοιμι τευθίδος 1155
δεόμενον, ἡ δ᾽ ὠπτημένη
σίζουσα πάραλος, ἐπὶ τραπέζῃ κειμένη,
ὀκέλλοι· κᾆτα μέλ-
λοντος λαβεῖν αὐτοῦ κύων
ἁρπάσασα φεύγοι. 1160

---

[a] *Exeunt Dic. and Lam.*, one to war the other to a banquet. They return 1189.
[b] In 1149 τὸ δεῖνα = τὸ αἰδοῖον: Schol.
[c] Otherwise unknown. He is called ὁ Ψακάδος " because always spitting ": Schol. The "shutting out" of Aristophanes may have been when he produced the Δαιταλεῖς two years before.
[d] A well-known dainty. Here it is supposed to come in on its table (W. 1216, " bring in the tables ") and to " come ashore " or " land " just close to Antimachus. πάραλος is explained by the Schol. either as " beside the salt " or " by the sea-shore." R. says it simply = " marine," and that " the cuttle gliding along on its table is likened to " the famous state trireme Paralus.

THE ACHARNIANS, 1142–1161

DI.   Take up the chest ; a suppery prospect mine.

CHOR.   Off to your duties, my heroes bold.[a]
Different truly the paths ye tread ;
One to drink with wreaths on his head ;
One to watch, and shiver with cold,
Lonely, the while his antagonist passes
The sweetest of hours with the sweetest
    of lasses.[b]

PRAY we that Zeus calmly reduce
            to destruction emphatic and utter
That meanest of poets and meanest of men,
            Antimachus,[c] offspring of Sputter ;
    The Choregus who sent me away
            without any supper at all
At the feast of Lenaea ; I pray,
            two Woes that Choregus befall.
May he hanker for a dish
            of the subtle cuttle-fish [d] ;
May he see the cuttle sailing
        through its brine and through its oil,
On its little table lying,
            hot and hissing from the frying,
Till it anchor close beside him,
            when alas ! and woe betide him !
As he reaches forth his hand
            for the meal the Gods provide him,
    May a dog snatch and carry off the spoil,
        off the spoil,
    May a dog snatch and carry off the spoil.

111

ARISTOPHANES

τοῦτο μὲν αὐτῷ κακὸν ἕν· κᾆθ' ἕτερον
νυκτερινὸν γένοιτο. [ἀντ.
ἠπιαλῶν γὰρ οἴκαδ' ἐξ ἱππασίας βαδίζων, 1165
εἶτα κατάξειέ τις αὐτοῦ μεθύων τὴν κεφαλὴν
Ὀρέστης
μαινόμενος· ὁ δὲ λίθον λαβεῖν
βουλόμενος, ἐν σκότῳ λάβοι
τῇ χειρὶ πέλεθον ἀρτίως κεχεσμένον· 1170
ἐπᾴξειεν δ' ἔχων
τὸν μάρμαρον, κᾆπειθ' ἁμαρ-
τὼν βάλοι Κρατῖνον.

ΘΕΡ. ὦ δμῶες οἳ κατ' οἶκόν ἐστε Λαμάχου,
ὕδωρ ὕδωρ ἐν χυτριδίῳ θερμαίνετε· 1175
ὀθόνια, κηρωτὴν παρασκευάζετε,
ἔρι' οἰσυπηρά, λαμπάδιον περὶ τὸ σφυρόν.
ἀνὴρ τέτρωται χάρακι διαπηδῶν τάφρον,
καὶ τὸ σφυρὸν παλίνορρον ἐξεκόκκισε,
καὶ τῆς κεφαλῆς κατέαγε περὶ λίθον πεσών, 1180
καὶ Γοργόν' ἐξήγειρεν ἐκ τῆς ἀσπίδος.
πτίλον δὲ τὸ μέγα κομπολακύθου πεσὸν

---

[a] A foot-pad; cf. B. 712, 1491.
[b] In 1172 μάρμαρος, "a stone of bright spar," is a Homeric word (Il. xii. 380; Od. ix. 499) purposely substituted for πέλεθος.
[c] See 849.
[d] Apparently the Gorgon on his shield is detachable.

THE ACHARNIANS, 1162–1182

Duly the first Woe is rehearsed ;
          attend whilst the other I'm telling.
It is night, and our gentleman, after a ride,
          is returning on foot to his dwelling ;
  With ague he's sorely bested,
          and he's feeling uncommonly ill,
When suddenly down on his head
          comes Orestes's [a] club with a will.
'Tis Orestes, hero mad,
          'tis the drunkard and the pad.
Then stooping in the darkness
          let him grope about the place,
If his hand can find a brickbat
          at Orestes to be flung ;
But instead of any brickbat
          may he grasp a podge of dung,
And rushing on with this,[b] Orestes may he
  miss,
    And hit young Cratinus [c] in the face, in the
      face,
    And hit young Cratinus in the face.

ATTENDANT. Varlets who dwell in Lamachus's halls,
  Heat water, knaves, heat water in a pot.
  Make ready lint, and salves, and greasy wool,
  And ankle-bandages. Your lord is hurt,
  Pierced by a stake whilst leaping o'er a trench.
  Then, twisting round, he wrenched his ankle
    out,
  And, falling, cracked his skull upon a stone ;
  And shocked the sleeping Gorgon from his
    shield.[d]
  Then the Great Boastard's plume being cast
    away

ARISTOPHANES

πρὸς ταῖς πέτραισι, δεινὸν ἐξηύδα μέλος·
"ὦ κλεινὸν ὄμμα, νῦν πανύστατόν σ' ἰδὼν
λείπω φάος τοὐράνιον· οὐκέτ' εἴμ' ἐγώ." 1185
τοσαῦτα λέξας εἰς ὑδορρόαν πεσὼν
ἀνίσταταί τε καὶ ξυναντᾷ δραπέταις,
λῃστὰς ἐλαύνων καὶ κατασπέρχων δορί.
ὁδὶ δὲ καὐτός· ἀλλ' ἄνοιγε τὴν θύραν.

ΛΑ. ἀτταταῖ, ἀτταταῖ. [στρ. 1190
στυγερὰ τάδε γε κρυερὰ πάθεα· τάλας ἐγώ.
διόλλυμαι δορὸς ὑπὸ πολεμίου τυπείς.
ἐκεῖνο δ' οὖν αἰακτὸν ἂν γένοιτο, 1195
Δικαιόπολις εἴ μ' ἴδοι τετρωμένον,
κᾆτ' ἐγχάνοι ταῖς ἐμαῖς τύχαισιν.
ΔΙ. ἀτταταῖ, ἀτταταῖ. [ἀντ.
τῶν τιτθίων, ὡς σκληρὰ καὶ κυδώνια.
φιλήσατόν με μαλθακῶς, ὦ χρυσίω, 1200
τὸ περιπεταστὸν κἀπιμανδαλωτόν.
τὸν γὰρ χόα πρῶτος ἐκπέπωκα.
ΛΑ. ὦ συμφορὰ τάλαινα τῶν ἐμῶν κακῶν.
ἰὼ ἰὼ τραυμάτων ἐπωδύνων. 1205
ΔΙ. ἰή, ἰή, χαῖρε Λαμαχίππιον.
ΛΑ. στυγερὸς ἐγώ.
ΔΙ.   μογερὸς ἐγώ.
ΛΑ. τί με σὺ κυνεῖς;
ΔΙ.   τί με σὺ δάκνεις;
ΛΑ. τάλας ἐγὼ τῆς ξυμβολῆς βαρείας. 1210
ΔΙ. τοῖς Χουσὶ γὰρ τίς ξυμβολάς σ' ἔπραττεν;
ΛΑ. ἰὼ ἰὼ Παιὰν ἰὼ Παιάν.
ΔΙ. ἀλλ' οὐχὶ τήμερον Παιώνια.

[a] *Re-enter L. wounded, supported by attendants, and Dic. jovial between two courtesans.*

THE ACHARNIANS, 1183-1213

Prone on the rocks, a dolorous cry he raised,
*O glorious Eye, with this my last fond look
The heavenly light I leave ; my day is done.*
He spake, and straightway falls into a ditch :
Jumps up again : confronts the runaways,
And prods the fleeing bandits with his spear.
But here he enters. Open wide the door.

LAM.[a] O lack-a-day ! O lack-a-day !
 I'm hacked, I'm killed, by hostile lances !
 But worse than wound or lance 'twill grieve me
 If Dicaeopolis perceive me
 And mock, and mock at my mischances.
DI. O lucky day ! O lucky day !
 What mortal ever can be richer,
 Than he who feels, my golden misses,
 Your softest, closest, loveliest kisses.[b]
 'Twas I, 'twas I, first drained the pitcher.
LAM. O me, my woful dolorous lot !
 O me, the gruesome wounds I've got !
DI. My darling Lamachippus, is it not ?
LAM. O doleful chance !
DI.   O cursed spite !
LAM. Why give me a kiss ?
DI.   Why give me a bite ?
LAM. O me the heavy, heavy charge [c] they tried.
DI. Who makes a charge this happy Pitcher-tide ?
LAM. O Paean, Healer ! heal me, Paean, pray.
DI. 'Tis not the Healer's festival to-day.

[b] In 1199 their breasts are compared to "quinces,"
μῆλα κυδώνια; and 1201 describes δύο εἴδη φιλημάτων ἐρωτικῶν:
Schol.
 [c] *Cf.* 1000-2. In 1210 ξυμβολή is "a hostile encounter";
in 1211 the "contribution" made by a guest to a common
entertainment.

ARISTOPHANES

ΛΑ. λάβεσθέ μου, λάβεσθε τοῦ σκέλους· παπαῖ,
προσλάβεσθ', ὦ φίλοι. 1215
ΔΙ. ἐμοῦ δέ γε σφὼ τοῦ πέους ἄμφω μέσου
προσλάβεσθ', ὦ φίλαι.
ΛΑ. ἰλιγγιῶ κάρα λίθῳ πεπληγμένος,
καὶ σκοτοδινιῶ.
ΔΙ. κἀγὼ καθεύδειν βούλομαι καὶ στύομαι 1220
καὶ σκοτοβινιῶ.
ΛΑ. θύραζέ μ' ἐξενέγκατ' ἐς τοῦ Πιττάλου
παιωνίαισι χερσίν.
ΔΙ. ὡς τοὺς κριτάς με φέρετε· ποῦ 'στιν ὁ
βασιλεύς;
ἀπόδοτέ μοι τὸν ἀσκόν. 1225
ΛΑ. λόγχη τις ἐμπέπηγέ μοι
δι' ὀστέων ὀδυρτά.
ΔΙ. ὁρᾶτε τουτονὶ κενόν.
τήνελλα καλλίνικος.
ΧΟ. τήνελλα δῆτ', εἴπερ καλεῖς γ',
ὦ πρέσβυ, καλλίνικος.
ΔΙ. καὶ πρός γ' ἄκρατον ἐγχέας
ἄμυστιν ἐξέλαψα.
ΧΟ. τήνελλά νυν, ὦ γεννάδα·
χώρει λαβὼν τὸν ἀσκόν. 1230
ΔΙ. ἕπεσθέ νυν ᾄδοντες ὦ
τήνελλα καλλίνικος.
ΧΟ. ἀλλ' ἑψόμεσθα σὴν χάριν
τήνελλα καλλίνικον ᾄ-
δοντες σὲ καὶ τὸν ἀσκόν.

[a] *i.e.* of the Pitcher-feast who are to award him the ἀσκὸς οἴνου as the best drinker. But Λ. is also appealing to

THE ACHARNIANS, 1214–1234

LAM. O lift me gently round the hips,
      My comrades true!
DI. O kiss me warmly on the lips,
      My darlings, do!
LAM. My brain is dizzy with the blow
      Of hostile stone.
DI. Mine's dizzy too: to bed I'll go,
      And not alone.
LAM. O take me in your healing hands, and bring
      To Pittalus this battered frame of mine.
DI. O take me to the judges.[a] Where's the King
      That rules the feast? hand me my skin of wine.
LAM. A lance has struck me through the bone
      So piteously! so piteously!
(*He is helped off the stage.*)
DI. I've drained the pitcher all alone;
      Sing ho! Sing ho! for Victory.[b]
CHOR. Sing ho! Sing ho! for Victory then,
      If so you bid, if so you bid.
DI. I filled it with neat wine, my men,
      And quaffed it at a gulp, I did.
CHOR. Sing ho! brave heart, the wineskin take,
      And onward go, and onward go.
DI. And ye must follow in my wake,
      And sing for Victory ho! sing ho!
CHOR. O yes, we'll follow for your sake
      Your wineskin and yourself, I trow.
      Sing ho! for Victory won, sing ho!

the πέντε κριταί of the theatrical contest to give the prize to him. βασιλεύς is the ἄρχων β. who presided at the Lenaea.
[b] τήνελλα κ.: the opening of a Song of Victory by Archilochus; *cf.* B. 1764.

THE KNIGHTS

INTRODUCTION

This play was exhibited at the Lenaean festival, in February 424 B.C., and obtained the prize, Cratinus being second with the *Satyrs*, and Aristomenes third with the *Woodcarriers*.

It was an attack on Cleon, then at the height of his power; for a few months before he had by a lucky and extraordinary chain of events gained an unequalled pre-eminence.

Cleon, a leather-seller, son of Cleaenetus, was a most persuasive orator, full of resource, but corrupt and rapacious beyond others; he amassed a huge fortune in his political life. His ignoble character is clear from the speech which Thucydides puts in his mouth, advocating the massacre of the people of Mitylene (iii. 36, iv. 21). He had long been a bitter assailant of Pericles; and when Pericles died, Cleon took his place as popular leader. But his success was due to the affair of Pylus.

Demosthenes, the Athenian general, had seized and fortified Pylus, a hill on the west of the Peloponnese, overlooking an important harbour which lay between the mainland and the island of Sphacteria. He intended to settle here the Messenian exiles who had settled at Naupactus, for this nation was the inveterate foe of Sparta. There his party was

THE KNIGHTS

attacked by the Spartans, who disembarked a large force upon the island opposite. The Athenian fleet came to the rescue, and blockaded this force in Sphacteria. The danger of their troops led the Spartans to sue for peace, which might then have been had upon honourable terms.

But Cleon, who was no statesman, demanded such terms as were really out of the Spartans' power to grant; and when they did not reject even those, but proposed a conference, he procured that they should be rebuffed with contumely. He expected that the troops in Sphacteria would now surrender; but time went on, winter approached, and yet they held out. Suddenly an accidental fire cleared the island of its wood, and Demosthenes seeing his opportunity, prepared to attack.

At Athens, disquieting rumours were rife; and Cleon accused the generals of cowardice; whereupon cries arose, asking why he did not go himself; and Nicias, who was present, offered to resign his post as Strategus in favour of Cleon. Thus driven into a corner, Cleon declared he would finish the business in twenty days; and taking a few hundred men with him, set sail for Sphacteria. When he arrived, he left Demosthenes to do all the work, to carry out, in fact, the scheme which he had already in hand; and when the general and his troops had won a complete victory, he returned with them and the prisoners to Athens, having himself done nothing whatever except to return within twenty days. This was in 425 B.C., and the *Knights* was exhibited at the Lenaea of the following year.

The "Knights" who compose the Chorus stand for the 1000 young men who constituted the

ARISTOPHANES

Athenian cavalry and, being drawn from the wealthier and more educated classes, are the natural enemies of demagogues. Demus is a respectable old householder who represents the sovereign people of Athens.

ΤΑ ΤΟΥ ΔΡΑΜΑΤΟΣ ΠΡΟΣΩΠΑ

ΔΗΜΟΣ
ΠΑΦΛΑΓΩΝ ⎫
ΝΙΚΙΑΣ ⎬ οἰκέται
ΔΗΜΟΣΘΕΝΗΣ ⎭
ΑΛΛΑΝΤΟΠΩΛΗΣ
ΧΟΡΟΣ ΙΠΠΕΩΝ

ΙΠΠΕΙΣ

ΔΗΜΟΣΘΕΝΗΣ. Ἰατταταιὰξ τῶν κακῶν, ἰατταταῖ.
κακῶς Παφλαγόνα τὸν νεώνητον κακὸν
αὐταῖσι βουλαῖς ἀπολέσειαν οἱ θεοί.
ἐξ οὗ γὰρ εἰσήρρησεν εἰς τὴν οἰκίαν,
πληγὰς ἀεὶ προστρίβεται τοῖς οἰκέταις. 5
ΝΙΚΙΑΣ. κάκιστα δῆθ' οὗτός γε πρῶτος Παφλαγόνων
αὐταῖς διαβολαῖς.
ΔΗ. ὦ κακόδαιμον, πῶς ἔχεις;
ΝΙ. κακῶς καθάπερ σύ.
ΔΗ. δεῦρό νυν πρόσελθ', ἵνα
ξυναυλίαν κλαύσωμεν Οὐλύμπου νόμον.
ΔΗ. καὶ ΝΙ. μῦ μῦ, μῦ μῦ, μῦ μῦ, μῦ μῦ, μῦ μῦ,
μῦ μῦ. 10
ΔΗ. τί κινυρόμεθ' ἄλλως; οὐκ ἐχρῆν ζητεῖν τινα
σωτηρίαν νῷν, ἀλλὰ μὴ κλάειν ἔτι;
ΝΙ. τίς οὖν γένοιτ' ἄν; λέγε σύ.
ΔΗ. σὺ μὲν οὖν μοι λέγε,
ἵνα μὴ μάχωμαι.

[a] In the foreground is a loose arrangement of stones, which will, later on, be taken to represent the Pnyx. Behind are three houses; the central one, with a harvest-wreath over the door, is the abode of Demus; whilst the others serve for Paphlagon, who is Cleon, and the Sausage-seller. Out of the house of Demus run two slaves, howling; their masks represent the two famous Athenian generals, Nicias and Demosthenes.

THE KNIGHTS

DEMOSTHENES.[a] O! O! This Paphlagon,[b] with all
    his wiles,
    This newly-purchased pest, I wish the Gods
    Would " utterly abolish and destroy "!
    For since he entered, by ill-luck, our house,
    He's always getting all the household flogged.
NICIAS. I wish they would, this chief[c] of Paphlagons,
    Him and his lies!
DE.   Ha! how feel *you*, poor fellow?
NIC. Bad, like yourself.
DE.   Then come, and let us wail
    A stave of old Olympus,[d] both together.
BOTH. (*Sobbing*) Mumu! Mumu! Mumu! Mumu!
    Mumu!
DE. Pah! What's the good of whimpering?
    Better far
    To dry our tears, and seek some way of safety.
NIC. Which way? You, tell me.
DE.   Rather, tell me you,
    Or else we'll fight.

   [b] Παφλαγών, a servile name describing the slave's country; but also = "a blusterer," from παφλάζω, *cf.* 919.
   [c] πρῶτος: "first," *i.e.* "worst." διαβολή and διαβάλλω are used regularly of C.'s "slanderous accusations"; *cf.* Thuc. ii. 27. 4.
   [d] A famous legendary flute-player; here, however, spoken of as a poet.

ARISTOPHANES

ΝΙ. μὰ τὸν Ἀπόλλω 'γὼ μὲν οὔ·
ἀλλ' εἰπὲ θαρρῶν, εἶτα κἀγώ σοι φράσω. 15
ΔΗ. πῶς ἂν σύ μοι λέξειας ἁμὲ χρὴ λέγειν;
ΝΙ. ἀλλ' οὐκ ἔνι μοι τὸ θρέττε. πῶς ἂν οὖν ποτε
εἴποιμ' ἂν αὐτὸ δῆτα κομψευριπικῶς;
ΔΗ. μή μοί γε, μή μοι, μὴ διασκανδικίσῃς·
ἀλλ' εὑρέ τιν' ἀπόκινον ἀπὸ τοῦ δεσπότου. 20
ΝΙ. λέγε δὴ "μόλωμεν" ξυνεχὲς ὡδὶ ξυλλαβών.
ΔΗ. καὶ δὴ λέγω· μόλωμεν.
ΝΙ.   ἐξόπισθε νῦν
"αὐτὸ" φαθὶ τοῦ "μόλωμεν."
ΔΗ.   αὐτό.
ΝΙ.   πάνυ καλῶς.
ὥσπερ δεφόμενος νῦν ἀτρέμα πρῶτον λέγε
τὸ "μόλωμεν," εἶτα δ' "αὐτό," κατεπάγων
πυκνόν. 25
ΔΗ. μόλωμεν αὐτὸ μόλωμεν αὐτομολῶμεν.
ΝΙ.   ἤν,
οὐχ ἡδύ;
ΔΗ.   νὴ Δία, πλήν γε περὶ τῷ δέρματι
δέδοικα τουτονὶ τὸν οἰωνόν.
ΝΙ.   τί δαί;
ΔΗ. ὁτιὴ τὸ δέρμα δεφομένων ἀπέρχεται.
ΝΙ. κράτιστα τοίνυν τῶν παρόντων ἐστὶ νῷν, 30
θεῶν ἰόντε προσπεσεῖν του πρὸς βρέτας.
ΔΗ. ποῖον βρετετέτας[1]; ἐτεὸν ἡγεῖ γὰρ θεούς;
ΝΙ. ἔγωγε.

[1] Most mss. βρέτας: VM βρεττέτας: Schol. βρετέττας:
Rogers βρετετέρας, suggested also by Neil.

[a] From Eur. *Hipp.* 345, where Phaedra urges the nurse to put in words what she shrank from saying herself.
[b] An allusion to E.'s mother selling potherbs; cf. *A.* 478.

THE KNIGHTS, 14-33

NIC.   By Apollo, no not I.
      You say it first, and then I'll say it after.
DE.   O that thou said'st the thing that I would say.[a]
NIC. I've not the pluck. I wish I could suggest
      Some plan in smart Euripidean style.
DE.   Don't do it! Don't! Pray don't be-chervil [b]
      me
      But find some caper-cutting trick [c] from
         master.
NIC. Will you say *sert*, like that, speaking it crisply?
DE.   Of course I'll say it, *sert*.
NIC.   Now, after *sert*
      Say *de*.
DE.   *De*.
NIC.   Yes, that's very nicely said.
      Now, first say *sert*, and then say *de*, beginning
      Slowly at first, but quickening as you go.
DE.   Aye; *sert-de, sert-de, sert, de-sert*.
NIC.   There 'tis!
      Do you not like it?
DE.   Like it, yes; but—
NIC.   What?
DE.   There's an uncanny sound about *desert*.
NIC. Uncanny? How?
DE.   They flog deserters so.
NIC. O then 'twere better that we both should go,
      And fall before the statues of the Gods.
DE.   Stat-at-ues [d] is it? What, do you really think
      That there *are* Gods?
NIC.   I know it.

    [c] ἀπόκινος: "a form of vulgar dance," Schol. The word also suggests " moving off."
    [d] The pious Nicias had in two tragic lines (*cf.* Aesch. *P.V.* 224; *S.a.T.* 92, 93) suggested a resort to prayer, but his teeth chattered as he pronounced βρέτας, and D. mocks him.

ARISTOPHANES

ΔΗ. ποίῳ χρώμενος τεκμηρίῳ;
ΝΙ. ὁτιὴ θεοῖσιν ἐχθρός εἰμ'. οὐκ εἰκότως;
ΔΗ. εὖ προσβιβάζεις μ'. ἀλλ' ἑτέρᾳ ποι σκεπτέον. 35
βούλει τὸ πρᾶγμα τοῖς θεαταῖσιν φράσω;
ΝΙ. οὐ χεῖρον· ἓν δ' αὐτοὺς παραιτησώμεθα,
ἐπίδηλον ἡμῖν τοῖς προσώποισιν ποιεῖν,
ἢν τοῖς ἔπεσι χαίρωσι καὶ τοῖς πράγμασι.
ΔΗ. λέγοιμ' ἂν ἤδη. νῶν γάρ ἐστι δεσπότης 40
ἄγροικος ὀργήν, κυαμοτρώξ, ἀκράχολος,
Δῆμος Πυκνίτης, δύσκολον γερόντιον,
ὑπόκωφον. οὗτος τῇ προτέρᾳ νουμηνίᾳ
ἐπρίατο δοῦλον, βυρσοδέψην, Παφλαγόνα,
πανουργότατον καὶ διαβολώτατόν τινα. 45
οὗτος καταγνοὺς τοῦ γέροντος τοὺς τρόπους,
ὁ βυρσοπαφλαγών, ὑποπεσὼν τὸν δεσπότην
ᾔκαλλ', ἐθώπευ', ἐκολάκευ', ἐξηπάτα
κοσκυλματίοις ἄκροισι, τοιαυτὶ λέγων·
ὦ Δῆμε, λοῦσαι πρῶτον ἐκδικάσας μίαν, 50
ἔνθου, ῥόφησον, ἔντραγ', ἔχε τριώβολον.
βούλει παραθῶ σοι δόρπον; εἶτ' ἀναρπάσας
ὅ τι ἄν τις ἡμῶν σκευάσῃ, τῷ δεσπότῃ
Παφλαγὼν κεχάρισται τοῦτο. καὶ πρώην γ'
ἐμοῦ
μᾶζαν μεμαχότος ἐν Πύλῳ Λακωνικήν, 55
πανουργότατά πως περιδραμὼν ὑφαρπάσας
αὐτὸς παρέθηκε τὴν ὑπ' ἐμοῦ μεμαγμένην.
ἡμᾶς δ' ἀπελαύνει, κοὐκ ἐᾷ τὸν δεσπότην

---

[a] ὅτι εἰ μὴ ἦσαν θεοί, οὐκ ἂν ἤμην θεοῖς ἐχθρός. Schol.
[b] Instead of his deme or place of residence, he is described as living in the Pnyx where public assemblies were held.
[c] Beans were used for voting purposes.
[d] Instead of " with little coaxing speeches " or the like.

THE KNIGHTS, 33-58

DE.   Know it! How?
NIC. I'm such a wretched God-detested chap.[a]
DE. Well urged indeed; but seek some other way.
     Would you I told the story to the audience?
NIC. Not a bad plan; but let us ask them first
     To show us plainly by their looks and cheer
     If they take pleasure in our words and acts.
DE. I'll tell them now. We two have got a master,
     Demus of Pnyx-borough,[b] such a sour old man,
     Quick-tempered, country-minded, bean-con-
         suming,[c]
     A trifle hard of hearing. Last new moon
     He bought a slave, a tanner, Paphlagon,
     The greatest rogue and liar in the world.
     This tanning-Paphlagon, he soon finds out
     Master's weak points; and cringing down
         before him
     Flatters, and fawns, and wheedles, and cajoles,
     With little apish leather-snippings,[d] thus;
     O Demus,[e] try one case, get the three-obol,
     Then take your bath, gorge, guzzle, eat your fill.
     Would you I set your supper? Then he'll seize
     A dish some other servant has prepared,
     And serve it up for master; and quite lately
     I'd baked [f] a rich Laconian cake at Pylus,
     When in runs Paphlagon, and bags my cake,
     And serves it up to Demus as his own.
     But us he drives away, and none but he

---

[a] Here Demus deserts the Assembly for his other favourite haunt, the δικαστήριον. There were 6000 dicasts and their fee was three obols a day (see *W.* Introd.). Here Demus is to get a full day's pay for trying a single suit.

[f] μᾶζαν μεμαχότος (from μάσσω, *knead*) is a play on μάχην μεμαχημένον. Cleon is accused of filching from Demosthenes the victory which he had all but gained.

ARISTOPHANES

ἄλλον θεραπεύειν, ἀλλὰ βυρσίνην ἔχων
δειπνοῦντος ἑστὼς ἀποσοβεῖ τοὺς ῥήτορας. 60
ᾄδει δὲ χρησμούς· ὁ δὲ γέρων σιβυλλιᾷ.
ὁ δ' αὐτὸν ὡς ὁρᾷ μεμακκοηκότα,
τέχνην πεποίηται. τοὺς γὰρ ἔνδον ἄντικρυς
ψευδῆ διαβάλλει· κᾆτα μαστιγούμεθα
ἡμεῖς· Παφλαγὼν δὲ περιθέων τοὺς οἰκέτας 65
αἰτεῖ, ταράττει, δωροδοκεῖ, λέγων τάδε·
ὁρᾶτε τὸν Ὕλαν δι' ἐμὲ μαστιγούμενον;
εἰ μή μ' ἀναπείσετ', ἀποθανεῖσθε τήμερον.
ἡμεῖς δὲ δίδομεν· εἰ δὲ μή, πατούμενοι
ὑπὸ τοῦ γέροντος ὀκταπλάσια χέζομεν. 70
νῦν οὖν ἀνύσαντε φροντίσωμεν, ὦγαθέ,
ποίαν ὁδὸν νῷ τρεπτέον καὶ πρὸς τίνα.
ΝΙ. κράτιστ' ἐκείνην τὴν "μόλωμεν," ὦγαθέ.
ΔΗ. ἀλλ' οὐχ οἷόν τε τὸν Παφλαγόν' οὐδὲν λαθεῖν·
ἐφορᾷ γὰρ αὐτὸς πάντ'. ἔχει γὰρ τὸ σκέλος 75
τὸ μὲν ἐν Πύλῳ, τὸ δ' ἕτερον ἐν τἠκκλησίᾳ.
τοσόνδε δ' αὐτοῦ βῆμα διαβεβηκότος
ὁ πρωκτός ἐστιν αὐτόχρημ' ἐν Χάοσι,
τὼ χεῖρ' ἐν Αἰτωλοῖς, ὁ δὲ νοῦς ἐν Κλωπιδῶν.
ΝΙ. κράτιστον οὖν νῷν ἀποθανεῖν. ἀλλὰ σκόπει, 80
ὅπως ἂν ἀποθάνωμεν ἀνδρικώτατα.

---

[a] For the vogue of oracles at this time *cf.* Thuc. ii. 8. 2; ii. 28. 3.
[b] The Χάονες are selected because the name suggests χαίνειν (ὡς εὐρύπρωκτον αὐτὸν διαβάλλει: Schol.) just as Αἰτωλοῖς suggests αἰτεῖν " to beg."
[c] Lit. "Thief-deme"; there was an actual deme Κρωπίδαι.

THE KNIGHTS, 59–81

    Must wait on master; there he stands through dinner
With leathern flap, and flicks away the speakers.
And he chants oracles,[a] till the dazed old man
Goes Sibyl-mad; then, when he sees him mooning,
He plies his trade. He slanders those within
With downright lies; so then we're flogged, poor wretches,
And Paphlagon runs round, extorting, begging,
Upsetting everyone; and *Mark*, says he,
*There's Hylas flogged; that's all my doing; better
Make friends with me, or you'll be trounced to-day.*
So then we bribe him off; or if we don't,
We're sure to catch it thrice as bad from master.
Now let's excogitate at once, good fellow,
Which way to turn our footsteps, and to whom.

NIC. There's nothing better than my *sert*, good fellow.

DE. But nought we do is hid from Paphlagon.
His eyes are everywhere; he straddles out,
One foot in Pylus, in the Assembly one.
So vast his stride, that at the self-same moment
His seat is in Chaonia,[b] and his hands
Are set on Begging, and his mind on Theft.[c]

NIC. Well then, we had better die; but just consider
How we can die the manliest sort of death.

ARISTOPHANES

ΔΗ. πῶς δῆτα πῶς γένοιτ᾽ ἂν ἀνδρικώτατα;
ΝΙ. βέλτιστον ἡμῖν αἷμα ταύρειον πιεῖν.
 ὁ Θεμιστοκλέους γὰρ θάνατος αἱρετώτερος.
ΔΗ. μὰ Δί᾽ ἀλλ᾽ ἄκρατον οἶνον ἀγαθοῦ δαίμονος. 85
 ἴσως γὰρ ἂν χρηστόν τι βουλευσαίμεθα.
ΝΙ. ἰδού γ᾽ ἄκρατον. περὶ ποτοῦ γοῦν ἐστί σοι;
 πῶς δ᾽ ἂν μεθύων χρηστόν τι βουλεύσαιτ᾽
 ἀνήρ;
ΔΗ. ἄληθες, οὗτος; κρουνοχυτρολήραιον εἶ.
 οἶνον σὺ τολμᾷς εἰς ἐπίνοιαν λοιδορεῖν; 90
 οἴνου γὰρ εὕροις ἄν τι πρακτικώτερον;
 ὁρᾷς; ὅταν πίνωσιν ἄνθρωποι, τότε
 πλουτοῦσι, διαπράττουσι, νικῶσιν δίκας,
 εὐδαιμονοῦσιν, ὠφελοῦσι τοὺς φίλους.
 ἀλλ᾽ ἐξένεγκέ μοι ταχέως οἴνου χόα, 95
 τὸν νοῦν ἵν᾽ ἄρδω καὶ λέγω τι δεξιόν.
ΝΙ. οἴμοι, τί ποθ᾽ ἡμᾶς ἐργάσει τῷ σῷ ποτῷ;
ΔΗ. ἀγάθ᾽· ἀλλ᾽ ἔνεγκ᾽· ἐγὼ δὲ κατακλινήσομαι.
 ἢν γὰρ μεθυσθῶ, πάντα ταυτὶ καταπάσω
 βουλευματίων καὶ γνωμιδίων καὶ νοϊδίων. 100
ΝΙ. ὡς εὐτυχῶς ὅτι οὐκ ἐλήφθην ἔνδοθεν
 κλέπτων τὸν οἶνον.
ΔΗ. εἰπέ μοι, Παφλαγὼν τί δρᾷ·
ΝΙ. ἐπίπαστα λείξας δημιόπραθ᾽ ὁ βάσκανος
 ῥέγκει μεθύων ἐν ταῖσι βύρσαις ὕπτιος.
ΔΗ. ἴθι νυν, ἄκρατον ἐγκάναξόν μοι πολὺν 105
 σπονδήν.
ΝΙ. λαβὲ δὴ καὶ σπεῖσον ἀγαθοῦ δαίμονος·

---

[a] He is said to have so poisoned himself when unable to fulfil his promises to the Persian king ; *cf.* Plut. *Them.* 31.
[b] Lit. "having licked up cakes made out of confiscation sales, sprinkled with honey."   [c] *i.e.* as a libation.

THE KNIGHTS, 82-106

DE. The manliest sort of death? Let's see; which is it?
NIC. Had we not better drink the blood of bulls? 'Twere fine to die Themistocles's death.[a]
DE. Blood? no : pure wine, to the toast of Happy Fortune!
From that we'll maybe get some happy thought.
NIC. Pure wine indeed! Is this a tippling matter?
How can one get, when drunk, a happy thought?
DE. Aye, say you so, you water-fountain-twaddler?
And dare you rail at wine's inventiveness?
I tell you nothing has such go as wine.
Why, look you now; 'tis when men drink, they thrive,
Grow wealthy, speed their business, win their suits,
Make themselves happy, benefit their friends.
Go, fetch me out a stoup of wine, and let me
Moisten my wits, and utter something bright.
NIC. O me, what good will all your tippling do?
DE. Much; bring it out; I'll lay me down awhile;
For when I'm drunk, I'll everything bespatter
With little scraps of schemes, and plots, and plans.
NIC. I've got the wine; nobody saw me take it.
Wasn't that luck?
DE. What's Paphlagon about?
NIC. Drunk! Snoring on his back amidst his hides,
The juggler; gorged with confiscation pasties.[b]
DE. Come, tinkle out a bumper of pure wine,
To pour.[c]
NIC. Here, take; and pour to Happy Fortune.

133

ARISTOPHANES

ἕλχ' ἕλκε τὴν τοῦ δαίμονος τοῦ Πραμνίου.
ΔΗ. ὦ δαῖμον ἀγαθέ, σὸν τὸ βούλευμ', οὐκ ἐμόν.
ΝΙ. εἴπ', ἀντιβολῶ, τί ἔστι;
ΔΗ.   τοὺς χρησμοὺς ταχὺ
κλέψας ἔνεγκε τοῦ Παφλαγόνος ἔνδοθεν,   110
ἕως καθεύδει.
ΝΙ.   ταῦτ'. ἀτὰρ τοῦ δαίμονος
δέδοιχ' ὅπως μὴ τεύξομαι κακοδαίμονος.
ΔΗ. φέρε νυν ἐγὼ 'μαυτῷ προσαγάγω τὸν χόα,
τὸν νοῦν ἵν' ἄρδω καὶ λέγω τι δεξιόν.
ΝΙ. ὡς μεγάλ' ὁ Παφλαγὼν πέρδεται καὶ ῥέγκεται, 115
ὥστ' ἔλαθον αὐτὸν τὸν ἱερὸν χρησμὸν λαβών,
ὅνπερ μάλιστ' ἐφύλαττεν.
ΔΗ.   ὦ σοφώτατε,
φέρ' αὐτόν, ἵν' ἀναγνῶ· σὺ δ' ἔγχεον πιεῖν
ἀνύσας τι. φέρ' ἴδω τί ἄρ' ἔνεστιν αὐτόθι.
ὦ λόγια. δός μοι δὸς τὸ ποτήριον ταχύ.   120
ΝΙ. ἰδού· τί φησ' ὁ χρησμός;
ΔΗ.   ἑτέραν ἔγχεον.
ΝΙ. ἐν τοῖς λογίοις ἔνεστιν " ἑτέραν ἔγχεον ";
ΔΗ. ὦ Βάκι.
ΝΙ.   τί ἔστι;
ΔΗ.   δὸς τὸ ποτήριον ταχύ.
ΝΙ. πολλῷ γ' ὁ Βάκις ἐχρῆτο τῷ ποτηρίῳ.
ΔΗ. ὦ μιαρὲ Παφλαγών, ταῦτ' ἄρ' ἐφυλάττου
πάλαι,   125
τὸν περὶ σεαυτοῦ χρησμὸν ὀρρωδῶν.
ΝΙ.   τιή;
ΔΗ. ἐνταῦθ' ἔνεστιν αὐτὸς ὡς ἀπόλλυται.

[a] He bids drink to " Good Luck " in good liquor. The fame of " Pramnian wine " is Homeric (*Il.* xi. 639 ; *Od.* iv. 235), but little else is known about it : see R.

THE KNIGHTS, 107-127

    Quaff, quaff the loving-cup of PRAMNIAN [a] Fortune.

DE. O Happy Fortune, thine's the thought, not mine!

NIC. Pray you, what is it?

DE.   Steal from Paphlagon, While yet he sleeps, those oracles of his, And bring them out.

NIC.   I will; and yet I'm fearful That I may meet with most *un*happy Fortune.

DE. Come now, I'll draw the pitcher to myself, Moisten my wits, and utter something bright.

NIC. Paphlagon's snoring so! He never saw me. I've got the sacred oracle which he keeps So snugly.

DE.   O you clever fellow you, I'll read it; hand it over; you the while Fill me the cup. Let's see: what have we here? O! Prophecies! Give me the cup directly.

NIC. Here! What do they say?

DE.   Fill me another cup.

NIC. *Fill me another?* Is that really there?

DE. O Bakis [b]!

NIC.   Well?

DE.   Give me the cup directly.

NIC. Bakis seems mighty partial to the cup.

DE. O villainous Paphlagon, this it was you feared, This oracle about yourself!

NIC.   What is it?

DE. Herein is written how himself shall perish.

[b] A Boeotian seer; *cf.* 1003 and Index.

ARISTOPHANES

ΝΙ. καὶ πῶς;
ΔΗ. ὅπως; ὁ χρησμὸς ἄντικρυς λέγει
ὡς πρῶτα μὲν στυππειοπώλης γίγνεται,
ὃς πρῶτος ἕξει τῆς πόλεως τὰ πράγματα. 130
ΝΙ. εἷς οὑτοσὶ πώλης. τί τοὐντεῦθεν; λέγε.
ΔΗ. μετὰ τοῦτον αὖθις προβατοπώλης, δεύτερος.
ΝΙ. δύο τώδε πώλα. καὶ τί τόνδε χρὴ παθεῖν;
ΔΗ. κρατεῖν, ἕως ἕτερος ἀνὴρ βδελυρώτερος
αὐτοῦ γένοιτο· μετὰ δὲ ταῦτ' ἀπόλλυται. 135
ἐπιγίγνεται γὰρ βυρσοπώλης ὁ Παφλαγών,
ἅρπαξ, κεκράκτης, Κυκλοβόρου φωνὴν ἔχων.
ΝΙ. τὸν προβατοπώλην ἦν ἄρ' ἀπολέσθαι χρεὼν
ὑπὸ βυρσοπώλου;
ΔΗ. νὴ Δί'.
ΝΙ. οἴμοι δείλαιος.
πόθεν οὖν ἂν ἔτι γένοιτο πώλης εἷς μόνος; 140
ΔΗ. ἔτ' ἐστὶν εἷς, ὑπερφυᾶ τέχνην ἔχων.
ΝΙ. εἴπ', ἀντιβολῶ, τίς ἐστιν;
ΔΗ. εἴπω;
ΝΙ. νὴ Δία.
ΔΗ. ἀλλαντοπώλης ἔσθ' ὁ τοῦτον ἐξελῶν.
ΝΙ. ἀλλαντοπώλης; ὦ Πόσειδον τῆς τέχνης.
φέρε ποῦ τὸν ἄνδρα τοῦτον ἐξευρήσομεν; 145
ΔΗ. ζητῶμεν αὐτόν.
ΝΙ. ἀλλ' ὁδὶ προσέρχεται
ὥσπερ κατὰ θεῖον εἰς ἀγοράν.
ΔΗ. ὦ μακάριε
ἀλλαντοπῶλα, δεῦρο δεῦρ', ὦ φίλτατε,

---

[a] A demagogue; called Eucrates by the Scholiast; cf. 254.
[b] Lysicles; married Aspasia after the death of Pericles;

THE KNIGHTS, 128-148

NIC. How shall he?
DE.   How? The oracle says straight out,
That first of all there comes an oakum-seller [a]
Who first shall manage all the State's affairs.
NIC. One something-seller; well, what follows,
pray?
DE. Next after him there comes a sheep-seller.[b]
NIC. Two something-sellers; what's this seller's
fortune?
DE. He'll hold the reins, till some more villainous
rogue
Arise than he; and thereupon he'll perish.
Then follows Paphlagon, our leather-seller,
Thief, brawler, roaring as Cycloborus[c] roars.
NIC. The leather-seller, then, shall overthrow
The sheep-seller?
DE.   He shall.
NIC.   O wretched me,
Is there no other something-seller left?
DE. There is yet one; a wondrous trade *he* has.
NIC. What, I beseech you?
DE.   Shall I tell you?
NIC.   Aye.
DE. A sausage-seller ousts the leather-seller.
NIC. A sausage-seller! Goodness, what a trade!
Wherever shall we find one?
DE.   That's the question.
NIC. Why here comes one, 'tis providential surely,
Bound for the agora.
DE.   Hi, come hither! here!
You dearest man, you blessed sausage-seller!

fell in battle with the Carians 428 B.C. (Thuc. iii. 19); mentioned again 765.   [c] *Cf. A.* 381.

ARISTOPHANES

ἀνάβαινε σωτὴρ τῇ πόλει καὶ νῷν φανείς.
ΑΛΛΑΝΤΟΠΩΛΗΣ. τί ἔστι; τί με καλεῖτε;
ΔΗ. δεῦρ' ἔλθ', ἵνα πύθῃ 150
ὡς εὐτυχὴς εἶ καὶ μεγάλως εὐδαιμονεῖς.
ΝΙ. ἴθι δή, κάθελ' αὐτοῦ τοὐλεόν, καὶ τοῦ θεοῦ
τὸν χρησμὸν ἀναδίδαξον αὐτὸν ὡς ἔχει·
ἐγὼ δ' ἰὼν προσκέψομαι τὸν Παφλαγόνα.
ΔΗ. ἄγε δὴ σὺ κατάθου πρῶτα τὰ σκεύη χαμαί· 155
ἔπειτα τὴν γῆν πρόσκυσον καὶ τοὺς θεούς.
ΑΛ. ἰδού· τί ἔστιν;
ΔΗ. ὦ μακάρι', ὦ πλούσιε,
ὦ νῦν μὲν οὐδείς, αὔριον δ' ὑπέρμεγας·
ὦ τῶν Ἀθηνῶν ταγὲ τῶν εὐδαιμόνων.
ΑΛ. τί μ', ὦγάθ', οὐ πλύνειν ἐᾷς τὰς κοιλίας 160
πωλεῖν τε τοὺς ἀλλᾶντας, ἀλλὰ καταγελᾷς;
ΔΗ. ὦ μῶρε, ποίας κοιλίας; δευρὶ βλέπε.
τὰς στίχας ὁρᾷς τὰς τῶνδε τῶν λαῶν;
ΑΛ. ὁρῶ.
ΔΗ. τούτων ἁπάντων αὐτὸς ἀρχέλας ἔσει,
καὶ τῆς ἀγορᾶς καὶ τῶν λιμένων καὶ τῆς
πυκνός· 165
βουλὴν πατήσεις καὶ στρατηγοὺς κλαστάσεις,
δήσεις, φυλάξεις, ἐν Πρυτανείῳ λαικάσεις.
ΑΛ. ἐγώ;
ΔΗ. σὺ μέντοι· κοὐδέπω γε πάνθ' ὁρᾷς.
ἀλλ' ἐπανάβηθι κἀπὶ τοὐλεὸν τοδὶ
καὶ κάτιδε τὰς νήσους ἁπάσας ἐν κύκλῳ. 170
ΑΛ. καθορῶ.
ΔΗ. τί δαί; τἀμπόρια καὶ τὰς ὁλκάδας;

---

[a] For ἀνάβαινε, which summons the second actor on to the stage, see R.   [b] Exit Nicias.
[c] λαικάσεις is a surprise instead of δειπνήσεις, the right

THE KNIGHTS, 149-171

	Arise,[a] a Saviour to the State and us.
SAUSAGE-SELLER.	Eh! What are you shouting at?
DE.	Come here this instant, And hear your wonderful amazing luck.
NIC.	Make him put down his dresser; tell him all The news about that oracle we've got. I'll keep an eye on Paphlagon the while.[b]
DE.	Come, put you down those cookery implements, Then make your reverence to the Gods and earth,—
S.S.	There! what's the row?
DE.	O happy man, and rich, Nothing to-day, to-morrow everything! O mighty ruler of Imperial Athens!
S.S.	Good fellow, let me wash the guts, and sell My sausages. What need to flout me so?
DE.	You fool! the guts indeed! Now look you here. You see those people on the tiers?
S.S.	I do.
DE.	You shall be over-lord of all those people, The Agora, and the Harbours, and the Pnyx. You'll trim the Generals, trample down the Council, Fetter, imprison, make the Hall your brothel.[c]
S.S.	What, I?
DE.	Yes, you yourself! And that's not all. For mount you up upon the dresser here And view the islands all around.
S.S.	I see.
DE.	And all the marts and merchant-ships?

to dine in the Prytaneum being a well-known reward of public service; cf. 766.

ARISTOPHANES

ΑΛ. ἔγωγε.
ΔΗ. πῶς οὖν οὐ μεγάλως εὐδαιμονεῖς;
ἔτι νῦν τὸν ὀφθαλμὸν παράβαλλ' εἰς Καρίαν
τὸν δεξιόν, τὸν δ' ἕτερον εἰς Καρχηδόνα.
ΑΛ. εὐδαιμονήσω γ', εἰ διαστραφήσομαι. 175
ΔΗ. οὔκ, ἀλλὰ διὰ σοῦ ταῦτα πάντα πέρναται.
γίγνει γάρ, ὡς ὁ χρησμὸς οὑτοσὶ λέγει,
ἀνὴρ μέγιστος.
ΑΛ. εἰπέ μοι, καὶ πῶς ἐγὼ
ἀλλαντοπώλης ὢν ἀνὴρ γενήσομαι;
ΔΗ. δι' αὐτὸ γάρ τοι τοῦτο καὶ γίγνει μέγας, 180
ὁτιὴ πονηρὸς κἀξ ἀγορᾶς εἶ καὶ θρασύς.
ΑΛ. οὐκ ἀξιῶ 'γὼ 'μαυτὸν ἰσχύειν μέγα.
ΔΗ. οἴμοι, τί ποτ' ἔσθ' ὅτι σαυτὸν οὐ φῂς ἄξιον;
ξυνειδέναι τί μοι δοκεῖς σαυτῷ καλόν.
μῶν ἐκ καλῶν εἶ κἀγαθῶν;
ΑΛ. μὰ τοὺς θεούς, 185
εἰ μὴ 'κ πονηρῶν γ'.
ΔΗ. ὦ μακάριε τῆς τύχης,
ὅσον πέπονθας ἀγαθὸν εἰς τὰ πράγματα.
ΑΛ. ἀλλ', ὦγάθ', οὐδὲ μουσικὴν ἐπίσταμαι,
πλὴν γραμμάτων, καὶ ταῦτα μέντοι κακὰ κακῶς.
ΔΗ. τουτὶ μόνον σ' ἔβλαψεν, ὅτι καὶ κακὰ κακῶς. 190
ἡ δημαγωγία γὰρ οὐ πρὸς μουσικοῦ
ἔτ' ἐστὶν ἀνδρὸς οὐδὲ χρηστοῦ τοὺς τρόπους,
ἀλλ' εἰς ἀμαθῆ καὶ βδελυρόν. ἀλλὰ μὴ παρῇς
ἅ σοι διδόασ' ἐν τοῖς λογίοισιν οἱ θεοί.
ΑΛ. πῶς δῆτά φησ' ὁ χρησμός;

THE KNIGHTS, 172-193

S.S. I see.
DE. And aren't you then a lucky man?
And *that's* not all. Just cast your eyes askew,
The right to Caria, and the left to Carthage.
S.S. A marvellous lucky man, to twist my neck [a]!
DE. Nay, but all these shall be your—perquisites.[b]
You shall become, this oracle declares,
A Man most mighty!
S.S. Humbug! How can I,
A sausage-selling chap, become a Man? [c]
DE. Why, that's the very thing will make you great,
Your roguery, impudence, and agora-training.
S.S. I am not worthy of great power, methinks.
DE. O me, not worthy! what's the matter now?
You've got, I fear, some good upon your conscience.
Spring you from gentlemen?
S.S. By the powers, not I.
From downright blackguards.
DE. Lucky, lucky man,
O what a start you've got for public life.
S.S. But I know nothing, friend, beyond my letters,
And even of them but little, and that badly.
DE. The mischief is that you know ANYTHING.
To be a Demus-leader is not now
For lettered men, nor yet for honest men,
But for the base and ignorant. Don't let slip
The bright occasion which the Gods provide you.
S.S. How goes the oracle?

[a] Or " get a squint "; *cf. B.* 677.
[b] πέρναται: δέον εἰπεῖν διοικεῖται. Schol. " Are sold " instead of " are administered through your agency."
[c] *Cf.* 1255.

ARISTOPHANES

ΔΗ. εὖ νὴ τοὺς θεοὺς 195
καὶ ποικίλως πως καὶ σοφῶς ᾐνιγμένος.
'Αλλ' ὁπόταν μάρψῃ βυρσαίετος ἀγκυλοχείλης
γαμφηλῇσι δράκοντα κοάλεμον αἱματοπώτην,
δὴ τότε Παφλαγόνων μὲν ἀπόλλυται ἡ σκοροδ-
άλμη,
κοιλιοπώλῃσιν δὲ θεὸς μέγα κῦδος ὀπάζει, 200
αἴ κεν μὴ πωλεῖν ἀλλᾶντας μᾶλλον ἕλωνται.
ΑΛ. πῶς οὖν πρὸς ἐμὲ ταῦτ' ἐστίν; ἀναδίδασκέ με.
ΔΗ. βυρσαίετος μὲν ὁ Παφλαγών ἐσθ' οὑτοσί.
ΑΛ. τί δ' ἀγκυλοχείλης ἐστίν;
ΔΗ. αὐτό που λέγει,
ὅτι ἀγκύλαις ταῖς χερσὶν ἁρπάζων φέρει. 205
ΑΛ. ὁ δράκων δὲ πρὸς τί;
ΔΗ. τοῦτο περιφανέστατον.
ὁ δράκων γάρ ἐστι μακρὸν ὅ τ' ἀλλᾶς αὖ
μακρόν·
εἶθ' αἱματοπώτης ἔσθ' ὅ τ' ἀλλᾶς χὡ δράκων.
τὸν οὖν δράκοντά φησι τὸν βυρσαίετον
ἤδη κρατήσειν, αἴ κε μὴ θαλφθῇ λόγοις. 210
ΑΛ. τὰ μὲν λόγι' αἰκάλλει με· θαυμάζω δ' ὅπως
τὸν δῆμον οἷός τ' ἐπιτροπεύειν εἴμ' ἐγώ.
ΔΗ. φαυλότατον ἔργον· ταῦθ' ἅπερ ποιεῖς ποίει·
τάραττε καὶ χόρδευ' ὁμοῦ τὰ πράγματα
ἅπαντα, καὶ τὸν δῆμον ἀεὶ προσποιοῦ 215
ὑπογλυκαίνων ῥηματίοις μαγειρικοῖς.
τὰ δ' ἄλλα σοι πρόσεστι δημαγωγικά,

---

[a] The oracles are written in the recognized oracular style.

THE KNIGHTS, 195–217

DE.   Full of promise good,
  Wrapped up in cunning enigmatic words.
 NAY, BUT IF ONCE THE EAGLE,[a]
     THE BLACK-TANNED MANDIBLE-CURVER,
  SEIZE WITH HIS BEAK THE SERPENT,
     THE DULLARD, THE DRINKER OF LIFE-BLOOD,
  THEN SHALL THE SHARP SOUR BRINE [b]
     OF THE PAPHLAGON-TRIBE BE EXTINGUISHED,
  THEN TO THE ENTRAIL-SELLERS
     SHALL GOD GREAT GLORY AND HONOUR
  RENDER, UNLESS THEY ELECT
     TO CONTINUE THE SALE OF THE SAUSAGE.
S.S. But what in the world has this to do with me?
DE. The black-tanned Eagle, that means Paphlagon.
S.S. And what the mandibles?
DE.   That's self-evident.
  His fingers, crooked to carry off their prey.
S.S. What does the Serpent mean?
DE.   That's plainer still.
  A serpent's long; a sausage too is long.
  Serpents drink blood, and sausages drink blood.
  The Serpent then, it says, shall overcome
  The black-tanned Eagle, if it's not talked over.
S.S. I like the lines: but how can I, I wonder,
  Contrive to manage Demus's affairs.
DE. Why nothing's easier. Do what now you do:
  Mince, hash, and mash up everything together.
  Win over Demus [c] with the savoury sauce
  Of little cookery phrases. You've already
  Whatever else a Demagogue requires.

 βυρσαίετος is formed on the analogy of χρυσαίετος "the golden eagle."
  [b] Used in tanning.
  [c] The Greek has a play on δῆμος, "people," and δημός, "fat."

ARISTOPHANES

φωνὴ μιαρά, γέγονας κακῶς, ἀγόραιος εἶ·
ἔχεις ἅπαντα πρὸς πολιτείαν ἃ δεῖ·
χρησμοί τε συμβαίνουσι καὶ τὸ Πυθικόν. 220
ἀλλὰ στεφανοῦ, καὶ σπένδε τῷ Κοαλέμῳ·
χὤπως ἀμυνεῖ τὸν ἄνδρα.

ΑΛ. καὶ τίς ξύμμαχος
γενήσεταί μοι; καὶ γὰρ οἵ τε πλούσιοι
δεδίασιν αὐτὸν ὅ τε πένης βδύλλει λεώς.

ΔΗ. ἀλλ' εἰσὶν ἱππεῖς ἄνδρες ἀγαθοὶ χίλιοι 225
μισοῦντες αὐτόν, οἳ βοηθήσουσί σοι,
καὶ τῶν πολιτῶν οἱ καλοί τε κἀγαθοί,
καὶ τῶν θεατῶν ὅστις ἐστὶ δεξιός,
κἀγὼ μετ' αὐτῶν· χὠ θεὸς ξυλλήψεται.
καὶ μὴ δέδιθ'· οὐ γάρ ἐστιν ἐξηκασμένος. 230
ὑπὸ τοῦ δέους γὰρ αὐτὸν οὐδεὶς ἤθελε
τῶν σκευοποιῶν εἰκάσαι. πάντως γε μὴν
γνωσθήσεται· τὸ γὰρ θέατρον δεξιόν.

ΝΙ. οἴμοι κακοδαίμων, ὁ Παφλαγὼν ἐξέρχεται.

ΠΑΦΛΑΓΩΝ. οὔ τοι μὰ τοὺς δώδεκα θεοὺς χαιρήσετον, 235
ὁτιὴ 'πὶ τῷ δήμῳ ξυνόμνυτον πάλαι.
τουτὶ τί δρᾷ τὸ Χαλκιδικὸν ποτήριον;
οὐκ ἔσθ' ὅπως οὐ Χαλκιδέας ἀφίστατον.
ἀπολεῖσθον, ἀποθανεῖσθον, ὦ μιαρωτάτω.

ΔΗ. οὗτος, τί φεύγεις; οὐ μενεῖς; ὦ γεννάδα 240
ἀλλαντοπῶλα, μὴ προδῷς τὰ πράγματα.

---

[a] The Athenian cavalry numbered 1000, each of the ten tribes contributing 100.
[b] This actor, unlike the representatives of Nicias and Demosthenes, wore no portrait mask, whatever the reason was.
[c] *Enter Nicias.* [d] *Enter Paphlagon.*

THE KNIGHTS, 218–241

        A brutal voice, low birth, an agora training;
Why you've got all one wants for public life.
The Pythian shrine and oracles concur.
Crown, crown your head; pour wine to mighty
  —Dulness;
Prepare to fight the man.

S.S.   But what ally
Will stand beside me, for the wealthy men
Tremble before him, and the poor folk blench.

DE.   A thousand Knights,[a] all honest men and true,
Detest the scoundrel, and will help the cause;
And whosoe'er is noblest in the State,
And whosoe'er is brightest in the tiers,
And I myself. And God will lend his aid.
And fear him not; he is not pictured really;[b]
For all the mask-providers feared to mould
His actual likeness; but our audience here
Are shrewd and bright; they'll recognize the
  man.[c]

NIC. Mercy upon us! here comes Paphlagon.[d]

PAPHLAGON. By the Twelve Gods,[e] you two shall pay
  for this,
Always conspiring, plotting ill to Demus!
What's this Chalcidian goblet doing here?
Hah! ye're inciting Chalcis[f] to revolt.
Villains and traitors! ye shall die the death.

DE.   (*To S.S.*) Hi! where are you off to? Stop!
  For goodness' sake,
Don't fail us now, most doughty Sausage-
  seller!

    [e] The Twelve Gods are Zeus, Poseidon, Apollo, Ares, Hephaestus, and Hermes; Hera, Athene, Artemis, Aphrodite, Demeter, and Hestia.
    [f] "The reference to the Chalcidians is doubtless to Chalcidice in Thrace": R.

ARISTOPHANES

ἄνδρες ἱππεῖς, παραγένεσθε· νῦν ὁ καιρός. ὦ
   Σίμων,
ὦ Παναίτι', οὐκ ἐλᾶτε πρὸς τὸ δεξιὸν κέρας;
ἄνδρες ἐγγύς· ἀλλ' ἀμύνου, κἀπαναστρέφου πάλιν.
ὁ κονιορτὸς δῆλος αὐτῶν ὡς ὁμοῦ προσκειμένων.
ἀλλ' ἀμύνου καὶ δίωκε καὶ τροπὴν αὐτοῦ ποιοῦ.
ΧΟΡΟΣ. παῖε παῖε τὸν πανοῦργον καὶ ταραξιππόστρατον
καὶ τελώνην καὶ φάραγγα καὶ Χάρυβδιν ἁρπαγῆς,
καὶ πανοῦργον καὶ πανοῦργον· πολλάκις γὰρ αὔτ'
   ἐρῶ,
καὶ γὰρ οὗτος ἦν πανοῦργος πολλάκις τῆς ἡμέρας.
ἀλλὰ παῖε καὶ δίωκε καὶ τάραττε καὶ κύκα
καὶ βδελύττου, καὶ γὰρ ἡμεῖς, κἀπικείμενος βόα·
εὐλαβοῦ δὲ μὴ 'κφύγῃ σε· καὶ γὰρ οἶδε τὰς ὁδούς,
ᾇσπερ Εὐκράτης ἔφευγεν εὐθὺ τῶν κυρηβίων.
ΠΑ. ὦ γέροντες ἡλιασταί, φράτορες τριωβόλου,
οὓς ἐγὼ βόσκω κεκραγὼς καὶ δίκαια κἄδικα,
παραβοηθεῖθ', ὡς ὑπ' ἀνδρῶν τύπτομαι ξυνωμοτῶν.
ΧΟ. ἐν δίκῃ γ', ἐπεὶ τὰ κοινὰ πρὶν λαχεῖν κατεσθίεις,

---

[a] *The Knights enter the orchestra.*
[b] The two Hipparchoi who commanded the two divisions of the Knights.
[c] Ταράξιππος seems to have been a title of Poseidon Hippios (Pausanias, vi. 20).
[d] The allusion is unknown, but the person Eucrates was a dealer in oakum, bran, and such things.
[e] The Heliasts were 6000 citizens, chosen by lot yearly from all citizens over 30. From these dicasts were chosen for each case. Three obols were the day's pay.

THE KNIGHTS, 242-258

Hasten up, my gallant horsemen,[a]
    now's the time your foe to fight.
Now then Simon, now Panactius,[b]
    charge with fury on the right.
Here they're coming! Worthy fellow,
    wheel about, commence the fray ;
Lo, the dust of many horsemen
    rushing on in close array!
Turn upon him, fight him, smite him,
    scout him, rout him, every way.

HORUS. Smite the rascal, smite him, smite him,
    troubler of our Knightly train,[c]
Foul extortioner, Charybdis,
    bottomless abyss of gain.
Smite the rascal ; smite the rascal ;
    many times the word I'll say,
For he proved himself a rascal
    many, many times a day.
Therefore smite him, chase him, pound him,
    rend and rattle and confound him!
Show your loathing, show as we do ;
    press with angry shouts around him.
Take you heed, or he'll evade you ;
    watch him closely, for the man
Knows how Eucrates[d] escaped us,
    fleeing to his stores of bran.

APH. O my Heliastic[e] veterans,
    of the great Triobol clan,
Whom through right and wrong I nourish,
    bawling, shouting all I can,
Help me, by conspiring traitors
    shamefully abused and beaten.

IOR. Rightly, for the public commons
    you before your turn have eaten,

ARISTOPHANES

κἀποσυκάζεις πιέζων τοὺς ὑπευθύνους, σκοπῶν
ὅστις αὐτῶν ὠμός ἐστιν ἢ πέπων ἢ μὴ πέπων·
κἄν τιν' αὐτῶν γνῷς ἀπράγμον' ὄντα καὶ κεχηνότα,
καταγαγὼν ἐκ Χερρονήσου, διαβαλών, ἀγκυρίσας,
εἶτ' ἀποστρέψας τὸν ὦμον, αὐτὸν ἐνεκολήβασας·
καὶ σκοπεῖς γε τῶν πολιτῶν ὅστις ἐστὶν ἀμνοκῶν,
πλούσιος καὶ μὴ πονηρὸς καὶ τρέμων τὰ πράγματα.

ΠΑ. ξυνεπίκεισθ' ὑμεῖς; ἐγὼ δ', ὦνδρες, δι' ὑμᾶς
τύπτομαι,
ὅτι λέγειν γνώμην ἔμελλον ὡς δίκαιον ἐν πόλει
ἱστάναι μνημεῖον ὑμῶν ἐστιν ἀνδρείας χάριν.

ΧΟ. ὡς δ' ἀλαζών, ὡς δὲ μάσθλης· εἶδες οἷ' ὑπέρχεται
ὡσπερεὶ γέροντας ἡμᾶς, κἀκκοβαλικεύεται;
ἀλλ' ἐὰν ταύτῃ παρέλθῃ, ταυτῃὶ πεπλήξεται·
ἢν δ' ὑπεκκλίνῃ γε δευρί, πρὸς σκέλος κυρηβάσει.

ΠΑ. ὦ πόλις καὶ δῆμ', ὑφ' οἵων θηρίων γαστρίζομαι.
ΧΟ. καὶ κέκραγας, ὥσπερ ἀεὶ τὴν πόλιν καταστρέφει;
ΑΛ. ἀλλ' ἐγώ σε τῇ βοῇ ταύτῃ γε πρῶτα τρέψομαι.

---

[a] The word is meant to recall συκοφάντης, sycophantes, the informer or blackmailer. This introduces the image of the fig (σῦκον), which is mixed later with terms of the wrestling-school. All public officials had their accounts scrutinized, or audited, at the end of their year of office.
[b] A play upon διαλαβών, "grasping," and διαβαλών, "calumniating." So 491, διαβολάς for διαλαβάς.
[c] The "hook" is a wrestling term.
[d] He tries to escape, head down (a stage direction, according to the Scholiast).

THE KNIGHTS, 259-275

  And you squeeze^a the audit-passers,
      pinching them like figs, to try
  Which is ripe, and which is ripening,
      which is very crude and dry.
  Find you one of easy temper,
      mouth agape, and vacant look,
  Back from Chersonese you bring him,
      grasp him firmly,^b fix your hook,^c
  Twist his shoulder back and, glibly,
      gulp the victim down at once.
  And you search amongst the townsmen
      for some lambkin-witted dunce,
  Wealthy, void of tricks and malice,
      shuddering at disputes and fuss.
PAPH. *You* assail me too, my masters?
      'tis for you they beat me thus;
  'Tis because I thought of moving
      that 'twere proper here to make
  Some memorial of your worships
      for your noble valour's sake.
CHOR. Hear him trying to cajole us!
      O the supple-bending sneak,
  Playing off his tricks upon us,
      as on dotards old and weak.
  Nay, but there my arm shall smite him
      if to pass you there he seek;
  If he dodge in this direction,
      here against my leg he butts.^d
PAPH. Athens! Demus! see the monsters,
      see them punch me in the guts.
CHOR. Shouting, are you? you who always
      by your shouts subvert the town.
S.S. But in this I'll first surpass him;
      thus I shout the fellow down.

ARISTOPHANES

ΧΟ. ἀλλ' ἐὰν μέντοι γε νικᾷς τῇ βοῇ, τήνελλος εἶ·
ἢν δ' ἀναιδείᾳ παρέλθῃς, ἡμέτερος ὁ πυραμοῦς.
ΠΑ. τουτονὶ τὸν ἄνδρ' ἐγὼ 'νδείκνυμι, καὶ φήμ' ἐξάγειν
ταῖσι Πελοποννησίων τριήρεσι ζωμεύματα.
ΑΛ. ναὶ μὰ Δία κἄγωγε τοῦτον, ὅτι κενῇ τῇ κοιλίᾳ
εἰσδραμὼν εἰς τὸ πρυτανεῖον, εἶτα πάλιν ἐκθεῖ πλέα.
ΔΗ. νὴ Δί', ἐξάγων γε τἀπόρρηθ', ἅμ' ἄρτον καὶ κρέας
καὶ τέμαχος, οὗ Περικλέης οὐκ ἠξιώθη πώποτε.
ΠΑ. ἀποθανεῖσθον αὐτίκα μάλα.
ΑΛ. τριπλάσιον κεκράξομαί σου.
ΠΑ. καταβοήσομαι βοῶν σε.
ΑΛ. κατακεκράξομαί σε κράζων.
ΠΑ. διαβαλῶ σ', ἐὰν στρατηγῇς.
ΑΛ. κυνοκοπήσω σου τὸ νῶτον.
ΠΑ. περιελῶ σ' ἀλαζονείαις.
ΑΛ. ὑποτεμοῦμαι τοὺς πόδας[1] σου.
ΠΑ. βλέψον εἴς μ' ἀσκαρδάμυκτος.
ΑΛ. ἐν ἀγορᾷ κἀγὼ τέθραμμαι.
ΠΑ. διαφορήσω σ', εἴ τι γρύξεις.
ΑΛ. κοπροφορήσω σ', εἰ λαλήσεις.
ΠΑ. ὁμολογῶ κλέπτειν· σὺ δ' οὐχί.
ΑΛ. νὴ τὸν Ἑρμῆν τὸν ἀγοραῖον,

[1] τοὺς πόδας, Rogers: τὰς ὁδούς MSS.

---

[a] A Greek proverb. A cake was the prize at drinking parties for the man who kept awake all night.
[b] A play upon ζωμεύματα, "sauces," and ὑποζώματα, "cables for under-girding a ship." Cf. the account of St. Paul's shipwreck, Acts xxvii. 17.
[c] To be a guest at the public dinner in the Prytaneum was a recognized honour. This was awarded to Cleon after his success at Sphacteria. At that time Cleon had bitterly attacked Nicias and Demosthenes.

THE KNIGHTS, 276-297

CHOR. If in bawling you defeat him,
        sing we ho! for Victory's sake.
    If in shamelessness you beat him,
        then indeed we take the cake.[a]

PAPH. I denounce this smuggling fellow;
        contraband of war he takes
    For the Peloponnesian galleys,
        frapping them with—girdle-cakes.[b]

S.S. I denounce this juggling fellow;
        at the Hall, from day to day,
    In he runs with empty belly,
        with a full one hies away.[c]

CHOR. Fish, and flesh, and bread exporting,
        and a hundred things like these,
    Contraband of peace, which never
        were allowed to Pericles.

PAPH.   Death awaits you at once, you two.
S.S.   Thrice as loud can I squall as you.
PAPH.   Now will I bawl you down by bawling.
S.S.   Now will I squall you down by squalling.
PAPH.   Lead our armies, and I'll backbite you.
S.S.   I'll with dog-whips slash you and smite you.
PAPH.   I'll outwit you by fraud and lying.
S.S.   I'll your pettitoes chop for frying.
PAPH.   Now unblinking regard me, you.
S.S.   I was bred in the agora too.
PAPH.   Say but g-r-r, and to strips I'll tear you.
S.S.   Speak one word, and as dung I'll bear you.
PAPH.   I confess that I steal. Do you?
S.S.   Agora Hermes[d]! yes, I do.

[d] An image of Hermes, as patron of commerce and of tricks, stood in the market-place.

ARISTOPHANES

ΠΑ.
κἀπιορκῶ γε βλεπόντων.
ἀλλότρια τοίνυν σοφίζει,
καί σε φαίνω τοῖς πρυτάνεσιν,
ἀδεκατεύτους τῶν θεῶν ἱε-
ρὰς ἔχοντα κοιλίας.

ΧΟ.
ὦ μιαρέ, καὶ βδελυρέ, καὶ κατακε- [στρ. α
κράκτα, τοῦ σοῦ θράσους
πᾶσα μὲν γῆ πλέα,
πᾶσα δ᾽ ἐκκλησία,
καὶ τέλη, καὶ γραφαί,
καὶ δικαστήρι᾽, ὦ
βορβοροτάραξι, καὶ
τὴν πόλιν ἅπασαν ἡ-
μῶν ἀνατετυρβακώς,
ὅστις ἡμῶν τὰς Ἀθήνας ἐκκεκώφωκας βοῶν,
κἀπὸ τῶν πετρῶν ἄνωθεν τοὺς φόρους θυννοσκοπῶν.
ΠΑ. οἶδ᾽ ἐγὼ τὸ πρᾶγμα τοῦθ᾽ ὅθεν πάλαι καττύεται.
ΑΛ. εἰ δὲ μὴ σύ γ᾽ οἶσθα κάττυμ᾽, οὐδ᾽ ἐγὼ χορδεύματα,
ὅστις ὑποτέμνων ἐπώλεις δέρμα μοχθηροῦ βοὸς
τοῖς ἀγροίκοισιν πανούργως, ὥστε φαίνεσθαι παχύ,
καὶ πρὶν ἡμέραν φορῆσαι, μεῖζον ἦν δυοῖν δοχμαῖν.
ΝΙ. νὴ Δία κἀμὲ τοῦτ᾽ ἔδρασε ταὐτόν, ὥστε καὶ γέλων

---

[a] *i.e.* "you are poaching on my preserves": R.
[b] Lit. "I denounce you to the Prytanes," who are sitting among the spectators; *cf.* 278.
[c] κοιλίας, "guts," for οὐσίας, "estates": Schol. Estates of certain offenders were confiscated, and a tithe paid to Athena. Tithes of their profits were also consecrated by private persons

THE KNIGHTS, 298-319

PAPH.   If I'm seen, I'm a perjurer too.
      Somebody else's tricks you're vaunting ;[a]
        Now to the Prytanes off I'll run,[b]
      Tell them you've got some holy pig-guts.
        Tell them you've paid no tithe thereon.[c]

CHOR. O villain, O shameless of heart,
        O Bawler and Brawler self-seeking,
    The land, the Assembly, the Tolls,
        are all with thine impudence reeking,
    And the Courts, and the actions at law ;
        they are full unto loathing and hate !
    Thou stirrest the mud to its depths,
        perturbing the whole of the State.
  Ruffian, who hast deafened Athens
        with thine everlasting din,
  Watching from the rocks the tribute,
        tunny-fashion, shoaling in.[d]

PAPH. Well I know the very quarter
      where they cobbled up the plot.
S.S.   You're a knowing hand at cobbling,
      else in mincing meat I'm not ;
    You who cheated all the rustics
      with a flabby bullock-hide,
    Cutting it aslant to make it
      look like leather firm and dried ;[e]
    In a day, the shoes you sold them
      wobbled half a foot too wide.
NIC.   That's the very trick the rascal
      played the other day on me,

in gratitude. Instances are recorded of butcher, baker, tanner, potter, fuller, and washerman. (*Greek Votive Offerings*, p. 59.)
  [d] An allusion to the watchers set to look out for shoals of tunny, who announce their advent with stentorian voice.
  [e] The slanting cut makes the leather seem thicker than it is.

ARISTOPHANES

πάμπολυν τοῖς δημόταισι καὶ φίλοις παρασχεθεῖν·
πρὶν γὰρ εἶναι Περγασῆσιν, ἔνεον ἐν ταῖς ἐμβάσιν.

XO. ἆρα δῆτ' οὐκ ἀπ' ἀρχῆς ἐδήλους ἀναί- [στρ. β
δειαν, ἥπερ μόνη προστατεῖ ῥητόρων;
ᾗ σὺ πιστεύων ἀμέλγεις τῶν ξένων τοὺς καρπίμους,
πρῶτος ὤν· ὁ δ' Ἱπποδάμου λείβεται θεώμενος.
ἀλλ' ἐφάνη γὰρ ἀνὴρ ἕτερος πολὺ
σοῦ μιαρώτερος, ὥστε με χαίρειν,
ὅς σε παύσει καὶ πάρεισι, δῆλός ἐστιν, αὐτόθεν,
πανουργίᾳ τε καὶ θράσει
καὶ κοβαλικεύμασιν.
ἀλλ' ὦ τραφεὶς ὅθενπέρ εἰσιν ἄνδρες οἵπερ εἰσί,
νῦν δεῖξον ὡς οὐδὲν λέγει τὸ σωφρόνως τραφῆναι.

ΑΛ. καὶ μὴν ἀκούσαθ' οἷός ἐστιν οὑτοσὶ πολίτης.
ΠΑ. οὐκ αὖ μ' ἐάσεις;
ΑΛ.   μὰ Δί', ἐπεὶ κἀγὼ πονηρός εἰμι.
ΧΟ. ἐὰν δὲ μὴ ταύτῃ γ' ὑπείκῃ, λέγ' ὅτι κἀκ πονηρῶν.
ΠΑ. οὐκ αὖ μ' ἐάσεις;
ΑΛ.   μὰ Δία.
ΠΑ.   ναὶ μὰ Δία.
ΑΛ.   μὰ τὸν Ποσειδῶ,
ἀλλ' αὐτὸ περὶ τοῦ πρότερος εἰπεῖν πρῶτα δια-
μαχοῦμαι.

---
[a] An Attic Deme.
[b] Archeptolemus, 794 below. He tried to end the war, but was foiled by Cleon. Being involved with the Four Hundred, he was afterwards condemned to death.

THE KNIGHTS, 320–339

      And my friends and fellow burghers
            laughed with undissembled glee,
      I was swimming in my slippers
            ere I got to Pergasae.[a]
CHOR. So then thou hast e'en from the first
            that shameless bravado displayed
      Which alone is the Orators' Patron.
            And foremost of all by its aid
      Thou the wealthy strangers milkest,
            draining off their rich supplies ;
      And the son of Hippodamus [b]
            watches thee with streaming eyes.
      Ah, but another has dawned on us now,
      Viler and fouler and coarser than thou,
      Viler and fouler and coarser by far,
      One who'll beat thee and defeat thee
            (therefore jubilant we are),
      Beat thee in jackanapes tricks and rascality,
      Beat thee in impudence, cheek, and brutality.
      O trained where Men are trained who best
            deserve that appellation,
      Now show us of how little worth
            is liberal education.
S.S. The sort of citizen he is, I'll first expose to view.
PAPH. Give *me* precedence.
S.S.   No, by Zeus, for I'm a blackguard too.
CHOR. And if to that he yield not, add " as all my fathers were."
PAPH. Give *me* precedence.
S.S.   No, by Zeus.
PAPH.   O yes, by Zeus.
S.S.   I swear
      I'll fight you on that very point ; you never *shall* be first.

ARISTOPHANES

ΠΑ. οἴμοι, διαρραγήσομαι.
ΑΛ. καὶ μὴν ἐγὼ οὐ παρήσω. 31(
ΧΟ. πάρες πάρες πρὸς τῶν θεῶν αὐτῷ διαρραγῆναι.
ΠΑ. τῷ καὶ πεποιθὼς ἀξιοῖς ἐμοῦ λέγειν ἔναντα;
ΑΛ. ὁτιὴ λέγειν οἷός τε κἀγὼ καὶ καρυκοποιεῖν.
ΠΑ. ἰδοὺ λέγειν. καλῶς γ' ἂν οὖν σὺ πρᾶγμα προσπεσόν σοι
ὠμοσπάρακτον παραλαβὼν μεταχειρίσαιο χρηστῶς. 34ἱ
ἀλλ' οἶσθ' ὅ μοι πεπονθέναι δοκεῖς; ὅπερ τὸ πλῆθος.
εἴ που δικίδιον εἶπας εὖ κατὰ ξένου μετοίκου,
τὴν νύκτα θρυλῶν καὶ λαλῶν ἐν ταῖς ὁδοῖς σεαυτῷ,
ὕδωρ τε πίνων, κἀπιδεικνὺς τοὺς φίλους τ' ἀνιῶν,
ᾤου δυνατὸς εἶναι λέγειν. ὦ μῶρε τῆς ἀνοίας. 35(
ΑΛ. τί δαὶ σὺ πίνων τὴν πόλιν πεποίηκας, ὥστε νυνὶ
ὑπὸ σοῦ μονωτάτου κατεγλωττισμένην σιωπᾶν;
ΠΑ. ἐμοὶ γὰρ ἀντέθηκας ἀνθρώπων τιν'; ὅστις εὐθὺς
θύννεια θερμὰ καταφαγών, κᾆτ' ἐπιπιὼν ἀκράτου
οἴνου χόα κασαλβάσω τοὺς ἐν Πύλῳ στρατηγούς. 35ἱ
ΑΛ. ἐγὼ δέ γ' ἤνυστρον βοὸς καὶ κοιλίαν ὑείαν

[a] The speaker intends this to repeat the words of 338, but the chorus misunderstand him to refer to "I shall burst."
[b] In later days, it was a gibe against the orator Demosthenes that he was a water-drinker; and something of the sort may be meant here.

THE KNIGHTS, 340-356

PAPH. O, I shall burst.
S.S. You never shall.[a]
CHOR. O let him, let him burst.
PAPH. How dare you try in speech to vie
                with ME ? On what rely you ?
S.S. Why I can speak first-rate, and eke
                with piquant sauce supply you.
PAPH. O speak you can ! and you're the man,
                I warrant, who is able
A mangled mess full well to dress,
                and serve it up to table.
I know your case, the common case ;
                against some alien folk
You had some petty suit to plead,
                and fairly well you spoke.
For oft you'd conned the speech by night,
                and in the streets discussed it,
And, quaffing water,[b] shown it off,
                and all your friends disgusted.
Now you're an orator, you think.
                O fool, the senseless thought !
S.S. Pray what's the draught which you have quaffed
                that Athens you have brought
Tongue-wheedled by yourself alone
                to sit so mute and still ?
PAPH. Who to compare with ME will dare ?
                I'll eat my tunny grill,
And quaff thereon a stoup of wine
                which water shall not touch,
And then with scurrilous abuse
                the Pylian generals smutch.
S.S. I'll eat the paunch of cow and swine,
                and quaff thereon their stew,

ARISTOPHANES

καταβροχθίσας, κἆτ' ἐπιπιὼν τὸν ζωμὸν ἀναπόνιπτος
λαρυγγιῶ τοὺς ῥήτορας καὶ Νικίαν ταράξω.
ΧΟ. τὰ μὲν ἄλλα μ' ἤρεσας λέγων· ἓν δ' οὐ προσίεταί με
τῶν πραγμάτων, ὁτιὴ μόνος τὸν ζωμὸν ἐκροφήσεις. 360
ΠΑ. ἀλλ' οὐ λάβρακας καταφαγὼν Μιλησίους κλονήσεις.
ΑΛ. ἀλλὰ σχελίδας ἐδηδοκὼς ὠνήσομαι μέταλλα.
ΠΑ. ἐγὼ δ' ἐπεισπηδῶν γε τὴν βουλὴν βίᾳ κυκήσω.
ΑΛ. ἐγὼ δὲ κινήσω γέ σου τὸν πρωκτὸν ἀντὶ φύσκης.
ΠΑ. ἐγὼ δέ γ' ἐξέλξω σε τῆς πυγῆς θύραζε κύβδα. 365
ΧΟ. νὴ τὸν Ποσειδῶ κἀμέ τἄρ', ἤνπερ γε τοῦτον ἕλκῃς.
ΠΑ. οἷόν σε δήσω 'ν τῷ ξύλῳ.
ΑΛ. διώξομαί σε δειλίας.
ΠΑ. ἡ βύρσα σου θρανεύσεται.
ΑΛ. δερῶ σε θύλακον κλοπῆς. 370
ΠΑ. διαπατταλευθήσει χαμαί.
ΑΛ. περικόμματ' ἔκ σου σκευάσω.
ΠΑ. τὰς βλεφαρίδας σου παρατιλῶ.
ΑΛ. τὸν πρηγορεῶνά σούκτεμῶ.
ΔΗ. καὶ νὴ Δί' ἐμβαλόντες αὐ- 375
τῷ πάτταλον μαγειρικῶς
ἐς τὸ στόμ', εἶτα δ' ἔνδοθεν
τὴν γλῶτταν ἐξείραντες αὐ-
τοῦ σκεψόμεσθ' εὖ κἀνδρικῶς
κεχηνότος 380
τὸν πρωκτόν, εἰ χαλαζᾷ.

---

[a] "The Milesian basse was a prime favourite with Hellenic epicures": R. Somehow Cleon had got money out of the Milesians, cf. 932.
[b] The reference is unknown.
[c] The terms in the following passage are drawn from the speakers' trades.

And rising from the board with hands
                which water never knew
I'll throttle all the orators, and flutter Nicias too.
CHOR. With all beside I'm satisfied,
                but one thing likes me not,
You speak as if you ate alone
                whatever stew you've got.
PAPH. You'll not consume your basse and then
                Miletus bring to grief.[a]
S.S. But mines I'll purchase [b] when I've first
                devoured my ribs of beef.
PAPH. I'll leap the Council-chamber in,
                and put them all to rout.
S.S. I'll treat you like a sausage-skin,
                and twirl your breech about.
PAPH. I'll hoist you by your crupper up,
                and thrust you through the gate, sir.
CHOR. If him you thrust, me too you must;
                you must as sure as fate, sir.
PAPH. Your feet in the stocks I'll fix full tight.
S.S. And you for your cowardice I'll indict.
PAPH. Outstretched on my board your hide I'll pin.[c]
S.S. "Pickpocket's purse" I'll make your skin.
PAPH. Your limbs on the tanhouse floor I'll stake.
S.S. Your flesh into force-meat balls I'll bake.
PAPH. I'll twitch the lashes off both your eyes.
S.S. I'll cut your gizzard out, poulterer-wise.
DE. Prop open his mouth with all your strength;
Insert the extender from jaw to jaw;
Pull out his tongue to its utmost length,
And, butcher-fashion, inspect his maw,
And whilst his gape is so broad and fine,
See if he's not   The symptoms got
Which show that he's nought but a measly swine.

ARISTOPHANES

ΧΟ. ἦν ἄρα πυρός γ' ἕτερα θερμότερα, [ἀντ.
καὶ λόγοι τῶν λόγων
ἐν πόλει τῶν ἀναι-
δῶν ἀναιδέστεροι· 385
καὶ τὸ πρᾶγμ' ἦν ἄρ' οὐ
φαῦλον ὧδ' [οὐδαμῶς].[1]
ἀλλ' ἔπιθι καὶ στρόβει,
μηδὲν ὀλίγον ποίει·
νῦν γὰρ ἔχεται μέσος.
ὡς ἐὰν νυνὶ μαλάξῃς αὐτὸν ἐν τῇ προσβολῇ,
δειλὸν εὑρήσεις· ἐγὼ γὰρ τοὺς τρόπους ἐπίσταμαι. 390
ΑΛ. ἀλλ' ὅμως οὗτος τοιοῦτος ὢν ἅπαντα τὸν βίον,
κᾆτ' ἀνὴρ ἔδοξεν εἶναι, τἀλλότριον ἀμῶν θέρος.
νῦν δὲ τοὺς στάχυς ἐκείνους, οὓς ἐκεῖθεν ἤγαγεν,
ἐν ξύλῳ δήσας ἀφαύει κἀποδόσθαι βούλεται.
ΠΑ. οὐ δέδοιχ' ὑμᾶς, ἕως ἂν ζῇ τὸ βουλευτήριον 395
καὶ τὸ τοῦ Δήμου πρόσωπον μακκοᾷ καθήμενον.

ΧΟ. ὡς δὲ πρὸς πᾶν ἀναιδεύεται κοὐ μεθί- [ἀντ.
στησι τοῦ χρώματος τοῦ παρεστηκότος.
εἴ σε μὴ μισῶ, γενοίμην ἐν Κρατίνου κῴδιον, 400
καὶ διδασκοίμην προσᾴδειν Μορσίμου τραγῳδίαν.

[1] οὐδαμῶς inserted by Rogers to complete the metre.

---

[a] "Cleon had done what he declared that the generals εἰ ΑΝΔΡΕΣ εἶεν would do, viz.: sail to Pylus and bring back the Spartans as captives, Thuc. iv. 27. He had reaped the harvest which Demosthenes had sown": R.
[b] Cratinus was a good bottle-man, and his sheepskin might be expected to fare ill. He was a competitor in this contest with Aristophanes.

THE KNIGHTS, 382-401

CHOR. There are things, then, hotter than fire ;
        there are speeches more shameless still
Than the shameless speeches of those
            who rule the City at will.
No trifling task is before you ;
        upon him and twist and garotte him.
Do nought that is little or mean ;
        for round the waist you have got him.
If in this assault you knead him
        limp and supple to your hand,
You will find the man a craven ;
        I his habits understand.
S.S. Truly for an arrant coward
        he has all his life been known ;
Yet a Man he seemed but lately,
        reaping where he had not sown.[a]
Now the ears of corn he brought us,
        he aspires to parch and dry,
Shuts them up in wood and fetters,
        hopes to sell them by and by
PAPH. You and your allies I fear not,
        while the Council lives, and while
Demus moons upon the benches
        with his own unmeaning smile.
CHOR. O see how he brazens it out !
        The colour remains as before
In his shameless impudent face.
        And O, if I hate you not sore,
Let me be a filthy sheepskin,
        that whereon Cratinus lay,[b]
Or let Morsimus[c] instruct me
        as the Chorus to his Play.

[c] Morsimus was a worthless tragedian.

ARISTOPHANES

ὦ περὶ πάντ' ἐπὶ πᾶσί τε πράγμασι
δωροδόκοισιν ἐπ' ἄνθεσιν ἵζων,
εἴθε φαύλως, ὥσπερ εὗρες, ἐκβάλοις τὴν ἔνθεσιν.
ἄσαιμι γὰρ τότ' ἂν μόνον· 40
πῖνε πῖν' ἐπὶ συμφοραῖς·
τὸν Ἰουλίου τ' ἂν οἴομαι, γέροντα πυροπίπην,
ἠσθέντ' ἰηπαιωνίσαι καὶ Βακχέβακχον ᾆσαι.

ΠΑ. οὔ τοί μ' ὑπερβαλεῖσθ' ἀναιδείᾳ μὰ τὸν Ποσειδῶ,
ἢ μή ποτ' ἀγοραίου Διὸς σπλάγχνοισι παρα-
γενοίμην. 41

ΑΛ. ἔγωγε νὴ τοὺς κονδύλους, οὓς πολλὰ δὴ 'πὶ πολλοῖς
ἠνεσχόμην ἐκ παιδίου, μαχαιρίδων τε πληγάς,
ὑπερβαλεῖσθαί σ' οἴομαι τούτοισιν, ἢ μάτην γ' ἂν
ἀπομαγδαλιὰς σιτούμενος τοσοῦτος ἐκτραφείην.

ΠΑ. ἀπομαγδαλιὰς ὥσπερ κύων; ὦ παμπόνηρε, πῶς οὖν 41
κυνὸς βορὰν σιτούμενος μάχει σὺ κυνοκεφάλλῳ;

ΑΛ. καὶ νὴ Δί' ἄλλα γ' ἐστί μου κόβαλα παιδὸς ὄντος.
ἐξηπάτων γὰρ τοὺς μαγείρους ἂν λέγων τοιαυτί·
σκέψασθε, παῖδες· οὐχ ὁρᾶθ'; ὥρα νέα, χελιδών.
οἱ δ' ἔβλεπον, κἀγὼ 'ν τοσούτῳ τῶν κρεῶν ἔκλεπτον. 42

---

[a] A ditty of Simonides.
[b] πυροπίπης, "one who keeps a loving eye on the bread" (cf. the Homeric παρθενοπίπης), was a nickname given by Cratinus to this old panther at the Prytaneum.
[c] A statue of Zeus under this title stood in the Agora, and another in the Pnyx.
[d] Pieces of dough used to clean the fingers, and then thrown to the dogs.
[e] See Baumeister, Denkmäler, fig. 2126, p. 1985.

THE KNIGHTS, 402-420

      Thou in all places, and thou at all hours,
      Flitting and sitting in bri-berry flowers,
      Sucking and sipping the gold they contain,
      Mayest thou lightly, as 'twas swallowed,
              cast thy mouthful up again.
      Then will I ever the roundelay sing
      Drink for the luck which the Destinies bring,[a]
      And old Iulius's son, the pantler Prytanean,[b]
      For joy will " Bacche-Bacchus " shout,
              and chant his Io-Pacan.

PAPH.   Think you in shamelessness to win ?
                          No, by Poseidon, no !
      Or may I evermore the feasts
                    of Agora Zeus [c] forgo.
S.S.   Now by the knuckles which in youth
                    would discipline my head,
      And those hard-handled butchers' knives
                    they often used instead,
      I think in shamelessness I'll win ;
                    else vainly in the slums
      Have I to such a bulk been reared
                  on finger-cleaning crumbs.[d]
PAPH.   On finger-pellets like a dog ?
                    And reared on these, you seek
      To fight a dog-faced fierce baboon !
                    I marvel at your cheek.
S.S.   And lots of other monkey-tricks
                    I practised as a boy.
      O how I used to chouse the cooks
                  by shrieking out *Ahoy !*
      Look lads, a swallow ! spring is here.
                  Look up, look up, I pray.[e]
      So up they looked whilst I purloined
                    a piece of meat away.

ARISTOPHANES

ΧΟ. ὦ δεξιώτατον κρέας, σοφῶς γε προὐνοήσω·
ὥσπερ ἀκαλήφας ἐσθίων πρὸ χελιδόνων ἔκλεπτες.
ΑΛ. καὶ ταῦτα δρῶν ἐλάνθανόν γ'· εἰ δ' οὖν ἴδοι τις
αὐτῶν,
ἀποκρυπτόμενος εἰς τὰ κοχώνα τοὺς θεοὺς ἀπ-
ώμνυν·
ὥστ' εἶπ' ἀνὴρ τῶν ῥητόρων ἰδών με τοῦτο δρῶντα·
οὐκ ἔσθ' ὅπως ὁ παῖς ὅδ' οὐ τὸν δῆμον ἐπιτροπεύσει.
ΧΟ. εὖ γε ξυνέβαλεν αὔτ'· ἀτὰρ δηλόν γ' ἀφ' οὗ
ξυνέγνω·
ὁτιὴ 'πιώρκεις θ' ἡρπακὼς καὶ κρέας ὁ πρωκτὸς
εἶχεν.
ΠΑ. ἐγώ σε παύσω τοῦ θράσους, οἶμαι δὲ μᾶλλον ἄμφω.
ἔξειμι γάρ σοι λαμπρὸς ἤδη καὶ μέγας καθιείς,
ὁμοῦ ταράττων τήν τε γῆν καὶ τὴν θάλατταν εἰκῇ.
ΑΛ. ἐγὼ δὲ συστείλας γε τοὺς ἀλλᾶντας εἶτ' ἀφήσω
κατὰ κῦμ' ἐμαυτὸν οὔριον, κλάειν σε μακρὰ
κελεύσας.
ΔΗ. κἄγωγ', ἐάν τι παραχαλᾷ, τὴν ἀντλίαν φυλάξω.
ΠΑ. οὔ τοι μὰ τὴν Δήμητρα καταπροίξει τάλαντα πολλὰ
κλέψας Ἀθηναίων.
ΧΟ. ἄθρει, καὶ τοῦ ποδὸς παρίει·
ὡς οὗτος ἤδη Καικίας καὶ Συκοφαντίας πνεῖ.

---

[a] Καικίας, the name of "the north-east wind, one of the most violent winds in the Mediterranean," was proverbially explained as "bringing evils" (ἕλκων κακά), and Aristophanes coins Συκοφαντίας on its analogy.

CHOR. Shrewd body, you were provident,
              and stole away your meat
      Before the vernal swallow came,
              as folk their nettles eat.
S.S. And no one caught me out, or else,
              if any saw me pot it,
      I clapped the meat between my thighs
              and vowed I hadn't got it;
      Whereat an orator observed,
              who watched me at my tricks,
      Some day this boy will make his mark
              as leader in the Pnyx.
CHOR. His inference was just; but still
              'tis plain from whence he drew it;
      He saw you filch the meat away,
              and swear you didn't do it.
PAPH. I'll stop your insolence, my man;
              your friend's and yours together.
      I'll swoop upon you like a gale
              of fresh and stormy weather,
      And all the land and all the sea
              in wild confusion throw.
S.S. But I will furl my sausages,
              and down the tide will go
      With prosperous seas, and favouring breeze,
              at you my fingers snapping.
DE.   And if your bark a leak should spring,
              the water I'll be tapping.
PAPH. Full many a talent have you filched,
              and dearly shall you pay,
      You public-treasury thief!
CHOR.   Look out, and slack the sheet away,
      I hear a loud Nor'-Easter there
              or Sycophanter [a] blow.

ARISTOPHANES

ΠΑ. σὲ δ᾽ ἐκ Ποτιδαίας ἔχοντ᾽ εὖ οἶδα δέκα τάλαντα.
ΑΛ. τί δῆτα; βούλει τῶν ταλάντων ἓν λαβὼν σιωπᾶν;
ΧΟ. ἀνὴρ ἂν ἡδέως λάβοι. τοὺς τερθρίους παρίει. 44
ΑΛ. τὸ πνεῦμ᾽ ἔλαττον γίγνεται.
ΠΑ. [δωροδοκίας]¹ φεύξει γραφὰς
    ἑκατονταλάντους τέτταρας.
ΑΛ. σὺ δ᾽ ἀστρατείας εἴκοσιν,
    κλοπῆς δὲ πλεῖν ἢ χιλίας.
ΠΑ. ἐκ τῶν ἀλιτηρίων σέ φη- 44
    μι γεγονέναι τῶν τῆς θεοῦ.
ΑΛ. τὸν πάππον εἶναί φημί σου
    τῶν δορυφόρων—
ΠΑ.   ποίων; φράσον.
ΑΛ. τῶν Βυρσίνης τῆς Ἱππίου.
ΠΑ. κόβαλος εἶ.
ΑΛ.   πανοῦργος εἶ. 45
ΧΟ. παῖ᾽ ἀνδρικῶς.
ΠΑ.   ἰοὺ ἰού,
    τύπτουσί μ᾽ οἱ ξυνωμόται.
ΧΟ. παῖ᾽ αὐτὸν ἀνδρικώτατα, καὶ
    γάστριζε καὶ τοῖς ἐντέροις
    καὶ τοῖς κόλοις, 45
    χὤπως κολᾷ τὸν ἄνδρα.

ὦ γεννικώτατον κρέας ψυχήν τ᾽ ἄριστε πάντων,
καὶ τῇ πόλει σωτὴρ φανεὶς ἡμῖν τε τοῖς πολίταις,

¹ Inserted by Rogers.

[a] Potidaea had surrendered on terms some five years before this, Thuc. ii. 70. No doubt Cleon had attacked the generals.
[b] The great family of the Alcmaeonidae was put under a curse for the murder of Cylon's friends in sanctuary, about 200 years before, Thuc. i. 126. The charge was revived against Cleisthenes, and later against Pericles, possibly also against Alcibiades. Here

PAPH. From Potidaea you received
　　　　　　　　ten talents, that I know.[a]
S.S. Will you take one, and hold your tongue?
CHOR. 　　　　　　　　He'd take it like a shot.
　　　Let out the yard-arm ropes a bit.
S.S. 　　　　　　　　The gale has milder got.
　　　The stormy blast is falling fast.
PAPH. You'll have, for bribery and deceit,
　　　Four hundred-talent writs to meet.
S.S. And you, for cowardliness a score,
　　　For theft a thousand writs and more.
PAPH. From that old sacrilegious race [b]
　　　I'll say that your descent you trace.
S.S. Your father's father marched, I'll swear,
　　　As body-guard to—
PAPH. 　　　　　　　　Whom? Declare!
S.S. To Hippias's Byrsine.[c]
PAPH. You jackanapes!
S.S. 　　　　　　　　You gallows-tree!
CHOR. Strike like a man!
PAPH. 　　　　　　　　O help me! Oh!
　　　These plotting traitors hurt me so.
CHOR. Strike, strike him, well and manfully,
　　　　And with those entrails beat him,
　　　And strings of sausage-meat, and try
　　　　Meet punishment to mete him.
　　O noblest flesh in all the world,
　　　　　　　　O spirit best and dearest,
　　To City and to citizens
　　　　　　　　a Saviour thou appearest.

it is used as a comic threat against the Sausage-seller, the last man to belong to such a family.

  [c] The wife of Hippias the tyrant was Myrsine; for which, to suit the tanner's trade, Aristophanes substitutes Βυρσίνη "a leather strap."

ARISTOPHANES

ὡς εὖ τὸν ἄνδρα ποικίλως θ' ὑπῆλθες ἐν λόγοισιν.
πῶς ἄν σ' ἐπαινέσαιμεν οὕτως ὥσπερ ἡδόμεσθα; 460
ΠΑ. ταυτὶ μὰ τὴν Δήμητρά μ' οὐκ ἐλάνθανεν
τεκταινόμενα τὰ πράγματ', ἀλλ' ἠπιστάμην
γομφούμεν' αὐτὰ πάντα καὶ κολλώμενα.
ΧΟ. οἴμοι, σὺ δ' οὐδὲν ἐξ ἁμαξουργοῦ λέγεις;
ΑΛ. οὔκουν μ' ἐν Ἄργει γ' οἷα πράττει λανθάνει. 465
πρόφασιν μὲν Ἀργείους φίλους ἡμῖν ποιεῖ·
ἰδίᾳ δ' ἐκεῖ Λακεδαιμονίοις ξυγγίγνεται.
καὶ ταῦτ' ἐφ' οἷσίν ἐστι συμφυσώμενα
ἐγῷδ'· ἐπὶ γὰρ τοῖς δεδεμένοις χαλκεύεται.
ΧΟ. εὖ γ' εὖ γε, χάλκευ' ἀντὶ τῶν κολλωμένων. 470
ΑΛ. καὶ ξυγκροτοῦσιν ἄνδρες αὖτ' ἐκεῖθεν αὖ,
καὶ ταῦτά μ' οὔτ' ἀργύριον οὔτε χρυσίον
διδοὺς ἀναπείσεις, οὔτε προσπέμπων φίλους,
ὅπως ἐγὼ ταῦτ' οὐκ Ἀθηναίοις φράσω.
ΠΑ. ἐγὼ μὲν οὖν αὐτίκα μάλ' εἰς βουλὴν ἰὼν 475
ὑμῶν ἁπάντων τὰς ξυνωμοσίας ἐρῶ,
καὶ τὰς ξυνόδους τὰς νυκτερινὰς ἐν τῇ πόλει,
καὶ πάνθ' ἃ Μήδοις καὶ βασιλεῖ ξυνόμνυτε,
καὶ τἀκ Βοιωτῶν ταῦτα συντυρούμενα.
ΑΛ. πῶς οὖν ὁ τυρὸς ἐν Βοιωτοῖς ὤνιος; 480
ΠΑ. ἐγώ σε νὴ τὸν Ἡρακλέα παραστορῶ.
ΧΟ. ἄγε δὴ σὺ τίνα νοῦν ἢ τίνα γνώμην ἔχεις;
νυνὶ διδάξεις, εἴπερ ἀπεκρύψω τότε

---

[a] A thirty years' truce between Sparta and Argos was running out; both Sparta and Athens were now bidding for the Argive support.
[b] The process for treason was impeachment before the Council, εἰσαγγελία.
[c] Demosthenes was intriguing with Boeotian cities to establish democracy there, Thuc. iv. 76. Cheese was an important product of Boeotia.

THE KNIGHTS, 459–483

   How well and with what varied skill
      thou foil'st him in debate !
   O would that I could praise you so,
      as our delight is great.
PAPH. Now, by Demeter, it escaped me not
   That these same plots were framing ; well I knew
   How they were pegged, and fixed, and glued together.
CHOR. O, me !
(*To S.S.*) Can't *you* say something from the cartwright's trade ?
S.S. These Argos doings have escaped me not.
   He goes, he says, to make a friend of Argos,[a]
   But 'tis with Sparta he's colloguing there.
   Aye and I know the anvil whereupon
   His plan is forged : 'tis welded on the captives.
CHOR. Good ! good ! return him welding for his glue.
S.S. And men from thence are hammering at it too.
   And not by bribes of silver or of gold
   Or sending friends, will you persuade me not
   To tell the Athenians how you are going on.
PAPH. I'll go this instant to the Council-board,[b]
   And all your vile conspiracies denounce,
   And all your nightly gatherings in the town,
   And how you plotted with the Medes and King,
   And all your cheese-pressed doings in Boeotia.[c]
S.S. Pray, how's cheese selling in Boeotia now ?
PAPH. I'll stretch you flat, by Heracles I will. [*Exit*
CHOR. Now then, what mean you ? what are you going to do ?
   Now shall you show us if in very truth

ARISTOPHANES

εἰς τὰ κοχώνα τὸ κρέας, ὡς αὐτὸς λέγεις.
θεύσει γὰρ ἄξας εἰς τὸ βουλευτήριον, 485
ὡς οὗτος εἰσπεσὼν ἐκεῖσε διαβαλεῖ
ἡμᾶς ἅπαντας καὶ κραγὸν κεκράξεται.

ΑΛ. ἀλλ' εἶμι· πρῶτον δ', ὡς ἔχω, τὰς κοιλίας
καὶ τὰς μαχαίρας ἐνθαδὶ καταθήσομαι.

ΔΗ. ἔχε νυν, ἄλειψον τὸν τράχηλον τουτῳί, 490
ἵν' ἐξολισθάνειν δύνῃ τὰς διαβολάς.

ΑΛ. ἀλλ' εὖ λέγεις καὶ παιδοτριβικῶς ταυταγί.

ΔΗ. ἔχε νυν, ἐπέγκαψον λαβὼν ταδί.

ΑΛ. τί δαί;

ΔΗ. ἵν' ἄμεινον, ὦ τᾶν, ἐσκοροδισμένος μάχῃ.
καὶ σπεῦδε ταχέως.

ΑΛ. ταῦτα δρῶ.

ΔΗ. μέμνησό νυν 495
δάκνειν, διαβάλλειν, τοὺς λόφους κατεσθίειν,
χὤπως τὰ κάλλαι' ἀποφαγὼν ἥξεις πάλιν.

ΧΟ. ἀλλ' ἴθι χαίρων, καὶ πράξειας
κατὰ νοῦν τὸν ἐμόν, καί σε φυλάττοι
Ζεὺς ἀγοραῖος· καὶ νικήσας 500
αὖθις ἐκεῖθεν πάλιν ὡς ἡμᾶς
ἔλθοις στεφάνοις κατάπαστος.
ὑμεῖς δ' ἡμῖν πρόσχετε τὸν νοῦν
τοῖς τ' ἀναπαίστοις, ὦ παντοίας
ἤδη Μούσης
πειραθέντες καθ' ἑαυτούς. 505

---

[a] The Scholiast says that he gives him lard ; but perhaps it is a draught of wine, 493. The garlic was to prime him like a fighting cock.

THE KNIGHTS, 484-506

      You stole the meat and hid it as you said.
      So to the Council-house you'll run, for he
      Will burst in thither, and against us all
      Utter his lies and bawl a mighty bawl.
S.S. Well, I will go ; but first I'll lay me down
      Here, as I am, these guts and butchers'-knives.
DE. Here take this ointment and anoint your neck,[a]
      So can you slip more easily through his lies.[b]
S.S. Well now, that's good and trainer-like advice.
DE. And next, take this and swallow it.
S.S.   What for ?
DE. Why, if you are garlie-primed, you'll fight
        much better.
      And now begone.
S.S.   I'm off.
DE.   And don't forget
      To peck, to lie, to gobble down his combs,
      And bite his wattles off. That done, return.

CHOR. Good-bye and good speed : may your daring
        succeed,
      And Zeus of the Agora help you in need.[c]
      May you conquer in fight, and return to our
        sight
      A Victor triumphant with garlands bedight.
      But YE[d] to our anapaests listen the while,
      And give us the heed that is due,
      Ye wits, who the Muse of each pattern and
        style
      Yourselves have attempted to woo.

---

[b] διαβολάς for διαλαβάς. So 496.
[c] 498-99 come from Sophocles, according to the Scholiast.
[d] Here the Chorus turns directly to the audience, and the Parabasis proper, 507-46, follows.

ARISTOPHANES

εἰ μέν τις ἀνὴρ τῶν ἀρχαίων κωμῳδοδιδάσκαλος ἡμᾶς
ἠνάγκαζεν λέξοντας ἔπη πρὸς τὸ θέατρον παραβῆναι,
οὐκ ἂν φαύλως ἔτυχεν τούτου· νῦν δ' ἄξιός ἐσθ' ὁ ποιητής,
ὅτι τοὺς αὐτοὺς ἡμῖν μισεῖ, τολμᾷ τε λέγειν τὰ δίκαια, 5]
καὶ γενναίως πρὸς τὸν Τυφῶ χωρεῖ καὶ τὴν ἐριώλην.
ἃ δὲ θαυμάζειν ὑμῶν φησιν πολλοὺς αὐτῷ προσιόντας,
καὶ βασανίζειν, ὡς οὐχὶ πάλαι χορὸν αἰτοίη καθ' ἑαυτόν,
ἡμᾶς ὑμῖν ἐκέλευε φράσαι περὶ τούτου. φησὶ γὰρ ἀνὴρ
οὐχ ὑπ' ἀνοίας τοῦτο πεπονθὼς διατρίβειν, ἀλλὰ νομίζων 5
κωμῳδοδιδασκαλίαν εἶναι χαλεπώτατον ἔργον ἁπάντων·
πολλῶν γὰρ δὴ πειρασάντων αὐτὴν ὀλίγοις χαρίσασθαι·
ὑμᾶς τε πάλαι διαγιγνώσκων ἐπετείους τὴν φύσιν ὄντας,
καὶ τοὺς προτέρους τῶν ποιητῶν ἅμα τῷ γήρᾳ προ-
διδόντας·
τοῦτο μὲν εἰδὼς ἅπαθε Μάγνης ἅμα ταῖς πολιαῖς κατ-
ιούσαις, 5

---

[a] A. had hitherto exhibited his plays in the name of Callistratus. The poet had to send in his play to the Archon, and "ask for a chorus"; if it was granted, the Archon chose a Choregus, who had to pay all expenses except the cost of the three actors provided by the state. These three divided the chief parts between them.
[b] Magnes, an early writer of comedy. The lines that follow allude to his plays, Βαρβιτισταί, *The Lute-players*, Ὄρνιθες, *The Birds*, Λυδοί, *The Lydians*, Ψῆνες, *The Gall-flies*, Βάτραχοι, *The Frogs*. The green dye, "frog-green," was smeared by actors upon their faces before the use of masks came in. Schol.

THE KNIGHTS, 507-520

If one of the old-fashioned Comedy-bards
    had our services sought to impress,
And make us before the spectators appear,
    to deliver the public address,
He would not have easily gained us ; but now,
    with pleasure we grant the request
Of a poet who ventures the truth to declare,
    and detests what we also detest,
And against the Tornado and Whirlwind, alone,
    with noble devotion advances.
But as for the question that puzzles you most,
    so that many inquire how it chances
That he never a Chorus had asked for himself,
    or attempted in person to vie, [a]
On this we're commissioned his views to explain,
    and this is the Poet's reply ;
That 'twas not from folly he lingered so long,
    but discerning by shrewd observation
That Comedy-Chorus-instruction is quite
    the most difficult thing in creation.
For out of the many who courted the Muse
    she has granted her favours to few,
While e'en as the plants that abide but a year,
    so shifting and changeful are you ;
And the Poets who flourished before him, he saw,
    ye were wont in their age to betray.
Observing the treatment which Magnes [b] received
    when his hair was besprinkled with grey,

ARISTOPHANES

ὃς πλεῖστα χορῶν τῶν ἀντιπάλων νίκης ἔστησε τρόπαια·
πάσας δ' ὑμῖν φωνὰς ἱεὶς καὶ ψάλλων καὶ πτερυγίζων
καὶ λυδίζων καὶ ψηνίζων καὶ βαπτόμενος βατραχείοις
οὐκ ἐξήρκεσεν, ἀλλὰ τελευτῶν ἐπὶ γήρως, οὐ γὰρ ἐφ'
ἥβης,
ἐξεβλήθη πρεσβύτης ὤν, ὅτι τοῦ σκώπτειν ἀπελείφθη· 5
εἶτα Κρατίνου μεμνημένος, ὃς πολλῷ ῥεύσας ποτ' ἐπαίνῳ
διὰ τῶν ἀφελῶν πεδίων ἔρρει, καὶ τῆς στάσεως παρασύρων
ἐφόρει τὰς δρῦς καὶ τὰς πλατάνους καὶ τοὺς ἐχθροὺς προθελύμνους·
ᾆσαι δ' οὐκ ἦν ἐν ξυμποσίῳ πλήν, Δωροῖ συκοπέδιλε,
καί, Τέκτονες εὐπαλάμων ὕμνων· οὕτως ἤνθησεν ἐκεῖνος. 5
νυνὶ δ' ὑμεῖς αὐτὸν ὁρῶντες παραληροῦντ' οὐκ ἐλεεῖτε,
ἐκπιπτουσῶν τῶν ἠλέκτρων, καὶ τοῦ τόνου οὐκ ἔτ' ἐνόντος,
τῶν θ' ἁρμονιῶν διαχασκουσῶν· ἀλλὰ γέρων ὢν περιέρρει,
ὥσπερ Κοννᾶς, στέφανον μὲν ἔχων αὖον, δίψῃ δ' ἀπολωλώς,

---

[a] Cratinus, another writer of comedies, now in his old age a toper and despised. He won the second place in this contest with *The Satyrs*. Next year he was again second to A., with the Χειμαζόμενοι, *The Storm-tossed*; and the year following he was first with Πυτίνη, *The Flagon*, A. being third with *The Clouds*.
[b] Songs of Cratinus from the *Eunidae*, a play full of parodies.

THE KNIGHTS, 521-534

Than whom there was none more trophies had won
        in the fields of dramatic display.
All voices he uttered, all forms he assumed,
        the Lydian, the fig-piercing Fly,
The Harp with its strings, the Bird with its wings,
        the Frog with its yellow-green dye.
Yet all was too little ; he failed in the end,
        when the freshness of youth was gone by,
And at last in his age he was hissed from the stage
        when lost was his talent for jeering.
Then he thought of Cratinus[a] who flowed through the plains
        'mid a tumult of plaudits and cheering ;
And sweeping on all that obstructed his course,
        with a swirl from their stations he tore them,
Oaks, rivals, and planes ; and away on his flood
        uprooted and prostrate he bore them.
And never a song at a banquet was sung
        but *Doro fig-sandaled and true*,[b]
Or *Framers of terse and artistical verse*,[b]
        such a popular poet he grew.
Yet now that he drivels and dotes in the streets,
        and Time of his ambers has reft him,
And his framework is gaping asunder with age,
        and his strings and his music have left him,
No pity ye show ; no assistance bestow ;
        but allow him to wander about
Like Connas,[c] with coronal withered and sere,
        and ready to perish with drought ;

"St. Bribitt with shoes of blackmail," recalls hymns to some goddess χρυσοπέδιλος, " with golden sandals."

[c] The Scholiast says Connas was " a flute-player and drunkard who used to go from feast to feast garlanded, and after winning many victories at Olympia, fell into poverty." The line embodies a proverb, Δελφὸς ἀνήρ, στέφανον μὲν ἔχων, δίψει δ' ἀπολωλώς, used of persons sacrificing while themselves in want.

ARISTOPHANES

ὃν χρῆν διὰ τὰς προτέρας νίκας πίνειν ἐν τῷ Πρυτανείῳ,
καὶ μὴ ληρεῖν, ἀλλὰ θεᾶσθαι λιπαρὸν παρὰ τῷ Διονύσῳ.
οἵας δὲ Κράτης ὀργὰς ὑμῶν ἠνέσχετο καὶ στυφελιγμούς·
ὃς ἀπὸ σμικρᾶς δαπάνης ὑμᾶς ἀριστίζων ἀπέπεμπεν,
ἀπὸ κραμβοτάτου στόματος μάττων ἀστειοτάτας ἐπι-
νοίας·
χοὖτος μέντοι μόνος ἀντήρκει, τότε μὲν πίπτων, τότε
δ' οὐχί.
ταῦτ' ὀρρωδῶν διέτριβεν ἀεί, καὶ πρὸς τούτοισιν
ἔφασκεν
ἐρέτην χρῆναι πρῶτα γενέσθαι, πρὶν πηδαλίοις ἐπιχειρεῖν,
κᾆτ' ἐντεῦθεν πρῳρατεῦσαι καὶ τοὺς ἀνέμους διαθρῆσαι,
κᾆτα κυβερνᾶν αὐτὸν ἑαυτῷ. τούτων οὖν οὕνεκα πάντων,
ὅτι σωφρονικῶς κοὐκ ἀνοήτως ἐσπηδήσας ἐφλυάρει,
αἴρεσθ' αὐτῷ πολὺ τὸ ῥόθιον, παραπέμψατ' ἐφ' ἕνδεκα
κώπαις

> θόρυβον χρηστὸν ληναΐτην,
> ἵν' ὁ ποιητὴς ἀπίῃ χαίρων,
> κατὰ νοῦν πράξας,
> φαιδρὸς λάμποντι μετώπῳ.

---

[a] A variation on the δειπνεῖν ἐν τῷ Πρυτανείῳ. "to dine in the Prytaneum," the reward for distinguished public service.
[b] His statue being placed in the theatre during the plays.
[c] Crates, like Magnes, was dead at this time. His subjects foreshadowed the New Comedy of manners.

THE KNIGHTS, 535–550

Who ought for his former achievements to DRINK [a]
   in the Hall, nor be laid on the shelf,
But to sit in the Theatre shining and bright,
   beside Dionysus himself.[b]
And then he remembered the stormy rebuffs
   which Crates [c] endured in his day,
Who a little repast at a little expense
   would provide you, then send you away;
Who the daintiest little devices would cook
   from the driest of mouths for you all;
Yet he, and he only held out to the end,
   now standing, now getting a fall.
So in fear of these dangers he lingered; besides,
   a sailor, he thought, should abide
And tug at the oar for a season, before
   he attempted the vessel to guide;
And next should be stationed awhile at the prow,
   the winds and the weather to scan;
And then be the Pilot, himself for himself.
   So seeing our Poet began
In a mood so discreet, nor with vulgar conceit
   rushed headlong before you at first,
Loud surges of praise to his honour upraise;
   salute him, all hands, with a burst [d]

  Of hearty triumphant Lenaean applause,
  That the bard may depart, all radiant and bright
  To the top of his forehead with joy and delight,
   Having gained, by your favour, his cause.

[d] " With eleven oars a side ": a phrase not understood. The explanations given are mere guesses.

ARISTOPHANES

ἵππι' ἄναξ Πόσειδον, ᾧ
χαλκοκρότων ἵππων κτύπος
καὶ χρεμετισμὸς ἀνδάνει,
καὶ κυανέμβολοι θοαὶ
μισθοφόροι τριήρεις, 555
μειρακίων θ' ἅμιλλα λαμ-
πρυνομένων ἐν ἅρμασιν
καὶ βαρυδαιμονούντων,
δεῦρ' ἔλθ' ἐς χορόν, ὦ χρυσοτρίαιν', ὦ
δελφίνων μεδέων, Σουνιάρατε, 560
ὦ Γεραίστιε παῖ Κρόνου,
Φορμίωνί τε φίλτατ', ἐκ
τῶν ἄλλων τε θεῶν Ἀθη-
ναίοις πρὸς τὸ παρεστός.

εὐλογῆσαι βουλόμεσθα τοὺς πατέρας ἡμῶν, ὅτι 565
ἄνδρες ἦσαν τῆσδε τῆς γῆς ἄξιοι καὶ τοῦ πέπλου,
οἵτινες πεζαῖς μάχαισιν ἔν τε ναυφράκτῳ στρατῷ
πανταχοῦ νικῶντες ἀεὶ τήνδ' ἐκόσμησαν πόλιν·
οὐ γὰρ οὐδεὶς πώποτ' αὐτῶν τοὺς ἐναντίους ἰδὼν
ἠρίθμησεν, ἀλλ' ὁ θυμὸς εὐθὺς ἦν ἀμυνίας· 570

---

[a] Geraestus, S.W. of Euboea, where was a temple of P.; Sunium, S. of Attica.

[b] Phormio, the Athenian naval commander, distinguished for courage, honesty, and patriotism, and a popular hero. See Thuc. ii. 68-69 on a late victory of his. He seems to have been dead at this time.

[c] An embroidered robe, raised like a sail upon the mast

THE KNIGHTS, 551-570

Dread Poseidon, the Horseman's King,
Thou who lovest the brazen clash,
Clash and neighing of warlike steeds ;
Pleased to watch where the trireme speeds
Purple-beaked, to the oar's long swing,
Winning glory (and pay) ; but chief
Where bright youths in their chariots flash
Racing (coming perchance to grief) ;
  Cronus's son,
Throned on Geraestus and Sunium [a] bold,
Swaying thy dolphins with trident of gold,
 Come, O come, at the call of us ;
  Dearest to Phormio [b] thou,
 Yea and dearest to all of us,
 Dearest to all of us now.

Let us praise our mighty fathers,
    men who ne'er would quake or quail,
Worthy of their native country,
    worthy of Athene's veil [c] ;
Men who with our fleets and armies
    everywhere the victory won,
And adorned our ancient city
    by achievements nobly done.
Never stayed they then to reckon
    what the numbers of the foe,
At the instant that they saw him,
    all their thought was *At him go* [d] *!*

of a ship, which was carried through the city at the great
Panathenaea, and dedicated to Athena Polias on the
Acropolis. The Knights took part in the procession, and
are so represented on the Parthenon frieze. See 1180, *B.* 827.
 [d] The word, which happens also to be a proper name, is
used as an epithet according to its verbal meaning.

ARISTOPHANES

εἰ δέ που πέσοιεν ἐς τὸν ὦμον ἐν μάχῃ τινί,
τοῦτ' ἀπεψήσαντ' ἄν, εἶτ' ἠρνοῦντο μὴ πεπτωκέναι,
ἀλλὰ διεπάλαιον αὖθις. καὶ στρατηγὸς οὐδ' ἂν εἶς
τῶν πρὸ τοῦ σίτησιν ᾔτησ' ἐρόμενος Κλεαίνετον·
νῦν δ' ἐὰν μὴ προεδρίαν φέρωσι καὶ τὰ σιτία, 575
οὐ μαχεῖσθαί φασιν. ἡμεῖς δ' ἀξιοῦμεν τῇ πόλει
προῖκα γενναίως ἀμύνειν καὶ θεοῖς ἐγχωρίοις.
καὶ πρὸς οὐκ αἰτοῦμεν οὐδέν, πλὴν τοσουτονὶ μόνον·
ἤν ποτ' εἰρήνη γένηται καὶ πόνων παυσώμεθα,
μὴ φθονεῖθ' ἡμῖν κομῶσι μηδ' ἀπεστλεγγισμένοις. 580

ὦ πολιοῦχε Παλλάς, ὦ
τῆς ἱερωτάτης ἁπα-
σῶν, πολέμῳ τε καὶ ποιη-
ταῖς δυνάμει θ' ὑπερφερού-
σης μεδέουσα χώρας, 585
δεῦρ' ἀφικοῦ λαβοῦσα τὴν
ἐν στρατιαῖς τε καὶ μάχαις
ἡμετέραν ξυνεργὸν
Νίκην, ἣ χορικῶν ἐστιν ἑταίρα,
τοῖς τ' ἐχθροῖσι μεθ' ἡμῶν στασιάζει. 590

---

[a] Cleaenetus, father of Cleon. Our fathers did not apply to his father.
[b] The Knights wore their hair long: see 1121. To do so was regarded as aristocratic, or as Spartan, and disliked. After gymnastics, a scraper or στλεγγίς was used to scrape off the oil.

THE KNIGHTS, 571-590

If they e'er in desperate struggling
                    on their shoulder chanced to fall,
Quick they wiped away the dust-mark,
                    swore they ne'er were thrown at all,
Closed again in deadly grapple.
                    None of all our generals brave
Then had stooped a public banquet
                    from Cleaenetus [a] to crave.
Now unless ye grant them banquets,
                    grant precedence as their right,
They will fight no more, they tell you.
                    Our ambition is to fight
Freely for our Gods and country,
                    as our fathers fought before,
No reward or pay receiving;
                    asking this and nothing more,
When returning Peace shall set us
                    free from all our warlike toil,
Grudge us not our flowing ringlets,[b]
                    grudge us not our baths and oil.

        Holy Pallas, our guardian Queen,
        Ruling over the holiest land,
        Land poetic, renowned, and strong,
        First in battle and first in song,
        Land whose equal never was seen,
        Come to prosper our Choral band!
        Bring thou with thee the Maiden bright,
        Her who greets us in every fight,
              VICTORY [c]!
She in the choir-competition abides with us,
Always against our antagonists sides with us.

   [c] The statue of Athene by Pheidias bore Victory in her hand.

ARISTOPHANES

νῦν οὖν δεῦρο φάνηθι· δεῖ
γὰρ τοῖς ἀνδράσι τοῖσδε πάσῃ τέχνῃ πορίσαι σε νί-
κην εἴπερ ποτὲ καὶ νῦν.

ἃ ξύνισμεν τοῖσιν ἵπποις, βουλόμεσθ' ἐπαινέσαι. 595
ἄξιοι δ' εἴσ' εὐλογεῖσθαι· πολλὰ γὰρ δὴ πράγματα
ξυνδιήνεγκαν μεθ' ἡμῶν, εἰσβολάς τε καὶ μάχας.
ἀλλὰ τἀν τῇ γῇ μὲν αὐτῶν οὐκ ἄγαν θαυμάζομεν,
ὡς ὅτ' εἰς τὰς ἱππαγωγοὺς εἰσεπήδων ἀνδρικῶς,
πριάμενοι κώθωνας, οἱ δὲ καὶ σκόροδα καὶ κρόμ-
μυα· 600
εἶτα τὰς κώπας λαβόντες ὥσπερ ἡμεῖς οἱ βροτοὶ
ἐμβαλόντες ἀνεβρύαξαν, ἱππαπαῖ, τίς ἐμβαλεῖ;
ληπτέον μᾶλλον. τί δρῶμεν; οὐκ ἐλᾷς, ὦ σαμφόρα;
ἐξεπήδων τ' ἐς Κόρινθον· εἶτα δ' οἱ νεώτατοι
ταῖς ὁπλαῖς ὤρυττον εὐνὰς καὶ μετῇσαν στρώματα· 605
ἤσθιον δὲ τοὺς παγούρους ἀντὶ ποίας Μηδικῆς,
εἴ τις ἐξέρποι θύραζε, κἀκ βυθοῦ θηρώμενοι·
ὥστ' ἔφη Θέωρος εἰπεῖν καρκίνον Κορίνθιον·

[a] A reference to the campaign of Nicias against Corinth in the year before : Thuc. iv. 42-45.
[b] ἱππαπαῖ, for the sailors' ῥυππαπαῖ (W. 909, F. 1073).
[c] Lit. "lucerne."
[d] Unknown : the Schol. says a poet.

THE KNIGHTS, 591–608

Come, great Goddess, appear to us,
Now, if ever, we pray,
Bring thou victory dear to us,
Crown thine Horsemen to-day.

What we witnessed with our horses
    we desire to eulogize.[a]
Worthy they of praise and honour !
    many a deed of high emprize,
Many a raid and battle-onset
    they with us have jointly shared.
Yet their feats ashore surprise not,
    with their feats afloat compared,
When they bought them cans and garlic,
    bought them strings of onions too,
Leapt at once aboard the transports,
    all with manful hearts and true,
Took their seats upon the benches,
    dipped their oar-blades in the sea,
Pulled like any human beings,
    neighing out their *Hippapae* [b]
Pull my hearties, pull your strongest,
    don't be shirking, Sigma-brand,
Then they leapt ashore at Corinth,
    and the youngest of the band
Hollowed with their hoofs their couches
    or for bedding searched about.
And they fed on crabs, for clover,[c]
    if they met one crawling out,
Or detected any lurking
    in the Ocean's deepest bed,
Till at length a crab of Corinth,
    so Theorus [d] tells us, said :

ARISTOPHANES

δεινά γ', ὦ Πόσειδον, εἰ μήτ' ἐν βυθῷ δυνήσομαι,
μήτε γῇ μήτ' ἐν θαλάττῃ, διαφυγεῖν τοὺς ἱππέας. 610

ΧΟ. ὦ φίλτατ' ἀνδρῶν καὶ νεανικώτατε,
ὅσην ἀπὼν παρέσχες ἡμῖν φροντίδα·
καὶ νῦν ἐπειδὴ σῶς ἐλήλυθας πάλιν,
ἄγγειλον ἡμῖν πῶς τὸ πρᾶγμ' ἠγωνίσω.
ΑΛ. τί δ' ἄλλο γ' εἰ μὴ Νικόβουλος ἐγενόμην;ᵃ 615

ΧΟ. νῦν ἄρ' ἄξιόν γε πᾶσίν ἐστιν ἐπολολύξαι.   [στρ
    ὦ καλὰ λέγων, πολὺ δ' ἀ-
    μεῖνον' ἔτι τῶν λόγων
    ἐργασάμεν', εἴθ' ἐπέλ-
    θοις ἅπαντά μοι σαφῶς·
    ὡς ἐγώ μοι δοκῶ   620
    κἂν μακρὰν ὁδὸν διελθεῖν
    ὥστ' ἀκοῦσαι. πρὸς τάδ', ὦ βέλ-
    τιστε, θαρρήσας λέγ', ὡς ἅ-
    παντες ἡδόμεσθά σοι.

ΑΛ. καὶ μὴν ἀκοῦσαί γ' ἄξιον τῶν πραγμάτων.ᵇ
    εὐθὺς γὰρ αὐτοῦ κατόπιν ἐνθένδ' ἱέμην·   625
    ὁ δ' ἄρ' ἔνδον ἐλασίβροντ' ἀναρρηγνὺς ἔπη
    τερατευόμενος ἤρειδε κατὰ τῶν ἱππέων,
    κρημνοὺς ἐρείδων καὶ ξυνωμότας λέγων
    πιθανώταθ'· ἡ βουλὴ δ' ἅπασ' ἀκροωμένη
    ἐγένεθ' ὑπ' αὐτοῦ ψευδατραφάξυος πλέα,   630

ᵃ *i.e.* "I am literally Nicobulus," which was an Athenian name.
ᵇ This passage parodies the style of a tragic messenger's speech.

THE KNIGHTS, 609-630

Hard it is, my Lord Poseidon,
             if the Knights we cannot flee
Even in the depths of Ocean, anywhere by land or sea.
             [*Enter the* SAUSAGE-SELLER

CHOR. Dearest of men, my lustiest, trustiest friend,
   Good lack! how anxious has your absence made us!
   But now that safe and sound you are come again,
   Say what has happened, and how went the fight.
S.S. How else but thus? The Council-victor I.[a]

CHOR. Now may we, joyous, raise the song of sacred praise.
   Fair the words you speak, but fairer
      Are the deeds you do.
   Far I'd go,   This I know,
      But to hear them through.
   Now then tell us all the story,
   All that, where you went, befell;
   Fearless be,   Sure that we
   All delight in all you tell.
S.S.[b] Aye and 'tis worth the hearing. When behind him
   I reached the Council-chamber, there was he
   Crashing and dashing, hurling at the Knights
   Strange wonder - working thunder - driving words,
   Calling them all, with all-persuading force,
   CONSPIRATORS! And all the Council, hearing,
   Grew full of lying orach[c] at his talk,

[c] Orach grows at a great pace; the hearers' minds are as quickly filled with Cleon's lies.

185

ARISTOPHANES

κἄβλεψε νᾶπυ, καὶ τὰ μέτωπ' ἀνέσπασεν.
κἄγωγ' ὅτε δὴ 'γνων ἐνδεχομένην τοὺς λόγους
καὶ τοῖς φενακισμοῖσιν ἐξαπατωμένην,
ἄγε δὴ Σκίταλοι καὶ Φένακες, ἦν δ' ἐγώ,
Βερέσχεθοί τε καὶ Κόβαλοι καὶ Μόθων, 635
ἀγορά τ', ἐν ᾗ παῖς ὢν ἐπαιδεύθην ἐγώ,
νῦν μοι θράσος καὶ γλῶτταν εὔπορον δότε
φωνήν τ' ἀναιδῆ. ταῦτα φροντίζοντί μοι
ἐκ δεξιᾶς ἀπέπαρδε καταπύγων ἀνήρ.
κἀγὼ προσέκυσα· κᾆτα τῷ πρωκτῷ θενὼν 640
τὴν κιγκλίδ' ἐξήραξα, κἀναχανὼν μέγα
ἀνέκραγον· ὦ βουλή, λόγους ἀγαθοὺς φέρων
εὐαγγελίσασθαι πρῶτον ὑμῖν βούλομαι·
ἐξ οὗ γὰρ ἡμῖν ὁ πόλεμος κατερράγη,
οὐπώποτ' ἀφύας εἶδον ἀξιωτέρας. 645
οἱ δ' εὐθέως τὰ πρόσωπα διεγαλήνισαν·
εἶτ' ἐστεφάνουν μ' εὐαγγέλια· κἀγὼ 'φρασα
αὐτοῖς ἀπόρρητον ποιησάμενος, ταχύ,
ἵνα τὰς ἀφύας ὠνοῖντο πολλὰς τοὐβολοῦ,
τῶν δημιουργῶν συλλαβεῖν τὰ τρύβλια. 650
οἱ δ' ἀνεκρότησαν καὶ πρὸς ἔμ' ἐκεχήνεσαν.
ὁ δ' ὑπονοήσας, ὁ Παφλαγών, εἰδώς θ' ἅμα
οἷς ἥδεθ' ἡ βουλὴ μάλιστα ῥήμασιν,
γνώμην ἔλεξεν· ἄνδρες, ἤδη μοι δοκεῖ
ἐπὶ συμφοραῖς ἀγαθαῖσιν εἰσηγγελμέναις 655
εὐαγγέλια θύειν ἑκατὸν βοῦς τῇ θεῷ.
ἐπένευσεν εἰς ἐκεῖνον ἡ βουλὴ πάλιν.
κἄγωγ' ὅτε δὴ 'γνων τοῖς βολίτοις ἡττημένος,

THE KNIGHTS, 631-658

Wore mustard looks, and puckered up their brows.
So when I saw them taking in his words,
Gulled by his knavish tricks, *Ye Gods*, said I,
Ye Gods of knavery, Skitals, and Phenaces,[a]
And ye Beresceths, Cobals, Mothon, and
Thou Agora, whence my youthful training came,
Now give me boldness and a ready tongue
And shameless voice ! And as I pondered thus,
I heard a loud explosion on my right,[b]
And made my reverence ; then I dashed apart
The railing-wicket, opened wide my mouth,
And cried aloud, *O Council, I have got*
Some lovely news which first I bring to you.
For never, never, since the War broke out,
Have I seen pilchards cheaper than to-day.
They calmed their brows and grew serene at once,
And crowned me for my news ; and I suggested,
Bidding them keep it secret, that forthwith,
To buy these pilchards, many for a penny,
'Twere best to seize the cups in all the shops.
They clapped their hands, and turned agape to me.
But Paphlagon perceived, and well aware
What kind of measures please the Council best,
Proposed a resolution ; *Sirs*, quoth he,
I move that for these happy tidings brought,
One hundred beeves be offered to Athene.
The Council instantly inclined to him.
So, overpowered with cow-dung, in a trice

[a] Goblin names ; nothing is known of Σκ. or Βερ., but Φένακες means spirits of treachery, Κόβαλοι, of vulgar impudence, Μόθωνες, of drunkenness and bestiality : *cf.* the English goblins, Flibbertigibbet, Fillpotts, Obidicut, Hobbididence.
[b] A sneeze on the right was lucky, and was greeted by a reverence.

ARISTOPHANES

διηκοσίῃσι βουσὶν ὑπερηκόντισα·
τῇ δ' Ἀγροτέρᾳ κατὰ χιλιῶν παρῄνεσα 660
εὐχὴν ποιήσασθαι χιμάρων εἰσαύριον,
αἱ τριχίδες εἰ γενοίαθ' ἑκατὸν τοὐβολοῦ.
ἐκαραδόκησεν εἰς ἔμ' ἡ βουλὴ πάλιν.
ὁ δὲ ταῦτ' ἀκούσας ἐκπλαγεὶς ἐφληνάφα.
κᾆθ' εἷλκον αὐτὸν οἱ πρυτάνεις χοἰ τοξόται. 665
οἱ δ' ἐθορύβουν περὶ τῶν ἀφύων ἑστηκότες·
ὁ δ' ἠντιβόλει γ' αὐτοὺς ὀλίγον μεῖναι χρόνον,
ἵν' ἄτθ' ὁ κῆρυξ οὐκ Λακεδαίμονος λέγει
πύθησθ'· ἀφῖκται γὰρ περὶ σπονδῶν, λέγων.
οἱ δ' ἐξ ἑνὸς στόματος ἅπαντες ἀνέκραγον· 670
νυνὶ περὶ σπονδῶν; ἐπειδή γ', ὦ μέλε,
ᾔσθοντο τὰς ἀφύας παρ' ἡμῖν ἀξίας;
οὐ δεόμεθα σπονδῶν· ὁ πόλεμος ἑρπέτω.
ἐκεκράγεσάν τε τοὺς πρυτάνεις ἀφιέναι·
εἶθ' ὑπερεπήδων τοὺς δρυφάκτους πανταχῇ. 675
ἐγὼ δὲ τὰ κορίανν' ἐπριάμην ὑποδραμὼν
ἅπαντα τά τε γήτει' ὅσ' ἦν ἐν τἀγορᾷ·
ἔπειτα ταῖς ἀφύαις ἐδίδουν ἡδύσματα
ἀπορούσιν αὐτοῖς προῖκα, κἀχαριζόμην.
οἱ δ' ὑπερεπῄνουν ὑπερεπύππαζόν τέ με 680
ἅπαντες οὕτως ὥστε τὴν βουλὴν ὅλην
ὀβολοῦ κοριάννοις ἀναλαβὼν ἐλήλυθα.

ΧΟ. πάντα τοι πέπραγας οἷα χρὴ τὸν εὐτυχοῦντα· [ἀντ
εὗρε δ' ὁ πανοῦργος ἕτε-
ρον πολὺ πανουργίαις
μείζοσι κεκασμένον, 685

---

[a] There was a temple of Athena Huntress on the Ilissus, where 500 goats were sacrificed yearly in memory of Marathon.

THE KNIGHTS, 659–685

I overshot him with *two hundred beeves*.
And *vow, said I, to slay to-morrow morn,*
If pilchards sell one hundred for an obol,
A thousand she-goats to our huntress Queen.[a]
Back came their heads, expectantly, to me.
He, dazed at this, went babbling idly on ;
So then the Prytanes and the Archers [b] seized him.
And *they* stood up, and raved about the pilchards ;
And *he* kept begging them to wait awhile
And hear the tale the Spartan envoy brings ;
He has just arrived about a peace, shrieked he.
But all the Council with one voice exclaimed,
What! now about a peace? No doubt, my man,
Now they've heard pilchards are so cheap at Athens!
We want no truces ; let the War go on!
With that, *Dismiss us, Prytanes!* shouted they ;
And overleaped the railings everywhere.
And I slipped out, and purchased all the leeks
And all the coriander in the market ;
And as they stood perplexed, I gave them all
Of my free bounty garnish for their fish.
And they so praised and purred about me, that
With just one obol's worth of coriander
I've all the Council won, and here I am.

CHOR. What rising men should do
                Has all been done by you
    He, the rascal, now has met a
        Bigger rascal still,

[b] Scythian archers were the Athenian police.

ARISTOPHANES

καὶ δόλοισι ποικίλοις,
ῥήμασίν θ' αἱμύλοις.
ἀλλ' ὅπως ἀγωνιεῖ φρόν-
τιζε τἀπίλοιπ' ἄριστα·
συμμάχους δ' ἡμᾶς ἔχων εὔνους ἐπίστασαι πάλαι. 690
ΑΛ. καὶ μὴν ὁ Παφλαγὼν οὑτοσὶ προσέρχεται,
ὠθῶν κολόκυμα καὶ ταράττων καὶ κυκῶν,
ὡς δὴ καταπιόμενός με. μορμὼ τοῦ θράσους.
ΠΑ. εἰ μή σ' ἀπολέσαιμ', εἴ τι τῶν αὐτῶν ἐμοὶ
ψευδῶν ἐνείη, διαπέσοιμι πανταχῇ. 695
ΑΛ. ἥσθην ἀπειλαῖς, ἐγέλασα ψολοκομπίαις,
ἀπεπυδάρισα μόθωνα, περιεκόκκυσα.
ΠΑ. οὔ τοι μὰ τὴν Δήμητρ', ἐὰν μή σ' ἐκφάγω
ἐκ τῆσδε τῆς γῆς, οὐδέποτε βιώσομαι.
ΑΛ. ἢν μὴ 'κφάγῃς; ἐγὼ δέ γ', ἢν μή σ' ἐκπίω, 700
κᾆτ' ἐκροφήσας αὐτὸς ἐπιδιαρραγῶ.
ΠΑ. ἀπολῶ σε νὴ τὴν προεδρίαν τὴν ἐκ Πύλου.
ΑΛ. ἰδοὺ προεδρίαν· οἷον ὄψομαί σ' ἐγὼ
ἐκ τῆς προεδρίας ἔσχατον θεώμενον.
ΠΑ. ἐν τῷ ξύλῳ δήσω σε νὴ τὸν οὐρανόν. 705
ΑΛ. ὡς ὀξύθυμος. φέρε τί σοι δῶ καταφαγεῖν;
ἐπὶ τῷ φάγοις ἥδιστ' ἄν; ἐπὶ βαλλαντίῳ;
ΠΑ. ἐξαρπάσομαί σου τοῖς ὄνυξι τἄντερα.
ΑΛ. ἀπονυχιῶ σου τὰν Πρυτανείῳ σιτία.
ΠΑ. ἕλξω σε πρὸς τὸν δῆμον, ἵνα δῷς μοι δίκην. 710
ΑΛ. κἀγὼ δέ σ' ἕλξω καὶ διαβαλῶ πλείονα.
ΠΑ. ἀλλ', ὦ πόνηρε, σοὶ μὲν οὐδὲν πείθεται·

[a] *i.e.* "to swallow me up," a sense which καταπίνω commonly bears.
[b] προεδρία, a front seat in the theatre, was often awarded as an honour for public service.

THE KNIGHTS, 686-712

   Full of guile Plot and wile,
      Full of knavish skill.
   Mind you carry through the conflict
   In the same undaunted guise.
   Well you know Long ago
   We're your faithful true allies.

S.S. See here comes Paphlagon, driving on before him
   A long ground-swell, all fuss and fury, thinking
   To drink me up.[a] Boh! for your impudent bluster.

PAPH. O if I've any of my old lies left,
   And don't destroy you, may I fall to bits!

S.S. I like your threats; I'm wonderfully tickled
   To hear you fume; I skip and cuckoo around you.

PAPH. O by Demeter, if I eat you not
   Out of the land, I'll never live at all.

S.S. You won't? Nor I, unless I drink you up,
   And swill you up, and burst myself withal.

PAPH. I'll crush you, by my Pylus-won precedence.[b]

S.S. Precedence, is it? I'm in hopes to see you
   In the last tier, instead of here in front.

PAPH. By Heaven, I'll clap you in the public stocks.

S.S. How fierce it's growing! what would it like to eat?
   What is its favourite dainty? Money-bags?[c]

PAPH. I'll tear your guts out with my nails, I will.

S.S. I'll scratch your Town Hall dinners out, I will.

PAPH. I'll hale you off to Demus; then you'll catch it.

S.S. Nay, I'll hale *you*, and then out-slander you.

PAPH. Alack, poor chap, he pays no heed to you,

---

[c] The Attic idiom is ἐσθίειν ὄψον ἐπὶ σίτῳ, etc., the last being the main fare.

191

ARISTOPHANES

ἐγὼ δ' ἐκείνου καταγελῶ γ' ὅσον θέλω.
ΑΛ. ὡς σφόδρα σὺ τὸν δῆμον σεαυτοῦ νενόμικας.
ΠΑ. ἐπίσταμαι γὰρ αὐτὸν οἷς ψωμίζεται. 715
ΑΛ. κᾆθ' ὥσπερ αἱ τίτθαι γε σιτίζεις κακῶς.
μασώμενος γὰρ τῷ μὲν ὀλίγον ἐντίθεις,
αὐτὸς δ' ἐκείνου τριπλάσιον κατέσπακας.
ΠΑ. καὶ νὴ Δί' ὑπό γε δεξιότητος τῆς ἐμῆς
δύναμαι ποιεῖν τὸν δῆμον εὐρὺν καὶ στενόν. 720
ΑΛ. χὠ πρωκτὸς οὑμὸς τουτογὶ σοφίζεται.
ΠΑ. οὐκ, ὦγάθ', ἐν βουλῇ με δόξεις καθυβρίσαι.
ἴωμεν εἰς τὸν δῆμον.
ΑΛ. οὐδὲν κωλύει·
ἰδού, βάδιζε, μηδὲν ἡμᾶς ἰσχέτω.
ΠΑ. ὦ Δῆμε, δεῦρ' ἔξελθε.
ΑΛ. νὴ Δί', ὦ πάτερ, 725
ἔξελθε δῆτ'·
ΠΑ. ὦ Δημίδιον, ὦ φίλτατον,
ἔξελθ', ἵν' εἰδῇς οἷα περιυβρίζομαι.
ΔΗΜΟΣ. τίνες οἱ βοῶντες; οὐκ ἄπιτ' ἀπὸ τῆς
θύρας;
τὴν εἰρεσιώνην μου κατεσπαράξατε.
τίς, ὦ Παφλαγών, ἀδικεῖ σε;
ΠΑ. διὰ σὲ τύπτομαι 730
ὑπὸ τουτουὶ καὶ τῶν νεανίσκων.
ΔΗΜΟΣ. τιή;
ΠΑ. ὁτιὴ φιλῶ σ', ὦ Δῆμ', ἐραστής τ' εἰμὶ σός
ΔΗΜΟΣ. σὺ δ' εἶ τίς ἐτεόν;
ΑΛ. ἀντεραστὴς τουτουί,
ἐρῶν πάλαι σου, βουλόμενός τέ σ' εὖ ποιεῖν,

---

[a] As nurses do for their children.
[b] An olive-branch decked out with wool and various

192

THE KNIGHTS, 713-734

   But I can fool him to my heart's content.
S.S. How sure you seem that Demus is your own!
PAPH. Because I know the titbits he prefers.
S.S. And feed him badly as the nurses do.
   You chew, and pop a morsel in his mouth,[a]
   But thrice as much you swallow down yourself.
PAPH. And I'm so dexterous-handed, I can make
   Demus expand, and then contract again.
S.S. I can do that with many things, I trow.
PAPH. 'Twon't be like bearding me in the Council
   now!
   No, come along to Demus.
S.S. Aye, why not?
   I'm ready; march; let nothing stop us now.
PAPH. O Demus, come out here.
S.S. O yes, by Zeus,
   Come out, my father.
PAPH. Dearest darling Demus,
   Come out, and hear how they're ill-treating
   me!
DEMUS. What's all this shouting? go away, you
   fellows.
   You've smashed my harvest-garland[b] all to
   bits!
   Who wrongs you, Paphlagon?
PAPH. He, and these young men,
   Keep beating me because of you.
DEMUS. Why so?
PAPH. Because I love you and adore you, Demus.
DEMUS. (*To S.S.*) And who are you?
S S. A rival for your love.
   Long have I loved, and sought to do you good,

harvest fruits, carried in the harvest procession and then
hung over the house door; *W*. 399.

ARISTOPHANES

ἄλλοι τε πολλοὶ καὶ καλοί τε κἀγαθοί.
ἀλλ' οὐχ οἷοί τ' ἐσμὲν διὰ τουτονί. σὺ γὰρ
ὅμοιος εἶ τοῖς παισὶ τοῖς ἐρωμένοις·
τοὺς μὲν καλούς τε κἀγαθοὺς οὐ προσδέχει,
σαυτὸν δὲ λυχνοπώλαισι καὶ νευρορράφοις
καὶ σκυτοτόμοις καὶ βυρσοπώλαισιν δίδως.

ΠΑ. εὖ γὰρ ποιῶ τὸν δῆμον.
ΑΛ. εἰπέ νυν, τί δρῶν;
ΠΑ. ὅ τι; τὸν στρατηγὸν ὑποδραμών, τοὺς ἐκ Πύλου,
πλεύσας ἐκεῖσε, τοὺς Λάκωνας ἤγαγον.
ΑΛ. ἐγὼ δὲ περιπατῶν γ' ἀπ' ἐργαστηρίου
ἕψοντος ἑτέρου τὴν χύτραν ὑφειλόμην.
ΓΑ. καὶ μὴν ποιήσας αὐτίκα μάλ' ἐκκλησίαν,
ὦ Δῆμ', ἵν' εἰδῇς ὁπότερος νῷν ἐστί σοι
εὐνούστερος, διάκρινον, ἵνα τοῦτον φιλῇς.
ΑΛ. ναὶ ναὶ διάκρινον δῆτα, πλὴν μὴ 'ν τῇ πυκνί.
ΔΗΜΟΣ. οὐκ ἂν καθιζοίμην ἐν ἄλλῳ χωρίῳ·
ἀλλ' εἰς τὸ πρόσθε χρὴ παριέν' ἐς τὴν πύκνα.
ΑΛ. οἴμοι κακοδαίμων, ὡς ἀπόλωλ'. ὁ γὰρ γέρων
οἴκοι μὲν ἀνδρῶν ἐστι δεξιώτατος,
ὅταν δ' ἐπὶ ταυτησὶ καθῆται τῆς πέτρας,
κέχηνεν ὥσπερ ἐμποδίζων ἰσχάδας.

[ο
ΧΟ. νῦν δή σε πάντα δεῖ κάλων ἐξιέναι σεαυτοῦ,
καὶ λῆμα θούριον φορεῖν καὶ λόγους ἀφύκτους,
ὅτοισι τόνδ' ὑπερβαλεῖ. ποικίλος γὰρ ἀνὴρ

---

^a An allusion to Hyperbolus: 1315, C. 1065.
^b πάριτ' ἐς τὸ πρόσθε was the formula of the Crier to summon citizens within the space purified for the sitting.
^c The meaning is differently explained, but remains uncertain: stringing figs, playing at bob-fig, or treading figs into cases.
^d Demus now takes his seat as the audience in the mimic Pnyx, and the orators take their places.

THE KNIGHTS, 735-758

        With many another honest gentleman,
        But Paphlagon won't let us. You yourself,
        Excuse me sir, are like the boys with lovers.
        The honest gentlemen you won't accept,
        Yet give yourself to lantern-selling chaps,[a]
        To sinew-stitchers, cobblers, aye and tanners.
PAPH. Because I am good to Demus.
S.S.   Tell me how.
PAPH. 'Twas I slipped in before the general there
        And sailed to Pylus, and brought back the
            Spartans.
S.S. And I walked round, and from the workshop
            stole
        A mess of pottage, cooked by someone else.
PAPH. Come, make a full Assembly out of hand,
        O Demus, do ; then find which loves you best,
        And so decide, and give that man your love.
S.S. O Demus, do. Not in the Pnyx however.
DEMUS. Aye, in the Pnyx, not elsewhere will I sit.
        So forward all, move forward to the Pnyx.[b]
S.S. O luckless me, I'm ruined ! The old fellow
        Is, when at home, the brightest man alive ;
        But once he sits upon his rock, he moons
        With open mouth, as one who gapes for figs.[c]

CHOR.[d] Now loosen every hawser,[e]
                      now speed your bark along,
        And mind your soul is eager,
                      and mind your words are strong,
        No subterfuge admitting ;
                      the man has many a trick

   [e] More accurately, loosen the ropes that hold up or reef the sail ; a long rope is still used to loop up the corner of the sail in the Levant.

ARISTOPHANES

κἀκ τῶν ἀμηχάνων πόρους εὐμήχανος πορίζειν.
πρὸς ταῦθ' ὅπως ἕξει πολὺς καὶ λαμπρὸς ἐς τὸν
ἄνδρα.
ἀλλὰ φυλάττου, καὶ πρὶν ἐκεῖνον προσκεῖσθαί σοι,
πρότερον σὺ
τοὺς δελφῖνας μετεωρίζου καὶ τὴν ἄκατον παρα-
βάλλου.

ΠΑ. τῇ μὲν δεσποίνῃ 'Αθηναίῃ, τῇ τῆς πόλεως μεδεούσῃ,
εὔχομαι, εἰ μὲν περὶ τὸν δῆμον τὸν 'Αθηναίων
γεγένημαι
βέλτιστος ἀνὴρ μετὰ Λυσικλέα καὶ Κύνναν καὶ
Σαλαβακχώ,
ὥσπερ νυνὶ μηδὲν δράσας δειπνεῖν ἐν τῷ Πρυτανείῳ·
εἰ δέ σε μισῶ καὶ μὴ περὶ σοῦ μάχομαι μόνος
ἀντιβεβηκώς,
ἀπολοίμην καὶ διαπρισθείην κατατμηθείην τε
λέπαδνα.

ΑΛ. κἄγωγ', ὦ Δῆμ', εἰ μή σε φιλῶ καὶ μὴ στέργω,
κατατμηθεὶς
ἑψοίμην ἐν περικομματίοις· κεἰ μὴ τούτοισι
πέποιθας,
ἐπὶ ταυτησὶ κατακνησθείην ἐν μυττωτῷ μετὰ τυροῦ,
καὶ τῇ κρεάγρᾳ τῶν ὀρχιπέδων ἑλκοίμην ἐς
Κεραμεικόν.

ΠΑ. καὶ πῶς ἂν ἐμοῦ μᾶλλόν σε φιλῶν, ὦ Δῆμε, γένοιτο
πολίτης;
ὃς πρῶτα μέν, ἡνίκ' ἐβούλευόν σοι, χρήματα πλεῖστ
ἀπέδειξα

---

[a] Masses of lead or iron in the shape of fish, hung from the yards and dropped upon the enemy ship : Thuc. vii. 41. 2.
[b] See note on 132. Instead of "the best since Pericles and Themistocles," he names a demagogue and two courtesans.

THE KNIGHTS, 759-774

      From hopeless things, in hopeless times,
                a hopeful course to pick.
      Upon him with a whirlwind's force,
                impetuous, fresh and quick.
      But keep on his movements a watch; and be sure
                that before he can deal you a blow,
      You hoist to the mast your dolphins,[a] and cast
                your vessel alongside the foe.

PAPH. To the Lady who over the city presides,
                to our mistress Athene, I pray
      If beyond all the rest I am stoutest and best,
                in the service of Demus to-day,
      Except Salabaccho, and Cynna the bold,
                and Lysicles [b]—then in the Hall
      May I dine as of late at the cost of the State
                for doing just nothing at all.
      But O if I hate you, nor stride to the van
                to protect you from woes and mishaps,
      Then slay me, and flay me, and saw me to bits,
                to be cut into martingale straps.[c]

S.S. And I, if I love you not, Demus, am game
             to be slaughtered by chopping and mincing,
      And boiled in a sausage-meat pie; and if THAT
                is, you think, not entirely convincing,
      Let me here, if you please, with a morsel of cheese,
                upon this to a salad be grated,
      Or to far Cerameicus be dragged through the streets
                with my flesh-hook, and there be cremated.

PAPH. O Demus, how can there be ever a man
                who loves you as dearly as I?
      When on *me* you relied your finances to guide,
                your Treasury never was dry,

    [c] The breast-bands fastening the yoke.

ARISTOPHANES

ἐν τῷ κοινῷ, τοὺς μὲν στρεβλῶν, τοὺς δ' ἄγχων,
τοὺς δὲ μεταιτῶν,
οὐ φροντίζων τῶν ἰδιωτῶν οὐδενός, εἰ σοὶ χαριοίμην.

ΑΛ. τοῦτο μέν, ὦ Δῆμ', οὐδὲν σεμνόν· κἀγὼ γὰρ τοῦτό
σε δράσω.
ἁρπάζων γὰρ τοὺς ἄρτους σοι τοὺς ἀλλοτρίους
παραθήσω.
ὡς δ' οὐχὶ φιλεῖ σ' οὐδ' ἔστ' εὔνους, τοῦτ' αὐτό σε
πρῶτα διδάξω,
ἀλλ' ἢ διὰ τοῦτ' αὔθ' ὁτιή σου τῆς ἀνθρακιᾶς
ἀπολαύει.
σὲ γάρ, ὃς Μήδοισι διεξιφίσω περὶ τῆς χώρας
Μαραθῶνι,
καὶ νικήσας ἡμῖν μεγάλως ἐγγλωττοτυπεῖν παρ-
έδωκας,
ἐπὶ ταῖσι πέτραις οὐ φροντίζει σκληρῶς σε καθήμενον οὕτως,
οὐχ ὥσπερ ἐγὼ ῥαψάμενός σοι τουτὶ φέρω. ἀλλ'
ἐπαναίρου,
κᾆτα καθίζου μαλακῶς, ἵνα μὴ τρίβῃς τὴν ἐν
Σαλαμῖνι.

ΔΗΜΟΣ. ἄνθρωπε, τίς εἶ; μῶν ἔγγονος εἶ τῶν Ἁρμοδίου τις ἐκείνων;
τοῦτό γέ τοί σου τοὔργον ἀληθῶς γενναῖον καὶ
φιλόδημον.

ΠΑ. ὡς ἀπὸ μικρῶν εὔνους αὐτῷ θωπευματίων γεγένησαι.

ΑΛ. καὶ σὺ γὰρ αὐτὸν πολὺ μικροτέροις τούτων δελεά-
σμασιν εἷλες.

---

[a] Literally, " to mint phrases about."   [b] The Pnyx.
[c] This passage satirizes the doles and indulgences by which
Cleon courted favour.

THE KNIGHTS, 775-789

I was begging of these, whilst those I would squeeze
    and rack to extort what was due,
And nought did I care how a townsman might fare,
    so long as I satisfied you.
s.s. Why, Demus, there's nothing to boast of in that ;
    to do it I'm perfectly able.
I've only to steal from my comrade a meal,
    and serve it up hot on your table.
And as for his loving and wishing you well,
    it isn't for you that he cares,
Excepting indeed for the gain that he gets,
    and the snug little fire that he shares.
Why you, who at Marathon fought with the Medes,
    for Athens and Hellas contending,
And won the great battle, and left us a theme
    for our songs and our speeches unending,[a]
He cares not a bit that so roughly you sit
    on the rocks,[b] nor has dreamed of providing
Those seats with the thing I have stitched you and bring.
    Just lift yourself up and subside in
This ease-giving cushion for fear you should gall
    what at Salamis sat by the oar.[c]
DEMUS. Who are you ? I opine you are sprung from the line
    of Harmodius [d] famous of yore ;
So noble and Demus-relieving [e] an act
    I never have witnessed before !
PAPH. O me, by what paltry attentions and gifts
    you contrive to attract and delude him !
s.s. 'Twas by baits that are smaller and poorer than mine,
    you rascal, you hooked and subdued him.

[d] Harmodius and Aristogeiton, the traditional founders of Athenian freedom.
[e] εὔνους τῷ δήμῳ is the regular phrase for a loyal citizen, used in honorific inscriptions.

ΠΑ. καὶ μὴν εἴ πού τις ἀνὴρ ἐφάνη τῷ δήμῳ μᾶλλον
ἀμύνων 79
ἢ μᾶλλον ἐμοῦ σε φιλῶν, ἐθέλω περὶ τῆς κεφαλῆς
περιδόσθαι.
ΑΛ. καὶ πῶς σὺ φιλεῖς, ὃς τοῦτον ὁρῶν οἰκοῦντ' ἐν ταῖς
πιθάκναισι
καὶ γυπαρίοις καὶ πυργιδίοις ἔτος ὄγδοον οὐκ
ἐλεαίρεις,
ἀλλὰ καθείρξας αὐτὸν βλίττεις· Ἀρχεπτολέμου δὲ
φέροντος
τὴν εἰρήνην ἐξεσκέδασας, τὰς πρεσβείας τ' ἀπ-
ελαύνεις 79
ἐκ τῆς πόλεως ῥαθαπυγίζων, αἳ τὰς σπονδὰς προ-
καλοῦνται.
ΠΑ. ἵνα γ' Ἑλλήνων ἄρξῃ πάντων. ἔστι γὰρ ἐν τοῖς
λογίοισιν
ὡς τοῦτον δεῖ ποτ' ἐν Ἀρκαδίᾳ πεντωβόλου
ἡλιάσασθαι,
ἢν ἀναμείνῃ· πάντως δ' αὐτὸν θρέψω 'γὼ καὶ
θεραπεύσω,
ἐξευρίσκων εὖ καὶ μιαρῶς ὁπόθεν τὸ τριώβολον ἕξει. 80
ΑΛ. οὐχ ἵνα γ' ἄρχῃ μὰ Δί' Ἀρκαδίας προνοούμενος,
ἀλλ' ἵνα μᾶλλον
σὺ μὲν ἁρπάζῃς καὶ δωροδοκῇς παρὰ τῶν πόλεων·
ὁ δὲ δῆμος

---

[a] The war began in 431 B.C., according to our historians; but the Athenian ideas as to the date were vague. See A. 266, 890, P. 990.
[b] An allusion to the crowding of refugees into Athens in the Peloponnesian War; Thuc. ii. 52.
[c] See 327: Spartan proposals for peace were rejected, when the Spartan troops were first shut up in Sphacteria, Thuc. iv. 21-22. We know nothing of A. in this debate, but his name makes a pun, "Delawarr offers peace."

THE KNIGHTS, 790-802

PAPH. Was there ever a man since the City began
        who for Demus has done such a lot,
Or fought for his welfare so stoutly as I ?
        I will wager my head there is not.
s.s. You love him right well who permit him to dwell
        eight [a] years in the clefts of the City,
In the nests of the vulture, in turrets and casks,[b]
        nor ever assist him or pity,
But keep him in durance to rifle his hive ;
        and that is the reason, no doubt,
Why the peace which, unsought, Archeptolemus[c] brought,
        you were quick from the city to scout
And as for the embassies coming to treat,
        you spanked them and chivied them out.
PAPH. That over all Hellas our Demus may rule ;
        for do not the oracles say,
He will surely his verdicts in Arcady give,
        receiving five obols a day,[d]
If he grow not aweary of fighting ? Meanwhile,
        it is I who will nourish and pet him,
And always the daily triobol he earns,
        unjustly or justly I'll get him.
s.s. No not that o'er Arcady Demus may rule,
        but rather that *you* might essay
To harry and plunder the cities at will,
        while Demus is looking away,

---

[d] Five obols was a common daily wage for labour. Cleon's glorious aim is to add two obols to the three obols of the dicasts' pay, and so make work unnecessary.

ARISTOPHANES

ὑπὸ τοῦ πολέμου καὶ τῆς ὁμίχλης ἃ πανουργεῖς μὴ
  καθορᾷ σου,
ἀλλ' ὑπ' ἀνάγκης ἅμα καὶ χρείας καὶ μισθοῦ πρός
  σε κεχήνῃ.
εἰ δέ ποτ' εἰς ἀγρὸν οὗτος ἀπελθὼν εἰρηναῖος
  διατρίψῃ, 80
καὶ χῖδρα φαγὼν ἀναθαρρήσῃ καὶ στεμφύλῳ εἰς
  λόγον ἔλθῃ,
γνώσεται οἵων ἀγαθῶν αὐτὸν τῇ μισθοφορᾷ
  παρεκόπτου,
εἶθ' ἥξει σοι δριμὺς ἄγροικος, κατὰ σοῦ τὴν ψῆφον
  ἰχνεύων.
ἃ σὺ γιγνώσκων τόνδ' ἐξαπατᾷς, καὶ ὀνειροπολεῖς
  περὶ σαυτοῦ.

ΠΑ. οὔκουν δεινὸν ταυτί σε λέγειν δῆτ' ἔστ' ἐμὲ καὶ
  διαβάλλειν 8]
πρὸς Ἀθηναίους καὶ τὸν δῆμον, πεποιηκότα πλείονα
  χρηστὰ
νὴ τὴν Δήμητρα Θεμιστοκλέους πολλῷ περὶ τὴν
  πόλιν ἤδη;

ΑΛ. ὦ πόλις Ἄργους, κλύεθ' οἷα λέγει. σὺ Θεμιστοκλεῖ ἀντιφερίζεις;
ὃς ἐποίησεν τὴν πόλιν ἡμῶν μεστήν, εὑρὼν ἐπιχειλῆ,
καὶ πρὸς τούτοις ἀριστώσῃ τὸν Πειραιᾶ προσέμαξεν, 8]

---

[a] This is just what Thucydides says, v. 16.
[b] The Greek means "countryman," but R. thinks ἀγρευτὴς should be read.
[c] Themistocles caused the Peiraeus to be founded, the walls of harbour and city to be built, and the fleet to be made great. No doubt the Long Walls were part of the plan; and T. is given credit for them in 815.
[d] This phrase is from Euripides' *Telephus*, and κλύεθ' οἷα λέγει from *Medea* 168.

THE KNIGHTS, 803-815

And the war with the haze and the dust that you raise
    is obscuring your actions from view,[a]
And Demus, constrained by his wants and his pay,
    is a gaping dependent on you.
But if once to the country in peace he returns,
    away from all fighting and fusses,
And strengthens his system with furmety there,
    and a confect of olive discusses,
He will know to your cost what a deal he has lost,
    while the pay you allowed him he drew,
And then, like a hunter,[b] irate he will come
    on the trail of a vote against you.
You KNOW it; and Demus you swindle with dreams,
    crammed full of yourself and your praises.

PAPH. It is really distressing to hear you presume
    to arraign with such scurrilous phrases
Before the Athenians and Demus a man
    who more for the city has done
Than e'er by Demeter Themistocles[c] did
    who glory undying has won.

S.S. O city of Argos ![d] yourself would you match
    with mighty Themistocles, him
Who made of our city a bumper indeed,
    though he found her scarce filled to the brim,[e]
Who, while she was lunching, Peiraeus threw in,
    as a dainty additional dish,[f]

---

[e] χεῖλος, the rim of a vessel, was of some depth; ἐπιχειλής, marks that the liquid touched the lower edges of the rim, ὑπερχειλής, that the cup is quite full (not running over).
[f] "Kneaded it into one with the city": a reference to the Long Walls. Scholiast.

ARISTOPHANES

ἀφελών τ' οὐδὲν τῶν ἀρχαίων ἰχθῦς καινοὺς παρέθηκε.
σὺ δ' Ἀθηναίους ἐζήτησας μικροπολίτας ἀποφῆναι διατειχίζων καὶ χρησμῳδῶν, ὁ Θεμιστοκλεῖ ἀντιφερίζων.
κἀκεῖνος μὲν φεύγει τὴν γῆν, σὺ δ' Ἀχιλλείων ἀπομάττει.

ΠΑ. οὔκουν ταυτὶ δεινὸν ἀκούειν, ὦ Δῆμ', ἐστίν μ' ὑπὸ τούτου, ὁτιή σε φιλῶ;

ΔΗΜΟΣ. παῦ παῦ', οὗτος, καὶ μὴ σκέρβολλε πονηρά.
πολλοῦ δὲ πολύν με χρόνον καὶ νῦν ἐλελήθεις ἐγκρυφιάζων.

ΑΛ. μιαρώτατος, ὦ Δημακίδιον, καὶ πλεῖστα πανοῦργα δεδρακώς,
ὁπόταν χασμᾷ, καὶ τοὺς καυλοὺς τῶν εὐθυνῶν ἐκκαυλίζων
καταβροχθίζει, κἀμφοῖν χειροῖν μυστιλᾶται τῶν δημοσίων.

ΠΑ. οὐ χαιρήσεις, ἀλλά σε κλέπτονθ' αἱρήσω 'γὼ τρεῖς μυριάδας.

ΑΛ. τί θαλαττοκοπεῖς καὶ πλατυγίζεις, μιαρώτατος ὢν περὶ τὸν δῆμον τὸν Ἀθηναίων; καί σ' ἐπιδείξω νὴ τὴν Δήμητρ', ἢ μὴ ζῴην,

---

[a] Some unknown building project of Cleon's. See *W.* 41.

THE KNIGHTS, 816-833

Who secured her the old, while providing untold
         and novel assortments of fish;
Whilst you, with your walls of partition forsooth,[a]
         and the oracle-chants which you hatch,
Would dwarf and belittle the city again,
         who yourself with Themistocles match!
And *he* was an exile, but *you* upon crumbs
         Achilléan[b] your fingers are cleaning.

PAPH. Now is it not monstrous that I must endure
         accusations so coarse and unmeaning,
And all for the love that I bear you?

DEMUS.   Forbear! no more of your wrangle and row!
Too long have your light-fingered tricks with my bread[c]
         my notice escaped until now.

S.S. He's the vilest of miscreants, Demus, and works
         more mischief than any, I vow.
While you're gaping about, he is picking from out
    Of the juiciest audit the juiciest sprout,
And devours it with zest; while deep in the chest
    Of the public exchequer both hands are addressed
To ladling out cash for himself, I protest.

PAPH. All this you'll deplore when it comes to the fore
That of drachmas you stole thirty thousand or more.

S.S. Why make such a dash with your oar-blades, and
      thrash
The waves into foam with your impotent splash?
'Tis but fury and sound; and you'll shortly be
      found
The worst of the toadies who Demus surround.
And proof I will give, or I ask not to live,

---

[b] Bread made from the finest barley; "the peerless Achilles" of barley, such as was served at the Prytaneium.

[c] ἄρτος ἐγκρυφίας was bread baked in the ashes, perhaps of an inferior kind.

ARISTOPHANES

δωροδοκήσαντ' ἐκ Μιτυλήνης
πλεῖν ἢ μνᾶς τετταράκοντα. 83

ΧΟ. ὦ πᾶσιν ἀνθρώποις φανεὶς μέγιστον ὠφέλημα, [ἂν
ζηλῶ σε τῆς εὐγλωττίας. εἰ γὰρ ὧδ' ἐποίσεις,
μέγιστος Ἑλλήνων ἔσει, καὶ μόνος καθέξεις
τὰν τῇ πόλει, τῶν ξυμμάχων τ' ἄρξεις ἔχων τρίαιναν,
ᾗ πολλὰ χρήματ' ἐργάσει σείων τε καὶ ταράττων. 8
καὶ μὴ μεθῇς τὸν ἄνδρ', ἐπειδή σοι λαβὴν δέδωκεν·
κατεργάσει γὰρ ῥᾳδίως, πλευρὰς ἔχων τοιαύτας.

ΠΑ. οὐκ, ὦγαθοί, ταῦτ' ἐστί πω ταύτῃ μὰ τὸν Ποσειδῶ.
ἐμοὶ γάρ ἐστ' εἰργασμένον τοιοῦτον ἔργον ὥστε
ἀπαξάπαντας τοὺς ἐμοὺς ἐχθροὺς ἐπιστομίζειν, 8
ἕως ἂν ᾖ τῶν ἀσπίδων τῶν ἐκ Πύλου τι λοιπόν.

ΑΛ. ἐπίσχες ἐν ταῖς ἀσπίσιν· λαβὴν γὰρ ἐνδέδωκας.
οὐ γάρ σ' ἐχρῆν, εἴπερ φιλεῖς τὸν δῆμον, ἐκ προνοίας
ταύτας ἐᾶν αὐτοῖσι τοῖς πόρπαξιν ἀνατεθῆναι.
ἀλλ' ἐστὶ τοῦτ', ὦ Δῆμε, μηχάνημ', ἵν', ἢν σὺ βούλῃ 8
τὸν ἄνδρα κολάσαι τουτονί, σοὶ τοῦτο μὴ 'γγένηται.

---

[a] Allusion unknown. After the M. revolt of 428, Cleon carried a motion to kill all the male population, afterwards partly rescinded : Thuc. iii. 50.
[b] A metaphor from wrestling.
[c] The shields of the Spartan prisoners from Sphacteria were hung up in the Painted Colonnade.

THE KNIGHTS, 834-851

CHOR.
That a bribe by the Mitylenaeans was sent,[a]
Forty minas and more ; to your pockets it went.
O sent to all the nation
                       a blessing and a boon !
O wondrous flow of language !
                       Fight thus, and you'll be soon
The greatest man in Hellas,
                       and all the State command,
And rule our faithful true allies,
                       a trident in your hand,
Wherewith you'll gather stores of wealth,
                       by shaking all the land.
And if he lend you once a hold,
                       then never let him go ;
With ribs like these you ought with ease
                       to subjugate the foe.

PAPH.
O matters have not come to that,
                       my very worthy friends !
I've done a deed, a noble deed,
                       a deed which so transcends
All other deeds, that all my foes
                       of speech are quite bereft,
While any shred of any shield,
                       from Pylus brought, is left.

S.S.
Halt at those Pylian shields of yours !
                       a lovely hold you're lending.[b]
For if you really Demus love,
                       what meant you by suspending
Those shields with all their handles on,
                       for action ready strapped ?[c]
O Demus, there's a dark design
                       within those handles wrapped,
And if to punish him you seek,
                       those shields will bar the way.

ARISTOPHANES

ὁρᾷς γὰρ αὐτῷ στῖφος οἷόν ἐστι βυρσοπωλῶν
νεανιῶν· τούτους δὲ περιοικοῦσι μελιτοπῶλαι
καὶ τυροπῶλαι· τοῦτο δ' εἰς ἕν ἐστι συγκεκυφός.
ὥστ' εἰ σὺ βριμήσαιο καὶ βλέψειας ὀστρακίνδα, 8
νύκτωρ κατασπάσαντες ἂν τὰς ἀσπίδας θέοντες
τὰς εἰσβολὰς τῶν ἀλφίτων ἂν καταλάβοιεν ἡμῶν.

ΔΗΜΟΣ. οἴμοι τάλας· ἔχουσι γὰρ πόρπακας; ὦ πόνηρε,
ὅσον με παρεκόπτου χρόνον τοιαῦτα κρουσιδημῶν.

ΠΑ. ὦ δαιμόνιε, μὴ τοῦ λέγοντος ἴσθι, μηδ' οἰηθῇς 8
ἐμοῦ ποθ' εὑρήσειν φίλον βελτίον'· ὅστις εἷς ὢν
ἔπαυσα τοὺς ξυνωμότας, καί μ' οὐ λέληθεν οὐδὲν
ἐν τῇ πόλει ξυνιστάμενον, ἀλλ' εὐθέως κέκραγα.

ΑΛ. ὅπερ γὰρ οἱ τὰς ἐγχέλεις θηρώμενοι πέπονθας.
ὅταν μὲν ἡ λίμνη καταστῇ, λαμβάνουσιν οὐδέν· 8
ἐὰν δ' ἄνω τε καὶ κάτω τὸν βόρβορον κυκῶσιν,
αἱροῦσι· καὶ σὺ λαμβάνεις, ἢν τὴν πόλιν ταράττῃς.
ἓν δ' εἰπέ μοι τοσουτονί· σκύτη τοσαῦτα πωλῶν,

---

[a] An allusion to the practice of "ostracizing" or banishing a too powerful citizen, in which the voting was carried out by inscribing the name on a potsherd. Aristophanes, however, by way of jest calls it ὀστρακίνδα, a game.

[b] εἰσβολαί would naturally refer to such "passes" as those between Boeotia and Attica. Here, however, "no very definite locality is indicated, but the general meaning would point to the gates through which the imported barley would enter Athens from the Peiraeus": R.

THE KNIGHTS, 852-868

You see the throng of tanner-lads
     he always keeps in pay,
And round them dwell the folk who sell
     their honey and their cheeses;
And these are all combined in one,
     to do whate'er he pleases.
And if the oyster-shelling game
     you seem inclined to play,[a]
They'll come by night with all their might
     and snatch those shields away,
And then with ease will run and seize
     the passes of—your wheat.[b]
DEMUS. Oh, are the handles really there?
     You rascal, what deceit
Have you so long been practising
     that Demus you may cheat?
PAPH. Pray don't be every speaker's gull,
     nor dream you'll ever get
A better friend than I, who all
     conspiracies upset.
Alone I crushed them all, and now,
     if any plots are brewing
Within the town, I scent them down,
     and raise a grand hallooing.
S.S. O ay, you're like the fisher-folk,
     the men who hunt for eels,
Who when the mere is still and clear
     catch nothing for their creels;
But when they rout the mud about
     and stir it up and down,
'Tis then they do; and so do you,
     when you perturb the town.
But answer me this single thing:
     you sell a lot of leather,

ARISTOPHANES

ἔδωκας ἤδη τουτῳὶ κάττυμα παρὰ σεαυτοῦ
ταῖς ἐμβάσιν, φάσκων φιλεῖν;
ΔΗΜΟΣ. οὐ δῆτα μὰ τὸν Ἀπόλλω.
ΑΛ. ἔγνωκας οὖν δῆτ' αὐτὸν οἷός ἐστιν; ἀλλ' ἐγώ σοι
ζεῦγος πριάμενος ἐμβάδων τουτὶ φορεῖν δίδωμι.
ΔΗΜΟΣ. κρίνω σ' ὅσων ἐγῷδα περὶ τὸν δῆμον ἄνδρ' ἄριστον
εὐνούστατόν τε τῇ πόλει καὶ τοῖσι δακτύλοισιν.
ΠΑ. οὐ δεινὸν οὖν δῆτ' ἐμβάδας τοσουτονὶ δύνασθαι,
ἐμοῦ δὲ μὴ μνείαν ἔχειν ὅσων πέπονθας; ὅστις
ἔπαυσα τοὺς βινουμένους, τὸν Γρύττον ἐξαλείψας.
ΑΛ. οὔκουν σε δῆτα ταῦτα δεινόν ἐστι πρωκτοτηρεῖν,
παῦσαί τε τοὺς βινουμένους; κοὐκ ἔσθ' ὅπως ἐκείνους
οὐχὶ φθονῶν ἔπαυσας, ἵνα μὴ ῥήτορες γένοιντο.
τονδὶ δ' ὁρῶν ἄνευ χιτῶνος ὄντα τηλικοῦτον,
οὐπώποτ' ἀμφιμασχάλου τὸν Δῆμον ἠξίωσας,
χειμῶνος ὄντος· ἀλλ' ἐγώ σοι τουτονὶ δίδωμι.
ΔΗΜΟΣ. τοιουτονὶ Θεμιστοκλῆς οὐπώποτ' ἐπενόησεν.
καίτοι σοφὸν κἀκεῖν' ὁ Πειραιεύς· ἔμοιγε μέντοι

---

[a] Unknown, but said by the Scholiast to be notorious for immorality. Conviction under a γραφὴ ἑταιρήσεως entailed loss of citizenship, and hence made it unlawful for the man to speak in the assembly.
[b] He wore the τρίβων or doubled χλαῖνα, like the poorer people.
[c] The Lenaean festival came in winter.
[d] The χιτών with one arm-hole (ἑτερομάσχαλος) was used by hand-workers, that with two arm-holes was the mark of a free man (Pollux, vii. 47).

THE KNIGHTS, 869-885

  You say you're passionately fond
      of Demus,—tell me whether
  You've given a clout to patch his shoes.
DEMUS.   No never, I declare.
S.S. You see the sort of man he is!
      but I, I've bought a pair
  Of good stout shoes, and here they are,
      I give them you to wear.
DEMUS. O worthy, patriotic gift!
      I really don't suppose
  There ever lived a man so kind
      to Demus and his toes.
PAPH. 'Tis shameful that a pair of shoes
      should have the power and might
  To put the favours I've conferred
      entirely out of sight,
  I who struck Gryttus [a] from the lists,
      and stopped the boy-loves quite.
S.S. 'Tis shameful, I with truth retort,
      that you should love to pry
  Into such vile degrading crimes
      as that you name. And why?
  Because you fear 'twill make the boys
      for public speaking fit.
  But Demus, at his age, you see
      without a tunic sit,[b]
  In winter [c] too; and nought from you
      his poverty relieves,
  But here's a tunic I have brought,
      well-lined, with double sleeves.[d]
DEMUS. O, why Themistocles himself
      ne'er thought of such a vest!
  Peiraeus was a clever thing,
      but yet, I do protest,

ARISTOPHANES

οὐ μεῖζον εἶναι φαίνετ' ἐξεύρημα τοῦ χιτῶνος.
ΠΑ. οἴμοι τάλας, οἵοις πιθηκισμοῖς με περιελαύνεις.
ΑΛ. οὔκ, ἀλλ' ὅπερ πίνων ἀνὴρ πέπονθ', ὅταν χεσείῃ,
τοῖσιν τρόποις τοῖς σοῖσιν ὥσπερ βλαυτίοισι χρῶμαι.
ΠΑ. ἀλλ' οὐχ ὑπερβαλεῖ με θωπείαις· ἐγὼ γὰρ αὐτὸν 8⟨
προσαμφιῶ τοδί· σὺ δ' οἴμωζ', ὦ πόνηρ'.
ΔΗΜΟΣ. ἰαιβοῖ.
οὐκ ἐς κόρακας ἀποφθερεῖ, βύρσης κάκιστον ὄζων;
ΑΛ. καὶ τοῦτό γ' ἐπίτηδές σε περιήμπισχ', ἵνα σ'
ἀποπνίξῃ·
καὶ πρότερον ἐπεβούλευσέ σοι. τὸν καυλὸν οἶσθ'
ἐκεῖνον
τοῦ σιλφίου τὸν ἄξιον γενόμενον;
ΔΗΜΟΣ. οἶδα μέντοι. 8
ΑΛ. ἐπίτηδες οὗτος αὐτὸν ἔσπευδ' ἄξιον γενέσθαι,
ἵν' ἐσθίοιτ' ὠνούμενοι, κἄπειτ' ἐν Ἡλιαίᾳ
βδέοντες ἀλλήλους ἀποκτείνειαν οἱ δικασταί.
ΔΗΜΟΣ. νὴ τὸν Ποσειδῶ καὶ πρὸς ἐμὲ τοῦτ' εἶπ' ἀνὴρ
Κόπρειος.
ΑΛ. οὐ γὰρ τόθ' ὑμεῖς βδεόμενοι δήπου 'γένεσθε πυρροί; 9
ΔΗΜΟΣ. καὶ νὴ Δί' ἦν γε τοῦτο Πυρράνδρου τὸ μηχάνημα.
ΠΑ. οἴοισί μ', ὦ πανοῦργε, βωμολοχεύμασιν ταράττεις.

---

[a] There was an Attic deme Κόπρος, adj. Κόπρειος. βδέοντες, "breaking wind." πυρροί, sc. τὸν πρωκτόν. The name Pyrrhander echoes this. Who he was, is unknown; some think Cleon is meant, and that his actor was decked up as a slave with red hair.

THE KNIGHTS, 886–902

      That on the whole, between the two,
                    I like the tunic best.
PAPH. (*To S.S.*) Pah! would you circumvent me thus,
                      with such an apish jest?
S.S.   Nay as one guest, at supper-time,
                    will take another's shoes,
      When dire occasion calls him out,
                    so I your methods use.
PAPH. Fawn on: you won't outdo me there.
                      I'll wrap him round about
      With this of mine. Now go and whine, you rascal.
DEMUS.   Pheugh! get out!
(*To P.'s wrapper*) Go to the crows, you brute, with that
                      disgusting smell of leather.
S.S.   He did it for the purpose, Sir;
                    to choke you altogether.
      He tried to do it once before:
                    don't you remember when
      A stalk of silphium sold so cheap?
DEMUS.   Remember? yes: what then?
S.S.   Why that was his contrivance too:
                  he managed there should be a
      Supply for all to buy and eat;
                    and in the Heliaea
      The dicasts one and all were seized
                    with violent diarrhoea.
DEMUS. O ay, a Coprolitish [a] man
                    described the sad affair.
S.S.   And worse and worse and worse you grew,
                    till yellow-tailed you were.
DEMUS. It must have been Pyrrhander's trick,
                    the fool with yellow hair.
PAPH. (*To S.S.*) With what tomfooleries, you rogue,
                    you harass and torment me.

ARISTOPHANES

ΑΛ. ἡ γὰρ θεός μ' ἐκέλευσε νικῆσαί σ' ἀλαζονείαις.
ΠΑ. ἀλλ' οὐχὶ νικήσεις. ἐγὼ γάρ φημί σοι παρέξειν,
ὦ Δῆμε, μηδὲν δρῶντι μισθοῦ τρύβλιον ῥοφῆσαι. 9(
ΑΛ. ἐγὼ δὲ κυλίχνιόν γέ σοι καὶ φάρμακον δίδωμι
τὰν τοῖσιν ἀντικνημίοις ἑλκύδρια περιαλείφειν.
ΠΑ. ἐγὼ δὲ τὰς πολιάς γέ σοὐκλέγων νέον ποιήσω.
ΑΛ. ἰδού, δέχου κέρκον λαγὼ τὠφθαλμιδίω περιψῆν.
ΠΑ. ἀπομυξάμενος ὦ Δῆμέ μου πρὸς τὴν κεφαλὴν ἀποψῶ. 9]
ΑΛ. ἐμοῦ μὲν οὖν, ἐμοῦ μὲν οὖν.
ΠΑ.   ἐγώ σε ποιήσω τριηρ-
    αρχεῖν, ἀναλίσκοντα τῶν
    σαυτοῦ, παλαιὰν ναῦν ἔχοντ',
    εἰς ἣν ἀναλῶν οὐκ ἐφέ-   9]
    ξεις οὐδὲ ναυπηγούμενος·
    διαμηχανήσομαί θ' ὅπως
    ἂν ἱστίον σαπρὸν λάβῃς.
ΧΟ. ἀνὴρ παφλάζει, παῦε παῦ',
    ὑπερζέων· ὑφελκτέον   9:
    τῶν δᾳδίων, ἀπαρυστέον
    τε τῶν ἀπειλῶν ταυτῃί.
ΠΑ. δώσεις ἐμοὶ καλὴν δίκην,
    ἱπούμενος ταῖς εἰσφοραῖς.
    ἐγὼ γὰρ εἰς τοὺς πλουσίους   9:
    σπεύσω σ' ὅπως ἂν ἐγγραφῇς.

---

[a] The "pay-soup" refers to the dicastic triobol (cf. 50) which he is to get for doing nothing.
[b] The diminutives imply: "Here is a nice little pot of medicine to cure your poor sores."
[c] The state provided the hulk, the trierarch had to fit it out for sea.   [d] ταυτηί: "with this ladle," holding one out.
[e] The εἰσφορά was a levy on property, the first class being assessed for the levy at twelve times a year's income, the second at ten times, the third at seven times.

THE KNIGHTS, 903–926

S.S. Yes, 'tis with humbug I'm to win ;
  for that the Goddess sent me
PAPH. You shall not win ! O Demus dear,
  be idle all the day,
And I'll provide you free, to swill,
  a foaming bowl of—pay.[a]
S.S. And I'll this gallipot provide,
  and healing cream within it ;[b]
Whereby the sores upon your shins
  you'll doctor in a minute.
PAPH. I'll pick these grey hairs neatly out,
  and make you young and fair.
S.S. See here ; this hare-scut take to wipe
  your darling eyes with care.
PAPH. Vouchsafe to blow your nose, and clean
  your fingers on my hair.
S.S. No, no ; on mine, on mine, on mine !
PAPH. A trierarch's office you shall fill,[c]
And by my influence I'll prevail
That you shall get, to test your skill,
A battered hull with tattered sail.
Your outlay and your building too
On such a ship will never end ;
No end of work you'll have to do,
No end of cash you'll have to spend.
CHOR. O see how foamy-full he gets.
Good Heavens, he's boiling over ; stay !
Some sticks beneath him draw away,
Bale out a ladleful of threats.[d]
PAPH. Rare punishment for this you'll taste ;
I'll make the taxes[e] weigh you down ;
Amongst the wealthiest of the town
I'll manage that your name is placed.

ARISTOPHANES

ΑΛ. ἐγὼ δ' ἀπειλήσω μὲν οὐδέν, εὔχομαι δέ σοι ταδί·
τὸ μὲν τάγηνον τευθίδων
ἐφεστάναι σίζον, σὲ δὲ 930
γνώμην ἐρεῖν μέλλοντα περὶ
Μιλησίων καὶ κερδανεῖν
τάλαντον, ἢν κατεργάσῃ,
σπεύδειν ὅπως τῶν τευθίδων
ἐμπλήμενος φθαίης ἔτ' εἰς 935
ἐκκλησίαν ἐλθών· ἔπει-
τα πρὶν φαγεῖν, ἀνὴρ μεθή-
κοι, καὶ σὺ τὸ τάλαντον λαβεῖν
βουλόμενος ἐ-
σθίων ἐπαποπνιγείης. 940
ΧΟ. εὖ γε νὴ τὸν Δία καὶ τὸν Ἀπόλλω καὶ τὴν
Δήμητρα.
ΔΗΜΟΣ. κἀμοὶ δοκεῖ καὶ τἄλλα γ' εἶναι καταφανῶς
ἀγαθὸς πολίτης, οἷος οὐδείς πω χρόνου
ἀνὴρ γεγένηται τοῖσι πολλοῖς τοὐβολοῦ. 945
σὺ δ', ὦ Παφλαγών, φάσκων φιλεῖν μ' ἐσκο-
ρόδισας.
καὶ νῦν ἀπόδος τὸν δακτύλιον, ὡς οὐκ ἔτι
ἐμοὶ ταμιεύσεις.
ΠΑ. ἔχε· τοσοῦτον δ' ἴσθ' ὅτι,
εἰ μή μ' ἐάσεις ἐπιτροπεύειν, ἕτερος αὖ
ἐμοῦ πανουργότερός τις ἀναφανήσεται. 950
ΔΗΜΟΣ. οὐκ ἔσθ' ὅπως ὁ δακτύλιός ἐσθ' οὑτοσὶ
οὑμός· τὸ γοῦν σημεῖον ἕτερον φαίνεται,
ἀλλ' ἢ οὐ καθορῶ;

THE KNIGHTS, 927-953

S.S.
I will not use a single threat;
I only most devoutly wish
That on your brazier may be set
A hissing pan of cuttle-fish;
And you the Assembly must address
About Miletus,—'tis a job
Which, if it meets entire success,
Will put a talent in your fob,—[a]
And O that ere your feast begin,
The Assembly waits your friend may cry,
And you, afire the fee to win
And very loth to lose the fry,
May strive in greedy haste to swallow
The cuttles and be CHOKED thereby.

CHOR. Good! Good! by Zeus, Demeter, and Apollo.[b]

DEMUS. Aye, and in all respects he seems to me
A worthy citizen. When lived a man
So good to the Many (the Many for a penny)?
You, Paphlagon, pretending that you loved me,
Primed me with garlic. Give me back my ring;
You shall no more be steward.

PAPH. Take the ring;
And be you sure, if I'm no more your guardian,
You'll get, instead, a greater rogue than I.

DEMUS. Bless me, this can't be mine, this signet-ring.
It's not the same device, it seems to me;
Or can't I see?

[a] The tribute of Miletus was raised in 424 B.C. from five talents to ten; Cleon may have been bribed to oppose this.

[b] This line is in prose; it is the solemn formula used in the heliastic oath (Pollux, viii. 122, so Demosth. *Callipp.* p. 1238).

ARISTOPHANES

ΑΛ. φέρ' ἴδω, τί σοι σημεῖον ἦν;
ΔΗΜΟΣ. δημοῦ βοείου θρῖον ἐξωπτημένον.
ΑΛ. οὐ τοῦτ' ἔνεστιν.
ΔΗΜΟΣ. οὐ τὸ θρῖον; ἀλλὰ τί; 955
ΑΛ. λάρος κεχηνὼς ἐπὶ πέτρας δημηγορῶν.
ΔΗΜΟΣ. αἰβοῖ τάλας.
ΑΛ. τί ἔστιν;
ΔΗΜΟΣ. ἀπόφερ' ἐκποδών.
οὐ τὸν ἐμὸν εἶχεν, ἀλλὰ τὸν Κλεωνύμου.
παρ' ἐμοῦ δὲ τουτονὶ λαβὼν ταμίευέ μοι.
ΠΑ. μὴ δῆτά πώ γ', ὦ δέσποτ', ἀντιβολῶ σ' ἐγώ, 960
πρὶν ἄν γε τῶν χρησμῶν ἀκούσῃς τῶν ἐμῶν.
ΑΛ. καὶ τῶν ἐμῶν νυν.
ΠΑ. ἀλλ' ἐὰν τούτῳ πίθῃ,
μολγὸν γενέσθαι δεῖ σε.
ΑΛ. κἄν γε τουτῳί,
ψωλὸν γενέσθαι δεῖ σε μέχρι τοῦ μυρρίνου.
ΠΑ. ἀλλ' οἵ γ' ἐμοὶ λέγουσιν ὡς ἄρξαι σε δεῖ 965
χώρας ἁπάσης ἐστεφανωμένον ῥόδοις.
ΑΛ. οὑμοὶ δέ γ' αὖ λέγουσιν ὡς ἁλουργίδα
ἔχων κατάπαστον καὶ στεφάνην ἐφ' ἅρματος
χρυσοῦ διώξεις Σμικύθην καὶ κύριον.
ΠΑ. καὶ μὴν ἔνεγκ' αὐτοὺς ἰών, ἵν' οὑτοσὶ 970
αὐτῶν ἀκούσῃ.
ΑΛ. πάνυ γε. καὶ σύ νυν φέρε.

---

[a] A play on δῆμος, "people," and δημός, "fat."
[b] The βῆμα or speaker's platform.
[c] A noted glutton; cf. 1290-9, and see Index.
[d] μολγός, "a black-jack," the slang equivalent of ἀσκός, "a wineskin." An oracle had promised that Athens should always keep above water like a skin bottle (Plutarch, *Theseus*, 24). [e] As a banqueter.

THE KNIGHTS, 953-971

S.S. What's the device on yours?
DEMUS. A leaf of beef-fat stuffing, roasted well.[a]
S.S. No, that's not here.
DEMUS. What then?
S.S. A cormorant
With open mouth haranguing on a rock.[b]
DEMUS. Pheugh!
S.S. What's the matter?
DEMUS. Throw the thing away.
He's got Cleonymus's [c] ring, not mine.
Take this from me, and you be steward now.
PAPH. O not yet, master, I beseech, not yet;
Wait till you've heard my oracles, I pray.
S.S. And mine as well.
PAPH. And if to *his* you listen,
You'll be a liquor-skin.[d]
S.S. And if to *his*,
You'll find yourself severely circumcised.
PAPH. Nay mine foretell that over all the land
Thyself shalt rule, with roses garlanded.[e]
S.S. And mine that crowned, in spangled purple robe,
Thou in thy golden chariot shalt pursue
And sue the lady Smicythe and her lord.[f]
PAPH. Well, go and fetch them hither, so that *he*
May hear them.
S.S. Certainly; and you fetch yours.

[f] A surprise, playing upon the double meaning of διώκω. Demus shall go hunting in oriental state, but his sport, to suit Athenian taste, shall be to "pursue," that is to "prosecute," a certain effeminate citizen (τὸν Σμικύθην κωμῳδεῖ ὡς κίναιδον· κύριον δὲ λέγει τὸν ἄνδρα: Schol.).

219

ARISTOPHANES

ΠΑ. ἰδού.
ΑΛ. ἰδοὺ νὴ τὸν Δί'· οὐδὲν κωλύει.

ΧΟ. ἥδιστον φάος ἡμέρας
ἔσται τοῖσι παροῦσι πᾶ-
σιν καὶ τοῖς ἀφικνουμένοις, 97
ἢν Κλέων ἀπόληται.
καίτοι πρεσβυτέρων τινῶν
οἵων ἀργαλεωτάτων
ἐν τῷ Δείγματι τῶν δικῶν
ἤκουσ' ἀντιλεγόντων, 98
ὡς εἰ μὴ 'γένεθ' οὗτος ἐν
τῇ πόλει μέγας, οὐκ ἂν ἤ-
στην σκεύη δύο χρησίμω,
δοῖδυξ οὐδὲ τορύνη.

ἀλλὰ καὶ τόδ' ἔγωγε θαυ- 98
μάζω τῆς ὑομουσίας
αὐτοῦ· φασὶ γὰρ αὐτὸν οἱ
παῖδες οἳ ξυνεφοίτων
τὴν Δωριστὶ μόνην ἂν ἁρ-
μόττεσθαι θαμὰ τὴν λύραν, 99
ἄλλην δ' οὐκ ἐθέλειν μαθεῖν·
κᾆτα τὸν κιθαριστὴν
ὀργισθέντ' ἀπάγειν κελεύ-
ειν, ὡς ἁρμονίαν ὁ παῖς
οὗτος οὐ δύναται μαθεῖν 99
ἢν μὴ Δωροδοκιστί.

ΠΑ. ἰδού, θέασαι, κοὐχ ἅπαντας ἐκφέρω.
ΑΛ. οἴμ' ὡς χεσείω, κοὐχ ἅπαντας ἐκφέρω.

---

[a] The opening lines are taken from Euripides.

THE KNIGHTS, 972-998

PAPH. Here goes.
S.S. Here goes, by Zeus. There's nought to stop us.

CHOR.[a] O bright and joyous day,
O day most sweet to all
Both near and far away,
The day of Cleon's fall.
Yet in our Action-mart [b]
I overheard by chance
Some ancient sires and tart
This counter-plea advance,
That but for him the State
Two things had ne'er possessed :—
A STIRRER-up of hate,
A PESTLE of unrest.

His swine-bred music we
With wondering hearts admire ;
At school, his mates agree,
He always tuned his lyre
In Dorian style to play.[c]
His master wrathful grew ;
He sent the boy away,
And this conclusion drew,
*This boy from all his friends
Donations seeks to wile,
His art begins and ends
In Dono-do-rian style.*

PAPH. Look at them, see ! and there are more behind.
S.S. O what a weight ! and there are more behind.

[b] The Deigma was the Exchange at the Peiraeus, " Sample Mart." Lawsuits are the staple product of Athens.
[c] The Dorian mode was a solemn and manly music ; it is chosen here as leading up to the pun in Δωροδοκιστί.

ARISTOPHANES

ΔΗΜΟΣ. ταυτὶ τί ἐστι;
ΠΑ. λόγια.
ΔΗΜΟΣ. πάντ';
ΠΑ. ἐθαύμασας;
καὶ νὴ Δί' ἔτι γέ μοῦστι κιβωτὸς πλέα. 10(
ΑΛ. ἐμοὶ δ' ὑπερῷον καὶ ξυνοικία δύο.
ΔΗΜΟΣ. φέρ' ἴδω, τίνος γάρ εἰσιν οἱ χρησμοί ποτε;
ΠΑ. οὑμοὶ μέν εἰσι Βάκιδος.
ΔΗΜΟΣ. οἱ δὲ σοὶ τίνος;
ΑΛ. Γλάνιδος, ἀδελφοῦ τοῦ Βάκιδος γεραιτέρου.
ΔΗΜΟΣ. εἰσὶν δὲ περὶ τοῦ;
ΠΑ. περὶ Ἀθηνῶν, περὶ Πύλου, 10(
περὶ σοῦ, περὶ ἐμοῦ, περὶ ἁπάντων πραγμάτων.
ΔΗΜΟΣ. οἱ σοὶ δὲ περὶ τοῦ;
ΑΛ. περὶ Ἀθηνῶν, περὶ φακῆς,
περὶ Λακεδαιμονίων, περὶ σκόμβρων νέων,
περὶ τῶν μετρούντων τἄλφιτ' ἐν ἀγορᾷ κακῶς,
περὶ σοῦ, περὶ ἐμοῦ. τὸ πέος οὑτοσὶ δάκοι. 10
ΔΗΜΟΣ. ἄγε νυν ὅπως αὐτοὺς ἀναγνώσεσθέ μοι,
καὶ τὸν περὶ ἐμοῦ 'κεῖνον ᾧπερ ἥδομαι,
ὡς ἐν νεφέλαισιν αἰετὸς γενήσομαι.
ΠΑ. ἄκουε δή νυν καὶ πρόσεχε τὸν νοῦν ἐμοί.
Φράζευ, Ἐρεχθείδη, λογίων ὁδόν, ἥν σοι Ἀπόλλων 10
ἴαχεν ἐξ ἀδύτοιο διὰ τριπόδων ἐριτίμων.
σώζεσθαί σ' ἐκέλευσ' ἱερὸν κύνα καρχαρόδοντα,

---

[a] An invented person.
[b] Refers to an oracle that foretells this for Athens. See *B.* 978.

Εὔδαιμον πτολίεθρον Ἀθηναίης ἀγελείης
πολλὰ ἰδόν, καὶ πολλὰ παθόν, καὶ πολλὰ μογῆσαν
αἰετὸς ἐν νεφέλῃσι γενήσεαι ἤματα πάντα.

THE KNIGHTS, 999–1017

DEMUS. What ARE they?
PAPH. Oracles!
DEMUS. All?
PAPH. You seem surprised;
By Zeus, I've got a chestful more at home.
S.S. And I a garret and two cellars full.
DEMUS. Come, let me see. Whose oracles are these?
PAPH. Mine are by Bakis.
DEMUS. (*To S.S.*) And by whom are yours?
S.S. Mine are by Glanis,[a] Bakis's elder brother.
DEMUS. What do they treat of?
PAPH. Mine? Of Athens, Pylus,
Of you, of me, of every blessed thing.
DEMUS. (*To S.S.*) And you; of what treat yours?
S.S. Of Athens, pottage,
Of Lacedaemon, mackerel freshly caught,
Of swindling barley-measurers in the mart,
Of you, of me. That nincompoop be hanged.
DEMUS. Well read them out; and prithee don't forget
The one I love to hear about myself,
That I'm to soar, an Eagle, in the clouds.[b]
PAPH. Now then give ear, and hearken to my words.
HEED THOU WELL, ERECHTHEIDES,
THE ORACLE'S DRIFT, WHICH APOLLO
OUT OF HIS SECRET SHRINE
THROUGH PRICELESS TRIPODS DELIVERED.
KEEP THOU SAFELY THE DOG,
THY JAG-TOOTHED HOLY PROTECTOR.[c]

O thou fortunate town
Of Athene, the Bringer of spoil,
Much shalt thou see, and much
Shalt thou suffer, and much shalt thou toil,
Then in the clouds thou shalt soar, as an Eagle, for ever and ever.

[c] Probably Cleon used to call himself the Watch-dog of the state. See *P.* 754, *W.* 1031.

ARISTOPHANES

ὃς πρὸ σέθεν χάσκων καὶ ὑπὲρ σοῦ δεινὰ κεκραγὼς
σοὶ μισθὸν ποριεῖ, κἂν μὴ δρᾷ ταῦτ', ἀπολεῖται.
πολλοὶ γὰρ μίσει σφε κατακρώζουσι κολοιοί. 10⟨5⟩
ΔΗΜΟΣ. ταυτὶ μὰ τὴν Δήμητρ' ἐγὼ οὐκ οἶδ' ὅ τι λέγει.
τί γάρ ἐστ' Ἐρεχθεῖ καὶ κολοιοῖς καὶ κυνί;
ΠΑ. ἐγὼ μέν εἰμ' ὁ κύων· πρὸ σοῦ γὰρ ἀπύω·
σοὶ δ' εἶπε σώζεσθαί μ' ὁ Φοῖβος τὸν κύνα.
ΑΛ. οὐ τοῦτό φησ' ὁ χρησμός, ἀλλ' ὁ κύων ὁδί, 10
ὥσπερ θύρας σοῦ, τῶν λογίων παρεσθίει.
ἐμοὶ γάρ ἐστ' ὀρθῶς περὶ τούτου τοῦ κυνός.
ΔΗΜΟΣ. λέγε νυν· ἐγὼ δὲ πρῶτα λήψομαι λίθον,
ἵνα μή μ' ὁ χρησμὸς ὁ περὶ τοῦ κυνὸς δάκῃ.
ΑΛ. Φράζευ, Ἐρεχθείδη, κύνα Κέρβερον ἀνδραπο-
διστήν, 10
ὃς κέρκῳ σαίνων σ', ὁπόταν δειπνῇς, ἐπιτηρῶν,
ἐξέδεταί σου τοὔψον, ὅταν σύ που ἄλλοσε χάσκῃς·
ἐσφοιτῶν τ' ἐς τοὐπτάνιον λήσει σε κυνηδὸν
νύκτωρ τὰς λοπάδας καὶ τὰς νήσους διαλείχων.
ΔΗΜΟΣ. νὴ τὸν Ποσειδῶ πολύ γ' ἄμεινον, ὦ Γλάνι. 1⟨0⟩
ΠΑ. ὦ τᾶν, ἄκουσον, εἶτα διάκρινον τότε.
Ἔστι γυνή, τέξει δὲ λέονθ' ἱεραῖς ἐν Ἀθήναις,
ὃς περὶ τοῦ δήμου πολλοῖς κώνωψι μαχεῖται,
ὥστε περὶ σκύμνοισι βεβηκώς· τὸν σὺ φυλάξαι,

---

[a] *i.e.* the islands of the Aegean which practically constituted the Athenian Empire.
[b] The words τέξει δὲ λέοντα are from an oracle quoted Herod. v. 92.

THE KNIGHTS, 1018–1039

    YAPPING BEFORE THY FEET,
           AND TERRIBLY ROARING TO GUARD THEE,
  HE THY PAY WILL PROVIDE :
          IF HE FAIL TO PROVIDE IT, HE'LL PERISH ;
    YEA, FOR MANY THE DAWS
          THAT ARE HATING AND CAWING AGAINST HIM.
DEMUS. This, by Demeter, beats me altogether.
    What does Erechtheus want with daws and dog ?
PAPH. I am the dog : I bark aloud for you.
    And Phoebus bids you guard the dog ; that's me.
S.S.   It says not that ; but this confounded dog
    Has gnawn the oracle, as he gnaws the door.
    I've the right reading here about the dog.
DEMUS. Let's hear ; but first I'll pick me up a stone
    Lest this dog-oracle take to gnawing *me*.
S.S. HEED THOU WELL, ERECHTHEIDES,
           THE KIDNAPPING CERBERUS BAN-DOG ;
  WAGGING HIS TAIL HE STANDS,
          AND FAWNING UPON THEE AT DINNER,
  WAITING THY SLICE TO DEVOUR
          WHEN AUGHT DISTRACT THINE ATTENTION.
  SOON AS THE NIGHT COMES ROUND
          HE STEALS UNSEEN TO THE KITCHEN
  DOG-WISE ; THEN WILL HIS TONGUE
          CLEAN OUT THE PLATES AND THE—ISLANDS.[a]
DEMUS. Aye, by Poseidon, Glanis, that's far better.
PAPH. Nay, listen first, my friend, and then decide.
  WOMAN SHE IS, BUT A LION
          SHE'LL BEAR[b] US IN ATHENS THE HOLY ;
  ONE WHO FOR DEMUS WILL FIGHT
          WITH AN ARMY OF STINGING MOSQUITOES,
  FIGHT, AS IF SHIELDING HIS WHELPS ;
          WHOM SEE THOU GUARD WITH DEVOTION

ARISTOPHANES

τεῖχος ποιήσας ξύλινον πύργους τε σιδηροῦς.
ταῦτ' οἶσθ' ὅ τι λέγει;
ΔΗΜΟΣ.   μὰ τὸν Ἀπόλλω 'γὼ μὲν οὔ.
ΠΑ. ἔφραζεν ὁ θεός σοι σαφῶς σώζειν ἐμέ·
    ἐγὼ γὰρ ἀντὶ τοῦ λέοντός εἰμί σοι.
ΔΗΜΟΣ. καὶ πῶς μ' ἐλελήθεις Ἀντιλέων γεγενημένος;
ΑΛ. ἐν οὐκ ἀναδιδάσκει σε τῶν λογίων ἑκών,
    ὃ μόνον σιδήρου τεῖχός ἐστι καὶ ξύλων,
    ἐν ᾧ σε σώζειν τόνδ' ἐκέλευσ' ὁ Λοξίας.
ΔΗΜΟΣ. πῶς δῆτα τοῦτ' ἔφραζεν ὁ θεός;
ΑΛ.   τουτονὶ
    δῆσαί σ' ἐκέλευσ' ἐν πεντεσυρίγγῳ ξύλῳ.
ΔΗΜΟΣ. ταυτὶ τελεῖσθαι τὰ λόγι' ἤδη μοι δοκεῖ.
ΠΑ. μὴ πείθου φθονεραὶ γὰρ ἐπικρώζουσι κορῶναι.
    ἀλλ' ἱέρακα φίλει, μεμνημένος ἐν φρεσίν, ὅς σοι
    ἤγαγε συνδήσας Λακεδαιμονίων κορακίνους.
ΑΛ. τοῦτό γέ τοι Παφλαγὼν παρεκινδύνευσε μεθυσθείς.
    Κεκροπίδη κακόβουλε, τί τοῦθ' ἡγεῖ μέγα τοὔργον;
    καί κε γυνὴ φέροι ἄχθος, ἐπεί κεν ἀνὴρ ἀναθείη·
    ἀλλ' οὐκ ἂν μαχέσαιτο· χέσαιτο γάρ, εἰ μαχέσαιτο.
ΠΑ. ἀλλὰ τόδε φράσσαι, πρὸ Πύλου Πύλον ἥν σοι ἔφραζεν,
    Ἔστι Πύλος πρὸ Πύλοιο.
ΔΗΜΟΣ.   τί τοῦτο λέγει, πρὸ Πύλοιο;

---

[a] From the famous oracle given to Athens before the battle of Salamis, Herod. vii. 141.
[b] Unknown.
[c] With holes for arms, legs, and head.
[d] A line from the Little Iliad of Lesches (Schol.). χέσαιτο in the next line is formed to echo μαχέσαιτο, making a complete vulgar burlesque.
[e] A well-known line runs ἔστι Πύλος πρὸ Πύλοιο, Πύλος γε μέν ἐστι καὶ ἄλλη. One was in N. Elis, one in S. Elis, one opposite Sphacteria. The words lead up to the play upon πύελος, a tub or trough.

THE KNIGHTS, 1040-1059

        BUILDING A WOODEN WALL [a]
                       AND AN IRON FORT TO SECURE HIM.
        Do you understand?
DEMUS.   By Apollo, no, not I.
PAPH.   The God, 'tis plain, would have you keep me safely,
        For I'm a valiant lion, for your sake.
DEMUS.   What, you Antileon [b] and I never knew it!
S.S.   One thing he purposely informs you not,
        What that oracular wall of wood and iron,
        Where Loxias bids you keep him safely, is.
DEMUS.   What means the God?
S.S.   He means that you're to clap
        Paphlagon in the five-holed pillory-stocks.[c]
DEMUS.   I shouldn't be surprised if that came true.
PAPH.   HEED NOT THE WORDS; FOR JEALOUS
                THE CROWS THAT ARE CROAKING AGAINST ME,
     CHERISH THE LORDLY FALCON,
                NOR EVER FORGET THAT HE BROUGHT THEE,
     BROUGHT THEE IN FETTERS AND CHAINS
                THE YOUNG LACONIAN MINNOWS.
S.S.   THIS DID PAPHLAGON DARE
                IN A MOMENT OF DRUNKEN BRAVADO.
     WHY THINK MUCH OF THE DEED,
                CECROPIDES FOOLISH IN COUNSEL?
     WEIGHT A WOMAN WILL BEAR,
                IF A MAN IMPOSE IT UPON HER,[d]
     FIGHT SHE WON'T AND SHE CAN'T:
                IN FIGHTING SHE'S ALWAYS A FRIGHT IN.
PAPH.   NAY, BUT REMEMBER THE WORD,
                HOW PYLUS, HE SAID, BEFORE PYLUS; [e]
     PYLUS THERE IS BEFORE PYLUS.
DEMUS.   What mean you by that "before Pylus"?

ARISTOPHANES

ΑΛ. τὰς πυέλους φησὶν καταλήψεσθ' ἐν βαλανείῳ.
ΔΗΜΟΣ. ἐγὼ δ' ἄλουτος τήμερον γενήσομαι.
ΑΛ. οὗτος γὰρ ἡμῶν τὰς πυέλους ἀφήρπασεν.
ἀλλ' οὑτοσὶ γάρ ἐστι περὶ τοῦ ναυτικοῦ
ὁ χρησμός, ᾧ σε δεῖ προσέχειν τὸν νοῦν πάνυ.
ΔΗΜΟΣ. προσέχω· σὺ δ' ἀναγίγνωσκε, τοῖς ναύταισί μου
ὅπως ὁ μισθὸς πρῶτον ἀποδοθήσεται.
ΑΛ. Αἰγείδη, φράσσαι κυναλώπεκα, μή σε δολώσῃ,
λαίθαργον, ταχύπουν, δολίαν κερδώ, πολύιδριν.
οἶσθ' ὅ τί ἐστιν τοῦτο;
ΔΗΜΟΣ. Φιλόστρατος ἡ κυναλώπηξ.
ΑΛ. οὐ τοῦτό φησιν, ἀλλὰ ναῦς ἑκάστοτε
αἰτεῖ ταχείας ἀργυρολόγους οὑτοσί·
ταύτας ἀπαυδᾷ μὴ διδόναι σ' ὁ Λοξίας.
ΔΗΜΟΣ. πῶς δὴ τριήρης ἐστὶ κυναλώπηξ;
ΑΛ. ὅπως;
ὅτι ἡ τριήρης ἐστὶ χὠ κύων ταχύ.
ΔΗΜΟΣ. πῶς οὖν ἀλώπηξ προσετέθη πρὸς τῷ κυνί;
ΑΛ. ἀλωπεκίοισι τοὺς στρατιώτας ᾔκασεν,
ὁτιὴ βότρυς τρώγουσιν ἐν τοῖς χωρίοις.
ΔΗΜΟΣ. εἶεν·
τούτοις ὁ μισθὸς τοῖς ἀλωπεκίοισι ποῦ;
ΑΛ. ἐγὼ ποριῶ καὶ τοῦτον ἡμερῶν τριῶν.
ἀλλ' ἔτι τόνδ' ἐπάκουσον, ὃν εἶπέ σοι ἐξαλέασθαι,
χρησμὸν Λητοΐδης, Κυλλήνην, μή σε δολώσῃ.
ΔΗΜΟΣ. ποίαν Κυλλήνην;
ΑΛ. τὴν τούτου χεῖρ' ἐποίησεν
Κυλλήνην ὀρθῶς, ὁτιή φησ', ἔμβαλε κυλλῇ.

---

[a] Philostratus, a pander, was nicknamed so: L. 957.
[b] Ships sent to collect the tribute: Thuc. ii. 69, iii. 19.
[c] Cyllene was the port of Elis. It is here used to suggest κυλλὴ χείρ, "the hollow hand" that welcomes a bride.

THE KNIGHTS, 1060-1083

S.S. Truly your pile of baths
    will he capture before you can take them.
DEMUS. O dear, then bathless must I go to-day
S.S. Because he has carried off our pile of baths.
    But here's an oracle about the fleet;
    Your best attention is required to this.
DEMUS. I'll give it too; but prithee, first of all,
    Read how my sailors are to get their pay.
S.S. O AEGEIDES, BEWARE
        OF THE HOUND-FOX, LEST HE DECEIVE THEE,
    STEALTHILY SNAPPING, THE CRAFTY,
            THE SWIFT, THE TRICKY MARAUDER.
    Know you the meaning of this?
DEMUS.   Philostratus, plainly, the hound-fox.[a]
S.S. Not so; but Paphlagon is evermore
    Asking swift triremes to collect the silver,[b]
    So Loxias bids you not to give him these.
DEMUS. Why is a trireme called a hound-fox?
S.S.   Why?
    A trireme's fleet; a hound is also fleet.
DEMUS. But for what reason adds he "fox" to "hound"?
S.S. The troops, he means, resemble little foxes,
    Because they scour the farms and eat the grapes.
DEMUS. Good.
    But where's the cash to pay these little foxes?
S.S. That I'll provide: within three days I'll do it.
    LIST THOU FURTHER THE REDE
            BY THE SON OF LETO DELIVERED;
    KEEP THOU ALOOF, SAID HE,
            FROM THE WILES OF HOLLOW CYLLENE.[c]
DEMUS. Hollow Cyllene! what's that?
S.S.   'Tis Paphlagon's hand he's describing.
    Paphlagon's outstretched hand,
            with his *Drop me a coin in the hollow.*

ARISTOPHANES

ΠΑ. οὐκ ὀρθῶς φράζει· τὴν Κυλλήνην γὰρ ὁ Φοῖβος
εἰς τὴν χεῖρ' ὀρθῶς ἠνίξατο τὴν Διοπείθους.
ἀλλὰ γάρ ἐστιν ἐμοὶ χρησμὸς περὶ σοῦ πτερυγωτός,
αἰετὸς ὡς γίγνει καὶ πάσης γῆς βασιλεύεις.

ΑΛ. καὶ γὰρ ἐμοί, καὶ γῆς καὶ τῆς ἐρυθρᾶς γε θαλάσσης,
χὤτι γ' ἐν Ἐκβατάνοις δικάσεις, λείχων ἐπίπαστα.

ΠΑ. ἀλλ' ἐγὼ εἶδον ὄναρ, καί μοὐδόκει ἡ θεὸς αὐτὴ
τοῦ δήμου καταχεῖν ἀρυταίνῃ πλουθυγίειαν.

ΑΛ. νὴ Δία καὶ γὰρ ἐγώ· καί μοὐδόκει ἡ θεὸς αὐτὴ
ἐκ πόλεως ἐλθεῖν καὶ γλαῦξ αὐτῇ 'πικαθῆσθαι·
εἶτα κατασπένδειν κατὰ τῆς κεφαλῆς ἀρυβάλλῳ
ἀμβροσίαν κατὰ σοῦ, κατὰ τούτου δὲ σκοροδάλμην.

ΔΗΜΟΣ. ἰοὺ ἰού.
οὐκ ἦν ἄρ' οὐδεὶς τοῦ Γλάνιδος σοφώτερος.
καὶ νῦν ἐμαυτὸν ἐπιτρέπω σοι τουτονὶ
γεροντεγωγεῖν κἀναπαιδεύειν πάλιν.

ΠΑ. μήπω γ', ἱκετεύω σ', ἀλλ' ἀνάμεινον, ὡς ἐγὼ
κριθὰς ποριῶ σοι καὶ βίον καθ' ἡμέραν.

ΔΗΜΟΣ. οὐκ ἀνέχομαι κριθῶν ἀκούων· πολλάκις
ἐξηπατήθην ὑπό τε σοῦ καὶ Θουφάνους.

ΠΑ. ἀλλ' ἄλφιτ' ἤδη σοι ποριῶ 'σκευασμένα.

ΑΛ. ἐγὼ δὲ μαζίσκας γε διαμεμαγμένας

---

[a] A crazy oracle-monger (cf. W. 380, B. 988), apparently with a crippled hand.
[b] A secretary under Cleon: Schol.

THE KNIGHTS, 1084–1105

PAPH. There this fellow is wrong.
  When he spake of the hollow Cyllene,
Phoebus was hinting, I ween,
    at the hand of the maimed Diopeithes.[a]
Nay, but I've got me, for you,
    a wingèd oracular message,
THOU SHALT AN EAGLE BECOME,
    AND RULE ALL LANDS AS A MONARCH.
S.S. Nay, but I've got me the same :—
    AND THE RED SEA TOO THOU SHALT GOVERN,
YEA IN ECBATANA JUDGE,
    RICH CAKES AS THOU JUDGEST DEVOURING.
PAPH. Nay, but I dreamed me a dream,
    and methought the Goddess Athene
Health and wealth was ladling
    in plentiful streams upon Demus.
S.S. Nay, but I dreamed one myself ;
    and methought of the Goddess Athene
Down from the Citadel stepped,
    and an owl sat perched on her shoulder ;
Then from a bucket she poured
    ambrosia down upon Demus,
Sweetest of scents upon *you*,
    upon Paphlagon sourest of pickles.
DEMUS. Good! Good!
  There never *was* a cleverer chap than Glanis.
  So now, my friend, I yield myself to you ;
  Be you the tutor of my thoughtless—Age.
PAPH. Not yet! pray wait awhile, and I'll provide
  Your barley-grain, and daily sustenance.
DEMUS. I can't abide your barley-talk ; too often
  Have I been duped by you and Thuphanes.[b]
PAPH. I'll give you barley-meal, all ready-made.
S.S. I'll give you barley-cakes, all ready-baked,

ARISTOPHANES

καὶ τοὔψον ὀπτόν· μηδὲν ἄλλ' εἰ μὴ 'σθιε.
ΔΗΜΟΣ. ἀνύσατέ νυν ὅ τι περ ποιήσεθ'· ὡς ἐγώ,
ὁπότερος ἂν σφῷν εὖ με μᾶλλον ἂν ποιῇ,
τούτῳ παραδώσω τῆς πυκνὸς τὰς ἡνίας.
ΠΑ. τρέχοιμ' ἂν εἴσω πρότερος.
ΑΛ. οὐ δῆτ', ἀλλ' ἐγώ. 1110

ΧΟ. ὦ Δῆμε, καλήν γ' ἔχεις
ἀρχήν, ὅτε πάντες ἄν-
θρωποι δεδίασί σ' ὥσ-
περ ἄνδρα τύραννον.
ἀλλ' εὐπαράγωγος εἶ, 1115
θωπευόμενός τε χαί-
ρεις κἀξαπατώμενος,
πρὸς τόν τε λέγοντ' ἀεὶ
κέχηνας· ὁ νοῦς δέ σου
παρὼν ἀποδημεῖ. 1120

ΔΗΜΟΣ. νοῦς οὐκ ἔνι ταῖς κόμαις
ὑμῶν, ὅτε μ' οὐ φρονεῖν
νομίζετ'· ἐγὼ δ' ἑκὼν
ταῦτ' ἠλιθιάζω.
αὐτός τε γὰρ ἥδομαι 1125
βρύλλων τὸ καθ' ἡμέραν,
κλέπτοντά τε βούλομαι
τρέφειν ἕνα προστάτην·
τοῦτον δ', ὅταν ᾖ πλέως,
ἄρας ἐπάταξα. 1130

ΧΟ. χοὔτω μὲν ἂν εὖ ποιοῖς,
εἴ σοι πυκνότης ἔνεστ'

---

[a] The προστάτης τοῦ δήμου was not an official, but the accepted democratic leader.

THE KNIGHTS, 1106-1132

        And well-broiled fish. Do nothing else but eat.
DEMUS. Make haste and do it then, remembering this,
        Whichever brings me most titbits to-day,
        To him alone I'll give the Pnyx's reins.
PAPH. O then I'll run in first.
S.S.   Not you, but I.

CHOR.   Proud, O Demus, thy sway.
          Thee, as Tyrant and King,
          All men fear and obey,
          Yet, O yet, 'tis a thing
          Easy, to lead thee astray.
          Empty fawning and praise
          Pleased thou art to receive;
          All each orator says
          Sure at once to believe;
          Wit thou hast, but 'tis roaming;
          Ne'er we find it its home in.

DEMUS. Wit there's none in your hair.
          What, you think me a fool!
          What, you know not I wear,
          Wear my motley by rule!
          Well all day do I fare,
          Nursed and cockered by all;
          Pleased to fatten and train
          One prime thief in my stall.[a]
          When full gorged with his gain,
          Up that instant I snatch him,[b]
          Strike one blow and dispatch him.

CHOR.   Art thou really so deep?
          Is such artfulness thine?

            [b] Hoist him up.

ARISTOPHANES

ἐν τῷ τρόπῳ, ὡς λέγεις,
τούτῳ πάνυ πολλή,
εἰ τούσδ' ἐπίτηδες ὥσ- 1135
περ δημοσίους τρέφεις
ἐν τῇ πυκνί, κᾆθ' ὅταν
μή σοι τύχῃ ὄψον ὄν,
τούτων ὃς ἂν ᾖ παχύς,
θύσας ἐπιδειπνεῖς. 1140

ΔΗΜΟΣ. σκέψασθε δέ μ', εἰ σοφῶς
αὐτοὺς περιέρχομαι,
τοὺς οἰομένους φρονεῖν
κἄμ' ἐξαπατύλλειν.
τηρῶ γὰρ ἑκάστοτ' αὐ- 1145
τούς, οὐδὲ δοκῶν ὁρᾶν,
κλέπτοντας· ἔπειτ' ἀναγ-
κάζω πάλιν ἐξεμεῖν
ἅττ' ἂν κεκλόφωσί μου,
κημὸν καταμηλῶν. 1150

ΠΑ. ἄπαγ' ἐς μακαρίαν ἐκποδών.
ΑΛ.   σύ γ', ὦ φθόρε.
ΠΑ. ὦ Δῆμ', ἐγὼ μέντοι παρεσκευασμένος
τρίπαλαι κάθημαι, βουλόμενός σ' εὐεργετεῖν.
ΑΛ. ἐγὼ δὲ δεκάπαλαί γε καὶ δωδεκάπαλαι
καὶ χιλιόπαλαι καὶ πρόπαλαι πάλαι πάλαι. 1155
ΔΗΜΟΣ. ἐγὼ δὲ προσδοκῶν γε τρισμυριόπαλαι
βδελύττομαι σφώ, καὶ πρόπαλαι πάλαι πάλαι.
ΑΛ. οἶσθ' οὖν ὃ δρᾶσον;
ΔΗΜΟΣ.   εἰ δὲ μή, φράσεις γε σύ.

THE KNIGHTS, 1133–1158

        Well for all if thou keep
        Firm to this thy design.
        Well for all if, as sheep
        Marked for victims, thou feed
        These thy knaves in the Pnyx,
        Then, if dainties thou need,
        Haste on a victim to fix ;
        Slay the fattest and finest ;
        There's thy meal when thou dinest.

DEMUS.   Ah ! they know not that I
        Watch them plunder and thieve.
        Ah ! *'tis easy*, they cry,
        Him to gull and deceive.
        Comes MY turn by and by !
        Down their gullet, full quick,
        Lo, my verdict-tube coils,[a]
        Turns them giddy and sick,
        Up they vomit their spoils :
        Such, with rogues, is my dealing,
        'Tis for MYSELF they are stealing.

PAPH. Go and be blest !
S.S.   Be blest yourself, you filth.
PAPH. O Demus, I've been sitting here prepared
      Three ages past, longing to do you good.
S.S.   And I ten ages, aye twelve ages, aye
      A thousand ages, ages, ages, ages.
DEMUS. And I've been waiting, till I loathe you both,
      For thirty thousand ages, ages, ages.
S.S.   Do—know you what ?
DEMUS.   And if I don't, you'll tell me.

[a] μήλη was a surgeon's probe, κημός the neck of the ballot-box: the phrase means pushing this down the throat to make them vomit.

ARISTOPHANES

ΑΛ. ἄφες ἀπὸ βαλβίδων ἐμέ τε καὶ τουτονί,
ἵνα σ' εὖ ποιῶμεν ἐξ ἴσου.
ΔΗΜΟΣ. δρᾶν ταῦτα χρή. 1160
ἄπιτον.
ΠΑ. καὶ ΑΛ. ἰδού.
ΔΗΜΟΣ. θέοιτ' ἄν.
ΑΛ. ὑποθεῖν οὐκ ἐῶ.
ΔΗΜΟΣ. ἀλλ' ἢ μεγάλως εὐδαιμονήσω τήμερον
ὑπὸ τῶν ἐραστῶν νὴ Δί' ἢ 'γὼ θρύψομαι.
ΠΑ. ὁρᾷς; ἐγώ σοι πρότερος ἐκφέρω δίφρον.
ΑΛ. ἀλλ' οὐ τράπεζαν, ἀλλ' ἐγὼ προτεραίτερος. 1165
ΠΑ. ἰδοὺ φέρω σοι τήνδε μαζίσκην ἐγὼ
ἐκ τῶν ὀλῶν τῶν ἐκ Πύλου μεμαγμένην.
ΑΛ. ἐγὼ δὲ μυστίλας μεμυστιλημένας
ὑπὸ τῆς θεοῦ τῇ χειρὶ τῇλεφαντίνῃ.
ΔΗΜΟΣ. ὡς μέγαν ἄρ' εἶχες, ὦ πότνια, τὸν δάκτυλον. 1170
ΠΑ. ἐγὼ δ' ἔτνος γε πίσινον εὔχρων καὶ καλόν·
ἐτόρυνε δ' αὔθ' ἡ Παλλὰς ἡ Πυλαιμάχος.
ΑΛ. ὦ Δῆμ', ἐναργῶς ἡ θεός σ' ἐπισκοπεῖ,
καὶ νῦν ὑπερέχει σου χύτραν ζωμοῦ πλέαν.
ΔΗΜΟΣ. οἴει γὰρ οἰκεῖσθ' ἂν ἔτι τήνδε τὴν πόλιν, 1175
εἰ μὴ φανερῶς ἡμῶν ὑπερεῖχε τὴν χύτραν;
ΠΑ. τουτὶ τέμαχός σοὔδωκεν ἡ Φοβεσιστράτη.
ΑΛ. ἡ δ' Ὀβριμοπάτρα γ' ἐφθὸν ἐκ ζωμοῦ κρέας
καὶ χόλικος ἡνύστρου τε καὶ γαστρὸς τόμον.
ΔΗΜΟΣ. καλῶς γ' ἐποίησε τοῦ πέπλου μεμνημένη. 1180
ΠΑ. ἡ Γοργολόφα σ' ἐκέλευε τουτουὶ φαγεῖν

---

[a] In the statue by Pheidias which stood in the Parthenon, the flesh was represented by ivory. μύστιλαι are pieces of bread hollowed out to serve as a sort of spoon.
[b] Lit. "that fights at the gates." The epithet is invented on the analogy of Πρόμαχος (the epithet of Athena as repre-

THE KNIGHTS, 1159-1181

S.S. Do start us from the signal-post, us two,
    All fair, no favour.
DEMUS.   Right you are ; move off.
PAPH. *and* S.S. Ready !
DEMUS.   Away !
S.S.   No " cutting in " allowed.
DEMUS. Zeus ! if I don't, with these two lovers, have
    A rare good time, 'tis dainty I must be.
PAPH. See, I'm the first to bring you out a chair.
S.S. But not a table ; I'm the firstlier there.
PAPH. Look, here's a jolly little cake I bring,
    Cooked from the barley-grain I brought from
        Pylus.
S.S. And here I'm bringing splendid scoops of
        bread,
    Scooped by the Goddess with her ivory hand.[a]
DEMUS. A mighty finger you must have, dread lady !
PAPH. And here's pease-porridge, beautiful and
        brown.
    Pallas Pylaemachus [b] it was that stirred it.
S.S. O Demus, plain it is the Goddess guards you,
    Holding above your head this—soup-tureen.
DEMUS. Why, think you Athens had survived, unless
    She plainly o'er us held her soup-tureen ?
PAPH. This slice of fish the Army-frightener sends
        you.
S.S. This boiled broth-meat the Nobly-fathered
        gives you,
    And this good cut of tripe and guts and paunch.
DEMUS. And well done she, to recollect the peplus.
PAPH. The Terror-crested bids you taste this cake

sented in the bronze statue which stood on the Acropolis),
and to Cleon means " who fought for me at Pylos." The
lines following contain titles of Athena.

237

ARISTOPHANES

ἐλατῆρος, ἵνα τὰς ναῦς ἐλαύνωμεν καλῶς.
ΑΛ. λαβὲ καὶ ταδί νυν.
ΔΗΜΟΣ. καὶ τί τούτοις χρήσομαι
τοῖς ἐντέροις;
ΑΛ. ἐπίτηδες αὔτ᾽ ἔπεμψέ σοι
εἰς τὰς τριήρεις ἐντερόνειαν ἡ θεός· 1185
ἐπισκοπεῖ γὰρ περιφανῶς τὸ ναυτικόν.
ἔχε καὶ πιεῖν κεκραμένον τρία καὶ δύο.
ΔΗΜΟΣ. ὡς ἡδύς, ὦ Ζεῦ, καὶ τὰ τρία φέρων καλῶς.
ΑΛ. ἡ Τριτογενὴς γὰρ αὐτὸν ἐνετριτώνισεν.
ΠΑ. λαβέ νυν πλακοῦντος πίονος παρ᾽ ἐμοῦ τόμον. 1190
ΑΛ. παρ᾽ ἐμοῦ δ᾽ ὅλον γε τὸν πλακοῦντα τουτονί.
ΠΑ. ἀλλ᾽ οὐ λαγῷ᾽ ἕξεις ὁπόθεν δῷς· ἀλλ᾽ ἐγώ.
ΑΛ. οἴμοι· πόθεν λαγῷά μοι γενήσεται;
ὦ θυμέ, νυνὶ βωμολόχον ἔξευρέ τι.
ΠΑ. ὁρᾷς τάδ᾽, ὦ κακόδαιμον;
ΑΛ. ὀλίγον μοι μέλει· 1195
ἐκεινοιὶ γὰρ ὡς ἔμ᾽ ἔρχονται.
ΠΑ. τίνες;
ΑΛ. πρέσβεις ἔχοντες ἀργυρίου βαλλάντια.
ΠΑ. ποῦ ποῦ;
ΑΛ. τί δέ σοι τοῦτ᾽; οὐκ ἐάσεις τοὺς ξένους;
ὦ Δημίδιον, ὁρᾷς τὰ λαγῷ᾽ ἅ σοι φέρω;
ΠΑ. οἴμοι τάλας, ἀδίκως γε τἄμ᾽ ὑφήρπασας. 1200
ΑΛ. νὴ τὸν Ποσειδῶ, καὶ σὺ γὰρ τοὺς ἐκ Πύλου.
ΔΗΜΟΣ. εἴπ᾽, ἀντιβολῶ, πῶς ἐπενόησας ἁρπάσαι;
ΑΛ. τὸ μὲν νόημα τῆς θεοῦ, τὸ δὲ κλέμμ᾽ ἐμόν.
ΔΗ. ἐγὼ δ᾽ ἐκινδύνευσ᾽.

ἔντερα, pig's " belly " to serve as " belly-timber " for the ships.
[b] Three parts of water to two of wine.
[c] A parody of some tragic line. All through this scene there are indications of parody.

THE KNIGHTS, 1182-1204

        With roe of fish, that we may row the better.
S.S.   And now take these.
DEMUS.   Whatever shall I do
        With these insides?
S.S.   The Goddess sends you these
        To serve as planks inside your ships of war.[a]
        Plainly she looks with favour on our fleet.
        Here, drink this also, mingled three and two.[b]
DEMUS. Zeus! but it's sweet and bears the three
        parts well.
S.S.   Tritogeneia 'twas that three'd and two'd it.
PAPH.   Accept from me this slice of luscious cake.
S.S.   And this whole luscious cake accept from me.
PAPH.   Ah, you've no hare to give him; that give I.
S.S.   O me, wherever can I get some hare?
        Now for some mountebank device, my soul.
PAPH.   Yah, see you this, poor Witless?
S.S.   What care I?
        For there they are! Yes, there they are coming!
PAPH.   Who?
S.S.   Envoys with bags of silver, all for me.
PAPH.   Where? Where?
S.S.   What's that to you? Let be the strangers.
        My darling Demus, take the hare I bring.
PAPH.   You thief, you've given what wasn't yours to
        give!
S.S.   Poseidon, yes; you did the same at Pylus.
DEMUS. Ha! Ha! what made you think of filching
        that?
S.S.   The thought's Athene's, but the theft was
        mine.[c]
DE.   'Twas I that ran the risk!

ARISTOPHANES

ΠΑ. ἐγὼ δ' ὤπτησά γε.
ΔΗΜΟΣ. ἄπιθ'. οὐ γὰρ ἀλλὰ τοῦ παραθέντος ἡ χάρις. 1205
ΠΑ. οἴμοι κακοδαίμων, ὑπεραναιδευθήσομαι.
ΑΛ. τί οὐ διακρίνεις, Δῆμ', ὁπότερός ἐστι νῷν
ἀνὴρ ἀμείνων περὶ σὲ καὶ τὴν γαστέρα;
ΔΗΜΟΣ. τῷ δῆτ' ἂν ὑμᾶς χρησάμενος τεκμηρίῳ
δόξαιμι κρίνειν τοῖς θεαταῖσιν σοφῶς; 1210
ΑΛ. ἐγὼ φράσω σοι. τὴν ἐμὴν κίστην ἰὼν
ξύλλαβε σιωπῇ, καὶ βασάνισον ἅττ' ἔνι,
καὶ τὴν Παφλαγόνος· κἀμέλει κρινεῖς καλῶς.
ΔΗΜΟΣ. φέρ' ἴδω, τί οὖν ἔνεστιν;
ΑΛ. οὐχ ὁρᾷς κενὴν
ὦ παππίδιον; ἅπαντα γάρ σοι παρεφόρουν. 1215
ΔΗΜΟΣ. αὕτη μὲν ἡ κίστη τὰ τοῦ δήμου φρονεῖ.
ΑΛ. βάδιζε γοῦν καὶ δεῦρο πρὸς τὴν Παφλαγόνος.
ὁρᾷς τάδ';
ΔΗΜΟΣ. οἴμοι τῶν ἀγαθῶν ὅσων πλέα.
ὅσον τὸ χρῆμα τοῦ πλακοῦντος ἀπέθετο·
ἐμοὶ δ' ἔδωκεν ἀποτεμὼν τυννουτονί. 1220
ΑΛ. τοιαῦτα μέντοι καὶ πρότερόν σ' εἰργάζετο·
σοὶ μὲν προσεδίδου μικρὸν ὧν ἐλάμβανεν,
αὐτὸς δ' ἑαυτῷ παρετίθει τὰ μείζονα.
ΔΗΜΟΣ. ὦ μιαρέ, κλέπτων δή με ταῦτ' ἐξηπάτας;
ἐγὼ δέ τυ ἐστεφάνιξα κἀδωρησάμην. 1225
ΠΑ. ἐγὼ δ' ἔκλεπτον ἐπ' ἀγαθῷ γε τῇ πόλει.
ΔΗΜΟΣ. κατάθου ταχέως τὸν στέφανον, ἵν' ἐγὼ
τουτῳὶ
αὐτὸν περιθῶ.

[a] In the Doric dialect; said to be quoted from some protest of the Helots that their Poseidon had not done his part for them. The Scholiast says that Cleon had been awarded a (golden) crown by the people for his services.

THE KNIGHTS, 1204-1228

PAPH.   'Twas I that cooked it!
DEMUS. Be off: the credit's his that served it up.
PAPH. Unhappy me! I'm over-impudenced.
S.S. Why not give judgement, Demus, of us two
      Which is the better towards your paunch and
      you?
DEMUS. Well, what's the test will make the audience
      think
      I give my judgement cleverly and well?
S.S. I'll tell you what; steal softly up, and search
      My hamper first, then Paphlagon's, and note
      What's in them; then you'll surely judge
      aright.
DEMUS. Well, what does *yours* contain?
S.S.   See here, it's empty.
      Dear Father mine, I served up all for you.
DEMUS. A Demus-loving hamper, sure enough.
S.S. Now come along, and look at Paphlagon's.
      Hey! only see!
DEMUS.   Why here's a store of dainties!
      Why, here's a splendid cheesecake he put by!
      And me he gave the tiniest slice, *so* big.
S.S. And, Demus, that is what he always does;
      Gives you the pettiest morsel of his gains,
      And keeps by far the largest share himself.
DEMUS. O miscreant, did you steal and gull me so,
      The while I crowned thy pow and gied thee
      gifties.[a]
PAPH. And if I stole 'twas for the public good.
DEMUS. Off with your crown this instant, and I'll place it
      On *him* instead.

ARISTOPHANES

ΑΛ. κατάθου ταχέως, μαστιγία.
ΠΑ. οὐ δῆτ', ἐπεί μοι χρησμός ἐστι Πυθικὸς
φράζων ὑφ' οὗ μ' ἐδέησεν ἡττᾶσθαι μόνου. 1230
ΑΛ. τοὐμόν γε φράζων ὄνομα καὶ λίαν σαφῶς.
ΠΑ. καὶ μήν σ' ἐλέγξαι βούλομαι τεκμηρίῳ,
εἴ τι ξυνοίσεις τοῦ θεοῦ τοῖς θεσφάτοις.
καί σου τοσοῦτο πρῶτον ἐκπειράσομαι·
παῖς ὢν ἐφοίτας ἐς τίνος διδασκάλου; 1235
ΑΛ. ἐν ταῖσιν εὔστραις κονδύλοις ἡρμοττόμην.
ΠΑ. πῶς εἶπας; ὥς μου χρησμὸς ἅπτεται φρενῶν.
εἶεν.
ἐν παιδοτρίβου δὲ τίνα πάλην ἐμάνθανες;
ΑΛ. κλέπτων ἐπιορκεῖν καὶ βλέπειν ἐναντίον.
ΠΑ. ὦ Φοῖβ' Ἄπολλον Λύκιε, τί ποτέ μ' ἐργάσει; 1240
τέχνην δὲ τίνα ποτ' εἶχες ἐξανδρούμενος;
ΑΛ. ἡλλαντοπώλουν—
ΠΑ. καὶ τί;
ΑΛ. καὶ βινεσκόμην.
ΠΑ. οἴμοι κακοδαίμων· οὐκέτ' οὐδέν εἰμ' ἐγώ.
λεπτή τις ἐλπίς ἐστ' ἐφ' ἧς ὀχούμεθα.
καί μοι τοσοῦτον εἰπέ· πότερον ἐν ἀγορᾷ 1245
ἠλλαντοπώλεις ἐτεὸν ἢ 'πὶ ταῖς πύλαις;
ΑΛ. ἐπὶ ταῖς πύλαισιν, οὗ τὸ τάριχος ὤνιον.
ΠΑ. οἴμοι πέπρακται τοῦ θεοῦ τὸ θέσφατον.
κυλίνδετ' εἴσω τόνδε τὸν δυσδαίμονα.
ὦ στέφανε, χαίρων ἄπιθι, καί σ' ἄκων ἐγὼ 1250
λείπω· σὲ δ' ἄλλος τις λαβὼν κεκτήσεται,
κλέπτης μὲν οὐκ ἂν μᾶλλον, εὐτυχὴς δ' ἴσως.

---

[a] From the *Telephus* of Euripides. Λύκιος is an epithet of Apollo.
[b] Eurip. *Bellerophon*, fr. 302 Nauck; but here κυλίνδετε is substituted for κομίζετε.
[c] Parodied from the farewell speech of the dying Alcestis

THE KNIGHTS, 1228-1252

S.S. Off with it, filth, this instant.
PAPH. Not so ; a Pythian oracle I've got
Describing him who only can defeat me.
S.S. Describing ME, without the slightest doubt.
PAPH. Well then I'll test and prove you, to discern
How far you tally with the God's predictions.
And first I ask this question,—when a boy
Tell me the teacher to whose school you went.
S.S. Hard knuckles drilled me in the singeing pits.
PAPH. How say you ? Heavens, the oracle's word
strikes home !
Well !
What at the trainer's did you learn to do ?
S.S. Forswear my thefts, and stare the accuser
down.
PAPH. Phoebus Apollo! Lycius ! what means this?[a]
Tell me what trade you practised when a man.
S.S. I sold sausages—
PAPH. Well ?
S.S. And sold myself.
PAPH. Unhappy me ! I'm done for. There remains
One slender hope whereon to anchor yet.
Where did you sell your sausages ? Did you
stand
Within the Agora, or beside the Gates ?
S.S. Beside the Gates, where the salt-fish is sold.
PAPH. O me, the oracle has all come true !
Roll in, roll in, this most unhappy man.[b]
O crown, farewell. Unwillingly I leave thee.
Begone, but thee some other will obtain,
A luckier man perchance, but not more—
thievish.[c]

to her marriage-bed, θνήσκω· σὲ δ' ἄλλη τις γυνὴ κεκτήσεται, |
σώφρων μὲν οὐκ ἂν μᾶλλον, εὐτυχὴς δ' ἴσως, Eur. *Alc.* 181.

243

ARISTOPHANES

ΑΛ. Ἑλλάνιε Ζεῦ, σὸν τὸ νικητήριον.
ΔΗ. ὢ χαῖρε καλλίνικε, καὶ μέμνησ' ὅτι
ἀνὴρ γεγένησαι δι' ἐμέ· καί σ' αἰτῶ βραχύ, 125
ὅπως ἔσομαί σοι Φανὸς ὑπογραφεὺς δικῶν.
ΔΗΜΟΣ. ἐμοὶ δέ γ' ὅ τι σοι τοὔνομ' εἴπ'.
ΑΛ. Ἀγοράκριτος·
ἐν τἀγορᾷ γὰρ κρινόμενος ἐβοσκόμην.
ΔΗΜΟΣ. Ἀγορακρίτῳ τοίνυν ἐμαυτὸν ἐπιτρέπω,
καὶ τὸν Παφλαγόνα παραδίδωμι τουτονί. 126
ΑΛ. καὶ μὴν ἐγώ σ', ὦ Δῆμε, θεραπεύσω καλῶς,
ὥσθ' ὁμολογεῖν σε μηδέν' ἀνθρώπων ἐμοῦ
ἰδεῖν ἀμείνω τῇ Κεχηναίων πόλει.

ΧΟ. τί κάλλιον ἀρχομένοισιν
ἢ καταπαυομένοισιν 126
ἢ θοᾶν ἵππων ἐλατῆρας ἀείδειν
μηδὲν ἐς Λυσίστρατον,
μηδὲ Θούμαντιν τὸν ἀνέστιον αὖ λυ-
πεῖν ἑκούσῃ καρδίᾳ;
καὶ γὰρ οὗτος, ὦ φίλ' Ἄπολλον, ἀεὶ 127
πεινῇ, θαλεροῖς δακρύοισιν
σᾶς ἁπτόμενος φαρέτρας Πυθῶνι δίᾳ
μὴ κακῶς πένεσθαι.

λοιδορῆσαι τοὺς πονηροὺς οὐδέν ἐστ' ἐπίφθονον,
ἀλλὰ τιμὴ τοῖσι χρηστοῖς, ὅστις εὖ λογίζεται. 127

[a] This was an Aeginetan title of Zeus, but it was used as a symbol of Greek unity. Cleon's fall means the triumph of Hellenism.
[b] A hanger-on of Cleon's (cf. W. 1220) who helped him in bringing actions.
[c] A surprise for Ἀθηναίων.
[d] A vicious wretch : A. 855-59, W. 787, 1300-17.

THE KNIGHTS, 1253–1275

S.S.   Hellanian [a] Zeus, the victory-prize is thine!
DE.   Hail, mighty Victor, nor forget 'twas I
       Made you a Man; and grant this small request,
       Make *me* your Phanus,[b] signer of your writs.
DEMUS. Your name, what is it?
S.S.   Agoracritus.
       An Agora-life I lived, and thrived by wrangling.
DEMUS. To Agoracritus I commit myself,
       And to *his* charge consign this Paphlagon.
S.S.   And, Demus, I will always tend you well,
       And you shall own there never lived a man
       Kinder than I to the Evergaping [c] City.

CHOR.   O what is a nobler thing,
             Beginning or ending a song,
            For horsemen who joy in driving
            Their fleet-foot coursers along,
Than—Never to launch a lampoon
                    at Lysistratus,[d] scurvy buffoon;
Or at heartless Thumantis [e] to gird,
                  poor starveling, in lightness of heart;
Who is weeping hot tears at thy shrine,
                Apollo, in Pytho [f] divine,
And, clutching thy quiver, implores
                  to be healed of his poverty's smart!

For lampooning worthless wretches,
                 none should bear the bard a grudge;
'Tis a sound and wholesome practice,
                 if the case you rightly judge.

[e] Noted for his leanness.   [f] Delphi.

ARISTOPHANES

εἰ μὲν οὖν ἄνθρωπος, ὃν δεῖ πόλλ' ἀκοῦσαι καὶ κακά,
αὐτὸς ἦν ἔνδηλος, οὐκ ἂν ἀνδρὸς ἐμνήσθην φίλου.
νῦν δ' Ἀρίγνωτον γὰρ οὐδεὶς ὅστις οὐκ ἐπίσταται,
ὅστις ἢ τὸ λευκὸν οἶδεν ἢ τὸν ὄρθιον νόμον.
ἔστιν οὖν ἀδελφὸς αὐτῷ τοὺς τρόπους οὐ συγγενής, 1280
Ἀριφράδης πονηρός. ἀλλὰ τοῦτο μὲν καὶ βούλεται·
ἐστὶ δ' οὐ μόνον πονηρός, οὐ γὰρ οὐδ' ἂν ᾐσθόμην,
οὐδὲ παμπόνηρος, ἀλλὰ καὶ προσεξεύρηκέ τι.
τὴν γὰρ αὑτοῦ γλῶτταν αἰσχραῖς ἡδοναῖς λυμαίνεται,
ἐν κασαυρείοισι λείχων τὴν ἀπόπτυστον δρόσον, 1285
καὶ μολύνων τὴν ὑπήνην, καὶ κυκῶν τὰς ἐσχάρας,
καὶ Πολυμνήστεια ποιῶν, καὶ ξυνὼν Οἰωνίχῳ.
ὅστις οὖν τοιοῦτον ἄνδρα μὴ σφόδρα βδελύττεται,
οὔ ποτ' ἐκ ταὐτοῦ μεθ' ἡμῶν πίεται ποτηρίου.

ἦ πολλάκις ἐννυχίαισι 1290
φροντίσι συγγεγένημαι,
καὶ διεζήτηχ' ὁπόθεν ποτὲ φαύλως
ἐσθίει Κλεώνυμος.

[a] Arignotus the harper, Ariphrades the vile creature here described, and a third, a famous actor, were sons of Automenes. See *W.* 1275-83, *P.* 883.
[b] A surprise for the ending of the proverb ὅστις οἶδε τὸ λευκὸν ἢ τὸ μέλαν, " who knows white from black."
[c] Polymnestus and Oeonichus were probably well-known wastrels ; but τὰ Πολυμνήστεια usually means the fine songs or tunes of Polymnestus, a musician.
[d] See 958 and Index.

THE KNIGHTS, 1276–1293

Now if he whose evil-doings
     I must needs expose to blame
Were himself a noted person,
     never had I named the name
Of a man I love and honour.
    Is there one who knows not well
Arignotus,[a] prince of harpers ?
     None, believe me, who can tell
How the whitest colour differs
     from the stirring tune he plays.[b]
Arignotus has a brother
     (not a brother in his ways)
Named Ariphrades, a rascal—
     nay, but that's the fellow's whim—
Not an ordinary rascal,
     or I had not noticed him.
Not a thorough rascal merely ;
     he's invented something more,
Novel forms of self-pollution,
     bestial tricks unknown before.
Yea, to nameless filth and horrors
     does the loathsome wretch descend,
Works the work of Polymnestus,[c]
     calls Oeonichus [c] his friend.
Whoso loathes not such a monster
     never shall be a friend of mine,
Never from the selfsame goblet
     quaff, with us, the rosy wine.
And oft in the watches of night
My spirit within me is thrilled,
To think of Cleonymus [d] eating
As though he would never be filled.
O whence could the fellow acquire
     that appetite deadly and dire ?

ARISTOPHANES

φασὶ μὲν γὰρ αὐτὸν ἐρεπτόμενον τὰ
τῶν ἐχόντων ἀνέρων   12
οὐκ ἂν ἐξελθεῖν ἀπὸ τῆς σιπύης,
τοὺς δ' ἀντιβολεῖν ἂν ὁμοίως·
ἴθ', ὦ ἄνα, πρὸς γονάτων, ἔξελθε καὶ σύγ-
γνωθι τῇ τραπέζῃ.

φασὶν ἀλλήλαις ξυνελθεῖν τὰς τριήρεις εἰς λόγον,   13
καὶ μίαν λέξαι τιν' αὐτῶν, ἥτις ἦν γεραιτέρα·
οὐδὲ πυνθάνεσθε ταῦτ', ὦ παρθένοι, τἀν τῇ πόλει;
φασὶν αἰτεῖσθαί τιν' ἡμῶν ἑκατὸν ἐς Καρχηδόνα
ἄνδρα μοχθηρόν, πολίτην ὀξίνην, Ὑπέρβολον·
ταῖς δὲ δόξαι δεινὸν εἶναι τοῦτο κοὐκ ἀνασχετόν,   13
καί τιν' εἰπεῖν, ἥτις ἀνδρῶν ἆσσον οὐκ ἐληλύθει·
ἀποτρόπαι', οὐ δῆτ' ἐμοῦ γ' ἄρξει ποτ', ἀλλ' ἐάν με χρῇ,
ὑπὸ τερηδόνων σαπεῖσ' ἐνταῦθα καταγηράσομαι.
οὐδὲ Ναυφάντης γε τῆς Ναύσωνος, οὐ δῆτ', ὦ θεοί,
εἴπερ ἐκ πεύκης γε κἀγὼ καὶ ξύλων ἐπηγνύμην.   13
ἢν δ' ἀρέσκῃ ταῦτ' Ἀθηναίοις, καθῆσθαί μοι δοκεῖ
εἰς τὸ Θησεῖον πλεούσας ἢ 'πὶ τῶν σεμνῶν θεῶν.

---

^a Don't eat the table too.
^b The names of Athenian ships were feminine: see *Corpus Inscr. Att.* ii. 789 ff.
^c From Euripides, *Alcmaeon*, fr. 66 Nauck.
^d Hyperbolus is called a μοχθηρὸς ἄνθρωπος by Thucydides, viii. 73. 3, and he became with Cleon a by-word. We do not know whether an expedition to Carthage was proposed by him.
^e Ἀποτρόπαιος, a title of Apollo, the "Averter," used in appeals.
^f Nauphante is the name of the trireme, and probably Nauson was meant for the builder.
^g To take sanctuary, as runaway slaves did in the Theseium. The Σεμναί were the Ἐρινύες or Furies. Both these shrines were in the city.

THE KNIGHTS, 1294-1312

They say when he grazes with those
    whose table with plenty is stored
That they never can get him away
    from the trencher, though humbly they pray
Have mercy, O King, and depart!
    O spare, we beseech thee, the board! ^a

Recently, 'tis said, our galleys
    met their prospects to discuss,
And an old experienced trireme
    introduced the subject thus;
" Have ye heard the news, my sisters? ^b
    'tis the talk in every street,^c
That Hyperbolus the worthless,
    vapid townsman, would a fleet
Of a hundred lovely galleys
    lead to Carthage far away." ^d
Over every prow there mantled
    deep resentment and dismay.
Up and spoke a little galley,
    yet from man's pollution free,
" Save us! ^e such a scurvy fellow
    never shall be lord of me.
Here I'd liefer rot and moulder,
    and be eaten up of worms."
" Nor Nauphante, Nauson's daughter,^f
    shall he board on any terms;
I, like you, can feel the insult;
    I'm of pine and timber knit.
Wherefore, if the measure passes,
    I propose we sail and sit
Suppliant at the shrine of Theseus,
    or the Dread Avenging Powers.^g

ARISTOPHANES

οὐ γὰρ ἡμῶν γε στρατηγῶν ἐγχανεῖται τῇ πόλει·
ἀλλὰ πλείτω χωρὶς αὐτὸς ἐς κόρακας, εἰ βούλεται
τὰς σκάφας, ἐν αἷς ἐπώλει τοὺς λύχνους, καθελκύσας. 135

ΑΛ. εὐφημεῖν χρὴ καὶ στόμα κλείειν, καὶ μαρτυριῶν
ἀπέχεσθαι,
καὶ τὰ δικαστήρια συγκλείειν, οἷς ἡ πόλις ἥδε
γέγηθεν,
ἐπὶ καιναῖσιν δ᾽ εὐτυχίαισιν παιωνίζειν τὸ θέατρον.

ΧΟ. ὦ ταῖς ἱεραῖς φέγγος Ἀθήναις καὶ ταῖς νήσοις
ἐπίκουρε,
τίν᾽ ἔχων φήμην ἀγαθὴν ἥκεις, ἐφ᾽ ὅτῳ κνισῶμεν
ἀγυιάς; 135

ΑΛ. τὸν Δῆμον ἀφεψήσας ὑμῖν καλὸν ἐξ αἰσχροῦ
πεποίηκα.

ΧΟ. καὶ ποῦ 'στιν νῦν, ὦ θαυμαστὰς ἐξευρίσκων
ἐπινοίας;

ΑΛ. ἐν ταῖσιν ἰοστεφάνοις οἰκεῖ ταῖς ἀρχαίαισιν
Ἀθήναις.

ΧΟ. πῶς ἂν ἴδοιμεν; ποίαν τιν᾽ ἔχει σκευήν; χοῖος
γεγένηται;

ΑΛ. οἷός περ Ἀριστείδῃ πρότερον καὶ Μιλτιάδῃ
ξυνεσίτει. 135
ὄψεσθε δέ· καὶ γὰρ ἀνοιγνυμένων ψόφος ἤδη τῶν
προπυλαίων.
ἀλλ᾽ ὀλολύξατε φαινομέναισιν ταῖς ἀρχαίαισιν
Ἀθήναις
καὶ θαυμασταῖς καὶ πολυύμνοις, ἵν᾽ ὁ κλεινὸς Δῆμος
ἐνοικεῖ.

---

[a] Suggested by the story of Medea. She boiled an old ram and made him young. Apollodorus, i. 9. 27.

250

THE KNIGHTS, 1313-1328

He shall ne'er, as our commander,
  fool it o'er this land of ours.
If he wants a little voyage,
  let him launch his sale-trays, those
Whereupon he sold his lanterns,
  steering to the kites and crows."

S.S. O let not a word of ill omen be heard ;
  away with all proof and citation,
And close for to-day the Law Courts, though they
  are the joy and delight of our nation.
At the news which I bring let the theatre ring
  with Paeans of loud acclamation.
CHOR. O Light of the City, O Helper and friend
  of the islands we guard with our fleets,
What news have you got ? O tell me for what
  shall the sacrifice blaze in our streets ?
S.S. Old Demus I've stewed till his youth is renewed,
  and his aspect most charming and nice is.[a]
CHOR. O where have you left him, and where is he now,
  you inventor of wondrous devices ?
S.S. He dwells in the City of ancient renown,
  which the violet chaplet is wearing.
CHOR. O would I could see him ! O what is his garb,
  and what his demeanour and bearing ?
S.S. As when, for his mess-mates, Miltiades bold
  and just Aristeides he chose.
But now ye shall see him, for, listen, the bars
  of the great Propylaea unclose.
Shout, shout to behold, as the portals unfold,
  fair Athens in splendour excelling,
The wondrous, the ancient, the famous in song,
  where the noble Demus is dwelling !

ARISTOPHANES

ΧΟ. ὦ ταὶ λιπαραὶ καὶ ἰοστέφανοι καὶ ἀριζήλωτοι
 Ἀθῆναι,
 δείξατε τὸν τῆς Ἑλλάδος ἡμῖν καὶ τῆς γῆς τῆσδε
 μόναρχον.
ΑΛ. ὅδ᾽ ἐκεῖνος ὁρᾶν τεττιγοφορῶν, ἀρχαίῳ σχήματι
 λαμπρός,
 οὐ χοιρινῶν ὄζων, ἀλλὰ σπονδῶν, σμύρνῃ κατά-
 λειπτος.
ΧΟ. χαῖρ᾽, ὦ βασιλεῦ τῶν Ἑλλήνων· καί σοι ξυγ-
 χαίρομεν ἡμεῖς.
 τῆς γὰρ πόλεως ἄξια πράττεις καὶ τοῦ Μαραθῶνι
 τροπαίου.
ΔΗΜΟΣ. ὦ φίλτατ᾽ ἀνδρῶν, ἐλθὲ δεῦρ᾽, Ἀγοράκριτε.
 ὅσα με δέδρακας ἀγάθ᾽ ἀφεψήσας.
ΑΛ. ἐγώ;
 ἀλλ᾽, ὦ μέλ᾽, οὐκ οἶσθ᾽ οἷος ἦσθ᾽ αὐτὸς πάρος,
 οὐδ᾽ οἷ᾽ ἔδρας· ἐμὲ γὰρ νομίζοις ἂν θεόν.
ΔΗΜΟΣ. τί δ᾽ ἔδρων πρὸ τοῦ, κάτειπε, καὶ ποῖός τις ἦ;
ΑΛ. πρῶτον μέν, ὁπότ᾽ εἴποι τις ἐν τἠκκλησίᾳ,
 ὦ Δῆμ᾽, ἐραστής τ᾽ εἰμὶ σὸς φιλῶ τέ σε
 καὶ κήδομαί σου καὶ προβουλεύω μόνος,
 τούτοις ὁπότε χρήσαιτό τις προοιμίοις,
 ἀνωρτάλιζες κἀκερουτίας.
ΔΗΜΟΣ. ἐγώ;
ΑΛ. εἶτ᾽ ἐξαπατήσας σ᾽ ἀντὶ τούτων ᾤχετο.
ΔΗΜΟΣ. τί φῄς;
 ταυτί μ᾽ ἔδρων, ἐγὼ δὲ τοῦτ᾽ οὐκ ᾐσθόμην;
ΑΛ. τὰ δ᾽ ὦτά γ᾽ ἄν σου νὴ Δί᾽ ἐξεπετάννυτο
 ὥσπερ σκιάδειον καὶ πάλιν ξυνήγετο.

THE KNIGHTS, 1329-1348

CHOR. O shining old town of the violet crown,
      O Athens the envied, display [a]
  The Sovereign of Hellas himself to our gaze,
      the monarch of all we survey.
S.S. See, see where he stands, no vote in his hands,
      but the golden cicala [b] his hair in,
  All splendid and fragrant with peace and with myrrh,
      and the grand old apparel he's wearing!
CHOR. Hail, Sovereign of Hellas! with thee we rejoice,
      right glad to behold thee again
  Enjoying a fate that is worthy the State
      and the trophy on Marathon's plain.[c]
DEMUS. O Agoracritus, my dearest friend,
  What good your stewing did me!
S.S.   Say you so?
  Why, if you knew the sort of man you were,
  And what you did, you'd reckon me a god.
DEMUS. What was I like? What did I do? Inform me.
S.S. First, if a speaker in the Assembly said
  O Demus, I'm your lover, I alone
  Care for you, scheme for you, tend and love you well,
  I say if anyone began like that
  You clapped your wings and tossed your horns.
DEMUS.   What, I?
S.S. Then in return he cheated you and left.
DEMUS. O did they treat me so, and I not know it!
S.S. Because, by Zeus, your ears would open wide
  And close again, like any parasol.

 [a] The opening words are quoted from Pindar, who first applied them to Athens in a dithyramb, Frag. 76 (Sandys).
 [b] Worn in old days by Athenians in their hair: Thuc. i. 6. 3.
 [c] A marble monument near the great barrow on the site of the battle: *W*. 711.

ARISTOPHANES

ΔΗΜΟΣ. οὕτως ἀνόητος ἐγεγενήμην καὶ γέρων;
ΑΛ. καὶ νὴ Δί' εἴ γε δύο λεγοίτην ῥήτορε, 1350
ὁ μὲν ποιεῖσθαι ναῦς λέγων, ὁ δ' ἕτερος αὖ
καταμισθοφορῆσαι τοῦθ', ὁ τὸν μισθὸν λέγων
τὸν τὰς τριήρεις παραδραμὼν ἂν ᾤχετο.
οὗτος, τί κύπτεις; οὐχὶ κατὰ χώραν μενεῖς;
ΔΗΜΟΣ. αἰσχύνομαί τοι ταῖς πρότερον ἁμαρτίαις. 1355
ΑΛ. ἀλλ' οὐ σὺ τούτων αἴτιος, μὴ φροντίσῃς,
ἀλλ' οἵ σε ταῦτ' ἐξηπάτων. νῦν δ' αὖ φράσον·
ἐάν τις εἴπῃ βωμολόχος ξυνήγορος,
οὐκ ἔστιν ὑμῖν τοῖς δικασταῖς ἄλφιτα,
εἰ μὴ καταγνώσεσθε ταύτην τὴν δίκην, 1360
τοῦτον τί δράσεις, εἰπέ, τὸν ξυνήγορον;
ΔΗΜΟΣ. ἄρας μετέωρον ἐς τὸ βάραθρον ἐμβαλῶ,
ἐκ τοῦ λάρυγγος ἐκκρεμάσας Ὑπέρβολον.
ΑΛ. τουτὶ μὲν ὀρθῶς καὶ φρονίμως ἤδη λέγεις·
τὰ δ' ἄλλα, φέρ' ἴδω, πῶς πολιτεύσει φράσον. 1365
ΔΗΜΟΣ. πρῶτον μὲν ὁπόσοι ναῦς ἐλαύνουσιν μακράς,
καταγομένοις τὸν μισθὸν ἀποδώσω 'ντελῆ.
ΑΛ. πολλοῖς γ' ὑπολίσποις πυγιδίοισιν ἐχαρίσω.
ΔΗΜΟΣ. ἔπειθ' ὁπλίτης ἐντεθεὶς ἐν καταλόγῳ
οὐδεὶς κατὰ σπουδὰς μετεγγραφήσεται, 1370
ἀλλ' ὥσπερ ἦν τὸ πρῶτον ἐγγεγράψεται.
ΑΛ. τοῦτ' ἔδακε τὸν πόρπακα τὸν Κλεωνύμου.
ΔΗΜΟΣ. οὐδ' ἀγοράσει γ' ἀγένειος οὐδεὶς ἐν ἀγορᾷ.
ΑΛ. ποῦ δῆτα Κλεισθένης ἀγοράσει καὶ Στράτων;
ΔΗΜΟΣ. τὰ μειράκια ταυτὶ λέγω, τἀν τῷ μύρῳ, 1375

---

[a] Lysias, 27. 1, says that similar threats were really made: εἰ μὴ καταψηφιεῖσθε ὧν κελεύουσιν ἐπιλείψει ὑμᾶς ἡ μισθοφορά.
"Barley" means "daily bread."
[b] Below a precipice of the rock of the Pnyx, in the corner between Town Wall and Long Wall, outside the city.

THE KNIGHTS, 1349–1375

DEMUS. Had I so old and witless grown as that?
s.s. And if, by Zeus, two orators proposed,
One to build ships of war, one to increase
Official salaries, the salary man
Would beat the ships-of-war man in a canter.
Hallo! why hang your head and shift your ground?
DEMUS. I am ashamed of all my former faults.
s.s. You're not to blame; pray don't imagine that.
'Twas they who tricked you so. But answer this;
If any scurvy advocate should say,
*Now please remember, justices, ye'll have
No barley, if the prisoner gets off free,*[a]
How would you treat that scurvy advocate?
DEMUS. I'd tie Hyperbolus about his neck,
And hurl him down into the Deadman's Pit.[b]
s.s. Why now you are speaking sensibly and well.
How else, in public business, will you act?
DEMUS. First, when the sailors from my ships of war
Come home, I'll pay them all arrears in full.
s.s. For that, full many a well-worn rump will bless you.
DEMUS. Next, when a hoplite's placed in any list,[c]
There shall he stay, and not for love or money
Shall he be shifted to some other list.
s.s. That bit the shield-strap of Cleonymus.[d]
DEMUS. No beardless boy shall haunt the agora now.
s.s. That's rough on Straton and on Cleisthenes.[e]
DEMUS. I mean those striplings in the perfume-mart,

[c] *i.e.* for service on some expedition; but influence might be used to get a name removed, P. 1180.
[d] Cleonymus had not yet thrown away his shield at Delium, but he must have been known as a coward.
[e] Two effeminates: A. 122.

ARISTOPHANES

ἃ στωμυλεῖται τοιαδὶ καθήμενα·
σοφός γ' ὁ Φαίαξ, δεξιῶς τ' οὐκ ἀπέθανε.
συνερκτικὸς γάρ ἐστι καὶ περαντικός,
καὶ γνωμοτυπικὸς καὶ σαφὴς καὶ κρουστικὸς
καταληπτικός τ' ἄριστα τοῦ θορυβητικοῦ. 1380
ΑΛ. οὔκουν καταδακτυλικὸς σὺ τοῦ λαλητικοῦ;
ΔΗΜΟΣ. μὰ Δί', ἀλλ' ἀναγκάσω κυνηγετεῖν ἐγὼ
τούτους ἅπαντας, παυσαμένους ψηφισμάτων.
ΑΛ. ἔχε νυν ἐπὶ τούτοις τουτονὶ τὸν ὀκλαδίαν,
καὶ παῖδ' ἐνόρχην, ὃς περιοίσει τόνδε σοι· 1385
κἄν που δοκῇ σοι, τοῦτον ὀκλαδίαν ποίει.
ΔΗΜΟΣ. μακάριος ἐς τἀρχαῖα δὴ καθίσταμαι.
ΑΛ. φήσεις γ', ἐπειδὰν τὰς τριακοντούτιδας
σπονδὰς παραδῶ σοι. δεῦρ' ἴθ' αἱ Σπονδαὶ
ταχύ.
ΔΗΜΟΣ. ὦ Ζεῦ πολυτίμηθ', ὡς καλαί· πρὸς τῶν
θεῶν, 1390
ἔξεστιν αὐτῶν κατατριακοντουτίσαι;
πῶς ἔλαβες αὐτὰς ἐτεόν;
ΑΛ. οὐ γὰρ ὁ Παφλαγὼν
ἀπέκρυπτε ταύτας ἔνδον, ἵνα σὺ μὴ λάβοις;
νῦν οὖν ἐγώ σοι παραδίδωμ' εἰς τοὺς ἀγροὺς
αὐτὰς ἰέναι λαβόντα.
ΔΗΜΟΣ. τὸν δὲ Παφλαγόνα, 1395
ὃς ταῦτ' ἔδρασεν, εἰφ' ὅ τι ποιήσεις κακόν.
ΑΛ. οὐδὲν μέγ' ἀλλ' ἢ τὴν ἐμὴν ἕξει τέχνην·
ἐπὶ ταῖς πύλαις ἀλλαντοπωλήσει μόνος,
τὰ κύνεια μιγνὺς τοῖς ὀνείοις πράγμασιν,

---

[a] The passage ridicules an affectation of using adjectives in -ικός. For Phaeax see Thuc. v. 4, and Plut. *Nic.* 11, *Alc.* 13. He was of some importance in politics. The Scholiast says he had been tried for his life and acquitted.

THE KNIGHTS, 1376–1399

Who sit them down and chatter stuff like this,
Sharp fellow, Phaeax ; wonderful defence ;
Coercive speaker ; most conclusive speaker ;
Effective ; argumentative ; incisive ;
Superlative against the combative.[a]

S.S. You're quite derisive of these talkatives.
DEMUS. I'll make them all give up their politics,
And go a-hunting with their hounds instead.
S.S. Then on these terms accept this folding-stool[b];
And here's a boy to carry it behind you.
No eunuch he !
DEMUS. O, I shall be once more
A happy Demus as in days gone by.
S.S. I think you'll think so when you get the sweet
Thirty-year treaties. Treaties dear, come
here.
DEMUS. Worshipful Zeus ! how beautiful they are.
Wouldn't I like to solemnize them all.
Whence got you these ?
S.S. Why, had not Paphlagon
Bottled them up that you might never see
them ?
Now then I freely give you them to take
Back to your farms, with you.
DEMUS. But Paphlagon
Who wrought all this, how will you punish
him ?
S.S. Not much : this only : he shall ply my trade,
Sole sausage-seller at the City gates.
There let him dogs'-meat mix with asses' flesh,

[b] It was the fashion in olden days for rich citizens to have these carried for them by attendants when they went to assemblies or the like.

ARISTOPHANES

μεθύων τε ταῖς πόρναισι λοιδορήσεται, 1400
κἀκ τῶν βαλανείων πίεται τὸ λούτριον.
ΔΗΜΟΣ. εὖ γ' ἐπενόησας οὗπέρ ἐστιν ἄξιος,
πόρναισι καὶ βαλανεῦσι διακεκραγέναι,
καί σ' ἀντὶ τούτων ἐς τὸ πρυτανεῖον καλῶ
ἐς τὴν ἕδραν θ', ἵν' ἐκεῖνος ἦν ὁ φαρμακός. 1405
ἕπου δὲ ταυτηνὶ λαβὼν τὴν βατραχίδα·
κἀκεῖνον ἐκφερέτω τις ὡς ἐπὶ τὴν τέχνην,
ἵν' ἴδωσιν αὐτόν, οἷς ἐλωβᾶθ', οἱ ξένοι.

THE KNIGHTS, 1400–1408

    There let him, tipsy, with the harlots wrangle,
    And drink the filthy scouring of the bath.
DEMUS. A happy thought ; and very fit he is
    To brawl with harlots and with bathmen there.
    But you I ask to dinner in the Hall,
    To take the place that scullion held before.
    Put on this frog-green robe and follow me.
    Whilst him they carry out to ply his trade,
    That so the strangers, whom he wronged, may see him.[a]

[a] Strangers were not present at the Lenaean festival.

THE CLOUDS

INTRODUCTION

The *Clouds* was produced at the Great Dionysia 423 B.C. The first prize was awarded to Cratinus with the *Wine-flagon*, the second to Ameipsias with the *Connos*, and Aristophanes was third and last.

The present is a revised edition published, but not exhibited, some years later, for in the New Parabasis the poet refers to the *Maricas* of Eupolis which was produced 421 B.C. In one of the Greek arguments prefixed to the play, it is stated that this revision (διόρθωσις) extends generally " through almost every part," but that it is " entire " (ὁλοσχερής) (1) in the Parabasis, (2) " where the Just Logic speaks to the Unjust," and (3) " where the school of Socrates is set on fire."

As to the Parabasis (518–562) where Aristophanes, speaking in the first person, expresses his indignation at his defeat, there can be no doubt. As regards (2) Mr. Rogers justly holds that this does not refer to the *whole* dispute between the Λόγοι (for this " is the very core of the play "), but to the magnificent anapaests in which the Just Logic describes " the ancient education," 961 *seq*. As regards (3) there can be little certainty.

The aim of the Comedy is to attack the Sophistical system of Education, which like " some subtle and insidious disease was sapping the very life of old

THE CLOUDS

Athenian character; which for a money payment taught men to argue not for Truth but for Victory; to assail all traditional beliefs; and to pride themselves on their ability to take up a bad cause and make it triumph over the right."[a]
In taking Socrates as "the representative and embodiment in a concrete form" of the Sophistic school Aristophanes is notoriously unjust. No one had less regard for speculation about τὰ μετέωρα and τὰ ὑπὸ τῆς γῆς than Socrates; to take money for teaching was in his eyes a crime; and the whole of his dialectic aimed not at "making the worse appear the better reason," but at the discovery of ethical truth. None the less, as Grote remarks, " if an Athenian had been asked 'Who are the principal Sophists in your city?' he would have named Socrates among the first," while he seemed to court caricature as he ambled round the agora and gymnasia, "bald-headed, with the countenance of a satyr and a protuberant belly, habitually barefoot, clad only in a shabby gaberdine (τρίβων) without even the usual undergarment (χιτών)."[b]

That the Athenians took the attack on him seriously, or that it had the least effect on his condemnation in 399, is wholly questionable. Plutarch (*De educat. puerorum*, c. 14, p. 10 c) relates that, when asked if he was not " indignant " at it, he replied, " No, not I; I am chaffed in the theatre as in a wine-party "; and Plato in the *Symposium* (221 b) not only brings in both Socrates and Aristophanes as guests who meet without offence, but makes Alcibiades quote the poet's own words (l. 362) as an

[a] Rogers, Introduction, p. xviii.
[b] *Ibid.* p. xxi.

ARISTOPHANES

admirable description of Socrates. Nor is it probable that, if he had held Aristophanes partly guilty for his master's execution, he would when dying have kept a copy of his comedies in his bed, or published his inimitable epigram:

αἱ Χάριτες, τέμενός τι λαβεῖν ὅπερ οὐχὶ πεσεῖται
ζητοῦσαι, ψυχὴν εὗρον Ἀριστοφανοῦς.[a]

In fact, when Socrates at the beginning of the *Apology* is made not only to quote the *Clouds* but to put phrases from it into an imaginary legal indictment, of which he says he is in more terror than of his actual accusers, it may well be that Plato— "putting into his mouth reflexions upon the *Clouds* which he, we may be sure, would never have uttered,"[b]—indicates with fine irony that it was a poor charge which was less weighty than the jibe of a comedian. But whether this be so or not, the fact of Plato introducing the quotations as well known and familiar proves—as do similar quotations in the *Oeconomicus* and *Symposium* of Xenophon—that when he wrote the *Clouds* had already that established fame which it has ever since maintained.

[a] The Graces sought a heavenly shrine, which ne'er
   Shall come to nought,
And in thy soul, Immortal Poet, found
   The shrine they sought.
                                                ROGERS.

[b] Rogers, Introd. p. xxiv.

ΤΑ ΤΟΥ ΔΡΑΜΑΤΟΣ ΠΡΟΣΩΠΑ

ΣΤΡΕΨΙΑΔΗΣ
ΦΕΙΔΙΠΠΙΔΗΣ
ΘΕΡΑΠΩΝ ΣΤΡΕΨΙΑΔΟΥ
ΜΑΘΗΤΑΙ ΣΩΚΡΑΤΟΥΣ
ΣΩΚΡΑΤΗΣ
ΧΟΡΟΣ ΝΕΦΕΛΩΝ
ΔΙΚΑΙΟΣ ΛΟΓΟΣ
ΑΔΙΚΟΣ ΛΟΓΟΣ
ΠΑΣΙΑΣ
ΑΜΥΝΙΑΣ
ΜΑΡΤΥΣ
ΧΑΙΡΕΦΩΝ

ΝΕΦΕΛΑΙ

ΣΤΡΕΨΙΑΔΗΣ. Ἰοὺ ἰού·
ὦ Ζεῦ βασιλεῦ, τὸ χρῆμα τῶν νυκτῶν ὅσον.
ἀπέραντον. οὐδέποθ' ἡμέρα γενήσεται;
καὶ μὴν πάλαι γ' ἀλεκτρυόνος ἤκουσ' ἐγώ·
οἱ δ' οἰκέται ῥέγκουσιν· ἀλλ' οὐκ ἂν πρὸ τοῦ. 5
ἀπόλοιο δῆτ', ὦ πόλεμε, πολλῶν οὕνεκα,
ὅτ' οὐδὲ κολάσ' ἔξεστί μοι τοὺς οἰκέτας.
ἀλλ' οὐδ' ὁ χρηστὸς οὑτοσὶ νεανίας
ἐγείρεται τῆς νυκτός, ἀλλὰ πέρδεται
ἐν πέντε σισύραις ἐγκεκορδυλημένος. 10
ἀλλ', εἰ δοκεῖ, ῥέγκωμεν ἐγκεκαλυμμένοι.

ἀλλ' οὐ δύναμαι δείλαιος εὕδειν δακνόμενος
ὑπὸ τῆς δαπάνης καὶ τῆς φάτνης καὶ τῶν χρεῶν,
διὰ τουτονὶ τὸν υἱόν. ὁ δὲ κόμην ἔχων
ἱππάζεταί τε καὶ ξυνωρικεύεται 15
ὀνειροπολεῖ θ' ἵππους· ἐγὼ δ' ἀπόλλυμαι,
ὁρῶν ἄγουσαν τὴν σελήνην εἰκάδας·
οἱ γὰρ τόκοι χωροῦσιν. ἅπτε, παῖ, λύχνον,
κἄκφερε τὸ γραμματεῖον, ἵν' ἀναγνῶ λαβὼν
ὁπόσοις ὀφείλω καὶ λογίσωμαι τοὺς τόκους. 20
φέρ' ἴδω, τί ὀφείλω; " δώδεκα μνᾶς Πασίᾳ."

[a] At the back of the stage are two buildings—the house of

THE CLOUDS[a]

STREPSIADES.   O dear! O dear!
O Lord! O Zeus! these nights, how long they are.
Will they ne'er pass? will the day never come?
Surely I heard the cock crow, hours ago.
Yet still my servants snore. These are new customs.
O 'ware of war for many various reasons;
One fears in war even to flog one's servants.
And here's this hopeful son of mine wrapped up
Snoring and sweating under five thick blankets.
Come, we'll wrap up and snore in opposition.
(*Tries to sleep*)
But I can't sleep a wink, devoured and bitten
By ticks, and bugbears, duns, and race-horses,
All through this son of mine. *He curls his hair*,[b]
And sports his thoroughbreds, and drives his tandem;
Even in dreams he rides: while I—I'm ruined,
Now that the Moon has reached her twentieths,
And paying-time comes on.[c] Boy! light a lamp,
And fetch my ledger: now I'll reckon up
Who are my creditors, and what I owe them.
Come, let me see then. *Fifty pounds to Pasias*!

---

[a] *Strepsiades and the Phrontisterion. The interior of the first is exposed to view by means of the eccyclema.*
[b] Like the Knights; *cf. K*. 580.
[c] Interest was payable on the first day of each new month, and the days after the twentieth mark its near approach.

ARISTOPHANES

τοῦ δώδεκα μνᾶς Πασίᾳ; τί ἐχρησάμην;
ὅτ' ἐπριάμην τὸν κοππατίαν. οἴμοι τάλας,
εἴθ' ἐξεκόπην πρότερον τὸν ὀφθαλμὸν λίθῳ.
ΦΕΙΔΙΠΠΙΔΗΣ. Φίλων, ἀδικεῖς· ἔλαυνε τὸν σαυτοῦ δρόμον.
ΣΤ. τοῦτ' ἔστι τουτὶ τὸ κακὸν ὅ μ' ἀπολώλεκεν·
ὀνειροπολεῖ γὰρ καὶ καθεύδων ἱππικήν.
ΦΕΙ. πόσους δρόμους ἐλᾷ τὰ πολεμιστήρια;
ΣΤ. ἐμὲ μὲν σὺ πολλοὺς τὸν πατέρ' ἐλαύνεις δρόμους.
ἀτὰρ " τί χρέος ἔβα " με μετὰ τὸν Πασίαν; 3(
" τρεῖς μναῖ διφρίσκου καὶ τροχοῖν 'Αμυνίᾳ."
ΦΕΙ. ἄπαγε τὸν ἵππον ἐξαλίσας οἴκαδε.
ΣΤ. ἀλλ', ὦ μέλ', ἐξήλικας ἐμέ γ' ἐκ τῶν ἐμῶν,
ὅτε καὶ δίκας ὤφληκα χἄτεροι τόκου
ἐνεχυράσεσθαί φασιν.
ΦΕΙ. ἐτεόν, ὦ πάτερ, 35
τί δυσκολαίνεις καὶ στρέφει τὴν νύχθ' ὅλην;
ΣΤ. δάκνει με δήμαρχός τις ἐκ τῶν στρωμάτων.
ΦΕΙ. ἔασον, ὦ δαιμόνιε, καταδαρθεῖν τί με.
ΣΤ. σὺ δ' οὖν κάθευδε· τὰ δὲ χρέα ταῦτ' ἴσθ' ὅτι
ἐς τὴν κεφαλὴν ἅπαντα τὴν σὴν τρέψεται. 40
φεῦ.
εἴθ' ὤφελ' ἡ προμνήστρι' ἀπολέσθαι κακῶς,
ἥτις με γῆμ' ἐπῆρε τὴν σὴν μητέρα·
ἐμοὶ γὰρ ἦν ἄγροικος ἥδιστος βίος,
εὐρωτιῶν, ἀκόρητος, εἰκῇ κείμενος,
βρύων μελίτταις καὶ προβάτοις καὶ στεμφύλοις. 45
ἔπειτ' ἔγημα Μεγακλέους τοῦ Μεγακλέους

---

[a] Lit. " the horse branded with a koppa (ϙ)," the symbol of Corinth, where the breed was supposed to descend from Pegasus.

THE CLOUDS, 22-46

Why fifty pounds to Pasias? what were they for?
O, for the hack [a] from Corinth. O dear! O dear!
I wish my eye had been hacked out before—
PHEIDIPPIDES. (*In his sleep*) You are cheating, Philon;
    keep to your own side.
ST. Ah! there it is! that's what has ruined me!
Even in his very sleep he thinks of horses.
PH. (*In his sleep*) How many heats do the war-chariots run?
ST. A pretty many heats you have run your father.
Now then, what debt assails me [b] after Pasias?
A curricle and wheels. Twelve pounds. Amynias.
PH. (*In his sleep*) Here, give the horse a roll, and take
    him home.
ST. You have rolled me *out* of house and home, my boy,
Cast in some suits already, while some swear
They'll seize my goods for payment.
PH.   Good, my father,
What makes you toss so restless all night long?
ST. There's a bumbailiff [c] from the mattress bites me.
PH. Come now, I prithee, let me sleep in peace.
ST. Well then, you sleep; only be sure of this,
These debts will fall on your own head at last.
Alas, alas!
For ever cursed be that same match-maker,
Who stirred me up to marry your poor mother.
Mine in the country was the pleasantest life,
Untidy, easy-going,[d] unrestrained,
Brimming with olives, sheepfolds, honey-bees.
Ah! then I married—I a rustic—her

---

[b] τί χρέος ἔβα με is from an unknown play of Euripides: Schol.
[c] δήμαρχος: a surprise instead of κόρις or ψύλλα. He was the headman of the deme, and also issued executions for unpaid debts.
[d] Lit. "mouldy, unswept."

ARISTOPHANES

ἀδελφιδῆν ἄγροικος ὢν ἐξ ἄστεως,
σεμνήν, τρυφῶσαν, ἐγκεκοισυρωμένην.
ταύτην ὅτ' ἐγάμουν, συγκατεκλινόμην ἐγὼ
ὄζων τρυγός, τρασιᾶς, ἐρίων περιουσίας,
ἡ δ' αὖ μύρου, κρόκου, καταγλωττισμάτων,
δαπάνης, λαφυγμοῦ, Κωλιάδος, Γενετυλλίδος.
οὐ μὴν ἐρῶ γ' ὡς ἀργὸς ἦν, ἀλλ' ἐσπάθα.
ἐγὼ δ' ἂν αὐτῇ θοἰμάτιον δεικνὺς τοδὶ
πρόφασιν ἔφασκον, " ὦ γύναι, λίαν σπαθᾷς."
ΘΕΡΑΠΩΝ. ἔλαιον ἡμῖν οὐκ ἔνεστ' ἐν τῷ λύχνῳ.
ΣΤ. οἴμοι· τί γάρ μοι τὸν πότην ἦπτες λύχνον;
δεῦρ' ἔλθ', ἵνα κλάῃς.
ΘΕ.   διὰ τί δῆτα κλαύσομαι;
ΣΤ. ὅτι τῶν παχειῶν ἐνετίθεις θρυαλλίδων.
μετὰ ταῦθ', ὅπως νῷν ἐγένεθ' υἱὸς οὑτοσί,
ἐμοί τε δὴ καὶ τῇ γυναικὶ τἀγαθῇ,
περὶ τοὐνόματος δὴ 'ντεῦθεν ἐλοιδορούμεθα·
ἡ μὲν γὰρ ἵππον προσετίθει πρὸς τοὔνομα,
Ξάνθιππον ἢ Χάριππον ἢ Καλλιππίδην,
ἐγὼ δὲ τοῦ πάππου 'τιθέμην Φειδωνίδην.
τέως μὲν οὖν ἐκρινόμεθ'· εἶτα τῷ χρόνῳ
κοινῇ ξυνέβημεν κἀθέμεθα Φειδιππίδην.
τοῦτον τὸν υἱὸν λαμβάνουσ' ἐκορίζετο,
ὅταν σὺ μέγας ὢν ἅρμ' ἐλαύνῃς πρὸς πόλιν,
ὥσπερ Μεγακλέης, ξυστίδ' ἔχων. ἐγὼ δ' ἔφην,
ὅταν μὲν οὖν τὰς αἶγας ἐκ τοῦ φελλέως,
ὥσπερ ὁ πατήρ σου, διφθέραν ἐνημμένος.
ἀλλ' οὐκ ἐπίθετο τοῖς ἐμοῖς οὐδὲν λόγοις,

---

[a] Lit. " of M. the son of M.," the repetition of the name being intended to enhance its importance. Megacles was a common name for the male, as Coesyra for the female, children of the aristocratic Alcmaeonid family.

THE CLOUDS, 47-73

A fine town-lady, niece of Megacles.[a]
A regular, proud, luxurious, Coesyra.
This wife I married, and we came together,
I rank with wine-lees, fig-boards,[b] greasy woolpacks;
She all with scents, and saffron, and tongue-kissings,
Feasting, expense, and lordly modes of loving.[c]
She was not idle though, she was too fast.[d]
I used to tell her, holding out my cloak,
Threadbare and worn; *Wife, you're too fast by half.*
SERVANT-BOY. Here's no more oil remaining in the lamp.
ST. O me! what made you light the tippling lamp?
Come and be whipp'd.
SERV.   Why, what would you whip me for?
ST. Why did you put one of those thick wicks in?
Well, when at last to me and my good woman
This hopeful son was born, our son and heir,
Why then we took to wrangle on the name.
She was for giving him some knightly name,
" Callippides," " Xanthippus," or " Charippus " :
I wished " Pheidonides," his grandsire's [e] name.
Thus for some time we argued: till at last
We compromised it in Pheidippides.
This boy she took, and used to spoil him, saying,
*Oh! when you are driving to the Acropolis, clad
Like Megacles, in your purple ;* whilst I said
*Oh! when the goats you are driving from the fells,
Clad like your father, in your sheepskin coat.*
Well, he cared nought for my advice, but soon

[b] On which they were dried in the sun.
[c] Κωλίας and Γενετυλλίς are names of love-deities.
[d] σπαθάω is literally " to ply the shuttle " (σπάθη), then as a slang term " to squander."
[e] Boys were regularly named after a grandfather; *cf. B.* 283. Pheidonides = " a son of thrift " (φειδώ).

ARISTOPHANES

ἀλλ' ἱππερόν μου κατέχεεν τῶν χρημάτων.
νῦν οὖν ὅλην τὴν νύκτα φροντίζων, ὁδὸν 75
μίαν εὗρον, ἀτραπὸν δαιμονίως ὑπερφυᾶ,
ἣν ἢν ἀναπείσω τουτονί, σωθήσομαι.
ἀλλ' ἐξεγεῖραι πρῶτον αὐτὸν βούλομαι.
πῶς δῆτ' ἂν ἥδιστ' αὐτὸν ἐπεγείραιμι; πῶς;
Φειδιππίδη, Φειδιππίδιον.
ΦΕΙ.   τί, ὦ πάτερ;   80
ΣΤ. κύσον με καὶ τὴν χεῖρα δὸς τὴν δεξιάν.
ΦΕΙ. ἰδού. τί ἔστιν;
ΣΤ.   εἰπέ μοι, φιλεῖς ἐμέ;
ΦΕΙ. νὴ τὸν Ποσειδῶ τουτονὶ τὸν ἵππιον.
ΣΤ. μή μοί γε τοῦτον μηδαμῶς τὸν ἵππιον·
οὗτος γὰρ ὁ θεὸς αἴτιός μοι τῶν κακῶν.   85
ἀλλ' εἴπερ ἐκ τῆς καρδίας μ' ὄντως φιλεῖς,
ὦ παῖ, πιθοῦ.
ΦΕΙ.   τί οὖν πίθωμαι δῆτά σοι;
ΣΤ. ἔκστρεψον ὡς τάχιστα τοὺς σαυτοῦ τρόπους,
καὶ μάνθαν' ἐλθὼν ἂν ἐγὼ παραινέσω.
ΦΕΙ. λέγε δή, τί κελεύεις;
ΣΤ.   καί τι πείσει;
ΦΕΙ.   πείσομαι, 90
νὴ τὸν Διόνυσον.
ΣΤ.   δεῦρό νυν ἀπόβλεπε.
ὁρᾷς τὸ θύριον τοῦτο καὶ τᾠκίδιον;
ΦΕΙ. ὁρῶ. τί οὖν τοῦτ' ἐστὶν ἐτεόν, ὦ πάτερ;
ΣΤ. ψυχῶν σοφῶν τοῦτ' ἐστὶ φροντιστήριον.
ἐνταῦθ' ἐνοικοῦσ' ἄνδρες οἳ τὸν οὐρανὸν   95
λέγοντες ἀναπείθουσιν ὡς ἔστιν πνιγεὺς

---

[a] Lit. " he poured a plague of horse-fever upon." ἵππερος is invented in imitation of ἴκτερος " jaundice."
[b] τουτονί : pointing to some statuette of Poseidon near his bed.

THE CLOUDS, 74-96

A galloping consumption caught *a* my fortunes.
Now cogitating all night long, I've found
One way, one marvellous transcendent way,
Which if he'll follow, we may yet be saved.
So,—but, however, I must rouse him first ;
But how to rouse him kindliest ? that's the rub.
Pheidippides, my sweet one.

PH.   Well, my father.
ST. Shake hands, Pheidippides, shake hands and kiss me.
PH. There ; what's the matter ?
ST.   Dost thou love me, boy ?
PH. Ay ! by Poseidon there,*b* the God of horses.
ST. No, no, not that : miss out the God of horses,
That God's the origin of all my evils.
But if you love me from your heart and soul,
My son, obey me.
PH.   Very well : what in ?
ST. Strip with all speed, strip off your present habits,
And go and learn what I'll advise you to.
PH. Name your commands.
ST.   Will you obey ?
PH.   I will,
By Dionysus !
ST.   Well then, look this way.
See you that wicket and the lodge beyond ?
PH. I see : and prithee what is that, my father ?
ST. That is the thinking-house *c* of sapient souls.
There dwell the men who teach—aye, who persuade us,
That Heaven is one vast fire-extinguisher *d*

---

c The word φροντιστήριον, " thinking-establishment," is apparently the invention of Aristophanes.
d So πνιγεύς is usually rendered. The Ravenna Scholiast gives three explanations, (1) " stove," (2) " the place where coals are crammed " (συμπνίγονται), and (3) " furnace " (φοῦρνος).

VOL. I   T   273

ARISTOPHANES

κἄστιν περὶ ἡμᾶς οὗτος, ἡμεῖς δ' ἄνθρακες.
οὗτοι διδάσκουσ', ἀργύριον ἤν τις διδῷ,
λέγοντα νικᾶν καὶ δίκαια κἄδικα.
ΦΕΙ. εἰσὶν δὲ τίνες;
ΣΤ. οὐκ οἶδ' ἀκριβῶς τοὔνομα·
μεριμνοφροντισταὶ καλοί τε κἀγαθοί.
ΦΕΙ. αἰβοῖ, πονηροί γ', οἶδα. τοὺς ἀλαζόνας,
τοὺς ὠχριῶντας, τοὺς ἀνυποδήτους λέγεις·
ὧν ὁ κακοδαίμων Σωκράτης καὶ Χαιρεφῶν.
ΣΤ. ἢ ἤ, σιώπα· μηδὲν εἴπῃς νήπιον.
ἀλλ' εἴ τι κήδει τῶν πατρῴων ἀλφίτων,
τούτων γενοῦ μοι, σχασάμενος τὴν ἱππικήν.
ΦΕΙ. οὐκ ἂν μὰ τὸν Διόνυσον, εἰ δοίης γέ μοι
τοὺς Φασιανοὺς οὓς τρέφει Λεωγόρας.
ΣΤ. ἴθ', ἀντιβολῶ σ', ὦ φίλτατ' ἀνθρώπων ἐμοί,
ἐλθὼν διδάσκου.
ΦΕΙ. καὶ τί σοι μαθήσομαι;
ΣΤ. εἶναι παρ' αὐτοῖς φασιν ἄμφω τὼ λόγω,
τὸν κρείττον', ὅστις ἐστί, καὶ τὸν ἥττονα.
τούτοιν τὸν ἕτερον τοῖν λόγοιν, τὸν ἥττονα,
νικᾶν λέγοντά φασι τἀδικώτερα.
ἢν οὖν μάθῃς μοι τὸν ἄδικον τοῦτον λόγον,
ἃ νῦν ὀφείλω διὰ σέ, τούτων τῶν χρεῶν
οὐκ ἂν ἀποδοίην οὐδ' ἂν ὀβολὸν οὐδενί.
ΦΕΙ. οὐκ ἂν πιθοίμην· οὐ γὰρ ἂν τλαίην ἰδεῖν
τοὺς ἱππέας τὸ χρῶμα διακεκναισμένος.
ΣΤ. οὐκ ἄρα μὰ τὴν Δήμητρα τῶν γ' ἐμῶν ἔδει,
οὔτ' αὐτὸς οὔθ' ὁ ζύγιος οὔθ' ὁ σαμφόρας·
ἀλλ' ἐξελῶ σ' ἐς κόρακας ἐκ τῆς οἰκίας.

---

[a] " Either horses or birds " (*i.e.* pheasants) says the Scholiast; but the former seem clearly indicated.
[b] To teach young men τὸν ἥττω λόγον κρείττω ποιεῖν was the

THE CLOUDS, 97-123

Placed round about us, and that we're the cinders.
Aye, and they'll teach (only they'll want some money),
How one may speak and conquer, right or wrong.
PH. Come, tell their names.
ST. Well, I can't quite remember,
But they're deep thinkers, and true gentlemen.
PH. Out on the rogues! I know them. Those rank pedants,
Those palefaced, barefoot vagabonds you mean :
That Socrates, poor wretch, and Chaerephon.
ST. Oh! Oh! hush! hush! don't use those foolish words;
But if the sorrows of my barley touch you,
Enter their Schools and cut the Turf for ever.
PH. I wouldn't go, so help me Dionysus,
For all Leogoras's breed of Phasians [a]!
ST. Go, I beseech you, dearest, dearest son,
Go and be taught.
PH. And what would you have me learn?
ST. 'Tis known that in their Schools they keep two Logics,[b]
The Worse, Zeus save the mark,[c] the Worse and
Better.
This Second Logic then, I mean the Worse one,
They teach to talk unjustly and—prevail.
Think then, you only learn that Unjust Logic,
And all the debts, which I have incurred through
you,—
I'll never pay, no, not one farthing of them.
PH. I will not go. How could I face the knights
With all my colour worn and torn away!
ST. O! then, by Earth, you have eat your last of mine,
You, and your coach-horse, and your sigma-brand :
Out with you! Go to the crows, for all I care.

famous " promise of Protagoras " (τὸ Π. ἐπάγγελμα, Arist. *Rhet.* ii. 24. 11), the sophist of Abdera.
[c] ὅστις ἐστί is " a sort of contemptuous dismissal ": R.

ARISTOPHANES

ΦΕΙ. ἀλλ' οὐ περιόψεταί μ' ὁ θεῖος Μεγακλέης
ἄνιππον. ἀλλ' εἴσειμι, σοῦ δ' οὐ φροντιῶ.

ΣΤ. ἀλλ' οὐδ' ἐγὼ μέντοι πεσών γε κείσομαι·
ἀλλ' εὐξάμενος τοῖσιν θεοῖς διδάξομαι
αὐτὸς βαδίζων εἰς τὸ φροντιστήριον.
πῶς οὖν γέρων ὢν κἀπιλήσμων καὶ βραδὺς
λόγων ἀκριβῶν σκινδαλάμους μαθήσομαι;
ἰτητέον. τί ταῦτ' ἔχων στραγγεύομαι,
ἀλλ' οὐχὶ κόπτω τὴν θύραν; παῖ, παιδίον.

ΜΑΘΗΤΗΣ. βάλλ' ἐς κόρακας· τίς ἐσθ' ὁ κόψας τὴν θύραν;

ΣΤ. Φείδωνος υἱὸς Στρεψιάδης Κικυννόθεν.

ΜΑ. ἀμαθής γε νὴ Δί', ὅστις οὑτωσὶ σφόδρα
ἀπεριμερίμνως τὴν θύραν λελάκτικας
καὶ φροντίδ' ἐξήμβλωκας ἐξευρημένην.

ΣΤ. σύγγνωθί μοι· τηλοῦ γὰρ οἰκῶ τῶν ἀγρῶν.
ἀλλ' εἰπέ μοι τὸ πρᾶγμα τοὐξημβλωμένον.

ΜΑ. ἀλλ' οὐ θέμις πλὴν τοῖς μαθηταῖσιν λέγειν.

ΣΤ. λέγε νυν ἐμοὶ θαρρῶν· ἐγὼ γὰρ οὑτοσὶ
ἥκω μαθητὴς εἰς τὸ φροντιστήριον.

ΜΑ. λέξω. νομίσαι δὲ ταῦτα χρὴ μυστήρια.
ἀνήρετ' ἄρτι Χαιρεφῶντα Σωκράτης
ψύλλαν ὁπόσους ἅλλοιτο τοὺς αὐτῆς πόδας·
δακοῦσα γὰρ τοῦ Χαιρεφῶντος τὴν ὀφρὺν
ἐπὶ τὴν κεφαλὴν τὴν Σωκράτους ἀφήλατο.

ΣΤ. πῶς δῆτα τοῦτ' ἐμέτρησε;

ΜΑ. δεξιώτατα.
κηρὸν διατήξας, εἶτα τὴν ψύλλαν λαβὼν
ἐνέβαψεν εἰς τὸν κηρὸν αὐτῆς τὼ πόδε,
κᾆτα ψυγείσῃ περιέφυσαν Περσικαί.
ταύτας ὑπολύσας ἀνεμέτρει τὸ χωρίον.

---

^a The name of a deme.

THE CLOUDS, 124–152

PH. But uncle Megacles won't leave me long
Without a horse : I'll go to him : good-bye.

ST. I'm thrown, by Zeus, but I won't long lie prostrate.
I'll pray the Gods and send myself to school :
I'll go at once and try their thinking-house.
Stay : how can I, forgetful, slow, old fool,
Learn the nice hair-splittings of subtle Logic ?
Well, go I must. 'Twont do to linger here.
Come on, I'll knock the door. Boy ! Ho there, boy!
STUDENT. (*Within*) O, hang it all! who's knocking at the door?
ST. Me ! Pheidon's son : Strepsiades of Cicynna.[a]
STU. Why, what a clown you are ! to kick our door,
In such a thoughtless, inconsiderate way !
You've made my cogitation to miscarry.[b]
ST. Forgive me : I'm an awkward country fool.
But tell me, what was that I made miscarry ?
STU. 'Tis not allowed : Students alone may hear.
ST. O that's all right : you may tell *me* : I'm come
To be a student in your thinking-house.
STU. Come then. But they're high mysteries, remember.
'Twas Socrates was asking Chaerephon,
How many feet of its own a flea could jump.
For one first bit the brow [c] of Chaerephon,
Then bounded off to Socrates's head.
ST. How did he measure this ?
STU.   Most cleverly.
He warmed some wax, and then he caught the flea,
And dipped its feet into the wax he'd melted :
Then let it cool, and there were Persian slippers !
These he took off, and so he found the distance.

[b] *Cf.* Plato, *Theaet.* 149 *seq.*, where Socrates describes himself as practising the art of intellectual midwifery (μαιευτικὴ τέχνη) and bringing thoughts to the birth.
[c] " C. had bushy eyebrows and S. was bald " : Schol.

ARISTOPHANES

ΣΤ. ὦ Ζεῦ βασιλεῦ, τῆς λεπτότητος τῶν φρενῶν.
ΜΑ. τί δῆτ' ἄν, ἕτερον εἰ πύθοιο Σωκράτους
φρόντισμα;
ΣΤ. ποῖον; ἀντιβολῶ, κάτειπέ μοι. 15ι
ΜΑ. ἀνήρετ' αὐτὸν Χαιρεφῶν ὁ Σφήττιος
ὁπότερα τὴν γνώμην ἔχοι, τὰς ἐμπίδας
κατὰ τὸ στόμ' ᾄδειν, ἢ κατὰ τοὐρροπύγιον.
ΣΤ. τί δῆτ' ἐκεῖνος εἶπε περὶ τῆς ἐμπίδος;
ΜΑ. ἔφασκεν εἶναι τοὔντερον τῆς ἐμπίδος 16ι
στενόν· διὰ λεπτοῦ δ' ὄντος αὐτοῦ τὴν πνοὴν
βίᾳ βαδίζειν εὐθὺ τοὐρροπυγίου·
ἔπειτα κοῖλον πρὸς στενῷ προσκείμενον
τὸν πρωκτὸν ἠχεῖν ὑπὸ βίας τοῦ πνεύματος.
ΣΤ. σάλπιγξ ὁ πρωκτός ἐστιν ἄρα τῶν ἐμπίδων. 16
ὦ τρισμακάριος τοῦ διεντερεύματος.
ἦ ῥᾳδίως φεύγων ἂν ἀποφύγοι δίκην
ὅστις δίοιδε τοὔντερον τῆς ἐμπίδος.
ΜΑ. πρώην δέ γε γνώμην μεγάλην ἀφῃρέθη
ὑπ' ἀσκαλαβώτου.
ΣΤ. τίνα τρόπον; κάτειπέ μοι. 17
ΜΑ. ζητοῦντος αὐτοῦ τῆς σελήνης τὰς ὁδοὺς
καὶ τὰς περιφοράς, εἶτ' ἄνω κεχηνότος
ἀπὸ τῆς ὀροφῆς νύκτωρ γαλεώτης κατέχεσεν.
ΣΤ. ἥσθην γαλεώτῃ καταχέσαντι Σωκράτους.
ΜΑ. ἐχθὲς δέ γ' ἡμῖν δεῖπνον οὐκ ἦν ἑσπέρας. 17
ΣΤ. εἶεν· τί οὖν πρὸς τἄλφιτ' ἐπαλαμήσατο;
ΜΑ. κατὰ τῆς τραπέζης καταπάσας λεπτὴν τέφραν,
κάμψας ὀβελίσκον, εἶτα διαβήτην λαβών,
ἐκ τῆς παλαίστρας θοἰμάτιον ὑφείλετο.

THE CLOUDS, 153-179

ST. O Zeus and king, what subtle intellects!
STU. What would you say then if you heard another,
    Our Master's own?
ST.   O come, do tell me that.
STU. Why, Chaerephon was asking him in turn,
    Which theory did he sanction; that the gnats
    Hummed through their mouth, or backwards, through
        the tail?
ST. Aye, and what said your Master of the gnat?
STU. He answered thus: the entrail of the gnat
    Is small: and through this narrow pipe the wind
    Rushes with violence straight towards the tail;
    There, close against the pipe, the hollow rump
    Receives the wind, and whistles to the blast.
ST. So then the rump is trumpet to the gnats!
    O happy, happy in your entrail-learning!
    Full surely need he fear nor debts nor duns,
    Who knows about the entrails of the gnats.
STU. And yet last night a mighty thought we lost
    Through a green lizard.
ST.   Tell me, how was that?
STU. Why, as Himself, with eyes and mouth wide open,
    Mused on the moon, her paths and revolutions,
    A lizard from the roof squirted full on him.
ST. He, he, he, he. I like the lizard's spattering Socrates.
STU. Then yesterday, poor we, we'd got no dinner.
ST. Hah! what did he devise to do for barley?
STU. He sprinkled on the table—some fine ash— [a]
    He bent a spit—he grasped it compass-wise—
    And—filched a mantle from the Wrestling School.

[a] As though he were going to solve some geometrical problem. Instead he uses the bent spit to hook away a cloak. The palaestra, like the market-place, was one of the usual haunts of Socrates.

ARISTOPHANES

ΣΤ. τί δῆτ' ἐκεῖνον τὸν Θαλῆν θαυμάζομεν;
ἄνοιγ' ἄνοιγ' ἀνύσας τὸ φροντιστήριον,
καὶ δεῖξον ὡς τάχιστά μοι τὸν Σωκράτην.
μαθητιῶ γάρ· ἀλλ' ἄνοιγε τὴν θύραν.
ὦ Ἡράκλεις, ταυτὶ ποδαπὰ τὰ θηρία;
ΜΑ. τί ἐθαύμασας; τῷ σοι δοκοῦσιν εἰκέναι;
ΣΤ. τοῖς ἐκ Πύλου ληφθεῖσι, τοῖς Λακωνικοῖς.
ἀτὰρ τί ποτ' ἐς τὴν γῆν βλέπουσιν οὑτοί;
ΜΑ. ζητοῦσιν οὗτοι τὰ κατὰ γῆς.
ΣΤ. βολβοὺς ἄρα
ζητοῦσι. μή νυν τουτογὶ φροντίζετε·
ἐγὼ γὰρ οἶδ' ἵν' εἰσὶ μεγάλοι καὶ καλοί.
τί γὰρ οἵδε δρῶσιν οἱ σφόδρ' ἐγκεκυφότες;
ΜΑ. οὗτοι δ' ἐρεβοδιφῶσιν ὑπὸ τὸν Τάρταρον.
ΣΤ. τί δῆθ' ὁ πρωκτὸς ἐς τὸν οὐρανὸν βλέπει;
ΜΑ. αὐτὸς καθ' αὑτὸν ἀστρονομεῖν διδάσκεται.
ἀλλ' εἴσιθ', ἵνα μὴ 'κεῖνος ἡμῖν ἐπιτύχῃ.
ΣΤ. μήπω γε μήπω γ', ἀλλ' ἐπιμεινάντων, ἵνα
αὐτοῖσι κοινώσω τι πραγμάτιον ἐμόν.
ΜΑ. ἀλλ' οὐχ οἷόν τ' αὐτοῖσι πρὸς τὸν ἀέρα
ἔξω διατρίβειν πολὺν ἄγαν ἐστὶν χρόνον.
ΣΤ. πρὸς τῶν θεῶν, τί γὰρ τάδ' ἐστίν; εἰπέ μοι.
ΜΑ. ἀστρονομία μὲν αὑτηί.
ΣΤ. τουτὶ δὲ τί;
ΜΑ. γεωμετρία.
ΣΤ. τοῦτ' οὖν τί ἐστι χρήσιμον;
ΜΑ. γῆν ἀναμετρεῖσθαι.

---

[a] Of Miletus, one of the seven wise men, constantly spoken of as the embodiment of wisdom; cf. B. 1009; Plaut. *Capt.* ii. 2. 24.

THE CLOUDS, 180-203

ST. Good heavens ! Why Thales [a] was a fool to this !
O open, open, wide the study door,
And show me, show me, show me Socrates.
I die to be a student. Open, open ! [b]
O Heracles, what kind of beasts are these !

STU. Why, what's the matter ? what do you think they're like ?

ST. Like ? why those Spartans whom we brought from Pylus [c] :
What makes them fix their eyes so on the ground ?

STU. They seek things underground.

ST. O ! to be sure,
Truffles ! You there, don't trouble about that !
I'll tell you where the best and finest grow.
Look ! why do those stoop down so very much ?

STU. They're diving deep into the deepest secrets.[d]

ST. Then why's their rump turned up towards the sky ?

STU. It's taking private lessons on the stars.
(*To the other Students*)
Come, come : get in : HE'll catch us presently.

ST. Not yet ! not yet ! just let them stop one moment,
While I impart a little matter to them.

STU. No, no : they must go in : 'twould never do
To expose themselves too long to the open air.

ST. O ! by the Gods, now, what are these ? do tell me.

STU. This is Astronomy.

ST. And what is this ?

STU. Geometry.

ST. Well, what's the use of that ?

STU. To mete out lands.

[b] " The entire front of the house is wheeled round . . . exposing the inner court of the Phrontisterion " : R.
[c] Captured by Cleon in Sphacteria and imprisoned at Athens; *cf.* K. 392.
[d] Lit. " Are searching into the darkness below Tartarus."

ARISTOPHANES

ΣΤ. πότερα τὴν κληρουχικήν;
ΜΑ. οὔκ, ἀλλὰ τὴν σύμπασαν.
ΣΤ. ἀστεῖον λέγεις.
τὸ γὰρ σόφισμα δημοτικὸν καὶ χρήσιμον.
ΜΑ. αὕτη δέ σοι γῆς περίοδος πάσης. ὁρᾷς;
αἵδε μὲν Ἀθῆναι.
ΣΤ. τί σὺ λέγεις; οὐ πείθομαι,
ἐπεὶ δικαστὰς οὐχ ὁρῶ καθημένους.
ΜΑ. ὡς τοῦτ' ἀληθῶς Ἀττικὸν τὸ χωρίον.
ΣΤ. καὶ ποῦ Κικυννῆς εἰσὶν οὑμοὶ δημόται;
ΜΑ. ἐνταῦθ' ἔνεισιν. ἡ δέ γ' Εὔβοι', ὡς ὁρᾷς,
ἡδὶ παρατέταται μακρὰ πόρρω πάνυ.
ΣΤ. οἶδ'· ὑπὸ γὰρ ἡμῶν παρετάθη καὶ Περικλέους.
ἀλλ' ἡ Λακεδαίμων ποῦ 'στιν;
ΜΑ. ὅπου 'στίν; αὑτηί.
ΣΤ. ὡς ἐγγὺς ἡμῶν. τοῦτο πάνυ φροντίζετε,
ταύτην ἀφ' ἡμῶν ἀπαγαγεῖν πόρρω πάνυ.
ΜΑ. ἀλλ' οὐχ οἷόν τε νὴ Δί'.
ΣΤ. οἰμώξεσθ' ἄρα.
φέρε τίς γὰρ οὗτος οὑπὶ τῆς κρεμάθρας ἀνήρ;
ΜΑ. αὐτός.
ΣΤ. τίς αὐτός;
ΜΑ. Σωκράτης.
ΣΤ. ὦ Σώκρατες.
ἴθ' οὗτος, ἀναβόησον αὐτόν μοι μέγα.
ΜΑ. αὐτὸς μὲν οὖν σὺ κάλεσον· οὐ γάρ μοι σχολή.
ΣΤ. ὦ Σώκρατες,
ὦ Σωκρατίδιον.

---
[a] γῆ κληρουχική is land taken from a conquered enemy and divided by lot among Athenian citizens.
[b] ἀστεῖον here is not merely = "choice," "elegant," but also almost = δημοτικός; cf. Plato, 227 D ἀστεῖοι καὶ δημωφελεῖς λόγοι. It is both *urbanum* and *urbi utile*.

THE CLOUDS, 203-223

ST. What, for allotment grounds [a]?
STU. No, but all lands.
ST. A choice idea,[b] truly.
Then every man may take his choice, you mean.
STU. Look; here's a chart of the whole world. Do you see?
This city's Athens.
ST. Athens? I like that.
I see no dicasts sitting. That's not Athens.
STU. In very truth, this is the Attic ground.
ST. And where then are my townsmen of Cicynna?
STU. Why, thereabouts; and here, you see, Euboea:
Here, reaching out a long way by the shore.
ST. Yes, overreached [c] by us and Pericles.
But now, where's Sparta?
STU. Let me see : O, here.
ST. Heavens! how near us. O do please manage this,
To shove her off from us, a long way further.
STU. We can't do that, by Zeus.
ST. The worse for you.
Hallo! who's that? that fellow in the basket?
STU. That's HE.[d]
ST. Who's HE?
STU. Socrates.
ST. Socrates!
You sir, call out to him as loud as you can.
STU. Call him yourself : I have not leisure now.
ST. Socrates! Socrates!
Sweet Socrates!

[c] Or "stretched on the rack"; there is a play on the secondary meaning of παρατείνω="exhaust," "do for." Euboea was reduced by Pericles 445 B.C.; cf. Thuc. i. 114.
[d] αὐτός="the Master," as in he Pythagorean αὐτὸς ἔφη, *Ipse dixit*.

ARISTOPHANES

ΣΩΚΡΑΤΗΣ. τί με καλεῖς, ὠφήμερε;
ΣΤ. πρῶτον μὲν ὅ τι δρᾷς, ἀντιβολῶ, κάτειπέ μοι.
ΣΩ. ἀεροβατῶ καὶ περιφρονῶ τὸν ἥλιον.
ΣΤ. ἔπειτ' ἀπὸ ταρροῦ τοὺς θεοὺς ὑπερφρονεῖς,
ἀλλ' οὐκ ἀπὸ τῆς γῆς, εἴπερ.
ΣΩ. οὐ γὰρ ἄν ποτε
ἐξεῦρον ὀρθῶς τὰ μετέωρα πράγματα,
εἰ μὴ κρεμάσας τὸ νόημα καὶ τὴν φροντίδα
λεπτὴν καταμίξας εἰς τὸν ὅμοιον ἀέρα.
εἰ δ' ὢν χαμαὶ τἄνω κάτωθεν ἐσκόπουν,
οὐκ ἄν ποθ' εὗρον· οὐ γὰρ ἀλλ' ἡ γῆ βίᾳ
ἕλκει πρὸς αὑτὴν τὴν ἰκμάδα τῆς φροντίδος.
πάσχει δὲ ταὐτὸ τοῦτο καὶ τὰ κάρδαμα.
ΣΤ. τί φῄς;
ἡ φροντὶς ἕλκει τὴν ἰκμάδ' εἰς τὰ κάρδαμα;
ἴθι νυν, κατάβηθ', ὦ Σωκρατίδιον, ὡς ἐμέ,
ἵνα με διδάξῃς ὦνπερ ἕνεκ' ἐλήλυθα.
ΣΩ. ἦλθες δὲ κατὰ τί;
ΣΤ. βουλόμενος μαθεῖν λέγειν.
ὑπὸ γὰρ τόκων χρήστων τε δυσκολωτάτων
ἄγομαι, φέρομαι, τὰ χρήματ' ἐνεχυράζομαι.
ΣΩ. πόθεν δ' ὑπόχρεως σαυτὸν ἔλαθες γενόμενος;
ΣΤ. νόσος μ' ἐπέτριψεν ἱππική, δεινὴ φαγεῖν.
ἀλλά με δίδαξον τὸν ἕτερον τοῖν σοῖν λόγοιν,
τὸν μηδὲν ἀποδιδόντα. μισθὸν δ' ὅντιν' ἂν
πράττῃ μ' ὀμοῦμαί σοι καταθήσειν τοὺς θεούς.
ΣΩ. ποίους θεοὺς ὀμεῖ σύ; πρῶτον γὰρ θεοὶ
ἡμῖν νόμισμ' οὐκ ἔστι.
ΣΤ. τῷ γὰρ ὄμνυτ'; ἢ
σιδαρέοισιν, ὥσπερ ἐν Βυζαντίῳ;

---

[a] εἴπερ: lit. " if so be " (that you do despise them).

THE CLOUDS, 223-249

SOCRATES. Mortal! why call'st thou me?
ST. O, first of all, please tell me what you are doing.
SO. I walk on air, and contem-plate the Sun.
ST. O then from a basket you contemn the Gods,
And not from the earth, at any rate [a]?
SO. Most true.
I could not have searched out celestial matters
Without suspending judgement, and infusing
My subtle spirit with the kindred air.
If from the ground I were to seek these things,
I could not find : so surely doth the earth
Draw to herself the essence of our thought.
The same too is the case with water-cress.[b]
ST. Hillo! what's that?
Thought draws the essence into water-cress?
Come down, sweet Socrates, more near my level,
And teach the lessons which I come to learn.
SO. And wherefore art thou come?
ST. To learn to speak.
For owing to my horrid debts and duns,
My goods are seized, I'm robbed, and mobbed, and plundered.
SO. How did you get involved with your eyes open?
ST. A galloping consumption seized my money.
Come now : do let me learn the unjust Logic
That can shirk debts : now do just let me learn it.
Name your own price, by all the Gods I'll pay it.
SO. The Gods! why you must know the Gods with us
Don't pass for current coin.
ST. Eh? what do you use then?
Have you got iron, as the Byzantines have [c]?

[b] An allusion to the homely imagery which Socrates constantly used.
[c] The Scholiast quotes Plato Comicus: χαλεπῶς ἂν οἰκήσαιμεν ἐν Βυζαντίοις, | ὅπου σιδαρέοισι τοῖς νομίσμασι | χρῶνται.

285

ARISTOPHANES

ΣΩ. βούλει τὰ θεῖα πράγματ' εἰδέναι σαφῶς 250
ἅττ' ἐστὶν ὀρθῶς;
ΣΤ. νὴ Δί', εἴπερ ἔστι γε.
ΣΩ. καὶ ξυγγενέσθαι ταῖς Νεφέλαισιν ἐς λόγους,
ταῖς ἡμετέραισι δαίμοσιν;
ΣΤ. μάλιστά γε.
ΣΩ. κάθιζε τοίνυν ἐπὶ τὸν ἱερὸν σκίμποδα.
ΣΤ. ἰδοὺ κάθημαι.
ΣΩ. τουτονὶ τοίνυν λαβὲ 255
τὸν στέφανον.
ΣΤ. ἐπὶ τί στέφανον; οἴμοι, Σώκρατες,
ὥσπερ με τὸν Ἀθάμανθ' ὅπως μὴ θύσετε.
ΣΩ. οὔκ, ἀλλὰ ταῦτα πάντα τοὺς τελουμένους
ἡμεῖς ποιοῦμεν.
ΣΤ. εἶτα δὴ τί κερδανῶ;
ΣΩ. λέγειν γενήσει τρῖμμα, κρόταλον, παιπάλη. 260
ἀλλ' ἔχ' ἀτρέμας.
ΣΤ. μὰ τὸν Δί' οὐ ψεύσει γε με·
καταπαττόμενος γὰρ παιπάλη γενήσομαι.

ΣΩ. εὐφημεῖν χρὴ τὸν πρεσβύτην καὶ τῆς εὐχῆς
ἐπακούειν.
ὦ δέσποτ' ἄναξ, ἀμέτρητ' Ἀήρ, ὃς ἔχεις τὴν γῆν
μετέωρον,
λαμπρός τ' Αἰθήρ, σεμναί τε θεαὶ Νεφέλαι
βρονπησικέραυνοι, 265
ἄρθητε, φάνητ', ὦ δέσποιναι, τῷ φροντιστῇ
μετέωροι.
ΣΤ. μήπω μήπω γε, πρὶν ἂν τουτὶ πτύξωμαι, μὴ
καταβρεχθῶ.

---

[a] He mistakes the chaplet which belongs to the ceremony of

286

THE CLOUDS, 250–267

so. Come, would you like to learn celestial matters,
How their truth stands?
st. Yes, if there's any truth.
so. And to hold intercourse with you bright Clouds,
Our virgin Goddesses?
st. Yes, that I should.
so. Then sit you down upon that sacred bed.
st. Well, I am sitting.
so. Here then, take this chaplet.
st. Chaplet? why? why? now, never, Socrates:
Don't sacrifice poor me, like Athamas.[a]
so. Fear not: our entrance-services require
All to do this.
st. But what am I to gain?
so. You'll be the flower[b] of talkers, prattlers, gossips:
Only keep quiet.
st. Zeus! your words come true!
I shall be flour indeed with all this peppering.

so. Old man sit you still, and attend to my will,
and hearken in peace to my prayer,
O Master and King, holding earth in your swing,
O measureless infinite Air;
And thou glowing Ether, and Clouds who enwreathe her
with thunder, and lightning, and storms,
Arise ye and shine, bright Ladies Divine,
to your student in bodily forms.
st. No, but stay, no, but stay, just one moment I pray,
while my cloak round my temples I wrap.

initiation for that used in sacrifice, and recalls how Athamas, who had married a Nephele (cf. the ambiguous ξυγ. ταῖς Νεφέλαισιν, 252), was introduced by Sophocles in a play crowned for sacrifice.
[b] παιπάλη, lit. "fine flour," stands for "subtlety" or "slimness." But in 261 Strepsiades refers to the actual flour or grain that is ceremonially sprinkled on him.

ARISTOPHANES

τὸ δὲ μηδὲ κυνῆν οἴκοθεν ἐλθεῖν ἐμὲ τὸν κακο-
δαίμον' ἔχοντα.

ΣΩ. ἔλθετε δῆτ', ὦ πολυτίμητοι Νεφέλαι, τῷδ' εἰς
ἐπίδειξιν·
εἴτ' ἐπ' Ὀλύμπου κορυφαῖς ἱεραῖς χιονοβλήτοισι
κάθησθε, 27
εἴτ' Ὠκεανοῦ πατρὸς ἐν κήποις ἱερὸν χορὸν
ἵστατε Νύμφαις,
εἴτ' ἄρα Νείλου προχοαῖς ὑδάτων χρυσέαις
ἀρύεσθε προχοῖσιν,
ἢ Μαιῶτιν λίμνην ἔχετ' ἢ σκόπελον νιφόεντα
Μίμαντος·
ὑπακούσατε δεξάμεναι θυσίαν καὶ τοῖς ἱεροῖσι
χαρεῖσαι.

ΧΟΡΟΣ. ἀέναοι Νεφέλαι, [στρ.
ἀρθῶμεν φανεραὶ δροσερὰν φύσιν εὐάγητον, 27
πατρὸς ἀπ' Ὠκεανοῦ βαρυαχέος
ὑψηλῶν ὀρέων κορυφὰς ἐπὶ
δενδροκόμους, ἵνα 28
τηλεφανεῖς σκοπιὰς ἀφορώμεθα,
καρπούς τ' ἀρδομέναν ἱερὰν χθόνα,
καὶ ποταμῶν ζαθέων κελαδήματα,
καὶ πόντον κελάδοντα βαρύβρομον·
ὄμμα γὰρ Αἰθέρος ἀκάματον σελαγεῖται 28
μαρμαρέαισιν ἐν αὐγαῖς.
ἀλλ' ἀποσεισάμεναι νέφος ὄμβριον
ἀθανάτας ἰδέας ἐπιδώμεθα
τηλεσκόπῳ ὄμματι γαῖαν. 29

THE CLOUDS, 268-290

  To think that I've come, stupid fool, from my home,
    with never a waterproof cap!
SO. Come forth, come forth, dread Clouds, and to earth
    your glorious majesty show;
Whether lightly ye rest on the time-honoured crest
    of Olympus environed in snow,
Or tread the soft dance 'mid the stately expanse
    of Ocean, the nymphs to beguile,
Or stoop to enfold with your pitchers of gold,
    the mystical waves of the Nile,[a]
Or around the white foam of Maeotis ye roam,
    or Mimas all wintry and bare,
O hear while we pray, and turn not away
    from the rites which your servants prepare.

CHORUS.[b]   Clouds of all hue,
Rise we aloft with our garments of dew.
Come from old Ocean's unchangeable bed,
Come, till the mountain's green summits we tread,
Come to the peaks with their landscapes untold,
Gaze on the Earth with her harvests of gold,[c]
Gaze on the rivers in majesty streaming,
  Gaze on the lordly, invincible Sea,
Come, for the Eye of the Ether is beaming,
  Come, for all Nature is flashing and free.
  Let us shake off this close-clinging dew
  From our members eternally new,
  And sail upwards the wide world to view.
    Come away! Come away!

  [a] Lit. "or at the outflow of the Nile are drawing up its waters with your golden pitchers."
  [b] The Clouds are still far away and out of sight; they do not enter until lines 323-8 and then in silence.
  [c] καρποὺς ἀρδομέναν, lit. "that has her crops watered."

ARISTOPHANES

ΣΩ. ὦ μέγα σεμναὶ Νεφέλαι, φανερῶς ἠκούσατέ μου
καλέσαντος.
ἤσθου φωνῆς ἅμα καὶ βροντῆς μυκησαμένης
θεοσέπτου;

ΣΤ. καὶ σέβομαί γ', ὦ πολυτίμητοι, καὶ βούλομαι
ἀνταποπαρδεῖν
πρὸς τὰς βροντάς· οὕτως αὐτὰς τετρεμαίνω καὶ
πεφόβημαι·
κεἰ θέμις ἐστίν, νυνί γ' ἤδη, κεἰ μὴ θέμις ἐστί,
χεσείω. 29

ΣΩ. οὐ μὴ σκώψῃς μηδὲ ποιήσῃς ἅπερ οἱ τρυγο-
δαίμονες οὗτοι,
ἀλλ' εὐφήμει· μέγα γάρ τι θεῶν κινεῖται σμῆνος
ἀοιδαῖς.

ΧΟ. παρθένοι ὀμβροφόροι, [ἀντ.
ἔλθωμεν λιπαρὰν χθόνα Παλλάδος, εὔανδρον γᾶν 30
Κέκροπος ὀψόμεναι πολυήρατον·
οὗ σέβας ἀρρήτων ἱερῶν, ἵνα
μυστοδόκος δόμος
ἐν τελεταῖς ἁγίαις ἀναδείκνυται,
οὐρανίοις τε θεοῖς δωρήματα, 30
ναοί θ' ὑψερεφεῖς καὶ ἀγάλματα,
καὶ πρόσοδοι μακάρων ἱερώταται,
εὐστέφανοί τε θεῶν θυσίαι θαλίαι τε,
παντοδαπαῖσιν ἐν ὥραις, 31
ἦρί τ' ἐπερχομένῳ Βρομία χάρις,
εὐκελάδων τε χορῶν ἐρεθίσματα,
καὶ Μοῦσα βαρύβρομος αὐλῶν.

ΣΤ. πρὸς τοῦ Διὸς ἀντιβολῶ σε, φράσον, τίνες εἴσ', ὦ
Σώκρατες, αὗται

THE CLOUDS, 291-314

so. O Goddesses mine, great Clouds and divine,
    ye have heeded and answered my prayer.
Heard ye their sound, and the thunder around,
    as it thrilled through the tremulous air?
st. Yes, by Zeus, and I shake, and I'm all of a quake,
    and I fear I must sound a reply,
Their thunders have made my soul so afraid,
    and those terrible voices so nigh:
So if lawful or not, I must run to a pot,
    by Zeus, if I stop I shall die.
so. Don't act in our schools like those Comedy-fools
    with their scurrilous scandalous ways.
Deep silence be thine: while this Cluster divine
    their soul-stirring melody raise.

ch.   Come then with me,
Daughters of Mist, to the land of the free.
Come to the people whom Pallas hath blest,
Come to the soil where the Mysteries rest;
Come, where the glorified Temple invites
The pure to partake of its mystical rites:
Holy the gifts that are brought to the Gods,
    Shrines with festoons and with garlands are crowned,
Pilgrims resort to the sacred abodes,
    Gorgeous the festivals all the year round.
    And the Bromian rejoicings in Spring,
    When the flutes with their deep music ring,
    And the sweetly-toned Choruses sing
        Come away! Come away!

st. O Socrates pray, by all the Gods, say,
    for I earnestly long to be told,

ARISTOPHANES

αἱ φθεγξάμεναι τοῦτο τὸ σεμνόν; μῶν ἡρῷναί
τινές εἰσιν; 315

ΣΩ. ἥκιστ', ἀλλ' οὐράνιαι Νεφέλαι, μεγάλαι θεαὶ
ἀνδράσιν ἀργοῖς·
αἵπερ γνώμην καὶ διάλεξιν καὶ νοῦν ἡμῖν παρέχουσι
καὶ τερατείαν καὶ περίλεξιν καὶ κροῦσιν καὶ
κατάληψιν.

ΣΤ. ταῦτ' ἄρ' ἀκούσασ' αὐτῶν τὸ φθέγμ' ἡ ψυχή μου
πεπότηται,
καὶ λεπτολογεῖν ἤδη ζητεῖ καὶ περὶ καπνοῦ
στενολεσχεῖν, 320
καὶ γνωμιδίῳ γνώμην νύξασ' ἑτέρῳ λόγῳ ἀντι-
λογῆσαι·
ὥστ', εἴ πως ἔστιν, ἰδεῖν αὐτὰς ἤδη φανερῶς
ἐπιθυμῶ.

ΣΩ. βλέπε νυν δευρὶ πρὸς τὴν Πάρνηθ'· ἤδη γὰρ ὁρῶ
κατιούσας
ἡσυχῇ αὐτάς.

ΣΤ. φέρε, ποῦ; δεῖξον.

ΣΩ. χωροῦσ' αὗται πάνυ πολλαί,
διὰ τῶν κοίλων καὶ τῶν δασέων, αὗται πλάγιαι.

ΣΤ. τί τὸ χρῆμα; 325
ὡς οὐ καθορῶ.

ΣΩ. παρὰ τὴν εἴσοδον.

ΣΤ. ἤδη νυνὶ μόλις οὕτως.

ΣΩ. νῦν γέ τοι ἤδη καθορᾷς αὐτάς, εἰ μὴ λημᾷς
κολοκύνταις.

[a] S. here runs through the attributes for which the sophists are indebted to the Clouds; γνώμην, "judgement"; διάλεξιν,

THE CLOUDS, 315-327

    Who are these that recite with such grandeur and might?
                  are they glorified mortals of old?
so. No mortals are there, but Clouds of the air,
             great Gods who the indolent fill:
These grant us discourse, and logical force,
             and the art of persuasion instil,
And periphrasis strange, and a power to arrange,
             and a marvellous judgement and skill.[a]
st. So then when I heard their omnipotent word,
             my spirit felt all of a flutter,
And it yearns to begin subtle cobwebs to spin
             and about metaphysics to stutter,
And together to glue an idea or two,
             and battle away in replies:
So if it's not wrong, I earnestly long
             to behold them myself with my eyes.
so. Look up in the air, towards Parnes out there,
             for I see they will pitch before long
These regions about.
st.   Where? point me them out.
so.   They are drifting, an infinite throng,
And their long shadows quake over valley and brake.
st.   Why, whatever's the matter to-day?
I can't see, I declare.
so.   By the Entrance[b]; look there!
st.   Ah, I just got a glimpse, by the way.
so. There, now you must see how resplendent they be,
             or your eyes must be pumpkins, I vow.

[a] "dialectical powers," skill in debate; νοῦν, "intelligence"; τερατείαν, "fanfaronade," the employment of grandiose thoughts and words; περίλεξιν, "periphrasis," circumlocution, the art of talking round a subject; κροῦσιν, "crushing force"; and κατάληψιν, "quickness of apprehension."

[b] By which the Chorus came into the orchestra.

ARISTOPHANES

ΣΤ. νὴ Δί' ἔγωγ', ὦ πολυτίμητοι, πάντα γὰρ ἤδη κατέχουσι.
ΣΩ. ταύτας μέντοι σὺ θεὰς οὔσας οὐκ ᾔδεις οὐδ' ἐνόμιζες;
ΣΤ. μὰ Δί', ἀλλ' ὀμίχλην καὶ δρόσον αὐτὰς ἡγούμην καὶ καπνὸν εἶναι. 330
ΣΩ. οὐ γὰρ μὰ Δί' οἶσθ' ὁτιὴ πλείστους αὗται βόσκουσι σοφιστάς,
Θουριομάντεις, ἰατροτέχνας, σφραγιδονυχαργοκομήτας,
κυκλίων τε χορῶν ᾀσματοκάμπτας, ἄνδρας μετεωροφένακας,
οὐδὲν δρῶντας βόσκουσ' ἀργούς, ὅτι ταύτας μουσοποιοῦσιν.
ΣΤ. ταῦτ' ἄρ' ἐποίουν " ὑγρᾶν Νεφελᾶν στρεπταιγλᾶν δάϊον ὁρμάν," 335
" πλοκάμους θ' ἑκατογκεφάλα Τυφῶ," "πρημαινούσας τε θυέλλας,"
εἶτ' "ἀερίας, διεράς," "γαμψοὺς οἰωνούς, ἀερονηχεῖς,"
" ὄμβρους θ' ὑδάτων δροσερᾶν Νεφελᾶν·" εἶτ' ἀντ' αὐτῶν κατέπινον
κεστρᾶν τεμάχη μεγαλᾶν ἀγαθᾶν, κρέα τ' ὀρνίθεια κιχηλᾶν.
ΣΩ. διὰ μέντοι τάσδ' οὐχὶ δικαίως;
ΣΤ. λέξον δή μοι, τί παθοῦσαι, 340
εἴπερ Νεφέλαι γ' εἰσὶν ἀληθῶς, θνηταῖς εἴξασι γυναιξίν;
οὐ γὰρ ἐκεῖναί γ' εἰσὶ τοιαῦται.

---

[a] Said by the Scholiast to refer to Lampon, one of the leaders of the colony which founded Thurii in 443 ; cf. B. 521.
[b] Along with the "tragic" and "comic" choruses at the

THE CLOUDS, 328-342

ST. Ah! I see them proceed; I should think so indeed:
    great powers! they fill everything now.
SO. So then till this day that celestials were they,
    you never imagined or knew?
ST. Why, no, on my word, for I always had heard
    they were nothing but vapour and dew.
SO. O, then I declare, you can't be aware
    that 'tis these who the sophists protect,
  Prophets sent beyond sea,[a] quacks of every degree,
    fops signet-and-jewel-bedecked,
  Astrological knaves, and fools who their staves
    of dithyrambs [b] proudly rehearse—
  'Tis the Clouds who all these support at their ease,
    because they exalt them in verse.
ST. 'Tis for this then they write of " the on-rushin' might
    o' the light-stappin' rain-drappin' Cloud,"
  And the " thousand black curls whilk the Tempest-
    lord whirls,"
      and the " thunder-blast stormy an' loud,"
  And " birds o' the sky floatin' upwards on high,"
    and " air-water leddies " which " droon
  Wi' their saft falling dew the gran' Ether sae blue," [c]
    and then in return they gulp doon
  Huge gobbets o' fishes [d] an' bountifu' dishes
    o' mavises prime in their season.
SO. And is it not right such praise to requite?
ST.   Ah, but tell me then what is the reason
  That if, as you say, they are Clouds, they to-day
    as women appear to our view?
  For the ones in the air are not women, I swear.

Dionysia, was one for dithyrambic contests, which is here called
κύκλιος χόρος.
  [c] " These are probably genuine quotations from the effusions
of dithyrambic poets " : R.
  [d] κέστρα is the muraena, esteemed a great delicacy.

295

ΣΩ. φέρε, ποῖαι γάρ τινές εἰσιν;
ΣΤ. οὐκ οἶδα σαφῶς· εἴξασιν γοῦν ἐρίοισιν πεπταμένοισι,
κοὐχὶ γυναιξίν, μὰ Δί', οὐδ' ὁτιοῦν· αὗται δὲ ῥῖνας ἔχουσιν.
ΣΩ. ἀπόκριναί νυν ἅττ' ἄν ἔρωμαι.
ΣΤ. λέγε νυν ταχέως ὅ τι βούλει. 345
ΣΩ. ἤδη ποτ' ἀναβλέψας εἶδες νεφέλην Κενταύρῳ ὁμοίαν
ἢ παρδάλει ἢ λύκῳ ἢ ταύρῳ;
ΣΤ. νὴ Δί' ἔγωγ'. εἶτα τί τοῦτο;
ΣΩ. γίγνονται πάνθ' ὅ τι βούλονται· κᾆτ' ἢν μὲν ἴδωσι κομήτην,
ἄγριόν τινα τῶν λασίων τούτων, οἷόνπερ τὸν Ξενοφάντου,
σκώπτουσαι τὴν μανίαν αὐτοῦ Κενταύροις ἤκασαν αὐτάς. 350
ΣΤ. τί γάρ, ἢν ἅρπαγα τῶν δημοσίων κατίδωσι Σίμωνα, τί δρῶσιν;
ΣΩ. ἀποφαίνουσαι τὴν φύσιν αὐτοῦ λύκοι ἐξαίφνης ἐγένοντο.
ΣΤ. ταῦτ' ἄρα, ταῦτα Κλεώνυμον αὗται τὸν ῥίψασπιν χθὲς ἰδοῦσαι,
ὅτι δειλότατον τοῦτον ἑώρων, ἔλαφοι διὰ τοῦτ' ἐγένοντο.
ΣΩ. καὶ νῦν γ' ὅτι Κλεισθένη εἶδον, ὁρᾷς, διὰ τοῦτ' ἐγένοντο γυναῖκες. 355
ΣΤ. χαίρετε τοίνυν, ὦ δέσποιναι· καὶ νῦν, εἴπερ τινὶ κἄλλῳ,
οὐρανομήκη ῥήξατε κἀμοὶ φωνήν, ὦ παμβασίλειαι.

THE CLOUDS, 342-357

SO.   Why, what do they seem then to you?
ST. I can't say very well, but they straggle and swell
                like fleeces spread out in the air;
Not like women they flit, no, by Zeus, not a bit,
                but these have got noses to wear.
SO. Well, now then, attend to this question, my friend.
ST.   Look sharp, and propound it to me.
SO. Didst thou never espy a Cloud in the sky,
             which a centaur or leopard might be,
Or a wolf, or a cow?
ST.   Very often, I vow:
              and show me the cause, I entreat.
SO. Why, I tell you that these become just what they please,
             and whenever they happen to meet
One shaggy and wild, like the tangle-haired child[a]
             of old Xenophantes, their rule
Is at once to appear like Centaurs, to jeer
              the ridiculous look of the fool.
ST. What then do they do if Simon[b] they view,
            that fraudulent harpy to shame?
SO. Why, his nature to show to us mortals below,
            a wolfish appearance they frame.
ST. O, they then I ween having yesterday seen
            Cleonymus quaking with fear,
(Him who threw off his shield as he fled from the field),
            metamorphosed themselves into deer.
SO. Yes, and now they espy soft Cleisthenes nigh,
            and therefore as women appear.
ST. O then without fail, All hail! and All hail!
            my welcome receive; and reply
With your voices so fine, so grand and divine,
            majestical Queens of the Sky!

[a] Hieronymus; cf. *A*. 389.   [b] Otherwise unknown.

ARISTOPHANES

ΧΟ. χαῖρ', ὦ πρεσβῦτα παλαιογενές, θηρατὰ λόγων
φιλομούσων·
σύ τε, λεπτοτάτων λήρων ἱερεῦ, φράζε πρὸς ἡμᾶς
ὅ τι χρῄζεις·
οὐ γὰρ ἂν ἄλλῳ γ' ὑπακούσαιμεν τῶν νῦν μετεωρο-
σοφιστῶν 360
πλὴν ἢ Προδίκῳ, τῷ μὲν σοφίας καὶ γνώμης
οὕνεκα, σοὶ δέ,
ὅτι βρενθύει τ' ἐν ταῖσιν ὁδοῖς καὶ τὠφθαλμὼ
παραβάλλεις,
κἀνυπόδητος κακὰ πόλλ' ἀνέχει κἀφ' ἡμῖν σεμνο-
προσωπεῖς.

ΣΤ. ὦ Γῆ τοῦ φθέγματος, ὡς ἱερὸν καὶ σεμνὸν καὶ
τερατῶδες.

ΣΩ. αὗται γάρ τοι μόναι εἰσὶ θεαί· τἄλλα δὲ πάντ'
ἐστὶ φλύαρος. 365

ΣΤ. ὁ Ζεὺς δ' ἡμῖν, φέρε, πρὸς τῆς Γῆς, οὑλύμπιος
οὐ θεός ἐστιν;

ΣΩ. ποῖος Ζεύς; οὐ μὴ ληρήσεις· οὐδ' ἔστι Ζεύς.

ΣΤ. τί λέγεις σύ;
ἀλλὰ τίς ὕει; τουτὶ γὰρ ἔμοιγ' ἀπόφηναι πρῶτον
ἁπάντων.

ΣΩ. αὗται δή που· μεγάλοις δέ σ' ἐγὼ σημείοις αὐτὸ
διδάξω.
φέρε, ποῦ γὰρ πώποτ' ἄνευ Νεφελῶν ὕοντ' ἤδη
τεθέασαι; 370
καίτοι χρῆν αἰθρίας ὕειν αὐτόν, ταύτας δ' ἀπο-
δημεῖν.

ΣΤ. νὴ τὸν Ἀπόλλω, τοῦτό γέ τοι δὴ τῷ νῦν λόγῳ
εὖ προσέφυσας·

THE CLOUDS, 358–372

CH. Our welcome to thee, old man, who wouldst see
                the marvels that science can show :
And thou, the high-priest of this subtlety feast,
                say what would you have us bestow ?
Since there is not a sage for whom we'd engage
                our wonders more freely to do,
Except, it may be, for Prodicus [a] ; he
            for his knowledge may claim them, but you,
For that sideways you throw your eyes as you go,
                and are all affectation and fuss ;
No shoes will you wear, but assume the grand air
                on the strength of your dealings with us.
ST. O Earth ! what a sound, how august and profound !
                it fills me with wonder and awe.
SO. These, these then alone, for true Deities own,
                the rest are all Godships of straw.
ST. Let Zeus be left out : He's a God beyond doubt :
                come, that you can scarcely deny.
SO. Zeus, indeed! there's no Zeus: don't you be so obtuse.
ST.   No Zeus up aloft in the sky !
Then, you first must explain, who it is sends the rain ;
                or I really must think you are wrong.
SO. Well then, be it known, these send it alone :
                I can prove it by arguments strong.
Was there ever a shower seen to fall in an hour
                when the sky was all cloudless and blue ?
Yet on a fine day, when the Clouds are away,
                he might send one, according to you.
ST. Well, it must be confessed, that chimes in with the rest:
                your words I am forced to believe.

[a] Of Ceos; "the most respectable of all the Sophists" (Müller) and author of *The Choice of Hercules*.

ARISTOPHANES

καίτοι πρότερον τὸν Δί' ἀληθῶς ᾤμην διὰ κοσκίνου
οὐρεῖν.
ἀλλ' ὅστις ὁ βροντῶν ἐστι φράσον· τοῦτό με ποιεῖ
τετρεμαίνειν.
ΣΩ. αὗται βροντῶσι κυλινδόμεναι.
ΣΤ. τῷ τρόπῳ, ὦ πάντα σὺ τολμῶν; 37
ΣΩ. ὅταν ἐμπλησθῶσ' ὕδατος πολλοῦ κἀναγκασθῶσι
φέρεσθαι,
κατακρημνάμεναι πλήρεις ὄμβρου δι' ἀνάγκην, εἶτα
βαρεῖαι
εἰς ἀλλήλας ἐμπίπτουσαι ῥήγνυνται καὶ πατα-
γοῦσιν.
ΣΤ. ὁ δ' ἀναγκάζων ἐστὶ τίς αὐτάς, οὐχ ὁ Ζεύς, ὥστε
φέρεσθαι;
ΣΩ. ἥκιστ', ἀλλ' αἰθέριος δῖνος.
ΣΤ. Δῖνος; τουτί μ' ἐλελήθει, 38
ὁ Ζεὺς οὐκ ὤν, ἀλλ' ἀντ' αὐτοῦ Δῖνος νυνὶ βασι-
λεύων.
ἀτὰρ οὐδέν πω περὶ τοῦ πατάγου καὶ τῆς βροντῆς
μ' ἐδίδαξας.
ΣΩ. οὐκ ἤκουσάς μου τὰς Νεφέλας ὕδατος μεστὰς ὅτι
φημὶ
ἐμπιπτούσας εἰς ἀλλήλας παταγεῖν διὰ τὴν πυκνό-
τητα;
ΣΤ. φέρε τουτὶ τῷ χρὴ πιστεύειν;
ΣΩ. ἀπὸ σαυτοῦ 'γώ σε διδάξω. 38
ἤδη ζωμοῦ Παναθηναίοις ἐμπλησθεὶς εἶτ' ἐταράχθης.

[a] *Cf.* Plato, *Phaedo* 99 B ὁ μέν τις δίνην περιτιθεὶς τῇ γῇ ὑπὸ
τοῦ οὐρανοῦ μένειν δὴ ποιεῖ τὴν γῆν, where the commentators refer

THE CLOUDS, 373-386

Yet before, I had dreamed that the rain-water streamed
  from Zeus and his chamber-pot sieve.
But whence then, my friend, does the thunder descend?
  that does make me quake with affright!
so. Why 'tis they, I declare, as they roll through the air.
st. What the Clouds? did I hear you aright?
so. Ay: for when to the brim filled with water they swim,
  by Necessity carried along,
They are hung up on high in the vault of the sky,
  and so by Necessity strong
In the midst of their course, they clash with great force,
  and thunder away without end.
st. But is it not He who compels this to be?
  does not Zeus this Necessity send?
so. No Zeus have we there, but a Vortex [a] of air.
st. What! Vortex? that's something, I own.
I knew not before, that Zeus was no more,
  but Vortex was placed on his throne!
But I have not yet heard to what cause you referred
  the thunder's majestical roar.
so. Yes, 'tis they, when on high full of water they fly,
  and then, as I told you before,
By Compression impelled, as they clash, are compelled
  a terrible clatter to make.
st. Come, how can that be? I really don't see.
so. Yourself as my proof I will take.
Have you never then eat the broth-puddings you get
  when the Panathenaea [b] comes round,

to Empedocles. But the Scholiast here says, "This is from Anaxagoras."
  [b] "At this feast all the colonial cities founded by Athens each sent an ox to sacrifice. There was thus no fear of meat failing . . . and some were tempted to eat more than was good for them": Schol.

301

ARISTOPHANES

τὴν γαστέρα, καὶ κλόνος ἐξαίφνης αὐτὴν διεκορκορύγησεν;

ΣΤ. νὴ τὸν Ἀπόλλω, καὶ δεινὰ ποιεῖ γ' εὐθύς μοι, καὶ τετάρακται
χὤσπερ βροντὴ τὸ ζωμίδιον παταγεῖ καὶ δεινὰ κέκραγεν·
ἀτρέμας πρῶτον παππὰξ παππάξ, κἄπειτ' ἐπάγει παπαπαππάξ, 390
χὤταν χέζω, κομιδῇ βροντᾷ παπαπαππάξ, ὥσπερ ἐκεῖναι.

ΣΩ. σκέψαι τοίνυν ἀπὸ γαστριδίου τυννουτουὶ οἷα πέπορδας·
τὸν δ' ἀέρα τόνδ' ὄντ' ἀπέραντον, πῶς οὐκ εἰκὸς μέγα βροντᾶν;
ταῦτ' ἄρα καὶ τὠνόματ' ἀλλήλοιν, βροντὴ καὶ πορδή, ὁμοίω.

ΣΤ. ἀλλ' ὁ κεραυνὸς πόθεν αὖ φέρεται λάμπων πυρί, τοῦτο δίδαξον, 395
καὶ καταφρύγει βάλλων ἡμᾶς, τοὺς δὲ ζῶντας περιφλύει.
τοῦτον γὰρ δὴ φανερῶς ὁ Ζεὺς ἵησ' ἐπὶ τοὺς ἐπιόρκους.

ΣΩ. καὶ πῶς, ὦ μῶρε σὺ καὶ Κρονίων ὄζων καὶ βεκκεσέληνε,
εἴπερ βάλλει τοὺς ἐπιόρκους, πῶς οὐχὶ Σίμων' ἐνέπρησεν
οὐδὲ Κλεώνυμον οὐδὲ Θέωρον; καίτοι σφόδρα γ' εἴσ' ἐπίορκοι· 400
ἀλλὰ τὸν αὑτοῦ γε νεὼν βάλλει καὶ " Σούνιον ἄκρον Ἀθηνέων "
καὶ τὰς δρῦς τὰς μεγάλας· τί μαθών; οὐ γὰρ δὴ δρῦς γ' ἐπιορκεῖ.

THE CLOUDS, 387–402

And felt with what might your bowels all night
    in turbulent tumult resound?
ST. By Apollo, 'tis true, there's a mighty to-do,
    and my belly keeps rumbling about;
And the puddings begin to clatter within
    and kick up a wonderful rout:
Quite gently at first, papapax, papapax,
    but soon pappapappax away,
Till at last, I'll be bound, I can thunder as loud,
    papapappappapappax, as They.
SO. Shalt thou then a sound so loud and profound
    from thy belly diminutive send,
And shall not the high and the infinite Sky
    go thundering on without end?
For both, you will find, on an impulse of wind
    and similar causes depend.
ST. Well, but tell me from Whom comes the bolt through
 the gloom, with its awful and terrible flashes;
And wherever it turns, some it singes and burns,
    and some it reduces to ashes!
For this 'tis quite plain, let who will send the rain,
    that Zeus against perjurers dashes.
SO. And how, you old fool of a dark-ages school,
    and an antediluvian wit,
If the perjured they strike, and not all men alike,
    have they never Cleonymus hit?
Then of Simon again, and Theorus explain:
    known perjurers, yet they escape.
But he smites his own shrine with his arrows divine,
    and " Sunium, Attica's cape," [a]
And the ancient gnarled oaks: now what prompted
 those strokes? *They* never forswore I should say.

[a] Hom. *Od.* iii. 278.

ARISTOPHANES

ΣΤ. οὐκ οἶδ᾽· ἀτὰρ εὖ σὺ λέγειν φαίνει. τί γάρ ἐστιν
 δῆθ᾽ ὁ κεραυνός;
ΣΩ. ὅταν εἰς ταύτας ἄνεμος ξηρὸς μετεωρισθεὶς κατα-
 κλεισθῇ,
 ἔνδοθεν αὐτὰς ὥσπερ κύστιν φυσᾷ, κἄπειθ᾽ ὑπ᾽ 40ι
 ἀνάγκης
 ῥήξας αὐτὰς ἔξω φέρεται σοβαρὸς διὰ τὴν πυκνό-
 τητα,
 ὑπὸ τοῦ ῥοίβδου καὶ τῆς ῥύμης αὐτὸς ἑαυτὸν
 κατακαίων.
ΣΤ. νὴ Δί᾽, ἐγὼ γοῦν ἀτεχνῶς ἔπαθον τουτί ποτε
 Διασίοισιν.
 ὤπτων γαστέρα τοῖς συγγενέσιν, κᾆτ᾽ οὐκ ἔσχων
 ἀμελήσας·
 ἡ δ᾽ ἄρ᾽ ἐφυσᾶτ᾽, εἶτ᾽ ἐξαίφνης διαλακήσασα πρὸς 41ι
 αὐτὼ
 τὠφθαλμώ μου προσετίλησεν καὶ κατέκαυσεν τὸ
 πρόσωπον.
ΧΟ. ὦ τῆς μεγάλης ἐπιθυμήσας σοφίας, ὤνθρωπε,
 παρ᾽ ἡμῶν,
 ὡς εὐδαίμων ἐν Ἀθηναίοις καὶ τοῖς Ἕλλησι
 γενήσει,
 εἰ μνήμων εἶ καὶ φροντιστὴς καὶ τὸ ταλαίπωρον
 ἔνεστιν
 ἐν τῇ ψυχῇ, καὶ μὴ κάμνεις μήθ᾽ ἑστὼς μήτε 41
 βαδίζων,
 μήτε ῥιγῶν ἄχθει λίαν, μήτ᾽ ἀριστᾶν ἐπιθυμεῖς,
 οἴνου τ᾽ ἀπέχει καὶ γυμνασίων καὶ τῶν ἄλλων
 ἀνοήτων,
 καὶ βέλτιστον τοῦτο νομίζεις, ὅπερ εἰκὸς δεξιὸν
 ἄνδρα,

THE CLOUDS, 403-418

. Can't say that they do : your words appear true.
   Whence comes then the thunderbolt, pray ?
. When a wind that is dry, being lifted on high,
   is suddenly pent into these,
It swells up their skin, like a bladder, within,
   by Necessity's changeless decrees :
Till, compressed very tight, it bursts them outright,
   and away with an impulse so strong,
That at last by the force and the swing of its course,
   it takes fire as it whizzes along.
. That's exactly the thing that I suffered one Spring,
   at the great feast of Zeus,[a] I admit :
I'd a paunch in the pot, but I wholly forgot
   about making the safety-valve slit.
So it spluttered and swelled, while the saucepan I held,
   till at last with a vengeance it flew :
Took me quite by surprise, dung-bespattered my eyes,
   and scalded my face black and blue !
ι. O thou who wouldst fain great wisdom attain,
   and comest to us in thy need,
All Hellas around shall thy glory resound,
   such a prosperous life thou shalt lead :
So thou art but endued with a memory good,
   and accustomed profoundly to think,
And thy soul wilt inure all wants to endure,
   and from no undertaking to shrink,
And art hardy and bold, to bear up against cold,
   and with patience a supper thou losest :
Nor too much dost incline to gymnastics and wine,
   but all lusts of the body refusest :
And esteemest it best, what is always the test
   of a truly intelligent brain,

---

[a] A great feast in honour of Ζεὺς Μειλίχιος, cf. Thuc. i. 126. 6.

ARISTOPHANES

νικᾶν πράττων καὶ βουλεύων καὶ τῇ γλώττῃ
πολεμίζων.
ΣΤ. ἀλλ' ἕνεκέν γε ψυχῆς στερρᾶς δυσκολοκοίτου τε
μερίμνης,
καὶ φειδωλοῦ καὶ τρυσιβίου γαστρὸς καὶ θυμ-
βρεπιδείπνου,
ἀμέλει θαρρῶν, οὕνεκα τούτων ἐπιχαλκεύειν παρ-
έχοιμ' ἄν.
ΣΩ. ἄλλο τι δῆτ' οὖν νομιεῖς ἤδη θεὸν οὐδένα πλὴν ἅπερ
ἡμεῖς,
τὸ Χάος τουτὶ καὶ τὰς Νεφέλας καὶ τὴν γλῶτταν,
τρία ταυτί;
ΣΤ. οὐδ' ἂν διαλεχθείην γ' ἀτεχνῶς τοῖς ἄλλοις, οὐδ'
ἂν ἀπαντῶν·
οὐδ' ἂν θύσαιμ', οὐδ' ἂν σπείσαιμ', οὐδ' ἐπιθείην
λιβανωτόν.
ΧΟ. λέγε νυν ἡμῖν ὅ τι σοι δρῶμεν θαρρῶν, ὡς οὐκ
ἀτυχήσεις,
ἡμᾶς τιμῶν καὶ θαυμάζων καὶ ζητῶν δεξιὸς εἶναι.
ΣΤ. ὦ δέσποιναι, δέομαι τοίνυν ὑμῶν τουτὶ πάνυ μικρόν,
τῶν Ἑλλήνων εἶναί με λέγειν ἑκατὸν σταδίοισιν
ἄριστον.
ΧΟ. ἀλλ' ἔσται σοι τοῦτο παρ' ἡμῶν· ὥστε τὸ λοιπόν
γ' ἀπὸ τουδὶ
ἐν τῷ δήμῳ γνώμας οὐδεὶς νικήσει πλείονας ἢ σύ.
ΣΤ. μή μοί γε λέγειν γνώμας μεγάλας· οὐ γὰρ τούτων
ἐπιθυμῶ,
ἀλλ' ὅσ' ἐμαυτῷ στρεψοδικῆσαι καὶ τοὺς χρήστας
διολισθεῖν.
ΧΟ. τεύξει τοίνυν ὧν ἱμείρεις· οὐ γὰρ μεγάλων ἐπιθυμεῖς.

THE CLOUDS, 419-435

  To prevail and succeed whensoever you plead,
      and hosts of tongue-conquests to gain.
ST. But as far as a sturdy soul is concerned
      and a horrible restless care,
  And a belly that pines and wears away
      on the wretchedest, frugalest fare,
  You may hammer and strike as long as you like ;
      I am quite invincible there.
SO. Now then you agree in rejecting with me
      the Gods you believed in when young,
  And *my* creed you'll embrace " *I believe in wide space,*
      in the Clouds, in the eloquent Tongue."
ST. If I happened to meet other Gods in the street,
      I'd show the cold shoulder, I vow.
  No libation I'll pour : not one victim more
      on their altars I'll sacrifice now.
CH. Now be honest and true, and say what we shall do :
      since you never shall fail of our aid,
  If you hold us most dear in devotion and fear,
      and will ply the philosopher's trade.
ST. O Ladies Divine, small ambition is mine :
      I only most modestly seek,
  Out and out for the rest of my life to be best
      of the children of Hellas to speak
CH. Say no more of your care, we have granted your prayer:
      and know from this moment, that none
  More acts shall pass through in the People than you :
      such favour from us you have won.
ST. Not acts, if you please : I want nothing of these :
      this gift you may quickly withdraw ;
  But I wish to succeed, just enough for my need,
      and to slip through the clutches of law.
CH. This then you shall do, for your wishes are few :
      not many nor great your demands,

ARISTOPHANES

ἀλλὰ σεαυτὸν θαρρῶν παράδος τοῖς ἡμετέροις προπόλοισι.

ΣΤ. δράσω ταῦθ' ὑμῖν πιστεύσας· ἡ γὰρ ἀνάγκη με πιέζει
διὰ τοὺς ἵππους τοὺς κοππατίας καὶ τὸν γάμον, ὅς
μ' ἐπέτριψεν.
νῦν οὖν χρήσθων ὅ τι βούλονται.
τουτὶ τό γ' ἐμὸν σῶμ' αὐτοῖσιν 440
παρέχω τύπτειν, πεινῆν, διψῆν,
αὐχμεῖν, ῥιγοῦν, ἀσκὸν δείρειν,
εἴπερ τὰ χρέα διαφευξοῦμαι,
τοῖς τ' ἀνθρώποις εἶναι δόξω
θρασύς, εὔγλωττος, τολμηρός, ἴτης, 445
βδελυρός, ψευδῶν συγκολλητής,
εὑρησιεπής, περίτριμμα δικῶν,
κύρβις, κρόταλον, κίναδος, τρύμη,
μάσθλης, εἴρων, γλοιός, ἀλαζών,
κέντρων, μιαρός, στρόφις, ἀργαλέος, 450
ματτυολοιχός.
ταῦτ' εἴ με καλοῦσ' ἀπαντῶντες,
δρώντων ἀτεχνῶς ὅ τι χρῄζουσιν·
κεἰ βούλονται
νὴ τὴν Δήμητρ' ἔκ μου χορδὴν 455
τοῖς φροντισταῖς παραθέντων.

ΧΟ. λῆμα μὲν πάρεστι τῷδέ γ'
οὐκ ἄτολμον, ἀλλ' ἕτοιμον. ἴσθι δ' ὡς
ταῦτα μαθὼν παρ' ἐμοῦ κλέος οὐρανόμηκες
ἐν βροτοῖσιν ἕξεις. 460

---

[a] 445-50 ἴτης, "a go-ahead fellow"; περίτριμμα, a superlative τρῖμμα (cf. 260); κύρβις, "a tablet of Law" τρύμη, "a carpenter's drill"; γλοιός, "well-oiled," "slippery"; κέντρων "quick to use the goad" (cf. 1300); στρόφις, "a weather-cock";

THE CLOUDS, 436-460

    So away with all care from henceforth, and prepare
                to be placed in our votaries' hands.
ST. This then will I do, confiding in you,
            for Necessity presses me sore,
    And so sad is my life, 'twixt my cobs and my wife,
            that I cannot put up with it more.
    So now, at your word, I give and afford
    My body to these, to treat as they please,
    To have and to hold, in squalor, in cold,
    In hunger and thirst, yea by Zeus, at the worst,
    To be flayed out of shape from my heels to my nape
    So along with my hide from my duns I escape,
    And to men may appear without conscience or fear,
    Bold,[a] hasty, and wise, a concocter of lies,
    A rattler to speak, a dodger, a sneak,
    A régular claw of the tables of law,
    A shuffler complete, well worn in deceit,
    A supple, unprincipled, troublesome cheat ;
    A hang-dog accurst, a bore with the worst,
    In the tricks of the jury-courts thoroughly versed.
    If all that I meet this praise shall repeat,
    Work away as you choose, I will nothing refuse,
    Without any reserve, from my head to my shoes.
    You shan't see me wince though my gutlets you mince,
    And these entrails of mine for a sausage combine,
    Served up for the gentlemen students to dine.

CH. Here's a spirit bold and high
    Ready-armed for any strife.
    (To Strepsiades)
    If you learn what I can teach
                Of the mysteries of speech,
    Your glory soon shall reach To the summit of the sky.

ματτυολοιχός (Bentley's emendation for ματιολοιχός) " a licker-up of hashed meat."

ARISTOPHANES

ΣΤ. τί πείσομαι;
ΧΟ.   τὸν πάντα χρόνον μετ' ἐμοῦ
    ζηλωτότατον βίον ἀνθρώπων διάξεις.   465
ΣΤ. ἆρά γε τοῦτ' ἄρ' ἐγώ ποτ' ὄψομαι;
ΧΟ. ὥστε γε σοῦ πολλοὺς ἐπὶ ταῖσι θύραις ἀεὶ καθῆσθαι,
    βουλομένους ἀνακοινοῦσθαί τε καὶ ἐς λόγον ἐλθεῖν, 470
    πράγματα κἀντιγραφὰς πολλῶν ταλάντων
    ἄξια σῇ φρενὶ συμβουλευσομένους μετὰ σοῦ.   475
    ἀλλ' ἐγχείρει τὸν πρεσβύτην ὅ τι περ μέλλεις προ-
    διδάσκειν,
    καὶ διακίνει τὸν νοῦν αὐτοῦ, καὶ τῆς γνώμης ἀπο-
    πειρῶ.

ΣΩ. ἄγε δή, κάτειπέ μοι σὺ τὸν σαυτοῦ τρόπον,
    ἵν' αὐτὸν εἰδὼς ὅστις ἐστὶ μηχανὰς
    ἤδη 'πὶ τούτοις πρὸς σὲ καινὰς προσφέρω.
ΣΤ. τί δέ; τειχομαχεῖν μοι διανοεῖ, πρὸς τῶν θεῶν; 480
ΣΩ. οὔκ, ἀλλὰ βραχέα σου πυθέσθαι βούλομαι,
    εἰ μνημονικὸς εἶ.
ΣΤ.   δύο τρόπω νὴ τὸν Δία·
    ἢν μὲν γὰρ ὀφείληταί τί μοι, μνήμων πάνυ,
    ἐὰν δ' ὀφείλω, σχέτλιος, ἐπιλήσμων πάνυ.
ΣΩ. ἔνεστι δῆτά σοι λέγειν ἐν τῇ φύσει;   485
ΣΤ. λέγειν μὲν οὐκ ἔνεστ', ἀποστερεῖν δ' ἔνι.
ΣΩ. πῶς οὖν δυνήσει μανθάνειν;
ΣΤ.   ἀμέλει, καλῶς.
ΣΩ. ἄγε νυν ὅπως, ὅταν τι προβάλω σοι σοφὸν
    περὶ τῶν μετεώρων, εὐθέως ὑφαρπάσει.
ΣΤ. τί δαί; κυνηδὸν τὴν σοφίαν σιτήσομαι;   490
ΣΩ. ἄνθρωπος ἀμαθὴς οὑτοσὶ καὶ βάρβαρος,
    δέδοικά σ', ὦ πρεσβῦτα, μὴ πληγῶν δέῃ.

THE CLOUDS, 461–493

ST. And what am I to gain?
CH.   With the Clouds you will obtain
The most happy, the most enviable life.
ST. Is it possible for me Such felicity to see?
CH. Yes, and men shall come and wait
                In their thousands at your gate,
Desiring consultations and advice
On an action or a pleading
              From the man of light and leading,
And you'll pocket many talents in a trice.
(*To Socrates*)
Here, take the old man, and do all that you can,
              your new-fashioned thoughts to instil,
And stir up his mind with your notions refined,
              and test him with judgement and skill.

SO. Come now, you tell me something of your habits:
For if I don't know them, I can't determine
What engines I must bring to bear upon you.
ST. Eh! what? Not going to storm me, by the Gods?
SO. No, no: I want to ask you a few questions.
First: is your memory good?
ST.   Two ways, by Zeus:
If I'm owed anything, I'm mindful, very:
But if I owe, (Oh, dear!) forgetful, very.
SO. Well then: have you the gift of speaking in you?
ST. The gift of speaking, no: of cheating, yes.
SO. No? how then can you learn?
ST.   Oh, well enough.
SO. Then when I throw you out some clever notion.
About the laws of nature, you must catch it.
ST. What! must I snap up sapience, in dog-fashion?
SO. Oh! why the man's an ignorant old savage:
I fear, my friend, that you'll require the whip.

ARISTOPHANES

ΣΤ. φέρ' ἴδω, τί δρᾷς, ἢν τίς σε τύπτῃ;
τύπτομαι,
ἔπειτ' ἐπισχὼν ὀλίγον ἐπιμαρτύρομαι, 495
εἶτ' αὖθις ἀκαρῆ διαλιπὼν δικάζομαι.
ΣΩ. ἴθι νυν, κατάθου θοἰμάτιον.
ΣΤ. ἠδίκηκά τι;
ΣΩ. οὔκ, ἀλλὰ γυμνοὺς εἰσιέναι νομίζεται.
ΣΤ. ἀλλ' οὐχὶ φωράσων ἔγωγ' εἰσέρχομαι.
ΣΩ. κατάθου. τί ληρεῖς;
ΣΤ. εἰπὲ δή νύν μοι τοδί· 500
ἢν ἐπιμελὴς ὦ καὶ προθύμως μανθάνω,
τῷ τῶν μαθητῶν ἐμφερὴς γενήσομαι;
ΣΩ. οὐδὲν διοίσεις Χαιρεφῶντος τὴν φύσιν.
ΣΤ. οἴμοι κακοδαίμων, ἡμιθνὴς γενήσομαι.
ΣΩ. οὐ μὴ λαλήσεις, ἀλλ' ἀκολουθήσεις ἐμοὶ 505
ἀνύσας τι δευρὶ θᾶττον;
ΣΤ. ἐς τὼ χεῖρέ νυν
δός μοι μελιτοῦτταν πρότερον· ὡς δέδοικ' ἐγὼ
εἴσω καταβαίνων ὥσπερ εἰς Τροφωνίου.
ΣΩ. χώρει· τί κυπτάζεις ἔχων περὶ τὴν θύραν;

ΧΟ. ἀλλ' ἴθι χαίρων τῆς ἀνδρείας 510
εἵνεκα ταύτης.
εὐτυχία γένοιτο τἀν-
θρώπῳ, ὅτι προήκων
ἐς βαθὺ τῆς ἡλικίας
νεωτέροις τὴν φύσιν αὑ- 515
τοῦ πράγμασιν χρωτίζεται
καὶ σοφίαν ἐπασκεῖ.

---

[a] Socrates wishes to appropriate it (cf. 179, 856), but Strepsiades thinks he is to be flogged.

THE CLOUDS, 494-517

Come, if one strikes you, what do you do?
ST. I'm struck :
Then in a little while I call my witness :
Then in another little while I summon him.
SO. Put off your cloak.^a
ST. Why, what have I done wrong?
SO. O, nothing, nothing : all go in here naked.
ST. Well, but I have not come with a search-warrant.^b
SO. Fool! throw it off.
ST. Well, tell me this one thing ;
If I'm extremely careful and attentive,
Which of your students shall I most resemble?
SO. Why, Chaerephon. You'll be his very image.
ST. What! I shall be half-dead! O luckless me!
SO. Don't chatter there, but come and follow me ;
Make haste now, quicker, here.
ST. Oh, but do first
Give me a honied cake : Zeus ! how I tremble,
To go down there, as if to see Trophonius.^c
SO. Go on! why keep you pottering round the door?

CH. Yes! go, and farewell ; as your courage is great,
  So bright be your fate.
May all good fortune his steps pursue,
  Who now, in his life's dim twilight haze,
Is game such venturesome things to do,
To steep his mind in discoveries new,
  To walk, a novice, in wisdom's ways.

^b The officer had to enter a house γυμνὸς ἢ χιτωνίσκον ἔχων (Plato, *Leg.* 954 A) so that he might not secretly carry in the thing asserted to be stolen.
^c The oracle of Trophonius was in a cave at Lebadea : the cakes were taken to appease " the serpent which haunted it " : Schol.

ARISTOPHANES

ὦ θεώμενοι, κατερῶ πρὸς ὑμᾶς ἐλευθέρως
τἀληθῆ, νὴ τὸν Διόνυσον τὸν ἐκθρέψαντά με.
οὕτω νικήσαιμί τ' ἐγὼ καὶ νομιζοίμην σοφός, 520
ὡς ὑμᾶς ἡγούμενος εἶναι θεατὰς δεξιοὺς
καὶ ταύτην σοφώτατ' ἔχειν τῶν ἐμῶν κωμῳδιῶν,
πρώτους ἠξίωσ' ἀναγεῦσ' ὑμᾶς, ἣ παρέσχε μοι
ἔργον πλεῖστον· εἶτ' ἀνεχώρουν ὑπ' ἀνδρῶν φορτικῶν
ἡττηθείς, οὐκ ἄξιος ὤν· ταῦτ' οὖν ὑμῖν μέμφομαι 525
τοῖς σοφοῖς, ὧν οὕνεκ' ἐγὼ ταῦτ' ἐπραγματευόμην.
ἀλλ' οὐδ' ὣς ὑμῶν ποθ' ἑκὼν προδώσω τοὺς δεξιούς.
ἐξ ὅτου γὰρ ἐνθάδ' ὑπ' ἀνδρῶν, οἷς ἡδὺ καὶ λέγειν,
ὁ σώφρων τε χὠ καταπύγων ἄριστ' ἠκουσάτην,
κἀγώ, παρθένος γὰρ ἔτ' ἦν, κοὐκ ἐξῆν πώ μοι τεκεῖν, 530
ἐξέθηκα, παῖς δ' ἑτέρα τις λαβοῦσ' ἀνείλετο,
ὑμεῖς δ' ἐξεθρέψατε γενναίως κἀπαιδεύσατε·
ἐκ τούτου μοι πιστὰ παρ' ὑμῖν γνώμης ἔσθ' ὅρκια.
νῦν οὖν Ἠλέκτραν κατ' ἐκείνην ἥδ' ἡ κωμῳδία

---

[a] 518-62 constitute the Parabasis of the revised Comedy.
[b] Two characters in his play the Banqueters.
[c] The Banqueters was exhibited in the name of Callistratus.
[d] The Choëphoroe of Aeschylus, where E. recognizes her brother's " lock of hair " on Agamemnon's tomb.

THE CLOUDS, 518-534

O Spectators,^a I will utter
    honest truths with accents free,
Yea! by mighty Dionysus,
    Him who bred and nurtured me.
So may I be deemed a poet,
    and this day obtain the prize,
As till that unhappy blunder
    I had always held you wise,
And of all my plays esteeming
    this the wisest and the best,
Served it up for your enjoyment,
    which had, more than all the rest,
Cost me thought, and time, and labour :
    then most scandalously treated,
I retired in mighty dudgeon,
    by unworthy foes defeated.
This is why I blame your critics,
    for whose sake I framed the play :
Yet the clever ones amongst you
    even now I won't betray.
No! for ever since from judges
    unto whom 'tis joy to speak,
Brothers Profligate and Modest ^b
    gained the praise we fondly seek,
When, for I was yet a Virgin,
    and it was not right to bear,
I exposed it, and Another
    did the foundling nurse with care,^c
But 'twas ye who nobly nurtured,
    ye who brought it up with skill ;—
From that hour I proudly cherish
    pledges of your sure good will.
Now then comes its sister hither,
    like Electra in the Play,^d

ARISTOPHANES

ζητοῦσ' ἦλθ', ἤν που 'πιτύχῃ θεαταῖς οὕτω σοφοῖς· 53.
γνώσεται γάρ, ἤνπερ ἴδῃ, τἀδελφοῦ τὸν βόστρυχον.
ὡς δὲ σώφρων ἐστὶ φύσει σκέψασθ'· ἥτις πρῶτα μὲν
οὐδὲν ἦλθε ῥαψαμένη σκύτινον καθειμένον,
ἐρυθρὸν ἐξ ἄκρου, παχύ, τοῖς παιδίοις ἵν' ᾖ γέλως·
οὐδ' ἔσκωψε τοὺς φαλακρούς, οὐδὲ κόρδαχ' εἵλκυσεν, 54(
οὐδὲ πρεσβύτης ὁ λέγων τἄπη τῇ βακτηρίᾳ
τύπτει τὸν παρόντ', ἀφανίζων πονηρὰ σκώμματα,
οὐδ' εἰσῇξε δᾷδας ἔχουσ', οὐδ' ἰοὺ ἰοὺ βοᾷ,
ἀλλ' αὑτῇ καὶ τοῖς ἔπεσιν πιστεύουσ' ἐλήλυθεν.
κἀγὼ μὲν τοιοῦτος ἀνὴρ ὢν ποιητὴς οὐ κομῶ, 54!
οὐδ' ὑμᾶς ζητῶ 'ξαπατᾶν δὶς καὶ τρὶς ταῦτ' εἰσάγων,
ἀλλ' ἀεὶ καινὰς ἰδέας εἰσφέρων σοφίζομαι,
οὐδὲν ἀλλήλαισιν ὁμοίας καὶ πάσας δεξιάς·
ὃς μέγιστον ὄντα Κλέων' ἔπαισ' εἰς τὴν γαστέρα,
κοὐκ ἐτόλμησ' αὖθις ἐπεμπηδῆσ' αὐτῷ κειμένῳ. 55(
οὗτοι δ', ὡς ἅπαξ παρέδωκεν λαβὴν Ὑπέρβολος,
τοῦτον δείλαιον κολετρῶσ' ἀεὶ καὶ τὴν μητέρα.

_a εἰσῇεσαν γὰρ οἱ κωμικοὶ διεζωσμένοι δερμάτινα αἰδοῖα, γελοίου χάριν : Schol.

THE CLOUDS, 535-552

Comes in earnest expectation
    kindred minds to meet to-day ;
She will recognize full surely,
    if she find, her brother's tress.
And observe how pure her morals :
    who, to notice her first dress,
Enters not with filthy symbols
    on her modest garments hung,[a]
Jeering bald-heads, dancing ballets,
    for the laughter of the young.
In this play no wretched greybeard
    with a staff his fellow pokes,
So obscuring from the audience
    all the poorness of his jokes.
No one rushes in with torches,
    no one groans, " *Oh, dear !* *Oh, dear !* "
Trusting in its genuine merits
    comes this play before you here.
Yet, though such a hero-poet,
    I, the bald-head, do not grow
Curling ringlets : neither do I
    twice or thrice my pieces show.
Always fresh ideas sparkle,
    always novel jests delight,
Nothing like each other, save that
    all are most exceeding bright.
I am he who floored the giant,
    Cleon, in his hour of pride,
Yet when down I scorned to strike him,
    and I left him when he died !
But the others, when a handle
    once Hyperbolus did lend,
Trample down the wretched caitiff,
    and his mother, without end.

ARISTOPHANES

Εὔπολις μὲν τὸν Μαρικᾶν πρώτιστον παρείλκυσεν
ἐκστρέψας τοὺς ἡμετέρους Ἱππέας κακὸς κακῶς,
προσθεὶς αὐτῷ γραῦν μεθύσην τοῦ κόρδακος οὕνεχ', ἣν 55
Φρύνιχος πάλαι πεποίηχ', ἣν τὸ κῆτος ἤσθιεν.
εἶθ' Ἕρμιππος αὖθις ἐποίησεν εἰς Ὑπέρβολον,
ἄλλοι τ' ἤδη πάντες ἐρείδουσιν εἰς Ὑπέρβολον,
τὰς εἰκοὺς τῶν ἐγχέλεων τὰς ἐμὰς μιμούμενοι.
ὅστις οὖν τούτοισι γελᾷ, τοῖς ἐμοῖς μὴ χαιρέτω· 56
ἣν δ' ἐμοὶ καὶ τοῖσιν ἐμοῖς εὐφραίνησθ' εὑρήμασιν,
ἐς τὰς ὥρας τὰς ἑτέρας εὖ φρονεῖν δοκήσετε.

ὑψιμέδοντα μὲν θεῶν
Ζῆνα τύραννον ἐς χορὸν
πρῶτα μέγαν κικλήσκω· 56
τόν τε μεγασθενῆ τριαί-
νης ταμίαν,
γῆς τε καὶ ἁλμυρᾶς θαλάσ-
σης ἄγριον μοχλευτήν·
καὶ μεγαλώνυμον ἡμέτερον πατέρ',
Αἰθέρα σεμνότατον, βιοθρέμμονα πάντων· 5·
τόν θ' ἱππονώμαν, ὃς ὑπερ-
λάμπροις ἀκτῖσιν κατέχει
γῆς πέδον, μέγας ἐν θεοῖς
ἐν θνητοῖσί τε δαίμων.

---

[a] Clearly the " mother of Hyperbolus."
[b] He seems to have travestied the story of Andromeda, bringing on a tipsy old woman to be devoured by the sea-monster.
[c] See K. 864-7.

THE CLOUDS, 553-574

In his Maricas the Drunkard,
                      Eupolis the charge began,
Shamefully my " Knights " distorting,
                      as he is a shameful man,
Tacking on the tipsy beldame,[a]
                      just the ballet-dance to keep,
Phrynichus's [b] prime invention,
                      eat by monsters of the deep.
Then Hermippus on the caitiff
                      opened all his little skill,
And the rest upon the caitiff
                      are their wit exhausting still ;
And my simile to pilfer
                      " of the Eels " [c] they all combine.
Whoso laughs at their productions,
                      let him not delight in mine.
But for you who praise my genius,
                      you who think my writings clever,
Ye shall gain a name for wisdom,
                      yea ! for ever and for ever.

    O mighty God, O heavenly King,
    First unto Thee my prayer I bring.
      O come, Lord Zeus, to my choral song ;—
And Thou, dread Power, whose resistless hand
Heaves up the sea and the trembling land,
    Lord of the trident, stern and strong ;—
And Thou who sustainest the life of us all
Come, Ether, our parent, O come to my call ;—
And Thou who floodest the world with light,
Guiding thy steeds through the glittering sky,
To men below and to Gods on high
    A Potentate heavenly-bright !

ARISTOPHANES

ὦ σοφώτατοι θεαταί, δεῦρο τὸν νοῦν πρόσχετε. 575
ἠδικημέναι γὰρ ὑμῖν μεμφόμεσθ' ἐναντίον·
πλεῖστα γὰρ θεῶν ἁπάντων ὠφελούσαις τὴν πόλιν,
δαιμόνων ἡμῖν μόναις οὐ θύετ' οὐδὲ σπένδετε,
αἵτινες τηροῦμεν ὑμᾶς. ἢν γὰρ ᾖ τις ἔξοδος
μηδενὶ ξὺν νῷ, τότ' ἢ βροντῶμεν ἢ ψακάζομεν. 580
εἶτα τὸν θεοῖσιν ἐχθρὸν βυρσοδέψην Παφλαγόνα
ἡνίχ' ᾑρεῖσθε στρατηγόν, τὰς ὀφρῦς συνήγομεν
κἀποιοῦμεν δεινά· "βροντὴ δ' ἐρράγη δι' ἀστραπῆς·"
ἡ σελήνη δ' ἐξέλειπε τὰς ὁδούς· ὁ δ' ἥλιος
τὴν θρυαλλίδ' εἰς ἑαυτὸν εὐθέως ξυνελκύσας 585
οὐ φανεῖν ἔφασκεν ὑμῖν, εἰ στρατηγήσει Κλέων.
ἀλλ' ὅμως εἵλεσθε τοῦτον. φασὶ γὰρ δυσβουλίαν
τῇδε τῇ πόλει προσεῖναι, ταῦτα μέντοι τοὺς θεοὺς
ἅττ' ἂν ὑμεῖς ἐξαμάρτητ' ἐπὶ τὸ βέλτιον τρέπειν.
ὡς δὲ καὶ τοῦτο ξυνοίσει ῥᾳδίως διδάξομεν. 590
ἢν Κλέωνα τὸν λάρον δώρων ἑλόντες καὶ κλοπῆς,

---

[a] From the *Teucer* of Sophocles : Schol.
[b] Nothing is known of this election.

THE CLOUDS, 575-591

O most sapient wise spectators,
                      hither turn attention due,
We complain of sad ill-treatment,
                      we've a bone to pick with you :
We have ever helped your city,
                      helped with all our might and main ;
Yet you pay us no devotion,
                      that is why we now complain.
We who always watch around you.
                      For if any project seems
Ill-concocted, then we thunder,
                      then the rain comes down in streams.
And, remember, very lately,
                      how we knit our brows together,
" Thunders crashing, lightnings flashing," [a]
                      never was such awful weather ;
And the Moon in haste eclipsed her,
                      and the Sun in anger swore
He would curl his wick within him
                      and give light to you no more,
Should you choose that mischief-worker,
                      Cleon, whom the Gods abhor,
Tanner, Slave, and Paphlagonian,
                      to lead out your hosts to war.[b]
Yet you chose him! yet you chose him!
                      For they say that Folly grows
Best and finest in this city,
                      but the gracious Gods dispose
Always all things for the better,
                      causing errors to succeed :
And how this sad job may profit,
                      surely he who runs may read.
Let the Cormorant be convicted,
                      in command, of bribes and theft,

ARISTOPHANES

εἶτα φιμώσητε τούτου τῷ ξύλῳ τὸν αὐχένα,
αὖθις ἐς τἀρχαῖον ὑμῖν, εἴ τι κἀξημάρτετε,
ἐπὶ τὸ βέλτιον τὸ πρᾶγμα τῇ πόλει συνοίσεται.

" ἀμφί μοι αὖτε," Φοῖβ' ἄναξ
Δήλιε, Κυνθίαν ἔχων
ὑψικέρατα πέτραν·
ἤ τ' Ἐφέσου μάκαιρα πάγ-
χρυσον ἔχεις
οἶκον ἐν ᾧ κόραι σε Λυ-
δῶν μεγάλως σέβουσιν·
ἤ τ' ἐπιχώριος ἡμετέρα θεός,
αἰγίδος ἡνίοχος, πολιοῦχος Ἀθάνα·
Παρνασσίαν θ' ὃς κατέχων
πέτραν σὺν πεύκαις σελαγεῖ
Βάκχαις Δελφίσιν ἐμπρέπων,
κωμαστὴς Διόνυσος.

ἡνίχ' ἡμεῖς δεῦρ' ἀφορμᾶσθαι παρεσκευάσμεθα,
ἡ Σελήνη συντυχοῦσ' ἡμῖν ἐπέστειλεν φράσαι,
πρῶτα μὲν χαίρειν Ἀθηναίοισι καὶ τοῖς ξυμμάχοις·
εἶτα θυμαίνειν ἔφασκε· δεινὰ γὰρ πεπονθέναι,
ὠφελοῦσ' ὑμᾶς ἅπαντας, οὐ λόγοις, ἀλλ' ἐμφανῶς.
πρῶτα μὲν τοῦ μηνὸς εἰς δᾷδ' οὐκ ἔλαττον ἢ δραχμήν,
ὥστε καὶ λέγειν ἅπαντας ἐξιόντας ἑσπέρας,

---

[a] ἀμφί μοι αὖτε was a common commencement of dithyrambic odes.

THE CLOUDS, 592-613

Let us have him gagged and muzzled,
      in the pillory chained and left,
Then again, in ancient fashion,
      all that ye have erred of late,
Will turn out your own advantage,
      and a blessing to the State.

  " Phoebus, my king, come to me still." [a]
  Thou who holdest the Cynthian hill,
   The lofty peak of the Delian isle ;—
  And Thou, his sister, to whom each day
  Lydian maidens devoutly pray
   In Thy stately gilded Ephesian pile ;—
  And Athene, our Lady, the queen of us all,
  With the Aegis of God, O come to my call ;—
  And Thou whose dancing torches of pine
  Flicker, Parnassian glades along,
  Dionysus, Star of Thy Maenad throng,
   Come, Reveller most divine !

We, when we had finished packing,
      and prepared our journey down,
Met the Lady Moon, who charged us
      with a message for your town.
First, All hail to noble Athens,
      and her faithful true Allies ;
Then, she said, your shameful conduct
      made her angry passions rise,
Treating her so ill who always
      aids you, not in words, but clearly ;
Saves you, first of all, in torchlight
      every month a drachma nearly,
So that each one says, if business
      calls him out from home by night,

ARISTOPHANES

μὴ πρίῃ, παῖ, δᾷδ', ἐπειδὴ φῶς Σεληναίης καλόν.
ἄλλα τ' εὖ δρᾶν φησιν, ὑμᾶς δ' οὐκ ἄγειν τὰς
ἡμέρας 615
οὐδὲν ὀρθῶς, ἀλλ' ἄνω τε καὶ κάτω κυδοιδοπᾶν·
ὥστ' ἀπειλεῖν φησιν αὐτῇ τοὺς θεοὺς ἑκάστοτε
ἡνίκ' ἂν ψευσθῶσι δείπνου, κἀπίωσιν οἴκαδε,
τῆς ἑορτῆς μὴ τυχόντες κατὰ λόγον τῶν ἡμερῶν.
κᾆθ' ὅταν θύειν δέῃ, στρεβλοῦτε καὶ δικάζετε· 620
πολλάκις δ' ἡμῶν ἀγόντων τῶν θεῶν ἀπαστίαν,
ἡνίκ' ἂν πενθῶμεν ἢ τὸν Μέμνον' ἢ Σαρπηδόνα,
σπένδεθ' ὑμεῖς καὶ γελᾶτ'· ἀνθ' ὧν λαχὼν Ὑπέρβολος
τῆτες ἱερομνημονεῖν, κἄπειθ' ὑφ' ἡμῶν τῶν θεῶν
τὸν στέφανον ἀφῃρέθη· μᾶλλον γὰρ οὕτως εἴσεται 625
κατὰ σελήνην ὡς ἄγειν χρὴ τοῦ βίου τὰς ἡμέρας.

ΣΩ. μὰ τὴν Ἀναπνοήν, μὰ τὸ Χάος, μὰ τὸν Ἀέρα,
οὐκ εἶδον οὕτως ἄνδρ' ἄγροικον οὐδένα
οὐδ' ἄπορον οὐδὲ σκαιὸν οὐδ' ἐπιλήσμονα·
ὅστις σκαλαθυρμάτι' ἄττα μικρὰ μανθάνων, 630
ταῦτ' ἐπιλέλησται πρὶν μαθεῖν· ὅμως γε μὴν
αὐτὸν καλῶ θύραζε δευρὶ πρὸς τὸ φῶς.
ποῦ Στρεψιάδης; ἕξει τὸν ἀσκάντην λαβών.

---

[a] The allusion is to alterations in the calendar introduced by the astronomer Meton about 432 B.C.
[b] Son of Eos (Aurora), slain by Achilles; for Sarpedon son of Zeus whom Patroclus slew see *Il.* xvi. 419 *seq.*
[c] An official sent with the three Pylagorae to the Amphictyonic Council. Nothing is known of the circumstance.
[d] *Socrates here comes out of the Phrontisterion where he has been endeavouring to teach Strepsiades.*

THE CLOUDS, 614–633

" Buy no link, my boy, this evening,
   for the Moon will lend her light."
Other blessings too she sends you,
   yet you will not mark your days
As she bids you, but confuse them,
   jumbling them all sorts of ways,[a]
And, she says, the Gods in chorus
   shower reproaches on her head,
When in bitter disappointment
   they go supperless to bed,
Not obtaining festal banquets
   duly on the festal day ;
Ye are badgering in the law-courts
   when ye should arise and slay !
And full oft when we celestials
   some strict fast are duly keeping,
For the fate of mighty Memnon,[b]
   or divine Sarpedon weeping,
Then you feast and pour libations :
   and Hyperbolus of late
Lost the crown he wore so proudly
   as Recorder [c] of the Gate,
Through the wrath of us immortals :
   so perchance he'll rather know
Always all his days in future
   by the Lady Moon to go.

so.[d] Never by Chaos, Air, and Respiration,
Never, no never have I seen a clown
So helpless, and forgetful, and absurd !
Why if he learns a quirk or two he clean
Forgets them ere he has learnt them : all the same,
I'll call him out of doors here to the light.
Take up your bed, Strepsiades, and come !

ARISTOPHANES

ΣΤ. ἀλλ' οὐκ ἐῶσί μ' ἐξενεγκεῖν οἱ κόρεις.
ΣΩ. ἀνύσας τι κατάθου, καὶ πρόσεχε τὸν νοῦν.
ΣΤ. ἰδού.
ΣΩ. ἄγε δή, τί βούλει πρῶτα νυνὶ μανθάνειν 635
ὧν οὐκ ἐδιδάχθης πώποτ' οὐδέν; εἰπέ μοι.
πότερον περὶ μέτρων ἢ περὶ ἐπῶν ἢ ῥυθμῶν;
ΣΤ. περὶ τῶν μέτρων ἔγωγ'· ἔναγχος γάρ ποτε
ὑπ' ἀλφιταμοιβοῦ παρεκόπην διχοινίκῳ. 640
ΣΩ. οὐ τοῦτ' ἐρωτῶ σ', ἀλλ' ὅ τι κάλλιστον μέτρον
ἡγεῖ· πότερον τὸ τρίμετρον ἢ τὸ τετράμετρον; 645
ΣΤ. ἐγὼ μὲν οὐδὲν πρότερον ἡμιεκτέου.
ΣΩ. οὐδὲν λέγεις, ὦνθρωπε.
ΣΤ. περίδου νυν ἐμοί,
εἰ μὴ τετράμετρόν ἐστιν ἡμιεκτέον.
ΣΩ. ἐς κόρακας, ὡς ἄγροικος εἶ καὶ δυσμαθής.
τάχα δ' ἂν δύναιο μανθάνειν περὶ ῥυθμῶν.
ΣΤ. τί δέ μ' ὠφελήσουσ' οἱ ῥυθμοὶ πρὸς τἄλφιτα;
ΣΩ. πρῶτον μὲν εἶναι κομψὸν ἐν συνουσίᾳ, 650
ἐπαΐονθ' ὁποῖός ἐστι τῶν ῥυθμῶν
κατ' ἐνόπλιον, χὠποῖος αὖ κατὰ δάκτυλον.
ΣΤ. κατὰ δάκτυλον; νὴ τὸν Δί', ἀλλ' οἶδ'.
ΣΩ. εἰπὲ δή.
ΣΤ. τίς ἄλλος ἀντὶ τουτουὶ τοῦ δακτύλου;
πρὸ τοῦ μέν, ἔτ' ἐμοῦ παιδὸς ὄντος, οὑτοσί.
ΣΩ. ἀγρεῖος εἶ καὶ σκαιός. 655
ΣΤ. οὐ γάρ, ὦζυρέ,
τούτων ἐπιθυμῶ μανθάνειν οὐδέν.
ΣΩ. τί δαί;
ΣΤ. ἐκεῖν' ἐκεῖνο, τὸν ἀδικώτατον λόγον.
ΣΩ. ἀλλ' ἕτερα δεῖ σε πρότερα τούτων μανθάνειν,

[a] The μέδιμνος = 48 χοίνικες, the ἑκτεύς = 8, and so the ἡμιεκτέον = 4, being therefore τετράμετρον. The joke, however, in

THE CLOUDS, 634-658

ST. By Zeus, I can't : the bugs make such resistance.
SO. Make haste. There, throw it down, and listen.
ST. Well !
SO. Attend to me : what shall I teach you first
That you've not learnt before ? Which will you have,
Measures or rhythms or the right use of words ?
ST. Oh ! measures to be sure : for very lately
A grocer swindled me of full three pints.
SO. I don't mean that : but which do you like the best
Of all the measures ; six feet, or eight feet ?
ST. Well, I like nothing better than the yard.
SO. Fool ! don't talk nonsense.
ST. What will you bet me now
That two yards don't exactly make six feet ?[a]
SO. Consume you ! what an ignorant clown you are !
Still, perhaps you can learn tunes more easily.
ST. But will tunes help me to repair my fortunes ?
SO. They'll help you to behave in company :
If you can tell which kind of tune is best
For the sword-dance, and which for finger music.[b]
ST. For fingers ! aye, but I know that.
SO. Say on, then.
ST. What is it but this finger ? though before,
Ere this was grown, I used to play with that.
SO. Insufferable dolt !
ST. Well but, you goose,
I don't want to learn this.
SO. What *do* you want then ?
ST. Teach me the Logic ! teach me the unjust Logic !
SO. But you must learn some other matters first :

the Greek consists largely in all the measures being measures of *capacity* (a μέδιμνος being about 12 gallons).
[b] Strepsiades knows nothing about " dactyl " but takes δάκτυλος in its literal sense, and makes indecent gestures with the middle finger (*infamis digitus*).

ARISTOPHANES

ΣΤ. τῶν τετραπόδων ἄττ' ἐστὶν ὀρθῶς ἄρρενα.
ἀλλ' οἶδ' ἔγωγε τἄρρεν', εἰ μὴ μαίνομαι· 660
κριός, τράγος, ταῦρος, κύων, ἀλεκτρυών.
ΣΩ. ὁρᾷς ἃ πάσχεις; τήν τε θήλειαν καλεῖς
ἀλεκτρυόνα κατὰ ταὐτὸ καὶ τὸν ἄρρενα.
ΣΤ. πῶς δή; φέρε.
ΣΩ. πῶς; ἀλεκτρυών· κἀλεκτρυών.
ΣΤ. νὴ τὸν Ποσειδῶ. νῦν δὲ πῶς με χρὴ καλεῖν; 665
ΣΩ. ἀλεκτρύαιναν, τὸν δ' ἕτερον ἀλέκτορα.
ΣΤ. ἀλεκτρύαιναν; εὖ γε νὴ τὸν Ἀέρα·
ὥστ' ἀντὶ τούτου τοῦ διδάγματος μόνου
διαλφιτώσω σου κύκλῳ τὴν κάρδοπον.
ΣΩ. ἰδοὺ μάλ' αὖθις τοῦθ' ἕτερον. τὴν κάρδοπον 670
ἄρρενα καλεῖς, θήλειαν οὖσαν.
ΣΤ. τῷ τρόπῳ
ἄρρενα καλῶ 'γὼ κάρδοπον;
ΣΩ. μάλιστά γε,
ὥσπερ γε καὶ Κλεώνυμον.
ΣΤ. πῶς δή; φράσον.
ΣΩ. ταὐτὸν δύναταί σοι κάρδοπος Κλεωνύμῳ.
ΣΤ. ἀλλ', ὦγάθ', οὐδ' ἦν κάρδοπος Κλεωνύμῳ, 675
ἀλλ' ἐν θυείᾳ στρογγύλῃ γ' ἀνεμάττετο.
ἀτὰρ τὸ λοιπὸν πῶς με χρὴ καλεῖν;
ΣΩ. ὅπως;
τὴν καρδόπην, ὥσπερ καλεῖς τὴν Σωστράτην.
ΣΤ. τὴν καρδόπην θήλειαν;
ΣΩ. ὀρθῶς γὰρ λέγεις.
ΣΤ. ἐκεῖνο δ' ἦν ἄν, καρδόπη, Κλεωνύμη. 680
ΣΩ. ἔτι δή γε περὶ τῶν ὀνομάτων μαθεῖν σε δεῖ,
ἅττ' ἄρρεν' ἐστίν, ἅττα δ' αὐτῶν θήλεα.
ΣΤ. ἀλλ' οἶδ' ἔγωγ' ἃ θήλε' ἐστίν.
ΣΩ. εἰπὲ δή.

THE CLOUDS, 659-683

As, what are males among the quadrupeds.
ST. I should be mad indeed not to know that.
The Ram, the Bull, the Goat, the Dog, the Fowl.
SO. Ah! there you are! there's a mistake at once!
You call the male and female fowl the same.
ST. How! tell me how.
SO. Why fowl and fowl of course.
ST. That's true though! what then shall I say in future?
SO. Call one a fowless and the other a fowl.
ST. A fowless? Good! Bravo! Bravo! by Air.
Now for that one bright piece of information
I'll give you a barley bumper in your trough.
SO. Look there, a fresh mistake; you called it trough,
Masculine, when it's feminine.
ST. How, pray?
How did I make it masculine?
SO. Why " trough,"
Just like " Cleonymus."
ST. I don't quite catch it.
SO. Why " trough," " Cleonymus," both masculine.
ST. Ah, but Cleonymus has got no trough,
His bread is kneaded in a rounded mortar : [a]
Still, what must I say in future?
SO. What! why call it
A " troughess," female, just as one says " an actress."
ST. A " troughess," female?
SO. That's the way to call it.
ST. O " troughess " then and Miss Cleonymus.
SO. Still you must learn some more about these names;
Which are the names of men and which of women.
ST. Oh, I know which are women.
SO. Well, repeat some.

[a] As being " a poor man " who had nothing better to use:
Schol. But there seems a reference " to the charge of effeminacy
which runs through these lines " : R.

ΣΤ. Λύσιλλα, Φίλιννα, Κλειταγόρα, Δημητρία.
ΣΩ. ἄρρενα δὲ ποῖα τῶν ὀνομάτων;
ΣΤ. μυρία. 685
   Φιλόξενος, Μελησίας, Ἀμυνίας.
ΣΩ. ἀλλ', ὦ πόνηρε, ταυτά γ' ἔστ' οὐκ ἄρρενα.
ΣΤ. οὐκ ἄρρεν' ἡμῖν ἐστιν;
ΣΩ. οὐδαμῶς γ', ἐπεὶ
   πῶς ἂν καλέσειας ἐντυχὼν Ἀμυνίᾳ;
ΣΤ. ὅπως ἄν; ὡδί, δεῦρο δεῦρ', Ἀμυνία. 690
ΣΩ. ὁρᾷς; γυναῖκα τὴν Ἀμυνίαν καλεῖς.
ΣΤ. οὔκουν δικαίως ἥτις οὐ στρατεύεται;
   ἀτὰρ τί ταῦθ' ἃ πάντες ἴσμεν μανθάνω;
ΣΩ. οὐδὲν μὰ Δί', ἀλλὰ κατακλινεὶς δευρί,
ΣΤ. τί δρῶ;
ΣΩ. ἐκφρόντισόν τι τῶν σεαυτοῦ πραγμάτων. 695
ΣΤ. μὴ δῆθ', ἱκετεύω σ', ἐνθάδ'· ἀλλ' εἴπερ γε χρή,
   χαμαί μ' ἔασον αὐτὰ ταῦτ' ἐκφροντίσαι.
ΣΩ. οὐκ ἔστι παρὰ ταῦτ' ἄλλα.
ΣΤ. κακοδαίμων ἐγώ,
   οἵαν δίκην τοῖς κόρεσι δώσω τήμερον.

ΣΩ. φρόντιζε δὴ καὶ διάθρει, πάντα τρόπον τε σαυτὸν 700
   στρόβει πυκνώσας.
   ταχὺς δ', ὅταν εἰς ἄπορον πέσῃς,
      ἐπ' ἄλλο πῆδα
   νόημα φρενός· ὕπνος δ' ἀπέστω γλυκύθυμος
      ὀμμάτων. 705
ΣΤ. ἰατταταῖ ἰατταταῖ.
ΧΟ. τί πάσχεις; τί κάμνεις;
ΣΤ. ἀπόλλυμαι δείλαιος· ἐκ τοῦ σκίμποδος

ST. Demetria, Cleitagora, Philinna.
SO. Now tell me some men's names.
ST.   O yes, ten thousand.
Philon, Melesias, Amynias.
SO. Hold! I said men's names : these are women's names.
ST. No, no, they're men's.
SO.   They are *not* men's, for how
Would you address Amynias if you met him?
ST. How? somehow thus : " Here, here, Amynia [a] ! "
SO. Amynia! a woman's name, you see.
ST. And rightly too ; a sneak who shirks all service!
But all know this : let's pass to something else.
SO. Well, then, you get into the bed.
ST.   And then?
SO. Excogitate about your own affairs.
ST. Not there : I do beseech, not there : at least
Let me excogitate on the bare ground.
SO. There is no way but this.
ST.   O luckless me!
How I shall suffer from the bugs to-day.

SO. Now then survey in every way,
      with airy judgement sharp and quick :
    Wrapping thoughts around you thick :
    And if so be in one you stick,
    Never stop to toil and bother,
      Lightly, lightly, lightly leap,
      To another, to another ;
      Far away be balmy sleep.
ST. Ugh! Ugh! Ugh! Ugh! Ugh!
CH. What's the matter? where's the pain?
ST. Friends! I'm dying. From the bed

---

[a] *Cf. W.* 466, 1267. The Greek vocative of " Amynias " becomes feminine in form.

ARISTOPHANES

δάκνουσί μ' ἐξέρποντες οἱ Κορίνθιοι, 710
καὶ τὰς πλευρὰς δαρδάπτουσιν
καὶ τὴν ψυχὴν ἐκπίνουσιν,
καὶ τοὺς ὄρχεις ἐξέλκουσιν,
καὶ τὸν πρωκτὸν διορύττουσιν,
καί μ' ἀπολοῦσιν. 71.

ΧΟ. μή νυν βαρέως ἄλγει λίαν.
ΣΤ. καὶ πῶς; ὅτε μου
φροῦδα τὰ χρήματα, φροῦδη χροιά,
φροῦδη ψυχή, φροῦδη δ' ἐμβάς·
καὶ πρὸς τούτοις ἔτι τοῖσι κακοῖς 720
φρουρᾶς ᾄδων
ὀλίγου φροῦδος γεγένημαι.

ΣΩ. οὗτος, τί ποιεῖς; οὐχὶ φροντίζεις;
ΣΤ. ἐγώ;
νὴ τὸν Ποσειδῶ.
ΣΩ. καὶ τί δῆτ' ἐφρόντισας;
ΣΤ. ὑπὸ τῶν κόρεων εἴ μού τι περιλειφθήσεται. 72
ΣΩ. ἀπολεῖ κάκιστ'.
ΣΤ. ἀλλ', ὦγάθ', ἀπόλωλ' ἀρτίως.
ΣΩ. οὐ μαλθακιστέ', ἀλλὰ περικαλυπτέα.
ἐξευρετέος γὰρ νοῦς ἀποστερητικὸς
κἀπαιόλημ'.
ΣΤ. οἴμοι, τίς ἂν δῆτ' ἐπιβάλοι
ἐξ ἀρνακίδων γνώμην ἀποστερητρίδα; 73
ΣΩ. φέρε νυν, ἀθρήσω πρῶτον, ὅ τι δρᾷ, τουτονί.
οὗτος, καθεύδεις;
ΣΤ. μὰ τὸν Ἀπόλλω 'γὼ μὲν οὔ.
ΣΩ. ἔχεις τι;

THE CLOUDS, 710–732

   Out creep bugbears [a] scantly fed,
   And my ribs they bite in twain,
   And my life-blood out they suck,
   And my manhood off they pluck,
   And my loins' they dig and drain,
   And I'm dying, once again.
CH. O take not the smart so deeply to heart.
ST.   Why, what can I do?
   Vanished my skin so ruddy of hue,
   Vanished my life-blood, vanished my shoe,
   Vanished my purse, and what is still worse
   As I hummed an old tune till my watch should
    be past,
   I had very near vanished myself at the last.

SO. Hallo there, are you pondering?
ST.   Eh! what? I?
 Yes to be sure.
SO.   And what have your ponderings come to?
ST. Whether these bugs will leave a bit of me.
SO. Consume you, wretch!
ST.   Faith, I'm consumed already.
SO. Come, come, don't flinch : pull up the clothes again :
 Search out and catch some very subtle dodge
 To fleece your creditors.
ST.   O me, how can I
 Fleece any one with all these fleeces on me?
 (*Puts his head under the clothes.*)
SO. Come, let me peep a moment what he's doing.
 Hey! he's asleep!
ST.   No, no! no fear of that!
SO. Caught anything?

---

[a] οἱ Κορίνθιοι (at this time the bitterest enemies of Athens) = οἱ κόρεις, "the bugs."

ARISTOPHANES

ΣΤ. μὰ Δί᾽ οὐ δῆτ᾽ ἔγωγ᾽.
ΣΩ. οὐδὲν πάνυ;
ΣΤ. οὐδέν γε πλὴν ἢ τὸ πέος ἐν τῇ δεξιᾷ.
ΣΩ. οὐκ ἐγκαλυψάμενος ταχέως τι φροντιεῖς; 735
ΣΤ. περὶ τοῦ; σὺ γάρ μοι τοῦτο φράσον, ὦ Σώκρατες.
ΣΩ. αὐτὸς ὅ τι βούλει πρῶτος ἐξευρὼν λέγε.
ΣΤ. ἀκήκοας μυριάκις ἁγὼ βούλομαι,
περὶ τῶν τόκων, ὅπως ἂν ἀποδῶ μηδενί.
ΣΩ. ἴθι νυν, καλύπτου καὶ σχάσας τὴν φροντίδα 740
λεπτὴν κατὰ μικρὸν περιφρόνει τὰ πράγματα,
ὀρθῶς διαιρῶν καὶ σκοπῶν.
ΣΤ. οἴμοι τάλας.
ΣΩ. ἔχ᾽ ἀτρέμα· κἂν ἀπορῇς τι τῶν νοημάτων,
ἀφεὶς ἄπελθε· κᾆτα τὴν γνώμην πάλιν
κίνησον αὖθις, αὐτὸ καὶ ζυγώθρισον. 74
ΣΤ. ὦ Σωκρατίδιον φίλτατον.
ΣΩ. τί, ὦ γέρον;
ΣΤ. ἔχω τόκου γνώμην ἀποστερητικήν.
ΣΩ. ἐπίδειξον αὐτήν.
ΣΤ. εἰπὲ δή νύν μοι,
ΣΩ. τὸ τί;
ΣΤ. γυναῖκα φαρμακίδ᾽ εἰ πριάμενος Θετταλήν,
καθέλοιμι νύκτωρ τὴν σελήνην, εἶτα δὲ 75
αὐτὴν καθείρξαιμ᾽ ἐς λοφεῖον στρογγύλον,
ὥσπερ κάτοπτρον, κᾆτα τηροίην ἔχων,
ΣΩ. τί δῆτα τοῦτ᾽ ἂν ὠφελήσειέν σ᾽;
ΣΤ. ὅ τι;
εἰ μηκέτ᾽ ἀνατέλλοι σελήνη μηδαμοῦ,
οὐκ ἂν ἀποδοίην τοὺς τόκους.
ΣΩ. ὁτιὴ τί δή; 75
ΣΤ. ὁτιὴ κατὰ μῆνα τἀργύριον δανείζεται.
ΣΩ. εὖ γ᾽· ἀλλ᾽ ἕτερον αὖ σοι προβαλῶ τι δεξιόν.

THE CLOUDS, 733-757

ST. No, nothing.
SO. Surely, something.
ST. Well, I had something in my hand, I'll own.
SO. Pull up the clothes again, and go on pondering.
ST. On what? now do please tell me, Socrates.
SO. What is it that you want? first tell me that.
ST. You have heard a million times what 'tis I want:
My debts! my debts! I want to shirk my debts.
SO. Come, come, pull up the clothes: refine your thoughts
With subtle wit: look at the case on all sides:
Mind you divide [a] correctly.
ST. Ugh! O me.
SO. Hush: if you meet with any difficulty
Leave it a moment: then return again
To the same thought: then lift and weigh it well.
ST. Oh, here, dear Socrates!
SO. Well, my old friend.
ST. I've found a notion how to shirk my debts.
SO. Well then, propound it.
ST. What do you think of this?
Suppose I hire some grand Thessalian witch
To conjure down the Moon, and then I take it
And clap it into some round helmet-box,
And keep it fast there, like a looking-glass,—
SO. But what's the use of that?
ST. The use, quotha:
Why if the Moon should never rise again,
I'd never pay one farthing.
SO. No! why not?
ST. Why, don't we pay our interest by the month?
SO. Good! now I'll proffer you another problem.

[a] διαίρεσις "division of genus into species" is a technical term in Logic.

335

ARISTOPHANES

εἴ σοι γράφοιτο πεντετάλαντός τις δίκη,
ὅπως ἂν αὐτὴν ἀφανίσειας εἰπέ μοι.
ΣΤ. ὅπως; ὅπως; οὐκ οἶδ'· ἀτὰρ ζητητέον. 76
ΣΩ. μή νυν περὶ σαυτὸν εἶλλε τὴν γνώμην ἀεί,
ἀλλ' ἀποχάλα τὴν φροντίδ' εἰς τὸν ἀέρα,
λινόδετον ὥσπερ μηλολόνθην τοῦ ποδός.
ΣΤ. εὕρηκ' ἀφάνισιν τῆς δίκης σοφωτάτην,
ὥστ' αὐτὸν ὁμολογεῖν σ' ἐμοί.
ΣΩ.   ποίαν τινά; 76
ΣΤ. ἤδη παρὰ τοῖσι φαρμακοπώλαις τὴν λίθον
ταύτην ἑόρακας, τὴν καλήν, τὴν διαφανῆ,
ἀφ' ἧς τὸ πῦρ ἅπτουσι;
ΣΩ.   τὴν ὕαλον λέγεις;
ΣΤ. ἔγωγε. φέρε, τί δῆτ' ἄν, εἰ ταύτην λαβών,
ὁπότε γράφοιτο τὴν δίκην ὁ γραμματεύς, 77(
ἀπωτέρω στὰς ὧδε πρὸς τὸν ἥλιον
τὰ γράμματ' ἐκτήξαιμι τῆς ἐμῆς δίκης;
ΣΩ. σοφῶς γε νὴ τὰς Χάριτας.
ΣΤ.   οἴμ' ὡς ἥδομαι
ὅτι πεντετάλαντος διαγέγραπταί μοι δίκη.
ΣΩ. ἄγε δὴ ταχέως τουτὶ ξυνάρπασον.
ΣΤ.   τὸ τί; 77(
ΣΩ. ὅπως ἀποστρέψαις ἂν ἀντιδίκων δίκην,
μέλλων ὀφλήσειν, μὴ παρόντων μαρτύρων.
ΣΤ. φαυλότατα καὶ ῥᾷστ'.
ΣΩ.   εἰπὲ δή.
ΣΤ.   καὶ δὴ λέγω.
εἰ πρόσθεν ἔτι μιᾶς ἐνεστώσης δίκης,
πρὶν τὴν ἐμὴν καλεῖσθ', ἀπαγξαίμην τρέχων. 78
ΣΩ. οὐδὲν λέγεις.
ΣΤ.   °νὴ τοὺς θεοὺς ἔγωγ', ἐπεὶ

THE CLOUDS, 758–781

      Suppose an action : damages, five talents :
      Now tell me how you can evade that same.
ST How ! how ! can't say at all : but I'll go seek.
SO. Don't wrap your mind for ever round yourself,
      But let your thoughts range freely through the air,
      Like chafers with a thread about their feet.[a]
ST. I've found a bright evasion of the action :
      Confess yourself, 'tis glorious.
SO.   But what is it ?
ST. I say, haven't you seen in druggists' shops
      That stone, that splendidly transparent stone,
      By which they kindle fire ?
SO.   The burning-glass ?
ST. That's it : well then, I'd get me one of these,
      And as the clerk was entering down my case,
      I'd stand, like this, some distance towards the sun,
      And burn out every line.
SO.   By the Three Graces,
      A clever dodge !
ST.   O me, how pleased I am
      To have a debt like that clean blotted out.
SO. Come, then, make haste and snap up this.
ST.   Well, what ?
SO. How to prevent an adversary's suit
      Supposing you were sure to lose it ; tell me.
ST. O, nothing easier.
SO.   How, pray ?
ST.   Why thus,
      While there was yet one trial intervening,
      Ere mine was cited, I'd go hang myself.
SO. Absurd !
ST.   No, by the Gods, it isn't though :

[a] To tie a thread round the leg of a cockchafer and then see it try to fly was apparently a common amusement of boys.

ARISTOPHANES

ουδεὶς κατ' ἐμοῦ τεθνεῶτος εἰσάξει δίκην.
ΣΩ. ὕθλεῖς· ἄπερρ', οὐκ ἂν διδαξαίμην σ' ἔτι.
ΣΤ. ὁτιὴ τί; ναὶ πρὸς τῶν θεῶν, ὦ Σώκρατες.
ΣΩ. ἀλλ' εὐθὺς ἐπιλήθει σύ γ' ἄττ' ἂν καὶ μάθῃς· 78
ἐπεὶ τί νυνὶ πρῶτον ἐδιδάχθης; λέγε.
ΣΤ. φέρ' ἴδω, τί μέντοι πρῶτον ἦν; τί πρῶτον ἦν;
τίς ἦν ἐν ᾗ ματτόμεθα μέντοι τἄλφιτα;
οἴμοι, τίς ἦν;
ΣΩ.   οὐκ ἐς κόρακας ἀποφθερεῖ,
ἐπιλησμότατον καὶ σκαιότατον γερόντιον; 79
ΣΤ. οἴμοι, τί οὖν δῆθ' ὁ κακοδαίμων πείσομαι;
ἀπὸ γὰρ ὀλοῦμαι μὴ μαθὼν γλωττοστροφεῖν.
ἀλλ', ὦ Νεφέλαι, χρηστόν τι συμβουλεύσατε.
ΧΟ. ἡμεῖς μέν, ὦ πρεσβῦτα, συμβουλεύομεν,
εἴ σοί τις υἱός ἐστιν ἐκτεθραμμένος, 79
πέμπειν ἐκεῖνον ἀντὶ σαυτοῦ μανθάνειν.
ΣΤ. ἀλλ' ἔστ' ἔμοιγ' υἱὸς καλός τε κἀγαθός·
ἀλλ' οὐκ ἐθέλει γὰρ μανθάνειν, τί ἐγὼ πάθω;
ΧΟ. σὺ δ' ἐπιτρέπεις;
ΣΤ.   εὐσωματεῖ γὰρ καὶ σφριγᾷ,
κἄστ' ἐκ γυναικῶν εὐπτέρων τῶν Κοισύρας. 80
ἀτὰρ μέτειμί γ' αὐτόν· ἢν δὲ μὴ θέλῃ,
οὐκ ἔσθ' ὅπως οὐκ ἐξελῶ 'κ τῆς οἰκίας.
ἀλλ' ἐπανάμεινόν μ' ὀλίγον εἰσελθὼν χρόνον.

ΧΟ. ἆρ' αἰσθάνει πλεῖστα δι' ἡμᾶς ἀγάθ' αὐτίχ' ἕξων [ἀντ.
μόνας θεῶν; ὡς
ἕτοιμος ὅδ' ἐστὶν ἅπαντα δρᾶν
ὅσ' ἂν κελεύῃς.
σὺ δ' ἀνδρὸς ἐκπεπληγμένου καὶ φανερῶς ἐπηρμένου 81

THE CLOUDS, 782–810

SO. They could not prosecute me were I dead.
Nonsense! Be off: I'll try no more to teach you.
ST. Why not? do, please: now, please do, Socrates.
SO. Why you forget all that you learn, directly.
Come, say what you learnt first: there's a chance for you.
ST. Ah! what was first?—Dear me: whatever was it?—
Whatever's that we knead the barley in?—
Bless us, what was it?
SO. Be off, and feed the crows,
You most forgetful, most absurd old dolt!
ST. O me! what will become of me, poor wretch!
I'm clean undone: I haven't learnt to speak.—
O gracious Clouds, now do advise me something.
CH. Our counsel, ancient friend, is simply this,
To send your son, if you have one at home,
And let him learn this wisdom in your stead.
ST. Yes! I've a son, quite a fine gentleman:
But he won't learn, so what am I to do?
CH. What! is he master?
ST. Well: he's strong and vigorous,
And he's got some of the Coesyra blood [a] within him:
Still I'll go for him, and if he won't come
By all the Gods I'll turn him out of doors.
Go in one moment, I'll be back directly.

CH. Dost thou not see how bounteous we our favours free
       Will shower on you,
    Since whatsoe'er your will prepare
       This dupe will do.
But now that you have dazzled and
                    elated so your man,

[a] γυναικῶν εὐπτέρων, lit. "high-flying women," "full of soaring notions."

ARISTOPHANES

γνοὺς ἀπολάψεις, ὅ τι πλεῖστον δύνασαι,
ταχέως· φιλεῖ γάρ πως τὰ τοιαῦθ' ἑτέρᾳ τρέπεσθαι.

ΣΤ. οὗτοι μὰ τὴν Ὁμίχλην ἔτ' ἐνταυθοῖ μενεῖς·
ἀλλ' ἔσθι' ἐλθὼν τοὺς Μεγακλέους κίονας. 81
ΦΕΙ. ὦ δαιμόνιε, τί χρῆμα πάσχεις, ὦ πάτερ;
οὐκ εὖ φρονεῖς μὰ τὸν Δία τὸν Ὀλύμπιον.
ΣΤ. ἰδού γ' ἰδοὺ Δί' Ὀλύμπιον· τῆς μωρίας·
τὸν Δία νομίζειν, ὄντα τηλικουτονί.
ΦΕΙ. τί δὲ τοῦτ' ἐγέλασας ἐτεόν;
ΣΤ. ἐνθυμούμενος 8⟨⟩
ὅτι παιδάριον εἶ καὶ φρονεῖς ἀρχαικά.
ὅμως γε μὴν πρόσελθ', ἵν' εἰδῇς πλείονα,
καί σοι φράσω πρᾶγμ' ὃ σὺ μαθὼν ἀνὴρ ἔσει.
ὅπως δὲ τοῦτο μὴ διδάξεις μηδένα.
ΦΕΙ. ἰδού· τί ἔστιν;
ΣΤ. ὤμοσας νυνὶ Δία. 8⟨⟩
ΦΕΙ. ἔγωγ'.
ΣΤ. ὁρᾷς οὖν ὡς ἀγαθὸν τὸ μανθάνειν;
οὐκ ἔστιν, ὦ Φειδιππίδη, Ζεύς.
ΦΕΙ. ἀλλὰ τίς;
ΣΤ. Δῖνος βασιλεύει, τὸν Δί' ἐξεληλακώς.
ΦΕΙ. αἰβοῖ, τί ληρεῖς;
ΣΤ. ἴσθι τοῦθ' οὕτως ἔχον.
ΦΕΙ. τίς φησι ταῦτα;
ΣΤ. Σωκράτης ὁ Μήλιος 8
καὶ Χαιρεφῶν, ὃς οἶδε τὰ ψυλλῶν ἴχνη.
ΦΕΙ. σὺ δ' εἰς τοσοῦτον τῶν μανιῶν ἐλήλυθας
ὥστ' ἀνδράσιν πείθει χολῶσιν;
ΣΤ. εὐστόμει,
καὶ μηδὲν εἴπῃς φλαῦρον ἄνδρας δεξιοὺς

THE CLOUDS, 811-834

    Make haste and seize whate'er you please
                      as quickly as you can,
    For cases such as these, my friend,
                    are very prone to change and bend.

ST. Get out! you shan't stop here : so help me Mist!
    Be off, and eat up Megacles's columns.
PH. How now, my father ? what's i' the wind to-day ?
    You're wandering ; by Olympian Zeus, you are.
ST. Look there ! Olympian Zeus ! you blockhead you,
    Come to *your* age, and yet believe in Zeus !
PH. Why prithee, what's the joke ?
ST.   'Tis so preposterous
    When babes like you hold antiquated notions.
    But come and I'll impart a thing or two,
    A wrinkle, making you a man indeed.
    But, mind : don't whisper this to any one.
PH. Well, what's the matter ?
ST.   Didn't you swear by Zeus ?
PH. I did.
ST.   See now, how good a thing is learning.
    There is no Zeus, Pheidippides.
PH.   Who then ?
ST. Why Vortex reigns, and he has turned out Zeus.
PH. Oh me, what stuff.
ST.   Be sure that this is so.
PH. Who says so, pray ?
ST.   The Melian [a]—Socrates,
    And Chaerephon, who knows about the flea-tracks.
PH. And are you come to such a pitch of madness
    As to put faith in brain-struck men ?
ST.   O hush !
    And don't blaspheme such very dexterous men

---

[a] The reference is to Diagoras the Melian, a notorious sceptic (θεομάχος, Schol.) ; *cf.* B. 1073.

ARISTOPHANES

καὶ νοῦν ἔχοντας· ὧν ὑπὸ τῆς φειδωλίας
ἀπεκείρατ᾽ οὐδεὶς πώποτ᾽ οὐδ᾽ ἠλείψατο
οὐδ᾽ εἰς βαλανεῖον ἦλθε λουσόμενος· σὺ δὲ
ὥσπερ τεθνεῶτός μου καταλούει τὸν βίον.
ἀλλ᾽ ὡς τάχιστ᾽ ἐλθὼν ὑπὲρ ἐμοῦ μάνθανε.
ΦΕΙ. τί δ᾽ ἂν παρ᾽ ἐκείνων καὶ μάθοι χρηστόν τις ἄν;
ΣΤ. ἄληθες; ὅσαπερ ἔστ᾽ ἐν ἀνθρώποις σοφά·
γνώσει δὲ σαυτὸν ὡς ἀμαθὴς εἶ καὶ παχύς.
ἀλλ᾽ ἐπανάμεινόν μ᾽ ὀλίγον ἐνταυθοῖ χρόνον.
ΦΕΙ. οἴμοι, τί δράσω παραφρονοῦντος τοῦ πατρός;
πότερα παρανοίας αὐτὸν εἰσαγαγὼν ἕλω,
ἢ τοῖς σοροπηγοῖς τὴν μανίαν αὐτοῦ φράσω;
ΣΤ. φέρ᾽ ἴδω, σὺ τουτονὶ τί νομίζεις; εἰπέ μοι.
ΦΕΙ. ἀλεκτρυόνα.
ΣΤ. καλῶς γε. ταυτηνὶ δὲ τί;
ΦΕΙ. ἀλεκτρυόν᾽.
ΣΤ. ἄμφω ταὐτό; καταγέλαστος εἶ.
μή νυν τὸ λοιπόν, ἀλλὰ τήνδε μὲν καλεῖν
ἀλεκτρύαιναν, τουτονὶ δ᾽ ἀλέκτορα.
ΦΕΙ. ἀλεκτρύαιναν; ταῦτ᾽ ἔμαθες τὰ δεξιὰ
εἴσω παρελθὼν ἄρτι παρὰ τοὺς γηγενεῖς;
ΣΤ. χἄτερά γε πόλλ᾽· ἀλλ᾽ ὅ τι μάθοιμ᾽ ἑκάστοτε,
ἐπελανθανόμην ἂν εὐθὺς ὑπὸ πλήθους ἐτῶν.
ΦΕΙ. διὰ ταῦτα δὴ καὶ θοἰμάτιον ἀπώλεσας;
ΣΤ. ἀλλ᾽ οὐκ ἀπολώλεκ᾽, ἀλλὰ καταπεφρόντικα.
ΦΕΙ. τὰς δ᾽ ἐμβάδας ποῖ τέτροφας, ὦνόητε σύ;
ΣΤ. ὥσπερ Περικλῆς εἰς τὸ δέον ἀπώλεσα.
ἀλλ᾽ ἴθι, βάδιζ᾽, ἴωμεν· εἶτα τῷ πατρὶ
πιθόμενος ἐξάμαρτε· κἀγώ τοί ποτε

---

[a] A son might bring an action to declare his father incapable of managing his affairs; cf. Plato, *Laws* 928 D, and the case of Iophon, son of Sophocles.

THE CLOUDS, 835-861

    And sapient too : men of such frugal habits
    They never shave, nor use your precious ointment,
    Nor go to baths to clean themselves : but you
    Have taken *me* for a corpse and cleaned me out.
    Come, come, make haste, do go and learn for me.
PH. What can one learn from them that is worth knowing?
ST. Learn! why, whatever's clever in the world :
    And you shall learn how gross and dense you are.
    But stop one moment : I'll be back directly.
PH. O me! what must I do with my mad father?
    Shall I indict him for his lunacy,[a]
    Or tell the undertakers of his symptoms?
ST. Now then! you see this, don't you? what do you call it?
PH. That? why a fowl.
ST.   Good! now then, what is this?
PH. That's a fowl too.
ST.   What both! Ridiculous!
    Never say that again, but mind you always
    Call this a fowless and the other a fowl.
PH. A fowless! These then are the mighty secrets
    You have picked up amongst those earth-born fellows.
ST. And lots besides : but everything I learn
    I straight forget : I am so old and stupid.
PH. And this is what you have lost your mantle for?
ST. It's very absent sometimes [b] : 'tisn't lost.
PH. And what have you done with your shoes, you dotard you?
ST. Like Pericles, all for the best,[c] I've lost them.
    Come, come ; go with me : humour me in this,
    And then do what you like. Ah! I remember

[b] καταπεφρόντικα, lit. " I have cogitated it away."
[c] εἰς τὸ δέον, "on the needful," a phrase used by Pericles when called to account for money spent " on secret service."

343

ARISTOPHANES

οἶδ' ἐξέτει σοι τραυλίσαντι πιθόμενος,
ὃν πρῶτον ὀβολὸν ἔλαβον Ἡλιαστικόν,
τούτου 'πριάμην σοι Διασίοις ἁμαξίδα.
ΦΕΙ. ἦ μὴν σὺ τούτοις τῷ χρόνῳ ποτ' ἀχθέσει. 865
ΣΤ. εὖ γ' ὅτι ἐπείσθης. δεῦρο δεῦρ', ὦ Σώκρατες,
ἔξελθ'· ἄγω γάρ σοι τὸν υἱὸν τουτονί,
ἄκοντ' ἀναπείσας.
ΣΩ.   νηπύτιος γάρ ἐστ' ἔτι,
καὶ τῶν κρεμαθρῶν οὐ τρίβων τῶν ἐνθάδε.
ΦΕΙ. αὐτὸς τρίβων εἴης ἄν, εἰ κρέμαιό γε. 870
ΣΤ. οὐκ ἐς κόρακας; καταρᾷ σὺ τῷ διδασκάλῳ;
ΣΩ. ἰδοὺ κρέμαι', ὡς ἠλίθιον ἐφθέγξατο
καὶ τοῖσι χείλεσιν διερρυηκόσιν.
πῶς ἂν μάθοι ποθ' οὗτος ἀπόφυξιν δίκης
ἢ κλῆσιν ἢ χαύνωσιν ἀναπειστηρίαν; 875
καίτοι ταλάντου τοῦτ' ἔμαθεν Ὑπέρβολος.
ΣΤ. ἀμέλει, δίδασκε· θυμόσοφός ἐστιν φύσει·
εὐθύς γέ τοι παιδάριον ὂν τυννουτονὶ
ἔπλαττεν ἔνδον οἰκίας, ναῦς τ' ἔγλυφεν,
ἁμαξίδας τε σκυτίνας εἰργάζετο, 880
κἀκ τῶν σιδίων βατράχους ἐποίει πῶς δοκεῖς.
ὅπως δ' ἐκείνω τὼ λόγω μαθήσεται,
τὸν κρείττον', ὅστις ἐστί, καὶ τὸν ἥττονα,
ὃς τἄδικα λέγων ἀνατρέπει τὸν κρείττονα·
ἐὰν δὲ μή, τὸν γοῦν ἄδικον πάσῃ τέχνῃ. 885
ΣΩ. αὐτὸς μαθήσεται παρ' αὐτοῖν τοῖν λόγοιν,
ἐγὼ δ' ἀπέσομαι.
ΣΤ.   τοῦτό νυν μέμνησ', ὅπως
πρὸς πάντα τὰ δίκαι' ἀντιλέγειν δυνήσεται.

344

THE CLOUDS, 862-888

      How I to humour you, a coaxing baby,
      With the first obol which my judgeship fetched me
      Bought you a go-cart at the great Diasia.[a]
PH. The time will come when you'll repent of this.
ST. Good boy to obey me. Hallo! Socrates.
      Come here; come here; I've brought this son of mine.
      Trouble enough, I'll warrant you.
SO.   Poor infant,
      Not yet aware of my suspension-wonders.[b]
PH. You'd make a wondrous piece of ware, suspended.
ST. Hey! Hang the lad! Do you abuse the Master?
SO. And look, " suthspended!" In what foolish fashion
      He mouthed the word with pouting lips agape.
      How can *he* learn evasion of a suit,
      Timely citation, damaging replies?
      Hyperbolus, though, learnt them for a talent.
ST. O never fear! he's very sharp, by nature.
      For when he was a little chap, *so* high,
      He used to build small baby-houses, boats,
      Go-carts of leather, darling little frogs
      Carved from pomegranates, you can't think how nicely!
      So now, I prithee, teach him both your Logics,
      The Better, as you call it, and the Worse
      Which with the worse cause can defeat the Better;
      Or if not both, at all events the Worse.
SO. Aye, with his own ears he shall hear them argue.
      I shan't be there.
ST.   But please remember this,
      Give him the knack of reasoning down all Justice.

    [a] *Cf.* 408 *n.*
    [b] Lit. "not versed in (the mysteries of) our baskets"; but 870 τρίβων is "a worn-out cloak" which Socrates would look like if hung upon a peg. For his wearing a τρίβων *cf.* Plato, *Symp.* 219 B.

ARISTOPHANES

ΔΙΚΑΙΟΣ ΛΟΓΟΣ. χώρει δευρί, δεῖξον σαυτὸν
τοῖσι θεαταῖς, καίπερ θρασὺς ὤν.
ΑΔΙΚΟΣ Λ. "ἴθ' ὅποι χρῄζεις." πολὺ γὰρ μᾶλλόν σ'
ἐν τοῖς πολλοῖσι λέγων ἀπολῶ.
ΔΙ. ἀπολεῖς σύ; τίς ὤν;
ΑΔ. λόγος.
ΔΙ. ἥττων γ' ὤν.
ΑΔ. ἀλλά σε νικῶ, τὸν ἐμοῦ κρείττω
φάσκοντ' εἶναι.
ΔΙ. τί σοφὸν ποιῶν;
ΑΔ. γνώμας καινὰς ἐξευρίσκων.
ΔΙ. ταῦτα γὰρ ἀνθεῖ διὰ τουτουσὶ
τοὺς ἀνοήτους.
ΑΔ. οὔκ, ἀλλὰ σοφούς.
ΔΙ. ἀπολῶ σε κακῶς.
ΑΔ. εἰπέ, τί ποιῶν;
ΔΙ. τὰ δίκαια λέγων.
ΑΔ. ἀλλ' ἀνατρέψω γ' αὔτ' ἀντιλέγων·
οὐδὲ γὰρ εἶναι πάνυ φημὶ δίκην.
ΔΙ. οὐκ εἶναι φῄς;
ΑΔ. φέρε γάρ, ποῦ 'στιν;
ΔΙ. παρὰ τοῖσι θεοῖς.
ΑΔ. πῶς δῆτα δίκης οὔσης ὁ Ζεὺς
οὐκ ἀπόλωλεν τὸν πατέρ' αὐτοῦ
δήσας;
ΔΙ. αἰβοῖ, τουτὶ καὶ δὴ
χωρεῖ τὸ κακόν· δότε μοι λεκάνην.
ΑΔ. τυφογέρων εἶ κἀνάρμοστος.
ΔΙ. καταπύγων εἶ κἀναίσχυντος.
ΑΔ. ῥόδα μ' εἴρηκας.

---

[a] From the *Telephus* of Euripides, ἴθ' ὅποι χρῇζεις· οὐκ ἀπ-

346

THE CLOUDS, 889-910

RIGHT LOGIC. Come show yourself now
                          with your confident brow.
               —To the stage, if you dare!
WRONG LOGIC. " Lead on where you please : " [a]
                     I shall smash you with ease,
                If an audience be there.
R.L. *You'll* smash me, you say! And who are *you*, pray?
W.L. A Logic, like you.
R.L.   But the Worst of the two.
W.L. Yet you I can drub whom my Better they dub.
R.L. By what artifice taught?
W.L.   By original thought.
R.L. Aye, truly your trade so successful is made.
  By means of these noodles of ours, I'm afraid.
W.L. Not noodles, but wise.
R.L.   I'll smash you and your lies!
W.L. By what method, forsooth?
R.L.   By speaking the Truth.
W.L. Your words I will meet, and entirely defeat:
  There never *was* Justice or Truth, I repeat.
R.L. No Justice! you say?
W.L.   Well, where does it stay?
R.L. With the Gods in the air.
W.L.   If Justice be there,
  How comes it that Zeus could his father reduce,
  Yet live with their Godships unpunished and loose?
R.L. Ugh! Ugh! These evils come thick,
                     I feel awfully sick,
  A basŏn, quick, quick!
W.L. You're a useless old drone with one foot in the grave!
R.L. You're a shameless, unprincipled, dissolute knave!
W.L. Hey! a rosy festoon.

ὀλοῦμαι | τῆς σῆς Ἑλένης οὕνεκα, where Agamemnon is quarrelling
with **Menelaus**.

ARISTOPHANES

ΔΙ. καὶ βωμολόχος. 910
ΑΔ. κρίνεσι στεφανοῖς.
ΔΙ. καὶ πατραλοίας.
ΑΔ. χρυσῷ πάττων μ' οὐ γιγνώσκεις.
ΔΙ. οὐ δῆτα πρὸ τοῦ γ', ἀλλὰ μολύβδῳ.
ΑΔ. νῦν δέ γε κόσμος τοῦτ' ἐστὶν ἐμοί.
ΔΙ. θρασὺς εἶ πολλοῦ.
ΑΔ. σὺ δέ γ' ἀρχαῖος. 915
ΔΙ. διὰ σὲ δὲ φοιτᾶν
οὐδεὶς ἐθέλει τῶν μειρακίων·
καὶ γνωσθήσει ποτ' Ἀθηναίοις
οἷα διδάσκεις τοὺς ἀνοήτους.
ΑΔ. αὐχμεῖς αἰσχρῶς.
ΔΙ. σὺ δέ γ' εὖ πράττεις. 920
καίτοι πρότερόν γ' ἐπτώχευες,
Τήλεφος εἶναι Μυσὸς φάσκων,
ἐκ πηριδίου
γνώμας τρώγων Πανδελετείους.
ΑΔ. ὤμοι σοφίας ἧς ἐμνήσθης. 925
ΔΙ. ὤμοι μανίας τῆς σῆς, πόλεώς θ',
ἥτις σε τρέφει
λυμαινόμενον τοῖς μειρακίοις.
ΑΔ. οὐχὶ διδάξεις τοῦτον Κρόνος ὤν.
ΔΙ. εἴπερ γ' αὐτὸν σωθῆναι χρὴ 930
καὶ μὴ λαλιὰν μόνον ἀσκῆσαι.
ΑΔ. δεῦρ' ἴθι, τοῦτον δ' ἔα μαίνεσθαι.
ΔΙ. κλαύσει, τὴν χεῖρ' ἢν ἐπιβάλλῃς.
ΧΟ. παύσασθε μάχης καὶ λοιδορίας.
ἀλλ' ἐπίδειξαι
σύ τε τοὺς προτέρους ἅττ' ἐδίδασκες, 935

R.L.   And a vulgar buffoon!
W.L. What! Lilies from *you*?
R.L.   And a parricide too!
W.L. 'Tis with gold (you don't know it) you sprinkle my
      head.
R.L. O gold is it now? but it used to be lead!
W.L. But now it's a grace and a glory instead.
R.L. You're a little too bold.
W.L.   You're a good deal too old.
R.L. 'Tis through you I well know not a stripling will go
      To attend to the rules which are taught in the Schools;
      But Athens one day shall be up to the fools.
W.L. How squalid your dress!
R.L.   Yours is fine, I confess.
      Yet of old, I declare, but a pauper you were;
      And passed yourself off, our compassion to draw
         As a Telephus, (Euripidéan)
      Well pleased from a beggarly wallet to gnaw
         At inanities Pandeletéan.[a]
W.L. O me! for the wisdom you've mentioned in jest!
R.L. O me! for the folly of you, and the rest
      Who you to destroy their children employ!
W.L. *Him* you never shall teach: you are quite out of date.
R.L. If not, he'll be lost, as he'll find to his cost:
      Taught nothing by you but to chatter and prate.
W.L. He raves, as you see: let him be, let him be.
R.L. Touch him if you dare! I bid you beware.
CH. Forbear, forbear to wrangle and scold!
      Each of you show
      You what you taught their fathers of old,

---

[a] Telephus in Euripides was introduced as a beggar and so carries a wallet, but here instead of scraps of food he is supposed to have in it sayings which Euripides stole from the scoundrel Pandeletus (συκοφάντης ἦν καὶ φιλόδικος Schol.).

ARISTOPHANES

σύ τε τὴν καινὴν
παίδευσιν, ὅπως ἂν ἀκούσας σφῷν
ἀντιλεγόντοιν κρίνας φοιτᾷ.
ΔΙ. δρᾶν ταῦτ' ἐθέλω.
ΑΔ. κἄγωγ' ἐθέλω.
ΧΟ. φέρε δὴ πότερος λέξει πρότερος; 940
ΑΔ. τούτῳ δώσω·
κᾆτ' ἐκ τούτων ὧν ἂν λέξῃ
ῥηματίοισιν καινοῖς αὐτὸν
καὶ διανοίαις κατατοξεύσω.
τὸ τελευταῖον δ', ἢν ἀναγρύζῃ,
τὸ πρόσωπον ἅπαν καὶ τὠφθαλμὼ 945
κεντούμενος ὥσπερ ὑπ' ἀνθρηνῶν
ὑπὸ τῶν γνωμῶν ἀπολεῖται.
ΧΟ. νῦν δείξετον τὼ πισύνω τοῖς περιδεξίοισι [στρ.
λόγοισι καὶ φροντίσι καὶ γνωμοτύποις μερίμναις,
λέγων ἀμείνων πότερος φανήσεται. νῦν γὰρ ἅπας
ἐνθάδε κίνδυνος ἀνεῖται σοφίας, 955
ἧς πέρι τοῖς ἐμοῖς φίλοις ἐστὶν ἀγὼν μέγιστος.
ἀλλ' ὦ πολλοῖς τοὺς πρεσβυτέρους ἤθεσι χρηστοῖς
στεφανώσας,
ῥῆξον φωνὴν ᾗτινι χαίρεις, καὶ τὴν σαυτοῦ φύσιν
εἰπέ. 960
ΔΙ. λέξω τοίνυν τὴν ἀρχαίαν παιδείαν, ὡς διέκειτο,
ὅτ' ἐγὼ τὰ δίκαια λέγων ἤνθουν καὶ σωφροσύνη
νενόμιστο.
πρῶτον μὲν ἔδει παιδὸς φωνὴν γρύξαντος μηδέν'
ἀκοῦσαι·
εἶτα βαδίζειν ἐν ταῖσιν ὁδοῖς εὐτάκτως εἰς κιθα-
ριστοῦ
τοὺς κωμήτας γυμνοὺς ἀθρόους, κεἰ κριμνώδη
κατανίφοι. 965

THE CLOUDS, 936-965

       You let us know
       Your system untried, that hearing each side
       From the lips of the Rivals the youth may decide
         To which of your schools he will go.
R.L. This then will I do.
W.L.   And so will I too.
CH. And who will put in his claim to begin?
W.L. If *he* wishes, he may : I kindly give way :
      And out of his argument quickly will I
      Draw facts and devices to fledge the reply
      Wherewith I will shoot him and smite and refute him.
      And at last if a word from his mouth shall be heard
      My sayings like fierce savage hornets shall pierce
        His forehead and eyes,
      Till in fear and distraction he yields and he—dies!
CH. With thoughts and words and maxims pondered well
        Now then in confidence let both begin :
        Try which his rival can in speech excel :
        Try which this perilous wordy war can win,
      Which all my votaries' hopes are fondly centred in.
O Thou who wert born our sires to adorn
                      with characters blameless and fair,
  Say on what you please, say on and to these
                      your glorious Nature declare.
R.L. To hear then prepare of the Discipline rare
                    which flourished in Athens of yore
  When Honour and Truth were in fashion with youth
                      and Sobriety bloomed on our shore ;
First of all the old rule was preserved in our school
                that " boys should be seen and not heard : "
And then to the home of the Harpist would come
                   decorous in action and word
All the lads of one town, though the snow peppered down,
                in spite of all wind and all weather :

ARISTOPHANES

εἶτ' αὖ προμαθεῖν ᾆσμ' ἐδίδασκεν, τὼ μηρὼ μὴ
 ξυνέχοντας,
ἢ " Παλλάδα περσέπολιν δεινάν," ἢ " Τηλέπορόν τι
 βόαμα,"
ἐντειναμένους τὴν ἁρμονίαν, ἣν οἱ πατέρες παρέδωκαν.
εἰ δέ τις αὐτῶν βωμολοχεύσαιτ' ἢ κάμψειέν τινα καμπήν,
οἵας οἱ νῦν τὰς κατὰ Φρῦνιν ταύτας τὰς δυσκολο-
 κάμπτους,
ἐπετρίβετο τυπτόμενος πολλὰς ὡς τὰς Μούσας ἀφανίζων.
ἐν παιδοτρίβου δὲ καθίζοντας τὸν μηρὸν ἔδει προ-
 βαλέσθαι
τοὺς παῖδας, ὅπως τοῖς ἔξωθεν μηδὲν δείξειαν ἀπηνές·
εἶτ' αὖ πάλιν αὖθις ἀνιστάμενον συμψῆσαι, καὶ προ-
 νοεῖσθαι
εἴδωλον τοῖσιν ἐρασταῖσιν τῆς ἥβης μὴ καταλείπειν.
ἠλείψατο δ' ἂν τοὐμφαλοῦ οὐδεὶς παῖς ὑπένερθεν τότ'
 ἄν, ὥστε
τοῖς αἰδοίοισι δρόσος καὶ χνοῦς ὥσπερ μήλοισιν ἐπήνθει·
οὐδ' ἂν μαλακὴν φυρασάμενος τὴν φωνὴν πρὸς τὸν
 ἐραστὴν
αὐτὸς ἑαυτὸν προαγωγεύων τοῖς ὀφθαλμοῖς ἐβάδιζεν,
οὐδ' ἂν ἑλέσθαι δειπνοῦντ' ἐξῆν κεφάλαιον τῆς ῥαφανῖδος,
οὐδ' ἄννηθον τῶν πρεσβυτέρων ἁρπάζειν οὐδὲ σέλινον,
οὐδ' ὀψοφαγεῖν, οὐδὲ κιχλίζειν, οὐδ' ἴσχειν τὼ πόδ'
 ἐναλλάξ.

---

[a] ἐντειναμένους τ. ἁ., "strenuously raising the air or tune."
The phrase " involves the idea of stretching out so as to keep the

THE CLOUDS, 966-983

And they sang an old song as they paced it along,
        not shambling with thighs glued together :
" *O the dread shout of War how it peals from afar,*"
        or " *Pallas the Stormer adore,*"
To some manly old air all simple and bare [a]
        which their fathers had chanted before.
And should anyone dare the tune to impair
        and with intricate twistings to fill,
Such as Phrynis is fain, and his long-winded train,
        perversely to quaver and trill,
Many stripes would he feel in return for his zeal,
        as to genuine Music a foe.
And every one's thigh was forward and high
        as they sat to be drilled in a row,
So that nothing the while indecent or vile
        the eye of a stranger might meet ;
And then with their hand they would smooth down the sand
        whenever they rose from their seat,
To leave not a trace of themselves in the place
        for a vigilant lover to view.
They never would soil their persons with oil
        but were inartificial and true.
Nor tempered their throat to a soft mincing note
        and sighs to their lovers addressed :
Nor laid themselves out, as they strutted about,
        to the wanton desires of the rest :
Nor would anyone dare such stimulant fare
        as the head of the radish to wish :
Nor to make over bold with the food of the old,
        the anise, and parsley, and fish :
Nor dainties to quaff, nor giggle and laugh,
        nor foot within foot to enfold.

line straight and tight ; the very reverse of κάμπτειν καμπήν in the next line " : R.

ARISTOPHANES

ΑΔ. ἀρχαῖά γε καὶ Διπολιώδη καὶ τεττίγων ἀνάμεστα,
καὶ Κηκείδου καὶ Βουφονίων.
ΔΙ. ἀλλ' οὖν ταῦτ' ἐστὶν ἐκεῖνα,
ἐξ ὧν ἄνδρας Μαραθωνομάχους ἡμὴ παίδευσις
ἔθρεψεν.
σὺ δὲ τοὺς νῦν εὐθὺς ἐν ἱματίοισι διδάσκεις
ἐντετυλίχθαι·
ὥστε μ' ἀπάγχεσθ', ὅταν ὀρχεῖσθαι Παναθηναίοις
δέον αὐτοὺς
τὴν ἀσπίδα τῆς κωλῆς προέχων ἀμελῇ τῆς
Τριτογενείας.
πρὸς ταῦτ', ὦ μειράκιον, θαρρῶν ἐμὲ τὸν κρείττω
λόγον αἱροῦ·
κἀπιστήσει μισεῖν ἀγορὰν καὶ βαλανείων ἀπέχεσθαι
καὶ τοῖς αἰσχροῖς αἰσχύνεσθαι, κἂν σκώπτῃ τίς σε,
φλέγεσθαι·
καὶ τῶν θάκων τοῖς πρεσβυτέροις ὑπανίστασθαι
προσιοῦσιν,
καὶ μὴ περὶ τοὺς σαυτοῦ γονέας σκαιουργεῖν,
ἄλλο τε μηδὲν
αἰσχρὸν ποιεῖν, ὅτι τῆς Αἰδοῦς μέλλεις τἄγαλμ'
ἀναπλάττειν·
μηδ' εἰς ὀρχηστρίδος εἰσᾴττειν, ἵνα μὴ πρὸς
ταῦτα κεχηνώς,
μήλῳ βληθεὶς ὑπὸ πορνιδίου, τῆς εὐκλείας ἀποθραυσθῇς·
μηδ' ἀντειπεῖν τῷ πατρὶ μηδέν, μηδ' Ἰαπετὸν
καλέσαντα

[a] The Διπόλεια was a festival of great antiquity, at which the slaughter of a steer (βουφόνια) was a distinguishing ceremony. For the τέττιγξ see K. 1331. Cecceides, says the Scholiast, was διθυράμβων ποιητὴς πάνυ ἀρχαῖος.

354

THE CLOUDS, 984–998

W.L. Faugh! this smells very strong of some musty old song,[a]
     and Chirrupers mounted in gold ;
 And Slaughter of beasts, and old-fashioned feasts.
R.L.   Yet these are the precepts which taught
 The heroes of old to be hardy and bold,
    and the Men who at Marathon fought !
 But now must the lad from his boyhood be clad
    in a Man's all-enveloping cloak : [b]
 So that, oft as the Panathenaea returns,
    I feel myself ready to choke
 When the dancers go by with their shields to their
  thigh,   not caring for Pallas a jot.
 You therefore, young man, choose me while you can;
    cast in with my Method your lot ;
 And then you shall learn the forum to spurn,
    and from dissolute baths to abstain,
 And fashions impure and shameful abjure,
    and scorners repel with disdain :
 And rise from your chair if an elder be there,
    and respectfully give him your place,
 And with love and with fear your parents revere,
    and shrink from the brand of Disgrace,
 And deep in your breast be the Image impressed
    of Modesty, simple and true,
 Nor resort any more to a dancing-girl's door,
    nor glance at the harlotry crew,
 Lest at length by the blow of the Apple they throw [c]
    from the hopes of your Manhood you fall.
 Nor dare to reply when your Father is nigh,
    nor " musty old Japhet " to call

---

 [b] *i.e.* he is not hardy enough to go without it ; the reverse of γυμνούς 965. So too in 989 even when dancing in armour the modern youth cover up any exposed part with their shields.
 [c] A regular form of love-challenge ; *cf.* Virg. *Ecl.* iii. 64.

ARISTOPHANES

μνησικακῆσαι τὴν ἡλικίαν, ἐξ ἧς ἐνεοττοτροφήθης.
ΑΔ. εἰ ταῦτ᾽, ὦ μειράκιον, πείσει τούτῳ, νὴ τὸν
Διόνυσον 1000
τοῖς Ἱπποκράτους υἱέσιν εἴξεις, καί σε καλοῦσι
βλιτομάμμιαν.
ΔΙ. ἀλλ᾽ οὖν λιπαρός γε καὶ εὐανθὴς ἐν γυμνασίοις
διατρίψεις,
οὐ στωμύλλων κατὰ τὴν ἀγορὰν τριβολεκτράπελ᾽,
οἷάπερ οἱ νῦν,
οὐδ᾽ ἑλκόμενος περὶ πραγματίου γλισχραντιλογεξεπιτρίπτου·
ἀλλ᾽ εἰς Ἀκαδήμειαν κατιὼν ὑπὸ ταῖς μορίαις
ἀποθρέξει 1005
στεφανωσάμενος καλάμῳ λευκῷ μετὰ σώφρονος
ἡλικιώτου,
μίλακος ὄζων καὶ ἀπραγμοσύνης καὶ λεύκης
φυλλοβολούσης,
ἦρος ἐν ὥρᾳ χαίρων, ὁπόταν πλάτανος πτελέᾳ
ψιθυρίζῃ.
ἢν ταῦτα ποιῇς ἁγὼ φράζω,
καὶ πρὸς τούτοις προσέχῃς τὸν νοῦν, 1010
ἕξεις ἀεὶ στῆθος λιπαρόν,
χροιὰν λαμπράν, ὤμους μεγάλους,
γλῶτταν βαιάν, πυγὴν μεγάλην,
πόσθην μικράν.
ἢν δ᾽ ἅπερ οἱ νῦν ἐπιτηδεύῃς, 1015
πρῶτα μὲν ἕξεις χροιὰν ὠχράν,
ὤμους μικρούς, στῆθος λεπτόν,
γλῶτταν μεγάλην, πυγὴν μικράν,

---

[a] Lit. "sons" but υἱέσιν is to be read as ὑσίν, and the Scholiast says they were ὑώδεις τινὲς καὶ ἀπαίδευτοι. Hippocrates

THE CLOUDS, 999–1018

  In your malice and rage that Sacred Old Age
     which lovingly cherished your youth.
W.L. Yes, yes, my young friend, if to him you attend,
     by Bacchus I swear of a truth
  You will scarce with the sty *a* of Hippocrates vie,
     as a mammy-suck known even there!
R.L. But then you'll excel in the games you love well,
     all blooming, athletic and fair:
  Not learning to prate as your idlers debate
     with marvellous prickly dispute,
  Nor dragged into Court day by day to make sport
     in some small disagreeable suit:
  But you will below to the Academe *b* go,
     and under the olives contend
  With your chaplet of reed, in a contest of speed
     with some excellent rival and friend:
  All fragrant with woodbine and peaceful content,
     and the leaf which the lime blossoms fling,
  When the plane whispers love to the elm in the grove
     in the beautiful season of Spring.
  If then you'll obey and do what I say,
  And follow with me the more excellent way,
  Your chest shall be white, your skin shall be bright,
  Your arms shall be tight, your tongue shall be slight,
  And everything else shall be proper and right.
  But if you pursue what men nowadays do,
  You will have, to begin, a cold pallid skin,
  Arms small and chest weak, tongue practised to speak,

is generally identified with an Athenian general who was slain in the battle of Delium.
 b Three-quarters of a mile N.W. of Athens; identified later with the school of Plato.

ARISTOPHANES

κωλῆν μεγάλην, ψήφισμα μακρόν,
καί σ' ἀναπείσει
τὸ μὲν αἰσχρὸν ἅπαν καλὸν ἡγεῖσθαι,   1020
τὸ καλὸν δ' αἰσχρόν·
καὶ πρὸς τούτοις τῆς Ἀντιμάχου
καταπυγοσύνης σ' ἀναπλήσει.

ΧΟ. ὦ καλλίπυργον σοφίαν κλεινοτάτην ἐπασκῶν, [ἀντ.
ὡς ἡδύ σου τοῖσι λόγοις σῶφρον ἔπεστιν ἄνθος.
εὐδαίμονες δ' ἦσαν ἄρ' οἱ ζῶντες ὅτ' ἦς τῶν προτέρων.
πρὸς οὖν τάδ', ὦ κομψοπρεπῆ μοῦσαν ἔχων,   1030
δεῖ σε λέγειν τι καινόν, ὡς εὐδοκίμηκεν ἀνήρ.
δεινῶν δέ σοι βουλευμάτων ἔοικε δεῖν πρὸς αὐτόν,
εἴπερ τὸν ἄνδρ' ὑπερβαλεῖ καὶ μὴ γέλωτ' ὀφλήσεις. 1035

ΑΔ. καὶ μὴν ἔγωγ' ἐπνιγόμην τὰ σπλάγχνα, κἀπεθύμουν
ἅπαντα ταῦτ' ἐναντίαις γνώμαισι συνταράξαι.
ἐγὼ γὰρ ἥττων μὲν λόγος δι' αὐτὸ τοῦτ' ἐκλήθην
ἐν τοῖσι φροντισταῖσιν, ὅτι πρώτιστος ἐπενόησα
τοῖσιν νόμοις καὶ ταῖς δίκαις τἀναντί' ἀντιλέξαι.   1040
καὶ τοῦτο πλεῖν ἢ μυρίων ἔστ' ἄξιον στατήρων,
αἱρούμενον τοὺς ἥττονας λόγους ἔπειτα νικᾶν.

---

a Some unknown effeminate.

THE CLOUDS, 1019-1042

    Special laws very long, and the symptoms all strong
Which show that your life is licentious and wrong.
And your mind he'll prepare so that foul to be fair
And fair to be foul you shall always declare ;
And you'll find yourself soon, if you listen to him,
With the filth of Antimachus^a filled to the brim!

CII.   O glorious Sage! with loveliest Wisdom teeming!
    Sweet on thy words does ancient Virtue rest!
    Thrice happy they who watched thy Youth's bright beaming!
    Thou of the vaunted genius, do thy best ;
    This man has gained applause : His Wisdom stands confessed.
And you with clever words and thoughts must needs your case adorn
Else he will surely win the day, and you retreat with scorn.

W.L. Aye, say you so ? why I have been
                         half-burst ; I do so long
To overthrow his arguments
                    with arguments more strong.
I am the Lesser Logic ? True :
                    these Schoolmen call me so,
Simply because I was the first
                     of all mankind to show
How old established rules and laws
                    might contradicted be :
And this, as you may guess, is worth
                    a thousand pounds to me,
To take the feebler cause, and yet
                    to win the disputation.

σκέψαι δὲ τὴν παίδευσιν ᾗ πέποιθεν ὡς ἐλέγξω·
ὅστις σε θερμῷ φησι λοῦσθαι πρῶτον οὐκ ἐάσειν.
καίτοι τίνα γνώμην ἔχων ψέγεις τὰ θερμὰ λουτρά;
ΔΙ. ὁτιὴ κάκιστόν ἐστι καὶ δειλὸν ποιεῖ τὸν ἄνδρα.
ΑΔ. ἐπίσχες· εὐθὺς γάρ σε μέσον ἔχω λαβὼν ἄφυκτον.
καί μοι φράσον, τῶν τοῦ Διὸς παίδων " τίν' ἄνδρ'
ἄριστον "
ψυχὴν νομίζεις, εἰπέ, καὶ πλείστους πόνους
πονῆσαι;
ΔΙ. ἐγὼ μὲν οὐδέν' Ἡρακλέους βελτίον' ἄνδρα κρίνω.
ΑΔ. ποῦ ψυχρὰ δῆτα πώποτ' εἶδες Ἡράκλεια λουτρά;
καίτοι τίς ἀνδρειότερος ἦν;
ΔΙ. ταῦτ' ἐστὶ ταῦτ' ἐκεῖνα,
ἃ τῶν νεανίσκων ἀεὶ δι' ἡμέρας λαλούντων
πλῆρες τὸ βαλανεῖον ποιεῖ, κενὰς δὲ τὰς παλαίστρας.
ΑΔ. εἶτ' ἐν ἀγορᾷ τὴν διατριβὴν ψέγεις, ἐγὼ δ' ἐπαινῶ.
εἰ γὰρ πονηρὸν ἦν, Ὅμηρος οὐδέποτ' ἂν ἐποίει
τὸν Νέστορ' ἀγορητὴν ἂν οὐδὲ τοὺς σοφοὺς
ἅπαντας.
ἄνειμι δῆτ' ἐντεῦθεν εἰς τὴν γλῶτταν, ἣν ὁδὶ μὲν
οὔ φησι χρῆναι τοὺς νέους ἀσκεῖν, ἐγὼ δέ φημί.

---

[a] "Athena made warm baths spring at Thermopylae for Heracles when very weary": Schol.
[b] He is λιγὺς Πυλίων ἀγορητής, Il. i. 248, iv. 293.

THE CLOUDS, 1043-1059

    And mark me now, how I'll confute
                his boasted Education!
    You said that always from warm baths
                the stripling must abstain :
    Why must he? on what grounds do you
                of these warm baths complain?
R.L. Why, it's the worst thing possible,
                it quite unstrings a man.
W.L. Hold there : I've got you round the waist :
                escape me if you can.
    And first : of all the sons of Zeus
                which think you was the best?
    Which was the manliest? which endured
                more toils than all the rest?
R.L. Well, I suppose that Heracles
                was bravest and most bold.
W.L. And are the baths of Heracles
                so wonderfully cold? [a]
    Aha! you blame warm baths, I think.
R.L.   This, this is what they say :
    This is the stuff our precious youths
                are chattering all the day!
    This is what makes them haunt the baths,
                and shun the manlier Games!
W.L. Well then, we'll take the Forum next :
                I praise it, and he blames.
    But if it *was* so bad, do you think
                old Homer would have made
    Nestor [b] and all his worthies ply
                a real forensic trade?
    Well : then he says a stripling's tongue
                should always idle be :
    I say it should be used of course :
                so there we disagree.

καὶ σωφρονεῖν αὖ φησὶ χρῆναι· δύο κακὼ μεγίστω. 1060
ἐπεὶ σὺ διὰ τὸ σωφρονεῖν τῷ πώποτ' εἶδες ἤδη
ἀγαθόν τι γενόμενον, φράσον, καί μ' ἐξέλεγξον
εἰπών.

ΔΙ. πολλοῖς. ὁ γοῦν Πηλεὺς ἔλαβε διὰ τοῦτο τὴν
μάχαιραν.

ΑΔ. μάχαιραν; ἀστεῖόν γε κέρδος ἔλαβεν ὁ κακοδαίμων.
Ὑπέρβολος δ' οὐκ τῶν λύχνων πλεῖν ἢ τάλαντα
πολλὰ 1065
εἴληφε διὰ πονηρίαν, ἀλλ' οὐ μὰ Δί' οὐ μάχαιραν.

ΔΙ. καὶ τὴν Θέτιν γ' ἔγημε διὰ τὸ σωφρονεῖν ὁ Πηλεύς.

ΑΔ. κᾆτ' ἀπολιποῦσά γ' αὐτὸν ᾤχετ'· οὐ γὰρ ἦν ὑβριστὴς
οὐδ' ἡδὺς ἐν τοῖς στρώμασιν τὴν νύκτα παννυχίζειν·
γυνὴ δὲ σιναμωρουμένη χαίρει· σὺ δ' εἶ κρόνιππος. 1070
σκέψαι γάρ, ὦ μειράκιον, ἐν τῷ σωφρονεῖν ἅπαντα
ἄνεστιν, ἡδονῶν θ' ὅσων μέλλεις ἀποστερεῖσθαι,
παίδων, γυναικῶν, κοττάβων, ὄψων, πότων, κι-
χλισμῶν.
καίτοι τί σοι ζῆν ἄξιον, τούτων ἐὰν στερηθῇς;
εἶεν. πάρειμ' ἐντεῦθεν ἐς τὰς τῆς φύσεως ἀνάγκας. 1075
ἥμαρτες, ἠράσθης, ἐμοίχευσάς τι, κᾆτ' ἐλήφθης·
ἀπόλωλας· ἀδύνατος γὰρ εἶ λέγειν. ἐμοὶ δ' ὁμιλῶν,

---

[a] Given to him by the gods when made an outcast because of his rejecting the advances of the wife of Acastus ; cf. Hor. Od. iii. 7. 17.

THE CLOUDS, 1060–1077

      And next he says you must be chaste.
                      A most preposterous plan!
      Come, tell me did you ever know
                      one single blessed man
      Gain the least good by chastity?
                  come, prove I'm wrong: make haste.
R.L. Yes, many, many! Peleus gained
                    a sword [a] by being chaste.
W.L. A sword indeed! a wondrous meed
                      the unlucky fool obtained.
      Hyperbolus the Lamp-maker
                    hath many a talent gained
      By knavish tricks which I have taught:
                    but not a sword, no, no!
R.L. Then Peleus did to his chaste life
                    the bed of Thetis owe.
W.L. And then she cut and ran away!
                      for nothing so engages
      A woman's heart as forward warmth,
                    old shred of those dark Ages!
      For take this chastity, young man:
                    sift it inside and out:
      Count all the pleasures, all the joys,
                    it bids you live without:
      No kind of dames, no kind of games,
                  no laughing, feasting, drinking,—
      Why, life itself is little worth
                  without these joys, I'm thinking.
      Well, I must notice now the wants
                  by Nature's self implanted;
      You love, seduce, you can't help that,
                you're caught, convicted. Granted.
      You're done for; you can't say one word:
                  while if you follow me

ARISTOPHANES

χρῶ τῇ φύσει, σκίρτα, γέλα, νόμιζε μηδὲν αἰσχρόν.
μοιχὸς γὰρ ἢν τύχῃς ἁλούς, τάδ' ἀντερεῖς πρὸς
αὐτόν,
ὡς οὐδὲν ἠδίκηκας· εἶτ' εἰς τὸν Δί' ἐπανενεγκεῖν,
κἀκεῖνος ὡς ἥττων ἔρωτός ἐστι καὶ γυναικῶν·
καίτοι σὺ θνητὸς ὢν θεοῦ πῶς μεῖζον ἂν δύναιο;
ΔΙ. τί δ' ἢν ῥαφανιδωθῇ πιθόμενός σοι τέφρᾳ τε τιλθῇ;
ἕξει τινὰ γνώμην λέγειν, τὸ μὴ εὐρύπρωκτος εἶναι;
ΑΔ. ἢν δ' εὐρύπρωκτος ᾖ, τί πείσεται κακόν;
ΔΙ. τί μὲν οὖν ἂν ἔτι μεῖζον πάθοι τούτου ποτέ;
ΑΔ. τί δῆτ' ἐρεῖς, ἢν τοῦτο νικηθῇς ἐμοῦ;
ΔΙ. σιγήσομαι. τί δ' ἄλλο;
ΑΔ. φέρε δή μοι φράσον·
συνηγοροῦσιν ἐκ τίνων;
ΔΙ. ἐξ εὐρυπρώκτων.
ΑΔ. πείθομαι.
τί δαί; τραγῳδοῦσ' ἐκ τίνων;
ΔΙ. ἐξ εὐρυπρώκτων.
ΑΔ. εὖ λέγεις.
δημηγοροῦσι δ' ἐκ τίνων;
ΔΙ. ἐξ εὐρυπρώκτων.
ΑΔ. ἆρα δῆτ'
ἔγνωκας ὡς οὐδὲν λέγεις;
καὶ τῶν θεατῶν ὁπότεροι
πλείους σκόπει.
ΔΙ. καὶ δὴ σκοπῶ.
ΑΔ. τί δῆθ' ὁρᾷς;

---

[a] Punishments of those taken in adultery: ῥαφανῖδας λαμ-
βάνοντες καθίεσαν εἰς τοὺς πρωκτοὺς αὐτῶν, καὶ παρατίλλοντες αὐτοὺς
τέφραν θερμὴν ἐπέπασσον· Schol.

THE CLOUDS, 1078-1098

        Indulge your genius, laugh and quaff,
                hold nothing base to be.
        Why if you're in adultery caught,
                your pleas will still be ample :
        You've done no wrong, you'll say, and then
                bring Zeus as your example.
        He fell before the wondrous powers
                by Love and Beauty wielded :
        And how can you, the Mortal, stand,
                where He, the Immortal, yielded ?

R.L.   Aye, but suppose in spite of all,
                he must be wedged and sanded.[a]
        Won't he be probed, or else can you
                prevent it ? now be candid.
W.L.   And what's the damage if it should be so ?
R.L.   What greater damage can the young man know ?
W.L.   What will you do, if this dispute I win ?
R.L.   I'll be for ever silent.
W.L.   Good, begin.
        The Counsellor : from whence comes he ?
R.L.   From probed adulterers.
W.L.   I agree.
        The Tragic Poets : whence are they ?
R.L.   From probed adulterers.
W.L.   So I say.
        The Orators : what class of men ?
R.L.   All probed adulterers.
W.L.   Right again.
        You feel your error, I'll engage,
        But look once more around the stage,
        Survey the audience, which they be,
        Probed or not Probed.
R.L.   I see, I see.
W.L.   Well, give your verdict.

ARISTOPHANES

ΔΙ. πολὺ πλείονας, νὴ τοὺς θεούς,
τοὺς εὐρυπρώκτους· τουτονὶ
γοῦν οἶδ' ἐγὼ κἀκεινονὶ
καὶ τὸν κομήτην τουτονί.
ΑΔ. τί δῆτ' ἐρεῖς;
ΔΙ. ἡττήμεθ', ὦ κινούμενοι,
πρὸς τῶν θεῶν δέξασθέ μου
θοἰμάτιον, ὡς
ἐξαυτομολῶ πρὸς ὑμᾶς.

ΣΩ. τί δῆτα; πότερα τοῦτον ἀπάγεσθαι λαβὼν
βούλει τὸν υἱόν, ἢ διδάσκω σοι λέγειν;
ΣΤ. δίδασκε καὶ κόλαζε, καὶ μέμνησ' ὅπως
εὖ μοι στομώσεις αὐτόν, ἐπὶ μὲν θἄτερα
οἵαν δικιδίοις, τὴν δ' ἑτέραν αὐτοῦ γνάθον
στόμωσον οἵαν ἐς τὰ μείζω πράγματα.
ΣΩ. ἀμέλει, κομιεῖ τοῦτον σοφιστὴν δεξιόν.
ΣΤ. ὠχρὸν μὲν οὖν ἔγωγε καὶ κακοδαίμονα.

ΧΟ. χωρεῖτέ νυν. οἶμαι δέ σοι ταῦτα μεταμελήσειν.
τοὺς κριτὰς ἃ κερδανοῦσιν, ἤν τι τόνδε τὸν χορὸν
ὠφελῶσ' ἐκ τῶν δικαίων, βουλόμεσθ' ἡμεῖς φράσαι.
πρῶτα μὲν γάρ, ἢν νεᾶν βούλησθ' ἐν ὥρᾳ τοὺς
  ἀγρούς,
ὕσομεν πρώτοισιν ὑμῖν, τοῖσι δ' ἄλλοις ὕστερον.
εἶτα τὸν καρπόν τε καὶ τὰς ἀμπέλους φυλάξομεν,
ὥστε μήτ' αὐχμὸν πιέζειν μήτ' ἄγαν ἐπομβρίαν.
ἢν δ' ἀτιμάσῃ τις ἡμᾶς θνητὸς ὢν οὔσας θεάς,

---

[a] *The two Logics go out, and enter Socrates from the Phrontisterium and Strepsiades from his own house to see how his son's education has been progressing. During the interval of the Chorus (1114–1130) that education is supposed to be completing.*

THE CLOUDS, 1098-1121

R.L.   It must go
For probed adulterers : him I know,
And him, and him : the Probed are most.
W.L.   How stand we then ?
R.L.   I own, I've lost.
O Cinaeds, Cinaeds, take my robe !
Your words have won, to you I run
To live and die with glorious Probe ! [a]

SO. Well, what do you want ? to take away your son
At once, or shall I teach him how to speak ?
ST. Teach him, and flog him, and be sure you well
Sharpen his mother wit, grind the one edge
Fit for my little law-suits, and the other,
Why, make that serve for more important matters.
SO. Oh, never fear ! He'll make a splendid sophist.
ST. Well, well, I hope he'll be a poor pale rascal.

CH. Go : but in us the thought is strong,
                 you will repent of this ere long.
Now we wish to tell the Judges
                 all the blessings they shall gain
If, as Justice plainly warrants,
                 we the worthy prize obtain.
First, whenever in the Season
                 ye would fain your fields renew,
All the world shall wait expectant
                 till we've poured our rain on you :
Then of all your crops and vineyards
                 we will take the utmost care
So that neither drought oppress them,
                 nor the heavy rain impair.
But if anyone amongst you
                 dare to treat our claims with scorn,

ARISTOPHANES

προσεχέτω τὸν νοῦν, πρὸς ἡμῶν οἷα πείσεται κακά,
λαμβάνων οὔτ' οἶνον οὔτ' ἀλλ' οὐδὲν ἐκ τοῦ χωρίου.
ἡνίκ' ἂν γὰρ αἵ τ' ἐλᾶαι βλαστάνωσ' αἵ τ' ἄμπελοι,
ἀποκεκόψονται· τοιαύταις σφενδόναις παιήσομεν. 1125
ἢν δὲ πλινθεύοντ' ἴδωμεν, ὕσομεν καὶ τοῦ τέγους
τὸν κέραμον αὐτοῦ χαλάζαις στρογγύλαις συν-
τρίψομεν.
κἂν γαμῇ ποτ' αὐτὸς ἢ τῶν ξυγγενῶν ἢ τῶν φίλων,
ὕσομεν τὴν νύκτα πᾶσαν· ὥστ' ἴσως βουλήσεται
κἂν ἐν Αἰγύπτῳ τυχεῖν ὢν μᾶλλον ἢ κρῖναι κακῶς. 1130

ΣΤ. πέμπτη, τετράς, τρίτη, μετὰ ταύτην δευτέρα,
εἶθ' ἣν ἐγὼ μάλιστα πασῶν ἡμερῶν
δέδοικα καὶ πέφρικα καὶ βδελύττομαι,
εὐθὺς μετὰ ταύτην ἔσθ' ἕνη τε καὶ νέα.
πᾶς γάρ τις ὄμνυσ', οἷς ὀφείλων τυγχάνω, 1135
θείς μοι πρυτανεῖ' ἀπολεῖν μέ φησι κἀξολεῖν,
ἐμοῦ μέτρι' ἄττα καὶ δίκαι' αἰτουμένου·
" ὦ δαιμόνιε, τὸ μέν τι νυνὶ μὴ λάβῃς,
τὸ δ' ἀναβαλοῦ μοι, τὸ δ' ἄφες," οὔ φασίν ποτε
οὕτως ἀπολήψεσθ', ἀλλὰ λοιδοροῦσί με 1140
ὡς ἄδικός εἰμι, καὶ δικάσεσθαί φασί μοι.
νῦν οὖν δικαζέσθων· ὀλίγον γάρ μοι μέλει,
εἴπερ μεμάθηκεν εὖ λέγειν Φειδιππίδης.

---

^a *i.e.* from the end of the month, when interest became due.
^b " When the Greek year was lunar, the months were alternately thirty and twenty-nine days each, so that the new Moon (the moon's orbit being 29½ days) always fell on the last day of the month. Hence that day was called the Old-and-New, because at the beginning of the day the moon was still on the wane, but before the close had begun to wax again ": R.

THE CLOUDS, 1122-1143

Mortal he, the Clouds immortal,
          better had he ne'er been born!
He from his estates shall gather
          neither corn, nor oil, nor wine,
For whenever blossoms sparkle
          on the olive or the vine
They shall all at once be blighted:
          we will ply our slings so true.
And if ever we behold him
          building up his mansions new,
With our tight and nipping hailstones
          we will all his tiles destroy.
But if he, his friends or kinsfolk,
          would a marriage-feast enjoy,
All night long we'll pour in torrents:
          so perchance he'll rather pray
To endure the drought of Egypt,
          than decide amiss to-day!

ST. The fifth,[a] the fourth, the third, and then the second,
And then that day which more than all the rest
I loathe and shrink from and abominate,
Then comes at once that hateful Old-and-New day.[b]
And every single blessed dun has sworn
He'll stake his gage,[c] and ruin and destroy me.
And when I make a modest small request,
"O my good friend, part don't exact at present,
And part defer, and part remit," they swear
So they shall never touch it, and abuse me
As a rank swindler, threatening me with actions.
Now let them bring their actions! Who's afraid?
Not I: if these have taught my son to speak.

[c] The sum deposited with the πρυτάνεις before commencing an action.

ARISTOPHANES

τάχα δ' εἴσομαι κόψας τὸ φροντιστήριον.
παῖ, ἠμί, παῖ παῖ.
ΣΩ. Στρεψιάδην ἀσπάζομαι. 11
ΣΤ. κἄγωγέ σ'. ἀλλὰ τουτονὶ πρῶτον λαβέ·
χρὴ γὰρ ἐπιθαυμάζειν τι τὸν διδάσκαλον.
καί μοι τὸν υἱόν, εἰ μεμάθηκε τὸν λόγον
ἐκεῖνον, εἴφ', ὃν ἀρτίως εἰσήγαγες.
ΣΩ. μεμάθηκεν.
ΣΤ. εὖ γ', ὦ παμβασίλει' 'Απαιόλη. 11
ΣΩ. ὥστ' ἀποφύγοις ἂν ἥντιν' ἂν βούλῃ δίκην.
ΣΤ. κεἰ μάρτυρες παρῆσαν, ὅτ' ἐδανειζόμην;
ΣΩ. πολλῷ γε μᾶλλον, κἂν παρῶσι χίλιοι.
ΣΤ. " βοάσομαί τἄρα τὰν ὑπέρτονον
βοάν." ἰώ, κλάετ' ὠβολοστάται, 11
αὐτοί τε καὶ τἀρχαῖα καὶ τόκοι τόκων·
οὐδὲν γὰρ ἄν με φλαῦρον ἐργάσαισθ' ἔτι·
οἷος ἐμοὶ τρέφεται
τοῖσδ' ἐνὶ δώμασι παῖς,
ἀμφήκει γλώττῃ λάμπων, 11
πρόβολος ἐμός, σωτὴρ δόμοις, ἐχθροῖς βλάβη,
λυσανίας πατρῴων μεγάλων κακῶν·
ὃν κάλεσον τρέχων ἔνδοθεν ὡς ἐμέ.
" ὦ τέκνον, ὦ παῖ, ἔξελθ' οἴκων,
ἄϊε " σοῦ πατρός. 11
ΣΩ. ὅδ' ἐκεῖνος ἀνήρ.
ΣΤ. ὦ φίλος, ὦ φίλος.
ΣΩ. ἄπιθι λαβὼν τὸν υἱόν.
ΣΤ. ἰὼ ἰὼ τέκνον.
ἰὼ ἰοῦ ἰοῦ. 11
ὡς ἥδομαί σου πρῶτα τὴν χροιὰν ἰδών.

^a From the *Satyrs* of Phrynichus; Schol.

THE CLOUDS, 1144-1171

But here's the door : I'll knock and soon find out.
Boy! Ho there, boy!
SO.   I clasp Strepsiades.
ST. And I clasp you : but take this meal-bag first.
'Tis meet and right to glorify one's Tutors.
But tell me, tell me, has my son yet learnt
That Second Logic which he saw just now?
SO. He hath.
ST.   Hurrah! great Sovereign Knavery!
SO. You may escape whatever suit you please.
ST. What, if I borrowed before witnesses?
SO. Before a thousand, and the more the merrier.
ST. " Then shall my song be loud and deep." [a]
Weep, obol-weighers, weep, weep, weep,
Ye, and your principals, and compound interests,
For ye shall never pester me again.
Such a son have I bred,
(He is within this door),
Born to inspire my foemen with dread,
Born his old father's house to restore :
Keen and polished of tongue is he,
He my Champion and Guard shall be,
He will set his old father free,
Run you, and call him forth to me.
" O my child! O my sweet! come out, I entreat;
'Tis the voice " [b] of your sire.
SO. Here's the man you require.
ST. Joy, joy of my heart!
SO. Take your son and depart.
ST. O come, O come, my son, my son,
O dear! O dear!
O joy, to see your beautiful complexion!

[b] A parody of Eur. *Hec.* 172, where Hecuba calls Polyxena from her tent.

ARISTOPHANES

νῦν μέν γ' ἰδεῖν εἰ πρῶτον ἐξαρνητικὸς
κἀντιλογικός, καὶ τοῦτο τοὐπιχώριον
ἀτεχνῶς ἐπανθεῖ, τὸ τί λέγεις σύ; καὶ δοκεῖν
ἀδικοῦντ' ἀδικεῖσθαι καὶ κακουργοῦντ' οἶδ' ὅτι. 117
ἐπὶ τοῦ προσώπου τ' ἐστὶν Ἀττικὸν βλέπος.
νῦν οὖν ὅπως σώσεις μ', ἐπεὶ κἀπώλεσας.
ΦΕΙ. φοβεῖ δὲ δὴ τί;
ΣΤ. τὴν ἕνην τε καὶ νέαν.
ΦΕΙ. ἕνη γάρ ἐστι καὶ νέα τις ἡμέρα;
ΣΤ. εἰς ἥν γε θήσειν τὰ πρυτανεῖά φασί μοι. 118
ΦΕΙ. ἀπολοῦσ' ἄρ' αὔθ' οἱ θέντες· οὐ γὰρ ἔσθ' ὅπως
μί' ἡμέρα γένοιτ' ἂν ἡμέραι δύο.
ΣΤ. οὐκ ἂν γένοιτο;
ΦΕΙ. πῶς γάρ; εἰ μή πέρ γ' ἅμα
αὐτὴ γένοιτ' ἂν γραῦς τε καὶ νέα γυνή.
ΣΤ. καὶ μὴν νενόμισταί γ'.
ΦΕΙ. οὐ γάρ, οἶμαι, τὸν νόμον 118
ἴσασιν ὀρθῶς ὅ τι νοεῖ.
ΣΤ. νοεῖ δὲ τί;
ΦΕΙ. ὁ Σόλων ὁ παλαιὸς ἦν φιλόδημος τὴν φύσιν.
ΣΤ. τουτὶ μὲν οὐδέν πω πρὸς ἕνην τε καὶ νέαν.
ΦΕΙ. ἐκεῖνος οὖν τὴν κλῆσιν εἰς δύ' ἡμέρας
ἔθηκεν, εἴς γε τὴν ἕνην τε καὶ νέαν, 119
ἵν' αἱ θέσεις γίγνοιντο τῇ νουμηνίᾳ.
ΣΤ. ἵνα δὴ τί τὴν ἕνην προσέθηκεν;
ΦΕΙ. ἵν', ὦ μέλε,
παρόντες οἱ φεύγοντες ἡμέρᾳ μιᾷ
πρότερον ἀπαλλάττοινθ' ἑκόντες, εἰ δὲ μή,
ἕωθεν ὑπανιῷντο τῇ νουμηνίᾳ. 119
ΣΤ. πῶς οὐ δέχονται δῆτα τῇ νουμηνίᾳ
ἀρχαὶ τὰ πρυτανεῖ', ἀλλ' ἕνῃ τε καὶ νέᾳ;

THE CLOUDS, 1172-1198

    Aye now you have an aspect Negative
    And Disputative, and our native query
    Shines forth there " What d'ye say ? " You've the
      true face
    Which rogues put on, of injured innocence.
    You have the regular Attic look about you.
    So now, you save me, for 'twas you undid me.
PH. What is it ails you ?
ST.   Why the Old-and-New day.
PH. And is there such a day as Old-and-New ?
ST. Yes : that's the day they mean to stake their gages.
PH. They'll lose them if they stake them. What ! do
      you think
    That one day can be two days, both together ?
ST. Why, can't it be so ?
PH.   Surely not ; or else
    A woman might at once be old and young.
ST. Still, the law says so.
PH.   True : but I believe
    They don't quite understand it.
ST.   You explain it.
PH. Old Solon had a democratic turn.
ST. Well, but that's nothing to the Old-and-New.
PH. Hence then he fixed that summonses be issued
    For these two days, the old one and the new one,
    So that the gage be staked on the New-month.
ST. What made him add " the old " then ?
PH.   I will tell you.
    He wished the litigants to meet on *that* day
    And compromise their quarrels : if they could not,
    Then let them fight it out on the New-month.
ST. Why then do Magistrates receive the stakes
    On the Old-and-New instead of the New-month ?

ARISTOPHANES

ΦΕΙ. ὅπερ οἱ προτένθαι γὰρ δοκοῦσί μοι ποιεῖν·
ἵν' ὡς τάχιστα τὰ πρυτανεῖ' ὑφελοίατο,
διὰ τοῦτο προὐτένθευσαν ἡμέρᾳ μιᾷ.
ΣΤ. εὖ γ', ὦ κακοδαίμονες, τί κάθησθ' ἀβέλτεροι,
ἡμέτερα κέρδη τῶν σοφῶν, ὄντες λίθοι,
ἀριθμός, πρόβατ', ἄλλως ἀμφορῆς νενησμένοι;
ὥστ' εἰς ἐμαυτὸν καὶ τὸν υἱὸν τουτονὶ
ἐπ' εὐτυχίαισιν ᾀστέον μοὔγκώμιον.
μάκαρ ὦ Στρεψίαδες,
αὐτός τ' ἔφυς ὡς σοφός,
χοῖον τὸν υἱὸν τρέφεις,
φήσουσι δή μ' οἱ φίλοι
χοἱ δημόται
ζηλοῦντες ἡνίκ' ἂν σὺ νικᾷς λέγων τὰς δίκας.
ἀλλ' εἰσάγων σε βούλομαι πρῶτον ἑστιᾶσαι.
ΠΑΣΙΑΣ. εἶτ' ἄνδρα τῶν αὑτοῦ τι χρὴ προϊέναι;
οὐδέποτέ γ', ἀλλὰ κρεῖττον ἦν εὐθὺς τότε
ἀπερυθριᾶσαι μᾶλλον ἢ σχεῖν πράγματα,
ὅτε τῶν ἐμαυτοῦ γ' ἕνεκα νυνὶ χρημάτων
ἕλκω σε κλητεύσοντα, καὶ γενήσομαι
ἐχθρὸς ἔτι πρὸς τούτοισιν ἀνδρὶ δημότῃ.
ἀτὰρ οὐδέποτέ γε τὴν πατρίδα καταισχυνῶ
ζῶν, ἀλλὰ καλοῦμαι Στρεψιάδην.
ΣΤ. τίς οὑτοσί;
ΠΑ. ἐς τὴν ἔνην τε καὶ νέαν.
ΣΤ. μαρτύρομαι,
ὅτι ἐς δύ' εἶπεν ἡμέρας. τοῦ χρήματος;
ΠΑ. τῶν δώδεκα μνῶν, ἃς ἔλαβες ὠνούμενος
τὸν ψαρὸν ἵππον.
ΣΤ. ἵππον; οὐκ ἀκούετε,
ὃν πάντες ὑμεῖς ἴστε μισοῦνθ' ἱππικήν;

---

[a] Apparently persons appointed to taste the viands to be

374

THE CLOUDS, 1199–1226

PH. Well, I believe they act like the Foretasters.[a]
 They wish to bag the gage as soon as possible,
 And thus they gain a whole day's foretaste of it.
ST. Aha! poor dupes, why sit ye mooning there,
 Game for us Artful Dodgers, you dull stones,
 You ciphers, lambkins, butts piled up together!
 Oh! my success inspires me, and I'll sing
 Glad eulogies on me and thee, my son.
  "*Man, most blessed, most divine,*
  What a wondrous wit is thine,
  What a son to grace thy line,"
   Friends and neighbours day by day
    Thus will say,
 When with envious eyes my suits they see you win:
 But first I'll feast you, so come in, my son, come in.

PASIAS.[b] What! must a man lose his own property!
 No: never, never. Better have refused
 With a bold face, than be so plagued as this.
 See! to get paid my own just debts, I'm forced
 To drag you to bear witness, and what's worse
 I needs must quarrel with my townsman here.
 Well, I won't shame my country, while I live,
 I'll go to law, I'll summon him.
ST.   Hallo!
PA. To the next Old-and-New.
ST.   Bear witness, all!
 He named two days. You'll summon me; what for?
PA. The fifty pounds I lent you when you bought
 That iron-grey.
ST.   Just listen to the fellow!
 The whole world knows that I detest all horses.

served at a public banquet, to see that everything was well cooked and wholesome.
 [b] *Enter Pasias,* the creditor mentioned l. 21.

ARISTOPHANES

ΠΑ. καὶ νὴ Δί' ἀποδώσειν γ' ἐπώμνυς τοὺς θεούς.
ΣΤ. μὰ τὸν Δί'· οὐ γάρ πω τότ' ἐξηπίστατο
Φειδιππίδης μοι τὸν ἀκατάβλητον λόγον.
ΠΑ. νῦν δὲ διὰ τοῦτ' ἔξαρνος εἶναι διανοεῖ; 12
ΣΤ. τί γὰρ ἄλλ' ἂν ἀπολαύσαιμι τοῦ μαθήματος;
ΠΑ. καὶ ταῦτ' ἐθελήσεις ἀπομόσαι μοι τοὺς θεούς;
ΣΤ. ποίους θεούς;
ΠΑ. τὸν Δία, τὸν Ἑρμῆν, τὸν Ποσειδῶ.
ΣΤ. νὴ Δία,
κἂν προσκαταθείην γ', ὥστ' ὀμόσαι, τριώβολον. 12
ΠΑ. ἀπόλοιο τοίνυν ἕνεκ' ἀναιδείας ἔτι.
ΣΤ. ἁλσὶν διασμηχθεὶς ὄναιτ' ἂν οὑτοσί.
ΠΑ. οἴμ' ὡς καταγελᾷς.
ΣΤ. ἓξ χόας χωρήσεται.
ΠΑ. οὔ τοι μὰ τὸν Δία τὸν μέγαν καὶ τοὺς θεοὺς
ἐμοῦ καταπροίξει.
ΣΤ. θαυμασίως ἥσθην θεοῖς, 12
καὶ Ζεὺς γέλοιος ὀμνύμενος τοῖς εἰδόσιν.
ΠΑ. ἦ μὴν σὺ τούτων τῷ χρόνῳ δώσεις δίκην.
ἀλλ' εἴτ' ἀποδώσεις μοι τὰ χρήματ' εἴτε μή,
ἀπόπεμψον ἀποκρινάμενος.
ΣΤ. ἔχε νυν ἥσυχος.
ἐγὼ γὰρ αὐτίκ' ἀποκρινοῦμαί σοι σαφῶς. 1ε
ΠΑ. τί σοι δοκεῖ δράσειν;
ΜΑΡΤΥΣ. ἀποδώσειν σοι δοκεῖ.
ΣΤ. ποῦ 'σθ' οὗτος ἀπαιτῶν με τἀργύριον; λέγε,
τουτὶ τί ἔστι;
ΠΑ. τοῦθ' ὅ τι ἐστί; κάρδοπος.
ΣΤ. ἔπειτ' ἀπαιτεῖς τἀργύριον τοιοῦτος ὤν;
οὐκ ἂν ἀποδοίην οὐδ' ἂν ὀβολὸν οὐδενί, 1ε
ὅστις καλέσειε κάρδοπον τὴν καρδόπην.

THE CLOUDS, 1227-1251

PA. I swear you swore by all the Gods to pay me.
ST. Well, now I swear I won't : Pheidippides
Has learnt since then the unanswerable Logic.
PA. And will you therefore shirk my just demand ?
ST. Of course I will : else why should he have learnt it ?
PA. And will you dare forswear it by the Gods ?
ST. The Gods indeed ! What Gods ?
PA. Poseidon, Hermes, Zeus.
ST. By Zeus I would,
Though I gave twopence halfpenny for the privilege.
PA. O then confound you for a shameless rogue !
ST. Hallo ! this butt should be rubbed down with salt.[a]
PA. Zounds ! you deride me !
ST. Why 'twill hold four gallons.
PA. You 'scape me not, by Mighty Zeus, and all
The Gods !
ST. I wonderfully like the Gods ;
An oath by Zeus is sport to knowing ones.
PA. Sooner or later you'll repent of this.
Come do you mean to pay your debts or don't you ?
Tell me, and I'll be off.
ST. Now do have patience ;
I'll give you a clear answer in one moment.
PA. What do you think he'll do ?
WITNESS. I think he'll pay you.
ST. Where is that horrid dun ? O here : now tell me
What you call this.
PA. What I call that ? a trough.
ST. Heavens ! what a fool : and do *you* want your money ?
I'd never pay one penny to a fellow
Who calls my troughess, trough. So there's your
answer.

[a] Pasias is apparently " a tun of a man " and wine-skins (ἀσκοί) were thus treated.

ARISTOPHANES

ΠΑ. οὐκ ἄρ' ἀποδώσεις;
ΣΤ. οὐχ, ὅσον γέ μ' εἰδέναι.
οὔκουν ἀνύσας τι θᾶττον ἀπολιταργιεῖς
ἀπὸ τῆς θύρας;
ΠΑ. ἄπειμι, καὶ τοῦτ' ἴσθ', ὅτι
θήσω πρυτανεῖ', ἢ μηκέτι ζώην ἐγώ. 1255
ΣΤ. προσαποβαλεῖς ἄρ' αὐτὰ πρὸς ταῖς δώδεκα.
καίτοι σε τοῦτό γ' οὐχὶ βούλομαι παθεῖν,
ὁτιὴ 'κάλεσας εὐηθικῶς τὴν κάρδοπον.

ΑΜΥΝΙΑΣ. ἰώ μοί μοι.
ΣΤ. ἔα. τίς οὑτοσί ποτ' ἔσθ' ὁ θρηνῶν; οὔ τί που 1260
τῶν Καρκίνου τις δαιμόνων ἐφθέγξατο;
ΑΜ. τί δ' ὅστις εἰμί, τοῦτο βούλεσθ' εἰδέναι;
ἀνὴρ κακοδαίμων.
ΣΤ. κατὰ σεαυτόν νυν τρέπου.
ΑΜ. "ὦ σκληρὲ δαῖμον, ὦ τύχαι θραυσάντυγες
ἵππων ἐμῶν·" "ὦ Παλλάς, ὥς μ' ἀπώλεσας." 1265
ΣΤ. τί δαί σε Τληπόλεμός ποτ' εἴργασται κακόν;
ΑΜ. μὴ σκῶπτέ μ', ὦ τᾶν, ἀλλά μοι τὰ χρήματα
τὸν υἱὸν ἀποδοῦναι κέλευσον ἅλαβεν,
ἄλλως τε μέντοι καὶ κακῶς πεπραγότι.
ΣΤ. τὰ ποῖα ταῦτα χρήμαθ';
ΑΜ. ἁδανείσατο. 1270
ΣΤ. κακῶς ἄρ' ὄντως εἶχες, ὥς γ' ἐμοὶ δοκεῖς.
ΑΜ. ἵππους ἐλαύνων ἐξέπεσον νὴ τοὺς θεούς.
ΣΤ. τί δῆτα ληρεῖς ὥσπερ ἀπ' ὄνου καταπεσών;
ΑΜ. ληρῶ, τὰ χρήματ' ἀπολαβεῖν εἰ βούλομαι;
ΣΤ. οὐκ ἔσθ' ὅπως σύ γ' αὐτὸς ὑγιαίνεις.

---
[a] *Enter Amynias*, the creditor mentioned l. 31.

378

THE CLOUDS, 1252-1275

PA. Then you won't pay me?
ST.   No, not if I know it.
Come put your best foot forward, and be off:
March off, I say, this instant!
PA.   May I die
If I don't go at once and stake my gage!
ST. No don't: the fifty pounds are loss enough:
And really on my word I would not wish you
To lose this too just for one silly blunder.

AMYNIAS.[a] Ah me! Oh! Oh! Oh!
ST. Hallo! who's that making that horrible noise?
Not one of Carcinus's snivelling Gods?
AM. Who cares to know what I am? what imports it?
An ill-starred man.
ST.   Then keep it to yourself.
AM. "O heavy fate!" "O Fortune, thou hast broken
My chariot wheels!" "Thou hast undone me,
Pallas!"[b]
ST. How! has Tlepolemus been at you, man?
AM. Jeer me not, friend, but tell your worthy son
To pay me back the money which I lent him:
I'm in a bad way and the times are pressing.
ST. What money do you mean?
AM.   Why what he borrowed.
ST. You *are* in a bad way, I really think.
AM. Driving my four-wheel out I fell, by Zeus.
ST. You rave as if you'd fall'n times out-of-mind.[c]
AM. I rave? how so? I only claim my own.
ST. You can't be quite right, surely.

[b] "These lines are from the *Licymnius* of Xenocles" (Schol.), a son of Carcinus (*cf. W.* 1511). In the play Tlepolemus accidentally kills Licymnius.

[c] ἀπ' ὄνου "from a donkey" can also be read ἀπὸ νοῦ "out of your mind."

ARISTOPHANES

ΑΜ. τί δαί; 1275
ΣΤ. τὸν ἐγκέφαλον ὥσπερ σεσεῖσθαί μοι δοκεῖς.
ΑΜ. σὺ δὲ νὴ τὸν Ἑρμῆν προσκεκλῆσθαί μοι δοκεῖς,
εἰ μὴ ἀποδώσεις τἀργύριον.
ΣΤ. κάτειπέ νυν,
πότερα νομίζεις καινὸν ἀεὶ τὸν Δία
ὕειν ὕδωρ ἑκάστοτ', ἢ τὸν ἥλιον 1280
ἕλκειν κάτωθεν ταὐτὸ τοῦθ' ὕδωρ πάλιν;
ΑΜ. οὐκ οἶδ' ἔγωγ' ὁπότερον, οὐδέ μοι μέλει.
ΣΤ. πῶς οὖν ἀπολαβεῖν τἀργύριον δίκαιος εἶ,
εἰ μηδὲν οἶσθα τῶν μετεώρων πραγμάτων;
ΑΜ. ἀλλ' εἰ σπανίζεις τἀργυρίου μοι τὸν τόκον 1285
ἀπόδος γε.
ΣΤ. τοῦτο δ' ἔσθ' ὁ τόκος τί θηρίον;
ΑΜ. τί δ' ἄλλο γ' ἢ κατὰ μῆνα καὶ καθ' ἡμέραν
πλέον πλέον τἀργύριον ἀεὶ γίγνεται,
ὑπορρέοντος τοῦ χρόνου;
ΣΤ. καλῶς λέγεις.
τί δῆτα; τὴν θάλατταν ἔσθ' ὅτι πλείονα 1290
νυνὶ νομίζεις ἢ πρὸ τοῦ;
ΑΜ. μὰ Δί', ἀλλ' ἴσην.
οὐ γὰρ δίκαιον πλείον' εἶναι.
ΣΤ. κᾆτα πῶς
αὕτη μέν, ὦ κακόδαιμον, οὐδὲν γίγνεται
ἐπιρρεόντων τῶν ποταμῶν πλείων, σὺ δὲ
ζητεῖς ποιῆσαι τἀργύριον πλεῖον τὸ σόν; 1295
οὐκ ἀποδιώξεις σαυτὸν ἀπὸ τῆς οἰκίας;
φέρε μοι τὸ κέντρον.
ΑΜ. ταῦτ' ἐγὼ μαρτύρομαι.
ΣΤ. ὕπαγε, τί μέλλεις; οὐκ ἐλᾷς, ὦ σαμφόρα;
ΑΜ. ταῦτ' οὐχ ὕβρις δῆτ' ἐστίν;
ΣΤ. ἄξεις; ἐπιαλῶ

THE CLOUDS, 1275-1299

AM.   Why, what mean you?
ST. I shrewdly guess your brain's received a shake.
AM. I shrewdly guess that you'll receive a summons
 If you don't pay my money.
ST.   Well then, tell me,
 Which theory do you side with, that the rain
 Falls fresh each time, or that the Sun draws back
 The same old rain, and sends it down again?
AM. I'm very sure I neither know nor care.
ST. Not care! good heavens! And do *you* claim your
  money,
 So unenlightened in the Laws of Nature?
AM. If you're hard up then, pay me back the Interest
 At least.
ST.   Int-er-est? what kind of a beast is that?
AM. What else than day by day and month by month
 Larger and larger still the silver grows
 As time sweeps by?
ST.   Finely and nobly said.
 What then! think you the Sea is larger now
 Than 'twas last year?
AM.   No surely, 'tis no larger:
 It is not right it should be.
ST.   And do you then,
 Insatiable grasper! when the Sea,
 Receiving all these Rivers, grows no larger,
 Do you desire your silver to grow larger?
 Come now, you prosecute your journey off!
 Here, fetch the whip.
AM.   Bear witness, I appeal.
ST. Be off! what, won't you? Gee up, sigma-brand!
AM. I say! a clear assault!
ST.   You won't be off?

ARISTOPHANES

κεντῶν ὑπὸ τὸν πρωκτόν σε τὸν σειραφόρον. 130(
φεύγεις; ἔμελλον ἄρα σε κινήσειν ἐγὼ
αὐτοῖς τροχοῖς τοῖς σοῖσι καὶ ξυνωρίσιν.

ΧΟ. οἷον τὸ πραγμάτων ἐρᾶν φλαύρων· ὁ γὰρ [στρ.
γέρων ὅδ' ἐρασθεὶς
ἀποστερῆσαι βούλεται 130ἰ
τὰ χρήμαθ' ἁδανείσατο·
κοὐκ ἔσθ' ὅπως οὐ τήμερον
λήψεταί τι πρᾶγμ', ὃ τοῦ-
τον ποιήσει τὸν σοφισ-
τὴν [γέροντ']
ἀνθ' ὧν πανουργεῖν ἤρξατ', ἐξαίφνης κακὸν λαβεῖν τι. 131(
οἶμαι γὰρ αὐτὸν αὐτίχ' εὑρήσειν ὅπερ [ἀντ.
πάλαι ποτ' ἐπῄτει,
εἶναι τὸν υἱὸν δεινόν οἱ
γνώμας ἐναντίας λέγειν
τοῖσιν δικαίοις, ὥστε νι-
κᾶν ἅπαντας οἷσπερ ἂν 131:
ξυγγένηται, κἂν λέγῃ
παμπόνηρ'.
ἴσως δ' ἴσως βουλήσεται κἄφωνον αὐτὸν εἶναι. 132

ΣΤ. ἰοὺ ἰού.
ὦ γείτονες καὶ ξυγγενεῖς καὶ δημόται,
ἀμυνάθετέ μοι τυπτομένῳ πάσῃ τέχνῃ.
οἴμοι κακοδαίμων τῆς κεφαλῆς καὶ τῆς γνάθου.
ὦ μιαρέ, τύπτεις τὸν πατέρα;
ΦΕΙ. φήμ', ὦ πάτερ. 132
ΣΤ. ὁρᾶθ' ὁμολογοῦνθ' ὅτι με τύπτει.
ΦΕΙ. καὶ μάλα.
ΣΤ. ὦ μιαρὲ καὶ πατραλοῖα καὶ τοιχωρύχε.

382

THE CLOUDS, 1300–1327

I'll stimulate you ; Zeus ! I'll goad your haunches.
Aha ! you run : I thought I'd stir you up
You and your phaetons, and wheels, and all !

CH. What a thing it is to long for matters which are wrong !
For you see how this old man
Is seeking, if he can
His creditors trepan :
And I confidently say
That he will this very day
Such a blow
Amid his prosperous cheats receive,
            that he will deeply deeply grieve.

For I think that he has won what he wanted for his son,
And the lad has learned the way
All justice to gainsay,
Be it what or where it may :
That he'll trump up any tale,
Right or wrong, and so prevail.
This I know.
Yea ! and perchance the time will come
        when he shall wish his son were dumb.

ST.   Oh ! Oh !
    Help ! Murder ! Help ! O neighbours, kinsfolk, townsmen,
    Help, one and all, against this base assault,
    Ah ! Ah ! my cheek ! my head ! O luckless me !
    Wretch ! do you strike your father ?
PH.   Yes, Papa.
ST.   See ! See ! he owns he struck me.
PH.   To be sure.
ST.   Scoundrel ! and parricide ! and house-breaker !

ARISTOPHANES

ΦΕΙ. αὖθίς με ταὐτὰ ταῦτα καὶ πλείω λέγε.
ἆρ' οἶσθ' ὅτι χαίρω πόλλ' ἀκούων καὶ κακά;
ΣΤ. ὦ λακκόπρωκτε.
ΦΕΙ. πάττε πολλοῖς τοῖς ῥόδοις. 1333
ΣΤ. τὸν πατέρα τύπτεις;
ΦΕΙ. κἀποφανῶ γε νὴ Δία
ὡς ἐν δίκῃ σ' ἔτυπτον.
ΣΤ. ὦ μιαρώτατε,
καὶ πῶς γένοιτ' ἂν πατέρα τύπτειν ἐν δίκῃ;
ΦΕΙ. ἔγωγ' ἀποδείξω, καί σε νικήσω λέγων.
ΣΤ. τουτὶ σὺ νικήσεις;
ΦΕΙ. πολύ γε καὶ ῥᾳδίως. 133
ἑλοῦ δ' ὁπότερον τοῖν λόγοιν βούλει λέγειν.
ΣΤ. ποίοιν λόγοιν;
ΦΕΙ. τὸν κρείττον', ἢ τὸν ἥττονα;
ΣΤ. ἐδιδαξάμην μέντοι σε νὴ Δί', ὦ μέλε,
τοῖσιν δικαίοις ἀντιλέγειν, εἰ ταῦτά γε
μέλλεις ἀναπείσειν, ὡς δίκαιον καὶ καλὸν 134
τὸν πατέρα τύπτεσθ' ἐστὶν ὑπὸ τῶν υἱέων.
ΦΕΙ. ἀλλ' οἴομαι μέντοι σ' ἀναπείσειν, ὥστε γε
οὐδ' αὐτὸς ἀκροασάμενος οὐδὲν ἀντερεῖς.
ΣΤ. καὶ μὴν ὅ τι καὶ λέξεις ἀκοῦσαι βούλομαι.
13
ΧΟ. σὸν ἔργον, ὦ πρεσβῦτα, φροντίζειν ὅπῃ [στρ.
τὸν ἄνδρα κρατήσεις,
ὡς οὗτος, εἰ μή τῳ ʼπεποίθειν, οὐκ ἂν ἦν
οὕτως ἀκόλαστος.
ἀλλ' ἔσθ' ὅτῳ θρασύνεται· δῆλόν γε τἀν- 13
θρώπου ʼστὶ τὸ λῆμα.

ἀλλ' ἐξ ὅτου τὸ πρῶτον ἤρξαθ' ἡ μάχη γενέσθαι
ἤδη λέγειν χρὴ πρὸς χορόν. πάντως δὲ τοῦτο δράσεις.

384

THE CLOUDS, 1328-1352

PH. Thank you : go on, go on : do please go on.
　　I am quite delighted to be called such names !
ST. O probed Adulterer.
PH. 　　　　　　　Roses from your lips.[a]
ST. Strike you your father ?
PH. 　　　　　　　O dear yes : what's more,
　　I'll prove I struck you justly.
ST. 　　　　　　　Struck me justly !
　　Villain ! how can you strike a father justly ?
PH. Yes, and I'll demonstrate it, if you please.
ST. Demonstrate this ?
PH. 　　　　　　　O yes, quite easily.
　　Come, take your choice, which Logic do you choose ?
ST. Which what ?
PH. 　　　Logic : the Better or the Worse ?
ST. Ah, then, in very truth I've had you taught
　　To reason down all Justice, if you think
　　You can prove this, that it is just and right
　　That fathers should be beaten by their sons !
PH. Well, well, I think I'll prove it, if you'll listen,
　　So that even you won't have one word to answer.
ST. Come, I should like to hear what you've to say.
CH. 'Tis yours, old man, some method to contrive
　　　　　This fight to win :
　　He would not without arms wherewith to strive
　　　　　So bold have been.
　　　　He knows, be sure, whereon to trust.
　　　　His eager bearing proves he must.

　　So come and tell us from what cause
　　　　　　　this sad dispute began ;
　　Come, tell us how it first arose :
　　　　　　　do tell us if you can.

[a] *Cf.* l. 910.

ARISTOPHANES

ΣΤ. καὶ μὴν ὅθεν γε πρῶτον ἠρξάμεσθα λοιδορεῖσθαι
ἐγὼ φράσω· 'πειδὴ γὰρ εἰστιώμεθ', ὥσπερ ἴστε,
πρῶτον μὲν αὐτὸν τὴν λύραν λαβόντ' ἐγὼ 'κέλευσα
ᾆσαι Σιμωνίδου μέλος, τὸν Κριόν, ὡς ἐπέχθη.
ὁ δ' εὐθέως ἀρχαῖον εἶν' ἔφασκε τὸ κιθαρίζειν
ᾄδειν τε πίνονθ', ὡσπερεὶ κάχρυς γυναῖκ' ἀλοῦσαν.

ΦΕΙ. οὐ γὰρ τότ' εὐθὺς χρῆν σε τύπτεσθαί τε καὶ
πατεῖσθαι,
ᾄδειν κελεύονθ', ὡσπερεὶ τέττιγας ἑστιῶντα;

ΣΤ. τοιαῦτα μέντοι καὶ τότ' ἔλεγεν ἔνδον, οἷάπερ νῦν,
καὶ τὸν Σιμωνίδην ἔφασκ' εἶναι κακὸν ποιητήν.
κἀγὼ μόλις μέν, ἀλλ' ὅμως ἠνεσχόμην τὸ πρῶτον.
ἔπειτα δ' ἐκέλευσ' αὐτὸν ἀλλὰ μυρρίνην λαβόντα
τῶν Αἰσχύλου λέξαι τί μοι· κᾆθ' οὗτος εὐθὺς εἶπεν,
" ἐγὼ γὰρ Αἰσχύλον νομίζω πρῶτον ἐν ποιηταῖς
ψόφου πλέων, ἀξύστατον, στόμφακα, κρημνο-
ποιόν·"
κἀνταῦθα πῶς οἴεσθέ μου τὴν καρδίαν ὀρεχθεῖν;
ὅμως δὲ τὸν θυμὸν δακὼν ἔφην, "σὺ δ' ἀλλὰ τούτων

---

[a] Crius was an Aeginetan wrestler on whose defeat at Olympia Simonides wrote an ode beginning "Ἐπέξαθ' ὁ Κριὸς οὐκ ἀεικέως," with a pun on κριός " a ram."
[b] Supposed to need no food but to live on dew.

THE CLOUDS, 1353-1369

ST. Well from the very first I will
                     the whole contention show :
'Twas when I went into the house
                     to feast him, as you know,
I bade him bring his lyre and sing,
                     the supper to adorn,
Some lay of old Simonides,
                     as, how the Ram was shorn : [a]
But he replied, to sing at meals
                     was coarse and obsolete ;
Like some old beldame humming airs
                     the while she grinds her wheat.
PH. And should you not be thrashed who told
                     your son, from food abstaining
To SING ! as though you were, forsooth
                     cicalas [b] entertaining.
ST. You hear him ! so he said just now
                     or e'er high words began :
And next he called Simonides
                     a very sorry man.
And when I heard him, I could scarce
                     my rising wrath command ;
Yet so I did, and him I bid
                     take myrtle in his hand
And chant some lines from Aeschylus,
                     but he replied with ire,
" Believe me, I'm not one of those
                     who Aeschylus admire,
That rough, unpolished, turgid bard,
                     that mouther of bombast ! "
When he said this, my heart began
                     to heave extremely fast ;
Yet still I kept my passion down,
                     and said, " Then prithee you,

ARISTOPHANES

λέξον τι τῶν νεωτέρων, ἅττ' ἐστὶ τὰ σοφὰ ταῦτα." 137
ὁ δ' εὐθὺς ἦσ' Εὐριπίδου ῥῆσίν τιν', ὡς ἐκίνει
ἀδελφός, ὠλεξίκακε, τὴν ὁμομητρίαν ἀδελφήν.ᵃ
κἀγὼ οὐκέτ' ἐξηνεσχόμην, ἀλλ' εὐθὺς ἐξαράττω
πολλοῖς κακοῖς καἰσχροῖσι· κᾆτ' ἐντεῦθεν, οἷον
εἰκός,
ἔπος πρὸς ἔπος ἠρειδόμεσθ'· εἶθ' οὗτος ἐπαναπηδᾷ, 137
κἄπειτ' ἔφλα με κἀσπόδει κἄπνιγε κἀπέθλιβεν.
ΦΕΙ. οὔκουν δικαίως, ὅστις οὐκ Εὐριπίδην ἐπαινεῖς,
σοφώτατον;
ΣΤ. σοφώτατόν γ' ἐκεῖνον, ὦ τί σ' εἴπω;
ἀλλ' αὖθις αὖ τυπτήσομαι.
ΦΕΙ. νὴ τὸν Δί', ἐν δίκῃ γ' ἄν.
ΣΤ. καὶ πῶς δικαίως; ὅστις ὠναίσχυντέ σ' ἐξέθρεψα, 138
αἰσθανόμενός σου πάντα τραυλίζοντος, ὅ τι νοοίης.
εἰ μέν γε βρῦν εἴποις, ἐγὼ γνοὺς ἂν πιεῖν ἐπέσχον.
μαμμᾶν δ' ἂν αἰτήσαντος ἧκόν σοι φέρων ἂν ἄρτον·
κακκᾶν δ' ἂν οὐκ ἔφθης φράσαι, κἀγὼ λαβὼν θύραζε
ἐξέφερον ἂν καὶ προὐσχόμην σε· σὺ δ' ἐμὲ νῦν
ἀπάγχων 138

ᵃ The reference is to the marriage of Macareus and Canace, the children of Aeolus.

THE CLOUDS, 1370-1385

    Sing one of those new-fangled songs
                    which modern striplings do."
And he began the shameful tale
                    Euripides has told
How a brother and a sister lived
                    incestuous lives of old.[a]
Then, then I could no more restrain,
                    but first I must confess
With strong abuse I loaded him,
                    and so, as you may guess,
We stormed and bandied threat for threat :
                    till out at last he flew,
And smashed and thrashed and thumped and bumped
                    and bruised me black and blue.
PH. And rightly too, who coolly dared
                    Euripides to blame,
Most sapient bard.
ST.   Most sapient bard !
                  you, what's your fitting name ?
Ah ! but he'll pummel me again.
PH.   He will : and justly too.
ST. What ! justly, heartless villain ! when
                    'twas I who nurtured you.
I knew your little lisping ways,
                    how soon, you'd hardly think,
If you cried " bree ! "[b] I guessed your wants,
                    and used to give you drink :
If you said " mamm ! " I fetched you bread
                    with fond discernment true,
And you could hardly say " Cacca ! "
                    when through the door I flew
And held you out a full arm's length
                    your little needs to do :

[b] βρῦν represents a child's cry for drink.

ARISTOPHANES

βοῶντα καὶ κεκραγόθ᾽ ὅτι
χεζητιῴην, οὐκ ἔτλης
ἔξω ᾽ξενεγκεῖν, ὦ μιαρέ,
θύραζέ μ᾽, ἀλλὰ πνιγόμενος
αὐτοῦ ᾽ποίησα κακκᾶν. 139

ΧΟ. οἶμαί γε τῶν νεωτέρων τὰς καρδίας [ἀντ.
πηδᾶν, ὅ τι λέξει.
εἰ γὰρ τοιαῦτά γ᾽ οὗτος ἐξειργασμένος
λαλῶν ἀναπείσει,
τὸ δέρμα τῶν γεραιτέρων λάβοιμεν ἄν 139
ἀλλ᾽ οὐδ᾽ ἐρεβίνθου.

σὸν ἔργον, ὦ καινῶν ἐπῶν κινητὰ καὶ μοχλευτά,
πειθώ τινα ζητεῖν, ὅπως δόξεις λέγειν δίκαια.
ΦΕΙ. ὡς ἡδὺ καινοῖς πράγμασιν καὶ δεξιοῖς ὁμιλεῖν,
καὶ τῶν καθεστώτων νόμων ὑπερφρονεῖν δύνασθαι. 14C
ἐγὼ γὰρ ὅτε μὲν ἱππικῇ τὸν νοῦν μόνῃ προσεῖχον,
οὐδ᾽ ἂν τρί᾽ εἰπεῖν ῥήμαθ᾽ οἷός τ᾽ ἦ πρὶν ἐξαμαρτεῖν·
νυνὶ δ᾽ ἐπειδή μ᾽ οὑτοσὶ τούτων ἔπαυσεν αὐτός,
γνώμαις δὲ λεπταῖς καὶ λόγοις ξύνειμι καὶ μερίμναις,
οἶμαι διδάξειν ὡς δίκαιον τὸν πατέρα κολάζειν. 14C
ΣΤ. ἵππευε τοίνυν νὴ Δί᾽, ὡς ἔμοιγε κρεῖττόν ἐστιν
ἵππων τρέφειν τέθριππον ἢ τυπτόμενον ἐπιτριβῆναι.

THE CLOUDS, 1386-1407

       But now when I was crying
       That I with pain was dying,
       You brute! you would not tarry
       Me out of doors to carry,
       But choking with despair
       I've been and done it there.

CH.   Sure all young hearts are palpitating now
           To hear him plead,
     Since if those lips with artful words avow
         The daring deed,
     And once a favouring verdict win,
     A fig for every old man's skin.
  O thou! who rakest up new thoughts
                 with daring hands profane.
  Try all you can, ingenious man,
                 that verdict to obtain.

PH. How sweet it is these novel arts,
               these clever words to know,
  And have the power established rules
               and laws to overthrow.
  Why in old times when horses were
               my sole delight, 'twas wonder
  If I could say a dozen words
               without some awful blunder!
  But now that he has made me quit
               that reckless mode of living,
  And I have been to subtle thoughts
               my whole attention giving,
  I hope to prove by logic strict
               'tis right to beat my father.

ST. O! buy your horses back, by Zeus,
               since I would ten times rather
  Have to support a four-in-hand,
               so I be struck no more.

ARISTOPHANES

ΦΕΙ. ἐκεῖσε δ' ὅθεν ἀπέσχισάς με τοῦ λόγου μέτειμι,
καὶ πρῶτ' ἐρήσομαί σε τουτί· παῖδά μ' ὄντ' ἔτυπτες;

ΣΤ. ἔγωγέ σ', εὐνοῶν τε καὶ κηδόμενος.

ΦΕΙ. εἰπὲ δή μοι,
οὐ κἀμέ σοι δίκαιόν ἐστιν εὐνοεῖν ὁμοίως,
τύπτειν τ', ἐπειδήπερ γε τοῦτ' ἔστ' εὐνοεῖν, τὸ
τύπτειν;
πῶς γὰρ τὸ μὲν σὸν σῶμα χρὴ πληγῶν ἀθῷον εἶναι,
τοὐμὸν δὲ μή; καὶ μὴν ἔφυν ἐλεύθερός γε κἀγώ.
" κλάουσι παῖδες, πατέρα δ' οὐ κλάειν δοκεῖς;"
φήσεις νομίζεσθαι σὺ παιδὸς τοῦτο τοὔργον εἶναι;
ἐγὼ δέ γ' ἀντείποιμ' ἂν ὡς δὶς παῖδες οἱ γέροντες,
εἰκός τε μᾶλλον τοὺς γέροντας ἢ νέους τι κλάειν,
ὅσῳπερ ἐξαμαρτάνειν ἧττον δίκαιον αὐτούς.

ΣΤ. ἀλλ' οὐδαμοῦ νομίζεται τὸν πατέρα τοῦτο πάσχειν.

ΦΕΙ. οὔκουν ἀνὴρ ὁ τὸν νόμον θεὶς τοῦτον ἦν τὸ πρῶτον,
ὥσπερ σὺ κἀγώ, καὶ λέγων ἔπειθε τοὺς παλαιούς;
ἧττόν τι δῆτ' ἔξεστι κἀμοὶ καινὸν αὖ τὸ λοιπὸν
θεῖναι νόμον τοῖς υἱέσιν, τοὺς πατέρας ἀντιτύπτειν;

---

[a] A parody of the famous line Eur. *Alcestis*, 691 χαίρεις ὁρῶν φῶς πατέρα δ' οὐ χαίρειν δοκεῖς; where Pheres addresses his son Admetus who had asked him to die in his stead.

THE CLOUDS, 1408-1424

PH. Peace. I will now resume the thread
  where I broke off before.
 And first I ask : when I was young,
  did you not strike me then ?
ST. Yea : for I loved and cherished you.
PH.   Well, solve me this again,
 Is it not just that I your son
  should cherish you alike,
 And strike you, since, as you observe,
  to cherish means to strike ?
 What ! must my body needs be scourged
  and pounded black and blue
 And yours be scathless ? was not I
  as much freeborn as you ?
 "Children are whipped, and shall not sires be whipped ? " [a]
 Perhaps you'll urge that children's minds
  alone are taught by blows :—
 Well : Age is Second Childhood then :
  that everybody knows.
 And as by old experience Age
  should guide its steps more clearly,
 So when they err, they surely should
  be punished more severely.
ST. But Law goes everywhere for me :
  deny it, if you can.
PH. Well was not he who made the law,
  a man, a mortal man,
 As you or I, who in old times
  talked over all the crowd ?
 And think you that to you or me
  the same is not allowed,
 To change it, so that sons by blows
  should keep their fathers steady ?

ARISTOPHANES

ὅσας δὲ πληγὰς εἴχομεν πρὶν τὸν νόμον τεθῆναι, 1421
ἀφίεμεν, καὶ δίδομεν αὐτοῖς προῖκα συγκεκόφθαι.
σκέψαι δὲ τοὺς ἀλεκτρυόνας καὶ τἄλλα τὰ βοτὰ
ταυτί,
ὡς τοὺς πατέρας ἀμύνεται· καίτοι τι διαφέρουσιν
ἡμῶν ἐκεῖνοι, πλὴν ὅτι ψηφίσματ' οὐ γράφουσιν;

ΣΤ. τί δῆτ', ἐπειδὴ τοὺς ἀλεκτρυόνας ἅπαντα μιμεῖ, 1430
οὐκ ἐσθίεις καὶ τὴν κόπρον κἀπὶ ξύλου καθεύδεις;

ΦΕΙ. οὐ ταυτόν, ὦ τᾶν, ἐστιν, οὐδ' ἂν Σωκράτει δοκοίη.

ΣΤ. πρὸς ταῦτα μὴ τύπτ'· εἰ δὲ μή, σαυτόν ποτ'
αἰτιάσει.

ΦΕΙ. καὶ πῶς;

ΣΤ. ἐπεὶ σὲ μὲν δίκαιός εἰμ' ἐγὼ κολάζειν,
σὺ δ', ἢν γένηταί σοι, τὸν υἱόν.

ΦΕΙ. ἢν δὲ μὴ γένηται, 143.
μάτην ἐμοὶ κεκλαύσεται, σὺ δ' ἐγχανὼν τεθνήξει.

ΣΤ. ἐμοὶ μέν, ὦνδρες ἥλικες, δοκεῖ λέγειν δίκαια·
κἄμοιγε συγχωρεῖν δοκεῖ τούτοισι τἀπιεικῆ.
κλάειν γὰρ ἡμᾶς εἰκός ἐστ', ἢν μὴ δίκαια δρῶμεν.

ΦΕΙ. σκέψαι δὲ χἀτέραν ἔτι γνώμην.

ΣΤ. ἀπὸ γὰρ ὀλοῦμαι. 1440

ΦΕΙ. καὶ μὴν ἴσως γ' οὐκ ἀχθέσει παθὼν ἃ νῦν πέπονθας.

THE CLOUDS, 1425–1441

  Still, we'll be liberal, and blows
        which we've received already
  We will forget, we'll have no ex-
          post-facto legislation.
  —Look at the game-cocks, look at all
         the animal creation,
  Do not *they* beat their parents? Aye:
         I say then, that in fact
  They are as we, except that they
         no special laws enact.
ST. Why don't you then, if always where
        the game-cock leads you follow,
  Ascend your perch to roost at night,
        and dirt and ordure swallow?
PH. The case is different there, old man,
        as Socrates would see.
ST. Well then you'll blame yourself at last,
        if you keep striking me.
PH. How so?
ST.   Why, if it's right for me to punish you my son,
  You can, if you have got one, yours.
PH.   Aye, but suppose I've none.
  Then having gulled me you will die,
        while I've been flogged in vain.
ST. Good friends! I really think he has
        some reason to complain.
  I must concede he has put the case
        in quite a novel light:
  I really think we should be flogged
        unless we act aright!
PH. Look to a fresh idea then.
ST.   He'll be my death I vow.
PH. Yet then perhaps you will not grudge
        ev'n what you suffer now.

ARISTOPHANES

ΣΤ. πῶς δή; δίδαξον γὰρ τί μ' ἐκ τούτων ἐπωφελήσεις.
ΦΕΙ. τὴν μητέρ' ὥσπερ καὶ σὲ τυπτήσω.
ΣΤ. τί φῄς; τί φῄς σύ;
τοῦθ' ἕτερον αὖ μεῖζον κακόν.
ΦΕΙ. τί δ', ἢν ἔχων τὸν ἥττω 144
λόγον σὲ νικήσω λέγων τὴν μητέρ' ὡς τύπτειν
χρεών;
ΣΤ. τί δ' ἄλλο γ'; ἢν ταυτὶ ποιῇς,
οὐδέν σε κωλύσει σεαυ-
τὸν ἐμβαλεῖν ἐς τὸ βάραθρον 145
μετὰ Σωκράτους
καὶ τὸν λόγον τὸν ἥττω.
ταυτὶ δι' ὑμᾶς, ὦ Νεφέλαι, πέπονθ' ἐγώ,
ὑμῖν ἀναθεὶς ἅπαντα τἀμὰ πράγματα.
ΧΟ. αὐτὸς μὲν οὖν σαυτῷ σὺ τούτων αἴτιος,
στρέψας σεαυτὸν ἐς πονηρὰ πράγματα. 145
ΣΤ. τί δῆτα ταῦτ' οὔ μοι τότ' ἠγορεύετε,
ἀλλ' ἄνδρ' ἄγροικον καὶ γέροντ' ἐπήρετε;
ΧΟ. ἡμεῖς ποιοῦμεν ταῦθ' ἑκάστοθ' ὅταν τινὰ
γνῶμεν πονηρῶν ὄντ' ἐραστὴν πραγμάτων,
ἕως ἂν αὐτὸν ἐμβάλωμεν εἰς κακόν, 146
ὅπως ἂν εἰδῇ τοὺς θεοὺς δεδοικέναι.
ΣΤ. οἴμοι, πονηρά γ', ὦ Νεφέλαι, δίκαια δέ.
οὐ γάρ μ' ἐχρῆν τὰ χρήμαθ' ἁδανεισάμην
ἀποστερεῖν. νῦν οὖν ὅπως, ὦ φίλτατε,
τὸν Χαιρεφῶντα τὸν μιαρὸν καὶ Σωκράτην 146
ἀπολεῖς, μετ' ἐμοῦ 'λθών, οἳ σὲ κἄμ' ἐξηπάτων.
ΦΕΙ. ἀλλ' οὐκ ἂν ἀδικήσαιμι τοὺς διδασκάλους.
ΣΤ. ναὶ ναί, καταιδέσθητι πατρῷον Δία.
ΦΕΙ. ἰδού γε Δία πατρῷον· ὡς ἀρχαῖος εἶ.
Ζεὺς γάρ τις ἔστιν;

THE CLOUDS, 1442-1470

ST. How! will you make me like the blows
                        which I've received to-day?
PH. Yes, for I'll beat my mother too.
ST.   What! What is that you say!
Why, this is worse than all.
PH.   But what, if as I proved the other,
By the same Logic I can prove
                        'tis right to beat my mother?
ST. Aye! what indeed! if this you plead,
    If this you think to win,
    Why then, for all I care, you may
    To the Accursed Pit convey
    Yourself with all your learning new,
    Your master, and your Logic too,
        And tumble headlong in.
    O Clouds! O Clouds! I owe all this to you!
    Why did I let you manage my affairs!
CH. Nay, nay, old man, you owe it to yourself.
    Why didst thou turn to wicked practices?
ST. Ah, but ye should have asked me that before,
    And not have spurred a poor old fool to evil.
CH. Such is our plan. We find a man
        On evil thoughts intent,
    Guide him along to shame and wrong,
        Then leave him to repent.
ST. Hard words, alas! yet not more hard than just.
    It was not right unfairly to keep back
    The money that I borrowed. Come, my darling,
    Come and destroy that filthy Chaerephon
    And Socrates; for they've deceived us both!
PH. No. I will lift no hand against my Tutors.
ST. Yes do, come, reverence Paternal Zeus.
PH. Look there! Paternal Zeus! what an old fool.
    Is there a Zeus?

ARISTOPHANES

ΣΤ. ἔστιν.
ΦΕΙ.   οὐκ ἔστ᾽ οὐκ ἐπεὶ
Δῖνος βασιλεύει, τὸν Δί᾽ ἐξεληλακώς.
ΣΤ. οὐκ ἐξελήλακ᾽ ἀλλ᾽ ἐγὼ τοῦτ᾽ ᾠόμην,
διὰ τουτονὶ τὸν Δῖνον. οἴμοι δείλαιος,
ὅτε καὶ σὲ χυτρεοῦν ὄντα θεὸν ἡγησάμην.
ΦΕΙ. ἐνταῦθα σαυτῷ παραφρόνει καὶ φληνάφα.
ΣΤ. οἴμοι παρανοίας· ὡς ἐμαινόμην ἄρα,
ὅτ᾽ ἐξέβαλλον τοὺς θεοὺς διὰ Σωκράτην.
ἀλλ᾽, ὦ φίλ᾽ Ἑρμῆ, μηδαμῶς θύμαινέ μοι,
μηδέ μ᾽ ἐπιτρίψῃς, ἀλλὰ συγγνώμην ἔχε
ἐμοῦ παρανοήσαντος ἀδολεσχίᾳ.
καί μοι γενοῦ ξύμβουλος, εἴτ᾽ αὐτοὺς γραφὴν
διωκάθω γραψάμενος, εἴθ᾽ ὅ τι σοι δοκεῖ.
ὀρθῶς παραινεῖς οὐκ ἐῶν δικορραφεῖν,
ἀλλ᾽ ὡς τάχιστ᾽ ἐμπιπράναι τὴν οἰκίαν
τῶν ἀδολεσχῶν. δεῦρο δεῦρ᾽, ὦ Ξανθία,
κλίμακα λαβὼν ἔξελθε καὶ σμινύην φέρων,
κἄπειτ᾽ ἐπαναβὰς ἐπὶ τὸ φροντιστήριον
τὸ τέγος κατάσκαπτ᾽, εἰ φιλεῖς τὸν δεσπότην,
ἕως ἂν αὐτοῖς ἐμβάλῃς τὴν οἰκίαν·
ἐμοὶ δὲ δᾷδ᾽ ἐνεγκάτω τις ἡμμένην,
κἀγώ τιν᾽ αὐτῶν τήμερον δοῦναι δίκην
ἐμοὶ ποιήσω, κεἰ σφόδρ᾽ εἴσ᾽ ἀλαζόνες.
ΜΑΘΗΤΗΣ Α. ἰοὺ ἰού.
ΣΤ. σὸν ἔργον, ὦ δᾴς, ἱέναι πολλὴν φλόγα.
Μ. Α. ἄνθρωπε, τί ποιεῖς;
ΣΤ.   ὅ τι ποιῶ; τί δ᾽ ἄλλο γ᾽ ἢ
διαλεπτολογοῦμαι ταῖς δοκοῖς τῆς οἰκίας.

---

[a] For δῖνος (spelt δεῖνος in Athenaeus) cf. W. 618. It is a "large bowl," but why it is on the stage or what the reference to it means is uncertain.

398

THE CLOUDS, 1470–1496

ST. There is.
PH. There is *no* Zeus.
Young Vortex reigns, and he has turned out Zeus.
ST. No Vortex reigns . that was my foolish thought
All through this vortex [a] here. Fool that I was,
To think a piece of earthenware a God.
PH. Well, rave away, talk nonsense to yourself.
ST. Oh! fool, fool, fool, how mad I must have been
To cast away the Gods, for Socrates.
Yet Hermes, gracious Hermes,[b] be not angry
Nor crush me utterly, but look with mercy
On faults to which his idle talk hath led me.
And lend thy counsel; tell me, had I better
Plague them with lawsuits, or how else annoy them.
(*Affects to listen.*)
Good : your advice is good : I'll have no lawsuits,
I'll go at once and set their house on fire,
The prating rascals. Here, here, Xanthias,
Quick, quick here, bring your ladder and your pitchfork,
Climb to the roof of their vile thinking-house,
Dig at their tiles, dig stoutly, an' thou lovest me.
Tumble the very house about their ears.
And someone fetch me here a lighted torch,
And I'll soon see if, boasters as they are,
They won't repent of what they've done to me.
STUDENT 1. O dear ! O dear !
ST. Now, now, my torch, send out a lusty flame.
S. 1. Man! what are you at there ?
ST. What am I at ? I'll tell you.
I'm splitting straws with your house-rafters here.

[b] A statue of Hermes Στροφαῖος placed at the door of the house ἐπὶ ἀποτροπῇ τῶν ἄλλων κλεπτῶν (Schol. on *Pl.* 1153).

ARISTOPHANES

Μ. Β. οἴμοι, τις ἡμῶν πυρπολεῖ τὴν οἰκίαν;
ΣΤ. ἐκεῖνος οὗπερ θοἰμάτιον εἰλήφατε.
Μ. Γ. ἀπολεῖς ἀπολεῖς.
ΣΤ.   τοῦτ' αὐτὸ γὰρ καὶ βούλομαι,
    ἢν ἡ σμινύη μοι μὴ προδῷ τὰς ἐλπίδας, 150
    ἢ 'γὼ πρότερόν πως ἐκτραχηλισθῶ πεσών.
ΣΩ. οὗτος, τί ποιεῖς ἐτεόν, οὑπὶ τοῦ τέγους;
ΣΤ. ἀεροβατῶ, καὶ περιφρονῶ τὸν ἥλιον.
ΣΩ. οἴμοι τάλας, δείλαιος ἀποπνιγήσομαι.
ΧΑΙΡΕΦΩΝ. ἐγὼ δὲ κακοδαίμων γε κατακαυθήσομαι. 150
ΣΤ. τί γὰρ μαθόντες τοὺς θεοὺς ὑβρίζετε,
    καὶ τῆς Σελήνης ἐσκοπεῖσθε τὴν ἕδραν;
    δίωκε, βάλλε, παῖε, πολλῶν οὕνεκα,
    μάλιστα δ' εἰδὼς τοὺς θεοὺς ὡς ἠδίκουν.
ΧΟ. ἡγεῖσθ' ἔξω· κεχόρευται γὰρ μετρίως τό γε
    τήμερον ἡμῖν. 151

THE CLOUDS, 1497–1510

s. 2. Oh me! who's been and set our house on fire?
ST. Who was it, think you, that you stole the cloak from?
s. 3. O Murder! Murder!
ST. That's the very thing,
 Unless this pick prove traitor to my hopes,
 Or I fall down, and break my blessed neck.
SO. Hallo! what are you at, up on our roof?
ST. I walk on air, and contemplate the Sun.
SO. O! I shall suffocate. O dear! O dear!
CHAEREPHON. And I, poor devil, shall be burnt to death.
ST. For with what aim did ye insult the Gods,
 And pry around the dwellings of the Moon?
 Strike, smite them, spare them not, for many reasons,
 BUT MOST BECAUSE THEY HAVE BLASPHEMED THE GODS!
CH. Lead out of the way: for I think we may say
 We have acted our part very fairly to-day.

THE WASPS

INTRODUCTION

The *Wasps* was produced at the Lenaean festival 422 B.C., gaining either the first or the second prize, and it is commonly regarded as " a criticism on the Athenian dicasteries," or, as Grote puts it, "The poet's purpose was to make the dicasts appear monsters of caprice and injustice."
Yet though " Aristophanes does not exempt them from his strokes of wit and satire (for once thoroughly in his comic vein, he spares neither friend nor foe)," [a] these old dicasts are none the less " representatives of his own favourite Μαραθωνομάχαι," and in the Epirrhema (1071-90) " he describes, in the noblest and most glowing eulogy that ever flowed from the lips of a Comedian, who and what these dicasts were," [b] his real object being to detach them from the demagogues, of whom they " were the main support and stay in the popular assembly." These poor old men who " have to grope their way through the mud in the dark," whose " talk is of pot-herbs," and who are " struck with consternation (309-12) at the audacity of a child who dares to ask for anything so far beyond the means of a dicast as a homely treat of common figs," [c] are yet under the delusion (592-600), carefully fostered by Cleon and his like, that they are masters of the State, and, while there is "no discussion

[a] Rogers, Introduction, p. xvii.
[b] *Ibid.* p. xvi. [c] *Ibid.* p. xviii.

THE WASPS

on the excellences or defects of the dicastic system " in the great Arbitration scene (521 *seq.*), " the whole of Philocleon's harangue is an elaborate argument . . . that the dicastic office is an ἀρχὴ μεγάλη, whilst Bdelycleon, on the contrary, exerts himself to prove that it is nothing more nor less than a μεγάλη δουλεία."[a]

As regards the Athenian jury-system, it may be noted that as the political affairs were in the hands of the ἐκκλησία, so judicial affairs were committed to an assembly called ἡλιαία. The numbers of this were limited to 6000, who must be over thirty years of age, and " in the full possession of their rights and privileges as Athenian citizens."[b] They were elected by lot, an equal number from each of the ten tribes, had to take the Heliastic oath, which included a declaration that " they would give a fair and impartial hearing to both sides " (*cf.* 725, 920), and from the time of Pericles received three obols a day as their fee.

After their election they were " distributed and marshalled," by ballot, into ten sections or committees,[c] which " sat each in a separate Hall or Court-house," distinguished by a particular colour, and every dicast received " a metallic or boxwood plate (πινάκιον) inscribed with his name, etc.," together with a staff of office (βακτηρία or σκίπων, 727). The average number of a sectional assembly was 500, and " each member, as he entered the Courthouse, was presented with a σύμβολον or ticket of attendance," which on the rising of the Court he handed to the Treasurer (κωλακρέτης), who thereupon paid him three obols."[d]

[a] *Ibid.* p. xix.   [b] *Ibid.* p. xxi.
[c] *Ibid.* p. xxvii.   [d] *Ibid.* p. xxxiv.

ARISTOPHANES

" An action at law was commenced by a summons (πρόσκλησις) served on the defendant by, or in the presence of a sompnour (κλητήρ)."[a] Both plaintiff and defendant made oath as to the truth of their case (these preliminary affidavits were called ἀντωμοσίαι), and evidence was produced by each. When the pleadings and documentary evidence (αἱ γραφαί) were complete, they were sealed up in an official vessel (ἐχῖνος), to be opened on the day of trial, and the cause was set down in the cause-lists (αἱ σανίδες). After considering the evidence, both documentary and oral, and hearing the speeches, the dicasts recorded their verdict by placing their votes in one or other of two urns (καδίσκοι, cf. 987), but when the verdict was " Guilty," and in cases where no particular penalty was annexed by law (δίκαι ἀτίμητοι), " it devolved upon the Court to determine its amount or nature," and " the prisoner was allowed to suggest a milder punishment than that demanded by the prosecution," in which event (as in the case of Socrates) a second vote had to be taken, and for this purpose " the dicasts had πινάκια τιμητικά (damage-cessing tablets), over the waxen surface of which they drew either a long line to mark the heavier, or a short line to mark the lighter penalty."[b]

" In addition to actions before a Court of Law the practice of referring a dispute to the decision of arbitrators (διαιτηταί) was as well known in Athens as it is in England,"[c] and the proceedings in 521 *seq.* are " a complete specimen " of such an arbitration.

[a] *Ibid.* p. xxxv. [b] *Ibid.* p. xxxvi. [c] *Ibid.* p. xliii.

ΤΑ ΤΟΥ ΔΡΑΜΑΤΟΣ ΠΡΟΣΩΠΑ

ΣΩΣΙΑΣ } οἰκέται
ΞΑΝΘΙΑΣ
ΒΔΕΛΥΚΛΕΩΝ
ΦΙΛΟΚΛΕΩΝ
ΧΟΡΟΣ ΓΕΡΟΝΤΩΝ ΣΦΗΚΩΝ
ΠΑΙΣ
ΚΥΩΝ
ΣΥΜΠΟΤΗΣ
ΑΡΤΟΠΩΛΙΣ
ΚΑΤΗΓΟΡΟΣ

ΣΦΗΚΕΣ

ΣΩΣΙΑΣ. Οὗτος, τί πάσχεις, ὦ κακόδαιμον Ξανθία;
ΞΑΝΘΙΑΣ. φυλακὴν καταλύειν νυκτερινὴν διδάσκομαι.
ΣΩ. κακὸν ἄρα ταῖς πλευραῖς τι προὐφείλεις μέγα.
ἆρ' οἶσθά γ' οἷον κνώδαλον φυλάττομεν;
ΞΑ. οἶδ'· ἀλλ' ἐπιθυμῶ σμικρὸν ἀπομερμηρίσαι. 5
ΣΩ. σὺ δ' οὖν παρακινδύνευ', ἐπεὶ καὐτοῦ γ' ἐμοῦ
κατὰ ταῖν κόραιν ὕπνου τι καταχεῖται γλυκύ.
ΞΑ. ἀλλ' ἦ παραφρονεῖς ἐτεὸν ἢ κορυβαντιᾷς;
ΣΩ. οὔκ, ἀλλ' ὕπνος μ' ἔχει τις ἐκ Σαβαζίου.
ΞΑ. τὸν αὐτὸν ἄρ' ἐμοὶ βουκολεῖς Σαβάζιον. 1
κἀμοὶ γὰρ ἀρτίως ἐπεστρατεύσατο
Μῆδός τις ἐπὶ τὰ βλέφαρα νυστακτὴς ὕπνος·
καὶ δῆτ' ὄναρ θαυμαστὸν εἶδον ἀρτίως.
ΣΩ. κἄγωγ' ἀληθῶς οἷον οὐδεπώποτε.
ἀτὰρ σὺ λέξον πρότερος.
ΞΑ. ἐδόκουν αἰετὸν]
καταπτάμενον εἰς τὴν ἀγορὰν μέγαν πάνυ
ἀναρπάσαντα τοῖς ὄνυξιν ἀσπίδα
φέρειν ἐπίχαλκον ἀνεκὰς εἰς τὸν οὐρανόν,

^a *The play opens with a dialogue between two drowsy slaves who have been keeping guard all night before* an *Athenian house. It is still dark, but the day is at hand.*

THE WASPS[a]

SOSIAS. You ill-starred Xanthias, what's the matter now?
XANTHIAS. The nightly watch I'm studying to relieve.[b]
SO. Why then, your ribs will have a score against you.
  Do you forget what sort of beast we're guarding?
XA. No, but I'd fain just drowse dull care away.
SO. Well, try your luck: for I too feel a sort
  Of drowsy sweetness settling o'er my eyes.
XA. Sure you're a maniac or a Corybant.
SO. (*Producing a wine flask*) Nay 'tis a sleep from great
  Sabazius holds me.[c]
XA. (*Producing another*) Aha! and I'm your fellow-votary
  there.
  My lids too felt just now the fierce assault
  Of a strong Median[d] nod-compelling sleep.
  And then I dreamed a dream; such a strange dream!
SO. And so did I: the strangest e'er I heard of.
  But tell yours first.
XA.   Methought a monstrous eagle
  Came flying towards the market-place, and there
  Seized in its claws a wriggling brassy shield,
  And bore it up in triumph to the sky,

[b] *i.e.* by going to sleep.
[c] X. denies that he is "a Corybant" but allows that he is almost one, being a devotee of Sabazius, the Phrygian Bacchus, and son of Cybele, of whom the Corybants were priests.
[d] *i.e.* as overwhelming as the host of Xerxes.

ARISTOPHANES

ΣΩ. κἄπειτα ταύτην ἀποβαλεῖν Κλεώνυμον.
ΣΩ. οὐδὲν ἄρα γρίφου διαφέρει Κλεώνυμος. 20
ΞΑ. πῶς δή;
ΣΩ. προσερεῖ τις τοῖσι συμπόταις λέγων,
τί ταὐτὸν ἐν γῇ τ' ἀπέβαλεν κἂν οὐρανῷ
κἂν τῇ θαλάττῃ θηρίον τὴν ἀσπίδα;
ΞΑ. οἴμοι, τί δῆτά μοι κακὸν γενήσεται
ἰδόντι τοιοῦτον ἐνύπνιον;
ΣΩ.   μὴ φροντίσῃς. 25
οὐδὲν γὰρ ἔσται δεινὸν οὐ μὰ τοὺς θεούς.
ΞΑ. δεινόν γέ πού 'στ' ἄνθρωπος ἀποβαλὼν ὅπλα.
ἀτὰρ σὺ τὸ σὸν αὖ λέξον.
ΣΩ.   ἀλλ' ἐστὶν μέγα.
περὶ τῆς πόλεως γάρ ἐστι τοῦ σκάφους ὅλου.
ΞΑ. λέγε νυν ἀνύσας τι τὴν τρόπιν τοῦ πράγματος. 30
ΣΩ. ἔδοξέ μοι περὶ πρῶτον ὕπνον ἐν τῇ πυκνὶ
ἐκκλησιάζειν πρόβατα συγκαθήμενα,
βακτηρίας ἔχοντα καὶ τριβώνια·
κἄπειτα τούτοις τοῖσι προβάτοις μοὐδόκει
δημηγορεῖν φάλαινα πανδοκεύτρια, 35
ἔχουσα φωνὴν ἐμπεπρημένης ὑός.
ΞΑ. αἰβοῖ.
ΣΩ.   τί ἔστι;
ΞΑ.   παῦε παῦε, μὴ λέγε·
ὄζει κάκιστον τοὐνύπνιον βύρσης σαπρᾶς.
ΣΩ. εἶθ' ἡ μιαρὰ φάλαιν' ἔχουσα τρυτάνην
ἵστη βόειον δημόν.

---

[a] The big eagle changes into bulky Cleonymus (cf. *A*. 88) the ῥίψασπις. There seems to be a play on ἀσπίς=(1) a shield, (2) a snake.
[b] The reference is to a well-known riddle (Athen. x. 78) τί ταὐτὸν ἐν οὐρανῷ, καὶ ἐπὶ γῆς, καὶ ἐν τῇ θαλάσσῃ; the answer

THE WASPS, 19-40

And then—Cleonymus fled off and dropped it.[a]
SO. Why then, Cleonymus is quite a riddle.
XA. How so?
SO. A man will ask his boon companions,
*What is that brute which throws away its shield
Alike in air, in ocean, in the field?*[b]
XA. O what mishap awaits me, that have seen
So strange a vision?
SO. Take it not to heart,
'Twill be no harm, I swear it by the Gods.
XA. No harm to see a man throw off his shield!
But now tell yours.
SO. Ah, mine's a big one, mine is;
About the whole great vessel of the state.
XA. Tell us at once the keel of the affair.
SO. 'Twas in my earliest sleep methought I saw
A flock of sheep assembled in the Pnyx,
Sitting close-packed, with little cloaks and staves;
Then to these sheep I heard, or seemed to hear
An all-receptive grampus [c] holding forth
In tone and accents like a sealded pig.
XA. Pheugh!
SO. Eh?
XA. Stop, stop, don't tell us any more.
Your dream smells horribly of putrid hides
SO. Then the vile grampus, scales in hand, weighed out
Bits of fat beef, cut up.[d]

being "a serpent" of which there are land and marine specimens, and which is also a constellation.
[c] Cleon; for his greed cf. *C*. 591, and for his voice *K*. 137.
[d] For the play on δημός "fat" and δῆμος "the people" cf. *K*. 954.

ARISTOPHANES

ΞΑ. οἴμοι δείλαιος.
τὸν Δῆμον ἡμῶν βούλεται διστάναι.
ΣΩ. ἐδόκει δέ μοι Θέωρος αὐτῆς πλησίον
χαμαὶ καθῆσθαι, τὴν κεφαλὴν κόρακος ἔχων.
εἶτ' Ἀλκιβιάδης εἶπε πρός με τραυλίσας·
ὁλᾶς; Θέωλος τὴν κεφαλὴν κόλακος ἔχει.
ΞΑ. ὀρθῶς γε τοῦτ' Ἀλκιβιάδης ἐτραύλισεν.
ΣΩ. οὔκουν ἐκεῖν' ἀλλόκοτον, ὁ Θέωρος κόραξ
γιγνόμενος;
ΞΑ. ἥκιστ', ἀλλ' ἄριστον.
ΣΩ. πῶς;
ΞΑ. ὅπως;
ἄνθρωπος ὢν εἶτ' ἐγένετ' ἐξαίφνης κόραξ·
οὔκουν ἐναργὲς τοῦτο συμβάλλειν, ὅτι
ἀρθεὶς ἀφ' ἡμῶν ἐς κόρακας οἰχήσεται;
ΣΩ. εἶτ' οὐκ ἐγὼ δοὺς δύ' ὀβολὼ μισθώσομαι
οὕτως ὑποκρινόμενον σοφῶς ὀνείρατα;
ΞΑ. φέρε νυν κατείπω τοῖς θεαταῖς τὸν λόγον,
ὀλίγ' ἄτθ' ὑπειπὼν πρῶτον αὐτοῖσιν ταδί,
μηδὲν παρ' ἡμῶν προσδοκᾶν λίαν μέγα,
μηδ' αὖ γέλωτα Μεγαρόθεν κεκλεμμένον.
ἡμῖν γὰρ οὐκ ἔστ' οὐδὲ κάρυ' ἐκ φορμίδος
δούλω διαρριπτοῦντε τοῖς θεωμένοις,
οὔθ' Ἡρακλῆς τὸ δεῖπνον ἐξαπατώμενος,
οὐδ' αὖθις ἀνασελγαινόμενος Εὐριπίδης·
οὐδ' εἰ Κλέων γ' ἔλαμψε τῆς τύχης χάριν,
αὖθις τὸν αὐτὸν ἄνδρα μυττωτεύσομεν
ἀλλ' ἔστιν ἡμῖν λογίδιον γνώμην ἔχον,

---

[a] For the play on κόραξ and κόλαξ cf. Diogenes (cited by Athenaeus vi. 65), πολὺ κρεῖττον ἐς κόρακας ἀπελθεῖν ἢ ἐς κόλακας. Theorus, who is here called a "flatterer," is jeered at as a

XA.   Woe worth the day!
He means to cut our city up in bits.
SO.   Methought beside him, on the ground, I saw
Theorus seated, with a raven's head.
Then Alcibiades lisped out to me,
Cwemark! Theocwus has a cwaven's[a] *head.*
XA.   Well lisped! and rightly, Alcibiades!
SO.   But is this not ill-omened, that a man
Turn to a crow?
XA.   Nay, excellent.
SO.   How?
XA.   How!
Being a man he straight becomes a crow:
Is it not obvious to conjecture that
He's going to leave us, going to the crows?
SO.   Shall I not pay two obols then, and hire
One who so cleverly interprets dreams?
XA.   Come, let me tell the story to the audience
With just these few remarks, by way of preface.
Expect not from us something mighty grand,
Nor yet some mirth purloined from Megara.[b]
We have no brace of servants here, to scatter
Nuts from their basket out among the audience,
No Heracles defrauded of his supper,
Nor yet Euripides besmirched again;
No, nor though Cleon shine, by fortune's favour,[c]
Will we to mincemeat chop the man again.
Ours is a little tale, with meaning in it,

"perjurer," *C.* 400. "To go to the crows" is the same as our "go to the dogs."
 [b] Susarion of Megara is said to have invented comedy, but "Megaric comedy" is often referred to as rude and vulgar; *cf. A.* 738.
 [c] He was in this year appointed commander-in-chief to oppose Brasidas in Thrace.

ARISTOPHANES

ὑμῶν μὲν αὐτῶν οὐχὶ δεξιώτερον, 65
κωμῳδίας δὲ φορτικῆς σοφώτερον.
ἔστιν γὰρ ἡμῖν· δεσπότης ἐκεινοσὶ
ἄνω καθεύδων, ὁ μέγας, οὑπὶ τοῦ τέγους.
οὗτος φυλάττειν τὸν πατέρ' ἐπέταξε νῷν,
ἔνδον καθείρξας, ἵνα θύραζε μὴ 'ξίῃ. 70
νόσον γὰρ ὁ πατὴρ ἀλλόκοτον αὐτοῦ νοσεῖ,
ἣν οὐδ' ἂν εἷς γνοίη ποτ' οὐδ' ἂν ξυμβάλοι,
εἰ μὴ πύθοιθ' ἡμῶν· ἐπεὶ τοπάζετε.
Ἀμυνίας μὲν ὁ Προνάπους φήσ' οὑτοσὶ
εἶναι φιλόκυβον αὐτόν· ἀλλ' οὐδὲν λέγει. 75
ΣΩ. μὰ Δί', ἀλλ' ἀφ' αὑτοῦ τὴν νόσον τεκμαίρεται.
ΞΑ. οὔκ, ἀλλὰ φιλο μέν ἐστιν ἀρχὴ τοῦ κακοῦ.
ὁδὶ δέ φησι Σωσίας πρὸς Δερκύλον
εἶναι φιλοπότην αὐτόν.
ΣΩ. οὐδαμῶς γ', ἐπεὶ
αὕτη γε χρηστῶν ἐστὶν ἀνδρῶν ἡ νόσος. 80
ΞΑ. Νικόστρατος δ' αὖ φησιν ὁ Σκαμβωνίδης
εἶναι φιλοθύτην αὐτὸν ἢ φιλόξενον.
ΣΩ. μὰ τὸν κύν', ὦ Νικόστρατ', οὐ φιλόξενος,
ἐπεὶ καταπύγων ἐστὶν ὅ γε Φιλόξενος.
ΞΑ. ἄλλως φλυαρεῖτ'· οὐ γὰρ ἐξευρήσετε. 85
εἰ δὴ 'πιθυμεῖτ' εἰδέναι, σιγᾶτε νῦν.
φράσω γὰρ ἤδη τὴν νόσον τοῦ δεσπότου.
φιληλιαστής ἐστιν ὡς οὐδεὶς ἀνήρ,
ἐρᾷ τε τούτου τοῦ δικάζειν, καὶ στένει,
ἢν μὴ 'πὶ τοῦ πρώτου καθίζηται ξύλου. 90
ὕπνου δ' ὁρᾷ τῆς νυκτὸς οὐδὲ πασπάλην.
ἢν δ' οὖν καταμύσῃ κἂν ἄχνην, ὅμως ἐκεῖ
ὁ νοῦς πέτεται τὴν νύκτα περὶ τὴν κλεψύδραν.
ὑπὸ τοῦ δὲ τὴν ψῆφόν γ' ἔχειν εἰωθέναι

THE WASPS, 65-94

Not too refined and exquisite for you,
Yet wittier far than vulgar comedy.
You see that great big man, the man asleep
Up on the roof, aloft : well, that's our master.
He keeps his father here, shut up within,
And bids us guard him that he stir not out.
For he, the father, has a strange disease,
Which none of you will know, or yet conjecture,
Unless we tell : else, if you think so, guess.
Amynias [a] there, the son of Pronapes,
Says he's a dice-lover : but he's quite out.
so. Ah, he conjectures from his own disease.
xa. Nay, but the word does really end with -lover.
Then Sosias here observes to Dercylus,
That 'tis a DRINK-lover.
so.   Confound it, no :
That's the disease of honest gentlemen.
xa. Then next, Nicostratus of Scambon says,
It is a sacrifice- [b] or stranger-lover.
so. What, like Philoxenus ? No, by the dog,
Not quite so lewd, Nicostratus, as that.
xa. Come, you waste words : you'll never find it out,
So all keep silence if you want to know.
I'll tell you the disease old master has.
He is a LAWCOURT-lover, no man like him.
Judging is what he dotes on, and he weeps
Unless he sit on the front bench of all.
At night he gets no sleep, no, not one grain,
Or if he doze the tiniest speck, his soul
Flutters in dreams around the water-clock.[c]
So used he is to holding votes, he wakes

[a] Here and below Aristophanes makes certain spectators credit Philocleon with their own special weakness.
[b] The Scholiast explains φιλοθύτης = δεισιδαίμων, "superstitious."
[c] By which the speeches of the advocates were timed.

ARISTOPHANES

τοὺς τρεῖς ξυνέχων τῶν δακτύλων ἀνίσταται, 95
ὥσπερ λιβανωτὸν ἐπιτιθεὶς νουμηνίᾳ.
καὶ νὴ Δί᾽ ἤν ἴδῃ γέ που γεγραμμένον
υἱὸν Πυριλάμπους ἐν θύρᾳ Δῆμον καλόν,
ἰὼν παρέγραψε πλησίον " κημὸς καλός."
τὸν ἀλεκτρυόνα δ᾽, ὃς ᾖδ᾽ ἀφ᾽ ἑσπέρας, ἔφη 100
ὄψ᾽ ἐξεγείρειν αὐτὸν ἀναπεπεισμένον,
παρὰ τῶν ὑπευθύνων ἔχοντα χρήματα.
εὐθὺς δ᾽ ἀπὸ δορπηστοῦ κέκραγεν ἐμβάδας,
κἄπειτ᾽ ἐκεῖσ᾽ ἐλθὼν προκαθεύδει πρῲ πάνυ,
ὥσπερ λεπὰς προσεχόμενος τῷ κίονι. 105
ὑπὸ δυσκολίας δ᾽ ἅπασι τιμῶν τὴν μακρὰν
ὥσπερ μέλιττ᾽ ἢ βομβυλιὸς εἰσέρχεται,
ὑπὸ τοῖς ὄνυξι κηρὸν ἀναπεπλασμένος.
ψήφων δὲ δείσας μὴ δεηθείη ποτέ,
ἵν᾽ ἔχοι δικάζειν, αἰγιαλὸν ἔνδον τρέφει. 110
τοιαῦτ᾽ ἀλύει· νουθετούμενος δ᾽ ἀεὶ
μᾶλλον δικάζει. τοῦτον οὖν φυλάττομεν
μοχλοῖσιν ἐνδήσαντες, ὡς ἂν μὴ 'ξίῃ.
ὁ γὰρ υἱὸς αὐτοῦ τὴν νόσον βαρέως φέρει.
καὶ πρῶτα μὲν λόγοισι παραμυθούμενος 115
ἀνέπειθεν αὐτὸν μὴ φορεῖν τριβώνιον
μηδ᾽ ἐξιέναι θύραζ᾽· ὁ δ᾽ οὐκ ἐπείθετο.
εἶτ᾽ αὐτὸν ἀπέλου κἀκάθαιρ᾽, ὁ δ᾽ οὐ μάλα.
μετὰ τοῦτ᾽ ἐκορυβάντιζ᾽· ὁ δ᾽ αὐτῷ τυμπάνῳ
ᾄξας ἐδίκαζεν εἰς τὸ Καινὸν ἐμπεσών. 120
ὅτε δὴ δὲ ταύταις ταῖς τελεταῖς οὐκ ὠφέλει,
διέπλευσεν εἰς Αἴγιναν· εἶτα ξυλλαβὼν

---

[a] For this practice of lovers *cf. A.* 144.
[b] Demus was a youth of eminent beauty; *cf.* Plato, *Gorg.*
481 D, where Socrates says ἐγὼ μὲν ἐρῶ Ἀλκιβιάδου τε τοῦ Κλεινίου καὶ φιλοσοφίας, σὺ δὲ τοῦ Ἀθηναίων δήμου καὶ τοῦ Πυριλάμπους.

THE WASPS, 95-122

With thumb and first two fingers closed, as one
That offers incense on a new moon's day.
If on a gate is written *Lovely Demus*,[a]
Meaning the son of Pyrilamp,[b] he goes
And writes beside it *Lovely Verdict-box*.
The cock which crew from eventide, he said,
Was tampered with, he knew, to call him late,
Bribed by officials whose accounts were due.[c]
Supper scarce done, he clamours for his shoes,
Hurries ere daybreak to the Court, and sleeps
Stuck like a limpet to the doorpost there.
So sour he is, the long condemning line [d]
He marks for all, then homeward like a bee
Laden with wax beneath his finger-nails.
Lest he lack votes, he keeps, to judge withal,
A private pebble-beach secure within.
Such is his frenzy, and the more you chide him
The more he judges : [e] so with bolts and bars
We guard him straitly that he stir not out.
For ill the young man brooks his sire's disease.
And first he tried by soft emollient words
To win him over, not to don the cloak
Or walk abroad : but never a jot he yielded.
He washed and purged him then : but never a jot.
A Corybant next he made him, but old master,
Timbrel and all, into the New Court bursts
And there sits judging. So when these rites failed,
We cross the Strait, and, in Aegina, place him,

[c] All officials at the close of their term of office had to submit to an account (εὔθυνη), and in cases where the public auditor was not satisfied the matter would come before the dicasteries ; *cf.* 571.
[d] See Introduction, p. 406.
[e] Said by the Scholiast to be a parody of Euripides : τοιαῦτ' ἀλύει· νουθετούμενος δ' Ἔρως | μᾶλλον πιέζει.

ARISTOPHANES

νύκτωρ κατέκλινεν αὐτὸν εἰς Ἀσκληπιοῦ·
ὁ δ' ἀνεφάνη κνεφαῖος ἐπὶ τῇ κιγκλίδι.
ἐντεῦθεν οὐκέτ' αὐτὸν ἐξεφρείομεν. 125
ὁ δ' ἐξεδίδρασκε διά τε τῶν ὑδορροῶν
καὶ τῶν ὀπῶν· ἡμεῖς δ' ὅσ' ἦν τετρημένα
ἐνεβύσαμεν ῥακίοισι κἀπακτώσαμεν·
ὁ δ' ὡσπερεὶ κολοιὸς αὑτῷ παττάλους
ἐνέκρουεν εἰς τὸν τοῖχον, εἶτ' ἐξήλλετο. 130
ἡμεῖς δὲ τὴν αὐλὴν ἅπασαν δικτύοις
καταπετάσαντες ἐν κύκλῳ φυλάττομεν.
ἔστιν δ' ὄνομα τῷ μὲν γέροντι Φιλοκλέων,
ναὶ μὰ Δία, τῷ δ' υἱεῖ γε τῳδὶ Βδελυκλέων,
ἔχων τρόπους φρυαγμοσεμνάκους τινάς. 135

ΒΔΕΛΥΚΛΕΩΝ. ὦ Ξανθία καὶ Σωσία, καθεύδετε;
ΞΑ. οἴμοι.
ΣΩ.   τί ἔστι;
ΞΑ.   Βδελυκλέων ἀνίσταται.
ΒΔ. οὐ περιδραμεῖται σφῷν ταχέως δεῦρ' ἅτερος;
ὁ γὰρ πατὴρ εἰς τὸν ἰπνὸν εἰσελήλυθεν
καὶ μυσπολεῖται καταδεδυκώς. ἀλλ' ἄθρει, 140
κατὰ τῆς πυέλου τὸ τρῆμ' ὅπως μὴ 'κδύσεται·
σὺ δὲ τῇ θύρᾳ πρόσκεισο.
ΣΩ.   ταῦτ', ὦ δέσποτα.
ΒΔ. ἄναξ Πόσειδον, τί ποτ' ἄρ' ἡ κάπνη ψοφεῖ;
οὗτος, τίς εἶ σύ;
ΦΙΛΟΚΛΕΩΝ.   καπνὸς ἔγωγ' ἐξέρχομαι.
ΒΔ. καπνός; φέρ' ἴδω ξύλου τίνος σύ.
ΦΙ.   συκίνου. 145
ΒΔ. νὴ τὸν Δί' ὅσπερ γ' ἐστὶ δριμύτατος καπνῶν.

[a] A common method of seeking a cure.
[b] i.e. "Cleon-lover."   [c] i.e. "Cleon-abhorrer."

418

THE WASPS, 123-146

To sleep the night inside Asclepius' temple :[a]
Lo! with the dawn he stands at the Court rails!
Then, after that, we let him out no more.
But he! he dodged along the pipes and gutters,
And so made off: we block up every cranny,
Stopping and stuffing them with clouts of rag :
Quick he drove pegs into the wall, and clambered
Up like an old jackdaw, and so hopped out.
Now then, we compass all the house with nets,
Spreading them round, and mew him safe within.
Well, sirs, Philocleon [b] is the old man's name ;
Ay truly ; and the son's, Bdelycleon [c] ;
A wondrous high-and-mighty mannered man.
BDELYCLEON. Xanthias and Sosias! are ye fast asleep?
XA. O dear!
SO. What now?
XA. Bdelycleon is up.
BD. One of you two run hither instantly,
For now my father's got into the kitchen,
Scurrying, mouselike, somewhere. Mind he don't
Slip through the hole for turning off the water.
And you, keep pressing at the door.
SO. Ay, ay, sir.
BD. O heavens! what's that? what makes the chimney
      rumble?
Hallo, sir! who are you?
PHILOCLEON. I'm smoke escaping.
BD. Smoke? of what wood?
PH. I'm of the fig-tree panel.
BD. Ay, and there's no more stinging smoke [d] than that.

[d] So too Theophrastus (*Hist. Plant.* v. 9. 5) δριμύτατος ὁ καπνὸς συκῆς. Philocleon selects a smoke that suits his own characters as a dicast; and there is also a reference to "informers" (συκοφάνται).

419

ARISTOPHANES

ἀτὰρ οὐκ ἐσερρήσεις γε; ποῦ 'σθ' ἡ τηλία;
δύου πάλιν· φέρ' ἐπαναθῶ σοι καὶ ξύλον.
ἐνταῦθα νῦν ζήτει τιν' ἄλλην μηχανήν.
ἀτὰρ ἄθλιός γ' εἴμ' ὡς ἕτερός γ' οὐδεὶς ἀνήρ, 15
ὅστις πατρὸς νῦν Καπνίου κεκλήσομαι.

ΣΩ. νῦν τὴν θύραν ὠθεῖ.
ΒΔ.   πίεζέ νυν σφόδρα
εὖ κἀνδρικῶς· κἀγὼ γὰρ ἐνταῦθ' ἔρχομαι.
καὶ τῆς κατακλεῖδος ἐπιμελοῦ καὶ τοῦ μοχλοῦ·
φύλαττέ θ' ὅπως μὴ τὴν βάλανον ἐκτρώξεται. 15
ΦΙ. τί δράσετ'; οὐκ ἐκφρήσετ', ὦ μιαρώτατοι,
δικάσοντά μ', ἀλλ' ἐκφεύξεται Δρακοντίδης;
ΒΔ. σὺ δὲ τοῦτο βαρέως ἂν φέροις;
ΦΙ.   ὁ γὰρ θεὸς
μαντευομένῳ μοὔχρησεν ἐν Δελφοῖς ποτέ,
ὅταν τις ἐκφύγῃ μ', ἀποσκλῆναι τότε. 16
ΒΔ. Ἄπολλον ἀποτρόπαιε, τοῦ μαντεύματος.
ΦΙ. ἴθ', ἀντιβολῶ σ', ἔκφρες με, μὴ διαρραγῶ.
ΒΔ. μὰ τὸν Ποσειδῶ, Φιλοκλέων, οὐδέποτέ γε.
ΦΙ. διατρώξομαι τοίνυν ὀδὰξ τὸ δίκτυον.
ΒΔ. ἀλλ' οὐκ ἔχεις ὀδόντας.
ΦΙ.   οἴμοι δείλαιος· 1
πῶς ἄν σ' ἀποκτείναιμι; πῶς; δότε μοι ξίφος
ὅπως τάχιστ', ἢ πινάκιον τιμητικόν.
ΒΔ. ἄνθρωπος οὗτος μέγα τι δρασείει κακόν.
ΦΙ. μὰ τὸν Δί' οὐ δῆτ', ἀλλ' ἀποδόσθαι βούλομαι
τὸν ὄνον ἄγων αὐτοῖσι τοῖς κανθηλίοις· 1
νουμηνία γάρ ἐστιν.
ΒΔ.   οὔκουν κἂν ἐγὼ
αὐτὸν ἀποδοίμην δῆτ' ἄν;
ΦΙ.   οὐχ ὥσπερ γ' ἐγώ.

Come, trundle back : what, won't you ? where's the
　　board ?
In with you ! nay, I'll clap this log on too.
There now, invent some other stratagem.
But I'm the wretchedest man that ever was ;
They'll call me now the son of Chimney-smoked.[a]
SO.　He's at the door now, pushing.
BD.　　　　　　　　　　　　　　Press it back then
With all your force : I'm coming there directly.
And O be careful of the bolt and bar,
And mind he does not nibble off the door-pin.
PH.　(*Within*) Let me out, villains ! let me out to judge.
What, shall Dracontides escape unpunished !
BD.　What if he should ?
PH.　　　　　　　　　　Why once, when I consulted
The Delphian oracle, the God replied,
That I should wither if a man escaped me.
BD.　Apollo shield us, what a prophecy !
PH.　O let me out, or I shall burst, I shall.
BD.　No, by Poseidon ! no, Philocleon, never !
PH.　O then by Zeus I'll nibble through the net.[b]
BD.　You've got no teeth, my beauty.
PH.　　　　　　　　　　　　　Fire and fury !
How shall I slay thee, how ? Give me a sword,
Quick, quick, or else a damage-cessing tablet.[c]
BD.　Hang it, he meditates some dreadful deed.
PH.　O no, I don't : I only want to take
And sell the donkey and his panniers too.
'Tis the new moon to-day.[d]
BD.　　　　　　　　　　　　And if it is,
　Cannot I sell them ?
PH.　　　　　　　　　Not so well as I.

[a] Some disreputable Athenian.　　　[b] See l. 131.
[c] See Introduction, p. 406.　　[d] A special market-day.

ΒΔ. μὰ Δί', ἀλλ' ἄμεινον. ἀλλὰ τὸν ὄνον ἔξαγε.
ΞΑ. οἵαν πρόφασιν καθῆκεν, ὡς εἰρωνικῶς,
ἵν' αὐτὸν ἐκπέμψειας.
ΒΔ. ἀλλ' οὐκ ἔσπασεν
ταύτῃ γ'· ἐγὼ γὰρ ᾐσθόμην τεχνωμένου.
ἀλλ' εἰσιών μοι τὸν ὄνον ἐξάγειν δοκῶ,
ὅπως ἂν ὁ γέρων μηδὲ παρακύψῃ πάλιν.
κάνθων, τί κλάεις; ὅτι πεπράσει τήμερον;
βάδιζε θᾶττον. τί στένεις, εἰ μὴ φέρεις
Ὀδυσσέα τιν';
ΞΑ. ἀλλὰ ναὶ μὰ Δία φέρει
κάτω γε τουτονί τιν' ὑποδεδυκότα.
ΒΔ. ποῖον; φέρ' ἴδωμαι.
ΞΑ. τουτονί.
ΒΔ. τουτὶ τί ἦν;
τίς εἶ ποτ', ὤνθρωπ', ἐτεόν;
ΦΙ. Οὖτις νὴ Δία.
ΒΔ. Οὖτις σύ; ποδαπός;
ΦΙ. Ἴθακος Ἀποδρασιππίδου.
ΒΔ. Οὖτις μὰ τὸν Δί' οὔ τι χαιρήσων γε σύ.
ὕφελκε θᾶττον αὐτόν. ὦ μιαρώτατος,
ἵν' ὑποδέδυκεν· ὥστ' ἔμοιγ' ἰνδάλλεται
ὁμοιότατος κλητῆρος εἶναι πωλίῳ.
ΦΙ. εἰ μή μ' ἐάσεθ' ἡσύχως, μαχούμεθα.
ΒΔ. περὶ τοῦ μαχεῖ νῷν δῆτα;
ΦΙ. περὶ ὄνου σκιᾶς.
ΒΔ. πονηρὸς εἶ πόρρω τέχνης καὶ παράβολος.
ΦΙ. ἐγὼ πονηρός; οὐ μὰ Δί', ἀλλ' οὐκ οἶσθα σὺ

---

[a] Odysseus escaped from the cave of Polyphemus, to whom he had given his name as Οὖτις (l. 184), by clinging to a ram's belly. The donkey here has his stable just inside the hall-door.

BD. No, but much better : drive the donkey out.
XA. How well and craftily he dropped the bait
   To make you let him through.
BD.   But he caught nothing
   That haul at least, for I perceived the trick.
   But I will in, and fetch the donkey out.
   No, no ; he shan't come slipping through again.
   Donkey, why grieve ? at being sold to-day ?
   Gee up ! why grunt and groan, unless you carry
   Some new Odysseus there ? [a]
XA.   And, in good truth,
   Here is a fellow clinging on beneath.
BD. Who ? where ?
XA.   Why, here.
BD.   Why, what in the world is this ?
   Who are you, sirrah ?
PH.   Noman I, by Zeus.
BD. Where from ?
PH.   From Ithaca, son of Runaway.
BD. Noman I promise to no good you'll be.
   Drag him out there from under. O the villain,
   The place he had crept to ! Now he seems to me
   The very image of a sompnour's [b] foal.
PH. Come now, hands off : or you and I shall fight.
BD. Fight ! what about ?
PH.   About a donkey's shadow.[c]
BD. You're a born bad one, with your tricks and fetches.
PH. Bad ! O my gracious ! then you don't know yet

[b] R. thinks that κλητήρ may not only = "one who calls or summons to court," but also be slang for a donkey = "the caller," from its bray.

[c] A man hired an ass to carry him from Athens to Megara, but finding the sun hot sat down in its shadow, which the driver said did not belong to him, so that finally they went to Law about the " donkey's shadow."

ARISTOPHANES

νῦν μ' ὄντ' ἄριστον· ἀλλ' ἴσως, ὅταν φάγῃς
ὑπογάστριον γέροντος ἡλιαστικοῦ.
ΒΔ. ὤθει τὸν ὄνον καὶ σαυτὸν εἰς τὴν οἰκίαν.
ΦΙ. ὦ ξυνδικασταὶ καὶ Κλέων, ἀμύνατε.
ΒΔ. ἔνδον κέκραχθι τῆς θύρας κεκλεισμένης.
ὤθει σὺ πολλοὺς τῶν λίθων πρὸς τὴν θύραν,
καὶ τὴν βάλανον ἔμβαλλε πάλιν εἰς τὸν μοχλόν,
καί, τῇ δοκῷ προσθείς, τὸν ὅλμον τὸν μέγαν
ἀνύσας τι προσκύλιέ γ'.
ΣΩ. οἴμοι δείλαιος·
πόθεν ποτ' ἐμπέπτωκέ μοι τὸ βώλιον;
ΞΑ. ἴσως ἄνωθεν μῦς ἐνέβαλέ σοί ποθεν.
ΣΩ. μῦς; οὐ μὰ Δί', ἀλλ' ὑποδυόμενός τις οὑτοσὶ
ὑπὸ τῶν κεραμίδων ἡλιαστὴς ὀροφίας.
ΒΔ. οἴμοι κακοδαίμων, στρουθὸς ἀνὴρ γίγνεται·
ἐκπτήσεται. ποῦ ποῦ 'στί μοι τὸ δίκτυον;
σοῦ σοῦ, πάλιν σοῦ. νὴ Δί' ἦ μοι κρεῖττον ἦν
τηρεῖν Σκιώνην ἀντὶ τούτου τοῦ πατρός.
ΣΩ. ἄγε νυν, ἐπειδὴ τουτονὶ σεσοβήκαμεν,
κοὐκ ἔσθ' ὅπως διαδὺς ἂν ἡμᾶς ἔτι λάθοι,
τί οὐκ ἀπεκοιμήθημεν ὅσον ὅσον στίλην;
ΒΔ. ἀλλ', ὦ πόνηρ', ἥξουσιν ὀλίγον ὕστερον
οἱ ξυνδικασταὶ παρακαλοῦντες τουτονὶ
τὸν πατέρα.
ΣΩ. τί λέγεις; ἀλλὰ νῦν ὄρθρος βαθύς.
ΒΔ. νὴ τὸν Δί', ὀψὲ γοῦν ἀνεστήκασι νῦν.
ὡς ἀπὸ μέσων νυκτῶν γε παρακαλοῦσ' ἀεί,
λύχνους ἔχοντες καὶ μινυρίζοντες μέλη
ἀρχαιομελισιδωνοφρυνιχήρατα,

---

[a] "The stuffed paunch of an ass was accounted a delicacy at Athens": R.

THE WASPS, 194-220

How good I am : but wait until you taste
The seasoned paunchlet of a prime old judge.[a]
BD. Get along in, you and your donkey too.
PH. O help me, fellow-dicasts : help me, Cleon !
BD. Bellow within there when the door is shut.
Now pile a heap of stones against the door,
And shoot the door-pin home into the bar,
And heave the beam athwart it, and roll up,
Quick, the great mortar-block.
SO. (*Starting*)   Save us ! what's that ?
Whence fell that clod of dirt upon my head ?
XA. Belike some mouse dislodged it from above.
SO. A mouse ? O, no, a rafter-haunting dicast,
Wriggling about behind the tiling there.
BD. Good lack ! the man is changing to a sparrow
Sure he'll fly off : where, where's the casting-net ?
Shoo ! shoo there ! shoo ! 'Fore Zeus, 'twere easier work
To guard Scione [b] than a sire like this.
SO. Well but at last we have fairly scared him in,
He can't slip out, he can't elude us now,
So why not slumber just a—just a—drop ?
BD. Slumber, you rogue ! when in a little while
His fellow-justices will come this way
Calling him up.
SO.   Why sir, 'tis twilight yet.
BD. Why then, by Zeus, they are very late to-day.
Soon after midnight is their usual time
To come here, carrying lights, and warbling tunes
Sweet-charming-old-Sidono-Phrynichéan [c]

[b] Scione, on the peninsula of Pallene, was at the time closely besieged by a large Athenian force.
[c] Lyrics from the *Phoenissae* of Phrynichus, published about fifty-five years earlier.

425

ARISTOPHANES

ΣΩ. οἷς ἐκκαλοῦνται τοῦτον.
οὐκοῦν, ἢν δέῃ,
ἤδη ποτ' αὐτοὺς τοῖς λίθοις βαλλήσομεν.
ΒΔ. ἀλλ', ὦ πόνηρε, τὸ γένος ἤν τις ὀργίσῃ
τὸ τῶν γερόντων, ἔσθ' ὅμοιον σφηκιᾷ.
ἔχουσι γὰρ καὶ κέντρον ἐκ τῆς ὀσφύος
ὀξύτατον, ᾧ κεντοῦσι, καὶ κεκραγότες
πηδῶσι καὶ βάλλουσιν ὥσπερ φέψαλοι.
ΣΩ. μὴ φροντίσῃς· ἐὰν ἐγὼ λίθους ἔχω,
πολλῶν δικαστῶν σφηκιὰν διασκεδῶ.

ΧΟΡΟΣ. χώρει, πρόβαιν' ἐρρωμένως. ὦ Κωμία, βραδύνεις;
μὰ τὸν Δί', οὐ μέντοι πρὸ τοῦ γ', ἀλλ' ἦσθ' ἱμὰς
κύνειος·
νυνὶ δὲ κρείττων ἐστὶ σοῦ Χαρινάδης βαδίζειν.
ὦ Στρυμόδωρε Κονθυλεῦ, βέλτιστε συνδικαστῶν,
Εὐεργίδης ἆρ' ἐστί που 'νταῦθ', ἢ Χάβης ὁ Φλυεύς;
πάρεσθ', ὃ δὴ λοιπόν γ' ἔτ' ἐστίν, ἀπαπαῖ παπαιάξ,
ἥβης ἐκείνης, ἡνίκ' ἐν Βυζαντίῳ ξυνῆμεν
φρουροῦντ' ἐγώ τε καὶ σύ· κᾆτα περιπατοῦντε
νύκτωρ
τῆς ἀρτοπώλιδος λαθόντ' ἐκλέψαμεν τὸν ὅλμον,
κᾆθ' ἥψομεν τοῦ κορκόρου, κατασχίσαντες αὐτόν.
ἀλλ' ἐγκονῶμεν, ὦνδρες, ὡς ἔσται Λάχητι νυνί·
σίμβλον δέ φασι χρημάτων ἔχειν ἅπαντες αὐτόν.

---

[a] "They are dressed up to resemble Wasps, armed with formidable stings": R.
[b] For the capture of Byzantium in 478 see Thuc. i. 94.
[c] Sent with 20 ships to Sicily in 427, but recalled two years later, and probably accused by Cleon of peculation.

Wherewith they call him out.

SO. And if they come.
Had we not better pelt them with some stones?

BD. Pelt them, you rogue! you might as well provoke
A nest of wasps as anger these old men.
Each wears beside his loins a deadly sting,[a]
Wherewith they smite, and on with yells and cries
They leap, and strike at you, like sparks of fire.

SO. Tut, never trouble, give me but some stones,
I'll chase the biggest wasps-nest of them all.

CHORUS. Step out, step out, my comrades stout:
    no loitering, Comias, pound along,
You're shirking now, you used, I vow,
    to pull as tough as leathern thong,
Yet now, with ease, Charinades
    can walk a brisker pace than you.
Ho! Strymodore of Conthylè,
    the best of all our dicast crew,
Has old Euergides appeared,
    and Chabes too from Phlya, pray?
Ah! here it strains, the poor remains,
    alas! alas! alack the day,
Of that mad set, I mind it yet,
    when once we paced our nightly round,
In years gone by, both you and I,
    along Byzantium's wall,[b] and found
And stole away the baker's tray,
    and sliced it up, and chopped it well,
A merry blaze therewith to raise,
    and so we cooked our pimpernel.
On, on again, with might and main:
    for Laches'[c] turn is come to-day:
Quick, look alive, a splendid hive
    of wealth the fellow's got, they say.

ARISTOPHANES

χθὲς οὖν Κλέων ὁ κηδεμὼν ἡμῖν ἐφεῖτ' ἐν ὥρᾳ
ἥκειν ἔχοντας ἡμερῶν ὀργὴν τριῶν πονηρὰν
ἐπ' αὐτόν, ὡς κολωμένους ὧν ἠδίκησεν. ἀλλὰ
σπεύδωμεν, ὦνδρες ἥλικες, πρὶν ἡμέραν γενέσθαι, 245
χωρῶμεν, ἅμα τε τῷ λύχνῳ πάντῃ διασκοπῶμεν.
μή που λίθων τις ἐμποδὼν ἡμᾶς κακόν τι δράσῃ.

ΠΑΙΣ. τὸν πηλόν, ὦ πάτερ πάτερ, τουτονὶ φύλαξαι.

ΧΟ. κάρφος χαμᾶθέν νυν λαβὼν τὸν λύχνον πρόβυσον.

ΠΑΙΣ. οὔκ, ἀλλὰ τῳδί μοι δοκῶ τὸν λύχνον προβύσειν. 250

ΧΟ. τί δὴ μαθὼν τῷ δακτύλῳ τὴν θρυαλλίδ' ὠθεῖς,
καὶ ταῦτα τοὐλαίου σπανίζοντος, ὦνόητε;
οὐ γὰρ δάκνει σ', ὅταν δέῃ τίμιον πρίασθαι.

ΠΑΙΣ. εἰ νὴ Δί' αὖθις κονδύλοις νουθετήσεθ' ἡμᾶς,
ἀποσβέσαντες τοὺς λύχνους ἄπιμεν οἴκαδ' αὐτοί· 255
κἄπειτ' ἴσως ἐν τῷ σκότῳ τουτονὶ στερηθεὶς
τὸν πηλὸν ὥσπερ ἀτταγᾶς τυρβάσεις βαδίζων.

ΧΟ. ἦ μὴν ἐγώ σοῦ χἀτέρους μείζονας κολάζω.

---

[a] Soldiers commonly carried three days' rations.

And Cleon too, our patron true,
  enjoined us each betimes to bring
Of anger sore an ample store,
  a good three days' provisioning [a]:
On all the man's unrighteous plans
  a vengeance well-deserved to take.
Come, every dear and tried compeer,
  come, quickly come, ere morning break,
And as you go, be sure you throw
  the light around on every side;
Lest somewhere nigh a stone may lie,
  and we therefrom be damnified.
BOY. O father, father, here's some mud!
  look sharp or in you'll go.
CH. Pick up a stick, and trim the wick,
  a better light to show.
BOY. Nay, father, with my finger, thus,
  I choose to trim the lamp.
CH. How dare you rout the wick about,
  you little wasteful scamp,
And that with oil so scarce? but no,
  it don't disturb *your* quiet,
However dear the oil may be,
  when I have got to buy it.
BOY. If with your knuckles once again
  you 'monish us, I swear
We'll douse the light, and take to flight,
  and leave you floundering there.
Then wading on without the lamp
  in darkness, I'll be bound
You'll stir and splash the mud about,
  like snipes in marshy ground.
CH. Ah, greater men than you, my boy,
  'tis often mine to beat.

ARISTOPHANES

ἀλλ' οὑτοσί μοι βόρβορος φαίνεται πατοῦντι·
κοὐκ ἔσθ' ὅπως οὐχ ἡμερῶν τεττάρων τὸ πλεῖστον 260
ὕδωρ ἀναγκαίως ἔχει τὸν θεὸν ποιῆσαι.
ἔπεισι γοῦν τοῖσιν λύχνοις οὑτοιὶ μύκητες·
φιλεῖ δ', ὅταν τοῦτ' ᾖ, ποιεῖν ὑετὸν μάλιστα.
δεῖται δὲ καὶ τῶν καρπίμων ἄττα μή 'στι πρῷα
ὕδωρ γενέσθαι κἀπιπνεῦσαι βόρειον αὐτοῖς. 265
τί χρῆμ' ἄρ' οὐκ τῆς οἰκίας τῆσδε συνδικαστὴς
πέπονθεν, ὡς οὐ φαίνεται δεῦρο πρὸς τὸ πλῆθος;
οὐ μὴν πρὸ τοῦ γ' ἐφολκὸς ἦν, ἀλλὰ πρῶτος ἡμῶν
ἡγεῖτ' ἂν ᾄδων Φρυνίχου· καὶ γάρ ἐστιν ἀνὴρ
φιλῳδός. ἀλλά μοι δοκεῖ στάντας ἐνθάδ', ὦνδρες, 270
ᾄδοντας αὐτὸν ἐκκαλεῖν, ἤν τί πως ἀκούσας
τοὐμοῦ μέλους ὑφ' ἡδονῆς ἑρπύσῃ θύραζε.

τί ποτ' οὐ πρὸ θυρῶν [στρ.
φαίνετ' ἄρ' ἡμῖν ὁ γέρων οὐδ' ὑπακούει;
μῶν ἀπολώλεκε τὰς
ἐμβάδας, ἢ προσέκοψ' 275

---

[a] For this sign of rain cf. Virg. *Georg.* i. 391 "testa quum ardente viderent | scintillare oleum, et putres concrescere fungos," where *fungos* exactly corresponds to μύκητες "mushrooms."

THE WASPS, 259-275

But, bless me, this is filth indeed
                    I feel beneath my feet :
Ay, and within four days from this,
                    or sooner, it is plain,
God will send down upon our town
                    a fresh supply of rain :
So dense and thick around the wick
                    these thieves collect and gather,[a]
And that's, as everybody knows,
                    a sign of heavy weather.
Well, well, 'tis useful for the fruits,
                    and all the backward trees,
To have a timely fall of rain,
                    and eke a good North breeze.
But how is this ? Our friend not here !
                    how comes it he's so slack ?
By Zeus, he never used to be
                    at all a hanger-back.
He always marched before us all,
                    on legal cares intent,
And some old tune of Phrynichus
                    he warbled as he went.
O he's a wonder for the songs !
                    Come, comrades, one and all,
Come stand around the house, and sing,
                    its master forth to call.
If once he hears me tuning up,
                    I know it won't be long
Before he comes creep, creeping out,
                    from pleasure at the song.

  How is it our friend is not here to receive us ?
    Why comes he not forth from his dwelling ?
  Can it be that he's had the misfortune to lose
      His one pair of shoes ;

ARISTOPHANES

ἐν τῷ σκότῳ τὸν δάκτυλόν που
[ποδός,] εἶτ' ἐφλέγμηνεν
τὸ σφυρὸν γέροντος ὄντος;
καὶ τάχ' ἂν βουβωνιῴη.
ἦ μὴν πολὺ δριμύτατός γ' ἦν τῶν παρ' ἡμῖν,
καὶ μόνος οὐκ ἂν ἐπείθετ',
ἀλλ' ὁπότ' ἀντιβολοίη
τις, κάτω κύπτων ἂν οὕτω,
" λίθον ἕψεις," ἔλεγεν.

τάχα δ' ἂν διὰ τὸν [ἀντ.
χθιζινὸν ἄνθρωπον, ὃς ἡμᾶς διεδύετ'
ἐξαπατῶν, ὁ λέγων
ὡς φιλαθήναιος ἦν
καὶ τἀν Σάμῳ πρῶτος κατείποι,
διὰ τοῦτ' ὀδυνηθεὶς
εἶτ' ἴσως κεῖται πυρέττων.
ἔστι γὰρ τοιοῦτος ἀνήρ.
ἀλλ', ὠγάθ', ἀνίστασο μηδ' οὕτω σεαυτὸν
ἔσθιε, μηδ' ἀγανάκτει.
καὶ γὰρ ἀνὴρ παχὺς ἥκει
τῶν προδόντων τἀπὶ Θρᾴκης·
ὃν ὅπως ἐγχυτριεῖς.

ὕπαγ', ὦ παῖ, ὕπαγε.

ΠΑΙΣ. ἐθελήσεις τί μοι οὖν, ὦ [στρ.
πάτερ, ἤν σού τι δεηθῶ;
ΧΟ. πάνυ γ', ὦ παιδίον. ἀλλ' εἰπὲ τί βούλει με πρίασθαι
καλόν; οἶμαι δέ σ' ἐρεῖν ἀ-
στραγάλους δήπουθεν, [ὦ παῖ.

THE WASPS, 276-296

Or striking his toe in the dark, by the grievous
Contusion is lamed, and his ankle inflamed?
   Or his groin has, it may be, a swelling.
     He of us all, I ween,
Was evermore the austerest, and most keen.
     Alone no prayers he heeded :
     Whene'er for grace they pleaded,
     He bent (like this) his head,
     You cook a stone, he said.

Is it all of that yesterday's man who cajoled us,
   And slipped through our hands, the deceiver,
Pretending a lover of Athens to be,
   Pretending that he
Was the first, of the Samian rebellion [a] that told us?
Our friend may be sick with disgust at the trick,
   And be now lying ill of a fever.
     That would be like him quite.
But now up, up, nor gnaw your soul with spite
     There comes a traitor base,
     A wealthy rogue from Thrace.[b]
     Safe in our toils we've got him,
     Up, up, old friend, and pot him!

On with you, boy, on with you.

BOY.   Father, if a boon I pray,
     Will you grant it, father, eh?
CH.   Certainly I will, my son.
     Tell me what you'd have me buy.
     Dibs,[c] my son? Hey, my son?
     Dibs it is, undoubtedly.

[a] "The Revolt of Samos in 440 which for a moment imperilled the whole fabric of Athenian power" : R.
[b] Where the Spartan general Brasidas was at the time causing great trouble.   [c] Lit. "knuckle-bones."

ARISTOPHANES

ΠΑΙΣ. μὰ Δί', ἀλλ' ἰσχάδας, ὦ παπ-
πία· ἥδιον γάρ.
ΧΟ. οὐκ ἂν
μὰ Δί', εἰ κρέμαισθέ γ' ὑμεῖς.
ΠΑΙΣ. μὰ Δί' οὔ τἄρα προπέμψω σε τὸ λοιπόν.
ΧΟ. ἀπὸ γὰρ τοῦδέ με τοῦ μισθαρίου 3
τρίτον αὐτὸν ἔχειν ἄλφιτα δεῖ καὶ
ξύλα κᾦψον·
σὺ δὲ σῦκά μ' αἰτεῖς.

ΠΑΙΣ. ἄγε νυν, ὦ πάτερ, ἢν μὴ [ἀντ.
τὸ δικαστήριον ἄρχων
καθίσῃ νῦν, πόθεν ὠνη- 3
σόμεθ' ἄριστον; ἔχεις ἐλ-
πίδα χρηστήν τινα νῷν ἢ
πόρον "Ελλας ἱερόν;
ΧΟ. ἀπαπαῖ, φεῦ, ἀπαπαῖ, φεῦ,
μὰ Δί' οὐκ ἔγωγε νῷν οἶδ' 3
ὁπόθεν γε δεῖπνον ἔσται.
ΠΑΙΣ. τί με δῆτ', ὦ μελέα μῆτερ, ἔτικτες,
ἵν' ἐμοὶ πράγματα βόσκειν παρέχῃς;
ΧΟ. ἀνόνητον ἄρ' ὦ θυλάκιόν σ' εἶχον ἄγαλμα. 3
ΠΑΙΣ. ἒ ἔ.
πάρα νῷν στενάζειν.

ΦΙ. φίλοι, τήκομαι μὲν
πάλαι διὰ τῆς ὀπῆς

[a] The boy uses πόρος in the sense of *resource*, and then " goes on humming some well-known words of Pindar in which πόρον means a *ford*, ' the sacred ford of Helle ' " : R.

434

THE WASPS, 296-317

BOY. Dibs, my father! No, my father!
FIGS! for they are sweeter far.
CH. You be hanged first: yet you shall not
Have them, monkey, when you are.
BOY. Then, my father, woe betide you!
Not another step I'll guide you.
CH. Is it not enough that I
With this paltry pay must buy
Fuel, bread, and sauce for three?
Must I needs buy figs for thee!

BOY. Father, if the Archon say
That the Court won't sit to-day,
Tell me truly, father mine,
Have we wherewithal to dine?
O my father, should not we
Then in " Straits of Helle " *a* be?
CH. Out upon it! out upon it!
Then, indeed, I should not know
For a little bit of supper
Whither in this world to go.
BOY. Why, my mother, didst thou breed me,
giving nothing else to feed me,*b*
But a store of legal woe?
CH. Empty scrip! O empty show,
Bootless, fruitless ornament!
BOY. O! O! woe! woe!
Ours to sorrow and lament.

PH. (*Appearing above*) Long my reins have been stirred,
Long through chinks have I heard,

b A parody of a θρῆνος from the *Theseus* of Euripides spoken by boys sent to be food for the Minotaur.

435

ARISTOPHANES

ὑμῶν ὑπακούων.
ἀλλὰ γὰρ οὐχ οἷός τ'
εἴμ' ἄδειν. τί ποιήσω;
τηροῦμαι δ' ὑπὸ τῶνδ', ἐπεὶ
βούλομαί γε πάλαι μεθ' ὑ-   32
μῶν ἐλθὼν ἐπὶ τοὺς καδί-
σκους κακόν τι ποιῆσαι.
ἀλλ', ὦ Ζεῦ μεγαβρόντα,
ἤ με ποίησον καπνὸν ἐξαίφνης,
ἢ Προξενίδην, ἢ τὸν Σέλλου   32
τοῦτον τὸν ψευδαμάμαξυν.
τόλμησον, ἄναξ, χαρίσασθαί μοι,
πάθος οἰκτείρας·
ἤ με κεραυνῷ διατινθαλέῳ
σπόδισον ταχέως·
κἄπειτ' ἀνελών μ' ἀποφυσήσας   33
εἰς ὀξάλμην ἔμβαλε θερμήν·
ἢ δῆτα λίθον με ποίησον ἐφ' οὗ
τὰς χοιρίνας ἀριθμοῦσιν.
ΧΟ. τίς γάρ ἐσθ' ὁ ταῦτά σ' εἴργων   [στρ.
κἀποκλείων τῇ θύρᾳ; λέξ-
ον· πρὸς εὔνους γὰρ φράσεις.   33
ΦΙ. οὑμὸς υἱός. ἀλλὰ μὴ βοᾶτε· καὶ γὰρ τυγχάνει
οὑτοσὶ πρόσθεν καθεύδων. ἀλλ' ὕφεσθε τοῦ τόνου.
ΧΟ. τοῦ δ' ἔφεξιν, ὦ μάταιε, ταῦτα δρᾶν σε βούλεται;
τίνα πρόφασίν τ' ἔχων;
ΦΙ. οὐκ ἐᾷ μ', ὦνδρες, δικάζειν οὐδὲ δρᾶν οὐδὲν κακόν, 34
ἀλλά μ' εὐωχεῖν ἕτοιμός ἐστ'· ἐγὼ δ' οὐ βούλομαι.

---
[a] An empty blusterer, cf. B. 1126.
[b] Aeschines, cf. 459, 1243, another empty boaster; "the *tree-vine* is adopted as his emblem, because of the prodigious splutter it makes while burning": R.

THE WASPS, 318-341

Heard your voices below.
Vain my efforts to sing,
These forbid me to go.
Vainly my sad heart yearns,
Yearns to be marching with you,
On to the judgement urns,
There some mischief to do.
O change to smoke by a lightning stroke,
Dread-thundering Zeus ! this body of mine,
Till I'm like Proxenides,[a] like the son
    Of Sellus,[b] that false tree-vine.
O Sovereign, pity my woeful lot,
Vouchsafe to grant me my heart's desire,
Fry me in dust with a glittering, hot,
    Red bolt of celestial fire,
Then take me up with thy hand divine,
And puff me, and plunge me in scalding brine.
Or turn me into the stone, whereon
They count the votes when the trial is done.

CH.   Who is he that thus detains you ?
    Who with bolted door restrains you ?
      Tell us, you will speak to friends.

PH. 'Tis my son, but don't be bawling :
              for he's slumbering now at ease
There, upon the roof before you :
              drop your tone a little, please.

CH. What's his object, idle trifler,
            that he does such things as these ?
    What's the motive he pretends ?

PH. He will let me do no mischief,
               and no more a lawsuit try.
True it is he'll feast and pet me,
            but with that I won't comply.

ΧΟ.   τοῦτ᾽ ἐτόλμησ᾽ ὁ μιαρὸς χα-
νεῖν ὁ Δημολογοκλέων ὅδ᾽,
ὅτι λέγεις σύ
τι περὶ τῶν νεῶν ἀληθές.
οὐ γὰρ ἄν ποθ᾽ οὗτος ἀνὴρ
τοῦτ᾽ ἐτόλμησεν λέγειν, εἰ
μὴ ξυνωμότης τις ἦν.   34
ἀλλ᾽ ἐκ τούτων ὥρα τινά σοι ζητεῖν καινὴν ἐπίνοιαν,
ἥτις σε λάθρα τἀνδρὸς τουδὶ καταβῆναι δεῦρο ποιήσει.
ΦΙ. τίς ἂν οὖν εἴη; ζητεῖθ᾽ ὑμεῖς, ὡς πᾶν ἂν ἔγωγε
ποιοίην·
οὕτω κιττῶ διὰ τῶν σανίδων μετὰ χοιρίνης
περιελθεῖν.
ΧΟ. ἔστιν ὀπὴ δῆθ᾽ ἥντιν᾽ ἂν ἔνδοθεν οἷός τ᾽ εἴης διορύξαι, 35
εἶτ᾽ ἐκδῦναι ῥάκεσιν κρυφθείς, ὥσπερ πολύμητις
Ὀδυσσεύς;
ΦΙ. πάντα πέφρακται κοὐκ ἔστιν ὀπῆς οὐδ᾽ εἰ σέρφῳ
διαδῦναι.
ἀλλ᾽ ἄλλο τι δεῖ ζητεῖν ὑμᾶς· ὀπίαν δ᾽ οὐκ ἔστι
γενέσθαι.
ΧΟ. μέμνησαι δῆθ᾽, ὅτ᾽ ἐπὶ στρατιᾶς κλέψας ποτὲ τοὺς
ὀβελίσκους
ἵεις σαυτὸν κατὰ τοῦ τείχους ταχέως, ὅτε Νάξος
ἑάλω;   35
ΦΙ. οἶδ᾽· ἀλλὰ τί τοῦτ᾽; οὐδὲν γὰρ τοῦτ᾽ ἐστὶν ἐκείνῳ
προσόμοιον.
ἥβων γὰρ κἀδυνάμην κλέπτειν, ἴσχυόν τ᾽ αὐτὸς
ἐμαυτοῦ,
κοὐδείς μ᾽ ἐφύλαττ᾽, ἀλλ᾽ ἐξῆν μοι

---

[a] The dicasts so call Bdelycleon in their anger, forgetting that the "obnoxious nickname snits their patron Cleon better": R.
[b] "Lists or notice-boards of the Court, probably suspended

CH. This the Demagogeleon [a] blared
 Out against you, since you dared
 Truth about the fleet to show.
 He must be involved, I see,
 In some dark CONSPIRACY,
 Else he durst not use you so.
  It is time some means of escape to find,
     some novel, ingenious plan, that so,
  Unseen of your son, you may get you down,
     alighting in safety here below.
PH. O what shall it be ? consider it ye !
     I'm ready to do whatever is planned :
  So sorely I'm longing a circuit to go,
  through the lists [b] of the Court, with a vote in my hand.
CH. Can you find no cranny or secret run,
     through which, from within, your path to urge,
  And then like wily Odysseus, here,
     disguised in tatters and rags,[c] emerge ?
PH. Each cranny is barred : there's never a run,
  thro' which though it were but a midge could squeeze.
  You must think, if you can, of a likelier plan :
     I can't run out like a runnet cheese.
CH. O don't you remember the old campaign,
     when you stole the spit, and let yourself down,
  And away by the side of the wall you hied ?
     'Twas when we had captured Naxos town.[d]
PH. Ah, well I remember ! but what of that ?
     it is quite another affair to-day.
  For then I was young, and then I could steal,
     and over myself I possessed full sway.
  And then none guarded my steps, but I

in some part of the building, along which the dicasts passed to record their votes " : R.
 [c] Such as Odysseus wore when he ventured into beleaguered Troy ; cf. Hom. Od. iv. 245.   [d] In 476 ; cf. Thuc. i. 98.

ARISTOPHANES

φεύγειν ἀδεῶς. νῦν δὲ ξὺν ὅπλοις
ἄνδρες ὁπλῖται διαταξάμενοι
κατὰ τὰς διόδους σκοπιωροῦνται,
τὼ δὲ δύ' αὐτῶν ἐπὶ ταῖσι θύραις
ὥσπερ με γαλῆν κρέα κλέψασαν
τηροῦσιν ἔχοντ' ὀβελίσκους.

ΧΟ. ἀλλὰ καὶ νῦν ἐκπόριζε   [ἀντ.
μηχανὴν ὅπως τάχισθ'· ἕ-
ως γάρ, ὦ μελίττιον.

ΦΙ. διατραγεῖν τοίνυν κράτιστον ἐστί μοι τὸ δίκτυον.
ἡ δέ μοι Δίκτυννα συγγνώμην ἔχοι τοῦ δικτύου.

ΧΟ. ταῦτα μὲν πρὸς ἀνδρός ἐστ' ἄνοντος ἐς σωτηρίαν.
ἀλλ' ἔπαγε τὴν γνάθον.

ΦΙ. διατέτρωκται τοῦτό γ'. ἀλλὰ μὴ βοᾶτε μηδαμῶς,
ἀλλὰ τηρώμεσθ', ὅπως μὴ Βδελυκλέων αἰσθήσεται.

ΧΟ. μηδέν, ὦ τᾶν, δέδιθι, μηδέν·
ὡς ἐγὼ τοῦτόν γ', ἐὰν γρύ-
ξῃ τι, ποιή-
σω δακεῖν τὴν καρδίαν καὶ
τὸν περὶ ψυχῆς δρόμον δρα-
μεῖν, ἵν' εἰδῇ μὴ πατεῖν τὰ
ταῖν θεαῖν ψηφίσματα.

ἀλλ' ἐξάψας διὰ τῆς θυρίδος τὸ καλώδιον εἶτα καθίμα
δήσας σαυτὸν καὶ τὴν ψυχὴν ἐμπλησάμενος Διοπείθους.

---

[a] *i.e.* Artemis. The name is here clearly connected with δίκτυον; elsewhere with Mt. Dicte in Crete.
[b] They formerly (l. 345) charged him with being a traitor; now they will accuse him of "violating the mysteries" (of Demeter

THE WASPS, 359-380

      Was free, wherever I chose, to fly;
      Whilst now, in every alley and street,
      Armed men with arms are stationed about,
      Watching with care that I steal not out.
      And there at the gate you may see those two
      Waiting with spits to spit me through,
      Like a cat that is running away with the meat.
CH.   Well but now be quickly shaping
      Some contrivance for escaping;
      Morning breaks, my honey-bee.
PH.   Then the best that I can think of,
              is to gnaw these meshes through.
      May Dictynna,[a] queen of hunters,
              pardon me the deed I do.
CH.   Spoken like a man whose efforts
              will salvation's goal ensue.
      Ply your jaw then lustily.
PH.   There, I've gnawn them through completely
            —Ah! but do not raise a shout,
      We must use the greatest caution,
              lest Bdelycleon find us out.
CH.   Fear not: fear not: if he speak,
         He shall gnaw his heart, and seek
         For his life to run amain.
         We will quickly make him learn
         Nevermore again to spurn
         Th' holy statutes of the Twain.[b]
      So now to the window lash the cord,
             and twine it securely your limbs around.
      With all Diopeithes[c] fill your soul,
            then let yourself cleverly down to the ground.

and Persephone) but, having a legal mind, substitute ψηφίσματα for μυστήρια.

  [c] *i.e.* with a fine frenzy like that of the soothsayer Diopeithes; for whom *cf. K.* 1085, *B.* 988.

ΦΙ. ἄγε νυν, ἢν αἰσθομένῳ τούτῳ ζητητόν μ' ἐσκαλαμᾶσθαι
κἀνασπαστὸν ποιεῖν εἴσω, τί ποιήσετε; φράζετε
νυνί.
ΧΟ. ἀμυνοῦμέν σοι τὸν πρινώδη θυμὸν ἅπαντες καλέσαντες,
ὥστ' οὐ δυνατόν σ' εἴργειν ἔσται· τοιαῦτα ποιήσομεν ἡμεῖς.
ΦΙ. δράσω τοίνυν ὑμῖν πίσυνος· καὶ μανθάνετ'· ἤν τι
πάθω 'γώ, 385
ἀνελόντες καὶ κατακλαύσαντες θεῖναί μ' ὑπὸ τοῖσι
δρυφάκτοις.
ΧΟ. οὐδὲν πείσει· μηδὲν δείσῃς. ἀλλ', ὦ βέλτιστε, καθίει
σαυτὸν θαρρῶν κἀπευξάμενος τοῖσι πατρῴοισι
θεοῖσιν.
ΦΙ. ὦ Λύκε δέσποτα, γείτων ἥρως· σὺ γὰρ οἷσπερ ἐγὼ
κεχάρησαι,
τοῖς δακρύοισιν τῶν φευγόντων ἀεὶ καὶ τοῖς
ὀλοφυρμοῖς· 390
ᾤκησας γοῦν ἐπίτηδες ἰὼν ἐνταῦθ', ἵνα ταῦτ'
ἀκροῷο,
κἀβουλήθης μόνος ἡρώων παρὰ τὸν κλάοντα
καθῆσθαι.
ἐλέησον καὶ σῶσον νυνὶ τὸν σαυτοῦ πλησιόχωρον·
κοὔ μή ποτέ σου παρὰ τὰς κάννας οὐρήσω μηδ'
ἀποπάρδω.
ΒΔ. οὗτος, ἐγείρου.
ΣΩ. τί τὸ πρᾶγμ';
ΒΔ. ὥσπερ φωνή μέ τις ἐγκεκύκλωται. 395
ΣΩ. μῶν ὁ γέρων πῃ διαδὺς ἔλαθεν;

THE WASPS, 381-396

PH. But suppose they catch me suspended here,
   and hoist me up by the line again,
 And angle me into the house once more,
   say what ye will do to deliver me then.
CH. Our hearts of oak we'll summon to aid,
   and all give battle at once for you.
 'Twere vain to attempt to detain you more :
   such wonderful feats we are going to do.
PH. This then will I do, confiding in you :
   and if anything happens to me, I implore
 That you take me up and bewail my fate,
   and bury me under the court-house floor.
CH. O nothing, nothing will happen to you :
   keep up, old comrade, your heart and hope ;
 First breathe a prayer to your father's gods :
   then let yourself down by the trusty rope.
PH. 'O Lycus,[a] neighbour and hero and lord !
   thou lovest the selfsame pleasures as I ;
 Day after day we both enjoy
   the suppliant's tears and his wailing cry.
 Thou camest here thine abode to fix,
   on purpose to listen to sounds so sweet,
 The only hero of all that deigns
   by the mourner's side to assume his seat :
 O pity thine old familiar friend :
   O save me and succour me, Power Divine !
 And never again will I do my needs
   by the osier matting that guards thy shrine.
BD. Get up, get up.[b]
SO.   Why, what's in the wind ?
BD. Some voice seems circling me round and round.
SO. Is the old man slipping away thro' a hole ?

[a] "The patron hero of all the Athenian dicasteries; *cf.* 819 ": R.
[b] *B. suddenly reappears and wakes up the slumbering slaves.*

ARISTOPHANES

ΒΔ. μὰ Δί᾽ οὐ δῆτ᾽, ἀλλὰ καθιμᾷ
αὐτὸν δήσας.
ΣΩ. ὦ μιαρώτατε, τί ποιεῖς; οὐ μὴ καταβήσει;
ΒΔ. ἀνάβαιν᾽ ἀνύσας κατὰ τὴν ἑτέραν καὶ ταῖσιν
φυλλάσι παῖε,
ἤν πως πρύμνην ἀνακρούσηται πληγεὶς ταῖς
εἰρεσιώναις.
ΦΙ. οὐ ξυλλήψεσθ᾽ ὁπόσοισι δίκαι τῆτες μέλλουσιν
ἔσεσθαι, 40
ὦ Σμικυθίων καὶ Τισιάδη καὶ Χρήμων καὶ
Φερέδειπνε;
πότε δ᾽, εἰ μὴ νῦν, ἐπαρήξετέ μοι, πρίν μ᾽ εἴσω
μᾶλλον ἄγεσθαι;
ΧΟ. εἰπέ μοι, τί μέλλομεν κινεῖν ἐκείνην τὴν χολήν,
ἤνπερ, ἡνίκ᾽ ἄν τις ἡμῶν ὀργίσῃ τὴν σφηκιάν;
νῦν ἐκεῖνο νῦν ἐκεῖνο [στρ. 40
τοὐξύθυμον, ᾧ κολαζό-
μεσθα, κέντρον ἐντέταται ὀξύ.
ἀλλὰ θαἰμάτια λαβόντες ὡς τάχιστα, παιδία,
θεῖτε καὶ βοᾶτε, καὶ Κλέωνι ταῦτ᾽ ἀγγέλλετε,
καὶ κελεύετ᾽ αὐτὸν ἥκειν 41
ὡς ἐπ᾽ ἄνδρα μισόπολιν
ὄντα κἀπολούμενον, ὅτι
τόνδε λόγον εἰσφέρει,
[ὡς χρὴ] μὴ δικάζειν δίκας.
ΒΔ. ὠγαθοί, τὸ πρᾶγμ᾽ ἀκούσατ᾽, ἀλλὰ μὴ κεκράγετε. 41
ΧΟ. νὴ Δί᾽ εἰς τὸν οὐρανόν γ᾽.
ΒΔ. ὡς τοῦδ᾽ ἐγὼ οὐ μεθήσομαι.

---

[a] Or "harvest-wreath," hanging about the door; cf. K. 729.

BD. No, by Zeus, but he lets himself down to the ground
Tied on to the rope.
SO. You infamous wretch !
what, won't you be quiet and not come down ?
BD. Climb up by the other window-sill,
and wallop him well with the harvest crown.
I warrant he'll speedily back stern first,
when he's thrashed with the branch of autumnal fruits.[a]
PH. Help ! help ! all those whoever propose
this year to busy themselves with suits.
Smicythion, help ! Tisiades, help !
Pheredeipnus, Chremon, the fray begin :
O now or never assist your friend,
before I'm carried away within
CH. Wherefore slumbers, wherefore slumbers,
that resentment in our breast,
Such as when a rash assailant
dares provoke our hornets-nest ?
Now protruding, now protruding,
Comes the fierce and dreadful sting,
Which we wield for punishing.
Children, hold these garments for us :
then away with all your speed,
Shout and run and bawl to Cleon,
tell him of this direful deed ;
Bid him quickly hither fly
As against a city-hater,
And a traitor doomed to die,
One who actually proposes
That we should no lawsuits try.
BD. Listen, worthy sirs, to reason :
goodness ! don't keep screaming so.
CH. Scream ! we'll scream as high as heaven.
BD. I don't intend to let him go.

445

ARISTOPHANES

ΧΟ. ταῦτα δῆτ' οὐ δεινὰ καὶ τυραννίς ἐστιν ἐμφανής;
ὦ πόλις καὶ Θεώρου θεοισεχθρία,
κεἴ τις ἄλλος προέστηκεν ὑμῶν κόλαξ.

ΞΑ. Ἡράκλεις, καὶ κέντρ' ἔχουσιν. οὐχ ὁρᾷς, ὦ
δέσποτα; 420

ΒΔ. οἷς γ' ἀπώλεσαν Φίλιππον ἐν δίκῃ τὸν Γοργίου.

ΧΟ. καὶ σέ γ' αὖθις ἐξολοῦμεν· ἀλλ' ἅπας ἐπίστρεφε
δεῦρο κἀξείρας τὸ κέντρον εἶτ' ἐπ' αὐτὸν ἵεσο,
ξυσταλείς, εὔτακτος, ὀργῆς καὶ μένους ἐμπλήμενος,
ὡς ἂν εὖ εἰδῇ τὸ λοιπὸν σμῆνος οἷον ὤργισεν. 425

ΞΑ. τοῦτο μέντοι δεινὸν ἤδη νὴ Δί', εἰ μαχούμεθα·
ὡς ἔγωγ' αὐτῶν ὁρῶν δέδοικα τὰς ἐγκεντρίδας.

ΧΟ. ἀλλ' ἀφίει τὸν ἄνδρ'. εἰ δὲ μή, φήμ' ἐγὼ
τὰς χελώνας μακαριεῖν σε τοῦ δέρματος.

ΦΙ. εἶά νυν, ὦ ξυνδικασταί, σφῆκες ὀξυκάρδιοι, 430
οἱ μὲν εἰς τὸν πρωκτὸν αὐτῶν εἰσπέτεσθ' ὠργισμένοι,
οἱ δὲ τὠφθαλμὼ 'ν κύκλῳ κεντεῖτε καὶ τοὺς
δακτύλους.

ΒΔ. ὦ Μίδα καὶ Φρὺξ βοήθει δεῦρο καὶ Μασυντία,

---

[a] See Index.
[b] "The hundred κόλακες who fluttered about Cleon, the chief προστάτης of the populace": R.
[c] Unknown.

THE WASPS, 417–433

CH. These be frightful things to see!
　　　　　　　　This is open TYRANNY!
　Rouse the State!　Rouse the great
　　　　　　God-abhorred　　Sneak Theorus [a]!
　And whoe'er [b]　Else is there,
　　　　　　Fawning lord　　Ruling o'er us.
XA. Heracles! they've stings beside them!
　　　　　　Master master, don't you see?
BD. Ay, which slew the son of Gorgias,
　　　　　　Philip,[c] with their sharp decree.
CH. You we'll also slay directly!
　　　　　　Wheel about him, every one,
　Draw your stings, and, all together,
　　　　　　　in upon the fellow run.
　Close your ranks, collect your forces,
　　　　　　brimming full of rage and hate,
　He shall know the sort of wasps-nest
　　　　　　he has dared to irritate.
XA. Now with such as these to combat
　　　　　　is, by Zeus, a serious thing :
　Verily I quake and tremble,
　　　　　　but to look upon their sting.
CH. Let him go!　Loose your hold!
　　　　　　If you don't　I declare
　You shall bless　Tortoise-backs
　　　　　　For the shells　Which they wear.
PH. On then, on, my fellow-dicasts,
　　　　　　brother wasps of heart severe,
　Some fly in with angry buzzings,
　　　　　　and attack them in the rear,
　Some surround them in a ring, and
　　　　　　both their eyes and fingers sting.
BD. Ho there! Midas! Phryx! Masyntias!
　　　　　　hither! hither! haste to me!

447

ARISTOPHANES

καὶ λάβεσθε τουτουὶ καὶ μὴ μεθῆσθε μηδενί·
εἰ δὲ μή, 'ν πέδαις παχείαις οὐδὲν ἀριστήσετε. 43
ὡς ἐγὼ πολλῶν ἀκούσας οἶδα θρίων τὸν ψόφον.

ΧΟ. εἰ δὲ μὴ τοῦτον μεθήσεις, ἔν τί σοι παγήσεται.

ΦΙ. ὦ Κέκροψ ἥρως ἄναξ, τὰ πρὸς ποδῶν Δρακοντίδη,
περιορᾷς οὕτω μ' ὑπ' ἀνδρῶν βαρβάρων χειρού-
μενον,
οὓς ἐγὼ 'δίδαξα κλάειν τέτταρ' ἐς τὴν χοίνικα; 44

ΧΟ. εἶτα δῆτ' οὐ πόλλ' ἔνεστι δεινὰ τῷ γήρᾳ κακά;
δηλαδή· καὶ νῦν γε τούτω τὸν παλαιὸν δεσπότην
πρὸς βίαν χειροῦσιν, οὐδὲν τῶν πάλαι μεμνημένοι
διφθερῶν κἀξωμίδων, ἃς οὗτος αὐτοῖς ἠμπόλα,
καὶ κυνᾶς, καὶ τοὺς πόδας χειμῶνος ὄντος ὠφέλει, 44
ὥστε μὴ ῥιγῶν γ' ἑκάστοτ'· ἀλλὰ τούτοις γ' οὐκ ἔνι
οὐδ' ἐν ὀφθαλμοῖσιν αἰδὼς τῶν παλαιῶν ἐμβάδων.

ΦΙ. οὐκ ἀφήσεις οὐδὲ νυνί μ', ὦ κάκιστον θηρίον;
οὐδ' ἀναμνησθεὶς ὅθ' εὑρὼν τοὺς βότρυς κλέπτοντά σε
προσαγαγὼν πρὸς τὴν ἐλάαν ἐξέδειρ' εὖ κἀνδρικῶς, 45

---

[a] The cracking and bouncing of fig-leaves when burning was used, says the Scholiast, proverbially in reference to empty threats and bluster.
[b] The legendary founder of Athens, shaped in the lower part like a serpent, and sometimes said to have sprung from a dragon's teeth.
[c] Lit. "quartern loaves, four to the choenix": the Scholiast notes that four *big* loaves went to the Choenix but eight *small* ones.
[d] ἐμβάδων is a surprise for δεσποτῶν.

THE WASPS, 434-450

    Take my father, guard him safely :
                  suffer none to set him free ;
    Else you both shall lunch off nothing,
                  clapped in fetters strong and stout.
    There's a sound of many fig-leaves
                  (well I know it) buzzed about.[a]
CH. This shall stand infixed within you
                  if you will not let him go.
PH. Mighty Cecrops[b] ! King and hero !
                  Dragon-born and -shaped below,
    Wilt thou let these rude barbarians
                  vex and maul me at their pleasure,
    Me who heretofore have made them
                  weep in full imperial measure[c] ?
CH. Truly, of abundant evils,
                  age is evermore the source:
    Only see how these two scoundrels
                  hold their ancient lord perforce,
    Clean forgetting how, aforetime,
                  he their daily wants supplied,
    Bought them little sleeveless jackets,
                  bought them caps and coats of hide,
    Clean forgetting all the kindness
                  shown their feet in wintry weather,
    How from chill and cold he kept them :
                  ah ! but these have altogether
    Banished from their eyes the reverence
                  owing to those dear old brogues.[d]
PH. Won't you even now unhand me,
                  shameless villain, worst of rogues ?
    When the grapes I caught you stealing,
                  O remember, if you can,
    How I tied you to the olive,
                  and I flogged you like a man,

ARISTOPHANES

ὥστε σε ζηλωτὸν εἶναι, σὺ δ' ἀχάριστος ἦσθ' ἄρα.
ἀλλ' ἄνες με καὶ σὺ καὶ σύ, πρὶν τὸν υἱὸν ἐκδραμεῖν.

ΧΟ. ἀλλὰ τούτων μὲν τάχ' ἡμῖν δώσετον καλὴν δίκην,
οὐκέτ' ἐς μακράν, ἵν' εἰδῆθ' οἷόν ἐστ' ἀνδρῶν τρόπος
ὀξυθύμων καὶ δικαίων καὶ βλεπόντων κάρδαμα. 4

ΒΔ. παῖε παῖ', ὦ Ξανθία, τοὺς σφῆκας ἀπὸ τῆς οἰκίας.
ΞΑ. ἀλλὰ δρῶ τοῦτ'.
ΒΔ. ἀλλὰ καὶ σὺ τῦφε πολλῷ τῷ καπνῷ.
οὐχὶ σοῦσθ', οὐκ ἐς κόρακας; οὐκ ἄπιτε; παῖε
τῷ ξύλῳ.
καὶ σὺ προσθεὶς Αἰσχίνην ἔντυφε τὸν Σελαρτίου.

ΣΩ. ἆρ' ἐμέλλομέν ποθ' ὑμᾶς ἀποσοβήσειν τῷ χρόνῳ; 4
ΒΔ. ἀλλὰ μὰ Δί' οὐ ῥᾳδίως οὕτως ἂν αὐτοὺς διέφυγες,
εἴπερ ἔτυχον τῶν μελῶν τῶν Φιλοκλέους βεβρω-
κότες.

ΧΟ. ἆρα δῆτ' οὐκ αὐτὰ δῆλα [ἀντ.
τοῖς πένησιν, ἡ τυραννὶς
ὡς λάθρᾳ γ' ἐλάνθαν' ὑπιοῦσα; 4
εἰ σύ γ', ὦ πόνῳ πόνηρε καὶ κομηταμυνία,
τῶν νόμων ἡμᾶς ἀπείργεις ὧν ἔθηκεν ἡ πόλις,
οὔτε τιν' ἔχων πρόφασιν

---

[a] " *Here B. suddenly issues from the house, followed by Xanthias and Sosias, the former armed with a stick, the latter carrying an apparatus for smoking-out wasps* " : R.
[b] *Cf.* 325 n.
[c] A tragic poet of the day, so bitter that he was nicknamed χολή, " gall."
[d] Long hair was considered a mark of aristocratic insolence, and also of sympathy with the long-haired and bearded (*cf.* 476) Spartans. Amynias was notorious for his (*cf.* 1267).

THE WASPS, 451-468

    So that all beheld with envy :
                but a grateful soul you lack !
    Oh, unhand me, you, and you,
                at once, before my son come back.
CH. But a famous retribution
                ye for this shall undergo,
    One that will not lag nor linger ;
                so that ye betimes shall know,
    Know the mood of angry-tempered,
                righteous, mustard-glancing men.
BD. Beat them, Xanthias,[a] from the door-way ;
                beat the wasps away again.
XA. That I will, sir.
BD.   Fume them, Sosias,
                drive the smoke in dense and thick.
    Shoo there, shoo ! be off, confound you.
                At them, Xanthias, with the stick !
    Smoke them, Sosias, smoke, infusing
                Aeschines, Selartius' son.[b]
SO. So then we at last were going,
                as it seems, to make you run.
BD. But you never would have managed
                thus to beat them off with ease,
    Had it chanced that they had eaten
                of the songs of Philocles.[c]
CH.   Creeping o'er us, creeping o'er us,
    Here at least the poor can see
    Stealthy-creeping TYRANNY !
    If you from the laws debar us,
                which the city has ordained,
    You, a curly-haired [d] Amynias,
                you, a rascal double-grained,
    Not by words of wit persuading,
    Not for weighty reasons shown,

451

ARISTOPHANES

οὔτε λόγον εὐτράπελον,
αὐτὸς ἄρχων μόνος.

ΒΔ. ἔσθ' ὅπως ἄνευ μάχης καὶ τῆς κατοξείας βοῆς
ἐς λόγους ἔλθοιμεν ἀλλήλοισι καὶ διαλλαγάς;

ΧΟ. σοὶ λόγους, ὦ μισόδημε καὶ μοναρχίας ἐραστά,
καὶ ξυνὼν Βρασίδᾳ, καὶ φορῶν κράσπεδα
στεμμάτων, τήν θ' ὑπήνην ἄκουρον τρέφων;

ΒΔ. νὴ Δί' ἦ μοι κρεῖττον ἐκστῆναι τὸ παράπαν τοῦ πατρὸς
μᾶλλον ἢ κακοῖς τοσούτοις ναυμαχεῖν ὁσημέραι.

ΧΟ. οὐδὲ μέν γ' οὐδ' ἐν σελίνῳ σοὐστὶν οὐδ' ἐν πηγάνῳ·
τοῦτο γὰρ παρεμβαλοῦμεν τῶν τριχοινίκων ἐπῶν.
ἀλλὰ νῦν μὲν οὐδὲν ἀλγεῖς, ἀλλ' ὅταν ξυνήγορος
ταὐτὰ ταῦτά σου καταντλῇ καὶ ξυνωμότας καλῇ.

ΒΔ. ἆρ' ἄν, ὦ πρὸς τῶν θεῶν, ὑμεῖς ἀπαλλαχθεῖτέ μου;
ἢ δέδοκταί μοι δέρεσθαι καὶ δέρειν δι' ἡμέρας;

ΧΟ. οὐδέποτέ γ', οὔχ, ἕως ἄν τί μου λοιπὸν ᾖ,
ὅστις ἡμῶν ἐπὶ τυραννίδι συνεστάλης.

ΒΔ. ὡς ἅπανθ' ὑμῖν τυραννίς ἐστι καὶ ξυνωμόται,

---

[a] Fringes or tassels of wool which edged the border of a Spartan cloak.
[b] The common border of Hellenic gardens. The meaning is "You have only entered on your troubles."

THE WASPS, 469-488

  But because, forsooth, you WILL it,
  Like an autocrat, alone.
BD. Can't we now, without this outcry,
      and this fierce denunciation,
  Come to peaceful terms together,
      terms of reconciliation?
CH. Terms with THEE, thou people-hater,
      and with Brasidas, thou traitor,
  Hand and glove! You who dare
      Woolly-fringed [a] Clothes to wear,
  Yes, and show Beard and hair
      Left to grow Everywhere.
BD. O, by Zeus, I'd really liefer
      drop my father altogether
  Than endure these daily conflicts,
      buffeting with waves and weather.
CH. Why, as yet you've hardly entered
      on the parsley and the rue [b]:
  (That we'll just throw in, a sample
      of our three-quart words for you.)
  Now you care not, wait a little,
      till the prosecutor trounce you,
  Sluicing out these selfsame charges,
      and CONSPIRATOR denounce you.
BD. O by all the gods I ask you,
      will ye never go away?
  Are ye quite resolved to linger,
      thwacked and thwacking all the day?
CH. Never more Will I while
      There's a grain Left of me
  Leave your door, Traitor vile
      Bent to gain TYRANNY.
BD. Ay "Conspiracy" and "Tyrant,"
      These with you are all in all,

ARISTOPHANES

ἤν τε μεῖζον ἤν τ' ἔλαττον πρᾶγμά τις κατηγορῇ,
ἧς ἐγὼ οὐκ ἤκουσα τοὔνομ' οὐδὲ πεντήκοντ' ἐτῶν· 49
νῦν δὲ πολλῷ τοῦ ταρίχους ἐστὶν ἀξιωτέρα·
ὥστε καὶ δὴ τοὔνομ' αὐτῆς ἐν ἀγορᾷ κυλίνδεται.
ἤν μὲν ὠνῆταί τις ὀρφῶς, μεμβράδας δὲ μὴ θέλῃ,
εὐθέως εἴρηχ' ὁ πωλῶν πλησίον τὰς μεμβράδας·
"οὗτος ὀψωνεῖν ἔοιχ' ἄνθρωπος ἐπὶ τυραννίδι." 49
ἤν δὲ γήτειον προσαιτῇ ταῖς ἀφύαις ἥδυσμά τι,
ἡ λαχανόπωλις παραβλέψασά φησι θατέρῳ·
"εἰπέ μοι, γήτειον αἰτεῖς, πότερον ἐπὶ τυραννίδι
ἢ νομίζεις τὰς Ἀθήνας σοὶ φέρειν ἡδύσματα;"

ΞΑ. κἀμέ γ' ἡ πόρνη χθὲς εἰσελθόντα τῆς μεσημβρίας, 50
ὅτι κελητίσαι 'κέλευον, ὀξυθυμηθεῖσά μοι
ἤρετ' εἰ τὴν Ἱππίου καθίσταμαι τυραννίδα.

ΒΔ. ταῦτα γὰρ τούτοις ἀκούειν ἡδέ', εἰ καὶ νῦν ἐγώ,
τὸν πατέρ' ὅτι βούλομαι τούτων ἀπαλλαχθέντα τῶν
ὀρθροφοιτοσυκοφαντοδικοταλαιπώρων τρόπων 50

---

^a κελητίσαι "to ride a horse" also describes a σχῆμα συνουσίας (cf. P. 900, L. 60), which is then jokingly called Ἱππίου τυραννίδα as in L. 618.

454

Whatsoe'er is brought before you,
    be the matter great or small.
Everywhere the name of Tyrant,
    now for fifty years unknown,
Is than cheap salt-fish at Athens
    commoner and cheaper grown.
Everywhere about the market
    it is bandied to and fro :
If you wish a basse to purchase,
    and without a pilchard go,
Straight the man who sells the pilchards
    grumbles from his stall hard by,
Here is plainly one that caters
    with a view to Tyranny.
If a leek, besides, you order,
    relish for your sprats perchance,
Says the potherb-girl directly,
    eyeing you with looks askance,
Leeks indeed ! and leeks I prithee !
    what, with Tyranny in view ?
Athens must be taxed, you fancy,
    relish to supply for YOU !

XA. Even so a naughty damsel
    yesternoon observed to me,
Just because I said her manners
    were a little bit too free,
She supposed that I was wishing
    Hippias's Tyranny.[a]

BD. Ay, by charges such as these
    our litigious friends they please.
Now because I'd have my father
    (quitting all this toil and strife,
This up-early-false-informing-
    troublesome-litigious life)

ARISTOPHANES

ζῆν βίον γενναῖον ὥσπερ Μόρυχος,[a] αἰτίαν ἔχω
ταῦτα δρᾶν ξυνωμότης ὢν καὶ φρονῶν τυραννικά.

ΦΙ. νὴ Δί' ἐν δίκῃ γ'· ἐγὼ γὰρ οὐδ' ἂν ὀρνίθων γάλα
ἀντὶ τοῦ βίου λάβοιμ' ἂν οὗ με νῦν ἀποστερεῖς·
οὐδὲ χαίρω βατίσιν οὐδ' ἐγχέλεσιν, ἀλλ' ἥδιον ἂν 51
δικίδιον σμικρὸν φάγοιμ' ἂν ἐν λοπάδι πεπνιγμένον.

ΒΔ. νὴ Δί' εἰθίσθης γὰρ ἤδεσθαι τοιούτοις πράγμασιν·
ἀλλ' ἐὰν σιγῶν ἀνάσχῃ καὶ μάθῃς ἁγὼ λέγω,
ἀναδιδάξειν οἴομαί σ' ὡς πάντα ταῦθ' ἁμαρτάνεις.

ΦΙ. ἐξαμαρτάνω δικάζων;

ΒΔ. καταγελώμενος μὲν οὖν 51
οὐκ ἐπαΐεις ὑπ' ἀνδρῶν, οὓς σὺ μόνον οὐ προσκυνεῖς.
ἀλλὰ δουλεύων λέληθας.

ΦΙ. παῦε δουλείαν λέγων,
ὅστις ἄρχω τῶν ἁπάντων.

ΒΔ. οὐ σύ γ', ἀλλ' ὑπηρετεῖς
οἰόμενος ἄρχειν· ἐπεὶ δίδαξον ἡμᾶς, ὦ πάτερ,
ἥτις ἡ τιμή 'στί σοι καρπουμένῳ τὴν Ἑλλάδα. 52

ΦΙ. πάνυ γε· καὶ τούτοισί γ' ἐπιτρέψαι θέλω.

ΒΔ. καὶ μὴν ἐγώ.
ἄφετέ νυν ἅπαντες αὐτόν.

ΦΙ. καὶ ξίφος γέ μοι δότε.

---

[a] A great epicure; cf. A. 887; P. 1008.

Live a life of ease and splendour,
                    live like Morychus,[a] you see
Straight I'm charged with Tyrant leanings,
                    charged with foul conspiracy.
PH. Yes, by Zeus, and very justly.
                    Not for pigeon's milk in store
I the pleasant life would barter
                    which you let me lead no more.
Nought I care for eels and rayfish :
                    daintier food to me would seem
Just a little, tiny lawsuit,
                    dished and stifled in its steam.
BD. Yes, for that's the sort of dainty
                    you, by Zeus, have loved so long.
Yet I think I'll soon convince you
                    that your mode of life is wrong,
If you can but once be silent,
                    and to what I say give heed
PH. I am wrong to be a dicast !
BD.   Laughed to utter scorn indeed,
Mocked by men you all but worship,
                    for you can't their treachery see,
You're a slave, and yet don't know it.
PH.   Name not slavery to me :
I am lord of all, I tell you.
BD.   You're the veriest drudge, I vow,
Thinking that you're lord of all.   For
                    come, my father, teach us now,
If you reap the fruits of Hellas.
                    what's the benefit to you ?
PH. Willingly.   Let these be umpires.
BD.   I'll accept their judgement too.
Now then all at once release him.
PH.   And besides a sword supply,

ARISTOPHANES

ἢν γὰρ ἡττηθῶ λέγων σου, περιπεσοῦμαι τῷ ξίφει.
ΒΔ. εἰπέ μοι, τί δ' ἦν, τὸ δεῖνα, τῇ διαίτῃ μὴ 'μμένῃς;
ΦΙ. μηδέποτε πίοιμ' ἄκρατον μισθὸν ἀγαθοῦ δαίμονος.ᵃ 52

ΧΟ. νῦν δὴ τὸν ἐκ θἠμετέρου   [στρ.
    γυμνασίου λέγειν τι δεῖ
    καινόν, ὅπως φανήσει
ΒΔ. ἐνεγκάτω μοι δεῦρο τὴν κίστην τις ὡς τάχιστα. 53
    ἀτὰρ φανεῖ ποῖός τις ὤν, ἢν ταῦτα παρακελεύῃ.
ΧΟ. μὴ κατὰ τὸν νεανίαν
    τόνδε λέγειν. ὁρᾷς γὰρ ὡς
    σοὶ μέγας ἔστ' ἀγὼν νῦν   53
    καὶ περὶ τῶν ἁπάντων,
    εἴπερ, ὃ μὴ γένοιθ', οὗ-
    τός σ' ἐθέλει κρατῆσαι.
ΒΔ. καὶ μὴν ὅσ' ἂν λέξῃ γ' ἁπλῶς μνημόσυνα γράψομαι
    'γώ.
ΦΙ. τί γὰρ φάθ' ὑμεῖς, ἢν ὁδί με τῷ λόγῳ κρατήσῃ;
ΧΟ. οὐκέτι πρεσβυτῶν ὄχλος   54
    χρήσιμος ἔστ' οὐδ' ἀκαρῆ·
    σκωπτόμενοι δ' ἐν ταῖς ὁδοῖς
    θαλλοφόροι καλούμεθ',ᵇ ἀν-
    τωμοσιῶν κελύφη.   54
    ἀλλ' ὦ περὶ τῆς πάσης μέλλων βασιλείας ἀντι-
      λογήσειν
    τῆς ἡμετέρας, νυνὶ θαρρῶν πᾶσαν γλῶτταν
      βασάνιζε.

ᵃ μισθόν is substituted for οἶνον ; a cup of undiluted wine to the toast of Happy Fortune was the final cup at a feast.
ᵇ " Alluding to the decrepit old men who carried olive branches in the Panathenaic processions ": R.
ᶜ ἀντωμοσίαι are preliminary affidavits, in which the prosecutor asserted, and the defendant denied, the truth of the charge.

THE WASPS, 523-547

If in this dispute I'm worsted,
   here upon this sword I'll die.
BD. But suppose you won't their final
   (what's the phrase) award obey?
PH. May I never drink thereafter,
   pure and neat, good fortune's—pay.[a]

CH. Now must the champion, going
  Out of our school, be showing
   Keen wit and genius new,
BD. Bring forth my memorandum-book :
   bring forth my desk to write in.
I'll quickly show you what you're like,
   if that's your style of fighting.
CH. In quite another fashion
   To aught this youth can do.
  Stern is the strife and anxious
   For all our earthly good,
  If he intends to conquer,
   Which Heaven forfend he should.
BD. Now I'll observe his arguments,
   and take a note of each.
PH. What would you say, if he to-day
   should make the conquering speech?
CH. Ah! should that mischance befall us,
  Our old troop were nothing worth :
  In the streets with ribald mirth
  Idle boys would dotards call us,
  Fit for nought but olive-bearing,[b]
  Shrivelled husks of counter swearing.[c]
O friend upon whom it devolves to plead
   the cause of our Sovereign Power to-day,
Now show us your best ; now bring to the test
   each trick that an eloquent tongue can play.

ARISTOPHANES

ΦΙ. καὶ μὴν εὐθύς γ' ἀπὸ βαλβίδων περὶ τῆς ἀρχῆς
ἀποδείξω
τῆς ἡμετέρας ὡς οὐδεμιᾶς ἥττων ἐστὶν βασιλείας.
τί γὰρ εὔδαιμον καὶ μακαριστὸν μᾶλλον νῦν ἐστὶ
δικαστοῦ,
ἢ τρυφερώτερον, ἢ δεινότερον ζῷον, καὶ ταῦτα
γέροντος;
ὃν πρῶτα μὲν ἕρποντ' ἐξ εὐνῆς τηροῦσ' ἐπὶ τοῖσι
δρυφάκτοις
ἄνδρες μεγάλοι καὶ τετραπήχεις· κἄπειτ' εὐθὺς
προσιόντι
ἐμβάλλει μοι τὴν χεῖρ' ἁπαλήν, τῶν δημοσίων
κεκλοφυῖαν·
ἱκετεύουσίν θ' ὑποκύπτοντες, τὴν φωνὴν οἰκτρο-
χοοῦντες·
"οἴκτειρόν μ', ὦ πάτερ, αἰτοῦμαί σ', εἰ καὐτὸς
πώποθ' ὑφείλου
ἀρχὴν ἄρξας ἢ 'πὶ στρατιᾶς τοῖς ξυσσίτοις
ἀγοράζων·"
ὃς ἔμ' οὐδ' ἂν ζῶντ' ᾔδειν, εἰ μὴ διὰ τὴν προτέραν
ἀπόφυξιν.

ΒΔ. τουτὶ περὶ τῶν ἀντιβολούντων ἔστω τὸ μνημόσυνόν
μοι.

ΦΙ. εἶτ' εἰσελθὼν ἀντιβοληθεὶς καὶ τὴν ὀργὴν ἀπο-
μορχθείς,
ἔνδον τούτων ὧν ἂν φάσκω πάντων οὐδὲν πεποίηκα,
ἀλλ' ἀκροῶμαι πάσας φωνὰς ἱέντων εἰς ἀπόφυξιν.
φέρ' ἴδω, τί γὰρ οὐκ ἔστιν ἀκοῦσαι θώπευμ'
ἐνταῦθα δικαστῇ;
οἱ μέν γ' ἀποκλάονται πενίαν αὑτῶν καὶ προστιθέασιν

---

[a] "In the next 180 lines Aristophanes sets before us the entire process of an Athenian *arbitration*": R.

THE WASPS, 548–564

PH. Away, away,^a like a racer gay,
   I start at once from the head of the lists,
To prove that no kinglier power than ours
   in any part of the world exists.
Is there any creature on earth more blest,
   more feared and petted from day to day,
Or that leads a happier, pleasanter life,
  than a Justice of Athens, though old and grey?
For first when rising from bed in the morn,
   to the criminal Court betimes I trudge,
Great six-foot fellows are there at the rails,
   in anxious haste to salute their Judge.
And the delicate hand, which has dipped so deep
   in the public purse, he claps into mine,
And he bows before me, and makes his prayer,
   and softens his voice to a pitiful whine:
O pity me, pity me, Sire, he cries,
   if you ever indulged your longing for pelf,
When you managed the mess on a far campaign,
   or served some office of state yourself.
The man would never have heard my name,
   if he had not been tried and acquitted before.
BD. (*Writing*) I'll take a note of the point you make,
   that *suppliant fellows your grace implore.*
PH. So when they have begged and implored me enough,
   and my angry temper is wiped away,
I enter in and I take my seat,
   and then I do none of the things I say.
I hear them utter all sorts of cries
   design'd expressly to win my grace,
What won't they utter, what don't they urge,
   to coax a Justice who tries their case?
Some vow they are needy and friendless men,
   and over their poverty wail and whine,

ARISTOPHANES

κακὰ πρὸς τοῖς οὖσιν, ἕως ἀνιὼν ἀνισώσῃ τοῖσιν
  ἐμοῖσιν· 56
οἱ δὲ λέγουσιν μύθους ἡμῖν, οἱ δ' Αἰσώπου τι
  γέλοιον·
οἱ δὲ σκώπτουσ', ἵν' ἐγὼ γελάσω καὶ τὸν θυμὸν
  κατάθωμαι.
κἂν μὴ τούτοις ἀναπειθώμεσθα, τὰ παιδάρι' εὐθὺς
  ἀνέλκει,
τὰς θηλείας καὶ τοὺς υἱεῖς, τῆς χειρός, ἐγὼ δ'
  ἀκροῶμαι·
τὰ δὲ συγκύπτονθ' ἅμα βληχᾶται· κἄπειθ' ὁ πατὴρ
  ὑπὲρ αὐτῶν 57(
ὥσπερ θεὸν ἀντιβολεῖ με τρέμων τῆς εὐθύνης
  ἀπολῦσαι·
" εἰ μὲν χαίρεις ἀρνὸς φωνῇ, παιδὸς φωνὴν
  ἐλεήσαις·"
εἰ δ' αὖ τοῖς χοιριδίοις χαίρω, θυγατρὸς φωνῇ με
  πιθέσθαι.
χἠμεῖς αὐτῷ τότε τῆς ὀργῆς ὀλίγον τὸν κόλλοπ'
  ἀνεῖμεν.
ἆρ' οὐ μεγάλη τοῦτ' ἔστ' ἀρχὴ καὶ τοῦ πλούτου
  καταχήνη; 57
ΒΔ. δεύτερον αὖ σου τουτὶ γράφομαι, τὴν τοῦ πλούτου
  καταχήνην·
καὶ τἀγαθά μοι μέμνησ' ἄχεις φάσκων τῆς Ἑλλάδος
  ἄρχειν.
ΦΙ. παίδων τοίνυν δοκιμαζομένων αἰδοῖα πάρεστι
  θεᾶσθαι.
κἂν Οἴαγρος εἰσέλθῃ φεύγων, οὐκ ἀποφεύγει πρὶν
  ἂν ἡμῖν

---

[a] He addresses the dicast as if he were a deity delighting in

THE WASPS, 565-579

And reckon up hardships, false and true,
    till he makes them out to be equal to mine.
Some tell us a legend of days gone by,
    or a joke from Aesop witty and sage,
Or jest and banter, to make me laugh,
    that so I may doff my terrible rage.
And if all this fails, and I stand unmoved,
    he leads by the hand his little ones near,
He brings his girls and he brings his boys ;
    and I, the Judge, am composed to hear.
They huddle together with piteous bleats :
    while trembling above them he prays to me,
Prays as to a God his accounts to pass,
    to give him a quittance, and leave him free.
If thou lovest a bleating male of the flock,[a]
    O lend thine ear to this boy of mine :
Or pity this sweet little delicate girl,
    if thy soul delights in the squeaking of swine.
So then we relax the pitch of our wrath,
    and screw it down to a peg more low.
Is THIS not a fine dominion of mine,
    a derision of wealth with its pride and show ?

BD. (*Writing*) A second point for my note-book that,
    a derision of wealth with its show and its pride.
Go on to mention the good you get
    by your empire of Hellas so vast and wide.

PH. 'Tis ours to inspect the Athenian youths,
    when we enter their names on the rolls of men.
And if ever Oeagrus [b] gets into a suit,
    be sure that he'll never get out again

---

the sacrifice of lambs and swine ; but ἀρνός is intended to suggest ἄρρενος and χοιρίδια the use of the word in 1353 ; *cf. A.* 769 n.

[b] An actor who took a part in the *Niobe* of Aeschylus or that of Sophocles.

ARISTOPHANES

ἐκ τῆς Νιόβης εἴπῃ ῥῆσιν τὴν καλλίστην ἀπολέξας. 58
κἂν αὐλητής γε δίκην νικᾷ, ταύτης ἡμῖν ἐπίχειρα
ἐν φορβειᾷ τοῖσι δικασταῖς ἔξοδον ηὔλησ' ἀπιοῦσιν.
κἂν ἀποθνῄσκων ὁ πατήρ τῳ δῷ καταλείπων παῖδ'
    ἐπίκληρον,
κλάειν ἡμεῖς μακρὰ τὴν κεφαλὴν εἰπόντες τῇ
    διαθήκῃ
καὶ τῇ κόγχῃ τῇ πάνυ σεμνῶς τοῖς σημείοισιν
    ἐπούσῃ, 58
ἔδομεν ταύτην ὅστις ἂν ἡμᾶς ἀντιβολήσας ἀναπείσῃ.
καὶ ταῦτ' ἀνυπεύθυνοι δρῶμεν· τῶν δ' ἄλλων
    οὐδεμί' ἀρχή.

ΒΔ. τουτὶ γάρ τοί σε μόνον τούτων ὧν εἴρηκας μα-
    καρίζω·
τῆς δ' ἐπικλήρου τὴν διαθήκην ἀδικεῖς ἀνα-
    κογχυλιάζων.

Φι. ἔτι δ' ἡ βουλὴ χὠ δῆμος ὅταν κρῖναι μέγα πρᾶγμ'
    ἀπορήσῃ, 59
ἐψήφισται τοὺς ἀδικοῦντας τοῖσι δικασταῖς παρα-
    δοῦναι·
εἶτ' Εὔαθλος χὠ μέγας οὗτος Κολακώνυμος
    ἀσπιδαποβλής
οὐχὶ προδώσειν ἡμᾶς φασίν, περὶ τοῦ πλήθους δὲ
    μαχεῖσθαι.
κἀν τῷ δήμῳ γνώμην οὐδεὶς πώποτ' ἐνίκησεν,
    ἐὰν μὴ
εἴπῃ τὰ δικαστήρι' ἀφεῖναι πρώτιστα μίαν δικά-
    σαντας· 59

---

[a] " κόγχαι were little cases or capsules which Athenian law-stationers placed over seals to preserve them from damage ": R.
[b] i.e. Cleonymus; cf. 16. He and Evathlus, like Theorus and Euphemius, are minor demagogues, satellites of Cleon.

THE WASPS, 580-595

Till he give us a speech from his Niobe part,
    selecting the best and the liveliest one.
And then if a piper gain his cause,
    he pays us our price for the kindness done,
By piping a tune with his mouth-band on,
    quick march as out of the Court we go.
And what if a father by will to a friend
    his daughter and heiress bequeath and bestow,
We care not a rap for the Will, or the cap *a*
    which is there on the seal so grand and sedate,
We bid them begone, and be hanged, and ourselves
    take charge of the girl and her worthy estate ;
And we give her away to whoever we choose,
    to whoever may chance to persuade us : yet we,
Whilst other officials must pass an account,
    alone from control and accounting are free.

BD. Ay that, and that only, of all you have said,
    I own is a privilege lucky and rare,
But uncapping the seal of the heiress's will
    seems rather a shabby and doubtful affair.

PH. And if ever the Council or People have got
    a knotty and difficult case to decide,
They pass a decree for the culprits to go
    to the able and popular Courts to be tried :
Evathlus, and He ! the loser of shields,
    the fawning, the great Cowardonymus *b* say
"They'll always be fighting away for the mob,"
    "the people of Athens they'll never betray."
And none in the People a measure can pass,
    unless he propose that the Courts shall be free,
Dismissed and discharged for the rest of the day
    when once we have settled a single decree.*c*

c Cf. K. 50 n.

ARISTOPHANES

αὐτὸς δ' ὁ Κλέων ὁ κεκραξιδάμας μόνον ἡμᾶς οὐ
περιτρώγει,
ἀλλὰ φυλάττει διὰ χειρὸς ἔχων καὶ τὰς μυίας
ἀπαμύνει.
σὺ δὲ τὸν πατέρ' οὐδ' ὁτιοῦν τούτων τὸν σαυτοῦ
πώποτ' ἔδρασας.
ἀλλὰ Θέωρος, καίτοὐστὶν ἀνὴρ Εὐφημίου οὐδὲν
ἐλάττων,
τὸν σπόγγον ἔχων ἐκ τῆς λεκάνης τἀμβάδι' ἡμῶν
περικωνεῖ. 6(
σκέψαι μ' ἀπὸ τῶν ἀγαθῶν οἵων ἀποκλείεις καὶ
κατερύκεις,
ἣν δουλείαν οὖσαν ἔφασκες καὶ ὑπηρεσίαν ἀποδείξειν.

ΒΔ. ἔμπλησο λέγων· πάντως γάρ τοι παύσει ποτὲ
κἀναφανήσει
πρωκτὸς λουτροῦ περιγιγνόμενος τῆς ἀρχῆς τῆς
περισέμνου.

ΦΙ. ὃ δέ γ' ἥδιστον τούτων ἐστὶν πάντων, οὗ 'γὼ
'πιλελήσμην, 6(
ὅταν οἴκαδ' ἴω τὸν μισθὸν ἔχων, κᾆτ' εἰσήκονθ'
ἅμα πάντες
ἀσπάζωνται διὰ τἀργύριον, καὶ πρῶτα μὲν ἡ
θυγάτηρ με
ἀπονίζῃ καὶ τὼ πόδ' ἀλείφῃ καὶ προσκύψασα
φιλήσῃ,
καὶ παππίζουσ' ἅμα τῇ γλώττῃ τὸ τριώβολον
ἐκκαλαμᾶται,
καὶ τὸ γύναιόν μ' ὑποθωπεῦσαν φυστὴν μᾶζαν
προσενέγκῃ, 6

466

THE WASPS, 596-610

Yea, Cleon the Bawler and Brawler himself,
    at us, and us only, to nibble forbears,
And sweeps off the flies that annoy us, and still
    with a vigilant hand for our dignity cares.
You never have shown such attention as this,
    or displayed such a zeal in your father's affairs.
Yet Theorus, a statesman as noble and grand
    as lordly Euphemius,[a] runs at our call
And whips out a sponge from his bottle, and stoops,
    to black and to polish the shoes of us all.
Such, such is the glory, the joy, the renown,
    from which you desire to retain and withhold me,
And THIS you will show, this Empire of mine,
    to be bondage and slavery merely, you told me.

BD. Ay, chatter your fill, you will cease before long :
    and then I will show that your boasted success
Is just the success of a tail that is washed,[b]
    going back to its filth and its slovenliness.

PH. But the nicest and pleasantest part of it all
    is this, which I'd wholly forgotten to say,
'Tis when with my fee in my wallet I come,
    returning home at the close of the day,
O then what a welcome I get for its sake ;
    my daughter, the darling, is foremost of all,
And she washes my feet and anoints them with care,
    and above them she stoops, and a kiss lets fall,
Till at last by the pretty Papas of her tongue
    she angles withal my three-obol away.
Then my dear little wife, she sets on the board
    nice manchets of bread in a tempting array,

[a] Unknown, but regarded by Aristophanes as "still more despicable than Theorus, who is obviously intended to be insulted by the comparison " : R.

[b] ὁ γὰρ πρωκτὸς πλυνόμενος περιγίνεται τῆς καθάρσεως καὶ ἔτι μολύνεται: Schol.

ARISTOPHANES

κἄπειτα καθεζομένη παρ' ἐμοὶ προσαναγκάζῃ,
"φάγε τουτί,
ἔντραγε τουτί·" τούτοισιν ἐγὼ γάνυμαι, καὶ μή
  με δεήσῃ
ἐς σὲ βλέψαι καὶ τὸν ταμίαν, ὁπότ' ἄριστον
  παραθήσει
καταρασάμενος καὶ τονθορύσας. ἀλλ' ἢν μή μοι
  ταχὺ μάξῃ,
τάδε κέκτημαι πρόβλημα κακῶν, σκευὴν βελέων
  ἀλεωρήν.   61
κἂν οἶνόν μοι μὴ 'γχῇς σὺ πιεῖν, τὸν ὄνον τόνδ'
  ἐσκεκόμισμαι
οἴνου μεστόν, κᾆτ' ἐγχέομαι κλίνας· οὗτος δὲ
  κεχηνὼς
βρωμησάμενος τοῦ σοῦ δίνου μέγα καὶ στράτιον
  κατέπαρδεν.
ἆρ' οὐ μεγάλην ἀρχὴν ἄρχω καὶ τοῦ Διὸς οὐδὲν
  ἐλάττω,   62
ὅστις ἀκούω ταῦθ' ἅπερ ὁ Ζεύς;
ἢν γοῦν ἡμεῖς θορυβήσωμεν,
πᾶς τίς φησιν τῶν παριόντων,
"οἷον βροντᾷ τὸ δικαστήριον,
ὦ Ζεῦ βασιλεῦ."   62
κἂν ἀστράψω, ποππύζουσιν,
κἀγκεχόδασίν μ' οἱ πλουτοῦντες
καὶ πάνυ σεμνοί.
καὶ σὺ δέδοικάς με μάλιστ' αὐτός·
νὴ τὴν Δήμητρα, δέδοικας. ἐγὼ δ'   63
ἀπολοίμην, εἴ σε δέδοικα.

THE WASPS, 611-630

And cosily taking a seat by my side,
  with loving entreaty constrains me to feed;
I beseech you taste this, I implore you try that.
 This, this I delight in, and ne'er may I need
To look to yourself and your pantler, a scrub
 who, whenever I ask him my breakfast to set,
Keeps grumbling and murmuring under his breath.
  No! no! if he haste not a manchet to get,
Lo here my defence from the evils of life,
 my armour of proof, my impregnable shield.
And what if you pour me no liquor to drink,
 yet here's an old Ass,[a] full of wine, that I wield,
And I tilt him, and pour for myself, and imbibe;
 whilst sturdy old Jack, as a bumper I drain,
Lets fly at your goblet a bray of contempt,
  a mighty and masterful snort of disdain.
 Is THIS not a fine dominion of mine?
 Is it less than the empire of Zeus?
Why the very same phrases, so grand and divine,
 For me, as for Him, are in use.
For when we are raging loud and high
 In stormy, tumultuous din,
O Lord! O Zeus! say the passers-by,
 How thunders the Court within!
The wealthy and great, when my lightnings glare,
Turn pale and sick, and mutter a prayer.[b]
You fear me too: I protest you do:
Yes, yes, by Demeter I vow 'tis true.
But hang me if I am afraid of you.

---

[a] A wine-flagon shaped like an ass, or an ass's head. In 617 κεχηνώς = " with its jaws wide open like a donkey braying ": R.
[b] " A Greek or Roman when alarmed by a thunderstorm was accustomed to make with his lips a clucking or popping noise, as a sort of charm to avert the danger ": R.

ARISTOPHANES

ΧΟ. οὐπώποθ' οὕτω καθαρῶς   [ἀντ.
     οὐδενὸς ἠκούσαμεν οὐ-
     δὲ ξυνετῶς λέγοντος.
ΦΙ. οὔκ, ἀλλ' ἐρήμας ᾤεθ' οὗτος ῥᾳδίως τρυγήσειν·
     καλῶς γὰρ ᾔδειν ὡς ἐγὼ ταύτῃ κράτιστός εἰμι. 63
ΧΟ. ὡς δ' ἐπὶ πάντ' ἐλήλυθεν
     κοὐδὲν παρῆλθεν, ὥστ' ἔγωγ'
     ηὐξανόμην ἀκούων,
     κἂν μακάρων δικάζειν
     αὐτὸς ἔδοξα νήσοις,   64
     ἡδόμενος λέγοντι.
ΦΙ. ὡς οὗτος ἤδη σκορδινᾶται κἄστιν οὐκ ἐν αὑτῷ.
     ἦ μὴν ἐγώ σε τήμερον σκύτη βλέπειν ποιήσω.
ΧΟ. δεῖ δέ σε παντοίας πλέκειν
     εἰς ἀπόφυξιν παλάμας.   64
     τὴν γὰρ ἐμὴν ὀργὴν πεπᾶ-
     ναι χαλεπὸν [νεανίᾳ]
     μὴ πρὸς ἐμοῦ λέγοντι.
     πρὸς ταῦτα μύλην ἀγαθὴν ὥρα ζητεῖν σοι καὶ
         νεόκοπτον
     (ἢν μή τι λέγῃς), ἥτις δυνατὴ τὸν ἐμὸν θυμὸν
         κατερεῖξαι.
ΒΔ. χαλεπὸν μὲν καὶ δεινῆς γνώμης καὶ μείζονος ἢ
         'πὶ τρυγῳδοῖς,   65
     ἰάσασθαι νόσον ἀρχαίαν ἐν τῇ πόλει ἐντετοκυῖαν.
     ἀτάρ, ὦ πάτερ ἡμέτερε Κρονίδη
ΦΙ.   παῦσαι καὶ μὴ πατέριζε.

---

[a] Philocleon (621 *seq.*) had arrogated to himself the attributes of Zeus, and so B. addresses him in the language Athene uses to Zeus in Homer (*Il.* viii. 313; *Od.* i. 45); but P. will have none of his " befathering."

THE WASPS, 631-652

CH. I never, no, I never
Have heard so clear and clever
And eloquent a speech—
PH. Ay, ay, he thought he'd steal my grapes,
         and pluck them undefended,
For well he knew that I'm in this
         particularly splendid.
CH. No topic he omitted,
But he duly went through each.
I waxed in size to hear him
Till with ecstasy possessed
Methought I sat a-judging
In the Islands of the Blest.
PH. See how uneasily he stands,
         and gapes, and shifts his ground.
I warrant, sir, before I've done,
         you'll look like a beaten hound.
CH. You must now, young man, be seeking
Every turn and every twist
Which can your defence assist.
To a youth against me speaking
Mine's a heart 'tis hard to render
(So you'll find it) soft and tender.
And therefore unless you can speak to the point,
         you must look for a millstone handy and good,
Fresh hewn from the rock, to shiver and shock
         the unyielding grit of my resolute mood.

BD. Hard were the task, and shrewd the intent,
         for a Comedy-poet all too great
To attempt to heal an inveterate, old
         disease engrained in the heart of the state.
Yet, O dread Cronides, Father and Lord,[a]
PH.   Stop, stop, don't talk in that father-me way,

ARISTOPHANES

εἰ μὴ γὰρ ὅπως δουλεύω 'γώ, τουτὶ ταχέως με διδάξεις,
οὐκ ἔστιν ὅπως οὐχὶ τεθνήξει, κἂν χρῇ σπλάγχνων μ' ἀπέχεσθαι.
ΒΔ. ἀκρόασαί νυν, ὦ παππίδιον, χαλάσας ὀλίγον τὸ μέτωπον· 65
καὶ πρῶτον μὲν λόγισαι φαύλως, μὴ ψήφοις, ἀλλ' ἀπὸ χειρός,
τὸν φόρον ἡμῖν ἀπὸ τῶν πόλεων συλλήβδην τὸν προσιόντα·
κἄξω τούτου τὰ τέλη χωρὶς καὶ τὰς πολλὰς ἑκατοστάς,
πρυτανεῖα, μέταλλ', ἀγοράς, λιμένας, μισθοὺς καὶ δημιόπρατα.
τούτων πλήρωμα τάλαντ' ἐγγὺς δισχίλια γίγνεται ἡμῖν. 60
ἀπὸ τούτου νυν κατάθες μισθὸν τοῖσι δικασταῖς ἐνιαυτοῦ,
ἓξ χιλιάσιν, κοὔπω πλείους ἐν τῇ χώρᾳ κατένασθεν,
γίγνεται ὑμῖν ἑκατὸν δήπου καὶ πεντήκοντα τάλαντα.
ΦΙ. οὐδ' ἡ δεκάτη τῶν προσιόντων ἡμῖν ἄρ' ἐγίγνεθ' ὁ μισθός.
ΒΔ. μὰ Δί' οὐ μέντοι.
ΦΙ. καὶ ποῖ τρέπεται δὴ 'πειτα τὰ χρήματα τἄλλα; 66
ΒΔ. ἐς τούτους τούς, "οὐχὶ προδώσω τὸν Ἀθηναίων κολοσυρτόν,
ἀλλὰ μαχοῦμαι περὶ τοῦ πλήθους ἀεί." σὺ γάρ, ὦ πάτερ, αὐτοὺς
ἄρχειν αἱρεῖ σαυτοῦ, τούτοις τοῖς ῥηματίοις περιπεφθείς.

---
^a *i.e.* as polluted by homicide.

472

THE WASPS, 653-668

Convince me at once that I'm only a slave,
  or else I protest you shall die this day
Albeit I then must ever abstain
  from the holy flesh of the victims slain.[a]

BD. Then listen my own little pet Papa,
  and smooth your brow from its frowns again.
And not with pebbles precisely ranged,
  but roughly thus on your fingers count
The tribute paid by the subject States,
  and just consider its whole amount ;
And then, in addition to this, compute
  the many taxes and one-per-cents,
The fees and the fines, and the silver mines,
  the markets and harbours and sales and rents.
If you take the total result of the lot,
  'twill reach two thousand talents or near.
And next put down the Justices' pay,
  and reckon the sums they receive a year :
Six thousand Justices, count them through,
  there dwell no more in the land as yet,
One hundred and fifty talents a year
  I think you will find is all they get.

PH. Then not one tithe of our income goes
  to furnish forth the Justices' pay.

BD. No, certainly not.

PH.   And what becomes
  of all the rest of the revenue, pray ?

BD. Why, bless you, it goes to the pockets of those,
  To the rabble of Athens I'll ever be true,
I'll always battle away for the mob.[b]
  O father, my father, 'tis owing to you :
By such small phrases as these cajoled,
  you lift them over yourselves to reign.

[b] He refers to P.'s words in 593.

ARISTOPHANES

κᾆθ' οὗτοι μὲν δωροδοκοῦσιν κατὰ πεντήκοντα
  τάλαντα
ἀπὸ τῶν πόλεων, ἐπαπειλοῦντες τοιαυτὶ κἀνα-
  φοβοῦντες,
" δώσετε τὸν φόρον, ἢ βροντήσας τὴν πόλιν ὑμῶν
  ἀνατρέψω."
σὺ δὲ τῆς ἀρχῆς ἀγαπᾷς τῆς σῆς τοὺς ἀργελόφους
  περιτρώγων.
οἱ δὲ ξύμμαχοι ὡς ᾔσθηνται τὸν μὲν σύρφακα τὸν
  ἄλλον
ἐκ κηθαρίου λαγαριζόμενον καὶ τραγαλίζοντα τὸ
  μηδέν,
σὲ μὲν ἡγοῦνται Κόννου ψῆφον, τούτοισι δὲ
  δωροφοροῦσιν
ὕρχας, οἶνον, δάπιδας, τυρόν, μέλι, σήσαμα,
  προσκεφάλαια,
φιάλας, χλανίδας, στεφάνους, ὅρμους, ἐκπώματα,
  πλουθυγιείαν·
σοὶ δ' ὧν ἄρχεις, πολλὰ μὲν ἐν γῇ, πολλὰ δ' ἐφ'
  ὑγρᾷ πιτυλεύσας,
οὐδεὶς οὐδὲ σκορόδου κεφαλὴν τοῖς ἑψητοῖσι
  δίδωσιν.

ΦΙ. μὰ Δί' ἀλλὰ παρ' Εὐχαρίδου καὐτὸς τρεῖς γ'
  ἄγλιθας μετέπεμψα.
ἀλλ' αὐτήν μοι τὴν δουλείαν οὐκ ἀποφαίνων
  ἀποκναίεις.

ΒΔ. οὐ γὰρ μεγάλη δουλεία 'στὶν τούτους μὲν ἅπαντας
  ἐν ἀρχαῖς
αὐτούς τ' εἶναι, καὶ τοὺς κόλακας τοὺς τούτων,
  μισθοφοροῦντας;
σοὶ δ' ἤν τις δῷ τοὺς τρεῖς ὀβολούς, ἀγαπᾷς· οὓς
  αὐτὸς ἐλαύνων

THE WASPS, 669-684

And then, believe me, they soon contrive
    some fifty talents in bribes to gain,
Extorting them out of the subject states,
    by hostile menace and angry frown :
Hand over, they say, *the tribute-pay,*
    or else my thunders shall crush your town.
You joy the while at the remnants vile,
    the trotters and tips of your power to gnaw.
So when our knowing, acute allies
    the rest, the scum of the Populace, saw
On a vote-box pine, and on nothingness dine,
    and marked how lanky and lean ye grow,
They count you all as a Connas's vote,[a]
    and ever and ever on these bestow
Wines, cheeses, necklaces, sesamè fruit,
    and jars of pickle and pots of honey,
Rugs, cushions, and mantles, and cups, and crowns,
    and health, and vigour, and lots of money.
Whilst you ! from out of the broad domain
    for which on the land and the wave you toiled,
None gives you so much as a garlic head,
    to flavour the dish when your sprats are boiled.
PH. That's true no doubt, for I just sent out,
    and bought, myself, from Eucharides three ;
But you wear me away by your long delay
    in proving my bondage and slavery.
BD. Why is it not slavery pure and neat,
    when these (themselves and their parasites too)
Are all in receipt of their pay, God wots,
    as high officials of state : whilst you
Must thankful be for your obols three,
    those obols which ye yourselves have won

---

[a] Apparently = something valueless. C. appears in K. 534 as a dissolute musician.

ARISTOPHANES

καὶ πεζομαχῶν καὶ πολιορκῶν ἐκτήσω, πολλὰ
ποιήσας.
καὶ πρὸς τούτοις ἐπιταττόμενος φοιτᾷς, ὃ μάλιστά
μ' ἀπάγχει,
ὅταν εἰσελθὸν μειράκιόν σοι κατάπυγον, Χαιρέου
υἱός,
ὡδὶ διαβάς, διακινηθεὶς τῷ σώματι καὶ τρυφε-
ρανθείς,
ἥκειν εἴπῃ πρῷ κἂν ὥρᾳ δικάσονθ', ὡς ὅστις ἂν
ὑμῶν
ὕστερος ἔλθῃ τοῦ σημείου, τὸ τριώβολον οὐ
κομιεῖται·
αὐτὸς δὲ φέρει τὸ συνηγορικόν, δραχμήν, κἂν
ὕστερος ἔλθῃ·
καὶ κοινωνῶν τῶν ἀρχόντων ἑτέρῳ τινὶ τῶν μεθ'
ἑαυτοῦ,
ἤν τίς τι διδῷ τῶν φευγόντων, ξυνθέντε τὸ πρᾶγμα
δύ' ὄντε
ἐσπουδάκατον, κᾆθ' ὡς πρίονθ' ὁ μὲν ἕλκει, ὁ δ'
ἀντενέδωκε·
σὺ δὲ χασκάζεις τὸν κωλακρέτην· τὸ δὲ πραττό-
μενόν σε λέληθεν.
ΦΙ. ταυτί με ποιοῦσ'; οἴμοι, τί λέγεις; ὥς μου τὸν
θῖνα ταράττεις,
καὶ τὸν νοῦν μου προσάγεις μᾶλλον, κοὐκ οἶδ' ὅ
τι χρῆμά με ποιεῖς.
ΒΔ. σκέψαι τοίνυν ὡς ἐξόν σοι πλουτεῖν καὶ τοῖσιν
ἅπασιν,
ὑπὸ τῶν ἀεὶ δημιζόντων οὐκ οἶδ' ὅποι ἐγκεκύ-
κλησαι·

In the battle's roar, by sea and by shore,
       'mid sieges and miseries many a one.
But O what throttles me most of all,
       is this, that under constraint you go,
When some young dissolute spark comes in,
       some son of a Chaereas,[a] straddling—so,
With his legs apart, and his body poised,
       and a mincing, soft, effeminate air,
And bids you Justices, one and all,
       betimes in the morn to the Court repair,
For that any who after the signal [b] come
       shall lose and forfeit their obols three.
Yet come as late as he choose himself,
       he pockets his drachma, " Counsel's fee." [c]
And then if a culprit give him a bribe,
       he gets his fellow the job to share,
And into each other's hands they play,
       and manage together the suit to square.
Just like two men at a saw they work,
       and one keeps pulling, and one gives way.
While you at the Treasurer [d] stare and gape,
       and never observe the tricks they play.
PH. Is THAT what they do ! O can it be true !
       Ah me, the depths of my being are stirred,
Your statements shake my soul, and I feel
       I know not how, at the things I've heard.
BD. And just consider when you and all
       might revel in affluence, free as air,
How these same demagogues wheel you round,
       and cabin and coop you I know not where.

[a] Unknown.
[b] A signal hoisted for the opening of the court.
[c] " A retaining fee paid to the 10 συνήγοροι appointed as public prosecutors " : R.
[d] One of the officers who paid the dicasts.

ARISTOPHANES

ὅστις πόλεων ἄρχων πλείστων, ἀπὸ τοῦ Πόντου
 μέχρι Σαρδοῦς,
οὐκ ἀπολαύεις πλὴν τοῦθ᾽ ὃ φέρεις ἀκαρῆ, καὶ
 τοῦτ᾽ ἐρίῳ σοι
ἐνστάζουσιν κατὰ μικρὸν ἀεί, τοῦ ζῆν ἔνεχ᾽,
 ὥσπερ ἔλαιον.
βούλονται γάρ σε πένητ᾽ εἶναι· καὶ τοῦθ᾽ ὧν
 εἵνεκ᾽, ἐρῶ σοι,
ἵνα γιγνώσκῃς τὸν τιθασευτήν· κᾆθ᾽ ὅταν οὗτός
 γ᾽ ἐπισίξῃ,
ἐπὶ τῶν ἐχθρῶν τιν᾽ ἐπιρρύξας, ἀγρίως αὐτοῖς
 ἐπιπηδᾷς.
εἰ γὰρ ἐβούλοντο βίον πορίσαι τῷ δήμῳ, ῥᾴδιον
 ἦν ἄν.
εἰσίν γε πόλεις χίλιαι, αἳ νῦν τὸν φόρον ἡμῖν
 ἀπάγουσιν·
τούτων εἴκοσιν ἄνδρας βόσκειν εἴ τις προσέταξεν
 ἑκάστῃ,
δύο μυριάδες τῶν δημοτικῶν ἔζων ἐν πᾶσι λαγῴοις
καὶ στεφάνοισιν παντοδαποῖσιν καὶ πυῷ καὶ
 πυριάτῃ,
ἄξια τῆς γῆς ἀπολαύοντες καὶ τοῦ Μαραθῶνι
 τροπαίου.
νῦν δ᾽ ὥσπερ ἐλαολόγοι χωρεῖθ᾽ ἅμα τῷ τὸν
 μισθὸν ἔχοντι.
ΦΙ. οἴμοι, τί ποθ᾽ ὥσπερ νάρκη μου κατὰ τῆς χειρὸς
 καταχεῖται,
καὶ τὸ ξίφος οὐ δύναμαι κατέχειν, ἀλλ᾽ ἤδη
 μαλθακός εἰμι.
ΒΔ. ἀλλ᾽ ὁπόταν μὲν δείσωσ᾽ αὐτοί, τὴν Εὔβοιαν
 διδόασιν

a Sardinia.

THE WASPS, 700-715

And you, the lord of such countless towns,
    from Pontus to Sardo,[a] nought obtain
Save this poor pittance you earn, and this
    they dole you in driblets, grain by grain,
As though they were dropping oil from wool,
    as much forsooth as will life sustain.
They MEAN you all to be poor and gaunt,
    and I'll tell you, father, the reason why.
They want you to know your keeper's hand ;
    and then if he hiss you on to fly
At some helpless foe, away you go,
    with eager vehemence ready and rough.
Since if they wished to maintain you well,
    the way to do it were plain enough.
A thousand cities our rule obey,
    a thousand cities their tribute pay,
Allot them twenty Athenians each,
    to feed and nourish from day to day,
And twice ten thousand citizens there,
    are living immersed in dishes of hare,
With creams and beestings and sumptuous fare,
    and garlands and coronals everywhere,
Enjoying a fate that is worthy the state,
    and worthy the trophy on Marathon plain.
Whilst now like gleaners [b] ye all are fain
    to follow along in the paymaster's train.
PH. O what can this strange sensation mean,
    this numbness that over my hand is stealing ?
My arm no longer can hold the sword :
    I yield, unmanned, to a womanish feeling.
BD. Let a panic possess them, they're ready to give
    Euboea at once for the State to divide,[c]

[b] Lit. " olive-gatherers " ; needy folk like our hop-pickers.
[c] *i.e.* to portion it out among you in " allotments " as κληροῦχοι.

ARISTOPHANES

ὑμῖν καὶ σῖτον ὑφίστανται κατὰ πεντήκοντα
  μεδίμνους
ποριεῖν· ἔδοσαν δ' οὐπώποτέ σοι, πλὴν πρώην
  πέντε μεδίμνους,
καὶ ταῦτα μόλις ξενίας φεύγων ἔλαβες κατὰ
  χοίνικα, κριθῶν.
ὧν εἵνεκ' ἐγώ σ' ἀπέκλειον ἀεί,
βόσκειν ἐθέλων καὶ μὴ τούτους
ἐγχάσκειν σοι στομφάζοντας.
καὶ νῦν ἀτεχνῶς ἐθέλω παρέχειν
ὅ τι βούλει σοι,
πλὴν κωλακρέτου γάλα πίνειν.

ΧΟ. ἦ που σοφὸς ἦν ὅστις ἔφασκεν, "πρὶν ἂν ἀμφοῖν
  μῦθον ἀκούσῃς,
οὐκ ἂν δικάσαις." σὺ γὰρ οὖν νῦν μοι νικᾶν
  πολλῷ δεδόκησαι·
ὥστ' ἤδη τὴν ὀργὴν χαλάσας τοὺς σκίπωνας
  καταβάλλω.
ἀλλ' ὦ τῆς ἡλικίας ἡμῖν τῆς αὐτῆς συνθιασῶτα,
  πιθοῦ πιθοῦ λόγοισι, μηδ' ἄφρων γένῃ, [στρ.
μηδ' ἀτενὴς ἄγαν ἀτεράμων τ' ἀνήρ.
εἴθ' ὤφελέν μοι κηδεμὼν ἢ ξυγγενὴς
εἶναί τις ὅστις τοιαῦτ' ἐνουθέτει.
σοὶ δὲ νῦν τις θεῶν
παρὼ νέμφανὴς
ξυλλαμβάνει τοῦ πράγματος,
καὶ δῆλός ἐστιν εὖ ποιῶν·
σὺ δὲ παρὼν δέχου.

ΒΔ. καὶ μὴν θρέψω γ' αὐτὸν παρέχων
ὅσα πρεσβύτῃ ξύμφορα, χόνδρον

THE WASPS, 716-738

And engage to supply for every man
        full fifty bushels of wheat beside.
But five poor bushels of barley each
        is all that you ever obtained in fact,
And that doled out by the quart, while first
        they worry you under the Alien Act.[a]
And therefore it was that I locked you away
To keep you in ease ; unwilling that these
With empty mouthings your age should bilk.
And now I offer you here to-day
Without any reserve whatever you please,
Save only a draught of—Treasurer's milk.

CH. 'Twas a very acute and intelligent man,
        whoever it was, that happened to say,
Don't make up your mind till you've heard both sides,
        for now I protest you have gained the fray.
Our staves of justice, our angry mood,
        for ever and ever aside we lay,
And we turn to talk to our old compeer,
        our choir-companion of many a day.
Don't be a fool : give in, give in,
Nor too perverse and stubborn be ;
I would to Heaven my kith and kin
Would show the like regard for me.
Some deity, 'tis plain, befriends
Your happy lot, believe, believe it ;
With open arms his aid he sends,
Do you with open arms receive it.
BD. I'll give him whatever his years require,
A basin of gruel, and soft attire,

[a] You have to establish your claim with as much trouble as if you were being prosecuted for fraudulently exercising the rights of citizenship.

ARISTOPHANES

      λείχειν, χλαῖναν μαλακήν, σισύραν,
      πόρνην, ἥτις τὸ πέος τρίψει
      καὶ τὴν ὀσφῦν.
      ἀλλ' ὅτι σιγᾷ κοὐδὲν γρύζει,
      τοῦτ' οὐ δύναταί με προσέσθαι.
ΧΟ. νενουθέτηκεν αὐτὸν ἐς τὰ πράγμαθ', οἷς [ἀντ.
      τότ' ἐπεμαίνετ'· ἔγνωκε γὰρ ἀρτίως,
      λογίζεταί τ' ἐκεῖνα πάνθ' ἁμαρτίας
      ἃ σοῦ κελεύοντος οὐκ ἐπείθετο.
      νῦν δ' ἴσως τοῖσι σοῖς
      λόγοις πείθεται,
      καὶ σωφρονεῖ μέντοι μεθι-
      στὰς ἐς τὸ λοιπὸν τὸν τρόπον
      πιθόμενός τέ σοι.
ΦΙ. ἰώ μοί μοι.
ΒΔ. οὗτος, τί βοᾷς;
ΦΙ. μή μοι τούτων μηδὲν ὑπισχνοῦ.
      κείνων ἔραμαι, κεῖθι γενοίμαν,
      ἵν' ὁ κῆρυξ φησί, "τίς ἀψήφι-
      στος; ἀνιστάσθω."
      κἀπισταίην ἐπὶ τοῖς κημοῖς
      ψηφιζομένων ὁ τελευταῖος.
      σπεῦδ', ὦ ψυχή. ποῦ μοι ψυχή;
      πάρες, ὦ σκιερά. μὰ τὸν Ἡρακλέα,
      μὴ νῦν ἔτ' ἐγὼ 'ν τοῖσι δικασταῖς
      κλέπτοντα Κλέωνα λάβοιμι.

ΒΔ. ἴθ', ὦ πάτερ, πρὸς τῶν θεῶν, ἐμοὶ πιθοῦ.
ΦΙ. τί σοι πίθωμαι; λέγ' ὅ τι βούλει, πλὴν ἑνός.
ΒΔ. ποίου; φέρ' ἴδω.
ΦΙ.   τοῦ μὴ δικάζειν. τοῦτο δὲ
      Ἅιδης διακρινεῖ πρότερον ἢ 'γὼ πείσομαι.

THE WASPS, 739-763

   And a good warm rug, and a handmaid fair,
   To chafe and cherish his limbs with care.
   —But I can't like this, that he stands so mute,
   And speaks not a word nor regards my suit.
CH. 'Tis that his soberer thoughts review
   The frenzy he indulged so long,
   And (what he would not yield to you)
   He feels his former life was wrong.
   Perchance he'll now amend his plan,
   Unbend his age to mirth and laughter,
   A better and a wiser man
   By your advice he'll live hereafter.
PH. O misery! O misery!
BD. O father, why that dolorous cry?
PH. Talk not of things like these to me![a]
   Those are my pleasures, *there* would I be
   Where the Usher cries
   Who has not voted? let him arise.
   And O that the last of the voting band
   By the verdict-box I could take my stand.
   On, on, my soul! why, where is she gone?
   Hah! by your leave, my shadowy one!
   Zounds, if I catch when in Court I'm sitting
   Cleon again a theft committing!

BD. O father, father, by the Gods comply.
PH. Comply with what? name any wish, save one.
BD. Save what, I prithee?
PH.   Not to judge; but that
   Hades shall settle ere my soul comply.

 [a] "P. breaks his tragic silence, and gives utterance to a cento of scraps from the *Hippolytus Velatus*, *Alcestis*, *Bellerophon*, and probably other plays of Euripides" R.

ARISTOPHANES

ΒΔ. σὺ δ' οὖν, ἐπειδὴ τοῦτο κεχάρηκας ποιῶν,
ἐκεῖσε μὲν μηκέτι βάδιζ', ἀλλ' ἐνθάδε
αὐτοῦ μένων δίκαζε τοῖσιν οἰκέταις.
ΦΙ. περὶ τοῦ; τί ληρεῖς;
ΒΔ. ταῦθ', ἅπερ ἐκεῖ πράττεται.
ὅτι τὴν θύραν ἀνέῳξεν ἡ σηκὶς λάθρᾳ,
ταύτης ἐπιβολὴν ψηφιεῖ μίαν μόνην.
πάντως δὲ κἀκεῖ ταῦτ' ἔδρας ἑκάστοτε.
καὶ ταῦτα μέν νυν εὐλόγως, ἢν ἐξέχῃ
εἴλη κατ' ὄρθρον, ἡλιάσει πρὸς ἥλιον·
ἐὰν δὲ νίφῃ, πρὸς τὸ πῦρ καθήμενος,
ὕοντος, εἴσει· κἂν ἔγρῃ μεσημβρινός,
οὐδείς σ' ἀποκλείσει θεσμοθέτης τῇ κιγκλίδι.
ΦΙ. τουτί μ' ἀρέσκει.
ΒΔ. πρὸς δὲ τούτοις γ', ἢν δίκην
λέγῃ μακράν τις, οὐχὶ πεινῶν ἀναμενεῖς,
δάκνων σεαυτὸν καὶ τὸν ἀπολογούμενον.
ΦΙ. πῶς οὖν διαγιγνώσκειν καλῶς δυνήσομαι
ὥσπερ πρότερον τὰ πράγματ', ἔτι μασώμενος;
ΒΔ. πολλῷ γ' ἄμεινον· καὶ λέγεται γὰρ τουτογί,
ὡς οἱ δικασταὶ ψευδομένων τῶν μαρτύρων
μόλις τὸ πρᾶγμ' ἔγνωσαν ἀναμασώμενοι.
ΦΙ. ἀνά τοί με πείθεις. ἀλλ' ἐκεῖν' οὔπω λέγεις,
τὸν μισθὸν ὁπόθεν λήψομαι.
ΒΔ. παρ' ἐμοῦ.
ΦΙ. καλῶς,
ὁτιὴ κατ' ἐμαυτὸν κοὐ μεθ' ἑτέρου λήψομαι.
αἴσχιστα γάρ τοί μ' εἰργάσατο Λυσίστρατος
ὁ σκωπτόλης. δραχμὴν μετ' ἐμοῦ πρώην λαβών,
ἐλθὼν διεκερματίζετ' ἐν τοῖς ἰχθύσιν,

---

^a εὐλόγως, "appropriately." A. is paving the way for a double
pun. "In fine weather ἡλιάσει (play the Heliast) πρὸς ἥλιον, in

484

THE WASPS, 764-789

BD. Well but if these are really your delights,
Yet why go *There*? why not remain at home
And sit and judge among your household here?
PH. Folly! judge what?
BD.   The same as There you do.
Suppose you catch your housemaid on the sly
Opening the door : fine her for that, one drachma.
That's what you did at every sitting There.
And very aptly,[a] if the morning's fine,
You'll fine your culprits, sitting in the sun.
In snow, enter your judgements by the fire
While it rains on : and—though you sleep till midday,
No archon here will close the door against you.
PH. Hah! I like that.
BD.   And then, however long
An orator proses on, no need to fast,
Worrying yourself (ay, and the prisoner too).
PH. But do you really think that I can judge
As well as now, whilst eating and digesting?
BD. As well? much better. When there's reckless
  swearing,
Don't people say, what time and thought and trouble
It took the judges to digest the case?
PH. I'm giving in. But you've not told me yet
How I'm to get my pay.
BD.   I'll pay you.
PH.   Good,
Then I shall have mine to myself, alone ;
For once Lysistratus, the funny fool,
Played me the scurviest trick. We'd got one drachma
Betwixt us two : he changed it at the fish-stall ;

---

wet weather εἴσει, which is really from εἴσομαι (*Pl.* 647) and is explained by the Scholiasts as δικάσεις, but upon which A. plays as if it were from εἴσειμι, ' you shall go indoors ' " : R.

ARISTOPHANES

κἄπειτ' ἐπέθηκε τρεῖς λοπίδας μοι κεστρέων·
κἀγὼ 'νέκαψ'· ὀβολοὺς γὰρ ᾠόμην λαβεῖν·
κᾆτα βδελυχθεὶς ὀσφρόμενος ἐξέπτυσα·
κᾆθ' εἷλκον αὐτόν.

ΒΔ.   ὁ δὲ τί πρὸς ταῦτ' εἶφ';
ΦΙ.   ὅ τι;
ἀλεκτρυόνος μ' ἔφασκε κοιλίαν ἔχειν·
" ταχὺ γοῦν καθέψεις τἀργύριον," ἦ δ' ὃς λέγων.
ΒΔ. ὁρᾷς ὅσον καὶ τοῦτο δῆτα κερδανεῖς;
ΦΙ. οὐ πάνυ τι μικρόν. ἀλλ' ὅπερ μέλλεις ποίει.
ΒΔ. ἀνάμενέ νυν· ἐγὼ δὲ ταῦθ' ἥξω φέρων.
ΦΙ. ὅρα τὸ χρῆμα· τὰ λόγι' ὡς περαίνεται.
ἠκηκόειν γὰρ ὡς Ἀθηναῖοί ποτε
δικάσοιεν ἐπὶ ταῖς οἰκίαισι τὰς δίκας,
κἀν τοῖς προθύροις ἀνοικοδομήσοι πᾶς ἀνὴρ
αὑτῷ δικαστηρίδιον μικρὸν πάνυ,
ὥσπερ Ἑκάταιον, πανταχοῦ πρὸ τῶν θυρῶν.
ΒΔ. ἰδού, τί ἔτ' ἐρεῖς; ὡς ἅπαντ' ἐγὼ φέρω
ὅσαπέρ γ' ἔφασκον, κἄτι πολλῷ πλείονα.
ἀμὶς μέν, ἢν οὐρητιάσῃς, αὑτηὶ
παρὰ σοὶ κρεμήσετ' ἐγγὺς ἐπὶ τοῦ παττάλου.
ΦΙ. σοφόν γε τουτὶ καὶ γέροντι πρόσφορον
ἐξεῦρες ἀτεχνῶς φάρμακον στραγγουρίας.
ΒΔ. καὶ πῦρ γε τουτί, καὶ προσέστηκεν φακῆ,
ῥοφεῖν ἐὰν δέῃ τι.
ΦΙ.   τοῦτ' αὖ δεξιόν·
κἂν γὰρ πυρέττω, τόν γε μισθὸν λήψομαι.
αὐτοῦ μένων γὰρ τὴν φακῆν ῥοφήσομαι.
ἀτὰρ τί τὸν ὄρνιν ὡς ἔμ' ἐξηνέγκατε;

THE WASPS, 790-815

    Then laid me down three mullet scales: and I,
    I thought them obols, popped them in my mouth [a];
    O the vile smell! O la! I spat them out
    And collared [b] him.
BD.   And what said he?
PH.   The rascal!
    He said I'd got the stomach of a cock.
    You'll soon digest hard coin, he says, says he.
BD. Then there again you'll get a great advantage.
PH. Ay, ay, that's something: let's begin at once.
BD. Then stop a moment whilst I fetch the traps.
PH. See here now, how the oracles come true.
    Oft have I heard it said that the Athenians
    One day would try their lawsuits in their homes,
    That each would have a little Courtlet built
    For his own use, in his own porch, before
    His entrance, like a shrine of Hecate.[c]
BD. (*Bustling in with a quantity of judicial properties*)
    Now then I hope you're satisfied: I've brought
    All that I promised, and a lot besides.
    See here I'll hang this vessel on a peg,
    In case you want it as the suit proceeds.
PH. Now that I call extremely kind and thoughtful,
    And wondrous handy for an old man's needs.
BD. And here's a fire, and gruel set beside it,
    All ready when you want it.
PH.   Good again.
    Now if I'm feverish I shan't lose my pay,
    For here I'll sit, and sip my gruel too.
    But why in the world have ye brought me out the
        cock?

    [a] For carrying money in the mouth *cf*. *B*. 503, *E*. 818.
    [b] εἷλκον = *in ius trahebam*.
    [c] Small images or shrines of Hecate set up before the doors that, as representing the Moon, she might guard them at night.

ARISTOPHANES

ΒΔ. ἵνα γ', ἢν καθεύδῃς ἀπολογουμένου τινός,
   ᾄδων ἄνωθεν ἐξεγείρῃ σ' οὑτοσί.
ΦΙ. ἐν ἔτι ποθῶ, τὰ δ' ἀλλ' ἀρέσκει μοι.
ΒΔ.   τὸ τί;
ΦΙ. θήρῶον εἴ πως ἐκκομίσαις τὸ τοῦ Λύκου.
ΒΔ. πάρεστι τουτί, καὐτὸς ἄναξ οὑτοσί. 82
ΦΙ. ὦ δέσποθ' ἥρως, ὡς χαλεπὸς ἄρ' ἦσθ' ἰδεῖν.
ΒΔ. οἷόσπερ ἡμῖν φαίνεται—Κλεώνυμος.
ΞΑ. οὔκουν ἔχει γ' οὐδ' αὐτὸς ἥρως ὧν ὅπλα.
ΒΔ. εἰ θᾶττον ἐκαθίζου σύ, θᾶττον ἂν δίκην
   ἐκάλουν.
ΦΙ.   κάλει νυν, ὡς κάθημαι 'γὼ πάλαι. 82
ΒΔ. φέρε νυν, τίν' αὐτῷ πρῶτον εἰσαγάγω δίκην;
   τί τίς κακὸν δέδρακε τῶν ἐν τῇ οἰκίᾳ;
   ἡ Θρᾷττα προσκαύσασα πρώην τὴν χύτραν
ΦΙ. ἐπίσχες οὗτος· ὡς ὀλίγου μ' ἀπώλεσας.
   ἄνευ δρυφάκτου τὴν δίκην μέλλεις καλεῖν, 83
   ὃ πρῶτον ἡμῖν τῶν ἱερῶν ἐφαίνετο;
ΒΔ. μὰ τὸν Δί' οὐ πάρεστιν.
ΦΙ.   ἀλλ' ἐγὼ δραμὼν
   αὐτὸς κομιοῦμαι τό γε παραυτίκ' ἔνδοθεν.
ΒΔ. τί ποτε τὸ χρῆμ'; ὡς δεινὸν ἡ φιλοχωρία.
ΞΑ. βάλλ' ἐς κόρακας. τοιουτονὶ τρέφειν κύνα. 83
ΒΔ. τί δ' ἔστιν ἐτεόν;
ΞΑ.   οὐ γὰρ ὁ Λάβης ἀρτίως
   ὁ κύων παράξας εἰς τὸν ἰπνὸν ἀναρπάσας
   τροφαλίδα τυροῦ Σικελικὴν κατεδήδοκεν;
ΒΔ. τοῦτ' ἄρα πρῶτον τἀδίκημα τῷ πατρὶ
   εἰσακτέον μοι· σὺ δὲ κατηγόρει παρών. 84

[a] *Cf.* 389. B. here produces a little image of him.
[b] A surprise; for C. was a notorious coward; *cf.* 19.
[c] φιλοχωρία describes the attachment to his old haunts which makes him run after "a railing" such as was used in the law

THE WASPS, 816-840

BD. To wake you, father, crowing over head
In case you're dozing whilst a prisoner pleads.
PH. One thing I miss, and only one.
BD. What's that?
PH. If you could somehow fetch the shrine of Lycus *a* !
BD. Here then it is, and here's the king in person.
PH. O hero lord, how stern you are to see !
BD. Almost, methinks, like our—Cleonymus.*b*
XA. Ay, and 'tis true the hero has no shield !
BD. If you got seated sooner, I should sooner
Call a suit on.
PH. Call on, I've sat for ages.
BD. Let's see : what matter shall I bring on first ?
Who's been at mischief of the household here ?
That careless Thratta now, she charred the pitcher.
PH. O stop, for goodness' sake ! you've all but killed me.
What ! call a suit on with no railing here,
Always the first of all our sacred things ?
BD. No more there is, by Zeus.
PH. I'll run myself
And forage out whatever comes to hand.
BD. Heyday ! where now ? The strange infatuation ! *c*
XA. Psha ! rot the dog ! To keep a cur like this !
BD. What's happened now ?
XA. Why, has not Labes *d* here
Got to the kitchen safe, and grabbed a cheese,
A rich Sicilian cheese, and bolted it ?
BD. Then that's the first indictment we'll bring on
Before my father : you shall prosecute.

courts to separate the dicasts from the general public. If the meaning is right, the "railing" is = *cancelli*, from which we derive "chancellor." While P. is gone a sudden scuffle takes place within and the voice of Xanthias is heard exclaiming at a dog.

d From λαμβάνω, like our " Grip " or " Pincher," and with a play on Laches (*cf.* 240).

489

ARISTOPHANES

ΞΑ. μὰ Δί' οὐκ ἔγωγ'· ἀλλ' ἅτερός φησιν Κύων[a]
κατηγορήσειν, ἥν τις εἰσάγῃ γραφήν.
ΒΔ. ἴθι νυν, ἄγ' αὐτὼ δεῦρο.
ΞΑ.   ταῦτα χρὴ ποιεῖν.
ΒΔ. τουτὶ τί ἐστι;
ΦΙ.   χοιροκομεῖον Ἑστίας.[b]
ΒΔ. εἶθ' ἱεροσυλήσας φέρεις;
ΦΙ.   οὔκ, ἀλλ' ἵνα   845
ἀφ' Ἑστίας ἀρχόμενος ἐπιτρίψω τινά.
ἀλλ' εἴσαγ' ἀνύσας· ὡς ἐγὼ τιμᾶν βλέπω.
ΒΔ. φέρε νυν, ἐνέγκω τὰς σανίδας καὶ τὰς γραφάς.
ΦΙ. οἴμοι, διατρίβεις κἀπολεῖς τριψημερῶν·
ἐγὼ δ' ἀλοκίζειν ἐδεόμην τὸ χωρίον.   850
ΒΔ. ἰδού.
ΦΙ.   κάλει νυν.
ΒΔ.   ταῦτα δή.
ΦΙ.   τίς οὑτοσὶ
ὁ πρῶτός ἐστιν;
ΒΔ.   ἐς κόρακας, ὡς ἄχθομαι,
ὁτιὴ 'πελαθόμην τοὺς καδίσκους ἐκφέρειν.
ΦΙ. οὗτος σὺ ποῖ θεῖς;
ΒΔ.   ἐπὶ καδίσκους.
ΦΙ.   μηδαμῶς.
ἐγὼ γὰρ εἶχον τούσδε τοὺς ἀρυστίχους.   855
ΒΔ. κάλλιστα τοίνυν· πάντα γὰρ πάρεστι νῷν
ὅσων δεόμεθα, πλήν γε δὴ τῆς κλεψύδρας.
ΦΙ. ἡδὶ δὲ δὴ τίς ἐστιν; οὐχὶ κλεψύδρα;
ΒΔ. εὖ γ' ἐκπορίζεις αὐτὰ κἀπιχωρίως.

---
[a] Κύων = Κλέων.
[b] That pigs might be kept within the precincts of the house is clear from *P*. 1106. How the fence which encloses them is specially connected with Ἑστία is not plain, but the name seems

THE WASPS, 841-859

XA. Thank you, not I. This other Cur ^a declares
    If there's a charge, he'll prosecute with pleasure.
BD. Bring them both here.
XA.   Yes, yes, sir, so I will.
BD. (*To Phil.*) Hallo, what's this?
PH.   Pig-railings from the hearth.
BD. Sacrilege, eh?
PH.   No, but I'd trounce some fellow
    (As the phrase goes) even from the very hearth.^b
    So call away : I'm keen for passing sentence.
BD. Then now I'll fetch the cause-lists and the pleadings.
PH. O these delays! You weary and wear me out.
    I've long been dying to commence my furrows.^c
BD. Now then!
PH.   Call on.
BD.   Yes, certainly.
PH.   And who
    Is first in order?
BD.   Dash it, what a bother!
    I quite forgot to bring the voting-urns.
PH. Goodness! where now?
BD.   After the urns.
PH.   Don't trouble,
    I'd thought of that. I've got these ladling-bowls.
BD. That's capital : then now methinks we have
    All that we want. No, there's no water-piece.
PH. Water-piece, quotha! pray what call you this? ^d
BD. Well thought on, father : and with shrewd home wit.

introduced because at festivals the first libation was poured and
the firstlings of the sacrifice were offered to Ἑστία. Hence the
phrase ἀφ' Ἑστίας ἄρχεσθαι came to mean " make a happy
beginning," and B. wishes to do this by " trouncing someone."
    ^c The condemning line on his πινάκιον, *cf.* 106 and Introd.
    ^d He points to the ἀμίς which his son had brought, 807, and
which is to take the place of the κλεψύδρα or water-clock by which
the orators spoke.

491

ARISTOPHANES

ἀλλ' ὡς τάχιστα πῦρ τις ἐξενεγκάτω 80
καὶ μυρρίνας καὶ τὸν λιβανωτὸν ἔνδοθεν,
ὅπως ἂν εὐξώμεσθα πρῶτα τοῖς θεοῖς.

ΧΟ. καὶ μὴν ἡμεῖς ἐπὶ ταῖς σπονδαῖς
καὶ ταῖς εὐχαῖς
φήμην ἀγαθὴν λέξομεν ὑμῖν, 86
ὅτι γενναίως ἐκ τοῦ πολέμου
καὶ τοῦ νείκους ξυνέβητον.
ΒΔ. εὐφημία μὲν πρῶτα νῦν ὑπαρχέτω. [στρ.
ΧΟ. ὦ Φοῖβ' Ἄπολλον Πύθι', ἐπ' ἀγαθῇ τύχῃ
τὸ πρᾶγμ' ὃ μηχανᾶται 87
ἔμπροσθεν οὗτος τῶν θυρῶν,
ἅπασιν ἡμῖν ἁρμόσαι
παυσαμένοις πλάνων.
Ἰήιε Παιάν.
ΒΔ. ὦ δέσποτ' ἄναξ, γεῖτον Ἀγυιεῦ τοὐμοῦ προθύρου
προπύλαιε, 87
δέξαι τελετὴν καινήν, ὦναξ, ἣν τῷ πατρὶ καινοτομοῦμεν·
παῦσόν τ' αὐτοῦ τοῦτο τὸ λίαν στρυφνὸν καὶ
πρίνινον ἦθος,
ἀντὶ σιραίου μέλιτος μικρὸν τῷ θυμιδίῳ παραμίξας·
ἤδη δ' εἶναι τοῖς ἀνθρώποις
ἤπιον αὐτόν,
τοὺς φεύγοντάς τ' ἐλεεῖν μᾶλλον 88
τῶν γραψαμένων
κἀπιδακρύειν ἀντιβολούντων,

---

[a] The obelisk in honour of Apollo which stood in the street (ἀγυιά) at the entrance.
[b] The difficulty is that σίραιον, a boiled down wine (*defrutum*),

THE WASPS, 860-882

Ho, there within! some person bring me out
A pan of coals, and frankincense, and myrtle,
That so our business may commence with prayer.

CH. We too, as ye offer the prayer and wine,
    We too will call on the Powers Divine
      To prosper the work begun ;
      For the battle is over and done,
    And out of the fray and the strife to-day
      Fair peace ye have nobly won.
BD. Now hush all idle words and sounds profane.
CH. O Pythian Phoebus, bright Apollo, deign
      To speed this youth's design
    Wrought here, these gates before,
    And give us from our wanderings rest
      And peace for evermore.
      (The shout of Io Paean is raised.)
BD. Aguieus [a]! my neighbour and hero and lord!
    who dwellest in front of my vestibule gate,
  I pray thee be graciously pleased to accept
      the rite that we new for my father create.
O bend to a pliant and flexible mood
      the stubborn and resolute oak of his will.
And into his heart, so crusty and tart,
      a trifle of honey for syrup [b] instil.
Endue him with sympathies wide,
    A sweet and humane disposition,
Which leans to the side of the wretch that is tried,
    And weeps at a culprit's petition.

is regularly described as "sweet." R. suggests that there is a play on θῡμίδιον "temper" and θῡμίδιον, the diminutive of θύμος, a herb much eaten by the Athenian poor (*Pl.* 253). "Mix," prays Bdelycleon, "honey with his temper, θῡμίδιον, as he is wont to mix mulled wine with his salad, θῡμίδιον."

ARISTOPHANES

καὶ παυσάμενον τῆς δυσκολίας
ἀπὸ τῆς ὀργῆς
τὴν ἀκαλήφην ἀφελέσθαι.
ΧΟ. ξυνευχόμεσθα [ταῦτά] σοι κἀπᾴδομεν   [ἀντ. 88
νέαισιν ἀρχαῖς, εἴνεκα τῶν προλελεγμένων.
εὖνοι γάρ ἐσμεν ἐξ οὗ
τὸν δῆμον ᾐσθόμεσθά σου
φιλοῦντος ὡς οὐδεὶς ἀνὴρ
τῶν γε νεωτέρων.   89
ΒΔ. εἴ τις θύρασιν ἡλιαστής, εἰσίτω·
ὡς ἡνίκ' ἂν λέγωσιν, οὐκ ἐσφρήσομεν.
ΦΙ. τίς ἆρ' ὁ φεύγων οὗτος; ὅσον ἁλώσεται.
ΒΔ. ἀκούετ' ἤδη τῆς γραφῆς. "ἐγράψατο
Κύων Κυδαθηναιεὺς Λάβητ' Αἰξωνέα,   89
τὸν τυρὸν ἀδικεῖν ὅτι μόνος κατήσθιεν
τὸν Σικελικόν. τίμημα κλῳὸς σύκινος."
ΦΙ. θάνατος μὲν οὖν κύνειος, ἢν ἅπαξ ἁλῷ.
ΒΔ. καὶ μὴν ὁ φεύγων οὑτοσὶ Λάβης πάρα.
ΦΙ. ὦ μιαρὸς οὗτος· ὡς δὲ καὶ κλέπτον βλέπει·   90
οἷον σεσηρὼς ἐξαπατήσειν μ' οἴεται.
ποῦ δ' οὖν ὁ διώκων, ὁ Κυδαθηναιεὺς Κύων;
ΚΥΩΝ. αὖ αὖ.
ΒΔ.   πάρεστιν.
ΞΑ.   ἕτερος οὗτος αὖ Λάβης,
ἀγαθός γ' ὑλακτεῖν καὶ διαλείχειν τὰς χύτρας.
ΒΔ. σίγα, κάθιζε, σὺ δ' ἀναβὰς κατηγόρει.   90
ΦΙ. φέρε νυν, ἅμα τήνδ' ἐγχεάμενος κἀγὼ ῥοφῶ.
ΞΑ. τῆς μὲν γραφῆς ἠκούσαθ' ἣν ἐγραψάμην,
ἄνδρες δικασταί, τουτονί. δεινότατα γὰρ

[a] After the solemn prayers, etc. (863 *seq.*) the judicial proceedings now commence, B. as the κῆρυξ or usher of the Court first making the customary proclamation.

THE WASPS, 883–908

    From harshness and anger to turn,
      May it now be his constant endeavour,
    And out of his temper the stern
      Sharp sting of the nettle to sever.
CH. We in thy prayers combine, and quite give in
    To the new rule, for the aforesaid reasons.
      Our heart has stood our friend
      And loved you, since we knew
      That you affect the people more
      Than other young men do.
BD. Is any Justice out there? let him enter.[a]
    We shan't admit him when they've once begun.
PH. Where is the prisoner fellow? won't he catch it!
BD. O yes! attention! (*Reads the indictment*)
                  Cur of Cydathon
*Hereby accuses Labes of Aexone,
For that, embezzling a Sicilian cheese,
Alone he ate it. Fine,[b] one fig-tree collar.*
PH. Nay, but a dog's death, an' he's once convicted.
BD. Here stands, to meet the charge, the prisoner Labes.
PH. O the vile wretch! O what a thievish look!
    See how he grins, and thinks to take me in.
    Where's the Accuser, Cur of Cydathon?
CUR. Bow!
BD.   Here he stands.
XA.   Another Labes this,
    Good dog to yelp and lick the platters clean.
BD. St! take your seat. (*To Cur*)
                        Go up and prosecute.
PH. Meanwhile I'll ladle out and sip my gruel.
XA.[c] Ye have heard the charge, most honourable judges,
    I bring against him. Scandalous the trick

      [b] The penalty proposed by the prosecutor.
      [c] Xanthias here speaks for Κύων (= Κλέων).

ARISTOPHANES

ἔργων δέδρακε κἀμὲ καὶ τὸ ῥυππαπαῖ.[a]
ἀποδρὰς γὰρ ἐς τὴν γωνίαν τυρὸν πολὺν
κατεσικέλιζε κἀνέπλητ' ἐν τῷ σκότῳ.

ΦΙ. νὴ τὸν Δί', ἀλλὰ δῆλός ἐστ'· ἔμοιγέ τοι
τυροῦ κάκιστον ἀρτίως ἐνήρυγεν
ὁ βδελυρὸς οὗτος.

ΞΑ. κοὐ μετέδωκ' αἰτοῦντί μοι.
καίτοι τίς ὑμᾶς εὖ ποιεῖν δυνήσεται,
ἢν μή τι κἀμοί τις προβάλλῃ τῷ κυνί;[b]

ΦΙ. οὐδὲν μετέδωκεν; οὐδὲ τῷ κοινῷ γ' ἐμοί.
θερμὸς γὰρ ἀνὴρ οὐδὲν ἧττον τῆς φακῆς.

ΒΔ. πρὸς τῶν θεῶν, μὴ προκαταγίγνωσκ', ὦ πάτερ,
πρὶν ἄν γ' ἀκούσῃς ἀμφοτέρων.

ΦΙ. ἀλλ', ὦγαθέ,
τὸ πρᾶγμα φανερόν ἐστιν· αὐτὸ γὰρ βοᾷ.

ΞΑ. μή νυν ἀφῆτέ γ' αὐτόν, ὡς ὄντ' αὖ πολὺ
κυνῶν ἁπάντων ἄνδρα μονοφαγίστατον,
ὅστις περιπλεύσας τὴν θυείαν ἐν κύκλῳ
ἐκ τῶν πόλεων τὸ σκῖρον ἐξεδήδοκεν.

ΦΙ. ἐμοὶ δέ γ' οὐκ ἔστ' οὐδὲ τὴν ὑδρίαν πλάσαι.

ΞΑ. πρὸς ταῦτα τοῦτον κολάσατ'· οὐ γὰρ ἄν ποτε
τρέφειν δύναιτ' ἂν μία λόχμη κλέπτα δύο·
ἵνα μὴ κεκλάγγω διὰ κενῆς ἄλλως ἐγώ·
ἐὰν δὲ μή, τὸ λοιπὸν οὐ κεκλάγξομαι.

ΦΙ. ἰοὺ ἰού.
ὅσας κατηγόρησε τὰς πανουργίας.
κλέπτον τὸ χρῆμα τἀνδρός· οὐ καὶ σοὶ δοκεῖ,
ὦλεκτρυόν; νὴ τὸν Δί', ἐπιμύει γέ τοι.

---

[a] τὸ ῥυππαπαῖ, the measured cry to which sailors rowed (cf. F. 1073): here put for the sailors themselves.
[b] Cf. K. 1017, where Cleon claims to be the " watch-dog " of

THE WASPS, 909-934

He played us all, me and the Sailor-laddies.[a]
Alone, in a corner, in the dark, he gorged,
And munched, and crunched, and Siliced the cheese!
PH. Pheugh! the thing's evident: the brute this instant
Breathed in my face the filthiest whiff of cheese.
O the foul skunk!
XA.   And would not give me any,
Not though I asked. Yet can *he* be your friend
Who won't throw anything to Me, the dog [b] ?
PH. Not give you any! No, nor Me, the state.
The man's a regular scorcher, (*burns his mouth*)
                                         like this gruel.
BD. Come don't decide against us, pray don't, father,
Before you've heard both sides.
PH.   But, my dear boy,
The thing's self-evident, speaks for itself.
XA. Don't let him off; upon my life he is
The most lone-eatingest dog that ever was.
The brute went coasting round and round the mortar,[c]
And snapped up all the rind off all the cities.
PH. And I've no mortar even to mend my pitcher!
XA. So then be sure you punish him. For why?
One bush, they say, can never keep two thieves.
Lest I should bark, and bark, and yet get nothing.
And if I do I'll never bark again.
PH. Soh! soh!
Here's a nice string of accusations truly!
A rare thief of a man! You think so too,
Old gamecock? Ay, he winks his eye, he thinks so.

the state. In the next line P. as a representative of the dicastery
claims to be the State itself.
  [c] Apparently here the pan in which the cheese was kept.
σκῖρον is some hard stuff from which cement could be made, and
also the rind of cheese. "In translating I have been obliged to
transfer the play on words from σκῖρον to θυεία": R.

ARISTOPHANES

ὁ θεσμοθέτης. ποῦ 'σθ' οὗτος; ἁμίδα μοι δότω.
ΒΔ. αὐτὸς καθελοῦ· τοὺς μάρτυρας γὰρ ἐσκαλῶ.
Λάβητι μάρτυρας παρεῖναι, τρύβλιον,
δοίδυκα, τυρόκνηστιν, ἐσχάραν, χύτραν,
καὶ τἄλλα τὰ σκεύη τὰ προσκεκαυμένα.
ἀλλ' ἔτι σύ γ' οὐρεῖς καὶ καθίζεις οὐδέπω;
ΦΙ. τοῦτον δέ γ' οἶμ' ἐγὼ χεσεῖσθαι τήμερον.
ΒΔ. οὐκ αὖ σὺ παύσει χαλεπὸς ὢν καὶ δύσκολος,
καὶ ταῦτα τοῖς φεύγουσιν, ἀλλ' ὀδὰξ ἔχει;
ἀνάβαιν', ἀπολογοῦ. τί σεσιώπηκας; λέγε.
ΦΙ. ἀλλ' οὐκ ἔχειν οὗτός γ' ἔοικεν ὅ τι λέγῃ.
ΒΔ. οὔκ, ἀλλ' ἐκεῖνό μοι δοκεῖ πεπονθέναι,
ὅπερ ποτὲ φεύγων ἔπαθε καὶ Θουκυδίδης·
ἀπόπληκτος ἐξαίφνης ἐγένετο τὰς γνάθους.
πάρεχ' ἐκποδών. ἐγὼ γὰρ ἀπολογήσομαι.
Χαλεπὸν μέν, ὦνδρες, ἐστὶ διαβεβλημένου
ὑπεραποκρίνεσθαι κυνός· λέξω δ' ὅμως.
ἀγαθὸς γάρ ἐστι καὶ διώκει τοὺς λύκους.
ΦΙ. κλέπτης μὲν οὖν οὗτός γε καὶ ξυνωμότης.
ΒΔ. μὰ Δί', ἀλλ' ἄριστός ἐστι τῶν νυνὶ κυνῶν,
οἷός τε πολλοῖς προβατίοις ἐφεστάναι.
ΦΙ. τί οὖν ὄφελος, τὸν τυρὸν εἰ κατεσθίει;
ΒΔ. ὅτι σοῦ προμάχεται καὶ φυλάττει τὴν θύραν
καὶ τἄλλ' ἄριστός ἐστιν· εἰ δ' ὑφείλετο,
ξύγγνωθι. κιθαρίζειν γὰρ οὐκ ἐπίσταται.
ΦΙ. ἐγὼ δ' ἐβουλόμην ἂν οὐδὲ γράμματα,
ἵνα μὴ κακουργῶν ἐνέγραφ' ἡμῖν τὸν λόγον.
ΒΔ. ἄκουσον ὦ δαιμόνιέ μου τῶν μαρτύρων.

---
[a] " Laches, a plain blunt man, and no orator as Cleon was, is so taken aback by the charges brought against him, that he has not a word to say ": R.   [b] Cf. A. 703.
[c] Apparently proverbial, for " he has never had much education " or the like.

THE WASPS, 935-962

Archon! Hi, fellow, hand me down the vessel.
BD. Reach it yourself; I'll call my witnesses.
The witnesses for Labes, please stand forward!
Pot, pestle, grater, brazier, water-jug,
And all the other scarred and charred utensils.
(*To Phil.*)
Good heavens, sir, finish there, and take your seat!
PH. I guess I'll finish *him* before I've done.
BD. What! always hard and pitiless, and that
To the prisoners, always keen to bite!
(*To Labes*)
Up, plead your cause: what, quite dumbfounded [a]?
speak.
PH. Seems he's got nothing in the world to say.
BD. Nay, 'tis a sudden seizure, such as once
Attacked Thucydides [b] when brought to trial.
'Tis tongue-paralysis that stops his jaws.
(*To Labes*)
Out of the way! I'll plead your cause myself.
O sirs, 'tis hard to argue for a dog
Assailed by slander: nevertheless, I'll try.
'Tis a good dog, and drives away the wolves.
PH. A thief I call him, and CONSPIRATOR.
BD. Nay, he's the best and worthiest dog alive,
Fit to take charge of any number o' sheep.
PH. What use in that, if he eat up the cheese?
BD. Use! why, he fights your battles, guards your door;
The best dog altogether. If he filched,
Yet O forgive: he never learnt the lyre.[c]
PH. I would to heaven he had never learned his letters,
Then he'd not given us all this tiresome speech.[d]
BD. Nay, nay, sir, hear my witnesses, I beg.

[d] The dog, says the Scholiast, is supposed to have " given his advocate a written speech."

ARISTOPHANES

ἀνάβηθι, τυρόκνηστι, καὶ λέξον μέγα·
σὺ γὰρ ταμιεύουσ' ἔτυχες. ἀπόκριναι σαφῶς,
εἰ μὴ κατέκνησας τοῖς στρατιώταις ἄλαβες.
φησὶ κατακνῆσαι.

ΦΙ. νὴ Δί', ἀλλὰ ψεύδεται.
ΒΔ. ὦ δαιμόνι', ἐλέει ταλαιπωρουμένους.
οὗτος γὰρ ὁ Λάβης καὶ τραχήλι' ἐσθίει
καὶ τὰς ἀκάνθας, κοὐδέποτ' ἐν ταὐτῷ μένει.
ὁ δ' ἕτερος οἷός ἐστιν οἰκουρὸς μόνον.
αὐτοῦ μένων γὰρ ἅττ' ἂν εἴσω τις φέρῃ,
τούτων μεταιτεῖ τὸ μέρος· εἰ δὲ μή, δάκνει.
ΦΙ. αἰβοῖ, τί κακόν ποτ' ἔσθ' ὅτῳ μαλάττομαι;
κακόν τι περιβαίνει με κἀναπείθομαι.
ΒΔ. ἴθ', ἀντιβολῶ σ', οἰκτείρατ' αὐτόν, ὦ πάτερ,
καὶ μὴ διαφθείρητε. ποῦ τὰ παιδία;
ἀναβαίνετ', ὦ πόνηρα, καὶ κνυζούμενα
αἰτεῖτε κἀντιβολεῖτε καὶ δακρύετε.
ΦΙ. κατάβα κατάβα κατάβα κατάβα.
ΒΔ. καταβήσομαι.
καίτοι τὸ κατάβα τοῦτο πολλοὺς δὴ πάνυ
ἐξηπάτηκεν. ἀτὰρ ὅμως καταβήσομαι.
ΦΙ. ἐς κόρακας. ὡς οὐκ ἀγαθόν ἐστι τὸ ῥοφεῖν.
ἐγὼ γὰρ ἀπεδάκρυσα νῦν, γνώμην ἐμήν,
οὐδέν ποτέ γ' ἀλλ' ἢ τῆς φακῆς ἐμπλήμενος.
ΒΔ. οὔκουν ἀποφεύγει δῆτα;
ΦΙ. χαλεπὸν εἰδέναι.
ΒΔ. ἴθ', ὦ πατρίδιον, ἐπὶ τὰ βελτίω τρέπου.
τηνδὶ λαβὼν τὴν ψῆφον ἐπὶ τὸν ὕστερον
μύσας παρᾷξον κἀπόλυσον, ὦ πάτερ.
ΦΙ. οὐ δῆτα· κιθαρίζειν γὰρ οὐκ ἐπίσταμαι.

---

[a] "The judges would say, *That will do, get down*: and the

THE WASPS, 963-989

Grater, get in the box, and speak well out.
You kept the mess ; I ask you, answer plainly,
Did you not grate the spoil between the soldiers ?
He says he did.
PH. Ay, but I vow he's lying.
BD. O sir, have pity upon poor toiling souls.
Our Labes here, he lives on odds and ends,
Bones, gristle : and is always on the go.
That other Cur is a mere stay-at-home,
Sits by the hearth, and when one brings aught in
Asks for a share : if he gets none, he bites.
PH. O me, what ails me that I grow so soft !
Some ill's afoot : I'm nearly giving in.
BD. O, I beseech you, father, show some pity,
Don't crush him quite. Where are his little cubs ?
Up, little wretches, up ; and whimpering there
Plead for your father : weep, implore, beseech.
PH. (*Deeply affected*) Get down, get down, get down, get down.
BD. I will.
Yet that " get down," I know, has taken in [a]
A many men. However I'll get down.
PH. Dash it ! this guzzling ain't the thing at all.
Here was I shedding tears, and seems to me
Only because I have gorged myself with gruel.
BD. Then will he not get off ?
PH. 'Tis hard to know.
BD. O take, dear father, take the kindlier turn.
Here, hold this vote : then with shut eyes dash by
To the Far Urn.[b] O father, do acquit him.
PH. No, no, my boy. I never learnt the lyre.[c]

prisoner would get down, expecting an acquittal and presently find himself condemned " : R.
[b] The one in which votes for acquittal were placed.
[c] *i.e.* " I know a judge's duty, and I know no more " : R. *Cf.* 959.

ΒΔ. φέρε νύν σε τῃδὶ τὴν ταχίστην περιάγω. 99
ΦΙ. ὅδ' ἔσθ' ὁ πρότερος;
ΒΔ. οὗτος.
ΦΙ. αὕτη 'ντευθενί.
ΒΔ. ἐξηπάτηται, κἀπολέλυκεν οὐχ ἑκών.
φέρ' ἐξεράσω.
ΦΙ. πῶς ἄρ' ἠγωνίσμεθα;
ΒΔ. δείξειν ἔοικεν· ἐκπέφευγας, ὦ Λάβης.
πάτερ πάτερ, τί πέπονθας;
ΦΙ. οἴμοι, ποῦ 'σθ' ὕδωρ; 99
ΒΔ. ἔπαιρε σαυτόν.
ΦΙ. εἰπέ νυν ἐκεῖνό μοι,
ὄντως ἀπέφυγε;
ΒΔ. νὴ Δί'·
ΦΙ. οὐδέν εἰμ' ἄρα.
ΒΔ. μὴ φροντίσῃς, ὦ δαιμόνι', ἀλλ' ἀνίστασο.
ΦΙ. πῶς οὖν ἐμαυτῷ τοῦτ' ἐγὼ ξυνείσομαι,
φεύγοντ' ἀπολύσας ἄνδρα; τί ποτε πείσομαι; 10
ἀλλ', ὦ πολυτίμητοι θεοί, ξύγγνωτέ μοι·
ἄκων γὰρ αὔτ' ἔδρασα κοὐ τοὐμοῦ τρόπου.
ΒΔ. καὶ μηδὲν ἀγανάκτει γ'. ἐγὼ γάρ σ', ὦ πάτερ,
θρέψω καλῶς, ἄγων μετ' ἐμαυτοῦ πανταχοῦ,
ἐπὶ δεῖπνον, εἰς ξυμπόσιον, ἐπὶ θεωρίαν, 10
ὥσθ' ἡδέως διάγειν σε τὸν λοιπὸν χρόνον·
κοὐκ ἐγχανεῖταί σ' ἐξαπατῶν Ὑπέρβολος.
ἀλλ' εἰσίωμεν.
ΦΙ. ταῦτα νῦν, εἴπερ δοκεῖ.
ΧΟ. ἀλλ' ἴτε χαίροντες ὅποι βούλεσθ'.

---

[a] The Chorus here dismiss the actors and address the audience in the Parabasis. This is here perfect in its seven parts as defined by Pollux (iv. 112)—(1) κομμάτιον a short prelude, 1009-

THE WASPS, 990–1009

BD. Here, let me lead you round the handiest way.
PH. Is this the Nearer?
BD.   This is.
PH.   In she goes.
BD. (*Aside*) Duped, as I live! acquits him by mistake!
(*Aloud*) I'll do the counting.
PH.   Well, how went the battle?
BD. We shall soon see. O Labes, you're acquitted!
Why, how now, father?
PH. (*Faintly*)   Water, give me water!
BD. Hold up, sir, do.
PH.   Just tell me only this,
Is he INDEED acquitted?
BD.   Yes.
PH.   I'm done for.
BD. Don't take it so to heart: stand up, sir, pray.
PH. How shall I bear this sin upon my soul?
A man acquitted! What awaits me now?
Yet, O great gods! I pray you pardon me,
Unwilled I did it, not from natural bent.
BD. And don't begrudge it; for I'll tend you well,
And take you, father, everywhere with me,
To feasts, to suppers, to the public games.
Henceforth in pleasure you shall spend your days,
And no Hyperbolus delude and mock you.
But go we in.
PH.   Yes, if you wish it, now.
CH.   Yea, go rejoicing your own good way,[a]
Wherever your path may be;

1014; (2) the Parabasis proper 1015-50, where the poet speaks in his own character, ending (3) with the Pnigos 1051-9 (so called because it was to be "sung without taking breath"). Then come (4) the στροφή 1060-70; (5) the ἐπίρρημα 1071-90; (6) ἀντίστροφος 1091-1101; and (7) ἀντεπίρρημα 1102-21, in which the Chorus explains its own character.

ARISTOPHANES

ὑμεῖς δὲ τέως, ὦ μυριάδες
ἀναρίθμητοι,
νῦν μὲν τὰ μέλλοντ' εὖ λέγε-
σθαι μὴ πέσῃ φαύλως χαμᾶζ'
εὐλαβεῖσθε.
τοῦτο γὰρ σκαιῶν θεατῶν
ἐστὶ πάσχειν, κοὐ πρὸς ὑμῶν.

νῦν αὖτε λεῷ πρόσχετε τὸν νοῦν, εἴπερ καθαρόν τι φιλεῖτε.
μέμψασθαι γὰρ τοῖσι θεαταῖς ὁ ποιητὴς νῦν ἐπιθυμεῖ.
ἀδικεῖσθαι γάρ φησιν πρότερος πόλλ' αὐτοὺς εὖ πεποιη-
κώς,
τὰ μὲν οὐ φανερῶς, ἀλλ' ἐπικουρῶν κρύβδην ἑτέροισι
ποιηταῖς,
μιμησάμενος τὴν Εὐρυκλέους μαντείαν καὶ διάνοιαν,
εἰς ἀλλοτρίας γαστέρας ἐνδὺς κωμῳδικὰ πολλὰ χέασθαι·
μετὰ τοῦτο δὲ καὶ φανερῶς ἤδη κινδυνεύων καθ' ἑαυτόν,
οὐκ ἀλλοτρίων, ἀλλ' οἰκείων Μουσῶν στόμαθ' ἡνιοχήσας.
ἀρθεὶς δὲ μέγας καὶ τιμηθεὶς ὡς οὐδεὶς πώποτ' ἐν ὑμῖν,
οὐκ ἐκτελέσαι φησὶν ἐπαρθεὶς οὐδ' ὀγκῶσαι τὸ φρόνημα,
οὐδὲ παλαίστρας περικωμάζειν πειρῶν· οὐδ' εἴ τις
ἐραστής,
κωμῳδεῖσθαι παιδίχ' ἑαυτοῦ μισῶν ἔσπευδε πρὸς αὐτόν,
οὐδενὶ πώποτέ φησι πιθέσθαι, γνώμην τιν' ἔχων ἐπιεικῆ,

---

[a] His early comedies, including the *Acharnians*, were exhibited in the name of Callistratus.

THE WASPS, 1010–1027

But you, ye numberless myriads, stay
    And listen the while to me.
Beware lest the truths I am going to say
    Unheeded to earth should fall ;
For that were the part of a fool to play,
    And not your part at all.

Now ALL ye people attend and hear,
    if ye love a simple and genuine strain,
For now our poet, with right good will,
    of you, spectators, must needs complain.
Ye have wronged him much, he protests, a bard
    who had served you often and well before ;
Partly, indeed, himself unseen,
    assisting others to please you more ; [a]
With the art of a Eurycles, weird and wild,
    he loved to dive in a stranger's breast,[b]
And pour from thence through a stranger's lips
    full many a sparkling comical jest ;
And partly at length in his own true form,
    as he challenged his fate by himself alone,
And the Muses whose bridled mouths he drave,
    were never another's, were all his own.
And thus he came to a height of fame
    which none had ever achieved before,
Yet waxed not high in his own conceit,
    nor ever an arrogant mind he bore.
He never was found in the exercise-ground,
    corrupting the boys : he never complied
With the suit of some dissolute knave, who loathed
    that the vigilant lash of the bard should chide
His vile effeminate boylove. No !
    he kept to his purpose pure and high,

[b] E. was an ἐγγαστρίμυθος or "ventriloquist."

ARISTOPHANES

ἵνα τὰς Μούσας αἷσιν χρῆται μὴ προαγωγοὺς ἀποφήνῃ.
οὐδ' ὅτε πρῶτόν γ' ἦρξε διδάσκειν, ἀνθρώποις φήσ' ἐπιθέσθαι,
ἀλλ' Ἡρακλέους ὀργήν τιν' ἔχων τοῖσι μεγίστοις ἐπιχειρεῖν,
θρασέως ξυστὰς εὐθὺς ἀπ' ἀρχῆς αὐτῷ τῷ καρχαρόδοντι,
οὗ δεινόταται μὲν ἀπ' ὀφθαλμῶν Κύννης ἀκτῖνες ἔλαμπον,
ἑκατὸν δὲ κύκλῳ κεφαλαὶ κολάκων οἰμωξομένων ἐλιχμῶντο
περὶ τὴν κεφαλήν, φωνὴν δ' εἶχεν χαράδρας ὄλεθρον τετοκυίας,
φώκης δ' ὀσμήν, Λαμίας δ' ὄρχεις ἀπλύτους, πρωκτὸν δὲ καμήλου.
τοιοῦτον ἰδὼν τέρας οὔ φησιν δείσας καταδωροδοκῆσαι,
ἀλλ' ὑπὲρ ὑμῶν ἔτι καὶ νυνὶ πολεμεῖ· φησίν τε μετ' αὐτοῦ
τοῖς ἠπιάλοις ἐπιχειρῆσαι πέρυσιν καὶ τοῖς πυρετοῖσιν,
οἳ τοὺς πατέρας τ' ἦγχον νύκτωρ καὶ τοὺς πάππους ἀπέπνιγον,
κατακλινόμενοί τ' ἐπὶ ταῖς κοίταις ἐπὶ τοῖσιν ἀπράγμοσιν ὑμῶν
ἀντωμοσίας καὶ προσκλήσεις καὶ μαρτυρίας συνεκόλλων,
ὥστ' ἀναπηδᾶν δειμαίνοντας πολλοὺς ὡς τὸν πολέμαρχον.
τοιόνδ' εὑρόντες ἀλεξίκακον, τῆς χώρας τῆσδε καθαρτήν,

[a] Lit. "began to teach" i.e. the Chorus supplied by the State, thus producing the play in his own name as κωμῳδοδιδάσκαλος, which he first did in the *Knights*.
[b] The epithet also applied to Cleon, *K.* 1017.
[c] A shameless prostitute.
[d] Lit. "heads"; the reference is to Typhoeus with his hundred snake-heads (κεφαλαὶ ὄφιος, Hes. *Theog.* 825).
[e] He refers to the attack on the Sophists made the year before in the *Clouds*. "As agues and fevers," says the Scholiast, "harm men's bodies, so do these men the city."

THE WASPS, 1028-1043

That never the Muse, whom he loved to use,
      the villainous trade of a bawd should ply.
When first he began to exhibit plays,[a]
      no paltry MEN for his mark he chose,
He came in the mood of a Heracles forth
      to grapple at once with the mightiest foes.
In the very front of his bold career
      with the jag-toothed [b] Monster he closed in fight,
Though out of its fierce eyes flashed and flamed
      the glare of Cynna's [c] detestable light,
And a hundred horrible sycophants' tongues [d]
      were twining and flickering over its head,
And a voice it had like the roar of a stream
      which has just brought forth destruction and dread,
And a Lamia's groin, and a camel's loin,
      and foul as the smell of a seal it smelt.
But He, when the monstrous form he saw,
      no bribe he took and no fear he felt,
For you he fought, and for you he fights :
      and then last year with adventurous hand
He grappled besides with the Spectral Shapes,
      the Agues and Fevers that plagued our land ; [e]
That loved in the darksome hours of night
      to throttle fathers, and grandsires choke,
That laid them down on their restless beds,
      and against your quiet and peaceable folk
Kept welding together proofs and writs
      and oath against oath, till many a man
Sprang up, distracted with wild affright,
      and off in haste to the Polemarch ran.[f]
Yet although such a champion [g] as this ye had found,
      to purge your land from sorrow and shame,

[f] *i.e.* for help ; *cf.* ὅσα τοῖς πολίταις ὁ ἄρχων, ταῦτα τοῖς μετοίκοις ὁ πολέμαρχος, Arist. *Pol. Ath.* 58.
[g] ἀλεξίκακος is a special epithet of Heracles ; *cf.* C. 1372.

ARISTOPHANES

πέρυσιν καταπρούδοτε καινοτάταις σπείραντ' αὐτὸν διανοίαις,
ἃς ὑπὸ τοῦ μὴ γνῶναι καθαρῶς ὑμεῖς ἐποιήσατ' ἀναλδεῖς· 10
καίτοι σπένδων πόλλ' ἐπὶ πολλοῖς ὄμνυσιν τὸν Διόνυσον
μὴ πώποτ' ἀμείνον' ἔπη τούτων κωμῳδικὰ μηδέν'
  ἀκοῦσαι.
τοῦτο μὲν οὖν ἔσθ' ὑμῖν αἰσχρὸν τοῖς μὴ γνοῦσιν παρα-
  χρῆμα,
ὁ δὲ ποιητὴς οὐδὲν χείρων παρὰ τοῖσι σοφοῖς νενόμισται,
εἰ παρελαύνων τοὺς ἀντιπάλους τὴν ἐπίνοιαν ξυνέτριψεν. 10

ἀλλὰ τὸ λοιπὸν τῶν ποιητῶν,
ὦ δαιμόνιοι, τοὺς ζητοῦντας
καινόν τι λέγειν κἀξευρίσκειν
στέργετε μᾶλλον καὶ θεραπεύετε,
καὶ τὰ νοήματα σώζεσθ' αὐτῶν·   1(
ἐσβάλλετέ τ' εἰς τὰς κιβωτοὺς
μετὰ τῶν μήλων.
κἂν ταῦτα ποιῆθ', ὑμῖν δι' ἔτους
τῶν ἱματίων
ὀζήσει δεξιότητος.

ὦ πάλαι ποτ' ὄντες ἡμεῖς ἄλκιμοι μὲν ἐν χοροῖς,   1(
  ἄλκιμοι δ' ἐν μάχαις,
καὶ κατ' αὐτὸ δὴ μόνον τοῦτ' ἄνδρες ἀλκιμώτατοι,
πρίν ποτ' ἦν, πρὶν ταῦτα· νῦν δ'
οἴχεται, κύκνου τέ γε πολιώτεραι δὴ
αἵδ' ἐπανθοῦσιν τρίχες.   1(

---

[a] *i.e.* when the *Clouds* was rejected.
[b] μήλων : " this is, I suppose, *citrons*, μῆλα Περσικά or Μηδικά
. . . commonly placed in wardrobes to preserve clothes from
moths and the like " : R.

THE WASPS, 1044-1065

Ye played him false when to reap, last year,
    the fruit of his novel designs he came,^a
Which, failing to see in their own true light,
    ye caused to fade and wither away.
And yet with many a deep libation,
    invoking Bacchus, he swears this day
That never a man, since the world began,
    has witnessed a cleverer comedy.
Yours is the shame that ye lacked the wit
    its infinite merit at first to see.
But none the less with the wise and skilled
    the bard his accustomed praise will get,
Though when he had distanced all his foes,
    his noble Play was at last upset.

  BUT O FOR the future, my Masters, pray
  Show more regard for a genuine Bard
  Who is ever inventing amusements new
  And fresh discoveries, all for you.
  Make much of his play, and store it away,
    And into your wardrobe throw it
  With the citrons ^b sweet : and if this you do,
  Your clothes will be fragrant, the whole year through,
    With the volatile wit of the Poet.

O OF OLD renowned and strong,
    in the choral dance and song,
  In the deadly battle throng,
And in this, our one distinction,
    manliest we, mankind among !
  Ah, but that was long ago :
  Those are days for ever past :
  Now my hairs are whitening fast,
  Whiter than the swan they grow.

ARISTOPHANES

ἀλλὰ κἀκ τῶν λειψάνων δεῖ
τῶνδε ῥώμην νεανικὴν σχεῖν·
ὡς ἐγὼ τοὐμὸν νομίζω
γῆρας εἶναι κρεῖττον ἢ πολλῶν κικίννους νεανιῶν καὶ
σχῆμα κεὐρυπρωκτίαν.

εἴ τις ὑμῶν, ὦ θεαταί, τὴν ἐμὴν ἰδὼν φύσιν
εἶτα θαυμάζει μ' ὁρῶν μέσον διεσφηκωμένον,
ἥτις ἡμῶν ἐστὶν ἡ 'πίνοια τῆς ἐγκεντρίδος,
ῥᾳδίως ἐγὼ διδάξω, "κἂν ἄμουσος ᾖ τὸ πρίν."
ἐσμὲν ἡμεῖς, οἷς πρόσεστι τοῦτο τοὐρροπύγιον,
Ἀττικοὶ μόνοι δικαίως ἐγγενεῖς αὐτόχθονες,
ἀνδρικώτατον γένος καὶ πλεῖστα τήνδε τὴν πόλιν
ὠφελῆσαν ἐν μάχαισιν, ἡνίκ' ἦλθ' ὁ βάρβαρος,
τῷ καπνῷ τύφων ἅπασαν τὴν πόλιν καὶ πυρπολῶν,
ἐξελεῖν ἡμῶν μενοινῶν πρὸς βίαν τἀνθρήνια.
εὐθέως γὰρ ἐκδραμόντες σὺν δόρει σὺν ἀσπίδι
ἐμαχόμεσθ' αὐτοῖσι, θυμὸν ὀξίνην πεπωκότες,
στὰς ἀνὴρ παρ' ἄνδρ', ὑπ' ὀργῆς τὴν χελύνην ἐσθίων·
ὑπὸ δὲ τῶν τοξευμάτων οὐκ ἦν ἰδεῖν τὸν οὐρανόν.

---

[a] The Chorus in what follows speak of themselves as veterans of the Persian war. But "in making them actually present at the battle of Marathon, 68 years before, . . . Aristophanes is treating them as types rather than individuals" : R.

[b] The Greek phrase is borrowed from the *Stheneboea* of Euripides, where it is Love that makes a man a poet "though he was not one before" ; *cf.* Plato, *Symp.* 196 E.

[c] Referring to the Spartan reply at Thermopylae when word was brought that the Persian arrows would "hide the sun"—"That is good news: we shall fight in the shade" ; *cf.* Herod. vii. 226.

THE WASPS, 1066-1084

Yet in these our embers low
        still some youthful fires must glow.
  Better far our old-world fashion,
    Better far our ancient truth,
  Than the curls and dissipation
    Of your modern youth.[a]

Do you wonder, O spectators,
        thus to see me spliced and braced,
Like a wasp in form and figure,
        tapering inwards at the waist?
Why I am so, what's the meaning
        of this sharp and pointed sting,
Easily I now will teach you,
        though you "knew not anything."[b]
We on whom this stern-appendage,
        this portentous tail is found,
Are the genuine old Autochthons,
        native children of the ground;
We the only true-born Attics,
        of the staunch heroic breed,
Many a time have fought for Athens,
        guarding her in hours of need;
When with smoke and fire and rapine
        forth the fierce Barbarian came,
Eager to destroy our wasps-nests,
        smothering all the town in flame,
Out at once we rushed to meet him:
        on with shield and spear we went,
Fought the memorable battle,
        primed with fiery hardiment;
Man to man we stood, and, grimly,
        gnawed for rage our under lips.
Hah! their arrows hail so densely,
        all the sun is in eclipse![c]

ARISTOPHANES

ἀλλ' ὅμως ἀπεωσάμεθα ξὺν θεοῖς πρὸς ἑσπέραν. 10
γλαῦξ γὰρ ἡμῶν πρὶν μάχεσθαι τὸν στρατὸν διέπτατο.
εἶτα δ' εἱπόμεσθα θυννάζοντες εἰς τοὺς θυλάκους,
οἱ δ' ἔφευγον τὰς γνάθους καὶ τὰς ὀφρῦς κεντούμενοι·
ὥστε παρὰ τοῖς βαρβάροισι πανταχοῦ καὶ νῦν ἔτι
μηδὲν Ἀττικοῦ καλεῖσθαι σφηκὸς ἀνδρικώτερον. 10

ἆρα δεινὸς ἦ τόθ' ὥστε πάντα μὴ δεδοικέναι,
καὶ κατεστρεψάμην
τοὺς ἐναντίους, πλέων ἐκεῖσε ταῖς τριήρεσιν.
οὐ γὰρ ἦν ἡμῖν ὅπως
ῥῆσιν εὖ λέξειν ἐμέλλομεν τότ', οὐδὲ 10
συκοφαντήσειν τινὰ
φροντίς, ἀλλ' ὅστις ἐρέτης ἔ-
σοιτ' ἄριστος. τοιγαροῦν πολλὰς πόλεις Μήδων ἑλόντες,
αἰτιώτατοι φέρεσθαι
τὸν φόρον δεῦρ' ἐσμέν, ὃν κλέ- 11
πτουσιν οἱ νεώτεροι.

πολλαχοῦ σκοποῦντες ἡμᾶς εἰς ἅπανθ' εὑρήσετε
τοὺς τρόπους καὶ τὴν δίαιταν σφηξὶν ἐμφερεστάτους.
πρῶτα μὲν γὰρ οὐδὲν ἡμῶν ζῷον ἠρεθισμένον

---

[a] The bird of Athene and the best of auguries for Athenians.
[b] The Epirrhema showed that the stinging wasp was no unfit emblem of the Chorus in their youth. "The Antepirrhema is designed to show that old and feeble as they have now become, there is yet much in their dicastic life and habits to remind the observer of that irritable and gregarious insect ": R.

THE WASPS, 1085-1104

Yet we drove their ranks before us,
  ere the fall of eventide:
As we closed, an owl ^a flew o'er us,
  and the Gods were on our side!
Stung in jaw, and cheek, and eyebrow,
  fearfully they took to flight,
We behind them, we harpooning
  at their slops with all our might :
So that in barbarian countries,
  even now the people call
Attic wasps the best, and bravest,
  yea, the manliest tribe of all!

MINE WAS then a life of glory,
  never craven fear came o'er me
  . Every foeman quailed before me
As across the merry waters,
  fast the eager galleys bore me.
'Twas not then our manhood's test,
Who can make a fine oration ?
Who is shrewd in litigation ?
It was, WHO CAN ROW THE BEST ?
Therefore did we batter down
  many a hostile Median town.
  And 'twas we who for the nation
  Gathered in the tribute pay,
  Which the younger generation
  Merely steal away.

You WILL find us very wasplike,^b
  if you scan us through and through,
In our general mode of living,
  and in all our habits too.
First, if any rash assailant dare provoke us, can there be

ARISTOPHANES

μᾶλλον ὀξύθυμόν ἐστιν οὐδὲ δυσκολώτερον·
εἶτα τἄλλ' ὅμοια πάντα σφηξὶ μηχανώμεθα.
ξυλλεγέντες γὰρ καθ' ἐσμούς, ὥσπερεὶ τἀνθρήνια,
οἱ μὲν ἡμῶν οὗπερ ἄρχων, οἱ δὲ παρὰ τοὺς ἕνδεκα,
οἱ δ' ἐν ᾠδείῳ δικάζουσ', οἱ δὲ πρὸς τοῖς τειχίοις,
ξυμβεβυσμένοι πυκνὸν νεύοντες εἰς τὴν γῆν, μόλις
ὥσπερ οἱ σκώληκες ἐν τοῖς κυττάροις κινούμενοι.
ἔς τε τὴν ἄλλην δίαιτάν ἐσμεν εὐπορώτατοι.
πάντα γὰρ κεντοῦμεν ἄνδρα κἀκπορίζομεν βίον.
ἀλλὰ γὰρ κηφῆνες ἡμῖν εἰσὶν ἐγκαθήμενοι,
οὐκ ἔχοντες κέντρον· οἳ μένοντες ἡμῶν τοῦ φόρου
τὸν γόνον κατεσθίουσιν, οὐ ταλαιπωρούμενοι.
τοῦτο δ' ἔστ' ἄλγιστον ἡμῖν, ἤν τις ἀστράτευτος ὢν
ἐκφορῇ τὸν μισθὸν ἡμῶν, τῆσδε τῆς χώρας ὕπερ
μήτε κώπην μήτε λόγχην μήτε φλύκταιναν λαβών.
ἀλλ' ἐμοὶ δοκεῖ τὸ λοιπὸν τῶν πολιτῶν ἐμβραχὺ
ὅστις ἂν μὴ 'χῃ τὸ κέντρον, μὴ φέρειν τριώβολον.

Φι. οὔ τοι ποτὲ ζῶν τοῦτον ἀποδυθήσομαι,

---

[a] The heads of the police. They seem to have had a special court-house called Παράβυστον. The various courts to which the dicasts might be summoned are mentioned to show how ubiquitous they were.

[b] Most explain as a reference to demagogues, but R. to men " who have never toiled or fought in the service of Athens " and ought therefore to be excluded from " dicastic pay and privileges."

[c] From here the play ceases to have a definite purpose. B. and P. re-enter, and the son tries to convert his father to the habits of " society " (to dress smartly, 1122-73, to talk fashionably, 1174-1207, and so on), with the result that Philocleon gets drunk and riotous, and the play ends as a mere farce so as to win the applause of the vulgar.

THE WASPS, 1105-1122

Any creature more vindictive,
     more irascible than we?
Then we manage all our business
     in a waspish sort of way,
Swarming in the Courts of Justice,
     gathering in from day to day,
Many where the Eleven [a] invite us,
     many where the Archon calls,
Many to the great Odeum, many to the city walls.
There we lay our heads together,
     densely packed, and stooping low,
Like the grubs within their cells, with
     movement tremulous and slow.
And for ways and means in general
     we're superlatively good,
Stinging every man about us,
     culling thence a livelihood.
Yet we've stingless drones [b] amongst us,
     idle knaves who sit them still,
Shrink from work, and toil, and labour,
     stop at home, and eat their fill,
Eat the golden tribute-honey
     our industrious care has wrought.
This is what extremely grieves us,
     that a man who never fought
Should contrive our fees to pilfer,
     one who for his native land
Never to this day had oar, or
     lance, or blister in his hand.
Therefore let us for the future
     pass a little short decree,
Whoso wears no sting shall never carry off the obols three.

PH. No! No! I'll never put this off alive.[c]

ἐπεὶ μόνος μ' ἔσωσε παρατεταγμένον,
ὅθ' ὁ βορέας ὁ μέγας ἐπεστρατεύσατο.
ΒΔ. ἀγαθὸν ἔοικας οὐδὲν ἐπιθυμεῖν παθεῖν.
ΦΙ. μὰ τὸν Δί', οὐ γὰρ οὐδαμῶς μοι ξύμφορον.
καὶ γὰρ πρότερον ἐπανθρακίδων ἐμπλήμενος
ἀπέδωκ' ὀφείλων τῷ γναφεῖ τριώβολον.
ΒΔ. ἀλλ' οὖν πεπειράσθω γ', ἐπειδήπερ γ' ἅπαξ
ἐμοὶ σεαυτὸν παραδέδωκας εὖ ποιεῖν.
ΦΙ. τί οὖν κελεύεις δρᾶν με;
ΒΔ. τὸν τρίβων' ἄφες·
τηνδὶ δὲ χλαῖναν ἀναβαλοῦ τριβωνικῶς.
ΦΙ. ἔπειτα παῖδας χρὴ φυτεύειν καὶ τρέφειν,
ὅθ' οὑτοσί με νῦν ἀποπνῖξαι βούλεται;
ΒΔ. ἔχ', ἀναβαλοῦ τηνδὶ λαβών, καὶ μὴ λάλει.
ΦΙ. τουτὶ τὸ κακὸν τί ἐστι πρὸς πάντων θεῶν;
ΒΔ. οἱ μὲν καλοῦσι Περσίδ', οἱ δὲ καυνάκην.
ΦΙ. ἐγὼ δὲ σισύραν ᾠόμην Θυμαιτίδα.
ΒΔ. κοὐ θαῦμά γ'· ἐς Σάρδεις γὰρ οὐκ ἐλήλυθας.
ἔγνως γὰρ ἄν· νῦν δ' οὐχὶ γιγνώσκεις.
ΦΙ. ἐγώ;
μὰ τὸν Δί' οὐ τοίνυν· ἀτὰρ δοκεῖ γέ μοι
ἐοικέναι μάλιστα Μορύχου σάγματι.
ΒΔ. οὔκ, ἀλλ' ἐν Ἐκβατάνοισι ταῦθ' ὑφαίνεται.
ΦΙ. ἐν Ἐκβατάνοισι γίγνεται κρόκης χόλιξ;
ΒΔ. πόθεν, ὦγάθ'; ἀλλὰ τοῦτο τοῖσι βαρβάροις
ὑφαίνεται πολλαῖς δαπάναις. αὕτη γέ τοι
ἐρίων τάλαντον καταπέπωκε ῥᾳδίως.
ΦΙ. οὔκουν ἐριώλην δῆτ' ἐχρῆν αὐτὴν καλεῖν
δικαιότερόν γ' ἢ καυνάκην;

---

[a] *i.e.* his mean unfashionable cloak (τριβών).
[b] A soft warm Persian robe of thick wool, with rough shaggy locks on one side, which in 1140 P. rudely compares to intestines.

THE WASPS, 1123-1149

With this [a] I was arrayed, and found my safety,
In the invasion of the great north wind.
BD. You seem unwilling to accept a good.
PH. 'Tis not expedient : no by Zeus it is not.
'Twas but the other day I gorged on sprats
And had to pay three obols to the fuller.
BD. Try it at all events : since once for all
Into my hands you have placed yourself for good.
PH. What would you have me do ?
BD.   Put off that cloak.
And wear this mantle in a cloak-like way.
PH. Should we beget and bring up children then,
When here my son is bent on smothering me ?
BD. Come, take and put it on, and don't keep chattering.
PH. Good heavens ! and what's this misery of a thing ?
BD. Some call it Persian, others Caunacès.[b]
PH. There ! and I thought it a Thymaetian [c] rug.
BD. No wonder : for you've never been to Sardis,
Else you'd have known it : now you don't.
PH.   Who ? I ?
No more I do by Zeus : it seemed to me
Most like an overwrap of Morychus.[d]
BD. Nay, in Ecbatana they weave this stuff.
PH. What ! have they wool-guts in Ecbatana ?
BD. Tut, man : they weave it in their foreign looms
At wondrous cost : this very article
Absorbed with ease a talent's weight of wool.
PH. Why, then, WOOL-GATHERER [e] were its proper name
Instead of Caunacès.

[c] Thymaetadae was an Attic deme on the coast; but nothing is known of these rugs.
[d] A voluptuary, cf. 506.
[e] ἐριώλη is " a hurricane " ; but P. invents a derivation from ἔριον and ὄλλυμι = " wool-destroyer."

ARISTOPHANES

ΒΔ. ἔχ', ὠγαθέ,
καὶ στῆθ' ἀναμπισχόμενος.
ΦΙ. οἴμοι δείλαιος·
ὡς θερμὸν ἡ μιαρά τί μου κατήρυγεν.
ΒΔ. οὐκ ἀναβαλεῖ;
ΦΙ. μὰ Δί' οὐκ ἔγωγ'. ἀλλ', ὠγαθέ,
εἴπερ γ' ἀνάγκη, κρίβανόν μ' ἀμπίσχετε.
ΒΔ. φέρ', ἀλλ' ἐγώ σε περιβαλῶ· σὺ δ' οὖν ἴθι.
ΦΙ. παράθου γε μέντοι καὶ κρεάγραν.
ΒΔ. τιὴ τί δή;
ΦΙ. ἵν' ἐξέλῃς με πρὶν διερρυηκέναι.
ΒΔ. ἄγε νυν, ὑπολύου τὰς καταράτους ἐμβάδας,
τασδὶ δ' ἀνύσας ὑπόδυθι τὰς Λακωνικάς.
ΦΙ. ἐγὼ γὰρ ἂν τλαίην ὑποδύσασθαί ποτε
ἐχθρῶν παρ' ἀνδρῶν δυσμενῆ καττύματα;
ΒΔ. ἔνθες πόδ', ὦ τᾶν, κἀπόβαιν' ἐρρωμένως
εἰς τὴν Λακωνικὴν ἀνύσας.
ΦΙ. ἀδικεῖς γέ με
εἰς γῆν πολεμίαν ἀποβιβάζων τὸν πόδα.
ΒΔ. φέρε καὶ τὸν ἕτερον.
ΦΙ. μηδαμῶς τοῦτόν γ', ἐπεὶ
πάνυ μισολάκων αὐτοῦ 'στιν εἷς τῶν δακτύλων.
ΒΔ. οὐκ ἔστι παρὰ ταῦτ' ἄλλα.
ΦΙ. κακοδαίμων ἐγώ,
ὅστις ἐπὶ γήρᾳ χίμετλον οὐδὲν λήψομαι.
ΒΔ. ἄνυσόν ποθ' ὑποδυσάμενος· εἶτα πλουσίως
ὡδὶ προβὰς τρυφερόν τι διασαλακώνισον.

---

[a] With which they struck into a cauldron or pot to bring up the meat ; cf. 1 Sam. ii. 14.

THE WASPS, 1149-1169

BD. Come, take it, take it,
Stand still and put it on.
PH. O dear, O dear,
O what a sultry puff the brute breathed o'er me!
BD. Quick, wrap it round you.
PH. No, I won't, that's flat.
You had better wrap me in a stove at once.
BD. Come then, I'll throw it round you.
    (*To the cloak*) You, begone.
PH. Do keep a flesh-hook *a* near.
BD. A flesh-hook! why?
PH. To pull me out before I melt away.
BD. Now off at once with those confounded shoes,
And on with these Laconians,*b* instantly.
PH. What I, my boy! I bring myself to wear
The hated foe's insufferable—cloutings!
BD. Come, sir, insert your foot, and step out firmly
In this Laconian.
PH. 'Tis too bad, it is,
To make a man set foot on hostile—leather.*c*
BD. Now for the other.
PH. O no, pray not that,
I've a toe there, a regular Lacon-hater.
BD. There is no way but this.
PH. O luckless I,
Why I shan't have, to bless my age, one—chilblain.
BD. Quick, father, get them on : and then move forward
Thus ; in an opulent swaggering sort of way.*d*

b Red shoes, fashionable, and of excellent quality.
c In 1162 ἐμβάδα is understood with Λακωνικήν, but P. supplies γῆν instead. "He speaks of the *soleam Laconicam* as if it were *solum Laconicum*": R.
d The Greek has a pun on Λάκων. "Wear your Λακωνικάς so as (not λακωνίζειν but) σαλακωνίζειν, to show yourself off with a fashionable strut": R.

ARISTOPHANES

ΦΙ. ἰδού. θεῶ τὸ σχῆμα, καὶ σκέψαι μ' ὅτῳ
μάλιστ' ἔοικα τὴν βάδισιν τῶν πλουσίων.
ΒΔ. ὅτῳ; δοθιῆνι σκόροδον ἠμφιεσμένῳ.
ΦΙ. καὶ μὴν προθυμοῦμαί γε σαυλοπρωκτιᾶν.
ΒΔ. ἄγε νυν, ἐπιστήσει λόγους σεμνοὺς λέγειν
ἀνδρῶν παρόντων πολυμαθῶν καὶ δεξιῶν;
ΦΙ. ἔγωγε.
ΒΔ.   τίνα δῆτ' ἂν λέγοις;
ΦΙ.   πολλοὺς πάνυ.
πρῶτον μὲν ὡς ἡ Λάμι' ἁλοῦσ' ἐπέρδετο,
ἔπειτα δ' ὡς ὁ Καρδοπίων τὴν μητέρα.
ΒΔ. μή μοί γε μύθους, ἀλλὰ τῶν ἀνθρωπίνων,
οἵους λέγομεν μάλιστα τοὺς κατ' οἰκίαν.
ΦΙ. ἐγᾦδα τοίνυν τῶν γε πάνυ κατ' οἰκίαν
ἐκεῖνον, ὡς "οὕτω ποτ' ἦν μῦς καὶ γαλῆ."
ΒΔ. ὦ σκαιὲ κἀπαίδευτε, Θεογένης ἔφη
τῷ κοπρολόγῳ, καὶ ταῦτα λοιδορούμενος,
μῦς καὶ γαλᾶς μέλλεις λέγειν ἐν ἀνδράσιν;
ΦΙ. ποίους τινὰς δὲ χρὴ λέγειν;
ΒΔ.   μεγαλοπρεπεῖς,
ὡς ξυνεθεώρεις Ἀνδροκλεῖ καὶ Κλεισθένει.
ΦΙ. ἐγὼ δὲ τεθεώρηκα πώποτ' οὐδαμοῦ
πλὴν ἐς Πάρον, καὶ ταῦτα δύ' ὀβολὼ φέρων.
ΒΔ. ἀλλ' οὖν λέγειν χρή σ' ὡς ἐμάχετό γ' αὐτίκα
Ἐφουδίων παγκράτιον Ἀσκώνδᾳ καλῶς,
ἤδη γέρων ὢν καὶ πολιός, ἔχων δέ τοι

---

[a] "The old man puffing himself out under his Persian robe is compared to a boil with a garlic plaster on it": R.

THE WASPS, 1170-1192

PH. Look then! observe my attitudes : think which
Of all your opulent friends I walk most like.
BD. Most like a pimple bandaged round with garlic.ᵃ
PH. Ay, ay, I warrant I've a mind for wriggling.
BD. Come, if you get with clever well-read men
Could you tell tales, good gentlemanly tales?
PH. Ay, that I could.
BD.   What sort of tales?
PH.   Why, lots,
As, first, how Lamia spluttered when they caught her,
And, next, Cardopion, how he swinged his mother.
BD. Pooh, pooh, no legends : give us something human,
Some what we call domestic incident.
PH. O, ay, I know a rare domestic tale,
How *once upon a time a cat and mouse*—
BD. *O fool and clown,* Theogenes replied
Rating the scavenger, what! would you tell
Tales of a cat and mouse, in company!ᵇ
PH. What, then?
BD.   Some stylish thing, as how you went
With Androcles and Cleisthenes, surveying.ᶜ
PH. Why, bless the boy, I never went surveying,
Save once to Paros, at two obols a day.ᵈ
BD. Still you must tell how splendidly, for instance,
Ephudion fought the pancratiastic fight
With young Ascondas : how the game old man

ᵇ B. apparently quotes to his father the rebuke addressed by T. to some dirty fellow who forgot where he was in telling a tale.
ᶜ θεωροί were men sent on special missions (*e.g.* to the Olympic games, *cf.* 1382) as representatives of the State. They went in great splendour and were usually men of distinction, so that A. and C., two noted rogues, are mentioned παρὰ προσδοκίαν.
ᵈ The regular pay of a common soldier. He had gone on a θεωρία only as one of the soldiers who formed an escort for the θεωροί.

521

ARISTOPHANES

πλευρὰν βαθυτάτην καὶ χέρας λαγόνας τε καὶ
θώρακ' ἄριστον.
ΦΙ. παῦε παῦ', οὐδὲν λέγεις.
πῶς ἂν μαχέσαιτο παγκράτιον θώρακ' ἔχων;
ΒΔ. οὕτω διηγεῖσθαι νομίζουσ' οἱ σοφοί.
ἀλλ' ἕτερον εἰπέ μοι· παρ' ἀνδράσι ξένοις
πίνων, σεαυτοῦ ποῖον ἂν λέξαι δοκεῖς
ἐπὶ νεότητος ἔργον ἀνδρικώτατον;
ΦΙ. ἐκεῖν' ἐκεῖν' ἀνδρειότατόν γε τῶν ἐμῶν,
ὅτ' Ἐργασίωνος τὰς χάρακας ὑφειλόμην.
ΒΔ. ἀπολεῖς με. ποίας χάρακας; ἀλλ' ὡς ἢ κάπρον
ἐδιώκαθές ποτ', ἢ λαγών, ἢ λαμπάδα
ἔδραμες, ἀνευρὼν ὅ τι νεανικώτατον.
ΦΙ. ἐγῷδα τοίνυν τό γε νεανικώτατον·
ὅτε τὸν δρομέα Φάϋλλον, ὢν βούπαις ἔτι,
εἷλον, διώκων λοιδορίας, ψήφοιν δυοῖν.
ΒΔ. παῦ'· ἀλλὰ δευρὶ κατακλινεὶς προσμάνθανε
ξυμποτικὸς εἶναι καὶ ξυνουσιαστικός.
ΦΙ. πῶς οὖν κατακλινῶ; φράζ' ἀνύσας.
ΒΔ. εὐσχημόνως.
ΦΙ. ὡδὶ κελεύεις κατακλιθῆναι,
ΒΔ. μηδαμῶς.
ΦΙ. πῶς δαί;
ΒΔ. τὰ γόνατ' ἔκτεινε, καὶ γυμναστικῶς
ὑγρὸν χύτλασον σεαυτὸν ἐν τοῖς στρώμασιν.
ἔπειτ' ἐπαίνεσόν τι τῶν χαλκωμάτων·
ὀροφὴν θέασαι, κρεκάδι' αὐλῆς θαύμασον·
ὕδωρ κατὰ χειρός· τὰς τραπέζας εἰσφέρειν·

---

[a] *i.e.* he is to talk like a "sportsman." In 1194 B. uses θώραξ ="breast," but P. understands it as "breastplate," whereas in the παγκράτιον (a form of wrestling and boxing) the combatants were unarmed.

THE WASPS, 1193–1216

    Though grey, had ample sides, strong hands, firm
      flanks,
    An iron chest.[a]
PH.   What humbug ! could a man
Fight the pancratium with an iron chest !
BD. This is the way our clever fellows talk.
But try another tack : suppose you sat
Drinking with strangers, what's the pluckiest feat,
Of all your young adventures, you could tell them ?
PH. My pluckiest feat ? O much my pluckiest, much,
Was when I stole away Ergasion's vine-poles.
BD. Tcha ! poles indeed ! Tell how you slew the boar,
Or coursed the hare, or ran the torch-race, tell
Your gayest, youthfullest act.
PH.   My youthfullest action ?
'Twas that I had, when quite a hobbledehoy,
With fleet Phaÿllus : and I caught him too :
Won by two—votes.[b] 'Twas for abuse, that action.
BD. No more of that : but lie down there, and learn
To be convivial and companionable.
PH. Yes ; how lie down ?
BD.   In an elegant graceful way.
PH. Like this, do you mean ?
BD.   No, not in the least like that.
PH. How then ?
BD.   Extend your knees, and let yourself
With practised ease subside along the cushions ;
Then praise some piece of plate : inspect the ceiling ;
Admire the woven hangings of the hall.
Ho ! water for our hands ! bring in the tables !

---

[b] B. had used νεανικός as = " high-spirited," and ἐδιώκαθες of literal " pursuit " ; but P. uses νεανικός = " in youth " and διώκειν as = " prosecute." Phaÿllus (cf. A. 215) was a noted runner, but at law P. had " caught " him.

ARISTOPHANES

δειπνοῦμεν· ἀπονενίμμεθ'· ἤδη σπένδομεν.
ΦΙ. πρὸς τῶν θεῶν, ἐνύπνιον ἑστιώμεθα;
ΒΔ. αὐλητρὶς ἐνεφύσησεν· οἱ δὲ συμπόται
εἰσὶν Θέωρος, Αἰσχίνης, Φανός, Κλέων,
ξένος τις ἕτερος πρὸς κεφαλῆς Ἀκέστορος.
τούτοις ξυνὼν τὰ σκόλι' ὅπως δέξει καλῶς.
ΦΙ. ἄληθες; ὡς οὐδεὶς Διακρίων δέξεται.
ΒΔ. ἐγὼ εἴσομαι· καὶ δὴ γάρ εἰμ' ἐγὼ Κλέων,
ᾄδω δὲ πρῶτος Ἁρμοδίου· δέξει δὲ σύ.
" οὐδεὶς πώποτ' ἀνὴρ ἔγεντ' Ἀθήναις "
ΦΙ. " οὐχ οὕτω γε πανοῦργος [ὡς σὺ] κλέπτης."
ΒΔ. τουτὶ σὺ δράσεις; παραπολεῖ βοώμενος·
φήσει γὰρ ἐξολεῖν σε καὶ διαφθερεῖν
καὶ τῆσδε τῆς γῆς ἐξελᾶν.
ΦΙ.   ἐγὼ δέ γε,
ἐὰν ἀπειλῇ, νὴ Δί' ἕτερον ᾄσομαι.
" ὤνθρωφ', οὗτος ὁ μαιόμενος τὸ μέγα κράτος,
ἀντρέψεις ἔτι τὰν πόλιν· ἁ δ' ἔχεται ῥοπᾶς."
ΒΔ. τί δ', ὅταν Θέωρος πρὸς ποδῶν κατακείμενος
ᾄδῃ Κλέωνος λαβόμενος τῆς δεξιᾶς,
" Ἀδμήτου λόγον, ὦταῖρε, μαθὼν τοὺς ἀγαθοὺς
φίλει."
τούτῳ τί λέξεις σκόλιον;
ΦΙ.   ᾠδικῶς ἐγώ,
" οὐκ ἔστιν ἀλωπεκίζειν,
οὐδ' ἀμφοτέροισι γίγνεσθαι φίλον."

---

[a] σκόλια were "catches" sung after dinner in turn, and each singer tried to link his own σκόλιον cleverly (cf. 1222) with the one before. Here in 1226 Cleon leads off with words which he expects to be "capped" with a compliment to himself only to

Dinner! the after-wash! now the libation.
PH. Good heavens! then is it in a dream we are feasting?
BD. The flute-girl has performed! our fellow-guests
Are Phanus, Aeschines, Theorus, Cleon,
Another stranger at Acestor's head.
Could you with these cap verses [a] properly?
PH. Could I? Ay, truly; no Diacrian [b] better.
BD. I'll put you to the proof. Suppose I'm Cleon.
I'll start the catch Harmodius.[c] You're to cap it.
  (*Singing*) " *Truly Athens never knew* "
PH. (*Singing*) " *Such a rascally thief as you.*"
BD. Will you do that? You'll perish in your noise.[d]
He'll swear he'll fell you, quell you, and expel you
Out of this realm.
PH.   Ay, truly, will he so?
And if he threaten, I've another strain.
  " *Mon, lustin' for power supreme, ye'll mak'*
  The city capseeze; she's noo on the shak'." [e]
BD. What if Theorus, lying at his feet,
Should grasp the hand of Cleon, and begin,
  " *From the story of Admetus learn, my friend, to love*
    the good." [f]
How will you take that on?
PH.   I, very neatly,
  " *It is not good the fox to play,*
  Nor to side with both in a false friend's way."

find the reverse. In 1239 the link seems very slight—φίλει and φίλον; so too in 1245—κἀμοί and κἀγώ.
[b] " The Highlanders—the poorest of the three parties into which Attica was divided in the days of Solon ": R. Why they are named here is obscure.
[c] *Cf. A.* 980.
[d] Many explain " being shouted down," *i.e.* by Cleon.
[e] Said by the Scholiast to be from Alcaeus.
[f] The Scholiast gives the second line as τῶν δειλῶν δ' ἀπέχου, γνοὺς ὅτι δειλῶν ὀλίγη χάρις.

ARISTOPHANES

ΒΔ. μετὰ τοῦτον Αἰσχίνης ὁ Σέλλου δέξεται,
ἀνὴρ σοφὸς καὶ μουσικός· κᾆτ' ᾄσεται·
"χρήματα καὶ βίαν
Κλειταγόρᾳ τε κἀ-
μοὶ μετὰ Θετταλῶν "
ΦΙ. "πολλὰ δὴ διεκόμπασας σὺ κἀγώ."
ΒΔ. τουτὶ μὲν ἐπιεικῶς σύ γ' ἐξεπίστασαι·
ὅπως δ' ἐπὶ δεῖπνον εἰς Φιλοκτήμονος ἴμεν.
παῖ παῖ, τὸ δεῖπνον, Χρυσέ, συσκεύαζε νῷν,
ἵνα καὶ μεθυσθῶμεν διὰ χρόνου.
ΦΙ. μηδαμῶς.
κακὸν τὸ πίνειν· ἀπὸ γὰρ οἴνου γίγνεται
καὶ θυροκοπῆσαι καὶ πατάξαι καὶ βαλεῖν,
κἄπειτ' ἀποτίνειν ἀργύριον ἐκ κραιπάλης.
ΒΔ. οὔκ, ἢν ξυνῇς γ' ἀνδράσι καλοῖς τε κἀγαθοῖς.
ἢ γὰρ παρῃτήσαντο τὸν πεπονθότα,
ἢ λόγον ἔλεξας αὐτὸς ἀστεῖόν τινα,
Αἰσωπικὸν γέλοιον ἢ Συβαριτικόν,
ὧν ἔμαθες ἐν τῷ συμποσίῳ· κᾆτ' ἐς γέλων
τὸ πρᾶγμ' ἔτρεψας, ὥστ' ἀφείς σ' ἀποίχεται.
ΦΙ. μαθητέον τἄρ' ἐστὶ πολλοὺς τῶν λόγων,
εἴπερ γ' ἀποτίσω μηδέν, ἤν τι δρῶ κακόν.
ἄγε νυν ἴωμεν· μηδὲν ἡμᾶς ἰσχέτω.

ΧΟ. πολλάκις δὴ 'δοξ' ἐμαυτῷ δεξιὸς πεφυκέναι,
καὶ σκαιὸς οὐδεπώποτε·
ἀλλ' Ἀμυνίας ὁ Σέλλου μᾶλλον οὑκ τῶν Κρωβύλου,

---

[a] The adjectives are ironical; cf. 349.
[b] "Nothing is known of the incident to which the lines refer": R.
[c] While the actors retire the Chorus indulge in a sort of second

THE WASPS, 1243-1267

BD. Next comes that son of Sellus, Aeschines,
　　Clever, accomplished [a] fellow, and he'll sing
　　" O the money, O the might,
　　How Cleitagora and I,
　　With the men of Thessaly "— [b]
PH. " How we boasted, you and I."
BD. Well, that will do : you're fairly up to that :
　　So come along : we'll dine at Philoctemon's.
　　Boy ! Chrysus ! pack our dinner up ; and now
　　For a rare drinking-bout at last.
PH. 　　　　　　　　　　　　　No, no,
　　Drinking ain't good : I know what comes of drinking,
　　Breaking of doors, assault, and battery,
　　And then, a headache and a fine to pay.
BD. Not if you drink with gentlemen, you know.
　　They'll go to the injured man, and beg you off,
　　Or you yourself will tell some merry tale,
　　A jest from Sybaris, or one of Aesop's,
　　Learned at the feast. And so the matter turns
　　Into a joke, and off he goes contented.
PH. O I'll learn plenty of those tales, if so
　　I can get off, whatever wrong I do.
　　Come, go we in : let nothing stop us now.[c]

CH. Often have I deemed myself
　　　　　　　　exceeding bright, acute, and clever,
　　　　Dull, obtuse, and awkward never.
　　　That is what Amynias is,
　　　　　　　　of Curling-borough,[d] Sellus' son ;

Parabasis. For Amynias, a fop noted for his long hair, cf. 466 ; C. 691. He had apparently come to poverty and was starving instead of dining with Leogoras, a well-known epicure and father of the orator Andocides.
　[d] For the κρώβυλος, an antique method of dressing the hair into some sort of topknot, cf. Thuc. i. 6.

527

ARISTOPHANES

οὗτος ὅν γ' ἐγώ ποτ' εἶδον ἀντὶ μήλου καὶ ῥοιᾶς
δειπνοῦντα μετὰ Λεωγόρου.
πεινῇ γὰρ ᾗπερ Ἀντιφῶν.
ἀλλὰ πρεσβεύων γὰρ ἐς Φάρσαλον ᾤχετ'· εἶτ' ἐκεῖ
μόνος μόνοις
τοῖς Πενέσταισι ξυνῆν τοῖς
Θετταλῶν, αὐτὸς πενέστης ὢν ἔλαττον οὐδενός.

ὦ μακάρι' Αὐτόμενες, ὥς σε μακαρίζομεν,
παῖδας ἐφύτευσας ὅτι χειροτεχνικωτάτους,
πρῶτα μὲν ἅπασι φίλον ἄνδρα τε σοφώτατον,
τὸν κιθαραοιδότατον, ᾧ χάρις ἐφέσπετο·
τὸν δ' ὑποκριτὴν ἕτερον, ἀργαλέον ὡς σοφόν·
εἶτ' Ἀριφράδην, πολύ τι θυμοσοφικώτατον,
ὅντινά ποτ' ὤμοσε μαθόντα παρὰ μηδενός,
ἀλλ' ἀπὸ σοφῆς φύσεος αὐτόματον ἐκμαθεῖν
γλωττοποιεῖν εἰς τὰ πορνεῖ' εἰσιόνθ' ἑκάστοτε.

εἰσί τινες οἵ μ' ἔλεγον ὡς καταδιηλλάγην,
ἡνίκα Κλέων μ' ὑπετάραττεν ἐπικείμενος
καί με κακίαις ἔκνισε· κᾆθ' ὅτ' ἀπεδειρόμην,
οὑκτὸς ἐγέλων μέγα κεκραγότα θεώμενοι,
οὐδὲν ἄρ' ἐμοῦ μέλον, ὅσον δὲ μόνον εἰδέναι
σκωμμάτιον εἴποτέ τι θλιβόμενος ἐκβαλῶ.

[a] "The villein race of Thessaly corresponding to the Helots of Laconia": R.
[b] His name was Arignotus, cf. K. 1278 where there is a similar attack on Ariphrades.
[c] "The general nature of the incident to which these lines refer is plain enough. Some attack had been made by Cleon upon A., who, finding that he did not receive from the people the support which he had expected, deemed it necessary to wriggle out of the scrape by patching up a hollow truce with his powerful opponent. Beyond this we are quite in the dark": R.

THE WASPS, 1268-1289

Him who now upon an apple
       and pomegranate dines, I saw
  At Leogoras's table
  Eat as hard as he was able,
  Goodness, what a hungry maw!
  Pinched and keen as Antiphon.
Once he travelled to Pharsalus, our ambassador to be,
  There a solitary guest, he
  Stayed with only the Penestae,[a]
Coming from the tribe himself,
       the kindred tribe, of Penury.

Fortunate Automenes, we envy your felicity;
Every son of yours is of an infinite dexterity:
First the Harper,[b] known to all, and loved of all excessively,
Grace and wit attend his steps, and elegant festivity,
Next the Actor, shrewd of wit beyond all credibility:
Last of all Ariphrades, that soul of ingenuity,
He who of his native wit, with rare originality,
Hit upon an undiscovered trick of bestiality:
All alone, the father tells us, striking out a novel line.

Some there are who said that I
       was reconciled in amity,
When upon me Cleon pressed,[c]
      and made me smart with injury,
Currying and tanning me:
      then as the stripes fell heavily
Th' outsiders laughed to see the sport,
      and hear me squalling lustily,
Caring not a whit for me, but only looking merrily,
To know if squeezed and pressed I chanced
       to drop some small buffoonery.

ARISTOPHANES

ταῦτα κατιδὼν ὑπό τι μικρὸν ἐπιθήκισα·
εἶτα νῦν ἐξηπάτησεν ἡ χάραξ τὴν ἄμπελον.

ΞΑ. ἰὼ χελῶναι μακάριαι τοῦ δέρματος,
καὶ τρισμακάριαι τοῦ 'πὶ ταῖς πλευραῖς τέγους.
ὡς εὖ κατηρέψασθε καὶ νουβυστικῶς
κεράμῳ τὸ νῶτον ὥστε τὰς πλευρὰς στέγειν.
ἐγὼ δ' ἀπόλωλα στιζόμενος βακτηρίᾳ.

ΧΟ. τί δ' ἔστιν, ὦ παῖ; παῖδα γάρ, κἂν ᾖ γέρων,
καλεῖν δίκαιον ὅστις ἂν πληγὰς λάβῃ.

ΞΑ. οὐ γὰρ ὁ γέρων ἀτηρότατον ἄρ' ἦν κακὸν
καὶ τῶν ξυνόντων πολὺ παροινικώτατος;
καίτοι παρῆν Ἵππυλλος, Ἀντιφῶν, Λύκων,
Λυσίστρατος, Θούφραστος, οἱ περὶ Φρύνιχον.
τούτων ἁπάντων ἦν ὑβριστότατος μακρῷ.
εὐθὺς γὰρ ὡς ἐνέπλητο πολλῶν κἀγαθῶν,
ἐνήλατ', ἐσκίρτα, πεπόρδει, κατεγέλα,
ὥσπερ καχρύων ὀνίδιον εὐωχημένον·
κἄτυπτε δή με νεανικῶς, παῖ παῖ καλῶν.
εἶτ' αὐτὸν ὡς εἶδ', ᾔκασεν Λυσίστρατος·
ἔοικας, ὦ πρεσβῦτα, νεοπλούτῳ τρυγὶ
κλητῆρί τ' εἰς ἀχυρῶνας ἀποδεδρακότι.
ὁ δ' ἀνακραγὼν ἀντῄκασ' αὐτὸν πάρνοπι
τὰ θρῖα τοῦ τρίβωνος ἀποβεβληκότι,
Σθενέλῳ τε τὰ σκευάρια διακεκαρμένῳ.
οἱ δ' ἀνεκρότησαν, πλήν γε Θουφράστου μόνου·
οὗτος δὲ διεμύλλαινεν, ὡς δὴ δεξιός.

[a] "A proverb used in reference to persons who find the support whereon they trusted giving way in the hour of need" : R. Here probably Aristophanes is the Vine, the people the Vine-pole.

530

THE WASPS, 1290-1315

Seeing this, I played the ape a little bit undoubtedly.
So then, after all, the Vine-pole
           proved unfaithful to the Vine.[a]

XA. O lucky tortoises, to have such skins,
Thrice lucky for the case upon your ribs :
How well and cunningly your backs are roofed
With tiling strong enough to keep out blows :
Whilst I, I'm cudgelled and tattooed to death.
CH. How now, my boy ? for though a man be old,
Still, if he's beaten, we may call him boy.
XA. Was not the old man the most outrageous nuisance,
Much the most drunk and riotous of all ?
And yet we'd Lycon, Antiphon, Hippyllus,
Lysistratus, Theophrastus, Phrynichus ;
But he was far the noisiest of the lot.
Soon as he'd gorged his fill of the good cheer,
He skipped, he leapt, and laughed, and frisked, and whinnied,
Just like a donkey on a feed of corn :
And slapped me youthfully, calling *Boy ! Boy !*
So then Lysistratus compared him thus :
Old man, says he, *you're like new wine fermenting,
Or like a sompnour, scampering to its bran.*[b]
But he shrieked back, *And you, you're like a locust
That has just shed the lappets of its cloak,
Or Sthenelus, shorn of his goods and chattels.*[c]
At this all clapped, save Theophrast ; but he
Made a wry face, being forsooth a wit.

[b] There was a proverb ὄνος εἰς ἀχυρῶνα ἀπέδρα and the phrase describes excitement. But the connexion with κλητήρ, " a summoner," is absent, unless " in Athenian slang a donkey was sometimes termed κλητήρ, caller " (R.) ; *cf.* 189.
[c] The similes are aimed at his shabby, threadbare appearance. Sthenelus was a tragic actor who had been reduced to poverty.

ARISTOPHANES

ὁ γέρων δὲ τὸν Θούφραστον ἤρετ', εἰπέ μοι,
ἐπὶ τῷ κομᾷς καὶ κομψὸς εἶναι προσποιεῖ,
κωμῳδολοιχῶν περὶ τὸν εὖ πράττοντ' ἀεί;
τοιαῦτα περιύβριζεν αὐτοὺς ἐν μέρει,
σκώπτων ἀγροίκως καὶ προσέτι λόγους λέγων 13
ἀμαθέστατ', οὐδὲν εἰκότας τῷ πράγματι.
ἔπειτ' ἐπειδὴ 'μέθυεν, οἴκαδ' ἔρχεται
τύπτων ἅπαντας, ἤν τις αὐτῷ ξυντύχῃ.
ὁδὶ δὲ δὴ καὶ σφαλλόμενος προσέρχεται.
ἀλλ' ἐκποδὼν ἄπειμι πρὶν πληγὰς λαβεῖν.   13

ΦΙ.   ἄνεχε, πάρεχε·
      κλαύσεταί τις τῶν ὄπισθεν
      ἐπακολουθούντων ἐμοί·
      οἷον, εἰ μὴ 'ρρήσεθ', ὑμᾶς,
      ὦ πόνηροι, ταυτηῒ τῇ   13
      δᾳδὶ φρυκτοὺς σκευάσω.

ΣΥΜΠΟΤΗΣ. ἦ μὴν σὺ δώσεις αὔριον τούτων δίκην
      ἡμῖν ἅπασι, κεἰ σφόδρ' εἶ νεανίας.
      ἀθρόοι γὰρ ἥξομέν σε προσκαλούμενοι.

ΦΙ.   ἰὴ ἰεῦ, καλούμενοι.   13
      ἀρχαῖά γ' ὑμῶν· ἆρά γ' ἴσθ'
      ὡς οὐδ' ἀκούων ἀνέχομαι
      δικῶν; ἰαιβοῖ αἰβοῖ.
      τάδε μ' ἀρέσκει· βάλλε κημούς.
      οὐκ ἄπεισι; ποῦ 'στιν   13
      ἡλιαστής; ἐκποδών.

---

[a] P. enters carrying a torch. ἄνεχε, πάρεχε are perhaps cries addressed to runners in the torch-races of the Cerameicus—" hold it up, hand it on."

[b] " The next 35 lines contain much that had been better

532

THE WASPS, 1316-1341

And pray, the old man asked him, *what makes you
Give yourself airs, and think yourself so grand,
You grinning flatterer of the well-to-do?*
Thus he kept bantering every guest in turn,
Making rude jokes, and telling idle tales,
In clownish fashion, relevant to nothing.
At last, well drunk, homeward he turns once more,
Aiming a blow at every one he meets.
Ah! here he's coming; stumbling, staggering on.
Methinks I'll vanish ere I'm slapped again.

PH.   Up ahoy! out ahoy![a]
    Some of you that follow me
      Shall ere long be crying.
    If they don't shog off, I swear
    I'll frizzle 'em all with the torch I bear,
      I'll set the rogues a-frying

GUEST. Zounds! we'll all make you pay for this to-morrow,
You vile old rake, however young you are!
We'll come and cite and summon you all together.

PH.   Yah! hah! summon and cite![b]
    The obsolete notion! don't you know
    I'm sick of the names of your suits and claims.
      Faugh! Faugh! Pheugh!
      Here's my delight!
    Away with the verdict-box! Won't he go?
    Where's the Heliast? out of my sight!

omitted: and the English is in many places necessarily a substitution for, rather than a translation of, the original text. These drunken scenes, and indeed the entire 200 lines from 1250 to 1449, were, in my opinion, a mere afterthought on the part of the poet, introduced when the defeat of the *Clouds* had taught him that he could not with impunity discard the broad farce, the coarse buffoonery, of other comedians": R.

ARISTOPHANES

ἀνάβαινε δεῦρο χρυσομηλολόνθιον,
τῇ χειρὶ τουδὶ λαβομένη τοῦ σχοινίου.
ἔχου· φυλάττου δ', ὡς σαπρὸν τὸ σχοινίον·
ὅμως γε μέντοι τριβόμενον οὐκ ἄχθεται.
ὁρᾷς ἐγώ σ' ὡς δεξιῶς ὑφειλόμην
μέλλουσαν ἤδη λεσβιεῖν τοὺς ξυμπότας·
ὧν εὕνεκ' ἀπόδος τῷ πέει τῳδὶ χάριν.
ἀλλ' οὐκ ἀποδώσεις οὐδ' ἐφιαλεῖς, οἶδ' ὅτι,
ἀλλ' ἐξαπατήσεις κἀγχανεῖ τούτῳ μέγα·
πολλοῖς γὰρ ἤδη χἀτέροις αὕτ' εἰργάσω.
ἐὰν γένῃ δὲ μὴ κακὴ νυνὶ γυνή,
ἐγώ σ', ἐπειδὰν οὑμὸς υἱὸς ἀποθάνῃ,
λυσάμενος ἕξω παλλακήν, ὦ χοιρίον.
νῦν δ' οὐ κρατῶ 'γὼ τῶν ἐμαυτοῦ χρημάτων.
νέος γάρ εἰμι καὶ φυλάττομαι σφόδρα.
τὸ γὰρ υἵδιον τηρεῖ με, κἄστι δύσκολον
κἄλλως κυμινοπριστοκαρδαμογλύφον.
ταῦτ' οὖν περί μου δέδοικε μὴ διαφθαρῶ.
πατὴρ γὰρ οὐδείς ἐστιν αὐτῷ πλὴν ἐμοῦ.
ὁδὶ δε καὐτός· ἐπὶ σὲ κἄμ' ἔοικε θεῖν.
ἀλλ' ὡς τάχιστα στῆθι τάσδε τὰς δετὰς
λαβοῦσ', ἵν' αὐτὸν τωθάσω νεανικῶς,
οἵως ποθ' οὗτος ἐμὲ πρὸ τῶν μυστηρίων.

ΒΔ. ὦ οὗτος οὗτος, τυφεδανὲ καὶ χοιρόθλιψ,
ποθεῖν ἐρᾶν τ' ἔοικας ὡραίας σοροῦ.
οὔ τοι καταπροίξει μὰ τὸν Ἀπόλλω τοῦτο δρῶν.

ΦΙ. ὡς ἡδέως φάγοις ἂν ἐξ ὄξους δίκην.

ΒΔ. οὐ δεινὰ τωθάζειν σε, τὴν αὐλητρίδα
τῶν ξυμποτῶν κλέψαντα;

THE WASPS, 1341-1369

My little golden chafer, come up here,
Hold by this rope,[a] a rotten one perchance,
But strong enough for you. Mount up, my dear.
See now, how cleverly I filched you off,
A wanton hussy, flirting with the guests.
You owe me, child, some gratitude for that.
But you're not one to pay your debts, I know.
O no! you'll laugh and chaff and slip away,
That's what you always do. But listen now,
Be a good girl, and don't be disobliging,
And when my son is dead, I'll ransom you,
And make you an honest woman. For indeed
I'm not yet master of my own affairs.
I am so young, and kept so very strict.
My son's my guardian, such a cross-grained man,
A cummin-splitting, mustard-scraping fellow.
He's so afraid that I should turn out badly,
For I'm in truth his only father now.[b]
But here he runs. Belike he's after us.
Quick, little lady, hold these links an instant;
And won't I quiz him boyishly and well,
As he did me before the initiation.[c]

BD. You there! you there! you old lascivious dotard!
Enamoured, eh? ay of a fine ripe coffin.[d]
Oh, by Apollo, you shall smart for this!
PH. Dear, dear, how keen to taste a suit in pickle!
BD. No quizzing, sir, when you have filched away
The flute-girl from our party.

[a] "Undoubtedly the σκύτινον καθειμένον described in *Clouds* 538, 539:" R.
[b] "A piece of pleasantry, for sons often say 'I am my father's only son'": Schol.
[c] *i.e.* my initiation into the mysteries of high life.
[d] σόρου is put unexpectedly for κόρης—*maturum funus* instead of *matura virgo*.

ARISTOPHANES

ΦΙ. ποίαν αὐλητρίδα;
τί ταῦτα ληρεῖς, ὥσπερ ἀπὸ τύμβου πεσών; 13
ΒΔ. νὴ τὸν Δί', αὕτη πού 'στί σοί γ' ἡ Δαρδανίς.
ΦΙ. οὔκ, ἀλλ' ἐν ἀγορᾷ τοῖς θεοῖς δᾷς κάεται.
ΒΔ. δᾷς ἥδε;
ΦΙ. δᾷς δῆτ'. οὐχ ὁρᾷς ἐστιγμένην;
ΒΔ. τί δὲ τὸ μέλαν τοῦτ' ἐστὶν αὐτῆς τοὐν μέσῳ;
ΦΙ. ἡ πίττα δήπου καομένης ἐξέρχεται. 13
ΒΔ. ὁ δ' ὄπισθεν οὐχὶ πρωκτός ἐστιν οὑτοσί;
ΦΙ. ὄζος μὲν οὖν τῆς δᾳδὸς οὗτος ἐξέχει.
ΒΔ. τί λέγεις σύ; ποῖος ὄζος; οὐκ εἶ δεῦρο σύ;
ΦΙ. ἆ ἆ, τί μέλλεις δρᾶν;
ΒΔ. ἄγειν ταύτην λαβὼν
ἀφελόμενός σε καὶ νομίσας εἶναι σαπρὸν 13ξ
κοὐδὲν δύνασθαι δρᾶν.
ΦΙ. ἄκουσόν νυν ἐμοῦ.
Ὀλυμπίασιν ἡνίκ' ἐθεώρουν ἐγώ,
Ἐφουδίων ἐμαχέσατ' Ἀσκώνδᾳ καλῶς,
ἤδη γέρων ὤν· εἶτα τῇ πυγμῇ θενὼν
ὁ πρεσβύτερος κατέβαλε τὸν νεώτερον. 13ξ
πρὸς ταῦτα τηροῦ μὴ λάβῃς ὑπώπια.
ΒΔ. νὴ τὸν Δί' ἐξέμαθές γε τὴν Ὀλυμπίαν.

ΑΡΤΟΠΩΛΙΣ. ἴθι μοι παράστηθ', ἀντιβολῶ πρὸς τῶν θεῶν.
ὁδὶ γὰρ ἀνήρ ἐστιν ὅς μ' ἀπώλεσεν
τῇ δᾳδὶ παίων, κἀξέβαλεν ἐντευθενὶ 13ξ
ἄρτους δέκ' ὀβολῶν κἀπιθήκην τέτταρας.
ΒΔ. ὁρᾷς ἃ δέδρακας; πράγματ' αὖ δεῖ καὶ δίκας
ἔχειν διὰ τὸν σὸν οἶνον.

---

[a] P. now treats his son as a half-dead dotard, and seems to invent this phrase on the analogy of ἀπ' ὄνου πεσών, cf. C. 1273.

[b] "This"=Dardanis. Torches, says the Scholiast, were

THE WASPS, 1369-1393

PH.   Eh ? what ? flute-girl ?
You're out of your mind, or out of your grave,[a] or
    something.
BD. Why, bless the fool, here's Dardanis beside you!
PH. What, this ? why, *this*[b] is a torch in the market-place!
BD. A torch, man ?
PH.   Clearly ; pray observe the punctures.
BD. Then what's this black here, on the top of her head ?
PH. Oh, that's the rosin, oozing while it burns.
BD. Then this of course is not a woman's arm ?
PH. Of course not ; that's a sprouting of the pine.
BD. Sprouting be hanged.
            (*To Dard.*) You come along with me.
PH. Hi ! hi ! what are you at ?
BD.   Marching her off
Out of your reach ; a rotten, as I think,
And impotent old man.
PH.   Now look ye here :
Once, when surveying at the Olympian games,
I saw how splendidly Ephudion fought
With young Ascondas : saw the game old man
Up with his fist, and knock the youngster down.
So mind your eye, or you'll be pummelled too.
BD. Troth, you have learned Olympia to some purpose.

BAKING-GIRL. Oh, there he is ! Oh, pray stand by me
    now !
There's the old rascal who misused me so,
Banged with his torch, and toppled down from here
Bread worth ten obols, and four loaves to boot.
BD. There now, you see ; troubles and suits once more
Your wine will bring us.

punctured and tattooed with figures, and Dardanis is compared
with one to introduce some coarse jokes.

ARISTOPHANES

ΦΙ. οὐδαμῶς γ', ἐπεὶ
λόγοι διαλλάξουσιν αὐτὰ δεξιοί·
ὥστ' οἶδ' ὁτιὴ ταύτῃ διαλλαχθήσομαι. 13
ΑΡ. οὔ τοι μὰ τὼ θεὼ καταπροίξει Μυρτίας
τῆς Ἀγκυλίωνος θυγατέρος καὶ Σωστράτης,
οὕτω διαφθείρας ἐμοῦ τὰ φορτία.
ΦΙ. ἄκουσον, ὦ γύναι· λόγον σοι βούλομαι
λέξαι χαρίεντα.
ΑΡ. μὰ Δία μή μοί γ', ὦ μέλε. 14
ΦΙ. Αἴσωπον ἀπὸ δείπνου βαδίζονθ' ἑσπέρας
θρασεῖα καὶ μεθύσῃ τις ὑλάκτει κύων.
κἄπειτ' ἐκεῖνος εἶπεν, ὦ κύον κύον,
εἰ νὴ Δί' ἀντὶ τῆς κακῆς γλώττης ποθὲν
πυροὺς πρίαιο, σωφρονεῖν ἄν μοι δοκεῖς. 14
ΑΡ. καὶ καταγελᾷς μου; προσκαλοῦμαί σ' ὅστις εἶ,
πρὸς τοὺς ἀγορανόμους βλάβης τῶν φορτίων,
κλητῆρ' ἔχουσα Χαιρεφῶντα τουτονί.
ΦΙ. μὰ Δί', ἀλλ' ἄκουσον, ἤν τί σοι δόξω λέγειν.
Λᾶσός ποτ' ἀντεδίδασκε καὶ Σιμωνίδης· 14
ἔπειθ' ὁ Λᾶσος εἶπεν, ὀλίγον μοι μέλει.
ΑΡ. ἄληθες, οὗτος;
ΦΙ. καὶ σὺ δή μοι, Χαιρεφῶν,
γυναικὶ κλητεύεις, ἐοικὼς θαψίνῃ
Ἰνοῖ κρεμαμένῃ πρὸς ποδῶν Εὐριπίδου;

---
[a] He has learned the lesson his son taught him, 1258.
[b] *i.e.* Demeter and Persephone, a regular female oath.
[c] ὥστε ἄρτους ποιῆσαι, ἐπεὶ ἀρτόπωλις : Schol.
[d] κλητήρ is the officer whose duty it was to see that the defendant was duly served with the citation to appear.

THE WASPS, 1393–1414

PH.   Troubles? Not at all.
A merry tale or two sets these things right.[a]
I'll soon set matters right with this young woman.

B.-G. No, by the Twain [b]! you shan't escape scot-free,
Doing such damage to the goods of Myrtia,
Sostrata's daughter, and Anchylion's, sir!

PH. Listen, good woman: I am going to tell you
A pleasant tale.

B.-G.   Not me, by Zeus, sir, no!

PH. At Aesop, as he walked one eve from supper,
There yapped an impudent and drunken bitch.
Then Aesop answered, *O you bitch! you bitch!*
If in the stead of that ungodly tongue
You'd buy some wheat,[c] methinks you'd have more sense.

B.-G. Insult me too? I summon you before
The Market Court for damage done my goods,
And for my sompnour [d] have this Chaerephon.

PH. Nay, nay, but listen if I speak not fair.
Simonides and Lasus [e] once were rivals.
Then Lasus says, *Pish, I don't care,* says he.

B-G.. You will, sir, will you?

PH.   And you, Chaerephon,
Are you her sompnour, you, like fear-blanched Ino
Pendent before Euripides's feet?[f]

---

[e] "Lasus of Hermione was a contemporary and rival of the great Simonides of Ceos, who was famous for the number of victories obtained by his dithyrambic choruses": R. P. like Lasus snaps his fingers at his opponent.

[f] "The story of Ino, who to escape her domestic miseries threw herself, with her youngest child Melicertes, into the sea, formed one of the most moving tragedies of Euripides": R. Doubtless she was represented in the tragedy as throwing herself at the feet of some deity or person, for whom A. here substitutes the poet himself. For Chaerephon the "cadaverous" (in Eupolis he is πύξινος) see Index.

ARISTOPHANES

ΒΔ. ὁδί τις ἕτερος, ὡς ἔοικεν, ἔρχεται
καλούμενός σε· τόν γέ τοι κλητῆρ' ἔχει.
ΚΑΤΗΓΟΡΟΣ. οἴμοι κακοδαίμων. προσκαλοῦμαί σ', ὦ
γέρον,
ὕβρεως.
ΒΔ. ὕβρεως; μή, μὴ καλέσῃς πρὸς τῶν θεῶν.
ἐγὼ γὰρ ὑπὲρ αὐτοῦ δίκην δίδωμί σοι,
ἣν ἂν σὺ τάξῃς, καὶ χάριν προσείσομαι.
ΦΙ. ἐγὼ μὲν οὖν αὐτῷ διαλλαχθήσομαι
ἑκών· ὁμολογῶ γὰρ πατάξαι καὶ βαλεῖν.
ἀλλ' ἐλθὲ δευρί, πότερον ἐπιτρέπεις ἐμοὶ
ὅ τι χρή μ' ἀποτίσαντ' ἀργύριον τοῦ πράγματος,
εἶναι φίλον τὸ λοιπόν, ἢ σύ μοι φράσεις;
ΚΑ. σὺ λέγε. δικῶν γὰρ οὐ δέομ' οὐδὲ πραγμάτων.
ΦΙ. ἀνὴρ Συβαρίτης ἐξέπεσεν ἐξ ἅρματος,
καί πως κατεάγη τῆς κεφαλῆς μέγα σφόδρα·
ἐτύγχανεν γὰρ οὐ τρίβων ὢν ἱππικῆς.
κᾆπειτ' ἐπιστὰς εἶπ' ἀνὴρ αὐτῷ φίλος·
ἔρδοι τις ἣν ἕκαστος εἰδείη τέχνην.
οὕτω δὲ καὶ σὺ παράτρεχ' εἰς τὰ Πιττάλου.
ΒΔ. ὅμοιά σου καὶ ταῦτα τοῖς ἄλλοις τρόποις.
ΚΑ. ἀλλ' οὖν σὺ μέμνησ' αὐτὸς ἀπεκρίνατο.
ΦΙ. ἄκουε, μὴ φεῦγ'. ἐν Συβάρει γυνή ποτε
κατέαξ' ἐχῖνον.
ΚΑ. ταῦτ' ἐγὼ μαρτύρομαι.
ΦΙ. οὑχῖνος οὖν ἔχων τιν' ἐπεμαρτύρατο·
εἶθ' ἡ Συβαρῖτις εἶπεν, εἰ ναὶ τὰν κόραν
τὴν μαρτυρίαν ταύτην ἐάσας ἐν τάχει
ἐπίδεσμον ἐπρίω, νοῦν ἂν εἶχες πλείονα.

---

[a] "The ὕβρεως γραφή was a very different matter from the βλάβης δίκη with which alone the baking-girl had threatened

540

BD. See, here's another coming, as I live,
　　To summon you : at least he has got his sompnour.
COMPLAINANT. O dear! O dear!　Old man, I summon you
　　For outrage.
BD.　　　　　　Outrage [a] ? no, by the Gods, pray don't.
　　I'll make amends for everything he has done
　　(Ask what you will), and thank you kindly too.
PH. Nay, I'll make friends myself without compulsion.
　　I quite admit the assault and battery.
　　So tell me which you'll do ; leave it to me
　　To name the compensation I must pay
　　To make us friends, or will you fix the sum ?
CO. Name it yourself : I want no suits nor troubles.
PH. There was a man of Sybaris,[b] do you know,
　　Thrown from his carriage, and he cracked his skull,
　　Quite badly too. Fact was, he could not drive.
　　There was a friend of his stood by, and said,
　　Let each man exercise the art he knows.
　　So you, run off to Doctor Pittalus.[c]
BD. Ay, this is like the rest of your behaviour.
CO. (*To Bd.*) You, sir, yourself, remember what he says.
PH. Stop, listen. Once in Sybaris a girl
　　Fractured a jug.
CO.　　　　　　　I call you, friend, to witness.
PH. Just so the jug : *it* called a friend to witness.
　　Then said the girl of Sybaris, *By'r Lady*,[d]
　　If you would leave off calling friends to witness,
　　And buy a rivet, you would show more brains.

him. It was so to say a criminal indictment, and not a mere civil action : and entailed a severe and speedy punishment " : R.
　[b] " P. reverts to his son's alternative prescription in 1259 and tries the effect of a Sybaritic apologue " : R.
　[c] *i.e.* Don't try litigation which you don't understand, but go to the famous doctor, Pittalus (*cf. A.* 1032).
　[d] *i.e.* Persephone.

ARISTOPHANES

ΚΑ. ὕβριζ', ἕως ἂν τὴν δίκην ἄρχων καλῇ.
ΒΔ. οὔ τοι μὰ τὴν Δήμητρ' ἔτ' ἐνταυθοῖ μενεῖς
ἀλλ' ἀράμενος οἴσω σε
ΦΙ. τί ποιεῖς;
ΒΔ. ὅ τι ποιῶ;
εἴσω φέρω σ' ἐντεῦθεν· εἰ δὲ μή, τάχα
κλητῆρες ἐπιλείψουσι τοὺς καλουμένους. 14⟨
ΦΙ. Αἴσωπον οἱ Δελφοί ποτ'
ΒΔ. ὀλίγον μοι μέλει.
ΦΙ. φιάλην ἐπῃτιῶντο κλέψαι τοῦ θεοῦ·
ὁ δ' ἔλεξεν αὐτοῖς, ὡς ὁ κάνθαρός ποτε
ΒΔ. οἴμ' ὡς ἀπολῶ σ' αὐτοῖσι τοῖσι κανθάροις.

ΧΟ. ζηλῶ γε τῆς εὐτυχίας [στρ. 14⟨
τὸν πρέσβυν, οἷ μετέστη
ξηρῶν τρόπων καὶ βιοτῆς·
ἕτερα δὲ νῦν ἀντιμαθὼν
ἤθη, μετά τι πεσεῖται
ἐπὶ τὸ τρυφερὸν καὶ μαλακόν. 14⟨
τάχα δ' ἂν ἴσως οὐκ ἐθέλοι.
τὸ γὰρ ἀποστῆναι χαλεπὸν
φύσεος, ἣν ἔχει τις ἀεί.
καίτοι πολλοὶ ταῦτ' ἔπαθον·
ξυνόντες γνώμαις ἑτέρων 14⟨
μετεβάλλοντο τοὺς τρόπους.

πολλοῦ δ' ἐπαίνου παρ' ἐμοὶ [ἀντ.
καὶ τοῖσιν εὖ φρονοῦσιν

---

[a] The Delphians brought a false charge against Aesop and,

542

THE WASPS, 1441-1463

CO. Jeer, till the Magistrate call on my case.
BD. No, by Demeter, but you shan't stop here,
I'll take and carry you—
PH. What now!
BD. What now?
Carry you in : or soon there won't be sompnours
Enough for all your summoning complainants.
PH. The Delphians once charged Aesop—
BD. I don't care.
PH. With having filched a vessel of their God.
But Aesop up and told them that a beetle [a]—
BD. Zounds! but I'll finish you, beetles and all.

CH.[b] I envy much his fortune
As he changes from his dry
Ungenial life and manners,
Another path to try.
Now all to soft indulgence
His eager soul will take,
And yet perchance it will not,
For, ah! 'tis hard to break
From all your lifelong habits ;
Yet some the change have made,
With other minds consorting,
By other counsels swayed.

With us and all good people
Great praise Philocleon's son

as he was being led to execution, he told them this fable, the moral of which is that evil-doers will in the end pay.

[b] This ode in which the Chorus " felicitates B. on the probable success of his experiment," after its demonstrable failure, seems " foreign to the original scheme of the Play." So too 1474 when Xanthias announces B.'s drunken behaviour " no one would gather that this is his second entrance on the self-same errand." See R. Introd. p. xiv and notes.

543

ARISTOPHANES

τυχὼν ἄπεισιν διὰ τὴν
φιλοπατρίαν καὶ σοφίαν
ὁ παῖς ὁ Φιλοκλέωνος.
οὐδενὶ γὰρ οὕτως ἀγανῷ
ξυνεγενόμην, οὐδὲ τρόποις
ἐπεμάνην, οὐδ' ἐξεχύθην.
τί γὰρ ἐκεῖνος ἀντιλέγων
οὐ κρείττων ἦν, βουλόμενος
τὸν φύσαντα σεμνοτέροις
κατακοσμῆσαι πράγμασι;

ΞΑ. νὴ τὸν Διόνυσον, ἄπορά γ' ἡμῖν πράγματα
δαίμων τις εἰσκεκύκληκεν εἰς τὴν οἰκίαν.
ὁ γὰρ γέρων ὡς ἔπιε διὰ πολλοῦ χρόνου
ἤκουσέ τ' αὐλοῦ, περιχαρὴς τῷ πράγματι
ὀρχούμενος τῆς νυκτὸς οὐδὲν παύεται
τἀρχαῖ' ἐκεῖν' οἷς Θέσπις ἠγωνίζετο·
καὶ τοὺς τραγῳδούς φησιν ἀποδείξειν κρόνους
τοὺς νῦν, διορχησάμενος ὀλίγον ὕστερον.

ΦΙ. τίς ἐπ' αὐλείοισι θύραις θάσσει;
ΞΑ. τουτὶ καὶ δὴ χωρεῖ τὸ κακόν.
ΦΙ. κλῇθρα χαλάσθω τάδε. καὶ δὴ γὰρ
σχήματος ἀρχὴ
ΞΑ. μᾶλλον δέ γ' ἴσως μανίας ἀρχή.
ΦΙ. πλευρὰν λυγίσαντος ὑπὸ ῥώμης,
οἷον μυκτὴρ μυκᾶται καὶ
σφόνδυλος ἀχεῖ.
ΞΑ. πῖθ' ἑλλέβορον.
ΦΙ. πτήσσει Φρύνιχος ὥς τις ἀλέκτωρ,

[a] The ancient writers for the stage, Thespis, Phrynichus (1490 seq.) and Carcinus (1501 seq.), introduced much dancing,

THE WASPS, 1464-1490

For filial love and genius
  In this affair has won.
Such sweet and gracious manners
  I never saw before,
Nor ever with such fondness
  My doting heart gushed o'er.
Where proved he not the victor
  In all this wordy strife,
Seeking to raise his father
  To higher paths of life?

XA. O Dionysus! here's a pretty mess
Into our house some power has whirligigged.
Soon as the old man heard the pipe, and drank
The long untasted wine, he grew so merry
He won't stop dancing all the whole night through
Those strange old dances such as Thespis taught; [a]
And your new bards he'll prove old fools, he says,
Dancing against them in the lists directly.

PH. Who sits, who waits at the entrance gates?
XA. More and more is this evil advancing!
PH. Be the bolts undone, we have just begun:
This, this is the first evolution of dancing.
XA. First evolution of madness, I think.
PH. With the strong contortion the ribs twist round,
And the nostril snorts, and the joints resound.
And the tendons crack.
XA.   O, hellebore drink! [b]
PH. Cocklike, Phrynichus crouches and cowers,[c]

and the old man remembers these dances. Bentley's full discussion of this passage is quoted in R.
  [b] Hellebore was a cure for madness.
  [c] Bentley emended πτήσσει to πλήσσει, but R. notes that "a cock crouches and sidles down immediately before it delivers a blow"; cf. 1491.

ARISTOPHANES

ΞΑ. τάχα βαλλήσεις.
ΦΙ. σκέλος οὐράνιόν γ' ἐκλακτίζων.
       πρωκτὸς χάσκει.
ΞΑ.   κατὰ σαυτὸν ὅρα.
ΦΙ. νῦν γὰρ ἐν ἄρθροις τοῖς ἡμετέροις
       στρέφεται χαλαρὰ κοτυληδών.
ΒΔ. οὐκ εὖ μὰ Δί' οὐ δῆτ', ἀλλὰ μανικὰ πράγματα.
ΦΙ. φέρε νυν ἀνείπω κἀνταγωνιστὰς καλῶ.
       εἴ τις τραγῳδός φησιν ὀρχεῖσθαι καλῶς,
       ἐμοὶ διορχησόμενος ἐνθάδ' εἰσίτω.
       φησίν τις, ἢ οὐδείς;
ΒΔ.   εἷς γ' ἐκεινοσὶ μόνος.
ΦΙ. τίς ὁ κακοδαίμων ἐστίν;
ΒΔ.   υἱὸς Καρκίνου
       ὁ μέσατος.
ΦΙ.   ἀλλ' οὗτός γε καταποθήσεται·
       ἀπολῶ γὰρ αὐτὸν ἐμμελείᾳ κονδύλου.
       ἐν τῷ ῥυθμῷ γὰρ οὐδέν ἐστ'.
ΒΔ.   ἀλλ', ὦζυρέ,
       ἕτερος τραγῳδὸς Καρκινίτης ἔρχεται,
       ἀδελφὸς αὐτοῦ.
ΦΙ.   νὴ Δί' ὠψώνηκ' ἄρα.
ΒΔ. μὰ τὸν Δί' οὐδέν γ' ἄλλο πλὴν γε καρκίνους.
       προσέρχεται γὰρ ἕτερος αὖ τῶν Καρκίνου.
ΦΙ. τουτὶ τί ἦν τὸ προσέρπον; ὀξίς, ἢ φάλαγξ;
ΒΔ. ὁ πιννοτήρης οὗτός ἐστι, τοῦ γένους
       ὁ σμικρότατος, ὃς τὴν τραγῳδίαν ποιεῖ.

---

[a] " P. holds the lists as the champion of the older tragic dances. Three representatives of the modern school of tragic dancing now enter, one by one, to accept his challenge. They are the three deformed and stunted sons of Carcinus, the constant butts of Aristophanes for their preposterous dances ": R.

THE WASPS, 1491-1511

XA. You'll strike by and by.
PH. Then he kicks his leg to the wondering sky,
XA. O look to yourself, look out, look out.
PH. For now in these sinewy joints of ours
The cup-like socket is twirled about.
BD. 'Twon't do, by Zeus : 'twon't do : 'tis downright madness.
PH. Come on, I challenge all the world to dance.
Now what tragedian thinks he dances well,
Let him come in and dance a match with me.
Well, is there one, or none ?
BD. Here's only one.
PH. Who's he, poor devil ?
BD. 'Tis the midmost son
Of poet Carcinus, the Crabbe.[a]
PH. I'll eat him.
'Sdeath ! I'll destroy him with a knuckle-dance.[b]
He's a born fool at rhythm.
BD. Nay, but look here !
Here comes a brother crab, another son
Of Carcinus.
PH. 'Faith, I've got crab enough.
BD. Nothing but crabs ! 'fore Zeus, nothing but crabs !
Here creeps a third of Carcinus's brood.
PH. Heyday ! what's this ? a vinaigrette, or spider ?
BD. This is the Pinnoteer,[c] of all the tribe
The tiniest crab : a tragic poet too !

[b] ἐμμέλεια is the technical word for a tragic dance; here P. promises to perform it with his fists.
[c] A tiny crustacean, about the size of a pea, a parasite of the pinna, a wedge-shaped bivalve. It was called " Pinna-watchman," because " the pinna having got its little guest safely lodged within, left its shell open : and so soon as any food came within the valves the pea-crab gave its host a nip, which caused it to close its shell and secure the prey " : R.

VOL. I   2 N 2   547

ARISTOPHANES

41. ὦ Καρκίν', ὦ μακάριε τῆς εὐπαιδίας·
ὅσον τὸ πλῆθος κατέπεσεν τῶν ὀρχίλων.
ἀτὰρ καταβατέον γ' ἐπ' αὐτούς μοι· σὺ δὲ
ἅλμην κύκα τούτοισιν, ἣν ἐγὼ κρατῶ.   15

ΧΟ. φέρε νυν ἡμεῖς αὐτοῖς ὀλίγον ξυγχωρήσωμεν
ἅπαντες,
ἵν' ἐφ' ἡσυχίας ἡμῶν πρόσθεν βεμβικίζωσιν
ἑαυτούς.
ἄγ', ὦ μεγαλώνυμα τέκνα τοῦ θαλασσίοιο,
πηδᾶτε παρὰ ψάμαθον   15
καὶ θῖν' ἁλὸς ἀτρυγέτοιο, καρίδων ἀδελφοί·
ταχὺν πόδα κυκλοσοβεῖτε, καὶ τὸ Φρυνίχειον
ἐκλακτισάτω τις, ὅπως   15
ἰδόντες ἄνω σκέλος [ὧδ'], ὤζωσιν οἱ θεαταί.
στρόβει, παράβαινε κύκλῳ καὶ γάστρισον σεαυτόν,
ῥῖπτε σκέλος οὐράνιον· βέμβικες ἐγγενέσθων.   15
καὐτὸς γὰρ ὁ ποντομέδων ἄναξ πατὴρ προσέρπει
ἡσθεὶς ἐπὶ τοῖσιν ἑαυτοῦ παισί, τοῖς τριόρχοις.
ἀλλ' ἐξάγετ', εἴ τι φιλεῖτ', ὀρχούμενοι θύραζε   15
ἡμᾶς ταχύ· τοῦτο γὰρ οὐδείς πω πάρος δέδρακεν
ὀρχούμενος, ὅστις ἀπήλλαξεν χορὸν τρυγῳδῶν.

---

[a] Lit. " golden-crested wrens." He calls them so because of their size, and perhaps with a suggestion of ὀρχηστῶν. In 1534 he calls them τρίορχοι (lit. " buzzards ")=" three-dancers."

[b] Their names are variously given by the Scholiast as Xenocles, Xenotimus, Diotimus, etc.

THE WASPS, 1512-1537

PH. O Carcinus! O proud and happy father!
Here's a fine troop of wrynecks [a] settling down.
Well, I must gird me to the fight: and you.
Mix pickles for these crabs, in case I beat them.

CH. Come draw we aside, and leave them a wide,
    a roomy and peaceable exercise-ground,
That before us therein like tops they may spin,
    revolving and whirling and twirling around.
O lofty-titled [b] sons of the ocean-roving sire,
Ye brethren of the shrimps, come and leap [c]
On the sand and on the strand
    of the salt and barren deep.[d]
Whisk nimble feet around you;
    kick out, till all admire,
The Phrynichean kick to the sky;
That the audience may applaud,
    as they view your leg on high.
On, on, in mazy circles; hit your stomach with your heel
Fling legs aloft to heaven,
    as like spinning-tops you wheel.
Your Sire is creeping onward, the Ruler of the Sea,
He gazes with delight at his hobby-dancers three.
Come, dancing as you are, if you like it, lead away,
For never yet, I warrant, has an actor till to-day
Led out a chorus, dancing, at the ending of the Play.

[c] R. quotes Paley for shrimps "bounding in the air from the shallow margin of the water, or from the wet sand."
[d] θῖν' ἁλός, etc., is from Hom. *Il.* i. 316, 327.

INDEX

Acestor, *W.* 1221
Achaia, a name of Demeter, *A.* 710
Acharnae, a deme of Athens, *A.* 180
Aegina, an island opposite the Peiraeus, *A.* 653, *W.* 122
Aeschines, a blusterer, *W.* 325, 459, 1220, 1243
Aeschylus, *C.* 1366
Aesop, *W.* 566, 1259
Aetolia, *K.* 79
Agoracritus, *K.* 1335
Agyieus, a title of Apollo, *W.* 875
Amphitheus, *A.* 46
Amynias, *C.* 31
Amynias, son of Sellus, *C.* 691, *W.* 74, 1266
Androcles, a rogue, *W.* 1187
Antimachus, an effeminate, *A.* 1150, *C.* 1022
Antiphon, *W.* 1270
Apaturia, a clan festival, *A.* 146
Arcadia, *K.* 798
Archeptolemus, *K.* 327, 794
Archilochus quoted, *A.* 1228
Argos, *K.* 465
Arignotus, son of Automenes, a harper, *K.* 1278, *W.* 1278
Ariphrades, son of Automenes, an evil man, *K.* 1281, *W.* 1280
Aristeides, son of Lysimachus "the Just," a statesman opposed to Themistocles, fought at Marathon, ostracized 483 B.C., but returned and took a great part in the political developments of Athens; died about 463, *K.* 1325.
Artemon, name of an effeminate who was carried about in a litter, hence called περιφόρητος, *A.* 85.
Asclepius, god of healing, *W.* 123.

Ascondas, *W.* 1383
Aspasia, mistress of Pericles, *A.* 527
Athamas, king of Orchomenus in Boeotia, married Nephele, and was father of Phrixus and Helle; he was stricken with madness, and fled into Thessaly, *C.* 257
Athens described, *A.* 639
Automenes, father of Arignotus and Ariphrades, *W.* 1275

Bakis, a Boeotian seer of Helicon; there was a collection current of his oracles, *K.* 123, 1003
Bellerophon, who rode the winged horse Pegasus; name of a play by Euripides, *A.* 427
Bereschethus, *K.* 635
Brasidas, a famous Spartan commander, son of Tellis, killed at Amphipolis 422 B.C., *W.* 475
Byzantium, the earlier city on the site of Constantinople, *C.* 249, *W.* 236

Caecias, the N.E. wind, *K.* 437
Camarina, a town in Sicily, *A.* 605
Carcinus, a comic poet, father of three dwarfish sons, *C.* 1261, *W.* 1508
Cardopion, *W.* 1178
Caria, *K.* 173
Carthage, *K.* 174, 1303
Caÿstrian plains, *A.* 68
Cecrops, *C.* 301, *W.* 438
Celeus, *A.* 49
Centaurs, *C.* 349
Cephisodemus, *A.* 705
Cerameicus, the potters' quarter

551

INDEX

at Athens, where public funerals took place, *K.* 772
Chaereas, *W.* 687
Chaerephon, a pupil of Socrates, *C.* 104, etc., *W.* 1408
Chaeris, a wretched Theban piper, *A.* 16
Chalcis, Chalcidice in Thrace, *K.* 238
Chaonia, in Epirus, *K.* 78, *A.* 613
Cherronesus, the peninsula of Gallipoli, *K.* 262
Choae, the Pitcher-feast, *A.* 961
Cicynna, an Attic deme, *C.* 134
Cleaenetus, father of Cleon, *K.* 574
Cleinias, father of Alcibiades, *A.* 716
Cleisthenes, "son of Sibyrtius," a coward and effeminate, *A.* 118, *W.* 1187, *K.* 1374, *C.* 355
Cleon, son of Cleaenetus, a tanner, demagogue and popular leader after the death of Pericles in 429 B.C. He opposed peace. In 424 took part in the surrender of the Spartans at Sphacteria, which he laid to his own credit. Killed by Brasidas at Amphipolis, 422. *A.* 6, 300, 378, 502, 659, *K.* 137, 976, *C.* 549, 586, 591, *W.* 35, 62, 197, 241, 596, 841, 895, 1220, 1224, 1237, 1285
Cleonymus, the butt of Athens for his bulk and his appetite, who cast away his shield at Delium, *A.* 88, 844, *K.* 958, 1293, 1372, *C.* 353, 450, 674, *W.* 20, 592, 822
Cobalus, *K.* 685
Coesyra, a name in the great Alcmaeonid family, *A.* 614, *C.* 48, 800
Colias, a love-deity, *C.* 52
Connas, a drunken flute-player, *K.* 534, *W.* 675
Copaïs, a lake in Boeotia, *A.* 880
Corinth, *K.* 603
Cranaan city, Athens, *A.* 75
Crates, a comic poet, flourished about 450 B.C., *K.* 536
Cratinus, a dandy, *A.* 849, 1173
Cratinus, a comic poet, 519-422 B.C., *K.* 400, 526
Cronus, father of Zeus, proverbial for things ancient and out of date, *C.* 929

Ctesias, an informer, *A.* 839
Cycloborus, a hill-torrent in Attica, *K.* 137
Cyllene, a port in Elis, *K.* 1081
Cynna, a courtesan, *K.* 765, *W.* 1032

DEIOMA, the Exchange at the Peiraeus, *K.* 979
Dexitheus, a good harpist, *A.* 14
Diasia, a feast in honour of Zeus Meilichius, *C.* 408, 864
Dictynna, a name of Artemis, *W.* 368
Diocles, an Athenian, who in some ancient battle had fought for Megara and given his life for a youth; a festival was held at his tomb, *A.* 774
Dionysia, a festival, *A.* 195
Diopeithes, a crazy oracle-monger, *K.* 1085, *W.* 380
Dracyllus, *A.* 612

ECBATANA, the old capital of the Medes, *A.* 64, *W.* 1143
Egypt, *C.* 1130
Electra of Aeschylus, *C.* 534
Ephudion, *W.* 1383
Erechtheus, a legendary king of Athens, *K.* 1022
Ergasion, *W.* 1201
Euathlus, *A.* 711, *W.* 592
Euboea, an island off Boeotia, *C.* 211, *W.* 715
Eucharides, *W.* 680
Eucrates, an oakum-seller, *K.* 129, 253
Euphemius, a politician, *W.* 599
Euphorides, *A.* 612
Eupolis, an early comic poet born about 446 B.C., died probably in 411, *C.* 553
Euripides, the tragic poet, son of a herb-seller, 480-406 B.C., *A.* 394, 452, *K.* 18, *C.* 1371, 1376, *W.* 61, 1414
Eurycles, a ventriloquist, *W.* 1019
Euthymenes, *A.* 67

GELA, a town in Sicily, *A.* 606
Genetyllis, a love-deity, *C.* 52
Geryones, a giant of legend, *A.* 1082
Gryttus, *K.* 877

INDEX

HADES, cap of, *A.* 390
Harmodius, lover of Aristogeiton; they are the traditional liberators of Athens from the tyrants, *A.* 980, 1093, *K.* 786, *W.* 1225
Heliaea, the supreme court of Athens, *K.* 897
Heracles, baths of, *C.* 1051
Hieronymus, a wild and hairy man, *A.* 389, *C.* 349
Hippias, the tyrant, *K.* 448, *W.* 502
Hippocrates and his sons, a dirty crew, *C.* 1001
Hippodamus, father of Archeptolemus, *K.* 327
Homer, *C.* 1056
Hyperbolus, a demagogue who succeeded Cleon, of servile origin, ostracized, finally killed by the oligarchs at Samos, 411 B.C., *A.* 846, *C.* 551, 876, *W.* 1007, *K.* 1304, 1363

IAPETUS, one of the Titans, proverbial for antiquity, *C.* 998
Ino, daughter of Cadmus, wife of Athamas, *A.* 434, *W.* 1414
Ismenichus, *A.* 861

LACHES, an Athenian commander in the Peloponnesian War, accused by Cleon of peculation; slain at Mantinea, *W.* 240, 836, 895
Lacrateides, an Athenian leader, possibly one of the accusers of Pericles, *A.* 220
Lamachus, son of Xenophanes, colleague of Alciblades and Nicias in the Sicilian expedition 415 B.C., a brave and honourable soldier. He was killed in the siege, *A.* 270, 567, 963
Lamia, a goblin, *W.* 1035, 1177
Lasus of Hermione, a lyric poet, contemporary with Simonides, *W.* 1410
Lenaea, a feast, at which the comedies were exhibited, *A.* 504
Leogoras, an epicure, *W.* 1269, *C.* 109
Loxias, a name of Apollo, *K.* 1072
Lycus, patron hero of the Athenian dicasteries, *W.* 389, 819

Lysicles, a sheep-seller, *K.* 132, 705
Lysistratus, a vicious man, *K.* 1267, *W.* 787

MAGNES, an early comedian, *K.* 520
Marathon, scene of the famous victory, 490 B.C., *A.* 697, *K.* 781, 1334
Marilades, *A.* 609
Marpsias, a contentious orator, *A.* 701
Megacles, a name in one of the great Athenian families, the Alcmaeonidae, *C.* 46, 815
Megara, a city near Athens, *A.* 519, 539, 738, *W.* 57
Memnon, son of Eos, slain by Achilles, *C.* 622
Miletus, an Ionian city in Asia Minor, *K.* 361, 932
Miltiades, the victor of Marathon, son of Cimon, and tyrant of the Chersonesus, *K.* 1325
Mitylene, in Lesbos, *K.* 834
Morsimus, a poor tragedian, *K.* 401
Morychus, an epicure, *A.* 887, *W.* 506, 1142
Moschus, a bad harpist, *A.* 13
Mothon, *K.* 635
Myrsine, wife of Hippias, *K.* 449

NICARCHUS, an informer, *A.* 908
Nicias, son of Niceratus, a distinguished general, of the aristocratic party, and an opponent of Cleon; he perished in the Sicilian expedition, 413 B.C., *K.* 358
Nicostratus, *W.* 81

ODEUM, a court in Athens, *W.* 1009
Odomantes, a Thracian tribe, *A.* 156
Odysseus, *W.* 181, 1351
Oeagrus, an actor, *W.* 579
Oeneus, king of Calydon, deposed and cast out by his nephews; name of a play by Euripides, *A.* 418
Oeonichus, a worthless man, *K.* 1287
Olympia in Elis, scene of the great games, *W.* 1382
Olympus, a legendary flute-player, *K.* 8
Orestes, a footpad, *A.* 1167
Orthian nome, *A.* 16

INDEX

Panaetius, *K*. 243
Panathenaea, a feast, *C*. 386, 988
Pandeletus, an informer, *C*. 924
Paphlagon, a servile name describing the slave's country, *K*. 1, etc.
Parnes, a hill near Athens, *A*. 348, *C*. 323
Paros, an island in the Cyclades, *W*. 1189
Pasias, *C*. 21
Pauson, a starveling painter, *A*. 854
Peiraeus, harbour of Athens, *K*. 815
Peleus, father of Achilles, *C*. 1063
Pergasae, an Attic deme, *K*. 321
Pericles, the great Athenian statesman, died 429 B.C., *A*. 530, *K*. 283, *C*. 213, 859
Phaeax, a politician, *K*. 1377
Phales, an imaginary name, *A*. 263
Phanus, a hanger-on of Cleon's, *K*. 1256, *W*. 1220
Pharsalus, a town in Thessaly, *W*. 1271
Phayllus, a famous Olympian victor, *A*. 215, *W*. 1206
Phibalus, a district of Megara, *A*. 802
Philip, son of Gorgias, *W*. 421
Philocles, son of Selartius, a bitter tragic poet, *W*. 462
Philoctetes, a famous archer in the Trojan war, bitten by a snake and left in Lemnos; name of a play by Euripides, exhibited 431 B.C., *A*. 424
Philostratus, a pander, *K*. 1069
Phoenix, accused by his father's wife of attempting her honour, was blinded by his father; name of a play by Euripides, *A*. 421
Phormio, a distinguished naval commander, *K*. 562
Phrynichus, an early comic poet, *W*. 220, 269, 1490
Phyle, a fort on the hills between Attica and Boeotia, *A*. 1023
Pindar quoted, *K*. 1329
Pittalus, probably a doctor, *A*. 1032, 1221, *W*. 1432
Pnyx, the place of assembly, *K*. 749
Polymnestus, a worthless man, also the name of a musician, *K*. 1287
Pontus, the N.E. district of Asia Minor, *W*. 700

Potidaia, on the peninsula of Pallene, revolted from Athens in 432 B.C., retaken 429, *K*. 438
Pramnian wine, *K*. 106
Prepis, a disolute man, *A*. 843
Prinides, *A*. 612
Prodicus of Ceos, a famous sophist, *C*. 361
Propylaea, the entrance to the Athenian acropolis, *K*. 1326
Proxenides, a blusterer, *W*. 325
Prytaneum, the town hall, *K*. 167
Pylus, a fort S.W. of Messenia, taken by Demosthenes in 425 B.C. and held for Athens, *K*. 55, 76, 355, 703, 846, 1058, 1167, *C*. 185
Pyrilampes, *W*. 98
Pyrrhandrus, *K*. 901 ·
Pytho=Delphi, *K*. 1272

Sabazius, the Phrygian Bacchus, *W*. 9
Salabaccho, a courtesan, *K*. 765
Salamis, scene of the naval victory over Xerxes in 480 B.C., *K*. 785
Samos, an island off the coast of Asia Minor, *W*. 282
Sardis, capital of Lyd a, *W*. 1139
Sardo=Sardinia, *W*. 700
Sarpedon, son of Zeus, slain by Patroclus, *C*. 622
Scione, on the peninsula of Pallene, *W*. 210
Scitalus, *K*. 634
Scythian wilderness, *A*. 704
Sellus, father of Aeschines, *W*. 325
Semnae, the Erinyes or Furies, *K*. 1312
Seriphus, a small island of the Cyclades, *A*. 542
Simaetha, a courtesan, *A*. 524
Simon, a dishonest politician, *C*. 351, *K*. 242
Simonides of Ceos, a lyric poet, 556-467 B.C., *W*. 1410, *C*. 1356, *K*. 406
Sisyphus, craftiest of mankind, a character in Greek legend, *A*. 391
Sitalces, king of the Odrysians in Thrace, allied with Athens, *A*. 134
Smicythes, an effeminate, *K*. 969
Socrates, the philosopher, son of Sophroniscus, born 469 B.C., put to death 499, *C*. 104, etc.

INDEX

Solon, the great lawgiver of Athens, born about 638 B.C., died about 558, *C.* 1187
Straton, an effeminate, *A.* 122, *K.* 1374
Strymodorus, *A.* 274
Sunium, a cape of Attica, *C.* 401
Sybaris, a luxurious city in S. Italy, *W.* 1435

TAENARUM, a promontory of Laconia, where stood a temple of Poseidon, *A.* 510
Telephus, a play by Euripides, acted 438 B.C. T. was son of Heracles and Auge, exposed as an infant, and brought up by a herd in poverty; he helped in the taking of Troy, *A.* 415, 432, 555, *C.* 922
Thales of Miletus, one of the Seven Wise Men, *C.* 180
Themistocles, the victor of Salamis, an Athenian statesman, *K.* 84, 813, 883
Theognis, a dull frigid poet, nicknamed Snow, *A.* 11, 140, *W.* 1183

Theorus, a politician, *A.* 134, *C.* 400, *W.* 42, 599, 1220
Theseum, the temple of Theseus, a sanctuary, *K.* 1312
Thetis, mother of Achilles, *C.* 1067
Thouphanes, a secretary under Cleon, *K.* 1103
Thucydides, son of Melesias, leader of the aristocratic party in opposition to Pericles, ostracized 444 B.C., *A.* 703, *W.* 947
Thyestes, brother of Atreus, son of Pelops; name of a play by Euripides, *A.* 433
Tithonus, husband of Aurora, made immortal, *A.* 688
Tlepolemus, *C.* 1266
Triptolemus, *A.* 48
Trophonius, a hero, who had an oracle in Lebadeia in Boeotia, *C.* 508

XANTHIAS, *A.* 243
Xenophantes, father of Hieronymus, *C.* 349

/

THE LOEB CLASSICAL LIBRARY

VOLUMES ALREADY PUBLISHED

LATIN AUTHORS

APULEIUS. THE GOLDEN ASS (METAMORPHOSES). Trans. by W. Adlington (1566). Revised by S. Gaselee. (*4th Impression.*)
AULUS GELLIUS. Trans. by J. C. Rolfe. 3 Vols.
AUSONIUS. Trans. by H. G. Evelyn White. 2 Vols.
BOETHIUS: TRACTATES and DE CONSOLATIONE PHILOSOPHIAE. Trans. by the Rev. H. F. Stewart and E. K. Rand. (*2nd Impression.*)
CAESAR: CIVIL WARS. Trans. by A. G. Peskett. (*3rd Impression.*)
CAESAR: GALLIC WAR. Trans. by H. J. Edwards. (*5th Impression.*)
CATULLUS. Trans. by F. W. Cornish; TIBULLUS. Trans. by J. P. Postgate; PERVIGILIUM VENERIS. Trans. by J. W. Mackail. (*8th Impression.*)
CICERO: DE FINIBUS. Trans. by H. Rackham. (*2nd Impression.*)
CICERO: DE OFFICIIS. Trans. by Walter Miller. (*3rd Impression.*)
CICERO: DE REPUBLICA and DE LEGIBUS. Trans. by Clinton Keyes.
CICERO: DE SENECTUTE, DE AMICITIA, DE DIVINATIONE. Trans. by W. A. Falconer. (*3rd Imp.*)
CICERO: LETTERS TO ATTICUS. Trans. by E. O. Winstedt. 3 Vols. (Vol. I. *4th*, II. *3rd*, and III. *2nd Imp.*)
CICERO: LETTERS TO HIS FRIENDS. Trans. by W. Glynn Williams. 3 Vols.
CICERO: PHILIPPICS. Trans. by W. C. A. Ker.
CICERO: PRO ARCHIA POETA, POST REDITUM IN SENATU, POST REDITUM AD QUIRITES, DE DOMO SUA, DE HARUSPICUM RESPONSIS, PRO PLANCIO. Trans. by N. H. Watts.
CICERO: PRO CAECINA, PRO LEGE MANILIA, PRO CLUENTIO, PRO RABIRIO. Trans. by H. Grose Hodge.
CICERO: PRO QUINCTIO, PRO ROSCIO AMERINO, PRO ROSCIO COMOEDO, CONTRA RULLUM. Trans. by J. H. Freese.

1

THE LOEB CLASSICAL LIBRARY

CICERO: TUSCULAN DISPUTATIONS. Trans. by J. E. King.
CICERO: VERRINE ORATIONS. Trans. by L. H. G. Greenwood. 2 Vols. Vol. I.
CLAUDIAN. Trans. by M. Platnauer. 2 Vols.
CONFESSIONS OF ST. AUGUSTINE. Trans. by W. Watts (1631). 2 Vols. (Vol. I. 4th, Vol. II. 3rd. Imp.)
FLORUS. Trans. by E. S. Forster: CORNELIUS NEPOS. Trans. by J. C. Rolfe.
FRONTINUS: STRATAGEMS AND AQUEDUCTS. Trans. by C. E. Bennett.
FRONTO: CORRESPONDENCE. Trans. by C. R. Haines. 2 Vols.
HORACE: ODES AND EPODES. Trans. by C. E. Bennett. (9th Impression revised.)
HORACE: SATIRES, EPISTLES, ARS POETICA. Trans. by H. R. Fairclough. (2nd Impression revised.)
JUVENAL AND PERSIUS. Trans. by G. G. Ramsay. (4th Impression.)
LIVY. Trans. by B. O. Foster. 13 Vols. Vols. I.-V. (Vol. I. 2nd Impression revised.)
LUCAN. Trans. by J. D. Duff.
LUCRETIUS. Trans. by W. H. D. Rouse. (2nd Edition.)
MARTIAL. Trans. by W. C. A. Ker. 2 Vols. (Vol. I. 3rd Impression, Vol. II. 2nd Impression revised.)
OVID: THE ART OF LOVE AND OTHER POEMS. Trans. by J. H. Mozley.
OVID: HEROIDES, AMORES. Trans. by Grant Showerman. (3rd Impression.)
OVID: METAMORPHOSES. Trans. by F. J. Miller. 2 Vols. (Vol. I. 5th Impression, II. 4th Impression.)
OVID: TRISTIA AND EX PONTO. Trans. by A. L. Wheeler.
PETRONIUS. Trans. by M. Heseltine: SENECA: APOCOLOCYNTOSIS. Trans. by W. H. D. Rouse. (5th Impression revised.)
PLAUTUS. Trans. by Paul Nixon. 5 Vols. Vols. I.-III. (Vol. I. 3rd Impression, Vol. III. 2nd Impression.)
PLINY: LETTERS. Melmoth's translation revised by W. M. L. Hutchinson. 2 Vols. (3rd Impression.)
PROPERTIUS. Trans. by H. E. Butler. (4th Impression.)
QUINTILIAN. Trans. by H. E. Butler. 4 Vols.

THE LOEB CLASSICAL LIBRARY

SAINT AUGUSTINE: SELECT LETTERS. Trans. by J. H. Baxter.
SALLUST. Trans. by J. C. Rolfe.
SCRIPTORES HISTORIAE AUGUSTAE. Trans. by D. Magie. 3 Vols. Vols. I. and II. (Vol. I. 2nd Impression revised.)
SENECA: EPISTULAE MORALES. Trans. by R. M. Gummere. 3 Vols. (Vols. I. and II. 2nd Impression, Vol. II. revised.)
SENECA: MORAL ESSAYS. Trans. by J. W. Basore. 3 Vols. Vol. I.
SENECA: TRAGEDIES. Trans. by F. J. Miller. 2 Vols. (2nd Impression revised.)
STATIUS. Trans. by J. H. Mozley. 2 Vols.
SUETONIUS. Trans. by J. C. Rolfe. 2 Vols. (4th Impression revised.)
TACITUS: DIALOGUS. Trans. by Sir Wm. Peterson; and AGRICOLA and GERMANIA. Trans. by Maurice Hutton. (3rd Impression.)
TACITUS: HISTORIES. Trans. by C. H. Moore. 2 Vols. Vol. I.
TERENCE. Trans. by John Sargeaunt. 2 Vols. (5th Imp.)
VELLEIUS PATERCULUS and RES GESTAE DIVI AUGUSTI. Trans. by F. W. Shipley.
VIRGIL. Trans. by H. R. Fairclough. 2 Vols. (Vol. I. 10th Impression, II. 8th Impression.)

GREEK AUTHORS

ACHILLES TATIUS. Trans. by S. Gaselee.
AENEAS TACTICUS, ASCLEPIODOTUS and ONASANDER. Trans. by The Illinois Greek Club.
AESCHINES. Trans. by C. D. Adams.
AESCHYLUS. Trans. by H. Weir Smyth. 2 Vols. (Vol. I. 3rd Impression, Vol. II. 2nd Impression revised.)
APOLLODORUS. Trans. by Sir James G. Frazer. 2 Vols.
APOLLONIUS RHODIUS. Trans. by R. C. Seaton. (3rd Impression.)
THE APOSTOLIC FATHERS. Trans. by Kirsopp Lake. 2 Vols. (Vol. I. 5th Impression, II. 4th Impression.)
APPIAN'S ROMAN HISTORY. Trans. by Horace White. 4 Vols. (Vols. I. and IV. 2nd Impression.)
ARISTOPHANES. Trans. by Benjamin Bickley Rogers. 3 Vols. (Verse translation.) (3rd Impression.)

THE LOEB CLASSICAL LIBRARY

ARISTOTLE: THE "ART" OF RHETORIC. Trans. by J. H. Freese.
ARISTOTLE: THE NICOMACHEAN ETHICS. Trans. by H. Rackham.
ARISTOTLE: THE PHYSICS. Trans. by the Rev. P. Wicksteed and F. M. Cornford. 2 Vols. Vol. I.
ARISTOTLE: POETICS: "LONGINUS": ON THE SUBLIME. Trans. by W. Hamilton Fyfe, AND DEMETRIUS: ON STYLE. Trans. by W. Rhys Roberts.
ARRIAN: HISTORY OF ALEXANDER AND INDICA. Trans. by the Rev. E. Iliffe Robson. 2 Vols. Vol. I.
ATHENAEUS: THE DEIPNOSOPHISTS. Trans. by C. B. Gulick. 7 Vols. Vols. I.-IV.
CALLIMACHUS AND LYCOPHRON. Trans. by A. W. Mair, AND ARATUS, trans. by G. R. Mair.
CLEMENT OF ALEXANDRIA. Trans. by the Rev. G. W. Butterworth.
DAPHNIS AND CHLOE. Thornley's translation revised by J. M. Edmonds: AND PARTHENIUS. Trans. by S. Gaselee. (*2nd Impression.*)
DEMOSTHENES: DE CORONA AND DE FALSA LEGATIONE. Trans. by C. A. Vince and J. H. Vince.
DIO CASSIUS: ROMAN HISTORY. Trans. by E. Cary. 9 Vols.
DIOGENES LAERTIUS. Trans. by R. D. Hicks. 2 Vols.
EPICTETUS. Trans. by W. A. Oldfather. 2 Vols.
EURIPIDES. Trans. by A. S. Way. 4 Vols. (Verse trans.) (Vols. I. and II. *5th*, III. *3rd*, IV. *4th Imp.*)
EUSEBIUS: ECCLESIASTICAL HISTORY. Trans. by Kirsopp Lake. 2 Vols. Vol. I.
GALEN: ON THE NATURAL FACULTIES. Trans. by A. J. Brock. (*2nd Impression.*)
THE GREEK ANTHOLOGY. Trans. by W. R. Paton. 5 Vols. (Vol. I. *3rd*, II. *2nd Impression.*)
THE GREEK BUCOLIC POETS (THEOCRITUS, BION, MOSCHUS). Trans. by J. M. Edmonds. (*5th Imp.*)
HERODOTUS. Trans. by A. D. Godley. 4 Vols. (Vols. I.-III. *2nd Impression.*)
HESIOD AND THE HOMERIC HYMNS. Trans. by H. G. Evelyn White. (*4th Impression.*)
HIPPOCRATES. Trans. by W. H. S. Jones and E. T Withington. 4 Vols. Vols. I.-III.

THE LOEB CLASSICAL LIBRARY

HOMER: ILIAD. Trans. by A. T. Murray. 2 Vols. (Vol. I. *3rd Impression*, Vol. II. *2nd Impression*.)
HOMER: ODYSSEY. Trans. by A. T. Murray. 2 Vols. (Vol. I. *4th Impression*, Vol. II. *3rd Impression*.)
ISAEUS. Trans. by E. S. Forster.
ISOCRATES. Trans. by G. Norlin. 3 Vols. Vols. I. and II.
JOSEPHUS. Trans. by H. St. J. Thackeray. 8 Vols. Vols. I.-IV.
JULIAN. Trans. by Wilmer Cave Wright. 3 Vols.
LUCIAN. Trans. by A. M. Harmon. 8 Vols. Vols. I.-IV. (Vols. I. and II. *3rd Impression*.)
LYRA GRAECA. Trans. by J. M. Edmonds. 3 Vols. (Vol. I. *2nd Edition revised and enlarged*.)
MARCUS AURELIUS. Trans. by C. R. Haines. (*3rd Impression revised*.)
MENANDER. Trans. by F. G. Allinson. (*2nd Imp. rev.*)
OPPIAN, COLLUTHUS AND TRYPHIODORUS. Trans. by A. W. Mair.
PAUSANIAS: DESCRIPTION OF GREECE. Trans. by W. H. S. Jones. 5 Vols. and Companion Vol. Vols. I. and II.
PHILO. Trans. by F. H. Colson and the Rev. G. H. Whitaker. 10 Vols. Vols. I. and II.
PHILOSTRATUS: THE LIFE OF APOLLONIUS OF TYANA. Trans. by F. C. Conybeare. 2 Vols. (Vol. I. *3rd*, II. *2nd Impression*.)
PHILOSTRATUS AND EUNAPIUS: LIVES OF THE SOPHISTS. Trans. by Wilmer Cave Wright.
PINDAR. Trans. by Sir J. E. Sandys. (*5th Imp. revised*.)
PLATO: CHARMIDES, ALCIBIADES I. and II., HIPPARCHUS, THE LOVERS, THEAGES, MINOS, EPINOMIS. Trans. by W. R. M. Lamb.
PLATO: CRATYLUS, PARMENIDES, GREATER AND LESSER HIPPIAS. Trans. by H. N. Fowler.
PLATO: EUTHYPHRO, APOLOGY, CRITO, PHAEDO, PHAEDRUS. Trans. by H. N. Fowler. (*6th Impression*.)
PLATO: LACHES, PROTAGORAS, MENO, EUTHYDEMUS. Trans. by W. R. M. Lamb.
PLATO: LAWS. Trans. by the Rev. R. G. Bury. 2 Vols.
PLATO: LYSIS, SYMPOSIUM, GORGIAS. Trans. by W. R. M. Lamb.

THE LOEB CLASSICAL LIBRARY

PLATO: REPUBLIC. Trans. by Paul Shorey. 2 Vols. Vol. I.
PLATO: STATESMAN, PHILEBUS. Trans. by H. N. Fowler; ION. Trans. by W. R. M. Lamb.
PLATO: THEAETETUS, SOPHIST. Trans. by H. N. Fowler. (2nd Impression.)
PLATO: TIMAEUS, CRITIAS, CLITOPHO, MENEXENUS, EPISTULAE. Trans. by the Rev. R. G. Bury.
PLUTARCH: THE PARALLEL LIVES. Trans. by B. Perrin. 11 Vols. (Vols. I., II. and VII. 2nd Imp.)
PLUTARCH: MORALIA. Trans. by F. C. Babbitt. 14 Vols. Vols. I. and II.
POLYBIUS. Trans. by W. R. Paton. 6 Vols.
PROCOPIUS; HISTORY OF THE WARS. Trans. by H. B. Dewing. 7 Vols. Vols. I.-V.
QUINTUS SMYRNAEUS. Trans. by A. S. Way. (Verse translation.)
ST. BASIL: THE LETTERS. Trans. by R. Deferrari. 4 Vols. Vols. I. and II.
ST. JOHN DAMASCENE: BARLAAM AND IOASAPH. Trans. by the Rev. G. R. Woodward and Harold Mattingly.
SOPHOCLES. Trans. by F. Storr. 2 Vols. (Verse translation.) (Vol. I. 5th Impression, II. 4th Impression.)
STRABO: GEOGRAPHY. Trans. by Horace L. Jones. 8 Vols. Vols. I.-VII.
THEOPHRASTUS: THE CHARACTERS. Trans. by J. M. Edmonds; HERODES, CERCIDAS AND THE GREEK CHOLIAMBIC POETS. Trans. by A. D. Knox.
THEOPHRASTUS: ENQUIRY INTO PLANTS. Trans. by Sir Arthur Hort, Bart. 2 Vols.
THUCYDIDES. Trans. by C. F. Smith. 4 Vols. (Vol. I. 2nd Impression revised.)
XENOPHON: CYROPAEDIA. Trans. by Walter Miller. 2 Vols. (Vol. I. 2nd Impression.)
XENOPHON: HELLENICA, ANABASIS, APOLOGY, AND SYMPOSIUM. Trans. by C. L. Brownson and O. J. Todd. 3 Vols. (Vol. I. 2nd Impression.)
XENOPHON: MEMORABILIA AND OECONOMICUS. Trans. by E. C. Marchant.
XENOPHON: SCRIPTA MINORA. Trans. by E. C. Marchant.

THE LOEB CLASSICAL LIBRARY

VOLUMES IN PREPARATION

GREEK AUTHORS

ARISTOTLE: METAPHYSICS, H. Tredennick.
ARISTOTLE: ON THE MOTION AND PROGRESSION OF ANIMALS, E. S. Forster.
ARISTOTLE: ORGANON, W. M. L. Hutchinson.
ARISTOTLE: POLITICS AND ATHENIAN CONSTITUTION, H. Rackham.
DEMOSTHENES: MEIDIAS, ANDROTION, ARISTOCRATES, TIMOCRATES, J. H. Vince.
DEMOSTHENES: OLYNTHIACS, PHILIPPICS, LEPTINES, MINOR SPEECHES, J. H. Vince.
DEMOSTHENES: PRIVATE ORATIONS, G. M. Calhoun.
DIO CHRYSOSTOM, J. W. Cohoon.
GREEK IAMBIC AND ELEGIAC POETRY, J. M. Edmonds.
LYSIAS, W. R. M. Lamb.
PAPYRI, A. S. Hunt.
PHILOSTRATUS: IMAGINES, Arthur Fairbanks.
SEXTUS EMPIRICUS, the Rev. R. G. Bury.

THE LOEB CLASSICAL LIBRARY

LATIN AUTHORS

AMMIANUS MARCELLINUS, J. C. Rolfe.
BEDE: ECCLESIASTICAL HISTORY, J. E. King.
CICERO: CATILINE ORATIONS, B. L. Ullman.
CICERO: DE NATURA DEORUM, H. Rackham.
CICERO: DE ORATORE, ORATOR, BRUTUS, Charles Stuttaford.
CICERO: IN PISONEM, PRO SCAURO, PRO FONTEIO, PRO MILONE, PRO RABIRIO POSTUMO, PRO MARCELLO, PRO LIGARIO, PRO REGE DEIOTARO, N. H. Watts.
CICERO: PRO SEXTIO, IN VATINIUM, PRO CAELIO, PRO PROVINCIIS CONSULARIBUS, PRO BALBO, J. H. Freese.
ENNIUS, LUCILIUS, AND OTHER SPECIMENS OF OLD LATIN, E. H. Warmington.
MINUCIUS FELIX, W. C. A. Ker.
OVID: FASTI, Sir J. G. Frazer.
PLINY: NATURAL HISTORY, W. H. S. Jones and L. F. Newman.
ST. JEROME'S LETTERS: F. A. Wright.
SIDONIUS, E. V. Arnold and W. B. Anderson.
TACITUS: ANNALS, John Jackson.
TERTULLIAN: APOLOGY, T. R. Glover.
VALERIUS FLACCUS, A. F. Scholfield.
VITRUVIUS: DE ARCHITECTURA, F. Granger.

DESCRIPTIVE PROSPECTUS ON APPLICATION

London	WILLIAM HEINEMANN LTD
New York	G. P. PUTNAM'S SONS

Lightning Source UK Ltd.
Milton Keynes UK
UKHW012010080920
369574UK00001B/79